SECOND EDITION

Hadoop: The Definitive Guide

Tom White

foreword by Doug Cutting

O'REILLY®

Beijing · Cambridge · Farnham · Köln · Sebastopol · Tokyo

Hadoop: The Definitive Guide, Second Edition

by Tom White

Published by O'Reilly Media, Inc., 1005 Gravenstein Highway North, Sebastopol, CA 95472.

O'Reilly books may be purchased for educational, business, or sales promotional use. Online editions are also available for most titles (*http://my.safaribooksonline.com*). For more information, contact our corporate/institutional sales department: (800) 998-9938 or *corporate@oreilly.com*.

Editor: Mike Loukides	**Indexer:** Jay Book Services
Production Editor: Adam Zaremba	**Cover Designer:** Karen Montgomery
Proofreader: Diane Il Grande	**Interior Designer:** David Futato
	Illustrator: Robert Romano

Printing History:

June 2009:	First Edition.
October 2010:	Second Edition.

ISBN: 978-1-449-38973-4

[LSI]   [2011-4-1]

1303397229

For Eliane, Emilia, and Lottie

Table of Contents

Foreword

Hadoop got its start in Nutch. A few of us were attempting to build an open source web search engine and having trouble managing computations running on even a handful of computers. Once Google published its GFS and MapReduce papers, the route became clear. They'd devised systems to solve precisely the problems we were having with Nutch. So we started, two of us, half-time, to try to re-create these systems as a part of Nutch.

We managed to get Nutch limping along on 20 machines, but it soon became clear that to handle the Web's massive scale, we'd need to run it on thousands of machines and, moreover, that the job was bigger than two half-time developers could handle.

Around that time, Yahoo! got interested, and quickly put together a team that I joined. We split off the distributed computing part of Nutch, naming it Hadoop. With the help of Yahoo!, Hadoop soon grew into a technology that could truly scale to the Web.

In 2006, Tom White started contributing to Hadoop. I already knew Tom through an excellent article he'd written about Nutch, so I knew he could present complex ideas in clear prose. I soon learned that he could also develop software that was as pleasant to read as his prose.

From the beginning, Tom's contributions to Hadoop showed his concern for users and for the project. Unlike most open source contributors, Tom is not primarily interested in tweaking the system to better meet his own needs, but rather in making it easier for anyone to use.

Initially, Tom specialized in making Hadoop run well on Amazon's EC2 and S3 services. Then he moved on to tackle a wide variety of problems, including improving the MapReduce APIs, enhancing the website, and devising an object serialization framework. In all cases, Tom presented his ideas precisely. In short order, Tom earned the role of Hadoop committer and soon thereafter became a member of the Hadoop Project Management Committee.

Tom is now a respected senior member of the Hadoop developer community. Though he's an expert in many technical corners of the project, his specialty is making Hadoop easier to use and understand.

Given this, I was very pleased when I learned that Tom intended to write a book about Hadoop. Who could be better qualified? Now you have the opportunity to learn about Hadoop from a master—not only of the technology, but also of common sense and plain talk.

—Doug Cutting
Shed in the Yard, California

Preface

Martin Gardner, the mathematics and science writer, once said in an interview:

> Beyond calculus, I am lost. That was the secret of my column's success. It took me so long to understand what I was writing about that I knew how to write in a way most readers would understand.[*]

In many ways, this is how I feel about Hadoop. Its inner workings are complex, resting as they do on a mixture of distributed systems theory, practical engineering, and common sense. And to the uninitiated, Hadoop can appear alien.

But it doesn't need to be like this. Stripped to its core, the tools that Hadoop provides for building distributed systems—for data storage, data analysis, and coordination—are simple. If there's a common theme, it is about raising the level of abstraction—to create building blocks for programmers who just happen to have lots of data to store, or lots of data to analyze, or lots of machines to coordinate, and who don't have the time, the skill, or the inclination to become distributed systems experts to build the infrastructure to handle it.

With such a simple and generally applicable feature set, it seemed obvious to me when I started using it that Hadoop deserved to be widely used. However, at the time (in early 2006), setting up, configuring, and writing programs to use Hadoop was an art. Things have certainly improved since then: there is more documentation, there are more examples, and there are thriving mailing lists to go to when you have questions. And yet the biggest hurdle for newcomers is understanding what this technology is capable of, where it excels, and how to use it. That is why I wrote this book.

The Apache Hadoop community has come a long way. Over the course of three years, the Hadoop project has blossomed and spun off half a dozen subprojects. In this time, the software has made great leaps in performance, reliability, scalability, and manageability. To gain even wider adoption, however, I believe we need to make Hadoop even easier to use. This will involve writing more tools; integrating with more systems; and

---

[*] "The science of fun," Alex Bellos, *The Guardian*, May 31, 2008, *http://www.guardian.co.uk/science/ 2008/may/31/maths.science*.

writing new, improved APIs. I'm looking forward to being a part of this, and I hope this book will encourage and enable others to do so, too.

Administrative Notes

During discussion of a particular Java class in the text, I often omit its package name, to reduce clutter. If you need to know which package a class is in, you can easily look it up in Hadoop's Java API documentation for the relevant subproject, linked to from the Apache Hadoop home page at *http://hadoop.apache.org/*. Or if you're using an IDE, it can help using its auto-complete mechanism.

Similarly, although it deviates from usual style guidelines, program listings that import multiple classes from the same package may use the asterisk wildcard character to save space (for example: import org.apache.hadoop.io.*).

The sample programs in this book are available for download from the website that accompanies this book: *http://www.hadoopbook.com/*. You will also find instructions there for obtaining the datasets that are used in examples throughout the book, as well as further notes for running the programs in the book, and links to updates, additional resources, and my blog.

What's in This Book?

The rest of this book is organized as follows. Chapter 1 emphasizes the need for Hadoop and sketches the history of the project. Chapter 2 provides an introduction to MapReduce. Chapter 3 looks at Hadoop filesystems, and in particular HDFS, in depth. Chapter 4 covers the fundamentals of I/O in Hadoop: data integrity, compression, serialization, and file-based data structures.

The next four chapters cover MapReduce in depth. Chapter 5 goes through the practical steps needed to develop a MapReduce application. Chapter 6 looks at how MapReduce is implemented in Hadoop, from the point of view of a user. Chapter 7 is about the MapReduce programming model, and the various data formats that MapReduce can work with. Chapter 8 is on advanced MapReduce topics, including sorting and joining data.

Chapters 9 and 10 are for Hadoop administrators, and describe how to set up and maintain a Hadoop cluster running HDFS and MapReduce.

Later chapters are dedicated to projects that build on Hadoop or are related to it. Chapters 11 and 12 present Pig and Hive, which are analytics platforms built on HDFS and MapReduce, whereas Chapters 13, 14, and 15 cover HBase, ZooKeeper, and Sqoop, respectively.

Finally, Chapter 16 is a collection of case studies contributed by members of the Apache Hadoop community.

What's New in the Second Edition?

The second edition has two new chapters on Hive and Sqoop (Chapters 12 and 15), a new section covering Avro (in Chapter 4), an introduction to the new security features in Hadoop (in Chapter 9), and a new case study on analyzing massive network graphs using Hadoop (in Chapter 16).

This edition continues to describe the 0.20 release series of Apache Hadoop, since this was the latest stable release at the time of writing. New features from later releases are occasionally mentioned in the text, however, with reference to the version that they were introduced in.

Conventions Used in This Book

The following typographical conventions are used in this book:

Italic
: Indicates new terms, URLs, email addresses, filenames, and file extensions.

`Constant width`
: Used for program listings, as well as within paragraphs to refer to program elements such as variable or function names, databases, data types, environment variables, statements, and keywords.

`Constant width bold`
: Shows commands or other text that should be typed literally by the user.

`Constant width italic`
: Shows text that should be replaced with user-supplied values or by values determined by context.

 This icon signifies a tip, suggestion, or general note.

 This icon indicates a warning or caution.

Using Code Examples

This book is here to help you get your job done. In general, you may use the code in this book in your programs and documentation. You do not need to contact us for permission unless you're reproducing a significant portion of the code. For example, writing a program that uses several chunks of code from this book does not require permission. Selling or distributing a CD-ROM of examples from O'Reilly books does require permission. Answering a question by citing this book and quoting example code does not require permission. Incorporating a significant amount of example code from this book into your product's documentation does require permission.

We appreciate, but do not require, attribution. An attribution usually includes the title, author, publisher, and ISBN. For example: "*Hadoop: The Definitive Guide*, Second Edition, by Tom White. Copyright 2011 Tom White, 978-1-449-38973-4."

If you feel your use of code examples falls outside fair use or the permission given above, feel free to contact us at *permissions@oreilly.com*.

Safari® Books Online

Safari Books Online is an on-demand digital library that lets you easily search over 7,500 technology and creative reference books and videos to find the answers you need quickly.

With a subscription, you can read any page and watch any video from our library online. Read books on your cell phone and mobile devices. Access new titles before they are available for print, and get exclusive access to manuscripts in development and post feedback for the authors. Copy and paste code samples, organize your favorites, download chapters, bookmark key sections, create notes, print out pages, and benefit from tons of other time-saving features.

O'Reilly Media has uploaded this book to the Safari Books Online service. To have full digital access to this book and others on similar topics from O'Reilly and other publishers, sign up for free at *http://my.safaribooksonline.com*.

How to Contact Us

Please address comments and questions concerning this book to the publisher:

> O'Reilly Media, Inc.
> 1005 Gravenstein Highway North
> Sebastopol, CA 95472
> 800-998-9938 (in the United States or Canada)
> 707-829-0515 (international or local)
> 707-829-0104 (fax)

We have a web page for this book, where we list errata, examples, and any additional information. You can access this page at:

> *http://oreilly.com/catalog/0636920010388/*

The author also has a site for this book at:

> *http://www.hadoopbook.com/*

To comment or ask technical questions about this book, send email to:

bookquestions@oreilly.com

For more information about our books, conferences, Resource Centers, and the O'Reilly Network, see our website at:

http://www.oreilly.com

Acknowledgments

I have relied on many people, both directly and indirectly, in writing this book. I would like to thank the Hadoop community, from whom I have learned, and continue to learn, a great deal.

In particular, I would like to thank Michael Stack and Jonathan Gray for writing the chapter on HBase. Also thanks go to Adrian Woodhead, Marc de Palol, Joydeep Sen Sarma, Ashish Thusoo, Andrzej Białecki, Stu Hood, Chris K. Wensel, and Owen O'Malley for contributing case studies for Chapter 16.

I would like to thank the following reviewers who contributed many helpful suggestions and improvements to my drafts: Raghu Angadi, Matt Biddulph, Christophe Bisciglia, Ryan Cox, Devaraj Das, Alex Dorman, Chris Douglas, Alan Gates, Lars George, Patrick Hunt, Aaron Kimball, Peter Krey, Hairong Kuang, Simon Maxen, Olga Natkovich, Benjamin Reed, Konstantin Shvachko, Allen Wittenauer, Matei Zaharia, and Philip Zeyliger. Ajay Anand kept the review process flowing smoothly. Philip ("flip") Kromer kindly helped me with the NCDC weather dataset featured in the examples in this book. Special thanks to Owen O'Malley and Arun C. Murthy for explaining the intricacies of the MapReduce shuffle to me. Any errors that remain are, of course, to be laid at my door.

For the second edition, I owe a debt of gratitude for the detailed review and feedback from Jeff Bean, Doug Cutting, Glynn Durham, Alan Gates, Jeff Hammerbacher, Alex Kozlov, Ken Krugler, Jimmy Lin, Todd Lipcon, Sarah Sproehnle, Vinithra Varadharajan, and Ian Wrigley, as well as all the readers who submitted errata for the first edition. I would also like to thank Aaron Kimball for contributing the chapter on Sqoop, and Philip ("flip") Kromer for the case study on graph processing.

I am particularly grateful to Doug Cutting for his encouragement, support, and friendship, and for contributing the foreword.

Thanks also go to the many others with whom I have had conversations or email discussions over the course of writing the book.

Halfway through writing this book, I joined Cloudera, and I want to thank my colleagues for being incredibly supportive in allowing me the time to write, and to get it finished promptly.

I am grateful to my editor, Mike Loukides, and his colleagues at O'Reilly for their help in the preparation of this book. Mike has been there throughout to answer my questions, to read my first drafts, and to keep me on schedule.

Finally, the writing of this book has been a great deal of work, and I couldn't have done it without the constant support of my family. My wife, Eliane, not only kept the home going, but also stepped in to help review, edit, and chase case studies. My daughters, Emilia and Lottie, have been very understanding, and I'm looking forward to spending lots more time with all of them.

## CHAPTER 1

Meet Hadoop

In pioneer days they used oxen for heavy pulling, and when one ox couldn't budge a log, they didn't try to grow a larger ox. We shouldn't be trying for bigger computers, but for more systems of computers.

—Grace Hopper

Data!

We live in the data age. It's not easy to measure the total volume of data stored electronically, but an IDC estimate put the size of the "digital universe" at 0.18 zettabytes in 2006, and is forecasting a tenfold growth by 2011 to 1.8 zettabytes.[*] A zettabyte is 10^{21} bytes, or equivalently one thousand exabytes, one million petabytes, or one billion terabytes. That's roughly the same order of magnitude as one disk drive for every person in the world.

This flood of data is coming from many sources. Consider the following:[†]

- The New York Stock Exchange generates about one terabyte of new trade data per day.
- Facebook hosts approximately 10 billion photos, taking up one petabyte of storage.
- Ancestry.com, the genealogy site, stores around 2.5 petabytes of data.
- The Internet Archive stores around 2 petabytes of data, and is growing at a rate of 20 terabytes per month.
- The Large Hadron Collider near Geneva, Switzerland, will produce about 15 petabytes of data per year.

---

[*] From Gantz et al., "The Diverse and Exploding Digital Universe," March 2008 (*http://www.emc.com/collateral/analyst-reports/diverse-exploding-digital-universe.pdf*).

[†] *http://www.intelligententerprise.com/showArticle.jhtml?articleID=207800705*, *http://mashable.com/2008/10/15/facebook-10-billion-photos/*, *http://blog.familytreemagazine.com/insider/Inside+Ancestrycoms+TopSecret+Data+Center.aspx*, and *http://www.archive.org/about/faqs.php*, *http://www.interactions.org/cms/?pid=1027032*.

So there's a lot of data out there. But you are probably wondering how it affects you. Most of the data is locked up in the largest web properties (like search engines), or scientific or financial institutions, isn't it? Does the advent of "Big Data," as it is being called, affect smaller organizations or individuals?

I argue that it does. Take photos, for example. My wife's grandfather was an avid photographer, and took photographs throughout his adult life. His entire corpus of medium format, slide, and 35mm film, when scanned in at high-resolution, occupies around 10 gigabytes. Compare this to the digital photos that my family took in 2008, which take up about 5 gigabytes of space. My family is producing photographic data at 35 times the rate my wife's grandfather's did, and the rate is increasing every year as it becomes easier to take more and more photos.

More generally, the digital streams that individuals are producing are growing apace. Microsoft Research's MyLifeBits project (*http://research.microsoft.com/en-us/projects/mylifebits/default.aspx*) gives a glimpse of archiving of personal information that may become commonplace in the near future. MyLifeBits was an experiment where an individual's interactions—phone calls, emails, documents—were captured electronically and stored for later access. The data gathered included a photo taken every minute, which resulted in an overall data volume of one gigabyte a month. When storage costs come down enough to make it feasible to store continuous audio and video, the data volume for a future MyLifeBits service will be many times that.

The trend is for every individual's data footprint to grow, but perhaps more important, the amount of data generated by machines will be even greater than that generated by people. Machine logs, RFID readers, sensor networks, vehicle GPS traces, retail transactions—all of these contribute to the growing mountain of data.

The volume of data being made publicly available increases every year, too. Organizations no longer have to merely manage their own data: success in the future will be dictated to a large extent by their ability to extract value from other organizations' data.

Initiatives such as Public Data Sets on Amazon Web Services (*http://aws.amazon.com/publicdatasets/*), Infochimps.org (*http://infochimps.org/*), and theinfo.org (*http://theinfo.org/*) exist to foster the "information commons," where data can be freely (or in the case of AWS, for a modest price) shared for anyone to download and analyze. Mashups between different information sources make for unexpected and hitherto unimaginable applications.

Take, for example, the Astrometry.net (*http://astrometry.net/*) project, which watches the Astrometry group on Flickr for new photos of the night sky. It analyzes each image and identifies which part of the sky it is from, as well as any interesting celestial bodies, such as stars or galaxies. This project shows the kind of things that are possible when data (in this case, tagged photographic images) is made available and used for something (image analysis) that was not anticipated by the creator.

It has been said that "More data usually beats better algorithms," which is to say that for some problems (such as recommending movies or music based on past preferences), however fiendish your algorithms are, they can often be beaten simply by having more data (and a less sophisticated algorithm).[‡]

The good news is that Big Data is here. The bad news is that we are struggling to store and analyze it.

Data Storage and Analysis

The problem is simple: while the storage capacities of hard drives have increased massively over the years, access speeds—the rate at which data can be read from drives—have not kept up. One typical drive from 1990 could store 1,370 MB of data and had a transfer speed of 4.4 MB/s,[§] so you could read all the data from a full drive in around five minutes. Over 20 years later, one terabyte drives are the norm, but the transfer speed is around 100 MB/s, so it takes more than two and a half hours to read all the data off the disk.

This is a long time to read all data on a single drive—and writing is even slower. The obvious way to reduce the time is to read from multiple disks at once. Imagine if we had 100 drives, each holding one hundredth of the data. Working in parallel, we could read the data in under two minutes.

Only using one hundredth of a disk may seem wasteful. But we can store one hundred datasets, each of which is one terabyte, and provide shared access to them. We can imagine that the users of such a system would be happy to share access in return for shorter analysis times, and, statistically, that their analysis jobs would be likely to be spread over time, so they wouldn't interfere with each other too much.

There's more to being able to read and write data in parallel to or from multiple disks, though.

The first problem to solve is hardware failure: as soon as you start using many pieces of hardware, the chance that one will fail is fairly high. A common way of avoiding data loss is through replication: redundant copies of the data are kept by the system so that in the event of failure, there is another copy available. This is how RAID works, for instance, although Hadoop's filesystem, the Hadoop Distributed Filesystem (HDFS), takes a slightly different approach, as you shall see later.

The second problem is that most analysis tasks need to be able to combine the data in some way; data read from one disk may need to be combined with the data from any of the other 99 disks. Various distributed systems allow data to be combined from

---

‡ The quote is from Anand Rajaraman writing about the Netflix Challenge (*http://anand.typepad.com/datawocky/2008/03/more-data-usual.html*). Alon Halevy, Peter Norvig, and Fernando Pereira make the same point in "The Unreasonable Effectiveness of Data," IEEE Intelligent Systems, March/April 2009.

§ These specifications are for the Seagate ST-41600n.

multiple sources, but doing this correctly is notoriously challenging. MapReduce provides a programming model that abstracts the problem from disk reads and writes, transforming it into a computation over sets of keys and values. We will look at the details of this model in later chapters, but the important point for the present discussion is that there are two parts to the computation, the map and the reduce, and it's the interface between the two where the "mixing" occurs. Like HDFS, MapReduce has built-in reliability.

This, in a nutshell, is what Hadoop provides: a reliable shared storage and analysis system. The storage is provided by HDFS and analysis by MapReduce. There are other parts to Hadoop, but these capabilities are its kernel.

Comparison with Other Systems

The approach taken by MapReduce may seem like a brute-force approach. The premise is that the entire dataset—or at least a good portion of it—is processed for each query. But this is its power. MapReduce is a *batch* query processor, and the ability to run an ad hoc query against your whole dataset and get the results in a reasonable time is transformative. It changes the way you think about data, and unlocks data that was previously archived on tape or disk. It gives people the opportunity to innovate with data. Questions that took too long to get answered before can now be answered, which in turn leads to new questions and new insights.

For example, Mailtrust, Rackspace's mail division, used Hadoop for processing email logs. One ad hoc query they wrote was to find the geographic distribution of their users. In their words:

> This data was so useful that we've scheduled the MapReduce job to run monthly and we will be using this data to help us decide which Rackspace data centers to place new mail servers in as we grow.

By bringing several hundred gigabytes of data together and having the tools to analyze it, the Rackspace engineers were able to gain an understanding of the data that they otherwise would never have had, and, furthermore, they were able to use what they had learned to improve the service for their customers. You can read more about how Rackspace uses Hadoop in Chapter 16.

RDBMS

Why can't we use databases with lots of disks to do large-scale batch analysis? Why is MapReduce needed?

The answer to these questions comes from another trend in disk drives: seek time is improving more slowly than transfer rate. Seeking is the process of moving the disk's head to a particular place on the disk to read or write data. It characterizes the latency of a disk operation, whereas the transfer rate corresponds to a disk's bandwidth.

If the data access pattern is dominated by seeks, it will take longer to read or write large portions of the dataset than streaming through it, which operates at the transfer rate. On the other hand, for updating a small proportion of records in a database, a traditional B-Tree (the data structure used in relational databases, which is limited by the rate it can perform seeks) works well. For updating the majority of a database, a B-Tree is less efficient than MapReduce, which uses Sort/Merge to rebuild the database.

In many ways, MapReduce can be seen as a complement to an RDBMS. (The differences between the two systems are shown in Table 1-1.) MapReduce is a good fit for problems that need to analyze the whole dataset, in a batch fashion, particularly for ad hoc analysis. An RDBMS is good for point queries or updates, where the dataset has been indexed to deliver low-latency retrieval and update times of a relatively small amount of data. MapReduce suits applications where the data is written once, and read many times, whereas a relational database is good for datasets that are continually updated.

Table 1-1. RDBMS compared to MapReduce

	Traditional RDBMS	MapReduce
Data size	Gigabytes	Petabytes
Access	Interactive and batch	Batch
Updates	Read and write many times	Write once, read many times
Structure	Static schema	Dynamic schema
Integrity	High	Low
Scaling	Nonlinear	Linear

Another difference between MapReduce and an RDBMS is the amount of structure in the datasets that they operate on. *Structured data* is data that is organized into entities that have a defined format, such as XML documents or database tables that conform to a particular predefined schema. This is the realm of the RDBMS. *Semi-structured data*, on the other hand, is looser, and though there may be a schema, it is often ignored, so it may be used only as a guide to the structure of the data: for example, a spreadsheet, in which the structure is the grid of cells, although the cells themselves may hold any form of data. *Unstructured data* does not have any particular internal structure: for example, plain text or image data. MapReduce works well on unstructured or semi-structured data, since it is designed to interpret the data at processing time. In other words, the input keys and values for MapReduce are not an intrinsic property of the data, but they are chosen by the person analyzing the data.

Relational data is often *normalized* to retain its integrity and remove redundancy. Normalization poses problems for MapReduce, since it makes reading a record a non-local operation, and one of the central assumptions that MapReduce makes is that it is possible to perform (high-speed) streaming reads and writes.

A web server log is a good example of a set of records that is *not* normalized (for example, the client hostnames are specified in full each time, even though the same client may appear many times), and this is one reason that logfiles of all kinds are particularly well-suited to analysis with MapReduce.

MapReduce is a linearly scalable programming model. The programmer writes two functions—a map function and a reduce function—each of which defines a mapping from one set of key-value pairs to another. These functions are oblivious to the size of the data or the cluster that they are operating on, so they can be used unchanged for a small dataset and for a massive one. More important, if you double the size of the input data, a job will run twice as slow. But if you also double the size of the cluster, a job will run as fast as the original one. This is not generally true of SQL queries.

Over time, however, the differences between relational databases and MapReduce systems are likely to blur—both as relational databases start incorporating some of the ideas from MapReduce (such as Aster Data's and Greenplum's databases) and, from the other direction, as higher-level query languages built on MapReduce (such as Pig and Hive) make MapReduce systems more approachable to traditional database programmers.‖

Grid Computing

The High Performance Computing (HPC) and Grid Computing communities have been doing large-scale data processing for years, using such APIs as Message Passing Interface (MPI). Broadly, the approach in HPC is to distribute the work across a cluster of machines, which access a shared filesystem, hosted by a SAN. This works well for predominantly compute-intensive jobs, but becomes a problem when nodes need to access larger data volumes (hundreds of gigabytes, the point at which MapReduce really starts to shine), since the network bandwidth is the bottleneck and compute nodes become idle.

‖ In January 2007, David J. DeWitt and Michael Stonebraker caused a stir by publishing "MapReduce: A major step backwards" (*http://databasecolumn.vertica.com/database-innovation/mapreduce-a-major-step-backwards*), in which they criticized MapReduce for being a poor substitute for relational databases. Many commentators argued that it was a false comparison (see, for example, Mark C. Chu-Carroll's "Databases are hammers; MapReduce is a screwdriver," *http://scienceblogs.com/goodmath/2008/01/databases_are_hammers_mapreduc.php*), and DeWitt and Stonebraker followed up with "MapReduce II" (*http://databasecolumn.vertica.com/database-innovation/mapreduce-ii*), where they addressed the main topics brought up by others.

MapReduce tries to collocate the data with the compute node, so data access is fast since it is local.# This feature, known as *data locality*, is at the heart of MapReduce and is the reason for its good performance. Recognizing that network bandwidth is the most precious resource in a data center environment (it is easy to saturate network links by copying data around), MapReduce implementations go to great lengths to conserve it by explicitly modelling network topology. Notice that this arrangement does not preclude high-CPU analyses in MapReduce.

MPI gives great control to the programmer, but requires that he or she explicitly handle the mechanics of the data flow, exposed via low-level C routines and constructs, such as sockets, as well as the higher-level algorithm for the analysis. MapReduce operates only at the higher level: the programmer thinks in terms of functions of key and value pairs, and the data flow is implicit.

Coordinating the processes in a large-scale distributed computation is a challenge. The hardest aspect is gracefully handling partial failure—when you don't know if a remote process has failed or not—and still making progress with the overall computation. MapReduce spares the programmer from having to think about failure, since the implementation detects failed map or reduce tasks and reschedules replacements on machines that are healthy. MapReduce is able to do this since it is a *shared-nothing* architecture, meaning that tasks have no dependence on one other. (This is a slight oversimplification, since the output from mappers is fed to the reducers, but this is under the control of the MapReduce system; in this case, it needs to take more care rerunning a failed reducer than rerunning a failed map, since it has to make sure it can retrieve the necessary map outputs, and if not, regenerate them by running the relevant maps again.) So from the programmer's point of view, the order in which the tasks run doesn't matter. By contrast, MPI programs have to explicitly manage their own checkpointing and recovery, which gives more control to the programmer, but makes them more difficult to write.

MapReduce might sound like quite a restrictive programming model, and in a sense it is: you are limited to key and value types that are related in specified ways, and mappers and reducers run with very limited coordination between one another (the mappers pass keys and values to reducers). A natural question to ask is: can you do anything useful or nontrivial with it?

The answer is yes. MapReduce was invented by engineers at Google as a system for building production search indexes because they found themselves solving the same problem over and over again (and MapReduce was inspired by older ideas from the functional programming, distributed computing, and database communities), but it has since been used for many other applications in many other industries. It is pleasantly surprising to see the range of algorithms that can be expressed in MapReduce, from

---

\# Jim Gray was an early advocate of putting the computation near the data. See "Distributed Computing Economics," March 2003, *http://research.microsoft.com/apps/pubs/default.aspx?id=70001*.

image analysis, to graph-based problems, to machine learning algorithms.* It can't solve every problem, of course, but it is a general data-processing tool.

You can see a sample of some of the applications that Hadoop has been used for in Chapter 16.

Volunteer Computing

When people first hear about Hadoop and MapReduce, they often ask, "How is it different from SETI@home?" SETI, the Search for Extra-Terrestrial Intelligence, runs a project called SETI@home (*http://setiathome.berkeley.edu/*) in which volunteers donate CPU time from their otherwise idle computers to analyze radio telescope data for signs of intelligent life outside earth. SETI@home is the most well-known of many *volunteer computing* projects; others include the Great Internet Mersenne Prime Search (to search for large prime numbers) and Folding@home (to understand protein folding and how it relates to disease).

Volunteer computing projects work by breaking the problem they are trying to solve into chunks called *work units*, which are sent to computers around the world to be analyzed. For example, a SETI@home work unit is about 0.35 MB of radio telescope data, and takes hours or days to analyze on a typical home computer. When the analysis is completed, the results are sent back to the server, and the client gets another work unit. As a precaution to combat cheating, each work unit is sent to three different machines and needs at least two results to agree to be accepted.

Although SETI@home may be superficially similar to MapReduce (breaking a problem into independent pieces to be worked on in parallel), there are some significant differences. The SETI@home problem is very CPU-intensive, which makes it suitable for running on hundreds of thousands of computers across the world,† since the time to transfer the work unit is dwarfed by the time to run the computation on it. Volunteers are donating CPU cycles, not bandwidth.

MapReduce is designed to run jobs that last minutes or hours on trusted, dedicated hardware running in a single data center with very high aggregate bandwidth interconnects. By contrast, SETI@home runs a perpetual computation on untrusted machines on the Internet with highly variable connection speeds and no data locality.

---

* Apache Mahout (*http://mahout.apache.org/*) is a project to build machine learning libraries (such as classification and clustering algorithms) that run on Hadoop.

† In January 2008, SETI@home was reported at *http://www.planetary.org/programs/projects/setiathome/ setiathome_20080115.html* to be processing 300 gigabytes a day, using 320,000 computers (most of which are not dedicated to SETI@home; they are used for other things, too).

A Brief History of Hadoop

Hadoop was created by Doug Cutting, the creator of Apache Lucene, the widely used text search library. Hadoop has its origins in Apache Nutch, an open source web search engine, itself a part of the Lucene project.

The Origin of the Name "Hadoop"

The name Hadoop is not an acronym; it's a made-up name. The project's creator, Doug Cutting, explains how the name came about:

> The name my kid gave a stuffed yellow elephant. Short, relatively easy to spell and pronounce, meaningless, and not used elsewhere: those are my naming criteria. Kids are good at generating such. Googol is a kid's term.

Subprojects and "contrib" modules in Hadoop also tend to have names that are unrelated to their function, often with an elephant or other animal theme ("Pig," for example). Smaller components are given more descriptive (and therefore more mundane) names. This is a good principle, as it means you can generally work out what something does from its name. For example, the jobtracker[‡] keeps track of MapReduce jobs.

Building a web search engine from scratch was an ambitious goal, for not only is the software required to crawl and index websites complex to write, but it is also a challenge to run without a dedicated operations team, since there are so many moving parts. It's expensive, too: Mike Cafarella and Doug Cutting estimated a system supporting a 1-billion-page index would cost around half a million dollars in hardware, with a monthly running cost of \$30,000.[§] Nevertheless, they believed it was a worthy goal, as it would open up and ultimately democratize search engine algorithms.

Nutch was started in 2002, and a working crawler and search system quickly emerged. However, they realized that their architecture wouldn't scale to the billions of pages on the Web. Help was at hand with the publication of a paper in 2003 that described the architecture of Google's distributed filesystem, called GFS, which was being used in production at Google.[‖] GFS, or something like it, would solve their storage needs for the very large files generated as a part of the web crawl and indexing process. In particular, GFS would free up time being spent on administrative tasks such as managing storage nodes. In 2004, they set about writing an open source implementation, the Nutch Distributed Filesystem (NDFS).

[‡] In this book, we use the lowercase form, "jobtracker," to denote the entity when it's being referred to generally, and the CamelCase form `JobTracker` to denote the Java class that implements it.

[§] Mike Cafarella and Doug Cutting, "Building Nutch: Open Source Search," *ACM Queue*, April 2004, *http://queue.acm.org/detail.cfm?id=988408*.

[‖] Sanjay Ghemawat, Howard Gobioff, and Shun-Tak Leung, "The Google File System," October 2003, *http://labs.google.com/papers/gfs.html*.

In 2004, Google published the paper that introduced MapReduce to the world.[#] Early in 2005, the Nutch developers had a working MapReduce implementation in Nutch, and by the middle of that year all the major Nutch algorithms had been ported to run using MapReduce and NDFS.

NDFS and the MapReduce implementation in Nutch were applicable beyond the realm of search, and in February 2006 they moved out of Nutch to form an independent subproject of Lucene called Hadoop. At around the same time, Doug Cutting joined Yahoo!, which provided a dedicated team and the resources to turn Hadoop into a system that ran at web scale (see sidebar). This was demonstrated in February 2008 when Yahoo! announced that its production search index was being generated by a 10,000-core Hadoop cluster.[*]

In January 2008, Hadoop was made its own top-level project at Apache, confirming its success and its diverse, active community. By this time, Hadoop was being used by many other companies besides Yahoo!, such as Last.fm, Facebook, and the *New York Times*. Some applications are covered in the case studies in Chapter 16 and on the Hadoop wiki (*http://wiki.apache.org/hadoop/PoweredBy*).

In one well-publicized feat, the *New York Times* used Amazon's EC2 compute cloud to crunch through four terabytes of scanned archives from the paper converting them to PDFs for the Web.[†] The processing took less than 24 hours to run using 100 machines, and the project probably wouldn't have been embarked on without the combination of Amazon's pay-by-the-hour model (which allowed the NYT to access a large number of machines for a short period) and Hadoop's easy-to-use parallel programming model.

In April 2008, Hadoop broke a world record to become the fastest system to sort a terabyte of data. Running on a 910-node cluster, Hadoop sorted one terabyte in 209 seconds (just under 3½ minutes), beating the previous year's winner of 297 seconds (described in detail in "TeraByte Sort on Apache Hadoop" on page 553). In November of the same year, Google reported that its MapReduce implementation sorted one terabyte in 68 seconds.[‡] As the first edition of this book was going to press (May 2009), it was announced that a team at Yahoo! used Hadoop to sort one terabyte in 62 seconds.

[#] Jeffrey Dean and Sanjay Ghemawat, "MapReduce: Simplified Data Processing on Large Clusters," December 2004, *http://labs.google.com/papers/mapreduce.html*.

[*] "Yahoo! Launches World's Largest Hadoop Production Application," 19 February 2008, *http://developer .yahoo.net/blogs/hadoop/2008/02/yahoo-worlds-largest-production-hadoop.html*.

[†] Derek Gottfrid, "Self-service, Prorated Super Computing Fun!" 1 November 2007, *http://open.blogs.nytimes .com/2007/11/01/self-service-prorated-super-computing-fun/*.

[‡] "Sorting 1PB with MapReduce," 21 November 2008, *http://googleblog.blogspot.com/2008/11/sorting-1pb -with-mapreduce.html*.

Hadoop at Yahoo!

Building Internet-scale search engines requires huge amounts of data and therefore large numbers of machines to process it. Yahoo! Search consists of four primary components: the *Crawler*, which downloads pages from web servers; the *WebMap*, which builds a graph of the known Web; the *Indexer*, which builds a reverse index to the best pages; and the *Runtime*, which answers users' queries. The WebMap is a graph that consists of roughly 1 trillion (10^{12}) edges each representing a web link and 100 billion (10^{11}) nodes each representing distinct URLs. Creating and analyzing such a large graph requires a large number of computers running for many days. In early 2005, the infrastructure for the WebMap, named *Dreadnaught*, needed to be redesigned to scale up to more nodes. Dreadnaught had successfully scaled from 20 to 600 nodes, but required a complete redesign to scale out further. Dreadnaught is similar to MapReduce in many ways, but provides more flexibility and less structure. In particular, each fragment in a Dreadnaught job can send output to each of the fragments in the next stage of the job, but the sort was all done in library code. In practice, most of the WebMap phases were pairs that corresponded to MapReduce. Therefore, the WebMap applications would not require extensive refactoring to fit into MapReduce.

Eric Baldeschwieler (Eric14) created a small team and we started designing and prototyping a new framework written in C++ modeled after GFS and MapReduce to replace Dreadnaught. Although the immediate need was for a new framework for WebMap, it was clear that standardization of the batch platform across Yahoo! Search was critical and by making the framework general enough to support other users, we could better leverage investment in the new platform.

At the same time, we were watching Hadoop, which was part of Nutch, and its progress. In January 2006, Yahoo! hired Doug Cutting, and a month later we decided to abandon our prototype and adopt Hadoop. The advantage of Hadoop over our prototype and design was that it was already working with a real application (Nutch) on 20 nodes. That allowed us to bring up a research cluster two months later and start helping real customers use the new framework much sooner than we could have otherwise. Another advantage, of course, was that since Hadoop was already open source, it was easier (although far from easy!) to get permission from Yahoo!'s legal department to work in open source. So we set up a 200-node cluster for the researchers in early 2006 and put the WebMap conversion plans on hold while we supported and improved Hadoop for the research users.

Here's a quick timeline of how things have progressed:

- 2004—Initial versions of what is now Hadoop Distributed Filesystem and MapReduce implemented by Doug Cutting and Mike Cafarella.
- December 2005—Nutch ported to the new framework. Hadoop runs reliably on 20 nodes.
- January 2006—Doug Cutting joins Yahoo!.
- February 2006—Apache Hadoop project officially started to support the standalone development of MapReduce and HDFS.

- February 2006—Adoption of Hadoop by Yahoo! Grid team.
- April 2006—Sort benchmark (10 GB/node) run on 188 nodes in 47.9 hours.
- May 2006—Yahoo! set up a Hadoop research cluster—300 nodes.
- May 2006—Sort benchmark run on 500 nodes in 42 hours (better hardware than April benchmark).
- October 2006—Research cluster reaches 600 nodes.
- December 2006—Sort benchmark run on 20 nodes in 1.8 hours, 100 nodes in 3.3 hours, 500 nodes in 5.2 hours, 900 nodes in 7.8 hours.
- January 2007—Research cluster reaches 900 nodes.
- April 2007—Research clusters—2 clusters of 1000 nodes.
- April 2008—Won the 1 terabyte sort benchmark in 209 seconds on 900 nodes.
- October 2008—Loading 10 terabytes of data per day on to research clusters.
- March 2009—17 clusters with a total of 24,000 nodes.
- April 2009—Won the minute sort by sorting 500 GB in 59 seconds (on 1,400 nodes) and the 100 terabyte sort in 173 minutes (on 3,400 nodes).

—Owen O'Malley

Apache Hadoop and the Hadoop Ecosystem

Although Hadoop is best known for MapReduce and its distributed filesystem (HDFS, renamed from NDFS), the term is also used for a family of related projects that fall under the umbrella of infrastructure for distributed computing and large-scale data processing.

Most of the core projects covered in this book are hosted by the Apache Software Foundation (*http://hadoop.apache.org/*), which provides support for a community of open source software projects, including the original HTTP Server from which it gets its name. As the Hadoop ecosystem grows, more projects are appearing, not necessarily hosted at Apache, which provide complementary services to Hadoop, or build on the core to add higher-level abstractions.

The Hadoop projects that are covered in this book are described briefly here:

Common
   A set of components and interfaces for distributed filesystems and general I/O (serialization, Java RPC, persistent data structures).

Avro
   A serialization system for efficient, cross-language RPC, and persistent data storage.

MapReduce
   A distributed data processing model and execution environment that runs on large clusters of commodity machines.

HDFS

A distributed filesystem that runs on large clusters of commodity machines.

Pig

A data flow language and execution environment for exploring very large datasets. Pig runs on HDFS and MapReduce clusters.

Hive

A distributed data warehouse. Hive manages data stored in HDFS and provides a query language based on SQL (and which is translated by the runtime engine to MapReduce jobs) for querying the data.

HBase

A distributed, column-oriented database. HBase uses HDFS for its underlying storage, and supports both batch-style computations using MapReduce and point queries (random reads).

ZooKeeper

A distributed, highly available coordination service. ZooKeeper provides primitives such as distributed locks that can be used for building distributed applications.

Sqoop

A tool for efficiently moving data between relational databases and HDFS.

## CHAPTER 2

MapReduce

MapReduce is a programming model for data processing. The model is simple, yet not too simple to express useful programs in. Hadoop can run MapReduce programs written in various languages; in this chapter, we shall look at the same program expressed in Java, Ruby, Python, and C++. Most important, MapReduce programs are inherently parallel, thus putting very large-scale data analysis into the hands of anyone with enough machines at their disposal. MapReduce comes into its own for large datasets, so let's start by looking at one.

A Weather Dataset

For our example, we will write a program that mines weather data. Weather sensors collecting data every hour at many locations across the globe gather a large volume of log data, which is a good candidate for analysis with MapReduce, since it is semi-structured and record-oriented.

Data Format

The data we will use is from the National Climatic Data Center (NCDC, *http://www .ncdc.noaa.gov/*). The data is stored using a line-oriented ASCII format, in which each line is a record. The format supports a rich set of meteorological elements, many of which are optional or with variable data lengths. For simplicity, we shall focus on the basic elements, such as temperature, which are always present and are of fixed width.

Example 2-1 shows a sample line with some of the salient fields highlighted. The line has been split into multiple lines to show each field: in the real file, fields are packed into one line with no delimiters.

Example 2-1. Format of a National Climate Data Center record

```
0057
332130  # USAF weather station identifier
99999   # WBAN weather station identifier
19500101 # observation date
0300    # observation time
4
+51317  # latitude (degrees x 1000)
+028783 # longitude (degrees x 1000)
FM-12
+0171   # elevation (meters)
99999
V020
320     # wind direction (degrees)
1       # quality code
N
0072
1
00450   # sky ceiling height (meters)
1       # quality code
C
N
010000  # visibility distance (meters)
1       # quality code
N
9
-0128   # air temperature (degrees Celsius x 10)
1       # quality code
-0139   # dew point temperature (degrees Celsius x 10)
1       # quality code
10268   # atmospheric pressure (hectopascals x 10)
1       # quality code
```

Data files are organized by date and weather station. There is a directory for each year from 1901 to 2001, each containing a gzipped file for each weather station with its readings for that year. For example, here are the first entries for 1990:

```
% ls raw/1990 | head
010010-99999-1990.gz
010014-99999-1990.gz
010015-99999-1990.gz
010016-99999-1990.gz
010017-99999-1990.gz
010030-99999-1990.gz
010040-99999-1990.gz
010080-99999-1990.gz
010100-99999-1990.gz
010150-99999-1990.gz
```

Since there are tens of thousands of weather stations, the whole dataset is made up of a large number of relatively small files. It's generally easier and more efficient to process a smaller number of relatively large files, so the data was preprocessed so that each year's readings were concatenated into a single file. (The means by which this was carried out is described in Appendix C.)

Analyzing the Data with Unix Tools

What's the highest recorded global temperature for each year in the dataset? We will answer this first without using Hadoop, as this information will provide a performance baseline, as well as a useful means to check our results.

The classic tool for processing line-oriented data is *awk*. Example 2-2 is a small script to calculate the maximum temperature for each year.

Example 2-2. A program for finding the maximum recorded temperature by year from NCDC weather records

```
#!/usr/bin/env bash
for year in all/*
do
  echo -ne `basename $year .gz`"\t"
  gunzip -c $year | \
    awk '{ temp = substr($0, 88, 5) + 0;
           q = substr($0, 93, 1);
           if (temp !=9999 && q ~ /[01459]/ && temp > max) max = temp }
         END { print max }'
done
```

The script loops through the compressed year files, first printing the year, and then processing each file using *awk*. The *awk* script extracts two fields from the data: the air temperature and the quality code. The air temperature value is turned into an integer by adding 0. Next, a test is applied to see if the temperature is valid (the value 9999 signifies a missing value in the NCDC dataset) and if the quality code indicates that the reading is not suspect or erroneous. If the reading is OK, the value is compared with the maximum value seen so far, which is updated if a new maximum is found. The END block is executed after all the lines in the file have been processed, and it prints the maximum value.

Here is the beginning of a run:

```
% ./max_temperature.sh
1901    317
1902    244
1903    289
1904    256
1905    283
...
```

The temperature values in the source file are scaled by a factor of 10, so this works out as a maximum temperature of 31.7°C for 1901 (there were very few readings at the beginning of the century, so this is plausible). The complete run for the century took 42 minutes in one run on a single EC2 High-CPU Extra Large Instance.

To speed up the processing, we need to run parts of the program in parallel. In theory, this is straightforward: we could process different years in different processes, using all the available hardware threads on a machine. There are a few problems with this, however.

First, dividing the work into equal-size pieces isn't always easy or obvious. In this case, the file size for different years varies widely, so some processes will finish much earlier than others. Even if they pick up further work, the whole run is dominated by the longest file. A better approach, although one that requires more work, is to split the input into fixed-size chunks and assign each chunk to a process.

Second, combining the results from independent processes may need further processing. In this case, the result for each year is independent of other years and may be combined by concatenating all the results, and sorting by year. If using the fixed-size chunk approach, the combination is more delicate. For this example, data for a particular year will typically be split into several chunks, each processed independently. We'll end up with the maximum temperature for each chunk, so the final step is to look for the highest of these maximums, for each year.

Third, you are still limited by the processing capacity of a single machine. If the best time you can achieve is 20 minutes with the number of processors you have, then that's it. You can't make it go faster. Also, some datasets grow beyond the capacity of a single machine. When we start using multiple machines, a whole host of other factors come into play, mainly falling in the category of coordination and reliability. Who runs the overall job? How do we deal with failed processes?

So, though it's feasible to parallelize the processing, in practice it's messy. Using a framework like Hadoop to take care of these issues is a great help.

Analyzing the Data with Hadoop

To take advantage of the parallel processing that Hadoop provides, we need to express our query as a MapReduce job. After some local, small-scale testing, we will be able to run it on a cluster of machines.

Map and Reduce

MapReduce works by breaking the processing into two phases: the map phase and the reduce phase. Each phase has key-value pairs as input and output, the types of which may be chosen by the programmer. The programmer also specifies two functions: the map function and the reduce function.

The input to our map phase is the raw NCDC data. We choose a text input format that gives us each line in the dataset as a text value. The key is the offset of the beginning of the line from the beginning of the file, but as we have no need for this, we ignore it.

Our map function is simple. We pull out the year and the air temperature, since these are the only fields we are interested in. In this case, the map function is just a data preparation phase, setting up the data in such a way that the reducer function can do its work on it: finding the maximum temperature for each year. The map function is also a good place to drop bad records: here we filter out temperatures that are missing, suspect, or erroneous.

To visualize the way the map works, consider the following sample lines of input data (some unused columns have been dropped to fit the page, indicated by ellipses):

```
0067011990999991950051507004...9999999N9+00001+99999999999...
0043011990999991950051512004...9999999N9+00221+99999999999...
0043011990999991950051518004...9999999N9-00111+99999999999...
0043012650999991949032412004...0500001N9+01111+99999999999...
0043012650999991949032418004...0500001N9+00781+99999999999...
```

These lines are presented to the map function as the key-value pairs:

```
(0, 0067011990999991950051507004...9999999N9+00001+99999999999...)
(106, 0043011990999991950051512004...9999999N9+00221+99999999999...)
(212, 0043011990999991950051518004...9999999N9-00111+99999999999...)
(318, 0043012650999991949032412004...0500001N9+01111+99999999999...)
(424, 0043012650999991949032418004...0500001N9+00781+99999999999...)
```

The keys are the line offsets within the file, which we ignore in our map function. The map function merely extracts the year and the air temperature (indicated in bold text), and emits them as its output (the temperature values have been interpreted as integers):

```
(1950, 0)
(1950, 22)
(1950, -11)
(1949, 111)
(1949, 78)
```

The output from the map function is processed by the MapReduce framework before being sent to the reduce function. This processing sorts and groups the key-value pairs by key. So, continuing the example, our reduce function sees the following input:

```
(1949, [111, 78])
(1950, [0, 22, -11])
```

Each year appears with a list of all its air temperature readings. All the reduce function has to do now is iterate through the list and pick up the maximum reading:

```
(1949, 111)
(1950, 22)
```

This is the final output: the maximum global temperature recorded in each year.

The whole data flow is illustrated in Figure 2-1. At the bottom of the diagram is a Unix pipeline, which mimics the whole MapReduce flow, and which we will see again later in the chapter when we look at Hadoop Streaming.

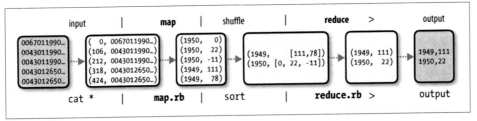

Figure 2-1. MapReduce logical data flow

Java MapReduce

Having run through how the MapReduce program works, the next step is to express it in code. We need three things: a map function, a reduce function, and some code to run the job. The map function is represented by an implementation of the Mapper interface, which declares a map() method. Example 2-3 shows the implementation of our map function.

Example 2-3. Mapper for maximum temperature example

```java
import java.io.IOException;

import org.apache.hadoop.io.IntWritable;
import org.apache.hadoop.io.LongWritable;
import org.apache.hadoop.io.Text;
import org.apache.hadoop.mapred.MapReduceBase;
import org.apache.hadoop.mapred.Mapper;
import org.apache.hadoop.mapred.OutputCollector;
import org.apache.hadoop.mapred.Reporter;

public class MaxTemperatureMapper extends MapReduceBase
  implements Mapper<LongWritable, Text, Text, IntWritable> {

  private static final int MISSING = 9999;

  public void map(LongWritable key, Text value,
      OutputCollector<Text, IntWritable> output, Reporter reporter)
      throws IOException {

    String line = value.toString();
    String year = line.substring(15, 19);
    int airTemperature;
    if (line.charAt(87) == '+') { // parseInt doesn't like leading plus signs
      airTemperature = Integer.parseInt(line.substring(88, 92));
    } else {
      airTemperature = Integer.parseInt(line.substring(87, 92));
    }
    String quality = line.substring(92, 93);
    if (airTemperature != MISSING && quality.matches("[01459]")) {
      output.collect(new Text(year), new IntWritable(airTemperature));
    }
  }
}
```

The Mapper interface is a generic type, with four formal type parameters that specify the input key, input value, output key, and output value types of the map function. For the present example, the input key is a long integer offset, the input value is a line of text, the output key is a year, and the output value is an air temperature (an integer). Rather than use built-in Java types, Hadoop provides its own set of basic types that are optimized for network serialization. These are found in the org.apache.hadoop.io package. Here we use LongWritable, which corresponds to a Java Long, Text (like Java String), and IntWritable (like Java Integer).

The map() method is passed a key and a value. We convert the Text value containing the line of input into a Java String, then use its substring() method to extract the columns we are interested in.

The map() method also provides an instance of OutputCollector to write the output to. In this case, we write the year as a Text object (since we are just using it as a key), and the temperature is wrapped in an IntWritable. We write an output record only if the temperature is present and the quality code indicates the temperature reading is OK.

The reduce function is similarly defined using a Reducer, as illustrated in Example 2-4.

Example 2-4. Reducer for maximum temperature example

```
import java.io.IOException;
import java.util.Iterator;

import org.apache.hadoop.io.IntWritable;
import org.apache.hadoop.io.Text;
import org.apache.hadoop.mapred.MapReduceBase;
import org.apache.hadoop.mapred.OutputCollector;
import org.apache.hadoop.mapred.Reducer;
import org.apache.hadoop.mapred.Reporter;

public class MaxTemperatureReducer extends MapReduceBase
  implements Reducer<Text, IntWritable, Text, IntWritable> {

  public void reduce(Text key, Iterator<IntWritable> values,
      OutputCollector<Text, IntWritable> output, Reporter reporter)
      throws IOException {

    int maxValue = Integer.MIN_VALUE;
    while (values.hasNext()) {
      maxValue = Math.max(maxValue, values.next().get());
    }
    output.collect(key, new IntWritable(maxValue));
  }
}
```

Again, four formal type parameters are used to specify the input and output types, this time for the reduce function. The input types of the reduce function must match the output types of the map function: Text and IntWritable. And in this case, the output types of the reduce function are Text and IntWritable, for a year and its maximum temperature, which we find by iterating through the temperatures and comparing each with a record of the highest found so far.

The third piece of code runs the MapReduce job (see Example 2-5).

Example 2-5. Application to find the maximum temperature in the weather dataset

```java
import java.io.IOException;

import org.apache.hadoop.fs.Path;
import org.apache.hadoop.io.IntWritable;
import org.apache.hadoop.io.Text;
import org.apache.hadoop.mapred.FileInputFormat;
import org.apache.hadoop.mapred.FileOutputFormat;
import org.apache.hadoop.mapred.JobClient;
import org.apache.hadoop.mapred.JobConf;

public class MaxTemperature {

  public static void main(String[] args) throws IOException {
    if (args.length != 2) {
      System.err.println("Usage: MaxTemperature <input path> <output path>");
      System.exit(-1);
    }

    JobConf conf = new JobConf(MaxTemperature.class);
    conf.setJobName("Max temperature");

    FileInputFormat.addInputPath(conf, new Path(args[0]));
    FileOutputFormat.setOutputPath(conf, new Path(args[1]));

    conf.setMapperClass(MaxTemperatureMapper.class);
    conf.setReducerClass(MaxTemperatureReducer.class);

    conf.setOutputKeyClass(Text.class);
    conf.setOutputValueClass(IntWritable.class);

    JobClient.runJob(conf);
  }
}
```

A JobConf object forms the specification of the job. It gives you control over how the job is run. When we run this job on a Hadoop cluster, we will package the code into a JAR file (which Hadoop will distribute around the cluster). Rather than explicitly specify the name of the JAR file, we can pass a class in the JobConf constructor, which Hadoop will use to locate the relevant JAR file by looking for the JAR file containing this class.

Having constructed a JobConf object, we specify the input and output paths. An input path is specified by calling the static addInputPath() method on FileInputFormat, and it can be a single file, a directory (in which case, the input forms all the files in that directory), or a file pattern. As the name suggests, addInputPath() can be called more than once to use input from multiple paths.

The output path (of which there is only one) is specified by the static setOutput Path() method on FileOutputFormat. It specifies a directory where the output files from the reducer functions are written. The directory shouldn't exist before running the job, as Hadoop will complain and not run the job. This precaution is to prevent data loss (it can be very annoying to accidentally overwrite the output of a long job with another).

Next, we specify the map and reduce types to use via the setMapperClass() and setReducerClass() methods.

The setOutputKeyClass() and setOutputValueClass() methods control the output types for the map and the reduce functions, which are often the same, as they are in our case. If they are different, then the map output types can be set using the methods setMapOutputKeyClass() and setMapOutputValueClass().

The input types are controlled via the input format, which we have not explicitly set since we are using the default TextInputFormat.

After setting the classes that define the map and reduce functions, we are ready to run the job. The static runJob() method on JobClient submits the job and waits for it to finish, writing information about its progress to the console.

A test run

After writing a MapReduce job, it's normal to try it out on a small dataset to flush out any immediate problems with the code. First install Hadoop in standalone mode— there are instructions for how to do this in Appendix A. This is the mode in which Hadoop runs using the local filesystem with a local job runner. Let's test it on the five-line sample discussed earlier (the output has been slightly reformatted to fit the page):

```
% export HADOOP_CLASSPATH=build/classes
% hadoop MaxTemperature input/ncdc/sample.txt output
09/04/07 12:34:35 INFO jvm.JvmMetrics: Initializing JVM Metrics with processName=Job
Tracker, sessionId=
09/04/07 12:34:35 WARN mapred.JobClient: Use GenericOptionsParser for parsing the
arguments. Applications should implement Tool for the same.
09/04/07 12:34:35 WARN mapred.JobClient: No job jar file set.  User classes may not
be found. See JobConf(Class) or JobConf#setJar(String).
09/04/07 12:34:35 INFO mapred.FileInputFormat: Total input paths to process : 1
09/04/07 12:34:35 INFO mapred.JobClient: Running job: job_local_0001
09/04/07 12:34:35 INFO mapred.FileInputFormat: Total input paths to process : 1
09/04/07 12:34:35 INFO mapred.MapTask: numReduceTasks: 1
09/04/07 12:34:35 INFO mapred.MapTask: io.sort.mb = 100
09/04/07 12:34:35 INFO mapred.MapTask: data buffer = 79691776/99614720
09/04/07 12:34:35 INFO mapred.MapTask: record buffer = 262144/327680
09/04/07 12:34:35 INFO mapred.MapTask: Starting flush of map output
09/04/07 12:34:36 INFO mapred.MapTask: Finished spill 0
09/04/07 12:34:36 INFO mapred.TaskRunner: Task:attempt_local_0001_m_000000_0 is
done. And is in the process of commiting
09/04/07 12:34:36 INFO mapred.LocalJobRunner: file:/Users/tom/workspace/htdg/input/n
cdc/sample.txt:0+529
09/04/07 12:34:36 INFO mapred.TaskRunner: Task 'attempt_local_0001_m_000000_0' done.
```

```
09/04/07 12:34:36 INFO mapred.LocalJobRunner:
09/04/07 12:34:36 INFO mapred.Merger: Merging 1 sorted segments
09/04/07 12:34:36 INFO mapred.Merger: Down to the last merge-pass, with 1 segments
left of total size: 57 bytes
09/04/07 12:34:36 INFO mapred.LocalJobRunner:
09/04/07 12:34:36 INFO mapred.TaskRunner: Task:attempt_local_0001_r_000000_0 is done.
And is in the process of commiting
09/04/07 12:34:36 INFO mapred.LocalJobRunner:
09/04/07 12:34:36 INFO mapred.TaskRunner: Task attempt_local_0001_r_000000_0 is
allowed to commit now
09/04/07 12:34:36 INFO mapred.FileOutputCommitter: Saved output of task
'attempt_local_0001_r_000000_0' to file:/Users/tom/workspace/htdg/output
09/04/07 12:34:36 INFO mapred.LocalJobRunner: reduce > reduce
09/04/07 12:34:36 INFO mapred.TaskRunner: Task 'attempt_local_0001_r_000000_0' done.
09/04/07 12:34:36 INFO mapred.JobClient:  map 100% reduce 100%
09/04/07 12:34:36 INFO mapred.JobClient: Job complete: job_local_0001
09/04/07 12:34:36 INFO mapred.JobClient: Counters: 13
09/04/07 12:34:36 INFO mapred.JobClient:   FileSystemCounters
09/04/07 12:34:36 INFO mapred.JobClient:     FILE_BYTES_READ=27571
09/04/07 12:34:36 INFO mapred.JobClient:     FILE_BYTES_WRITTEN=53907
09/04/07 12:34:36 INFO mapred.JobClient:   Map-Reduce Framework
09/04/07 12:34:36 INFO mapred.JobClient:     Reduce input groups=2
09/04/07 12:34:36 INFO mapred.JobClient:     Combine output records=0
09/04/07 12:34:36 INFO mapred.JobClient:     Map input records=5
09/04/07 12:34:36 INFO mapred.JobClient:     Reduce shuffle bytes=0
09/04/07 12:34:36 INFO mapred.JobClient:     Reduce output records=2
09/04/07 12:34:36 INFO mapred.JobClient:     Spilled Records=10
09/04/07 12:34:36 INFO mapred.JobClient:     Map output bytes=45
09/04/07 12:34:36 INFO mapred.JobClient:     Map input bytes=529
09/04/07 12:34:36 INFO mapred.JobClient:     Combine input records=0
09/04/07 12:34:36 INFO mapred.JobClient:     Map output records=5
09/04/07 12:34:36 INFO mapred.JobClient:     Reduce input records=5
```

When the hadoop command is invoked with a classname as the first argument, it launches a JVM to run the class. It is more convenient to use hadoop than straight java since the former adds the Hadoop libraries (and their dependencies) to the classpath and picks up the Hadoop configuration, too. To add the application classes to the classpath, we've defined an environment variable called HADOOP_CLASSPATH, which the hadoop script picks up.

When running in local (standalone) mode, the programs in this book all assume that you have set the HADOOP_CLASSPATH in this way. The commands should be run from the directory that the example code is installed in.

The output from running the job provides some useful information. (The warning about the job JAR file not being found is expected, since we are running in local mode without a JAR. We won't see this warning when we run on a cluster.) For example, we can see that the job was given an ID of job_local_0001, and it ran one map task and one reduce task (with the IDs attempt_local_0001_m_000000_0 and attempt_local_0001_r_000000_0). Knowing the job and task IDs can be very useful when debugging MapReduce jobs.

The last section of the output, titled "Counters," shows the statistics that Hadoop generates for each job it runs. These are very useful for checking whether the amount of data processed is what you expected. For example, we can follow the number of records that went through the system: five map inputs produced five map outputs, then five reduce inputs in two groups produced two reduce outputs.

The output was written to the *output* directory, which contains one output file per reducer. The job had a single reducer, so we find a single file, named *part-00000*:

```
% cat output/part-00000
1949    111
1950    22
```

This result is the same as when we went through it by hand earlier. We interpret this as saying that the maximum temperature recorded in 1949 was 11.1°C, and in 1950 it was 2.2°C.

The new Java MapReduce API

Release 0.20.0 of Hadoop included a new Java MapReduce API, sometimes referred to as "Context Objects," designed to make the API easier to evolve in the future. The new API is type-incompatible with the old, however, so applications need to be rewritten to take advantage of it.[*]

There are several notable differences between the two APIs:

- The new API favors abstract classes over interfaces, since these are easier to evolve. For example, you can add a method (with a default implementation) to an abstract class without breaking old implementations of the class. In the new API, the Mapper and Reducer interfaces are now abstract classes.

- The new API is in the org.apache.hadoop.mapreduce package (and subpackages). The old API can still be found in org.apache.hadoop.mapred.

- The new API makes extensive use of context objects that allow the user code to communicate with the MapReduce system. The MapContext, for example, essentially unifies the role of the JobConf, the OutputCollector, and the Reporter.

- The new API supports both a "push" and a "pull" style of iteration. In both APIs, key-value record pairs are pushed to the mapper, but in addition, the new API allows a mapper to pull records from within the map() method. The same goes for the reducer. An example of how the "pull" style can be useful is processing records in batches, rather than one by one.

---

[*] The new API is not complete (or stable) in the 0.20 release series (the latest available at the time of writing). This book uses the old API for this reason. However, a copy of all of the examples in this book, rewritten to use the new API (for releases 0.21.0 and later), will be made available on the book's website.

- Configuration has been unified. The old API has a special `JobConf` object for job configuration, which is an extension of Hadoop's vanilla `Configuration` object (used for configuring daemons; see "The Configuration API" on page 130). In the new API, this distinction is dropped, so job configuration is done through a `Configuration`.
- Job control is performed through the `Job` class, rather than `JobClient`, which no longer exists in the new API.
- Output files are named slightly differently: *part-m-nnnnn* for map outputs, and *part-r-nnnnn* for reduce outputs (where *nnnnn* is an integer designating the part number, starting from zero).

Example 2-6 shows the `MaxTemperature` application rewritten to use the new API. The differences are highlighted in bold.

 When converting your `Mapper` and `Reducer` classes to the new API, don't forget to change the signature of the `map()` and `reduce()` methods to the new form. Just changing your class to extend the new `Mapper` or `Reducer` classes will *not* produce a compilation error or warning, since these classes provide an identity form of the `map()` or `reduce()` method (respectively). Your mapper or reducer code, however, will not be invoked, which can lead to some hard-to-diagnose errors.

Example 2-6. Application to find the maximum temperature in the weather dataset using the new context objects MapReduce API

```
public class NewMaxTemperature {

  static class NewMaxTemperatureMapper
    extends Mapper<LongWritable, Text, Text, IntWritable> {

    private static final int MISSING = 9999;

    public void map(LongWritable key, Text value, Context context)
        throws IOException, InterruptedException {

      String line = value.toString();
      String year = line.substring(15, 19);
      int airTemperature;
      if (line.charAt(87) == '+') { // parseInt doesn't like leading plus signs
        airTemperature = Integer.parseInt(line.substring(88, 92));
      } else {
        airTemperature = Integer.parseInt(line.substring(87, 92));
      }
      String quality = line.substring(92, 93);
      if (airTemperature != MISSING && quality.matches("[01459]")) {
        context.write(new Text(year), new IntWritable(airTemperature));
      }
    }
  }
```

```
  static class NewMaxTemperatureReducer
    extends Reducer<Text, IntWritable, Text, IntWritable> {

    public void reduce(Text key, Iterable<IntWritable> values,
        Context context)
        throws IOException, InterruptedException {

      int maxValue = Integer.MIN_VALUE;
      for (IntWritable value : values) {
        maxValue = Math.max(maxValue, value.get());
      }
      context.write(key, new IntWritable(maxValue));
    }
  }

  public static void main(String[] args) throws Exception {
    if (args.length != 2) {
      System.err.println("Usage: NewMaxTemperature <input path> <output path>");
      System.exit(-1);
    }

    Job job = new Job();
    job.setJarByClass(NewMaxTemperature.class);

    FileInputFormat.addInputPath(job, new Path(args[0]));
    FileOutputFormat.setOutputPath(job, new Path(args[1]));

    job.setMapperClass(NewMaxTemperatureMapper.class);
    job.setReducerClass(NewMaxTemperatureReducer.class);

    job.setOutputKeyClass(Text.class);
    job.setOutputValueClass(IntWritable.class);

    System.exit(job.waitForCompletion(true) ? 0 : 1);
  }
}
```

Scaling Out

You've seen how MapReduce works for small inputs; now it's time to take a bird's-eye view of the system and look at the data flow for large inputs. For simplicity, the examples so far have used files on the local filesystem. However, to scale out, we need to store the data in a distributed filesystem, typically HDFS (which you'll learn about in the next chapter), to allow Hadoop to move the MapReduce computation to each machine hosting a part of the data. Let's see how this works.

Data Flow

First, some terminology. A MapReduce *job* is a unit of work that the client wants to be performed: it consists of the input data, the MapReduce program, and configuration information. Hadoop runs the job by dividing it into *tasks*, of which there are two types: *map tasks* and *reduce tasks*.

There are two types of nodes that control the job execution process: a *jobtracker* and a number of *tasktrackers*. The jobtracker coordinates all the jobs run on the system by scheduling tasks to run on tasktrackers. Tasktrackers run tasks and send progress reports to the jobtracker, which keeps a record of the overall progress of each job. If a task fails, the jobtracker can reschedule it on a different tasktracker.

Hadoop divides the input to a MapReduce job into fixed-size pieces called *input splits*, or just *splits*. Hadoop creates one map task for each split, which runs the user-defined map function for each *record* in the split.

Having many splits means the time taken to process each split is small compared to the time to process the whole input. So if we are processing the splits in parallel, the processing is better load-balanced if the splits are small, since a faster machine will be able to process proportionally more splits over the course of the job than a slower machine. Even if the machines are identical, failed processes or other jobs running concurrently make load balancing desirable, and the quality of the load balancing increases as the splits become more fine-grained.

On the other hand, if splits are too small, then the overhead of managing the splits and of map task creation begins to dominate the total job execution time. For most jobs, a good split size tends to be the size of an HDFS block, 64 MB by default, although this can be changed for the cluster (for all newly created files), or specified when each file is created.

Hadoop does its best to run the map task on a node where the input data resides in HDFS. This is called the *data locality optimization*. It should now be clear why the optimal split size is the same as the block size: it is the largest size of input that can be guaranteed to be stored on a single node. If the split spanned two blocks, it would be unlikely that any HDFS node stored both blocks, so some of the split would have to be transferred across the network to the node running the map task, which is clearly less efficient than running the whole map task using local data.

Map tasks write their output to the local disk, not to HDFS. Why is this? Map output is intermediate output: it's processed by reduce tasks to produce the final output, and once the job is complete the map output can be thrown away. So storing it in HDFS, with replication, would be overkill. If the node running the map task fails before the map output has been consumed by the reduce task, then Hadoop will automatically rerun the map task on another node to re-create the map output.

Reduce tasks don't have the advantage of data locality—the input to a single reduce task is normally the output from all mappers. In the present example, we have a single reduce task that is fed by all of the map tasks. Therefore, the sorted map outputs have to be transferred across the network to the node where the reduce task is running, where they are merged and then passed to the user-defined reduce function. The output of the reduce is normally stored in HDFS for reliability. As explained in Chapter 3, for each HDFS block of the reduce output, the first replica is stored on the local node, with other replicas being stored on off-rack nodes. Thus, writing the reduce output does consume network bandwidth, but only as much as a normal HDFS write pipeline consumes.

The whole data flow with a single reduce task is illustrated in Figure 2-2. The dotted boxes indicate nodes, the light arrows show data transfers on a node, and the heavy arrows show data transfers between nodes.

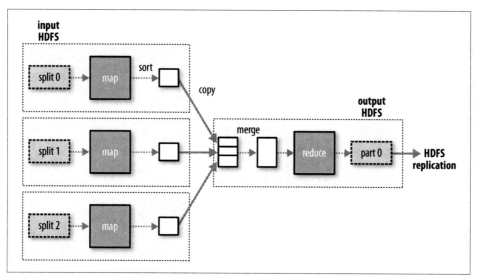

Figure 2-2. MapReduce data flow with a single reduce task

The number of reduce tasks is not governed by the size of the input, but is specified independently. In "The Default MapReduce Job" on page 191, you will see how to choose the number of reduce tasks for a given job.

When there are multiple reducers, the map tasks *partition* their output, each creating one partition for each reduce task. There can be many keys (and their associated values) in each partition, but the records for any given key are all in a single partition. The partitioning can be controlled by a user-defined partitioning function, but normally the default partitioner—which buckets keys using a hash function—works very well.

The data flow for the general case of multiple reduce tasks is illustrated in Figure 2-3. This diagram makes it clear why the data flow between map and reduce tasks is colloquially known as "the shuffle," as each reduce task is fed by many map tasks. The shuffle is more complicated than this diagram suggests, and tuning it can have a big impact on job execution time, as you will see in "Shuffle and Sort" on page 177.

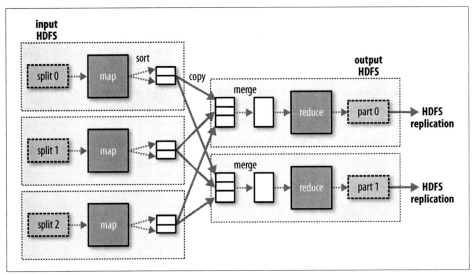

Figure 2-3. MapReduce data flow with multiple reduce tasks

Finally, it's also possible to have zero reduce tasks. This can be appropriate when you don't need the shuffle since the processing can be carried out entirely in parallel (a few examples are discussed in "NLineInputFormat" on page 211). In this case, the only off-node data transfer is when the map tasks write to HDFS (see Figure 2-4).

Combiner Functions

Many MapReduce jobs are limited by the bandwidth available on the cluster, so it pays to minimize the data transferred between map and reduce tasks. Hadoop allows the user to specify a *combiner function* to be run on the map output—the combiner function's output forms the input to the reduce function. Since the combiner function is an optimization, Hadoop does not provide a guarantee of how many times it will call it for a particular map output record, if at all. In other words, calling the combiner function zero, one, or many times should produce the same output from the reducer.

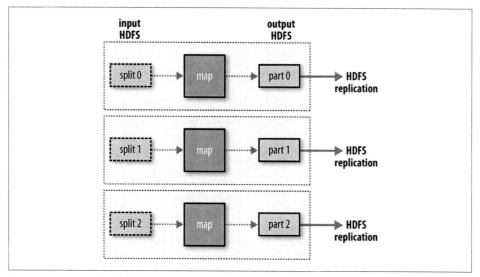

Figure 2-4. MapReduce data flow with no reduce tasks

The contract for the combiner function constrains the type of function that may be used. This is best illustrated with an example. Suppose that for the maximum temperature example, readings for the year 1950 were processed by two maps (because they were in different splits). Imagine the first map produced the output:

```
(1950, 0)
(1950, 20)
(1950, 10)
```

And the second produced:

```
(1950, 25)
(1950, 15)
```

The reduce function would be called with a list of all the values:

```
(1950, [0, 20, 10, 25, 15])
```

with output:

```
(1950, 25)
```

since 25 is the maximum value in the list. We could use a combiner function that, just like the reduce function, finds the maximum temperature for each map output. The reduce would then be called with:

```
(1950, [20, 25])
```

and the reduce would produce the same output as before. More succinctly, we may express the function calls on the temperature values in this case as follows:

$$max(0, 20, 10, 25, 15) = max(max(0, 20, 10), max(25, 15)) = max(20, 25) = 25$$

Not all functions possess this property.[†] For example, if we were calculating mean temperatures, then we couldn't use the mean as our combiner function, since:

mean(0, 20, 10, 25, 15) = 14

but:

mean(mean(0, 20, 10), mean(25, 15)) = mean(10, 20) = 15

The combiner function doesn't replace the reduce function. (How could it? The reduce function is still needed to process records with the same key from different maps.) But it can help cut down the amount of data shuffled between the maps and the reduces, and for this reason alone it is always worth considering whether you can use a combiner function in your MapReduce job.

Specifying a combiner function

Going back to the Java MapReduce program, the combiner function is defined using the Reducer interface, and for this application, it is the same implementation as the reducer function in MaxTemperatureReducer. The only change we need to make is to set the combiner class on the JobConf (see Example 2-7).

Example 2-7. Application to find the maximum temperature, using a combiner function for efficiency

```
public class MaxTemperatureWithCombiner {

  public static void main(String[] args) throws IOException {
    if (args.length != 2) {
      System.err.println("Usage: MaxTemperatureWithCombiner <input path> " +
              "<output path>");
      System.exit(-1);
    }

    JobConf conf = new JobConf(MaxTemperatureWithCombiner.class);
    conf.setJobName("Max temperature");

    FileInputFormat.addInputPath(conf, new Path(args[0]));
    FileOutputFormat.setOutputPath(conf, new Path(args[1]));

    conf.setMapperClass(MaxTemperatureMapper.class);
    conf.setCombinerClass(MaxTemperatureReducer.class);
    conf.setReducerClass(MaxTemperatureReducer.class);

    conf.setOutputKeyClass(Text.class);
    conf.setOutputValueClass(IntWritable.class);

    JobClient.runJob(conf);
  }
}
```

[†] Functions with this property are called *distributive* in the paper "Data Cube: A Relational Aggregation Operator Generalizing Group-By, Cross-Tab, and Sub-Totals," Gray et al. (1995).

Running a Distributed MapReduce Job

The same program will run, without alteration, on a full dataset. This is the point of MapReduce: it scales to the size of your data and the size of your hardware. Here's one data point: on a 10-node EC2 cluster running High-CPU Extra Large Instances, the program took six minutes to run.‡

We'll go through the mechanics of running programs on a cluster in Chapter 5.

Hadoop Streaming

Hadoop provides an API to MapReduce that allows you to write your map and reduce functions in languages other than Java. *Hadoop Streaming* uses Unix standard streams as the interface between Hadoop and your program, so you can use any language that can read standard input and write to standard output to write your MapReduce program.

Streaming is naturally suited for text processing (although, as of version 0.21.0, it can handle binary streams, too), and when used in text mode, it has a line-oriented view of data. Map input data is passed over standard input to your map function, which processes it line by line and writes lines to standard output. A map output key-value pair is written as a single tab-delimited line. Input to the reduce function is in the same format—a tab-separated key-value pair—passed over standard input. The reduce function reads lines from standard input, which the framework guarantees are sorted by key, and writes its results to standard output.

Let's illustrate this by rewriting our MapReduce program for finding maximum temperatures by year in Streaming.

Ruby

The map function can be expressed in Ruby as shown in Example 2-8.

Example 2-8. Map function for maximum temperature in Ruby

```ruby
#!/usr/bin/env ruby

STDIN.each_line do |line|
  val = line
  year, temp, q = val[15,4], val[87,5], val[92,1]
  puts "#{year}\t#{temp}" if (temp != "+9999" && q =~ /[01459]/)
end
```

---

‡ This is a factor of seven faster than the serial run on one machine using *awk*. The main reason it wasn't proportionately faster is because the input data wasn't evenly partitioned. For convenience, the input files were gzipped by year, resulting in large files for later years in the dataset, when the number of weather records was much higher.

The program iterates over lines from standard input by executing a block for each line from STDIN (a global constant of type IO). The block pulls out the relevant fields from each input line, and, if the temperature is valid, writes the year and the temperature separated by a tab character \t to standard output (using puts).

 It's worth drawing out a design difference between Streaming and the Java MapReduce API. The Java API is geared toward processing your map function one record at a time. The framework calls the map() method on your Mapper for each record in the input, whereas with Streaming the map program can decide how to process the input—for example, it could easily read and process multiple lines at a time since it's in control of the reading. The user's Java map implementation is "pushed" records, but it's still possible to consider multiple lines at a time by accumulating previous lines in an instance variable in the Mapper.§ In this case, you need to implement the close() method so that you know when the last record has been read, so you can finish processing the last group of lines.

Since the script just operates on standard input and output, it's trivial to test the script without using Hadoop, simply using Unix pipes:

```
% cat input/ncdc/sample.txt | ch02/src/main/ruby/max_temperature_map.rb
1950    +0000
1950    +0022
1950    -0011
1949    +0111
1949    +0078
```

The reduce function shown in Example 2-9 is a little more complex.

Example 2-9. Reduce function for maximum temperature in Ruby

```ruby
#!/usr/bin/env ruby

last_key, max_val = nil, 0
STDIN.each_line do |line|
  key, val = line.split("\t")
  if last_key && last_key != key
    puts "#{last_key}\t#{max_val}"
    last_key, max_val = key, val.to_i
  else
    last_key, max_val = key, [max_val, val.to_i].max
  end
end
puts "#{last_key}\t#{max_val}" if last_key
```

§ Alternatively, you could use "pull" style processing in the new MapReduce API—see "The new Java MapReduce API" on page 25.

Again, the program iterates over lines from standard input, but this time we have to store some state as we process each key group. In this case, the keys are weather station identifiers, and we store the last key seen and the maximum temperature seen so far for that key. The MapReduce framework ensures that the keys are ordered, so we know that if a key is different from the previous one, we have moved into a new key group. In contrast to the Java API, where you are provided an iterator over each key group, in Streaming you have to find key group boundaries in your program.

For each line, we pull out the key and value, then if we've just finished a group (last_key && last_key != key), we write the key and the maximum temperature for that group, separated by a tab character, before resetting the maximum temperature for the new key. If we haven't just finished a group, we just update the maximum temperature for the current key.

The last line of the program ensures that a line is written for the last key group in the input.

We can now simulate the whole MapReduce pipeline with a Unix pipeline (which is equivalent to the Unix pipeline shown in Figure 2-1):

```
% cat input/ncdc/sample.txt | ch02/src/main/ruby/max_temperature_map.rb | \
  sort | ch02/src/main/ruby/max_temperature_reduce.rb
1949    111
1950    22
```

The output is the same as the Java program, so the next step is to run it using Hadoop itself.

The hadoop command doesn't support a Streaming option; instead, you specify the Streaming JAR file along with the jar option. Options to the Streaming program specify the input and output paths, and the map and reduce scripts. This is what it looks like:

```
% hadoop jar $HADOOP_INSTALL/contrib/streaming/hadoop-*-streaming.jar \
  -input input/ncdc/sample.txt \
  -output output \
  -mapper ch02/src/main/ruby/max_temperature_map.rb \
  -reducer ch02/src/main/ruby/max_temperature_reduce.rb
```

When running on a large dataset on a cluster, we should set the combiner, using the -combiner option.

From release 0.21.0, the combiner can be any Streaming command. For earlier releases, the combiner had to be written in Java, so as a workaround it was common to do manual combining in the mapper, without having to resort to Java. In this case, we could change the mapper to be a pipeline:

```
% hadoop jar $HADOOP_INSTALL/contrib/streaming/hadoop-*-streaming.jar \
  -input input/ncdc/all \
  -output output \
  -mapper "ch02/src/main/ruby/max_temperature_map.rb | sort | \
    ch02/src/main/ruby/max_temperature_reduce.rb" \
  -reducer ch02/src/main/ruby/max_temperature_reduce.rb \
```

```
    -file ch02/src/main/ruby/max_temperature_map.rb \
    -file ch02/src/main/ruby/max_temperature_reduce.rb
```

Note also the use of -file, which we use when running Streaming programs on the cluster to ship the scripts to the cluster.

Python

Streaming supports any programming language that can read from standard input, and write to standard output, so for readers more familiar with Python, here's the same example again.‖ The map script is in Example 2-10, and the reduce script is in Example 2-11.

Example 2-10. Map function for maximum temperature in Python

```python
#!/usr/bin/env python

import re
import sys

for line in sys.stdin:
  val = line.strip()
  (year, temp, q) = (val[15:19], val[87:92], val[92:93])
  if (temp != "+9999" and re.match("[01459]", q)):
    print "%s\t%s" % (year, temp)
```

Example 2-11. Reduce function for maximum temperature in Python

```python
#!/usr/bin/env python

import sys

(last_key, max_val) = (None, 0)
for line in sys.stdin:
  (key, val) = line.strip().split("\t")
  if last_key and last_key != key:
    print "%s\t%s" % (last_key, max_val)
    (last_key, max_val) = (key, int(val))
  else:
    (last_key, max_val) = (key, max(max_val, int(val)))

if last_key:
  print "%s\t%s" % (last_key, max_val)
```

‖ As an alternative to Streaming, Python programmers should consider Dumbo (*http://www.last.fm/dumbo*), which makes the Streaming MapReduce interface more Pythonic and easier to use.

We can test the programs and run the job in the same way we did in Ruby. For example, to run a test:

```
% cat input/ncdc/sample.txt | ch02/src/main/python/max_temperature_map.py | \
  sort | ch02/src/main/python/max_temperature_reduce.py
1949    111
1950    22
```

Hadoop Pipes

Hadoop Pipes is the name of the C++ interface to Hadoop MapReduce. Unlike Streaming, which uses standard input and output to communicate with the map and reduce code, Pipes uses sockets as the channel over which the tasktracker communicates with the process running the C++ map or reduce function. JNI is not used.

We'll rewrite the example running through the chapter in C++, and then we'll see how to run it using Pipes. Example 2-12 shows the source code for the map and reduce functions in C++.

Example 2-12. Maximum temperature in C++

```cpp
#include <algorithm>
#include <limits>
#include <stdint.h>
#include <string>

#include "hadoop/Pipes.hh"
#include "hadoop/TemplateFactory.hh"
#include "hadoop/StringUtils.hh"

class MaxTemperatureMapper : public HadoopPipes::Mapper {
public:
  MaxTemperatureMapper(HadoopPipes::TaskContext& context) {
  }
  void map(HadoopPipes::MapContext& context) {
    std::string line = context.getInputValue();
    std::string year = line.substr(15, 4);
    std::string airTemperature = line.substr(87, 5);
    std::string q = line.substr(92, 1);
    if (airTemperature != "+9999" &&
        (q == "0" || q == "1" || q == "4" || q == "5" || q == "9")) {
      context.emit(year, airTemperature);
    }
  }
};

class MapTemperatureReducer : public HadoopPipes::Reducer {
public:
  MapTemperatureReducer(HadoopPipes::TaskContext& context) {
  }
  void reduce(HadoopPipes::ReduceContext& context) {
    int maxValue = INT_MIN;
    while (context.nextValue()) {
```

```
        maxValue = std::max(maxValue, HadoopUtils::toInt(context.getInputValue()));
      }
      context.emit(context.getInputKey(), HadoopUtils::toString(maxValue));
    }
};

int main(int argc, char *argv[]) {
  return HadoopPipes::runTask(HadoopPipes::TemplateFactory<MaxTemperatureMapper,
                              MapTemperatureReducer>());
}
```

The application links against the Hadoop C++ library, which is a thin wrapper for communicating with the tasktracker child process. The map and reduce functions are defined by extending the Mapper and Reducer classes defined in the HadoopPipes namespace and providing implementations of the map() and reduce() methods in each case. These methods take a context object (of type MapContext or ReduceContext), which provides the means for reading input and writing output, as well as accessing job configuration information via the JobConf class. The processing in this example is very similar to the Java equivalent.

Unlike the Java interface, keys and values in the C++ interface are byte buffers, represented as Standard Template Library (STL) strings. This makes the interface simpler, although it does put a slightly greater burden on the application developer, who has to convert to and from richer domain-level types. This is evident in MapTempera tureReducer where we have to convert the input value into an integer (using a convenience method in HadoopUtils) and then the maximum value back into a string before it's written out. In some cases, we can save on doing the conversion, such as in MaxTem peratureMapper where the airTemperature value is never converted to an integer since it is never processed as a number in the map() method.

The main() method is the application entry point. It calls HadoopPipes::runTask, which connects to the Java parent process and marshals data to and from the Mapper or Reducer. The runTask() method is passed a Factory so that it can create instances of the Mapper or Reducer. Which one it creates is controlled by the Java parent over the socket connection. There are overloaded template factory methods for setting a combiner, partitioner, record reader, or record writer.

Compiling and Running

Now we can compile and link our program using the Makefile in Example 2-13.

Example 2-13. Makefile for C++ MapReduce program

```
CC = g++
CPPFLAGS = -m32 -I$(HADOOP_INSTALL)/c++/$(PLATFORM)/include

max_temperature: max_temperature.cpp
	$(CC) $(CPPFLAGS) $< -Wall -L$(HADOOP_INSTALL)/c++/$(PLATFORM)/lib -lhadooppipes \
	-lhadooputils -lpthread -g -O2 -o $@
```

The Makefile expects a couple of environment variables to be set. Apart from `HADOOP_INSTALL` (which you should already have set if you followed the installation instructions in Appendix A), you need to define `PLATFORM`, which specifies the operating system, architecture, and data model (e.g., 32- or 64-bit). I ran it on a 32-bit Linux system with the following:

```
% export PLATFORM=Linux-i386-32
% make
```

On successful completion, you'll find the `max_temperature` executable in the current directory.

To run a Pipes job, we need to run Hadoop in *pseudo-distributed* mode (where all the daemons run on the local machine), for which there are setup instructions in Appendix A. Pipes doesn't run in standalone (local) mode, since it relies on Hadoop's distributed cache mechanism, which works only when HDFS is running.

With the Hadoop daemons now running, the first step is to copy the executable to HDFS so that it can be picked up by tasktrackers when they launch map and reduce tasks:

```
% hadoop fs -put max_temperature bin/max_temperature
```

The sample data also needs to be copied from the local filesystem into HDFS:

```
% hadoop fs -put input/ncdc/sample.txt sample.txt
```

Now we can run the job. For this, we use the Hadoop `pipes` command, passing the URI of the executable in HDFS using the `-program` argument:

```
% hadoop pipes \
    -D hadoop.pipes.java.recordreader=true \
    -D hadoop.pipes.java.recordwriter=true \
    -input sample.txt \
    -output output \
    -program bin/max_temperature
```

We specify two properties using the `-D` option: `hadoop.pipes.java.recordreader` and `hadoop.pipes.java.recordwriter`, setting both to `true` to say that we have not specified a C++ record reader or writer, but that we want to use the default Java ones (which are for text input and output). Pipes also allows you to set a Java mapper, reducer, combiner, or partitioner. In fact, you can have a mixture of Java or C++ classes within any one job.

The result is the same as the other versions of the same program that we ran.

## CHAPTER 3

The Hadoop Distributed Filesystem

When a dataset outgrows the storage capacity of a single physical machine, it becomes necessary to partition it across a number of separate machines. Filesystems that manage the storage across a network of machines are called *distributed filesystems*. Since they are network-based, all the complications of network programming kick in, thus making distributed filesystems more complex than regular disk filesystems. For example, one of the biggest challenges is making the filesystem tolerate node failure without suffering data loss.

Hadoop comes with a distributed filesystem called HDFS, which stands for *Hadoop Distributed Filesystem*. (You may sometimes see references to "DFS"—informally or in older documentation or configurations—which is the same thing.) HDFS is Hadoop's flagship filesystem and is the focus of this chapter, but Hadoop actually has a general-purpose filesystem abstraction, so we'll see along the way how Hadoop integrates with other storage systems (such as the local filesystem and Amazon S3).

The Design of HDFS

HDFS is a filesystem designed for storing very large files with streaming data access patterns, running on clusters of commodity hardware.[*] Let's examine this statement in more detail:

Very large files
> "Very large" in this context means files that are hundreds of megabytes, gigabytes, or terabytes in size. There are Hadoop clusters running today that store petabytes of data.[†]

---

[*] The architecture of HDFS is described in "The Hadoop Distributed File System" by Konstantin Shvachko, Hairong Kuang, Sanjay Radia, and Robert Chansler (Proceedings of MSST2010, May 2010, *http://storageconference.org/2010/Papers/MSST/Shvachko.pdf*).

[†] "Scaling Hadoop to 4000 nodes at Yahoo!," *http://developer.yahoo.net/blogs/hadoop/2008/09/scaling_hadoop_to_4000_nodes_a.html*.

Streaming data access

> HDFS is built around the idea that the most efficient data processing pattern is a write-once, read-many-times pattern. A dataset is typically generated or copied from source, then various analyses are performed on that dataset over time. Each analysis will involve a large proportion, if not all, of the dataset, so the time to read the whole dataset is more important than the latency in reading the first record.

Commodity hardware

> Hadoop doesn't require expensive, highly reliable hardware to run on. It's designed to run on clusters of commodity hardware (commonly available hardware available from multiple vendors[‡]) for which the chance of node failure across the cluster is high, at least for large clusters. HDFS is designed to carry on working without a noticeable interruption to the user in the face of such failure.

It is also worth examining the applications for which using HDFS does not work so well. While this may change in the future, these are areas where HDFS is not a good fit today:

Low-latency data access

> Applications that require low-latency access to data, in the tens of milliseconds range, will not work well with HDFS. Remember, HDFS is optimized for delivering a high throughput of data, and this may be at the expense of latency. HBase (Chapter 13) is currently a better choice for low-latency access.

Lots of small files

> Since the namenode holds filesystem metadata in memory, the limit to the number of files in a filesystem is governed by the amount of memory on the namenode. As a rule of thumb, each file, directory, and block takes about 150 bytes. So, for example, if you had one million files, each taking one block, you would need at least 300 MB of memory. While storing millions of files is feasible, billions is beyond the capability of current hardware.[§]

Multiple writers, arbitrary file modifications

> Files in HDFS may be written to by a single writer. Writes are always made at the end of the file. There is no support for multiple writers, or for modifications at arbitrary offsets in the file. (These might be supported in the future, but they are likely to be relatively inefficient.)

[‡] See Chapter 9 for a typical machine specification.

[§] For an in-depth exposition of the scalability limits of HDFS, see Konstantin V. Shvachko's "Scalability of the Hadoop Distributed File System," (*http://developer.yahoo.net/blogs/hadoop/2010/05/scalability_of_the_hadoop_dist.html*) and the companion paper "HDFS Scalability: The limits to growth," (April 2010, pp. 6–16. *http://www.usenix.org/publications/login/2010-04/openpdfs/shvachko.pdf*) by the same author.

HDFS Concepts

Blocks

A disk has a block size, which is the minimum amount of data that it can read or write. Filesystems for a single disk build on this by dealing with data in blocks, which are an integral multiple of the disk block size. Filesystem blocks are typically a few kilobytes in size, while disk blocks are normally 512 bytes. This is generally transparent to the filesystem user who is simply reading or writing a file—of whatever length. However, there are tools to perform filesystem maintenance, such as *df* and *fsck*, that operate on the filesystem block level.

HDFS, too, has the concept of a block, but it is a much larger unit—64 MB by default. Like in a filesystem for a single disk, files in HDFS are broken into block-sized chunks, which are stored as independent units. Unlike a filesystem for a single disk, a file in HDFS that is smaller than a single block does not occupy a full block's worth of underlying storage. When unqualified, the term "block" in this book refers to a block in HDFS.

Why Is a Block in HDFS So Large?

HDFS blocks are large compared to disk blocks, and the reason is to minimize the cost of seeks. By making a block large enough, the time to transfer the data from the disk can be made to be significantly larger than the time to seek to the start of the block. Thus the time to transfer a large file made of multiple blocks operates at the disk transfer rate.

A quick calculation shows that if the seek time is around 10 ms, and the transfer rate is 100 MB/s, then to make the seek time 1% of the transfer time, we need to make the block size around 100 MB. The default is actually 64 MB, although many HDFS installations use 128 MB blocks. This figure will continue to be revised upward as transfer speeds grow with new generations of disk drives.

This argument shouldn't be taken too far, however. Map tasks in MapReduce normally operate on one block at a time, so if you have too few tasks (fewer than nodes in the cluster), your jobs will run slower than they could otherwise.

Having a block abstraction for a distributed filesystem brings several benefits. The first benefit is the most obvious: a file can be larger than any single disk in the network. There's nothing that requires the blocks from a file to be stored on the same disk, so they can take advantage of any of the disks in the cluster. In fact, it would be possible, if unusual, to store a single file on an HDFS cluster whose blocks filled all the disks in the cluster.

Second, making the unit of abstraction a block rather than a file simplifies the storage subsystem. Simplicity is something to strive for all in all systems, but is especially important for a distributed system in which the failure modes are so varied. The storage subsystem deals with blocks, simplifying storage management (since blocks are a fixed size, it is easy to calculate how many can be stored on a given disk) and eliminating metadata concerns (blocks are just a chunk of data to be stored—file metadata such as permissions information does not need to be stored with the blocks, so another system can handle metadata separately).

Furthermore, blocks fit well with replication for providing fault tolerance and availability. To insure against corrupted blocks and disk and machine failure, each block is replicated to a small number of physically separate machines (typically three). If a block becomes unavailable, a copy can be read from another location in a way that is transparent to the client. A block that is no longer available due to corruption or machine failure can be replicated from its alternative locations to other live machines to bring the replication factor back to the normal level. (See "Data Integrity" on page 75 for more on guarding against corrupt data.) Similarly, some applications may choose to set a high replication factor for the blocks in a popular file to spread the read load on the cluster.

Like its disk filesystem cousin, HDFS's fsck command understands blocks. For example, running:

```
% hadoop fsck / -files -blocks
```

will list the blocks that make up each file in the filesystem. (See also "Filesystem check (fsck)" on page 301.)

Namenodes and Datanodes

An HDFS cluster has two types of node operating in a master-worker pattern: a *namenode* (the master) and a number of *datanodes* (workers). The namenode manages the filesystem namespace. It maintains the filesystem tree and the metadata for all the files and directories in the tree. This information is stored persistently on the local disk in the form of two files: the namespace image and the edit log. The namenode also knows the datanodes on which all the blocks for a given file are located, however, it does not store block locations persistently, since this information is reconstructed from datanodes when the system starts.

A *client* accesses the filesystem on behalf of the user by communicating with the namenode and datanodes. The client presents a POSIX-like filesystem interface, so the user code does not need to know about the namenode and datanode to function.

Datanodes are the workhorses of the filesystem. They store and retrieve blocks when they are told to (by clients or the namenode), and they report back to the namenode periodically with lists of blocks that they are storing.

Without the namenode, the filesystem cannot be used. In fact, if the machine running the namenode were obliterated, all the files on the filesystem would be lost since there would be no way of knowing how to reconstruct the files from the blocks on the datanodes. For this reason, it is important to make the namenode resilient to failure, and Hadoop provides two mechanisms for this.

The first way is to back up the files that make up the persistent state of the filesystem metadata. Hadoop can be configured so that the namenode writes its persistent state to multiple filesystems. These writes are synchronous and atomic. The usual configuration choice is to write to local disk as well as a remote NFS mount.

It is also possible to run a *secondary namenode*, which despite its name does not act as a namenode. Its main role is to periodically merge the namespace image with the edit log to prevent the edit log from becoming too large. The secondary namenode usually runs on a separate physical machine, since it requires plenty of CPU and as much memory as the namenode to perform the merge. It keeps a copy of the merged namespace image, which can be used in the event of the namenode failing. However, the state of the secondary namenode lags that of the primary, so in the event of total failure of the primary, data loss is almost certain. The usual course of action in this case is to copy the namenode's metadata files that are on NFS to the secondary and run it as the new primary.

See "The filesystem image and edit log" on page 294 for more details.

The Command-Line Interface

We're going to have a look at HDFS by interacting with it from the command line. There are many other interfaces to HDFS, but the command line is one of the simplest and, to many developers, the most familiar.

We are going to run HDFS on one machine, so first follow the instructions for setting up Hadoop in pseudo-distributed mode in Appendix A. Later you'll see how to run on a cluster of machines to give us scalability and fault tolerance.

There are two properties that we set in the pseudo-distributed configuration that deserve further explanation. The first is `fs.default.name`, set to *hdfs://localhost/*, which is used to set a default filesystem for Hadoop. Filesystems are specified by a URI, and here we have used an `hdfs` URI to configure Hadoop to use HDFS by default. The HDFS daemons will use this property to determine the host and port for the HDFS namenode. We'll be running it on `localhost`, on the default HDFS port, 8020. And HDFS clients will use this property to work out where the namenode is running so they can connect to it.

We set the second property, dfs.replication, to 1 so that HDFS doesn't replicate filesystem blocks by the default factor of three. When running with a single datanode, HDFS can't replicate blocks to three datanodes, so it would perpetually warn about blocks being under-replicated. This setting solves that problem.

Basic Filesystem Operations

The filesystem is ready to be used, and we can do all of the usual filesystem operations such as reading files, creating directories, moving files, deleting data, and listing directories. You can type hadoop fs -help to get detailed help on every command.

Start by copying a file from the local filesystem to HDFS:

```
% hadoop fs -copyFromLocal input/docs/quangle.txt hdfs://localhost/user/tom/
    quangle.txt
```

This command invokes Hadoop's filesystem shell command fs, which supports a number of subcommands—in this case, we are running -copyFromLocal. The local file *quangle.txt* is copied to the file */user/tom/quangle.txt* on the HDFS instance running on localhost. In fact, we could have omitted the scheme and host of the URI and picked up the default, hdfs://localhost, as specified in *core-site.xml*:

```
% hadoop fs -copyFromLocal input/docs/quangle.txt /user/tom/quangle.txt
```

We could also have used a relative path and copied the file to our home directory in HDFS, which in this case is */user/tom*:

```
% hadoop fs -copyFromLocal input/docs/quangle.txt quangle.txt
```

Let's copy the file back to the local filesystem and check whether it's the same:

```
% hadoop fs -copyToLocal quangle.txt quangle.copy.txt
% md5 input/docs/quangle.txt quangle.copy.txt
MD5 (input/docs/quangle.txt) = a16f231da6b05e2ba7a339320e7dacd9
MD5 (quangle.copy.txt) = a16f231da6b05e2ba7a339320e7dacd9
```

The MD5 digests are the same, showing that the file survived its trip to HDFS and is back intact.

Finally, let's look at an HDFS file listing. We create a directory first just to see how it is displayed in the listing:

```
% hadoop fs -mkdir books
% hadoop fs -ls .
Found 2 items
drwxr-xr-x   - tom supergroup          0 2009-04-02 22:41 /user/tom/books
-rw-r--r--   1 tom supergroup        118 2009-04-02 22:29 /user/tom/quangle.txt
```

The information returned is very similar to the Unix command ls -l, with a few minor differences. The first column shows the file mode. The second column is the replication factor of the file (something a traditional Unix filesystem does not have). Remember we set the default replication factor in the site-wide configuration to be 1, which is why we see the same value here. The entry in this column is empty for directories since the concept of replication does not apply to them—directories are treated as metadata and stored by the namenode, not the datanodes. The third and fourth columns show the file owner and group. The fifth column is the size of the file in bytes, or zero for directories. The sixth and seventh columns are the last modified date and time. Finally, the eighth column is the absolute name of the file or directory.

File Permissions in HDFS

HDFS has a permissions model for files and directories that is much like POSIX.

There are three types of permission: the read permission (r), the write permission (w), and the execute permission (x). The read permission is required to read files or list the contents of a directory. The write permission is required to write a file, or for a directory, to create or delete files or directories in it. The execute permission is ignored for a file since you can't execute a file on HDFS (unlike POSIX), and for a directory it is required to access its children.

Each file and directory has an *owner*, a *group*, and a *mode*. The mode is made up of the permissions for the user who is the owner, the permissions for the users who are members of the group, and the permissions for users who are neither the owners nor members of the group.

By default, a client's identity is determined by the username and groups of the process it is running in. Because clients are remote, this makes it possible to become an arbitrary user, simply by creating an account of that name on the remote system. Thus, permissions should be used only in a cooperative community of users, as a mechanism for sharing filesystem resources and for avoiding accidental data loss, and not for securing resources in a hostile environment. (Note, however, that the latest versions of Hadoop support Kerberos authentication, which removes these restrictions, see "Security" on page 281.) Despite these limitations, it is worthwhile having permissions enabled (as it is by default; see the dfs.permissions property), to avoid accidental modification or deletion of substantial parts of the filesystem, either by users or by automated tools or programs.

When permissions checking is enabled, the owner permissions are checked if the client's username matches the owner, and the group permissions are checked if the client is a member of the group; otherwise, the other permissions are checked.

There is a concept of a super-user, which is the identity of the namenode process. Permissions checks are not performed for the super-user.

Hadoop Filesystems

Hadoop has an abstract notion of filesystem, of which HDFS is just one implementation. The Java abstract class org.apache.hadoop.fs.FileSystem represents a filesystem in Hadoop, and there are several concrete implementations, which are described in Table 3-1.

Table 3-1. Hadoop filesystems

Filesystem	URI scheme	Java implementation (all under org.apache.hadoop)	Description
Local	*file*	`fs.LocalFileSystem`	A filesystem for a locally connected disk with client-side checksums. Use `RawLocalFileSystem` for a local filesystem with no checksums. See "LocalFileSystem" on page 76.
HDFS	*hdfs*	`hdfs.DistributedFileSystem`	Hadoop's distributed filesystem. HDFS is designed to work efficiently in conjunction with MapReduce.
HFTP	*hftp*	`hdfs.HftpFileSystem`	A filesystem providing read-only access to HDFS over HTTP. (Despite its name, HFTP has no connection with FTP.) Often used with *distcp* (see "Parallel Copying with distcp" on page 70) to copy data between HDFS clusters running different versions.
HSFTP	*hsftp*	`hdfs.HsftpFileSystem`	A filesystem providing read-only access to HDFS over HTTPS. (Again, this has no connection with FTP.)
HAR	*har*	`fs.HarFileSystem`	A filesystem layered on another filesystem for archiving files. Hadoop Archives are typically used for archiving files in HDFS to reduce the namenode's memory usage. See "Hadoop Archives" on page 71.
KFS (Cloud-Store)	*kfs*	`fs.kfs.KosmosFileSystem`	CloudStore (formerly Kosmos filesystem) is a distributed filesystem like HDFS or Google's GFS, written in C++. Find more information about it at *http://kosmosfs.sourceforge.net/*.
FTP	*ftp*	`fs.ftp.FTPFileSystem`	A filesystem backed by an FTP server.
S3 (native)	*s3n*	`fs.s3native.NativeS3FileSystem`	A filesystem backed by Amazon S3. See *http://wiki.apache.org/hadoop/AmazonS3*.
S3 (block-based)	*s3*	`fs.s3.S3FileSystem`	A filesystem backed by Amazon S3, which stores files in blocks (much like HDFS) to overcome S3's 5 GB file size limit.

Hadoop provides many interfaces to its filesystems, and it generally uses the URI scheme to pick the correct filesystem instance to communicate with. For example, the filesystem shell that we met in the previous section operates with all Hadoop filesystems. To list the files in the root directory of the local filesystem, type:

```
% hadoop fs -ls file:///
```

Although it is possible (and sometimes very convenient) to run MapReduce programs that access any of these filesystems, when you are processing large volumes of data, you should choose a distributed filesystem that has the data locality optimization, such as HDFS or KFS (see "Scaling Out" on page 27).

Interfaces

Hadoop is written in Java, and all Hadoop filesystem interactions are mediated through the Java API.[||] The filesystem shell, for example, is a Java application that uses the Java `FileSystem` class to provide filesystem operations. The other filesystem interfaces are discussed briefly in this section. These interfaces are most commonly used with HDFS, since the other filesystems in Hadoop typically have existing tools to access the underlying filesystem (FTP clients for FTP, S3 tools for S3, etc.), but many of them will work with any Hadoop filesystem.

Thrift

By exposing its filesystem interface as a Java API, Hadoop makes it awkward for non-Java applications to access Hadoop filesystems. The Thrift API in the "thriftfs" contrib module remedies this deficiency by exposing Hadoop filesystems as an Apache Thrift service, making it easy for any language that has Thrift bindings to interact with a Hadoop filesystem, such as HDFS.

To use the Thrift API, run a Java server that exposes the Thrift service and acts as a proxy to the Hadoop filesystem. Your application accesses the Thrift service, which is typically running on the same machine as your application.

The Thrift API comes with a number of pregenerated stubs for a variety of languages, including C++, Perl, PHP, Python, and Ruby. Thrift has support for versioning, so it's a good choice if you want to access different versions of a Hadoop filesystem from the same client code (you will need to run a proxy for each version of Hadoop to achieve this, however).

For installation and usage instructions, please refer to the documentation in the *src/contrib/thriftfs* directory of the Hadoop distribution.

C

Hadoop provides a C library called *libhdfs* that mirrors the Java `FileSystem` interface (it was written as a C library for accessing HDFS, but despite its name it can be used to access any Hadoop filesystem). It works using the *Java Native Interface* (JNI) to call a Java filesystem client.

The C API is very similar to the Java one, but it typically lags the Java one, so newer features may not be supported. You can find the generated documentation for the C API in the *libhdfs/docs/api* directory of the Hadoop distribution.

[||] The RPC interfaces in Hadoop are based on Hadoop's `Writable` interface, which is Java-centric. In the future, Hadoop will adopt Avro, a cross-language, RPC framework, which will allow native HDFS clients to be written in languages other than Java.

Hadoop comes with prebuilt *libhdfs* binaries for 32-bit Linux, but for other platforms, you will need to build them yourself using the instructions at *http://wiki.apache.org/hadoop/LibHDFS*.

FUSE

Filesystem in Userspace (FUSE) allows filesystems that are implemented in user space to be integrated as a Unix filesystem. Hadoop's Fuse-DFS contrib module allows any Hadoop filesystem (but typically HDFS) to be mounted as a standard filesystem. You can then use Unix utilities (such as `ls` and `cat`) to interact with the filesystem, as well as POSIX libraries to access the filesystem from any programming language.

Fuse-DFS is implemented in C using *libhdfs* as the interface to HDFS. Documentation for compiling and running Fuse-DFS is located in the *src/contrib/fuse-dfs* directory of the Hadoop distribution.

WebDAV

WebDAV is a set of extensions to HTTP to support editing and updating files. WebDAV shares can be mounted as filesystems on most operating systems, so by exposing HDFS (or other Hadoop filesystems) over WebDAV, it's possible to access HDFS as a standard filesystem.

At the time of this writing, WebDAV support in Hadoop (which is implemented by calling the Java API to Hadoop) is still under development, and can be tracked at *https://issues.apache.org/jira/browse/HADOOP-496*.

Other HDFS Interfaces

There are two interfaces that are specific to HDFS:

HTTP
> HDFS defines a read-only interface for retrieving directory listings and data over HTTP. Directory listings are served by the namenode's embedded web server (which runs on port 50070) in XML format, while file data is streamed from datanodes by their web servers (running on port 50075). This protocol is not tied to a specific HDFS version, making it possible to write clients that can use HTTP to read data from HDFS clusters that run different versions of Hadoop. `HftpFileSystem` is a such a client: it is a Hadoop filesystem that talks to HDFS over HTTP (`HsftpFileSystem` is the HTTPS variant).

FTP
> Although not complete at the time of this writing (*https://issues.apache.org/jira/browse/HADOOP-3199*), there is an FTP interface to HDFS, which permits the use of the FTP protocol to interact with HDFS. This interface is a convenient way to transfer data into and out of HDFS using existing FTP clients.

The FTP interface to HDFS is not to be confused with `FTPFileSystem`, which exposes any FTP server as a Hadoop filesystem.

The Java Interface

In this section, we dig into the Hadoop's `FileSystem` class: the API for interacting with one of Hadoop's filesystems.# While we focus mainly on the HDFS implementation, `DistributedFileSystem`, in general you should strive to write your code against the `FileSystem` abstract class, to retain portability across filesystems. This is very useful when testing your program, for example, since you can rapidly run tests using data stored on the local filesystem.

Reading Data from a Hadoop URL

One of the simplest ways to read a file from a Hadoop filesystem is by using a `java.net.URL` object to open a stream to read the data from. The general idiom is:

```
InputStream in = null;
try {
  in = new URL("hdfs://host/path").openStream();
  // process in
} finally {
  IOUtils.closeStream(in);
}
```

There's a little bit more work required to make Java recognize Hadoop's `hdfs` URL scheme. This is achieved by calling the `setURLStreamHandlerFactory` method on `URL` with an instance of `FsUrlStreamHandlerFactory`. This method can only be called once per JVM, so it is typically executed in a static block. This limitation means that if some other part of your program—perhaps a third-party component outside your control—sets a `URLStreamHandlerFactory`, you won't be able to use this approach for reading data from Hadoop. The next section discusses an alternative.

Example 3-1 shows a program for displaying files from Hadoop filesystems on standard output, like the Unix cat command.

Example 3-1. Displaying files from a Hadoop filesystem on standard output using a URLStreamHandler

```
public class URLCat {

  static {
    URL.setURLStreamHandlerFactory(new FsUrlStreamHandlerFactory());
  }
```

\#From release 0.21.0, there is a new filesystem interface called `FileContext` with better handling of multiple filesystems (so a single `FileContext` can resolve multiple filesystem schemes, for example) and a cleaner, more consistent interface.

```
public static void main(String[] args) throws Exception {
  InputStream in = null;
  try {
    in = new URL(args[0]).openStream();
    IOUtils.copyBytes(in, System.out, 4096, false);
  } finally {
    IOUtils.closeStream(in);
  }
}
}
```

We make use of the handy IOUtils class that comes with Hadoop for closing the stream in the finally clause, and also for copying bytes between the input stream and the output stream (System.out in this case). The last two arguments to the copyBytes method are the buffer size used for copying and whether to close the streams when the copy is complete. We close the input stream ourselves, and System.out doesn't need to be closed.

Here's a sample run:[*]

```
% hadoop URLCat hdfs://localhost/user/tom/quangle.txt
On the top of the Crumpetty Tree
The Quangle Wangle sat,
But his face you could not see,
On account of his Beaver Hat.
```

Reading Data Using the FileSystem API

As the previous section explained, sometimes it is impossible to set a URLStreamHand lerFactory for your application. In this case, you will need to use the FileSystem API to open an input stream for a file.

A file in a Hadoop filesystem is represented by a Hadoop Path object (and not a java.io.File object, since its semantics are too closely tied to the local filesystem). You can think of a Path as a Hadoop filesystem URI, such as *hdfs://localhost/user/tom/quangle.txt*.

FileSystem is a general filesystem API, so the first step is to retrieve an instance for the filesystem we want to use—HDFS in this case. There are two static factory methods for getting a FileSystem instance:

```
public static FileSystem get(Configuration conf) throws IOException
public static FileSystem get(URI uri, Configuration conf) throws IOException
```

A Configuration object encapsulates a client or server's configuration, which is set using configuration files read from the classpath, such as *conf/core-site.xml*. The first method returns the default filesystem (as specified in the file *conf/core-site.xml*, or the default local filesystem if not specified there). The second uses the given URI's scheme and

---

[*] The text is from *The Quangle Wangle's Hat* by Edward Lear.

authority to determine the filesystem to use, falling back to the default filesystem if no scheme is specified in the given URI.

With a FileSystem instance in hand, we invoke an open() method to get the input stream for a file:

```
public FSDataInputStream open(Path f) throws IOException
public abstract FSDataInputStream open(Path f, int bufferSize) throws IOException
```

The first method uses a default buffer size of 4 K.

Putting this together, we can rewrite Example 3-1 as shown in Example 3-2.

Example 3-2. Displaying files from a Hadoop filesystem on standard output by using the FileSystem directly

```
public class FileSystemCat {

  public static void main(String[] args) throws Exception {
    String uri = args[0];
    Configuration conf = new Configuration();
    FileSystem fs = FileSystem.get(URI.create(uri), conf);
    InputStream in = null;
    try {
      in = fs.open(new Path(uri));
      IOUtils.copyBytes(in, System.out, 4096, false);
    } finally {
      IOUtils.closeStream(in);
    }
  }
}
```

The program runs as follows:

```
% hadoop FileSystemCat hdfs://localhost/user/tom/quangle.txt
On the top of the Crumpetty Tree
The Quangle Wangle sat,
But his face you could not see,
On account of his Beaver Hat.
```

FSDataInputStream

The open() method on FileSystem actually returns a FSDataInputStream rather than a standard java.io class. This class is a specialization of java.io.DataInputStream with support for random access, so you can read from any part of the stream:

```
package org.apache.hadoop.fs;

public class FSDataInputStream extends DataInputStream
    implements Seekable, PositionedReadable {
  // implementation elided
}
```

The Seekable interface permits seeking to a position in the file and a query method for the current offset from the start of the file (getPos()):

```
public interface Seekable {
  void seek(long pos) throws IOException;
  long getPos() throws IOException;
}
```

Calling seek() with a position that is greater than the length of the file will result in an IOException. Unlike the skip() method of java.io.InputStream that positions the stream at a point later than the current position, seek() can move to an arbitrary, absolute position in the file.

Example 3-3 is a simple extension of Example 3-2 that writes a file to standard out twice: after writing it once, it seeks to the start of the file and streams through it once again.

Example 3-3. Displaying files from a Hadoop filesystem on standard output twice, by using seek

```
public class FileSystemDoubleCat {

  public static void main(String[] args) throws Exception {
    String uri = args[0];
    Configuration conf = new Configuration();
    FileSystem fs = FileSystem.get(URI.create(uri), conf);
    FSDataInputStream in = null;
    try {
      in = fs.open(new Path(uri));
      IOUtils.copyBytes(in, System.out, 4096, false);
      in.seek(0); // go back to the start of the file
      IOUtils.copyBytes(in, System.out, 4096, false);
    } finally {
      IOUtils.closeStream(in);
    }
  }
}
```

Here's the result of running it on a small file:

```
% hadoop FileSystemDoubleCat hdfs://localhost/user/tom/quangle.txt
On the top of the Crumpetty Tree
The Quangle Wangle sat,
But his face you could not see,
On account of his Beaver Hat.
On the top of the Crumpetty Tree
The Quangle Wangle sat,
But his face you could not see,
On account of his Beaver Hat.
```

FSDataInputStream also implements the PositionedReadable interface for reading parts of a file at a given offset:

```
public interface PositionedReadable {

  public int read(long position, byte[] buffer, int offset, int length)
```

```
    throws IOException;

  public void readFully(long position, byte[] buffer, int offset, int length)
    throws IOException;

  public void readFully(long position, byte[] buffer) throws IOException;
}
```

The read() method reads up to length bytes from the given position in the file into the buffer at the given offset in the buffer. The return value is the number of bytes actually read: callers should check this value as it may be less than length. The readFully() methods will read length bytes into the buffer (or buffer.length bytes for the version that just takes a byte array buffer), unless the end of the file is reached, in which case an EOFException is thrown.

All of these methods preserve the current offset in the file and are thread-safe, so they provide a convenient way to access another part of the file—metadata perhaps—while reading the main body of the file. In fact, they are just implemented using the Seekable interface using the following pattern:

```
long oldPos = getPos();
try {
  seek(position);
  // read data
} finally {
  seek(oldPos);
}
```

Finally, bear in mind that calling seek() is a relatively expensive operation and should be used sparingly. You should structure your application access patterns to rely on streaming data, (by using MapReduce, for example) rather than performing a large number of seeks.

Writing Data

The FileSystem class has a number of methods for creating a file. The simplest is the method that takes a Path object for the file to be created and returns an output stream to write to:

```
public FSDataOutputStream create(Path f) throws IOException
```

There are overloaded versions of this method that allow you to specify whether to forcibly overwrite existing files, the replication factor of the file, the buffer size to use when writing the file, the block size for the file, and file permissions.

 The create() methods create any parent directories of the file to be written that don't already exist. Though convenient, this behavior may be unexpected. If you want the write to fail if the parent directory doesn't exist, then you should check for the existence of the parent directory first by calling the exists() method.

There's also an overloaded method for passing a callback interface, `Progressable`, so your application can be notified of the progress of the data being written to the datanodes:

```
package org.apache.hadoop.util;

public interface Progressable {
  public void progress();
}
```

As an alternative to creating a new file, you can append to an existing file using the `append()` method (there are also some other overloaded versions):

```
public FSDataOutputStream append(Path f) throws IOException
```

The append operation allows a single writer to modify an already written file by opening it and writing data from the final offset in the file. With this API, applications that produce unbounded files, such as logfiles, can write to an existing file after a restart, for example. The append operation is optional and not implemented by all Hadoop filesystems. For example, HDFS supports append, but S3 filesystems don't.

Example 3-4 shows how to copy a local file to a Hadoop filesystem. We illustrate progress by printing a period every time the `progress()` method is called by Hadoop, which is after each 64 K packet of data is written to the datanode pipeline. (Note that this particular behavior is not specified by the API, so it is subject to change in later versions of Hadoop. The API merely allows you to infer that "something is happening.")

Example 3-4. Copying a local file to a Hadoop filesystem

```
public class FileCopyWithProgress {
  public static void main(String[] args) throws Exception {
    String localSrc = args[0];
    String dst = args[1];

    InputStream in = new BufferedInputStream(new FileInputStream(localSrc));

    Configuration conf = new Configuration();
    FileSystem fs = FileSystem.get(URI.create(dst), conf);
    OutputStream out = fs.create(new Path(dst), new Progressable() {
      public void progress() {
        System.out.print(".");
      }
    });

    IOUtils.copyBytes(in, out, 4096, true);
  }
}
```

Typical usage:

```
% hadoop FileCopyWithProgress input/docs/1400-8.txt hdfs://localhost/user/tom/
    1400-8.txt
    . . . . . . . . . . . . . .
```

Currently, none of the other Hadoop filesystems call progress() during writes. Progress is important in MapReduce applications, as you will see in later chapters.

FSDataOutputStream

The create() method on FileSystem returns an FSDataOutputStream, which, like FSDataInputStream, has a method for querying the current position in the file:

```
package org.apache.hadoop.fs;

public class FSDataOutputStream extends DataOutputStream implements Syncable {

    public long getPos() throws IOException {
      // implementation elided
    }

    // implementation elided

}
```

However, unlike FSDataInputStream, FSDataOutputStream does not permit seeking. This is because HDFS allows only sequential writes to an open file or appends to an already written file. In other words, there is no support for writing to anywhere other than the end of the file, so there is no value in being able to seek while writing.

Directories

FileSystem provides a method to create a directory:

```
public boolean mkdirs(Path f) throws IOException
```

This method creates all of the necessary parent directories if they don't already exist, just like the java.io.File's mkdirs() method. It returns true if the directory (and all parent directories) was (were) successfully created.

Often, you don't need to explicitly create a directory, since writing a file, by calling create(), will automatically create any parent directories.

Querying the Filesystem

File metadata: FileStatus

An important feature of any filesystem is the ability to navigate its directory structure and retrieve information about the files and directories that it stores. The FileStatus class encapsulates filesystem metadata for files and directories, including file length, block size, replication, modification time, ownership, and permission information.

The method getFileStatus() on FileSystem provides a way of getting a FileStatus object for a single file or directory. Example 3-5 shows an example of its use.

Example 3-5. Demonstrating file status information

```java
public class ShowFileStatusTest {

  private MiniDFSCluster cluster; // use an in-process HDFS cluster for testing
  private FileSystem fs;

  @Before
  public void setUp() throws IOException {
    Configuration conf = new Configuration();
    if (System.getProperty("test.build.data") == null) {
      System.setProperty("test.build.data", "/tmp");
    }
    cluster = new MiniDFSCluster(conf, 1, true, null);
    fs = cluster.getFileSystem();
    OutputStream out = fs.create(new Path("/dir/file"));
    out.write("content".getBytes("UTF-8"));
    out.close();
  }

  @After
  public void tearDown() throws IOException {
    if (fs != null) { fs.close(); }
    if (cluster != null) { cluster.shutdown(); }
  }

  @Test(expected = FileNotFoundException.class)
  public void throwsFileNotFoundForNonExistentFile() throws IOException {
    fs.getFileStatus(new Path("no-such-file"));
  }

  @Test
  public void fileStatusForFile() throws IOException {
    Path file = new Path("/dir/file");
    FileStatus stat = fs.getFileStatus(file);
    assertThat(stat.getPath().toUri().getPath(), is("/dir/file"));
    assertThat(stat.isDir(), is(false));
    assertThat(stat.getLen(), is(7L));
    assertThat(stat.getModificationTime(),
        is(lessThanOrEqualTo(System.currentTimeMillis())));
    assertThat(stat.getReplication(), is((short) 1));
    assertThat(stat.getBlockSize(), is(64 * 1024 * 1024L));
    assertThat(stat.getOwner(), is("tom"));
    assertThat(stat.getGroup(), is("supergroup"));
    assertThat(stat.getPermission().toString(), is("rw-r--r--"));
  }

  @Test
  public void fileStatusForDirectory() throws IOException {
    Path dir = new Path("/dir");
    FileStatus stat = fs.getFileStatus(dir);
    assertThat(stat.getPath().toUri().getPath(), is("/dir"));
    assertThat(stat.isDir(), is(true));
    assertThat(stat.getLen(), is(0L));
    assertThat(stat.getModificationTime(),
        is(lessThanOrEqualTo(System.currentTimeMillis())));
```

```
    assertThat(stat.getReplication(), is((short) 0));
    assertThat(stat.getBlockSize(), is(0L));
    assertThat(stat.getOwner(), is("tom"));
    assertThat(stat.getGroup(), is("supergroup"));
    assertThat(stat.getPermission().toString(), is("rwxr-xr-x"));
  }

}
```

If no file or directory exists, a `FileNotFoundException` is thrown. However, if you are interested only in the existence of a file or directory, then the `exists()` method on FileSystem is more convenient:

```
    public boolean exists(Path f) throws IOException
```

Listing files

Finding information on a single file or directory is useful, but you also often need to be able to list the contents of a directory. That's what FileSystem's `listStatus()` methods are for:

```
    public FileStatus[] listStatus(Path f) throws IOException
    public FileStatus[] listStatus(Path f, PathFilter filter) throws IOException
    public FileStatus[] listStatus(Path[] files) throws IOException
    public FileStatus[] listStatus(Path[] files, PathFilter filter) throws IOException
```

When the argument is a file, the simplest variant returns an array of `FileStatus` objects of length 1. When the argument is a directory, it returns zero or more `FileStatus` objects representing the files and directories contained in the directory.

Overloaded variants allow a `PathFilter` to be supplied to restrict the files and directories to match—you will see an example in section "PathFilter" on page 61. Finally, if you specify an array of paths, the result is a shortcut for calling the equivalent single-path `listStatus` method for each path in turn and accumulating the `FileStatus` object arrays in a single array. This can be useful for building up lists of input files to process from distinct parts of the filesystem tree. Example 3-6 is a simple demonstration of this idea. Note the use of `stat2Paths()` in `FileUtil` for turning an array of `FileStatus` objects to an array of `Path` objects.

Example 3-6. Showing the file statuses for a collection of paths in a Hadoop filesystem

```
public class ListStatus {

  public static void main(String[] args) throws Exception {
    String uri = args[0];
    Configuration conf = new Configuration();
    FileSystem fs = FileSystem.get(URI.create(uri), conf);

    Path[] paths = new Path[args.length];
    for (int i = 0; i < paths.length; i++) {
      paths[i] = new Path(args[i]);
    }
```

```
    FileStatus[] status = fs.listStatus(paths);
    Path[] listedPaths = FileUtil.stat2Paths(status);
    for (Path p : listedPaths) {
      System.out.println(p);
    }
  }
}
```

We can use this program to find the union of directory listings for a collection of paths:

```
% hadoop ListStatus hdfs://localhost/ hdfs://localhost/user/tom
hdfs://localhost/user
hdfs://localhost/user/tom/books
hdfs://localhost/user/tom/quangle.txt
```

File patterns

It is a common requirement to process sets of files in a single operation. For example, a MapReduce job for log processing might analyze a month's worth of files contained in a number of directories. Rather than having to enumerate each file and directory to specify the input, it is convenient to use wildcard characters to match multiple files with a single expression, an operation that is known as *globbing*. Hadoop provides two FileSystem method for processing globs:

```
public FileStatus[] globStatus(Path pathPattern) throws IOException
public FileStatus[] globStatus(Path pathPattern, PathFilter filter) throws
    IOException
```

The globStatus() method returns an array of FileStatus objects whose paths match the supplied pattern, sorted by path. An optional PathFilter can be specified to restrict the matches further.

Hadoop supports the same set of glob characters as Unix *bash* (see Table 3-2).

Table 3-2. Glob characters and their meanings

Glob	Name	Matches
*	asterisk	Matches zero or more characters
?	question mark	Matches a single character
[ab]	character class	Matches a single character in the set {a, b}
[^ab]	negated character class	Matches a single character that is not in the set {a, b}
[a-b]	character range	Matches a single character in the (closed) range [a, b], where a is lexicographically less than or equal to b
[^a-b]	negated character range	Matches a single character that is not in the (closed) range [a, b], where a is lexicographically less than or equal to b
{a,b}	alternation	Matches either expression a or b
\c	escaped character	Matches character c when it is a metacharacter

Imagine that logfiles are stored in a directory structure organized hierarchically by date. So, for example, logfiles for the last day of 2007 would go in a directory named */2007/12/31*. Suppose that the full file listing is:

- */2007/12/30*
- */2007/12/31*
- */2008/01/01*
- */2008/01/02*

Here are some file globs and their expansions:

Glob	Expansion
/*	/2007 /2008
/*/*	/2007/12 /2008/01
/*/12/*	/2007/12/30 /2007/12/31
/200?	/2007 /2008
/200[78]	/2007 /2008
/200[7-8]	/2007 /2008
/200[^01234569]	/2007 /2008
/*/*/{31,01}	/2007/12/31 /2008/01/01
/*/*/3{0,1}	/2007/12/30 /2007/12/31
/*/{12/31,01/01}	/2007/12/31 /2008/01/01

PathFilter

Glob patterns are not always powerful enough to describe a set of files you want to access. For example, it is not generally possible to exclude a particular file using a glob pattern. The listStatus() and globStatus() methods of FileSystem take an optional PathFilter, which allows programmatic control over matching:

```
package org.apache.hadoop.fs;

public interface PathFilter {
  boolean accept(Path path);
}
```

PathFilter is the equivalent of java.io.FileFilter for Path objects rather than File objects.

Example 3-7 shows a PathFilter for excluding paths that match a regular expression.

Example 3-7. A PathFilter for excluding paths that match a regular expression

```
public class RegexExcludePathFilter implements PathFilter {

  private final String regex;

  public RegexExcludePathFilter(String regex) {
    this.regex = regex;
  }

  public boolean accept(Path path) {
    return !path.toString().matches(regex);
  }
}
```

The filter passes only files that *don't* match the regular expression. We use the filter in conjunction with a glob that picks out an initial set of files to include: the filter is used to refine the results. For example:

```
fs.globStatus(new Path("/2007/*/*"), new RegexExcludeFilter("^.*/2007/12/31$"))
```

will expand to */2007/12/30*.

Filters can only act on a file's name, as represented by a Path. They can't use a file's properties, such as creation time, as the basis of the filter. Nevertheless, they can perform matching that neither glob patterns nor regular expressions can achieve. For example, if you store files in a directory structure that is laid out by date (like in the previous section), then you can write a PathFilter to pick out files that fall in a given date range.

Deleting Data

Use the delete() method on FileSystem to permanently remove files or directories:

```
public boolean delete(Path f, boolean recursive) throws IOException
```

If f is a file or an empty directory, then the value of recursive is ignored. A nonempty directory is only deleted, along with its contents, if recursive is true (otherwise an IOException is thrown).

Data Flow

Anatomy of a File Read

To get an idea of how data flows between the client interacting with HDFS, the name-node and the datanodes, consider Figure 3-1, which shows the main sequence of events when reading a file.

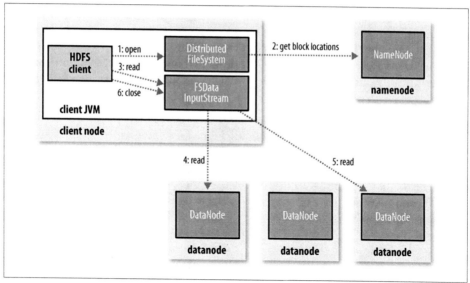

Figure 3-1. A client reading data from HDFS

The client opens the file it wishes to read by calling open() on the FileSystem object, which for HDFS is an instance of DistributedFileSystem (step 1 in Figure 3-1). DistributedFileSystem calls the namenode, using RPC, to determine the locations of the blocks for the first few blocks in the file (step 2). For each block, the namenode returns the addresses of the datanodes that have a copy of that block. Furthermore, the datanodes are sorted according to their proximity to the client (according to the topology of the cluster's network; see "Network Topology and Hadoop" on page 64). If the client is itself a datanode (in the case of a MapReduce task, for instance), then it will read from the local datanode, if it hosts a copy of the block.

The DistributedFileSystem returns an FSDataInputStream (an input stream that supports file seeks) to the client for it to read data from. FSDataInputStream in turn wraps a DFSInputStream, which manages the datanode and namenode I/O.

The client then calls read() on the stream (step 3). DFSInputStream, which has stored the datanode addresses for the first few blocks in the file, then connects to the first (closest) datanode for the first block in the file. Data is streamed from the datanode back to the client, which calls read() repeatedly on the stream (step 4). When the end of the block is reached, DFSInputStream will close the connection to the datanode, then find the best datanode for the next block (step 5). This happens transparently to the client, which from its point of view is just reading a continuous stream.

Blocks are read in order with the DFSInputStream opening new connections to datanodes as the client reads through the stream. It will also call the namenode to retrieve the datanode locations for the next batch of blocks as needed. When the client has finished reading, it calls close() on the FSDataInputStream (step 6).

During reading, if the DFSInputStream encounters an error while communicating with a datanode, then it will try the next closest one for that block. It will also remember datanodes that have failed so that it doesn't needlessly retry them for later blocks. The DFSInputStream also verifies checksums for the data transferred to it from the datanode. If a corrupted block is found, it is reported to the namenode before the DFSInput Stream attempts to read a replica of the block from another datanode.

One important aspect of this design is that the client contacts datanodes directly to retrieve data and is guided by the namenode to the best datanode for each block. This design allows HDFS to scale to a large number of concurrent clients, since the data traffic is spread across all the datanodes in the cluster. The namenode meanwhile merely has to service block location requests (which it stores in memory, making them very efficient) and does not, for example, serve data, which would quickly become a bottleneck as the number of clients grew.

Network Topology and Hadoop

What does it mean for two nodes in a local network to be "close" to each other? In the context of high-volume data processing, the limiting factor is the rate at which we can transfer data between nodes—bandwidth is a scarce commodity. The idea is to use the bandwidth between two nodes as a measure of distance.

Rather than measuring bandwidth between nodes, which can be difficult to do in practice (it requires a quiet cluster, and the number of pairs of nodes in a cluster grows as the square of the number of nodes), Hadoop takes a simple approach in which the network is represented as a tree and the distance between two nodes is the sum of their distances to their closest common ancestor. Levels in the tree are not predefined, but it is common to have levels that correspond to the data center, the rack, and the node that a process is running on. The idea is that the bandwidth available for each of the following scenarios becomes progressively less:

- Processes on the same node
- Different nodes on the same rack
- Nodes on different racks in the same data center
- Nodes in different data centers[†]

For example, imagine a node *n1* on rack *r1* in data center *d1*. This can be represented as */d1/r1/n1*. Using this notation, here are the distances for the four scenarios:

- *distance(/d1/r1/n1, /d1/r1/n1)* = 0 (processes on the same node)
- *distance(/d1/r1/n1, /d1/r1/n2)* = 2 (different nodes on the same rack)
- *distance(/d1/r1/n1, /d1/r2/n3)* = 4 (nodes on different racks in the same data center)
- *distance(/d1/r1/n1, /d2/r3/n4)* = 6 (nodes in different data centers)

[†] At the time of this writing, Hadoop is not suited for running across data centers.

This is illustrated schematically in Figure 3-2. (Mathematically inclined readers will notice that this is an example of a distance metric.)

Finally, it is important to realize that Hadoop cannot divine your network topology for you. It needs some help; we'll cover how to configure topology in "Network Topology" on page 261. By default though, it assumes that the network is flat—a single-level hierarchy—or in other words, that all nodes are on a single rack in a single data center. For small clusters, this may actually be the case, and no further configuration is required.

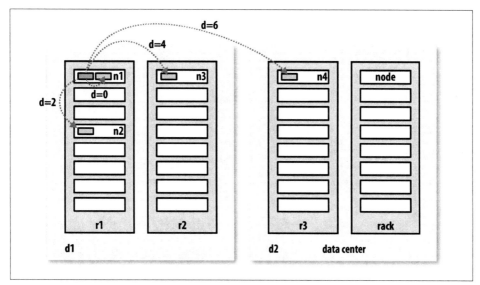

Figure 3-2. Network distance in Hadoop

Anatomy of a File Write

Next we'll look at how files are written to HDFS. Although quite detailed, it is instructive to understand the data flow since it clarifies HDFS's coherency model.

The case we're going to consider is the case of creating a new file, writing data to it, then closing the file. See Figure 3-3.

The client creates the file by calling create() on DistributedFileSystem (step 1 in Figure 3-3). DistributedFileSystem makes an RPC call to the namenode to create a new file in the filesystem's namespace, with no blocks associated with it (step 2). The namenode performs various checks to make sure the file doesn't already exist, and that the client has the right permissions to create the file. If these checks pass, the namenode makes a record of the new file; otherwise, file creation fails and the client is thrown an IOException. The DistributedFileSystem returns an FSDataOutputStream for the client

to start writing data to. Just as in the read case, FSDataOutputStream wraps a DFSOutput
Stream, which handles communication with the datanodes and namenode.

As the client writes data (step 3), DFSOutputStream splits it into packets, which it writes
to an internal queue, called the *data queue*. The data queue is consumed by the Data
Streamer, whose responsibility it is to ask the namenode to allocate new blocks by
picking a list of suitable datanodes to store the replicas. The list of datanodes forms a
pipeline—we'll assume the replication level is three, so there are three nodes in the
pipeline. The DataStreamer streams the packets to the first datanode in the pipeline,
which stores the packet and forwards it to the second datanode in the pipeline. Similarly, the second datanode stores the packet and forwards it to the third (and last)
datanode in the pipeline (step 4).

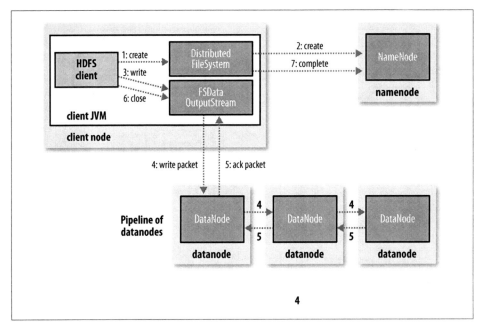

Figure 3-3. A client writing data to HDFS

DFSOutputStream also maintains an internal queue of packets that are waiting to be
acknowledged by datanodes, called the *ack queue*. A packet is removed from the ack
queue only when it has been acknowledged by all the datanodes in the pipeline (step 5).

If a datanode fails while data is being written to it, then the following actions are taken,
which are transparent to the client writing the data. First the pipeline is closed, and any
packets in the ack queue are added to the front of the data queue so that datanodes
that are downstream from the failed node will not miss any packets. The current block
on the good datanodes is given a new identity, which is communicated to the namenode, so that the partial block on the failed datanode will be deleted if the failed

datanode recovers later on. The failed datanode is removed from the pipeline and the remainder of the block's data is written to the two good datanodes in the pipeline. The namenode notices that the block is under-replicated, and it arranges for a further replica to be created on another node. Subsequent blocks are then treated as normal.

It's possible, but unlikely, that multiple datanodes fail while a block is being written. As long as dfs.replication.min replicas (default one) are written, the write will succeed, and the block will be asynchronously replicated across the cluster until its target replication factor is reached (dfs.replication, which defaults to three).

When the client has finished writing data, it calls close() on the stream (step 6). This action flushes all the remaining packets to the datanode pipeline and waits for acknowledgments before contacting the namenode to signal that the file is complete (step 7). The namenode already knows which blocks the file is made up of (via Data Streamer asking for block allocations), so it only has to wait for blocks to be minimally replicated before returning successfully.

Replica Placement

How does the namenode choose which datanodes to store replicas on? There's a trade-off between reliability and write bandwidth and read bandwidth here. For example, placing all replicas on a single node incurs the lowest write bandwidth penalty since the replication pipeline runs on a single node, but this offers no real redundancy (if the node fails, the data for that block is lost). Also, the read bandwidth is high for off-rack reads. At the other extreme, placing replicas in different data centers may maximize redundancy, but at the cost of bandwidth. Even in the same data center (which is what all Hadoop clusters to date have run in), there are a variety of placement strategies. Indeed, Hadoop changed its placement strategy in release 0.17.0 to one that helps keep a fairly even distribution of blocks across the cluster. (See "balancer" on page 304 for details on keeping a cluster balanced.) And from 0.21.0, block placement policies are pluggable.

Hadoop's default strategy is to place the first replica on the same node as the client (for clients running outside the cluster, a node is chosen at random, although the system tries not to pick nodes that are too full or too busy). The second replica is placed on a different rack from the first (*off-rack*), chosen at random. The third replica is placed on the same rack as the second, but on a different node chosen at random. Further replicas are placed on random nodes on the cluster, although the system tries to avoid placing too many replicas on the same rack.

Once the replica locations have been chosen, a pipeline is built, taking network topology into account. For a replication factor of 3, the pipeline might look like Figure 3-4.

Overall, this strategy gives a good balance among reliability (blocks are stored on two racks), write bandwidth (writes only have to traverse a single network switch), read performance (there's a choice of two racks to read from), and block distribution across the cluster (clients only write a single block on the local rack).

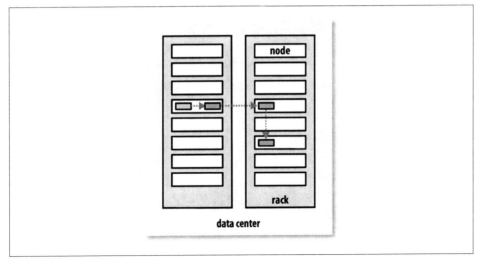

Figure 3-4. A typical replica pipeline

Coherency Model

A coherency model for a filesystem describes the data visibility of reads and writes for a file. HDFS trades off some POSIX requirements for performance, so some operations may behave differently than you expect them to.

After creating a file, it is visible in the filesystem namespace, as expected:

```
Path p = new Path("p");
fs.create(p);
assertThat(fs.exists(p), is(true));
```

However, any content written to the file is not guaranteed to be visible, even if the stream is flushed. So the file appears to have a length of zero:

```
Path p = new Path("p");
OutputStream out = fs.create(p);
out.write("content".getBytes("UTF-8"));
out.flush();
assertThat(fs.getFileStatus(p).getLen(), is(0L));
```

Once more than a block's worth of data has been written, the first block will be visible to new readers. This is true of subsequent blocks, too: it is always the current block being written that is not visible to other readers.

HDFS provides a method for forcing all buffers to be synchronized to the datanodes via the sync() method on FSDataOutputStream. After a successful return from sync(), HDFS guarantees that the data written up to that point in the file is persisted and visible to all new readers:‡

```
Path p = new Path("p");
FSDataOutputStream out = fs.create(p);
out.write("content".getBytes("UTF-8"));
out.flush();
out.sync();
assertThat(fs.getFileStatus(p).getLen(), is(((long) "content".length())));
```

This behavior is similar to the fsync system call in POSIX that commits buffered data for a file descriptor. For example, using the standard Java API to write a local file, we are guaranteed to see the content after flushing the stream and synchronizing:

```
FileOutputStream out = new FileOutputStream(localFile);
out.write("content".getBytes("UTF-8"));
out.flush(); // flush to operating system
out.getFD().sync(); // sync to disk
assertThat(localFile.length(), is(((long) "content".length())));
```

Closing a file in HDFS performs an implicit sync(), too:

```
Path p = new Path("p");
OutputStream out = fs.create(p);
out.write("content".getBytes("UTF-8"));
out.close();
assertThat(fs.getFileStatus(p).getLen(), is(((long) "content".length())));
```

Consequences for application design

This coherency model has implications for the way you design applications. With no calls to sync(), you should be prepared to lose up to a block of data in the event of client or system failure. For many applications, this is unacceptable, so you should call sync() at suitable points, such as after writing a certain number of records or number of bytes. Though the sync() operation is designed to not unduly tax HDFS, it does have some overhead, so there is a trade-off between data robustness and throughput. What is an acceptable trade-off is application-dependent, and suitable values can be selected after measuring your application's performance with different sync() frequencies.

‡ Releases of Hadoop up to and including 0.20 do not have a working implementation of sync(); however, this has been remedied from 0.21.0 onward. Also, from that version, sync() is deprecated in favor of hflush(), which only guarantees that new readers will see all data written to that point, and hsync(), which makes a stronger guarantee that the operating system has flushed the data to disk (like POSIX fsync), although data may still be in the disk cache.

Parallel Copying with distcp

The HDFS access patterns that we have seen so far focus on single-threaded access. It's possible to act on a collection of files, by specifying file globs, for example, but for efficient, parallel processing of these files you would have to write a program yourself. Hadoop comes with a useful program called *distcp* for copying large amounts of data to and from Hadoop filesystems in parallel.

The canonical use case for *distcp* is for transferring data between two HDFS clusters. If the clusters are running identical versions of Hadoop, the *hdfs* scheme is appropriate:

```
% hadoop distcp hdfs://namenode1/foo hdfs://namenode2/bar
```

This will copy the */foo* directory (and its contents) from the first cluster to the */bar* directory on the second cluster, so the second cluster ends up with the directory structure */bar/foo*. If */bar* doesn't exist, it will be created first. You can specify multiple source paths, and all will be copied to the destination. Source paths must be absolute.

By default, *distcp* will skip files that already exist in the destination, but they can be overwritten by supplying the -overwrite option. You can also update only files that have changed using the -update option.

> Using either (or both) of -overwrite or -update changes how the source and destination paths are interpreted. This is best shown with an example. If we changed a file in the */foo* subtree on the first cluster from the previous example, then we could synchronize the change with the second cluster by running:
>
> ```
> % hadoop distcp -update hdfs://namenode1/foo hdfs://namenode2/bar/foo
> ```
>
> The extra trailing */foo* subdirectory is needed on the destination, as now the *contents* of the source directory are copied to the *contents* of the destination directory. (If you are familiar with *rsync*, you can think of the -overwrite or -update options as adding an implicit trailing slash to the source.)
>
> If you are unsure of the effect of a *distcp* operation, it is a good idea to try it out on a small test directory tree first.

There are more options to control the behavior of *distcp*, including ones to preserve file attributes, ignore failures, and limit the number of files or total data copied. Run it with no options to see the usage instructions.

distcp is implemented as a MapReduce job where the work of copying is done by the maps that run in parallel across the cluster. There are no reducers. Each file is copied by a single map, and *distcp* tries to give each map approximately the same amount of data, by bucketing files into roughly equal allocations.

The number of maps is decided as follows. Since it's a good idea to get each map to copy a reasonable amount of data to minimize overheads in task setup, each map copies at least 256 MB (unless the total size of the input is less, in which case one map handles it all). For example, 1 GB of files will be given four map tasks. When the data size is very large, it becomes necessary to limit the number of maps in order to limit bandwidth and cluster utilization. By default, the maximum number of maps is 20 per (tasktracker) cluster node. For example, copying 1,000 GB of files to a 100-node cluster will allocate 2,000 maps (20 per node), so each will copy 512 MB on average. This can be reduced by specifying the -m argument to *distcp*. For example, -m 1000 would allocate 1,000 maps, each copying 1 GB on average.

If you try to use *distcp* between two HDFS clusters that are running different versions, the copy will fail if you use the *hdfs* protocol, since the RPC systems are incompatible. To remedy this, you can use the read-only HTTP-based HFTP filesystem to read from the source. The job must run on the destination cluster so that the HDFS RPC versions are compatible. To repeat the previous example using HFTP:

```
% hadoop distcp hftp://namenode1:50070/foo hdfs://namenode2/bar
```

Note that you need to specify the namenode's web port in the source URI. This is determined by the dfs.http.address property, which defaults to 50070.

Keeping an HDFS Cluster Balanced

When copying data into HDFS, it's important to consider cluster balance. HDFS works best when the file blocks are evenly spread across the cluster, so you want to ensure that *distcp* doesn't disrupt this. Going back to the 1,000 GB example, by specifying -m 1 a single map would do the copy, which—apart from being slow and not using the cluster resources efficiently—would mean that the first replica of each block would reside on the node running the map (until the disk filled up). The second and third replicas would be spread across the cluster, but this one node would be unbalanced. By having more maps than nodes in the cluster, this problem is avoided—for this reason, it's best to start by running *distcp* with the default of 20 maps per node.

However, it's not always possible to prevent a cluster from becoming unbalanced. Perhaps you want to limit the number of maps so that some of the nodes can be used by other jobs. In this case, you can use the *balancer* tool (see "balancer" on page 304) to subsequently even out the block distribution across the cluster.

Hadoop Archives

HDFS stores small files inefficiently, since each file is stored in a block, and block metadata is held in memory by the namenode. Thus, a large number of small files can eat up a lot of memory on the namenode. (Note, however, that small files do not take up any more disk space than is required to store the raw contents of the file. For example, a 1 MB file stored with a block size of 128 MB uses 1 MB of disk space, not 128 MB.)

Hadoop Archives, or HAR files, are a file archiving facility that packs files into HDFS blocks more efficiently, thereby reducing namenode memory usage while still allowing transparent access to files. In particular, Hadoop Archives can be used as input to MapReduce.

Using Hadoop Archives

A Hadoop Archive is created from a collection of files using the *archive* tool. The tool runs a MapReduce job to process the input files in parallel, so to run it, you need a MapReduce cluster running to use it. Here are some files in HDFS that we would like to archive:

```
% hadoop fs -lsr /my/files
-rw-r--r--   1 tom supergroup          1 2009-04-09 19:13 /my/files/a
drwxr-xr-x   - tom supergroup          0 2009-04-09 19:13 /my/files/dir
-rw-r--r--   1 tom supergroup          1 2009-04-09 19:13 /my/files/dir/b
```

Now we can run the `archive` command:

```
%
hadoop archive -archiveName files.har /my/files /my
```

The first option is the name of the archive, here *files.har*. HAR files always have a *.har* extension, which is mandatory for reasons we shall see later. Next comes the files to put in the archive. Here we are archiving only one source tree, the files in */my/files* in HDFS, but the tool accepts multiple source trees. The final argument is the output directory for the HAR file. Let's see what the archive has created:

```
% hadoop fs -ls /my
Found 2 items
drwxr-xr-x   - tom supergroup          0 2009-04-09 19:13 /my/files
drwxr-xr-x   - tom supergroup          0 2009-04-09 19:13 /my/files.har
% hadoop fs -ls /my/files.har
Found 3 items
-rw-r--r--  10 tom supergroup        165 2009-04-09 19:13 /my/files.har/_index
-rw-r--r--  10 tom supergroup         23 2009-04-09 19:13 /my/files.har/_masterindex
-rw-r--r--   1 tom supergroup          2 2009-04-09 19:13 /my/files.har/part-0
```

The directory listing shows what a HAR file is made of: two index files and a collection of part files—just one in this example. The part files contain the contents of a number of the original files concatenated together, and the indexes make it possible to look up the part file that an archived file is contained in, and its offset and length. All these details are hidden from the application, however, which uses the *har* URI scheme to interact with HAR files, using a HAR filesystem that is layered on top of the underlying filesystem (HDFS in this case). The following command recursively lists the files in the archive:

```
% hadoop fs -lsr har:///my/files.har
drw-r--r--   - tom supergroup          0 2009-04-09 19:13 /my/files.har/my
drw-r--r--   - tom supergroup          0 2009-04-09 19:13 /my/files.har/my/files
-rw-r--r--  10 tom supergroup          1 2009-04-09 19:13 /my/files.har/my/files/a
drw-r--r--   - tom supergroup          0 2009-04-09 19:13 /my/files.har/my/files/dir
-rw-r--r--  10 tom supergroup          1 2009-04-09 19:13 /my/files.har/my/files/dir/b
```

This is quite straightforward if the filesystem that the HAR file is on is the default filesystem. On the other hand, if you want to refer to a HAR file on a different filesystem, then you need to use a different form of the path URI to normal. These two commands have the same effect, for example:

```
% hadoop fs -lsr har:///my/files.har/my/files/dir
% hadoop fs -lsr har://hdfs-localhost:8020/my/files.har/my/files/dir
```

Notice in the second form that the scheme is still *har* to signify a HAR filesystem, but the authority is *hdfs* to specify the underlying filesystem's scheme, followed by a dash and the HDFS host (localhost) and port (8020). We can now see why HAR files have to have a *.har* extension. The HAR filesystem translates the *har* URI into a URI for the underlying filesystem, by looking at the authority and path up to and including the component with the *.har* extension. In this case, it is *hdfs://localhost:8020/my/files .har*. The remaining part of the path is the path of the file in the archive: */my/files/dir*.

To delete a HAR file, you need to use the recursive form of delete, since from the underlying filesystem's point of view the HAR file is a directory:

```
%
hadoop fs -rmr /my/files.har
```

Limitations

There are a few limitations to be aware of with HAR files. Creating an archive creates a copy of the original files, so you need as much disk space as the files you are archiving to create the archive (although you can delete the originals once you have created the archive). There is currently no support for archive compression, although the files that go into the archive can be compressed (HAR files are like *tar* files in this respect).

Archives are immutable once they have been created. To add or remove files, you must re-create the archive. In practice, this is not a problem for files that don't change after being written, since they can be archived in batches on a regular basis, such as daily or weekly.

As noted earlier, HAR files can be used as input to MapReduce. However, there is no archive-aware InputFormat that can pack multiple files into a single MapReduce split, so processing lots of small files, even in a HAR file, can still be inefficient. "Small files and CombineFileInputFormat" on page 203 discusses another approach to this problem.

## CHAPTER 4

Hadoop I/O

Hadoop comes with a set of primitives for data I/O. Some of these are techniques that are more general than Hadoop, such as data integrity and compression, but deserve special consideration when dealing with multiterabyte datasets. Others are Hadoop tools or APIs that form the building blocks for developing distributed systems, such as serialization frameworks and on-disk data structures.

Data Integrity

Users of Hadoop rightly expect that no data will be lost or corrupted during storage or processing. However, since every I/O operation on the disk or network carries with it a small chance of introducing errors into the data that it is reading or writing, when the volumes of data flowing through the system are as large as the ones Hadoop is capable of handling, the chance of data corruption occurring is high.

The usual way of detecting corrupted data is by computing a *checksum* for the data when it first enters the system, and again whenever it is transmitted across a channel that is unreliable and hence capable of corrupting the data. The data is deemed to be corrupt if the newly generated checksum doesn't exactly match the original. This technique doesn't offer any way to fix the data—merely error detection. (And this is a reason for not using low-end hardware; in particular, be sure to use ECC memory.) Note that it is possible that it's the checksum that is corrupt, not the data, but this is very unlikely, since the checksum is much smaller than the data.

A commonly used error-detecting code is CRC-32 (cyclic redundancy check), which computes a 32-bit integer checksum for input of any size.

Data Integrity in HDFS

HDFS transparently checksums all data written to it and by default verifies checksums when reading data. A separate checksum is created for every io.bytes.per.checksum bytes of data. The default is 512 bytes, and since a CRC-32 checksum is 4 bytes long, the storage overhead is less than 1%.

Datanodes are responsible for verifying the data they receive before storing the data and its checksum. This applies to data that they receive from clients and from other datanodes during replication. A client writing data sends it to a pipeline of datanodes (as explained in Chapter 3), and the last datanode in the pipeline verifies the checksum. If it detects an error, the client receives a `ChecksumException`, a subclass of `IOExcep tion`, which it should handle in an application-specific manner, by retrying the operation, for example.

When clients read data from datanodes, they verify checksums as well, comparing them with the ones stored at the datanode. Each datanode keeps a persistent log of checksum verifications, so it knows the last time each of its blocks was verified. When a client successfully verifies a block, it tells the datanode, which updates its log. Keeping statistics such as these is valuable in detecting bad disks.

Aside from block verification on client reads, each datanode runs a `DataBlockScanner` in a background thread that periodically verifies all the blocks stored on the datanode. This is to guard against corruption due to "bit rot" in the physical storage media. See "Datanode block scanner" on page 303 for details on how to access the scanner reports.

Since HDFS stores replicas of blocks, it can "heal" corrupted blocks by copying one of the good replicas to produce a new, uncorrupt replica. The way this works is that if a client detects an error when reading a block, it reports the bad block and the datanode it was trying to read from to the namenode before throwing a `ChecksumException`. The namenode marks the block replica as corrupt, so it doesn't direct clients to it, or try to copy this replica to another datanode. It then schedules a copy of the block to be replicated on another datanode, so its replication factor is back at the expected level. Once this has happened, the corrupt replica is deleted.

It is possible to disable verification of checksums by passing `false` to the `setVerify Checksum()` method on `FileSystem`, before using the `open()` method to read a file. The same effect is possible from the shell by using the `-ignoreCrc` option with the `-get` or the equivalent `-copyToLocal` command. This feature is useful if you have a corrupt file that you want to inspect so you can decide what to do with it. For example, you might want to see whether it can be salvaged before you delete it.

LocalFileSystem

The Hadoop `LocalFileSystem` performs client-side checksumming. This means that when you write a file called *filename*, the filesystem client transparently creates a hidden file, *.filename.crc*, in the same directory containing the checksums for each chunk of the file. Like HDFS, the chunk size is controlled by the `io.bytes.per.checksum` property, which defaults to 512 bytes. The chunk size is stored as metadata in the *.crc* file, so the file can be read back correctly even if the setting for the chunk size has changed. Checksums are verified when the file is read, and if an error is detected, LocalFileSystem throws a ChecksumException.

Checksums are fairly cheap to compute (in Java, they are implemented in native code), typically adding a few percent overhead to the time to read or write a file. For most applications, this is an acceptable price to pay for data integrity. It is, however, possible to disable checksums: typically when the underlying filesystem supports checksums natively. This is accomplished by using RawLocalFileSystem in place of Local FileSystem. To do this globally in an application, it suffices to remap the implementation for *file* URIs by setting the property fs.file.impl to the value org.apache.hadoop.fs.RawLocalFileSystem. Alternatively, you can directly create a Raw LocalFileSystem instance, which may be useful if you want to disable checksum verification for only some reads; for example:

```
Configuration conf = ...
FileSystem fs = new RawLocalFileSystem();
fs.initialize(null, conf);
```

ChecksumFileSystem

LocalFileSystem uses ChecksumFileSystem to do its work, and this class makes it easy to add checksumming to other (nonchecksummed) filesystems, as Checksum FileSystem is just a wrapper around FileSystem. The general idiom is as follows:

```
FileSystem rawFs = ...
FileSystem checksummedFs = new ChecksumFileSystem(rawFs);
```

The underlying filesystem is called the *raw* filesystem, and may be retrieved using the getRawFileSystem() method on ChecksumFileSystem. ChecksumFileSystem has a few more useful methods for working with checksums, such as getChecksumFile() for getting the path of a checksum file for any file. Check the documentation for the others.

If an error is detected by ChecksumFileSystem when reading a file, it will call its reportChecksumFailure() method. The default implementation does nothing, but LocalFileSystem moves the offending file and its checksum to a side directory on the same device called *bad_files*. Administrators should periodically check for these bad files and take action on them.

Compression

File compression brings two major benefits: it reduces the space needed to store files, and it speeds up data transfer across the network, or to or from disk. When dealing with large volumes of data, both of these savings can be significant, so it pays to carefully consider how to use compression in Hadoop.

There are many different compression formats, tools and algorithms, each with different characteristics. Table 4-1 lists some of the more common ones that can be used with Hadoop.*

Table 4-1. A summary of compression formats

Compression format	Tool	Algorithm	Filename extension	Multiple files	Splittable
DEFLATE[a]	N/A	DEFLATE	.deflate	No	No
gzip	gzip	DEFLATE	.gz	No	No
bzip2	bzip2	bzip2	.bz2	No	Yes
LZO	lzop	LZO	.lzo	No	No

[a] DEFLATE is a compression algorithm whose standard implementation is zlib. There is no commonly available command-line tool for producing files in DEFLATE format, as gzip is normally used. (Note that the gzip file format is DEFLATE with extra headers and a footer.) The *.deflate* filename extension is a Hadoop convention.

All compression algorithms exhibit a space/time trade-off: faster compression and decompression speeds usually come at the expense of smaller space savings. All of the tools listed in Table 4-1 give some control over this trade-off at compression time by offering nine different options: -1 means optimize for speed and -9 means optimize for space. For example, the following command creates a compressed file *file.gz* using the fastest compression method:

```
gzip -1 file
```

The different tools have very different compression characteristics. Gzip is a general-purpose compressor, and sits in the middle of the space/time trade-off. Bzip2 compresses more effectively than gzip, but is slower. Bzip2's decompression speed is faster than its compression speed, but it is still slower than the other formats. LZO, on the other hand, optimizes for speed: it is faster than gzip (or any other compression or decompression tool[†]), but compresses slightly less effectively.

The "Splittable" column in Table 4-1 indicates whether the compression format supports splitting; that is, whether you can seek to any point in the stream and start reading from some point further on. Splittable compression formats are especially suitable for MapReduce; see "Compression and Input Splits" on page 83 for further discussion.

Codecs

A *codec* is the implementation of a compression-decompression algorithm. In Hadoop, a codec is represented by an implementation of the CompressionCodec interface. So, for

---

* At the time of this writing, Hadoop does not support ZIP compression. See *https://issues.apache.org/jira/browse/MAPREDUCE-210*.

† Jeff Gilchrist's Archive Comparison Test at *http://compression.ca/act/act-summary.html* contains benchmarks for compression and decompression speed, and compression ratio for a wide range of tools.

example, GzipCodec encapsulates the compression and decompression algorithm for gzip. Table 4-2 lists the codecs that are available for Hadoop.

Table 4-2. Hadoop compression codecs

Compression format	Hadoop CompressionCodec
DEFLATE	org.apache.hadoop.io.compress.DefaultCodec
gzip	org.apache.hadoop.io.compress.GzipCodec
bzip2	org.apache.hadoop.io.compress.BZip2Codec
LZO	com.hadoop.compression.lzo.LzopCodec

The LZO libraries are GPL-licensed and may not be included in Apache distributions, so for this reason the Hadoop codecs must be downloaded separately from *http://code .google.com/p/hadoop-gpl-compression/* (or *http://github.com/kevinweil/hadoop-lzo*, which includes bugfixes and more tools). The LzopCodec is compatible with the lzop tool, which is essentially the LZO format with extra headers, and is the one you normally want. There is also a LzoCodec for the pure LZO format, which uses the *.lzo_de-flate* filename extension (by analogy with DEFLATE, which is gzip without the headers).

Compressing and decompressing streams with CompressionCodec

CompressionCodec has two methods that allow you to easily compress or decompress data. To compress data being written to an output stream, use the createOutput Stream(OutputStream out) method to create a CompressionOutputStream to which you write your uncompressed data to have it written in compressed form to the underlying stream. Conversely, to decompress data being read from an input stream, call createInputStream(InputStream in) to obtain a CompressionInputStream, which allows you to read uncompressed data from the underlying stream.

CompressionOutputStream and CompressionInputStream are similar to java.util.zip.DeflaterOutputStream and java.util.zip.DeflaterInputStream, except that both of the former provide the ability to reset their underlying compressor or decompressor, which is important for applications that compress sections of the data stream as separate blocks, such as SequenceFile, described in "Sequence-File" on page 116.

Example 4-1 illustrates how to use the API to compress data read from standard input and write it to standard output.

Example 4-1. A program to compress data read from standard input and write it to standard output

```
public class StreamCompressor {

  public static void main(String[] args) throws Exception {
    String codecClassname = args[0];
    Class<?> codecClass = Class.forName(codecClassname);
```

```
    Configuration conf = new Configuration();
    CompressionCodec codec = (CompressionCodec)
      ReflectionUtils.newInstance(codecClass, conf);

    CompressionOutputStream out = codec.createOutputStream(System.out);
    IOUtils.copyBytes(System.in, out, 4096, false);
    out.finish();
  }
}
```

The application expects the fully qualified name of the CompressionCodec implementation as the first command-line argument. We use ReflectionUtils to construct a new instance of the codec, then obtain a compression wrapper around System.out. Then we call the utility method copyBytes() on IOUtils to copy the input to the output, which is compressed by the CompressionOutputStream. Finally, we call finish() on CompressionOutputStream, which tells the compressor to finish writing to the compressed stream, but doesn't close the stream. We can try it out with the following command line, which compresses the string "Text" using the StreamCompressor program with the GzipCodec, then decompresses it from standard input using *gunzip*:

```
% echo "Text" | hadoop StreamCompressor org.apache.hadoop.io.compress.GzipCodec \
  | gunzip -
Text
```

Inferring CompressionCodecs using CompressionCodecFactory

If you are reading a compressed file, you can normally infer the codec to use by looking at its filename extension. A file ending in *.gz* can be read with GzipCodec, and so on. The extension for each compression format is listed in Table 4-1.

CompressionCodecFactory provides a way of mapping a filename extension to a CompressionCodec using its getCodec() method, which takes a Path object for the file in question. Example 4-2 shows an application that uses this feature to decompress files.

Example 4-2. A program to decompress a compressed file using a codec inferred from the file's extension

```
public class FileDecompressor {

  public static void main(String[] args) throws Exception {
    String uri = args[0];
    Configuration conf = new Configuration();
    FileSystem fs = FileSystem.get(URI.create(uri), conf);

    Path inputPath = new Path(uri);
    CompressionCodecFactory factory = new CompressionCodecFactory(conf);
    CompressionCodec codec = factory.getCodec(inputPath);
    if (codec == null) {
      System.err.println("No codec found for " + uri);
      System.exit(1);
    }
```

```
String outputUri =
  CompressionCodecFactory.removeSuffix(uri, codec.getDefaultExtension());

InputStream in = null;
OutputStream out = null;
try {
  in = codec.createInputStream(fs.open(inputPath));
  out = fs.create(new Path(outputUri));
  IOUtils.copyBytes(in, out, conf);
} finally {
  IOUtils.closeStream(in);
  IOUtils.closeStream(out);
}
  }
}
```

Once the codec has been found, it is used to strip off the file suffix to form the output filename (via the `removeSuffix()` static method of `CompressionCodecFactory`). In this way, a file named *file.gz* is decompressed to *file* by invoking the program as follows:

```
% hadoop FileDecompressor file.gz
```

`CompressionCodecFactory` finds codecs from a list defined by the `io.compression.codecs` configuration property. By default, this lists all the codecs provided by Hadoop (see Table 4-3), so you would need to alter it only if you have a custom codec that you wish to register (such as the externally hosted LZO codecs). Each codec knows its default filename extension, thus permitting `CompressionCodecFactory` to search through the registered codecs to find a match for a given extension (if any).

Table 4-3. Compression codec properties

Property name	Type	Default value	Description
io.compression.codecs	comma-separated Class names	org.apache.hadoop.io. compress.DefaultCodec, org.apache.hadoop.io. compress.GzipCodec, org.apache.hadoop.io. compress.Bzip2Codec	A list of the CompressionCodec classes for compression/ decompression.

Native libraries

For performance, it is preferable to use a native library for compression and decompression. For example, in one test, using the native gzip libraries reduced decompression times by up to 50% and compression times by around 10% (compared to the built-in Java implementation). Table 4-4 shows the availability of Java and native implementations for each compression format. Not all formats have native implementations (bzip2, for example), whereas others are only available as a native implementation (LZO, for example).

Table 4-4. Compression library implementations

Compression format	Java implementation	Native implementation
DEFLATE	Yes	Yes
gzip	Yes	Yes
bzip2	Yes	No
LZO	No	Yes

Hadoop comes with prebuilt native compression libraries for 32- and 64-bit Linux, which you can find in the *lib/native* directory. For other platforms, you will need to compile the libraries yourself, following the instructions on the Hadoop wiki at *http://wiki.apache.org/hadoop/NativeHadoop*.

The native libraries are picked up using the Java system property java.library.path. The *hadoop* script in the *bin* directory sets this property for you, but if you don't use this script, you will need to set the property in your application.

By default, Hadoop looks for native libraries for the platform it is running on, and loads them automatically if they are found. This means you don't have to change any configuration settings to use the native libraries. In some circumstances, however, you may wish to disable use of native libraries, such as when you are debugging a compression-related problem. You can achieve this by setting the property hadoop.native.lib to false, which ensures that the built-in Java equivalents will be used (if they are available).

CodecPool. If you are using a native library and you are doing a lot of compression or decompression in your application, consider using CodecPool, which allows you to reuse compressors and decompressors, thereby amortizing the cost of creating these objects.

The code in Example 4-3 shows the API, although in this program, which only creates a single Compressor, there is really no need to use a pool.

Example 4-3. A program to compress data read from standard input and write it to standard output using a pooled compressor

```
public class PooledStreamCompressor {

  public static void main(String[] args) throws Exception {
    String codecClassname = args[0];
    Class<?> codecClass = Class.forName(codecClassname);
    Configuration conf = new Configuration();
    CompressionCodec codec = (CompressionCodec)
      ReflectionUtils.newInstance(codecClass, conf);
    Compressor compressor = null;
    try {
      compressor = CodecPool.getCompressor(codec);
      CompressionOutputStream out =
        codec.createOutputStream(System.out, compressor);
      IOUtils.copyBytes(System.in, out, 4096, false);
      out.finish();
```

```
    } finally {
      CodecPool.returnCompressor(compressor);
    }
  }
}
```

We retrieve a Compressor instance from the pool for a given CompressionCodec, which we use in the codec's overloaded createOutputStream() method. By using a finally block, we ensure that the compressor is returned to the pool even if there is an IOException while copying the bytes between the streams.

Compression and Input Splits

When considering how to compress data that will be processed by MapReduce, it is important to understand whether the compression format supports splitting. Consider an uncompressed file stored in HDFS whose size is 1 GB. With an HDFS block size of 64 MB, the file will be stored as 16 blocks, and a MapReduce job using this file as input will create 16 input splits, each processed independently as input to a separate map task.

Imagine now the file is a gzip-compressed file whose compressed size is 1 GB. As before, HDFS will store the file as 16 blocks. However, creating a split for each block won't work since it is impossible to start reading at an arbitrary point in the gzip stream, and therefore impossible for a map task to read its split independently of the others. The gzip format uses DEFLATE to store the compressed data, and DEFLATE stores data as a series of compressed blocks. The problem is that the start of each block is not distinguished in any way that would allow a reader positioned at an arbitrary point in the stream to advance to the beginning of the next block, thereby synchronizing itself with the stream. For this reason, gzip does not support splitting.

In this case, MapReduce will do the right thing and not try to split the gzipped file, since it knows that the input is gzip-compressed (by looking at the filename extension) and that gzip does not support splitting. This will work, but at the expense of locality: a single map will process the 16 HDFS blocks, most of which will not be local to the map. Also, with fewer maps, the job is less granular, and so may take longer to run.

If the file in our hypothetical example were an LZO file, we would have the same problem since the underlying compression format does not provide a way for a reader to synchronize itself with the stream.[‡] A bzip2 file, however, does provide a synchronization marker between blocks (a 48-bit approximation of pi), so it does support splitting. (Table 4-1 lists whether each compression format supports splitting.)

[‡] It is possible to preprocess gzip and LZO files to build an index of split points, effectively making them splittable. See *https://issues.apache.org/jira/browse/MAPREDUCE-491* for gzip. For LZO, there is an indexer tool available with the Hadoop LZO libraries, which you can obtain from the site listed in "Codecs" on page 78.

> ## Which Compression Format Should I Use?
>
> Which compression format you should use depends on your application. Do you want to maximize the speed of your application or are you more concerned about keeping storage costs down? In general, you should try different strategies for your application, and benchmark them with representative datasets to find the best approach.
>
> For large, unbounded files, like logfiles, the options are:
>
> - Store the files uncompressed.
> - Use a compression format that supports splitting, like bzip2.
> - Split the file into chunks in the application and compress each chunk separately using any supported compression format (it doesn't matter whether it is splittable). In this case, you should choose the chunk size so that the compressed chunks are approximately the size of an HDFS block.
> - Use Sequence File, which supports compression and splitting. See "Sequence-File" on page 116.
> - Use an Avro data file, which supports compression and splitting, just like Sequence File, but has the added advantage of being readable and writable from many languages, not just Java. See "Avro data files" on page 109.
>
> For large files, you should *not* use a compression format that does not support splitting on the whole file, since you lose locality and make MapReduce applications very inefficient.
>
> For archival purposes, consider the Hadoop archive format (see "Hadoop Archives" on page 71), although it does not support compression.

Using Compression in MapReduce

As described in "Inferring CompressionCodecs using CompressionCodecFactory" on page 80, if your input files are compressed, they will be automatically decompressed as they are read by MapReduce, using the filename extension to determine the codec to use.

To compress the output of a MapReduce job, in the job configuration, set the `mapred.output.compress` property to `true` and the `mapred.output.compression.codec` property to the classname of the compression codec you want to use, as shown in Example 4-4.

Example 4-4. Application to run the maximum temperature job producing compressed output

```
public class MaxTemperatureWithCompression {

  public static void main(String[] args) throws IOException {
    if (args.length != 2) {
      System.err.println("Usage: MaxTemperatureWithCompression <input path> " +
          "<output path>");
```

```
      System.exit(-1);
    }

    JobConf conf = new JobConf(MaxTemperatureWithCompression.class);
    conf.setJobName("Max temperature with output compression");

    FileInputFormat.addInputPath(conf, new Path(args[0]));
    FileOutputFormat.setOutputPath(conf, new Path(args[1]));

    conf.setOutputKeyClass(Text.class);
    conf.setOutputValueClass(IntWritable.class);

    conf.setBoolean("mapred.output.compress", true);
    conf.setClass("mapred.output.compression.codec", GzipCodec.class,
        CompressionCodec.class);

    conf.setMapperClass(MaxTemperatureMapper.class);
    conf.setCombinerClass(MaxTemperatureReducer.class);
    conf.setReducerClass(MaxTemperatureReducer.class);

    JobClient.runJob(conf);
  }
}
```

We run the program over compressed input (which doesn't have to use the same compression format as the output, although it does in this example) as follows:

```
% hadoop MaxTemperatureWithCompression input/ncdc/sample.txt.gz output
```

Each part of the final output is compressed; in this case, there is a single part:

```
% gunzip -c output/part-00000.gz
1949    111
1950    22
```

If you are emitting sequence files for your output, then you can set the `mapred.out put.compression.type` property to control the type of compression to use. The default is `RECORD`, which compresses individual records. Changing this to `BLOCK`, which compresses groups of records, is recommended since it compresses better (see "The SequenceFile format" on page 122).

Compressing map output

Even if your MapReduce application reads and writes uncompressed data, it may benefit from compressing the intermediate output of the map phase. Since the map output is written to disk and transferred across the network to the reducer nodes, by using a fast compressor such as LZO, you can get performance gains simply because the volume of data to transfer is reduced. The configuration properties to enable compression for map outputs and to set the compression format are shown in Table 4-5.

Table 4-5. Map output compression properties

Property name	Type	Default value	Description
mapred.compress.map.output	boolean	false	Compress map outputs.
mapred.map.output. compression.codec	Class	org.apache.hadoop.io. compress.DefaultCodec	The compression codec to use for map outputs.

Here are the lines to add to enable gzip map output compression in your job:

```
conf.setCompressMapOutput(true);
conf.setMapOutputCompressorClass(GzipCodec.class);
```

Serialization

Serialization is the process of turning structured objects into a byte stream for transmission over a network or for writing to persistent storage. *Deserialization* is the reverse process of turning a byte stream back into a series of structured objects.

Serialization appears in two quite distinct areas of distributed data processing: for interprocess communication and for persistent storage.

In Hadoop, interprocess communication between nodes in the system is implemented using *remote procedure calls* (RPCs). The RPC protocol uses serialization to render the message into a binary stream to be sent to the remote node, which then deserializes the binary stream into the original message. In general, it is desirable that an RPC serialization format is:

Compact
> A compact format makes the best use of network bandwidth, which is the most scarce resource in a data center.

Fast
> Interprocess communication forms the backbone for a distributed system, so it is essential that there is as little performance overhead as possible for the serialization and deserialization process.

Extensible
> Protocols change over time to meet new requirements, so it should be straightforward to evolve the protocol in a controlled manner for clients and servers. For example, it should be possible to add a new argument to a method call, and have the new servers accept messages in the old format (without the new argument) from old clients.

Interoperable
> For some systems, it is desirable to be able to support clients that are written in different languages to the server, so the format needs to be designed to make this possible.

On the face of it, the data format chosen for persistent storage would have different requirements from a serialization framework. After all, the lifespan of an RPC is less than a second, whereas persistent data may be read years after it was written. As it turns out, the four desirable properties of an RPC's serialization format are also crucial for a persistent storage format. We want the storage format to be compact (to make efficient use of storage space), fast (so the overhead in reading or writing terabytes of data is minimal), extensible (so we can transparently read data written in an older format), and interoperable (so we can read or write persistent data using different languages).

Hadoop uses its own serialization format, Writables, which is certainly compact and fast, but not so easy to extend or use from languages other than Java. Since Writables are central to Hadoop (most MapReduce programs use them for their key and value types), we look at them in some depth in the next three sections, before looking at serialization frameworks in general, and then Avro (a serialization system that was designed to overcome some of the limitations of Writables) in more detail.

The Writable Interface

The Writable interface defines two methods: one for writing its state to a DataOutput binary stream, and one for reading its state from a DataInput binary stream:

```
package org.apache.hadoop.io;

import java.io.DataOutput;
import java.io.DataInput;
import java.io.IOException;

public interface Writable {
  void write(DataOutput out) throws IOException;
  void readFields(DataInput in) throws IOException;
}
```

Let's look at a particular Writable to see what we can do with it. We will use IntWritable, a wrapper for a Java int. We can create one and set its value using the set() method:

```
IntWritable writable = new IntWritable();
writable.set(163);
```

Equivalently, we can use the constructor that takes the integer value:

```
IntWritable writable = new IntWritable(163);
```

To examine the serialized form of the IntWritable, we write a small helper method that wraps a java.io.ByteArrayOutputStream in a java.io.DataOutputStream (an implementation of java.io.DataOutput) to capture the bytes in the serialized stream:

```
public static byte[] serialize(Writable writable) throws IOException {
  ByteArrayOutputStream out = new ByteArrayOutputStream();
  DataOutputStream dataOut = new DataOutputStream(out);
  writable.write(dataOut);
  dataOut.close();
```

```
        return out.toByteArray();
    }
```

An integer is written using four bytes (as we see using JUnit 4 assertions):

```
    byte[] bytes = serialize(writable);
    assertThat(bytes.length, is(4));
```

The bytes are written in big-endian order (so the most significant byte is written to the stream first, this is dictated by the java.io.DataOutput interface), and we can see their hexadecimal representation by using a method on Hadoop's StringUtils:

```
    assertThat(StringUtils.byteToHexString(bytes), is("000000a3"));
```

Let's try deserialization. Again, we create a helper method to read a Writable object from a byte array:

```
    public static byte[] deserialize(Writable writable, byte[] bytes)
        throws IOException {
      ByteArrayInputStream in = new ByteArrayInputStream(bytes);
      DataInputStream dataIn = new DataInputStream(in);
      writable.readFields(dataIn);
      dataIn.close();
      return bytes;
    }
```

We construct a new, value-less, IntWritable, then call deserialize() to read from the output data that we just wrote. Then we check that its value, retrieved using the get() method, is the original value, 163:

```
    IntWritable newWritable = new IntWritable();
    deserialize(newWritable, bytes);
    assertThat(newWritable.get(), is(163));
```

WritableComparable and comparators

IntWritable implements the WritableComparable interface, which is just a subinterface of the Writable and java.lang.Comparable interfaces:

```
    package org.apache.hadoop.io;

    public interface WritableComparable<T> extends Writable, Comparable<T> {
    }
```

Comparison of types is crucial for MapReduce, where there is a sorting phase during which keys are compared with one another. One optimization that Hadoop provides is the RawComparator extension of Java's Comparator:

```
package org.apache.hadoop.io;

import java.util.Comparator;

public interface RawComparator<T> extends Comparator<T> {

  public int compare(byte[] b1, int s1, int l1, byte[] b2, int s2, int l2);

}
```

This interface permits implementors to compare records read from a stream without deserializing them into objects, thereby avoiding any overhead of object creation. For example, the comparator for IntWritables implements the raw compare() method by reading an integer from each of the byte arrays b1 and b2 and comparing them directly, from the given start positions (s1 and s2) and lengths (l1 and l2).

WritableComparator is a general-purpose implementation of RawComparator for WritableComparable classes. It provides two main functions. First, it provides a default implementation of the raw compare() method that deserializes the objects to be compared from the stream and invokes the object compare() method. Second, it acts as a factory for RawComparator instances (that Writable implementations have registered). For example, to obtain a comparator for IntWritable, we just use:

```
RawComparator<IntWritable> comparator = WritableComparator.get(IntWritable.class);
```

The comparator can be used to compare two IntWritable objects:

```
IntWritable w1 = new IntWritable(163);
IntWritable w2 = new IntWritable(67);
assertThat(comparator.compare(w1, w2), greaterThan(0));
```

or their serialized representations:

```
byte[] b1 = serialize(w1);
byte[] b2 = serialize(w2);
assertThat(comparator.compare(b1, 0, b1.length, b2, 0, b2.length),
    greaterThan(0));
```

Writable Classes

Hadoop comes with a large selection of Writable classes in the org.apache.hadoop.io package. They form the class hierarchy shown in Figure 4-1.

Writable wrappers for Java primitives

There are Writable wrappers for all the Java primitive types (see Table 4-6) except short and char (both of which can be stored in an IntWritable). All have a get() and a set() method for retrieving and storing the wrapped value.

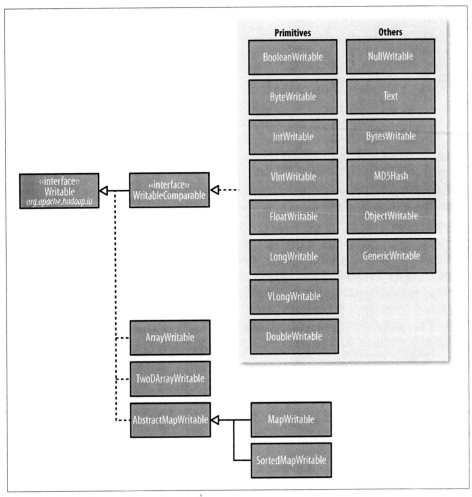

Figure 4-1. Writable class hierarchy

Table 4-6. Writable wrapper classes for Java primitives

Java primitive	Writable implementation	Serialized size (bytes)
boolean	BooleanWritable	1
byte	ByteWritable	1
int	IntWritable	4
	VIntWritable	1–5
float	FloatWritable	4
long	LongWritable	8
	VLongWritable	1–9

Java primitive	Writable implementation	Serialized size (bytes)
double	DoubleWritable	8

When it comes to encoding integers, there is a choice between the fixed-length formats (IntWritable and LongWritable) and the variable-length formats (VIntWritable and VLongWritable). The variable-length formats use only a single byte to encode the value if it is small enough (between −112 and 127, inclusive); otherwise, they use the first byte to indicate whether the value is positive or negative, and how many bytes follow. For example, 163 requires two bytes:

```
byte[] data = serialize(new VIntWritable(163));
assertThat(StringUtils.byteToHexString(data), is("8fa3"));
```

How do you choose between a fixed-length and a variable-length encoding? Fixed-length encodings are good when the distribution of values is fairly uniform across the whole value space, such as a (well-designed) hash function. Most numeric variables tend to have nonuniform distributions, and on average the variable-length encoding will save space. Another advantage of variable-length encodings is that you can switch from VIntWritable to VLongWritable, since their encodings are actually the same. So by choosing a variable-length representation, you have room to grow without committing to an 8-byte long representation from the beginning.

Text

Text is a Writable for UTF-8 sequences. It can be thought of as the Writable equivalent of java.lang.String. Text is a replacement for the UTF8 class, which was deprecated because it didn't support strings whose encoding was over 32,767 bytes, and because it used Java's modified UTF-8.

The Text class uses an int (with a variable-length encoding) to store the number of bytes in the string encoding, so the maximum value is 2 GB. Furthermore, Text uses standard UTF-8, which makes it potentially easier to interoperate with other tools that understand UTF-8.

Indexing. Because of its emphasis on using standard UTF-8, there are some differences between Text and the Java String class. Indexing for the Text class is in terms of position in the encoded byte sequence, not the Unicode character in the string, or the Java char code unit (as it is for String). For ASCII strings, these three concepts of index position coincide. Here is an example to demonstrate the use of the charAt() method:

```
Text t = new Text("hadoop");
assertThat(t.getLength(), is(6));
assertThat(t.getBytes().length, is(6));

assertThat(t.charAt(2), is((int) 'd'));
assertThat("Out of bounds", t.charAt(100), is(-1));
```

Notice that charAt() returns an int representing a Unicode code point, unlike the String variant that returns a char. Text also has a find() method, which is analogous to String's indexOf():

```
Text t = new Text("hadoop");
assertThat("Find a substring", t.find("do"), is(2));
assertThat("Finds first 'o'", t.find("o"), is(3));
assertThat("Finds 'o' from position 4 or later", t.find("o", 4), is(4));
assertThat("No match", t.find("pig"), is(-1));
```

Unicode. When we start using characters that are encoded with more than a single byte, the differences between Text and String become clear. Consider the Unicode characters shown in Table 4-7.[§]

Table 4-7. Unicode characters

Unicode code point	U+0041	U+00DF	U+6771	U+10400
Name	LATIN CAPITAL LETTER A	LATIN SMALL LETTER SHARP S	N/A (a unified Han ideograph)	DESERET CAPITAL LETTER LONG I
UTF-8 code units	41	c3 9f	e6 9d b1	f0 90 90 80
Java representation	\u0041	\u00DF	\u6771	\uuD801\uDC00

All but the last character in the table, U+10400, can be expressed using a single Java char. U+10400 is a supplementary character and is represented by two Java chars, known as a surrogate pair. The tests in Example 4-5 show the differences between String and Text when processing a string of the four characters from Table 4-7.

Example 4-5. Tests showing the differences between the String and Text classes

```
public class StringTextComparisonTest {

  @Test
  public void string() throws UnsupportedEncodingException {

    String s = "\u0041\u00DF\u6771\uD801\uDC00";
    assertThat(s.length(), is(5));
    assertThat(s.getBytes("UTF-8").length, is(10));

    assertThat(s.indexOf("\u0041"), is(0));
    assertThat(s.indexOf("\u00DF"), is(1));
    assertThat(s.indexOf("\u6771"), is(2));
    assertThat(s.indexOf("\uD801\uDC00"), is(3));

    assertThat(s.charAt(0), is('\u0041'));
    assertThat(s.charAt(1), is('\u00DF'));
    assertThat(s.charAt(2), is('\u6771'));
    assertThat(s.charAt(3), is('\uD801'));
    assertThat(s.charAt(4), is('\uDC00'));
```

[§] This example is based on one from the article Supplementary Characters in the Java Platform (*http://java.sun.com/developer/technicalArticles/Intl/Supplementary/*).

```
    assertThat(s.codePointAt(0), is(0x0041));
    assertThat(s.codePointAt(1), is(0x00DF));
    assertThat(s.codePointAt(2), is(0x6771));
    assertThat(s.codePointAt(3), is(0x10400));
  }

  @Test
  public void text() {

    Text t = new Text("\u0041\u00DF\u6771\uD801\uDC00");
    assertThat(t.getLength(), is(10));

    assertThat(t.find("\u0041"), is(0));
    assertThat(t.find("\u00DF"), is(1));
    assertThat(t.find("\u6771"), is(3));
    assertThat(t.find("\uD801\uDC00"), is(6));

    assertThat(t.charAt(0), is(0x0041));
    assertThat(t.charAt(1), is(0x00DF));
    assertThat(t.charAt(3), is(0x6771));
    assertThat(t.charAt(6), is(0x10400));
  }
}
```

The test confirms that the length of a String is the number of char code units it contains
(5, one from each of the first three characters in the string, and a surrogate pair from
the last), whereas the length of a Text object is the number of bytes in its UTF-8 encoding
(10 = 1+2+3+4). Similarly, the indexOf() method in String returns an index in char
code units, and find() for Text is a byte offset.

The charAt() method in String returns the char code unit for the given index, which
in the case of a surrogate pair will not represent a whole Unicode character. The code
PointAt() method, indexed by char code unit, is needed to retrieve a single Unicode
character represented as an int. In fact, the charAt() method in Text is more like the
codePointAt() method than its namesake in String. The only difference is that it is
indexed by byte offset.

Iteration. Iterating over the Unicode characters in Text is complicated by the use of byte
offsets for indexing, since you can't just increment the index. The idiom for iteration
is a little obscure (see Example 4-6): turn the Text object into a java.nio.ByteBuffer,
then repeatedly call the bytesToCodePoint() static method on Text with the buffer. This
method extracts the next code point as an int and updates the position in the buffer.
The end of the string is detected when bytesToCodePoint() returns −1.

Example 4-6. Iterating over the characters in a Text object

```
public class TextIterator {

  public static void main(String[] args) {
    Text t = new Text("\u0041\u00DF\u6771\uD801\uDC00");
```

```
    ByteBuffer buf = ByteBuffer.wrap(t.getBytes(), 0, t.getLength());
    int cp;
    while (buf.hasRemaining() && (cp = Text.bytesToCodePoint(buf)) != -1) {
      System.out.println(Integer.toHexString(cp));
    }
  }
}
```

Running the program prints the code points for the four characters in the string:

```
% hadoop TextIterator
41
df
6771
10400
```

Mutability. Another difference with `String` is that `Text` is mutable (like all `Writable` implementations in Hadoop, except `NullWritable`, which is a singleton). You can reuse a `Text` instance by calling one of the `set()` methods on it. For example:

```
Text t = new Text("hadoop");
t.set("pig");
assertThat(t.getLength(), is(3));
assertThat(t.getBytes().length, is(3));
```

In some situations, the byte array returned by the `getBytes()` method may be longer than the length returned by `getLength()`:

```
Text t = new Text("hadoop");
t.set(new Text("pig"));
assertThat(t.getLength(), is(3));
assertThat("Byte length not shortened", t.getBytes().length,
  is(6));
```

This shows why it is imperative that you always call `getLength()` when calling `getBytes()`, so you know how much of the byte array is valid data.

Resorting to String. `Text` doesn't have as rich an API for manipulating strings as `java.lang.String`, so in many cases, you need to convert the `Text` object to a `String`. This is done in the usual way, using the `toString()` method:

```
assertThat(new Text("hadoop").toString(), is("hadoop"));
```

BytesWritable

`BytesWritable` is a wrapper for an array of binary data. Its serialized format is an integer field (4 bytes) that specifies the number of bytes to follow, followed by the bytes themselves. For example, the byte array of length two with values 3 and 5 is serialized as a 4-byte integer (00000002) followed by the two bytes from the array (03 and 05):

```
BytesWritable b = new BytesWritable(new byte[] { 3, 5 });
byte[] bytes = serialize(b);
assertThat(StringUtils.byteToHexString(bytes), is("000000020305"));
```

BytesWritable is mutable, and its value may be changed by calling its set() method. As with Text, the size of the byte array returned from the getBytes() method for Byte sWritable—the capacity—may not reflect the actual size of the data stored in the BytesWritable. You can determine the size of the BytesWritable by calling get Length(). To demonstrate:

```
b.setCapacity(11);
assertThat(b.getLength(), is(2));
assertThat(b.getBytes().length, is(11));
```

NullWritable

NullWritable is a special type of Writable, as it has a zero-length serialization. No bytes are written to, or read from, the stream. It is used as a placeholder; for example, in MapReduce, a key or a value can be declared as a NullWritable when you don't need to use that position—it effectively stores a constant empty value. NullWritable can also be useful as a key in SequenceFile when you want to store a list of values, as opposed to key-value pairs. It is an immutable singleton: the instance can be retrieved by calling NullWritable.get().

ObjectWritable and GenericWritable

ObjectWritable is a general-purpose wrapper for the following: Java primitives, String, enum, Writable, null, or arrays of any of these types. It is used in Hadoop RPC to marshal and unmarshal method arguments and return types.

ObjectWritable is useful when a field can be of more than one type: for example, if the values in a SequenceFile have multiple types, then you can declare the value type as an ObjectWritable and wrap each type in an ObjectWritable. Being a general-purpose mechanism, it's fairly wasteful of space since it writes the classname of the wrapped type every time it is serialized. In cases where the number of types is small and known ahead of time, this can be improved by having a static array of types, and using the index into the array as the serialized reference to the type. This is the approach that GenericWritable takes, and you have to subclass it to specify the types to support.

Writable collections

There are four Writable collection types in the org.apache.hadoop.io package: Array Writable, TwoDArrayWritable, MapWritable, and SortedMapWritable.

ArrayWritable and TwoDArrayWritable are Writable implementations for arrays and two-dimensional arrays (array of arrays) of Writable instances. All the elements of an ArrayWritable or a TwoDArrayWritable must be instances of the same class, which is specified at construction, as follows:

```
ArrayWritable writable = new ArrayWritable(Text.class);
```

In contexts where the `Writable` is defined by type, such as in `SequenceFile` keys or values, or as input to MapReduce in general, you need to subclass `ArrayWritable` (or `TwoDArrayWritable`, as appropriate) to set the type statically. For example:

```
public class TextArrayWritable extends ArrayWritable {
  public TextArrayWritable() {
    super(Text.class);
  }
}
```

`ArrayWritable` and `TwoDArrayWritable` both have `get()` and `set()` methods, as well as a `toArray()` method, which creates a shallow copy of the array (or 2D array).

`MapWritable` and `SortedMapWritable` are implementations of `java.util.Map<Writable, Writable>` and `java.util.SortedMap<WritableComparable, Writable>`, respectively. The type of each key and value field is a part of the serialization format for that field. The type is stored as a single byte that acts as an index into an array of types. The array is populated with the standard types in the `org.apache.hadoop.io` package, but custom `Writable` types are accommodated, too, by writing a header that encodes the type array for nonstandard types. As they are implemented, `MapWritable` and `SortedMapWritable` use positive `byte` values for custom types, so a maximum of 127 distinct nonstandard `Writable` classes can be used in any particular `MapWritable` or `SortedMapWritable` instance. Here's a demonstration of using a `MapWritable` with different types for keys and values:

```
MapWritable src = new MapWritable();
src.put(new IntWritable(1), new Text("cat"));
src.put(new VIntWritable(2), new LongWritable(163));

MapWritable dest = new MapWritable();
WritableUtils.cloneInto(dest, src);
assertThat((Text) dest.get(new IntWritable(1)), is(new Text("cat")));
assertThat((LongWritable) dest.get(new VIntWritable(2)), is(new
  LongWritable(163)));
```

Conspicuous by their absence are `Writable` collection implementations for sets and lists. A set can be emulated by using a `MapWritable` (or a `SortedMapWritable` for a sorted set), with `NullWritable` values. For lists of a single type of `Writable`, `ArrayWritable` is adequate, but to store different types of `Writable` in a single list, you can use `GenericWritable` to wrap the elements in an `ArrayWritable`. Alternatively, you could write a general `ListWritable` using the ideas from `MapWritable`.

Implementing a Custom Writable

Hadoop comes with a useful set of `Writable` implementations that serve most purposes; however, on occasion, you may need to write your own custom implementation. With a custom `Writable`, you have full control over the binary representation and the sort order. Because `Writable`s are at the heart of the MapReduce data path, tuning the binary representation can have a significant effect on performance. The stock `Writable` implementations that come with Hadoop are well-tuned, but for more elaborate structures, it is often better to create a new Writable type, rather than compose the stock types.

To demonstrate how to create a custom Writable, we shall write an implementation that represents a pair of strings, called TextPair. The basic implementation is shown in Example 4-7.

Example 4-7. A Writable implementation that stores a pair of Text objects

```
import java.io.*;

import org.apache.hadoop.io.*;

public class TextPair implements WritableComparable<TextPair> {

  private Text first;
  private Text second;

  public TextPair() {
    set(new Text(), new Text());
  }

  public TextPair(String first, String second) {
    set(new Text(first), new Text(second));
  }

  public TextPair(Text first, Text second) {
    set(first, second);
  }

  public void set(Text first, Text second) {
    this.first = first;
    this.second = second;
  }

  public Text getFirst() {
    return first;
  }

  public Text getSecond() {
    return second;
  }

  @Override
  public void write(DataOutput out) throws IOException {
    first.write(out);
    second.write(out);
  }

  @Override
  public void readFields(DataInput in) throws IOException {
    first.readFields(in);
    second.readFields(in);
```

```
    }

    @Override
    public int hashCode() {
      return first.hashCode() * 163 + second.hashCode();
    }

    @Override
    public boolean equals(Object o) {
      if (o instanceof TextPair) {
        TextPair tp = (TextPair) o;
        return first.equals(tp.first) && second.equals(tp.second);
      }
      return false;
    }

    @Override
    public String toString() {
      return first + "\t" + second;
    }

    @Override
    public int compareTo(TextPair tp) {
      int cmp = first.compareTo(tp.first);
      if (cmp != 0) {
        return cmp;
      }
      return second.compareTo(tp.second);
    }
  }
```

The first part of the implementation is straightforward: there are two Text instance variables, first and second, and associated constructors, getters, and setters. All Writable implementations must have a default constructor so that the MapReduce framework can instantiate them, then populate their fields by calling readFields(). Writable instances are mutable and often reused, so you should take care to avoid allocating objects in the write() or readFields() methods.

TextPair's write() method serializes each Text object in turn to the output stream, by delegating to the Text objects themselves. Similarly, readFields() deserializes the bytes from the input stream by delegating to each Text object. The DataOutput and DataInput interfaces have a rich set of methods for serializing and deserializing Java primitives, so, in general, you have complete control over the wire format of your Writable object.

Just as you would for any value object you write in Java, you should override the hashCode(), equals(), and toString() methods from java.lang.Object. The hash Code() method is used by the HashPartitioner (the default partitioner in MapReduce) to choose a reduce partition, so you should make sure that you write a good hash function that mixes well to ensure reduce partitions are of a similar size.

If you ever plan to use your custom Writable with TextOutputFormat, then you must implement its toString() method. TextOutputFormat calls toString() on keys and values for their output representation. For Text Pair, we write the underlying Text objects as strings separated by a tab character.

TextPair is an implementation of WritableComparable, so it provides an implementation of the compareTo() method that imposes the ordering you would expect: it sorts by the first string followed by the second. Notice that TextPair differs from TextArrayWrita ble from the previous section (apart from the number of Text objects it can store), since TextArrayWritable is only a Writable, not a WritableComparable.

Implementing a RawComparator for speed

The code for TextPair in Example 4-7 will work as it stands; however, there is a further optimization we can make. As explained in "WritableComparable and comparators" on page 88, when TextPair is being used as a key in MapReduce, it will have to be deserialized into an object for the compareTo() method to be invoked. What if it were possible to compare two TextPair objects just by looking at their serialized representations?

It turns out that we can do this, since TextPair is the concatenation of two Text objects, and the binary representation of a Text object is a variable-length integer containing the number of bytes in the UTF-8 representation of the string, followed by the UTF-8 bytes themselves. The trick is to read the initial length, so we know how long the first Text object's byte representation is; then we can delegate to Text's RawComparator, and invoke it with the appropriate offsets for the first or second string. Example 4-8 gives the details (note that this code is nested in the TextPair class).

Example 4-8. A RawComparator for comparing TextPair byte representations

```
public static class Comparator extends WritableComparator {

  private static final Text.Comparator TEXT_COMPARATOR = new Text.Comparator();

  public Comparator() {
    super(TextPair.class);
  }

  @Override
  public int compare(byte[] b1, int s1, int l1,
                     byte[] b2, int s2, int l2) {

    try {
      int firstL1 = WritableUtils.decodeVIntSize(b1[s1]) + readVInt(b1, s1);
      int firstL2 = WritableUtils.decodeVIntSize(b2[s2]) + readVInt(b2, s2);
      int cmp = TEXT_COMPARATOR.compare(b1, s1, firstL1, b2, s2, firstL2);
      if (cmp != 0) {
        return cmp;
      }
```

```
      return TEXT_COMPARATOR.compare(b1, s1 + firstL1, l1 - firstL1,
                                     b2, s2 + firstL2, l2 - firstL2);
    } catch (IOException e) {
      throw new IllegalArgumentException(e);
    }
  }
}

static {
  WritableComparator.define(TextPair.class, new Comparator());
}
```

We actually subclass WritableComparator rather than implement RawComparator directly, since it provides some convenience methods and default implementations. The subtle part of this code is calculating firstL1 and firstL2, the lengths of the first Text field in each byte stream. Each is made up of the length of the variable-length integer (returned by decodeVIntSize() on WritableUtils) and the value it is encoding (returned by readVInt()).

The static block registers the raw comparator so that whenever MapReduce sees the TextPair class, it knows to use the raw comparator as its default comparator.

Custom comparators

As we can see with TextPair, writing raw comparators takes some care, since you have to deal with details at the byte level. It is worth looking at some of the implementations of Writable in the org.apache.hadoop.io package for further ideas, if you need to write your own. The utility methods on WritableUtils are very handy, too.

Custom comparators should also be written to be RawComparators, if possible. These are comparators that implement a different sort order to the natural sort order defined by the default comparator. Example 4-9 shows a comparator for TextPair, called First Comparator, that considers only the first string of the pair. Note that we override the compare() method that takes objects so both compare() methods have the same semantics.

We will make use of this comparator in Chapter 8, when we look at joins and secondary sorting in MapReduce (see "Joins" on page 247).

Example 4-9. A custom RawComparator for comparing the first field of TextPair byte representations

```
public static class FirstComparator extends WritableComparator {

  private static final Text.Comparator TEXT_COMPARATOR = new Text.Comparator();

  public FirstComparator() {
    super(TextPair.class);
  }

  @Override
  public int compare(byte[] b1, int s1, int l1,
                     byte[] b2, int s2, int l2) {
```

```
    try {
      int firstL1 = WritableUtils.decodeVIntSize(b1[s1]) + readVInt(b1, s1);
      int firstL2 = WritableUtils.decodeVIntSize(b2[s2]) + readVInt(b2, s2);
      return TEXT_COMPARATOR.compare(b1, s1, firstL1, b2, s2, firstL2);
    } catch (IOException e) {
      throw new IllegalArgumentException(e);
    }
  }

  @Override
  public int compare(WritableComparable a, WritableComparable b) {
    if (a instanceof TextPair && b instanceof TextPair) {
      return ((TextPair) a).first.compareTo(((TextPair) b).first);
    }
    return super.compare(a, b);
  }
}
```

Serialization Frameworks

Although most MapReduce programs use Writable key and value types, this isn't mandated by the MapReduce API. In fact, any types can be used; the only requirement is that there be a mechanism that translates to and from a binary representation of each type.

To support this, Hadoop has an API for pluggable serialization frameworks. A serialization framework is represented by an implementation of Serialization (in the org.apache.hadoop.io.serializer package). WritableSerialization, for example, is the implementation of Serialization for Writable types.

A Serialization defines a mapping from types to Serializer instances (for turning an object into a byte stream) and Deserializer instances (for turning a byte stream into an object).

Set the io.serializations property to a comma-separated list of classnames to register Serialization implementations. Its default value is org.apache.hadoop.io.serial izer.WritableSerialization, which means that only Writable objects can be serialized or deserialized out of the box.

Hadoop includes a class called JavaSerialization that uses Java Object Serialization. Although it makes it convenient to be able to use standard Java types in MapReduce programs, like Integer or String, Java Object Serialization is not as efficient as Writables, so it's not worth making this trade-off (see the sidebar on the next page).

Why Not Use Java Object Serialization?

Java comes with its own serialization mechanism, called Java Object Serialization (often referred to simply as "Java Serialization"), that is tightly integrated with the language, so it's natural to ask why this wasn't used in Hadoop. Here's what Doug Cutting said in response to that question:

> Why didn't I use Serialization when we first started Hadoop? Because it looked big and hairy and I thought we needed something lean and mean, where we had precise control over exactly how objects are written and read, since that is central to Hadoop. With Serialization you can get some control, but you have to fight for it.
>
> The logic for not using RMI was similar. Effective, high-performance inter-process communications are critical to Hadoop. I felt like we'd need to precisely control how things like connections, timeouts and buffers are handled, and RMI gives you little control over those.

The problem is that Java Serialization doesn't meet the criteria for a serialization format listed earlier: compact, fast, extensible, and interoperable.

Java Serialization is not compact: it writes the classname of each object being written to the stream—this is true of classes that implement `java.io.Serializable` or `java.io.Externalizable`. Subsequent instances of the same class write a reference handle to the first occurrence, which occupies only 5 bytes. However, reference handles don't work well with random access, since the referent class may occur at any point in the preceding stream—that is, there is state stored in the stream. Even worse, reference handles play havoc with sorting records in a serialized stream, since the first record of a particular class is distinguished and must be treated as a special case.

All these problems are avoided by not writing the classname to the stream at all, which is the approach that Writable takes. This makes the assumption that the client knows the expected type. The result is that the format is considerably more compact than Java Serialization, and random access and sorting work as expected since each record is independent of the others (so there is no stream state).

Java Serialization is a general-purpose mechanism for serializing graphs of objects, so it necessarily has some overhead for serialization and deserialization operations. What's more, the deserialization procedure creates a new instance for each object deserialized from the stream. Writable objects, on the other hand, can be (and often are) reused. For example, for a MapReduce job, which at its core serializes and deserializes billions of records of just a handful of different types, the savings gained by not having to allocate new objects are significant.

In terms of extensibility, Java Serialization has some support for evolving a type, but it is brittle and hard to use effectively (Writables have no support: the programmer has to manage them himself).

In principle, other languages could interpret the Java Serialization stream protocol (defined by the Java Object Serialization Specification), but in practice there are no widely used implementations in other languages, so it is a Java-only solution. The situation is the same for Writables.

Serialization IDL

There are a number of other serialization frameworks that approach the problem in a different way: rather than defining types through code, you define them in a language-neutral, declarative fashion, using an *interface description language* (IDL). The system can then generate types for different languages, which is good for interoperability. They also typically define versioning schemes that make type evolution straightforward.

Hadoop's own Record I/O (found in the `org.apache.hadoop.record` package) has an IDL that is compiled into Writable objects, which makes it convenient for generating types that are compatible with MapReduce. For whatever reason, however, Record I/O was not widely used, and has been deprecated in favor of Avro.

Apache Thrift (*http://incubator.apache.org/thrift/*) and Google Protocol Buffers (*http://code.google.com/p/protobuf/*) are both popular serialization frameworks, and they are commonly used as a format for persistent binary data. There is limited support for these as MapReduce formats;[∥] however, Thrift is used in parts of Hadoop to provide cross-language APIs, such as the "thriftfs" contrib module, where it is used to expose an API to Hadoop filesystems (see "Thrift" on page 49).

In the next section, we look at Avro, an IDL-based serialization framework designed to work well with large-scale data processing in Hadoop.

Avro

Apache Avro (*http://avro.apache.org/*)[#] is a language-neutral data serialization system. The project was created by Doug Cutting (the creator of Hadoop) to address the major downside of Hadoop Writables: lack of language portability. Having a data format that can be processed by many languages (currently C, C++, Java, Python, and Ruby) makes it easier to share datasets with a wider audience than one tied to a single language. It is also more future-proof, allowing data to potentially outlive the language used to read and write it.

But why a new data serialization system? Avro has a set of features that, taken together, differentiate it from other systems like Apache Thrift or Google's Protocol Buffers.[*] Like

---

∥ You can find the latest status for a Thrift `Serialization` at *https://issues.apache.org/jira/browse/HADOOP-3787*, and a Protocol Buffers `Serialization` at *https://issues.apache.org/jira/browse/HADOOP-3788*. Twitter's Elephant Bird project (*http://github.com/kevinweil/elephant-bird*) includes tools for working with Protocol Buffers in Hadoop.

\# Named after the British aircraft manufacturer from the 20th century.

* Avro also performs favorably compared to other serialization libraries, as the benchmarks at *http://code.google.com/p/thrift-protobuf-compare/* demonstrate.

these systems and others, Avro data is described using a language-independent *schema*. However, unlike some other systems, code generation is optional in Avro, which means you can read and write data that conforms to a given schema even if your code has not seen that particular schema before. To achieve this, Avro assumes that the schema is always present—at both read and write time—which makes for a very compact encoding, since encoded values do not need to be tagged with a field identifier.

Avro schemas are usually written in JSON, and data is usually encoded using a binary format, but there are other options, too. There is a higher-level language called Avro IDL, for writing schemas in a C-like language that is more familiar to developers. There is also a JSON-based data encoder, which, being human-readable, is useful for prototyping and debugging Avro data.

The *Avro specification (http://avro.apache.org/docs/current/spec.html)* precisely defines the binary format that all implementations must support. It also specifies many of the other features of Avro that implementations should support. One area that the specification does not rule on, however, is APIs: implementations have complete latitude in the API they expose for working with Avro data, since each one is necessarily language-specific. The fact that there is only one binary format is significant, since it means the barrier for implementing a new language binding is lower, and avoids the problem of a combinatorial explosion of languages and formats, which would harm interoperability.

Avro has rich *schema resolution* capabilities. Within certain carefully defined constraints, the schema used to read data need not be identical to the schema that was used to write the data. This is the mechanism by which Avro supports schema evolution. For example, a new, optional field may be added to a record by declaring it in the schema used to read the old data. New and old clients alike will be able to read the old data, while new clients can write new data that uses the new field. Conversely, if an old client sees newly encoded data, it will gracefully ignore the new field and carry on processing as it would have done with old data.

Avro specifies an *object container format* for sequences of objects—similar to Hadoop's sequence file. An *Avro data file* has a metadata section where the schema is stored, which makes the file self-describing. Avro data files support compression and are splittable, which is crucial for a MapReduce data input format. Furthermore, since Avro was designed with MapReduce in mind, in the future it will be possible to use Avro to bring first-class MapReduce APIs (that is, ones that are richer than Streaming, like the Java API, or C++ Pipes) to languages that speak Avro.

Avro can be used for *RPC*, too, although this isn't covered here. The Hadoop project has plans to migrate to Avro RPC, which will have several benefits, including supporting rolling upgrades, and the possibility of multilanguage clients, such as an HDFS client implemented entirely in C.

Avro data types and schemas

Avro defines a small number of data types, which can be used to build application-specific data structures by writing schemas. For interoperability, implementations must support all Avro types.

Avro's primitive types are listed in Table 4-8. Each primitive type may also be specified using a more verbose form, using the type attribute, such as:

```
{ "type": "null" }
```

Table 4-8. Avro primitive types

Type	Description	Schema
null	The absence of a value	"null"
boolean	A binary value	"boolean"
int	32-bit signed integer	"int"
long	64-bit signed integer	"long"
float	Single precision (32-bit) IEEE 754 floating-point number	"float"
double	Double precision (64-bit) IEEE 754 floating-point number	"double"
bytes	Sequence of 8-bit unsigned bytes	"bytes"
string	Sequence of Unicode characters	"string"

Avro also defines the complex types listed in Table 4-9, along with a representative example of a schema of each type.

Table 4-9. Avro complex types

Type	Description	Schema example
array	An ordered collection of objects. All objects in a particular array must have the same schema.	```{ "type": "array", "items": "long" }```
map	An unordered collection of key-value pairs. Keys must be strings, values may be any type, although within a particular map all values must have the same schema.	```{ "type": "map", "values": "string" }```
record	A collection of named fields of any type.	```{ "type": "record", "name": "WeatherRecord", "doc": "A weather reading.", "fields": [{"name": "year", "type": "int"}, {"name": "temperature", "type": "int"}, {"name": "stationId", "type": "string"}] }```
enum	A set of named values.	```{ "type": "enum", "name": "Cutlery", "doc": "An eating utensil.",```

Type	Description	Schema example
		`"symbols": ["KNIFE", "FORK", "SPOON"]` `}`

fixed	A fixed number of 8-bit unsigned bytes.	`{`
		`  "type": "fixed",`
		`  "name": "Md5Hash",`
		`  "size": 16`
		`}`

union	A union of schemas. A union is represented by a JSON array, where each element in the array is a schema. Data represented by a union must match one of the schemas in the union.	`[`
		`  "null",`
		`  "string",`
		`  {"type": "map", "values": "string"}`
		`]`

Each Avro language API has a representation for each Avro type that is specific to the language. For example, Avro's double type is represented in C, C++, and Java by a double, in Python by a float, and in Ruby by a Float.

What's more, there may be more than one representation, or mapping, for a language. All languages support a dynamic mapping, which can be used even when the schema is not known ahead of run time. Java calls this the *generic* mapping.

In addition, the Java and C++ implementations can generate code to represent the data for an Avro schema. Code generation, which is called the *specific* mapping in Java, is an optimization that is useful when you have a copy of the schema before you read or write data. Generated classes also provide a more domain-oriented API for user code than generic ones.

Java has a third mapping, the *reflect* mapping, which maps Avro types onto preexisting Java types, using reflection. It is slower than the generic and specific mappings, and is not generally recommended for new applications.

Java's type mappings are shown in Table 4-10. As the table shows, the specific mapping is the same as the generic one unless otherwise noted (and the reflect one is the same as the specific one unless noted). The specific mapping only differs from the generic one for record, enum, and fixed, all of which have generated classes (the name of which is controlled by the name and optional namespace attribute).

> Why don't the Java generic and specific mappings use Java String to represent an Avro string? The answer is efficiency: the Avro Utf8 type is mutable, so it may be reused for reading or writing a series of values. Also, Java String decodes UTF-8 at object construction time, while Avro Utf8 does it lazily, which can increase performance in some cases. Note that the Java reflect mapping does use Java's String class, since it is designed for Java compatibility, not performance.

Table 4-10. Avro Java type mappings

Avro type	Generic Java mapping	Specific Java mapping	Reflect Java mapping
null	null type		
boolean	boolean		
int	int		short or int
long	long		
float	float		
double	double		
bytes	java.nio.ByteBuffer		Array of byte
string	org.apache.avro.util.Utf8		java.lang.String
array	org.apache.avro.generic.GenericArray		Array or java.util.Collection
map	java.util.Map		
record	org.apache.avro.generic.Generic Record	Generated class implementing org.apache.avro.specific.Specific Record.	Arbitrary user class with a zero-argument constructor. All inherited nontransient instance fields are used.
enum	java.lang.String	Generated Java enum	Arbitrary Java enum
fixed	org.apache.avro.generic.GenericFixed	Generated class implementing org.apache.avro.specific.SpecificFixed.	org.apache.avro.generic.GenericFixed
union	java.lang.Object		

In-memory serialization and deserialization

Avro provides APIs for serialization and deserialization, which are useful when you want to integrate Avro with an existing system, such as a messaging system where the framing format is already defined. In other cases, consider using Avro's data file format.

Let's write a Java program to read and write Avro data to and from streams. We'll start with a simple Avro schema for representing a pair of strings as a record:

```
{
  "type": "record",
  "name": "Pair",
  "doc": "A pair of strings.",
  "fields": [
    {"name": "left", "type": "string"},
    {"name": "right", "type": "string"}
  ]
}
```

If this schema is saved in a file on the classpath called *Pair.avsc* (.avsc is the conventional extension for an Avro schema), then we can load it using the following statement:

```
Schema schema = Schema.parse(getClass().getResourceAsStream("Pair.avsc"));
```

We can create an instance of an Avro record using the generic API as follows:

```
GenericRecord datum = new GenericData.Record(schema);
datum.put("left", new Utf8("L"));
datum.put("right", new Utf8("R"));
```

Notice that we construct Avro Utf8 instances for the record's string fields.

Next, we serialize the record to an output stream:

```
ByteArrayOutputStream out = new ByteArrayOutputStream();
DatumWriter<GenericRecord> writer = new GenericDatumWriter<GenericRecord>(schema);
Encoder encoder = new BinaryEncoder(out);
writer.write(datum, encoder);
encoder.flush();
out.close();
```

There are two important objects here: the DatumWriter and the Encoder. A DatumWriter translates data objects into the types understood by an Encoder, which the latter writes to the output stream. Here we are using a GenericDatumWriter, which passes the fields of GenericRecord to the Encoder, in this case the BinaryEncoder.

In this example only one object is written to the stream, but we could call write() with more objects before closing the stream if we wanted to.

The GenericDatumWriter needs to be passed the schema since it follows the schema to determine which values from the data objects to write out. After we have called the writer's write() method, we flush the encoder, then close the output stream.

We can reverse the process and read the object back from the byte buffer:

```
DatumReader<GenericRecord> reader = new GenericDatumReader<GenericRecord>(schema);
Decoder decoder = DecoderFactory.defaultFactory()
  .createBinaryDecoder(out.toByteArray(), null);
GenericRecord result = reader.read(null, decoder);
assertThat(result.get("left").toString(), is("L"));
assertThat(result.get("right").toString(), is("R"));
```

We pass null to the calls to createBinaryDecoder() and read() since we are not reusing objects here (the decoder or the record, respectively).

Let's look briefly at the equivalent code using the specific API. We can generate the Pair class from the schema file, by using the Avro tools JAR file:[†]

```
% java -jar $AVRO_HOME/avro-tools-*.jar compile schema \
> avro/src/main/resources/Pair.avsc avro/src/main/java
```

---

† Avro can be downloaded in both source and binary forms from *http://avro.apache.org/releases.html*.

Then instead of a GenericRecord we construct a Pair instance, which we write to the stream using a SpecificDatumWriter, and read back using a SpecificDatumReader:

```
Pair datum = new Pair();
datum.left = new Utf8("L");
datum.right = new Utf8("R");

ByteArrayOutputStream out = new ByteArrayOutputStream();
DatumWriter<Pair> writer = new SpecificDatumWriter<Pair>(Pair.class);
Encoder encoder = new BinaryEncoder(out);
writer.write(datum, encoder);
encoder.flush();
out.close();

DatumReader<Pair> reader = new SpecificDatumReader<Pair>(Pair.class);
Decoder decoder = DecoderFactory.defaultFactory()
  .createBinaryDecoder(out.toByteArray(), null);
Pair result = reader.read(null, decoder);
assertThat(result.left.toString(), is("L"));
assertThat(result.right.toString(), is("R"));
```

Avro data files

Avro's object container file format is for storing sequences of Avro objects. It is very similar in design to Hadoop's sequence files, which are described in "Sequence-File" on page 116. The main difference is that Avro data files are designed to be portable across languages, so, for example, you can write a file in Python and read it in C (we will do exactly this in the next section).

A data file has a header containing metadata, including the Avro schema and a *sync marker*, followed by a series of (optionally compressed) blocks containing the serialized Avro objects. Blocks are separated by a sync marker that is unique to the file (the marker for a particular file is found in the header) and that permits rapid resynchronization with a block boundary after seeking to an arbitrary point in the file, such as an HDFS block boundary. Thus, Avro data files are splittable, which makes them amenable to efficient MapReduce processing.

Writing Avro objects to a data file is similar to writing to a stream. We use a DatumWriter, as before, but instead of using an Encoder, we create a DataFileWriter instance with the DatumWriter. Then we can create a new data file (which, by convention, has a .avro extension) and append objects to it:

```
File file = new File("data.avro");
DatumWriter<GenericRecord> writer = new GenericDatumWriter<GenericRecord>(schema);
DataFileWriter<GenericRecord> dataFileWriter =
  new DataFileWriter<GenericRecord>(writer);
dataFileWriter.create(schema, file);
dataFileWriter.append(datum);
dataFileWriter.close();
```

The objects that we write to the data file must conform to the file's schema, otherwise an exception will be thrown when we call append().

This example demonstrates writing to a local file (java.io.File in the previous snippet), but we can write to any java.io.OutputStream by using the overloaded create() method on DataFileWriter. To write a file to HDFS, for example, get an OutputStream by calling create() on FileSystem (see "Writing Data" on page 55).

Reading back objects from a data file is similar to the earlier case of reading objects from an in-memory stream, with one important difference: we don't have to specify a schema since it is read from the file metadata. Indeed, we can get the schema from the DataFileReader instance, using getSchema(), and verify that it is the same as the one we used to write the original object with:

```
DatumReader<GenericRecord> reader = new GenericDatumReader<GenericRecord>();
DataFileReader<GenericRecord> dataFileReader =
  new DataFileReader<GenericRecord>(file, reader);
assertThat("Schema is the same", schema, is(dataFileReader.getSchema()));
```

DataFileReader is a regular Java iterator, so we can iterate through its data objects by calling its hasNext() and next() methods. The following snippet checks that there is only one record, and that it has the expected field values:

```
assertThat(dataFileReader.hasNext(), is(true));
GenericRecord result = dataFileReader.next();
assertThat(result.get("left").toString(), is("L"));
assertThat(result.get("right").toString(), is("R"));
assertThat(dataFileReader.hasNext(), is(false));
```

Rather than using the usual next() method, however, it is preferable to use the overloaded form that takes an instance of the object to be returned (in this case, GenericRecord), since it will reuse the object and save allocation and garbage collection costs for files containing many objects. The following is idiomatic:

```
GenericRecord record = null;
while (dataFileReader.hasNext()) {
  record = dataFileReader.next(record);
  // process record
}
```

If object reuse is not important, you can use this shorter form:

```
for (GenericRecord record : dataFileReader) {
  // process record
}
```

For the general case of reading a file on a Hadoop file system, use Avro's FsInput to specify the input file using a Hadoop Path object. DataFileReader actually offers random access to Avro data file (via its seek() and sync() methods); however, in many cases, sequential streaming access is sufficient, for which DataFileStream should be used. DataFileStream can read from any Java InputStream.

Interoperability

To demonstrate Avro's language interoperability, let's write a data file using one language (Python) and read it back with another (C).

Python API. The program in Example 4-10 reads comma-separated strings from standard input and writes them as `Pair` records to an Avro data file. Like the Java code for writing a data file, we create a `DatumWriter` and a `DataFileWriter` object. Notice that we have embedded the Avro schema in the code, although we could equally well have read it from a file.

Python represents Avro records as dictionaries; each line that is read from standard in is turned into a `dict` object and appended to the `DataFileWriter`.

Example 4-10. A Python program for writing Avro record pairs to a data file

```python
import os
import string
import sys

from avro import schema
from avro import io
from avro import datafile

if __name__ == '__main__':
  if len(sys.argv) != 2:
    sys.exit('Usage: %s <data_file>' % sys.argv[0])
  avro_file = sys.argv[1]
  writer = open(avro_file, 'wb')
  datum_writer = io.DatumWriter()
  schema_object = schema.parse("""\
{ "type": "record",
  "name": "Pair",
  "doc": "A pair of strings.",
  "fields": [
    {"name": "left", "type": "string"},
    {"name": "right", "type": "string"}
  ]
}""")
  dfw = datafile.DataFileWriter(writer, datum_writer, schema_object)
  for line in sys.stdin.readlines():
    (left, right) = string.split(line.strip(), ',')
    dfw.append({'left':left, 'right':right});
  dfw.close()
```

Before we can run the program, we need to install Avro for Python:

```
% easy_install avro
```

To run the program, we specify the name of the file to write output to (*pairs.avro*) and send input pairs over standard in, marking the end of file by typing Control-D:

```
% python avro/src/main/py/write_pairs.py pairs.avro
a,1
c,2
b,3
b,2
^D
```

C API. Next we'll turn to the C API and write a program to display the contents of *pairs.avro*; see Example 4-11.‡

Example 4-11. A C program for reading Avro record pairs from a data file

```c
#include <avro.h>
#include <stdio.h>
#include <stdlib.h>

int main(int argc, char *argv[]) {
  if (argc != 2) {
    fprintf(stderr, "Usage: dump_pairs <data_file>\n");
    exit(EXIT_FAILURE);
  }

  const char *avrofile = argv[1];
  avro_schema_error_t error;
  avro_file_reader_t filereader;
  avro_datum_t pair;
  avro_datum_t left;
  avro_datum_t right;
  int rval;
  char *p;

  avro_file_reader(avrofile, &filereader);
  while (1) {
    rval = avro_file_reader_read(filereader, NULL, &pair);
    if (rval) break;
    if (avro_record_get(pair, "left", &left) == 0) {
      avro_string_get(left, &p);
      fprintf(stdout, "%s,", p);
    }
    if (avro_record_get(pair, "right", &right) == 0) {
      avro_string_get(right, &p);
      fprintf(stdout, "%s\n", p);
    }
  }
  avro_file_reader_close(filereader);
  return 0;
}
```

The core of the program does three things:

1. opens a file reader of type `avro_file_reader_t` by calling Avro's `avro_file_reader` function,§

2. reads Avro data from the file reader with the `avro_file_reader_read` function in a while loop until there are no pairs left (as determined by the return value `rval`), and

3. closes the file reader with `avro_file_reader_close`.

---

‡ For the general case, the Avro tools JAR file has a `tojson` command that dumps the contents of a Avro data file as JSON.

§ Avro functions and types have a `avro_` prefix and are defined in the *avro.h* header file.

The `avro_file_reader_read` function accepts a schema as its second argument to support the case where the schema for reading is different to the one used when the file was written (this is explained in the next section), but we simply pass in `NULL`, which tells Avro to use the data file's schema. The third argument is a pointer to a `avro_datum_t` object, which is populated with the contents of the next record read from the file. We unpack the pair structure into its fields by calling `avro_record_get`, and then we extract the value of these fields as strings using `avro_string_get`, which we print to the console.

Running the program using the output of the Python program prints the original input:

```
% ./dump_pairs pairs.avro
a,1
c,2
b,3
b,2
```

We have successfully exchanged complex data between two Avro implementations.

Schema resolution

We can choose to use a different schema for reading the data back (the *reader's schema*) to the one we used to write it (the *writer's schema*). This is a powerful tool, since it enables schema evolution. To illustrate, consider a new schema for string pairs, with an added `description` field:

```
{
  "type": "record",
  "name": "Pair",
  "doc": "A pair of strings with an added field.",
  "fields": [
    {"name": "left", "type": "string"},
    {"name": "right", "type": "string"},
    {"name": "description", "type": "string", "default": ""}
  ]
}
```

We can use this schema to read the data we serialized earlier, since, crucially, we have given the `description` field a default value (the empty string‖), which Avro will use when there is no field defined in the records it is reading. Had we omitted the `default` attribute, we would get an error when trying to read the old data.

 To make the default value `null`, rather than the empty string, we would instead define the description field using a union with the `null` Avro type:

```
{"name": "description", "type": ["null", "string"], "default": "null"}
```

‖ Default values for fields are encoded using JSON. See the Avro specification for a description of this encoding for each data type.

When the reader's schema is different from the writer's, we use the constructor for
GenericDatumReader that takes two schema objects, the writer's and the reader's, in that
order:

```
DatumReader<GenericRecord> reader =
  new GenericDatumReader<GenericRecord>(schema, newSchema);
Decoder decoder = DecoderFactory.defaultFactory()
  .createBinaryDecoder(out.toByteArray(), null);
GenericRecord result = reader.read(null, decoder);
assertThat(result.get("left").toString(), is("L"));
assertThat(result.get("right").toString(), is("R"));
assertThat(result.get("description").toString(), is(""));
```

For data files, which have the writer's schema stored in the metadata, we only need to
specify the readers's schema explicitly, which we can do by passing null for the writer's
schema:

```
DatumReader<GenericRecord> reader =
  new GenericDatumReader<GenericRecord>(null, newSchema);
```

Another common use of a different reader's schema is to drop fields in a record, an
operation called *projection*. This is useful when you have records with a large number
of fields and you only want to read some of them. For example, this schema can be
used to get only the right field of a Pair:

```
{
  "type": "record",
  "name": "Pair",
  "doc": "The right field of a pair of strings.",
  "fields": [
    {"name": "right", "type": "string"}
  ]
}
```

The rules for schema resolution have a direct bearing on how schemas may evolve from
one version to the next, and are spelled out in the Avro specification for all Avro types.
A summary of the rules for record evolution from the point of view of readers and
writers (or servers and clients) is presented in Table 4-11.

Table 4-11. Schema resolution of records

New schema	Writer	Reader	Action
Added field	Old	New	The reader uses the default value of the new field, since it is not written by the writer.
	New	Old	The reader does not know about the new field written by the writer, so it is ignored. (Projection).
Removed field	Old	New	The reader ignores the removed field. (Projection).
	New	Old	The removed field is not written by the writer. If the old schema had a default defined for the field, then the reader uses this, otherwise it gets an error. In this case, it is best to update the reader's schema at the same time as, or before, the writer's.

Sort order

Avro defines a sort order for objects. For most Avro types, the order is the natural one you would expect—for example, numeric types are ordered by ascending numeric value. Others are a little more subtle—enums are compared by the order in which the symbol is defined and not by the value of the symbol string, for instance.

All types except `record` have preordained rules for their sort order as described in the Avro specification; they cannot be overridden by the user. For records, however, you can control the sort order by specifying the `order` attribute for a field. It takes one of three values: `ascending` (the default), `descending` (to reverse the order), or `ignore` (so the field is skipped for comparison purposes).

For example, the following schema (*SortedPair.avsc*) defines an ordering of `Pair` records by the `right` field in descending order. The `left` field is ignored for the purposes of ordering, but it is still present in the projection:

```
{
  "type": "record",
  "name": "Pair",
  "doc": "A pair of strings, sorted by right field descending.",
  "fields": [
    {"name": "left", "type": "string", "order": "ignore"},
    {"name": "right", "type": "string", "order": "descending"}
  ]
}
```

The record's fields are compared pairwise in the document order of the reader's schema. Thus, by specifying an appropriate reader's schema, you can impose an arbitrary ordering on data records. This schema (*SwitchedPair.avsc*) defines a sort order by the `right` field, then the `left`:

```
{
  "type": "record",
  "name": "Pair",
  "doc": "A pair of strings, sorted by right then left.",
  "fields": [
    {"name": "right", "type": "string"},
    {"name": "left", "type": "string"}
  ]
}
```

Avro implements efficient binary comparisons. That is to say, Avro does not have to deserialize a binary data into objects to perform the comparison, since it can instead work directly on the byte streams.# In the case of the original `Pair` schema (with no `order` attributes), for example, Avro implements the binary comparison as follows.

#A useful consequence of this property is that you can compute an Avro datum's hash code from either the object or the binary representation (the latter by using the static `hashCode()` method on `BinaryData`) and get the same result in both cases.

The first field, left, is a UTF-8-encoded string, for which Avro can compare the bytes lexicographically. If they differ, then the order is determined, and Avro can stop the comparison there. Otherwise, if the two byte sequences are the same, it compares the second two (right) fields, again lexicographically at the byte level since the field is another UTF-8 string.

Notice that this description of a comparison function has exactly the same logic as the binary comparator we wrote for Writables in "Implementing a RawComparator for speed" on page 99. The great thing is that Avro provides the comparator for us, so we don't have to write and maintain this code. It's also easy to change the sort order just by changing the reader's schema. For the *SortedPair.avsc* or *SwitchedPair.avsc* schemas, the comparison function Avro uses is essentially the same as the one just described: the difference is in which fields are considered, the order in which they are considered, and whether the order is ascending or descending.

Avro MapReduce

Avro provides a number of classes for making it easy to run MapReduce programs on Avro data. For example, AvroMapper and AvroReducer in the org.apache.avro.mapred package are specializations of Hadoop's (old style) Mapper and Reducer classes. They eliminate the key-value distinction for inputs and outputs, since Avro data files are just a sequence of values. However, intermediate data is still divided into key-value pairs for the shuffle. Avro's MapReduce integration was being added as this edition went to press, but you can find example code at the website accompanying this book.

For languages other than Java, Avro provides a connector framework (in the org.apache.avro.mapred.tether package). At the time of writing, there are no bindings for other languages, but it is expected these will be added in future releases.

File-Based Data Structures

For some applications, you need a specialized data structure to hold your data. For doing MapReduce-based processing, putting each blob of binary data into its own file doesn't scale, so Hadoop developed a number of higher-level containers for these situations.

SequenceFile

Imagine a logfile, where each log record is a new line of text. If you want to log binary types, plain text isn't a suitable format. Hadoop's SequenceFile class fits the bill in this situation, providing a persistent data structure for binary key-value pairs. To use it as a logfile format, you would choose a key, such as timestamp represented by a LongWritable, and the value is a Writable that represents the quantity being logged.

SequenceFiles also work well as containers for smaller files. HDFS and MapReduce are optimized for large files, so packing files into a SequenceFile makes storing and processing the smaller files more efficient. ("Processing a whole file as a record" on page 206 contains a program to pack files into a SequenceFile.*)

Writing a SequenceFile

To create a SequenceFile, use one of its createWriter() static methods, which returns a SequenceFile.Writer instance. There are several overloaded versions, but they all require you to specify a stream to write to (either a FSDataOutputStream or a FileSystem and Path pairing), a Configuration object, and the key and value types. Optional arguments include the compression type and codec, a Progressable callback to be informed of write progress, and a Metadata instance to be stored in the SequenceFile header.

The keys and values stored in a SequenceFile do not necessarily need to be Writable. Any types that can be serialized and deserialized by a Serialization may be used.

Once you have a SequenceFile.Writer, you then write key-value pairs, using the append() method. Then when you've finished, you call the close() method (Sequence File.Writer implements java.io.Closeable).

Example 4-12 shows a short program to write some key-value pairs to a Sequence File, using the API just described.

Example 4-12. Writing a SequenceFile

```
public class SequenceFileWriteDemo {

  private static final String[] DATA = {
    "One, two, buckle my shoe",
    "Three, four, shut the door",
    "Five, six, pick up sticks",
    "Seven, eight, lay them straight",
    "Nine, ten, a big fat hen"
  };

  public static void main(String[] args) throws IOException {
    String uri = args[0];
    Configuration conf = new Configuration();
    FileSystem fs = FileSystem.get(URI.create(uri), conf);
    Path path = new Path(uri);

    IntWritable key = new IntWritable();
    Text value = new Text();
    SequenceFile.Writer writer = null;
    try {
      writer = SequenceFile.createWriter(fs, conf, path,
```

---

* In a similar vein, the blog post "A Million Little Files" by Stuart Sierra includes code for converting a *tar* file into a SequenceFile, *http://stuartsierra.com/2008/04/24/a-million-little-files*.

```
        key.getClass(), value.getClass());

    for (int i = 0; i < 100; i++) {
      key.set(100 - i);
      value.set(DATA[i % DATA.length]);
      System.out.printf("[%s]\t%s\t%s\n", writer.getLength(), key, value);
      writer.append(key, value);
    }
  } finally {
    IOUtils.closeStream(writer);
  }
}
}
```

The keys in the sequence file are integers counting down from 100 to 1, represented as
IntWritable objects. The values are Text objects. Before each record is appended to the
SequenceFile.Writer, we call the getLength() method to discover the current position
in the file. (We will use this information about record boundaries in the next section
when we read the file nonsequentially.) We write the position out to the console, along
with the key and value pairs. The result of running it is shown here:

```
% hadoop SequenceFileWriteDemo numbers.seq
[128]   100   One, two, buckle my shoe
[173]   99    Three, four, shut the door
[220]   98    Five, six, pick up sticks
[264]   97    Seven, eight, lay them straight
[314]   96    Nine, ten, a big fat hen
[359]   95    One, two, buckle my shoe
[404]   94    Three, four, shut the door
[451]   93    Five, six, pick up sticks
[495]   92    Seven, eight, lay them straight
[545]   91    Nine, ten, a big fat hen
...
[1976]  60    One, two, buckle my shoe
[2021]  59    Three, four, shut the door
[2088]  58    Five, six, pick up sticks
[2132]  57    Seven, eight, lay them straight
[2182]  56    Nine, ten, a big fat hen
...
[4557]  5     One, two, buckle my shoe
[4602]  4     Three, four, shut the door
[4649]  3     Five, six, pick up sticks
[4693]  2     Seven, eight, lay them straight
[4743]  1     Nine, ten, a big fat hen
```

Reading a SequenceFile

Reading sequence files from beginning to end is a matter of creating an instance of
SequenceFile.Reader and iterating over records by repeatedly invoking one of the
next() methods. Which one you use depends on the serialization framework you are
using. If you are using Writable types, you can use the next() method that takes a key

and a value argument, and reads the next key and value in the stream into these variables:

```
public boolean next(Writable key, Writable val)
```

The return value is true if a key-value pair was read and false if the end of the file has been reached.

For other, nonWritable serialization frameworks (such as Apache Thrift), you should use these two methods:

```
public Object next(Object key) throws IOException
public Object getCurrentValue(Object val) throws IOException
```

In this case, you need to make sure that the serialization you want to use has been set in the io.serializations property; see "Serialization Frameworks" on page 101.

If the next() method returns a non-null object, a key-value pair was read from the stream, and the value can be retrieved using the getCurrentValue() method. Otherwise, if next() returns null, the end of the file has been reached.

The program in Example 4-13 demonstrates how to read a sequence file that has Writable keys and values. Note how the types are discovered from the Sequence File.Reader via calls to getKeyClass() and getValueClass(), then ReflectionUtils is used to create an instance for the key and an instance for the value. By using this technique, the program can be used with any sequence file that has Writable keys and values.

Example 4-13. Reading a SequenceFile

```
public class SequenceFileReadDemo {

  public static void main(String[] args) throws IOException {
    String uri = args[0];
    Configuration conf = new Configuration();
    FileSystem fs = FileSystem.get(URI.create(uri), conf);
    Path path = new Path(uri);

    SequenceFile.Reader reader = null;
    try {
      reader = new SequenceFile.Reader(fs, path, conf);
      Writable key = (Writable)
        ReflectionUtils.newInstance(reader.getKeyClass(), conf);
      Writable value = (Writable)
        ReflectionUtils.newInstance(reader.getValueClass(), conf);
      long position = reader.getPosition();
      while (reader.next(key, value)) {
        String syncSeen = reader.syncSeen() ? "*" : "";
        System.out.printf("[%s%s]\t%s\t%s\n", position, syncSeen, key, value);
        position = reader.getPosition(); // beginning of next record
      }
    } finally {
      IOUtils.closeStream(reader);
    }
```

```
    }
}
```

Another feature of the program is that it displays the position of the *sync points* in the sequence file. A sync point is a point in the stream that can be used to resynchronize with a record boundary if the reader is "lost"—for example, after seeking to an arbitrary position in the stream. Sync points are recorded by `SequenceFile.Writer`, which inserts a special entry to mark the sync point every few records as a sequence file is being written. Such entries are small enough to incur only a modest storage overhead—less than 1%. Sync points always align with record boundaries.

Running the program in Example 4-13 shows the sync points in the sequence file as asterisks. The first one occurs at position 2021 (the second one occurs at position 4075, but is not shown in the output):

```
% hadoop SequenceFileReadDemo numbers.seq
[128]    100    One, two, buckle my shoe
[173]    99     Three, four, shut the door
[220]    98     Five, six, pick up sticks
[264]    97     Seven, eight, lay them straight
[314]    96     Nine, ten, a big fat hen
[359]    95     One, two, buckle my shoe
[404]    94     Three, four, shut the door
[451]    93     Five, six, pick up sticks
[495]    92     Seven, eight, lay them straight
[545]    91     Nine, ten, a big fat hen
[590]    90     One, two, buckle my shoe
...
[1976]   60     One, two, buckle my shoe
[2021*]  59     Three, four, shut the door
[2088]   58     Five, six, pick up sticks
[2132]   57     Seven, eight, lay them straight
[2182]   56     Nine, ten, a big fat hen
...
[4557]   5      One, two, buckle my shoe
[4602]   4      Three, four, shut the door
[4649]   3      Five, six, pick up sticks
[4693]   2      Seven, eight, lay them straight
[4743]   1      Nine, ten, a big fat hen
```

There are two ways to seek to a given position in a sequence file. The first is the `seek()` method, which positions the reader at the given point in the file. For example, seeking to a record boundary works as expected:

```
reader.seek(359);
assertThat(reader.next(key, value), is(true));
assertThat(((IntWritable) key).get(), is(95));
```

But if the position in the file is not at a record boundary, the reader fails when the `next()` method is called:

```
reader.seek(360);
reader.next(key, value); // fails with IOException
```

The second way to find a record boundary makes use of sync points. The sync(long position) method on SequenceFile.Reader positions the reader at the next sync point after position. (If there are no sync points in the file after this position, then the reader will be positioned at the end of the file.) Thus, we can call sync() with any position in the stream—a nonrecord boundary, for example—and the reader will reestablish itself at the next sync point so reading can continue:

```
reader.sync(360);
assertThat(reader.getPosition(), is(2021L));
assertThat(reader.next(key, value), is(true));
assertThat(((IntWritable) key).get(), is(59));
```

 SequenceFile.Writer has a method called sync() for inserting a sync point at the current position in the stream. This is not to be confused with the identically named but otherwise unrelated sync() method defined by the Syncable interface for synchronizing buffers to the underlying device.

Sync points come into their own when using sequence files as input to MapReduce, since they permit the file to be split, so different portions of it can be processed independently by separate map tasks. See "SequenceFileInputFormat" on page 213.

Displaying a SequenceFile with the command-line interface

The hadoop fs command has a -text option to display sequence files in textual form. It looks at a file's magic number so that it can attempt to detect the type of the file and appropriately convert it to text. It can recognize gzipped files and sequence files; otherwise, it assumes the input is plain text.

For sequence files, this command is really useful only if the keys and values have a meaningful string representation (as defined by the toString() method). Also, if you have your own key or value classes, then you will need to make sure they are on Hadoop's classpath.

Running it on the sequence file we created in the previous section gives the following output:

```
% hadoop fs -text numbers.seq | head
100     One, two, buckle my shoe
99      Three, four, shut the door
98      Five, six, pick up sticks
97      Seven, eight, lay them straight
96      Nine, ten, a big fat hen
95      One, two, buckle my shoe
94      Three, four, shut the door
93      Five, six, pick up sticks
92      Seven, eight, lay them straight
91      Nine, ten, a big fat hen
```

Sorting and merging SequenceFiles

The most powerful way of sorting (and merging) one or more sequence files is to use MapReduce. MapReduce is inherently parallel and will let you specify the number of reducers to use, which determines the number of output partitions. For example, by specifying one reducer, you get a single output file. We can use the sort example that comes with Hadoop by specifying that the input and output are sequence files, and by setting the key and value types:

```
% hadoop jar $HADOOP_INSTALL/hadoop-*-examples.jar sort -r 1 \
  -inFormat org.apache.hadoop.mapred.SequenceFileInputFormat \
  -outFormat org.apache.hadoop.mapred.SequenceFileOutputFormat \
  -outKey org.apache.hadoop.io.IntWritable \
  -outValue org.apache.hadoop.io.Text \
  numbers.seq sorted
% hadoop fs -text sorted/part-00000 | head
1       Nine, ten, a big fat hen
2       Seven, eight, lay them straight
3       Five, six, pick up sticks
4       Three, four, shut the door
5       One, two, buckle my shoe
6       Nine, ten, a big fat hen
7       Seven, eight, lay them straight
8       Five, six, pick up sticks
9       Three, four, shut the door
10      One, two, buckle my shoe
```

Sorting is covered in more detail in "Sorting" on page 232.

As an alternative to using MapReduce for sort/merge, there is a `SequenceFile.Sorter` class that has a number of `sort()` and `merge()` methods. These functions predate Map-Reduce and are lower-level functions than MapReduce (for example, to get parallelism, you need to partition your data manually), so in general MapReduce is the preferred approach to sort and merge sequence files.

The SequenceFile format

A sequence file consists of a header followed by one or more records (see Figure 4-2). The first three bytes of a sequence file are the bytes `SEQ`, which acts a magic number, followed by a single byte representing the version number. The header contains other fields including the names of the key and value classes, compression details, user-defined metadata, and the sync marker.[†] Recall that the sync marker is used to allow a reader to synchronize to a record boundary from any position in the file. Each file has a randomly generated sync marker, whose value is stored in the header. Sync markers appear between records in the sequence file. They are designed to incur less than a 1% storage overhead, so they don't necessarily appear between every pair of records (such is the case for short records).

---

† Full details of the format of these fields may be found in `SequenceFile`'s documentation (*http://hadoop.apache .org/common/docs/current/api/org/apache/hadoop/io/SequenceFile.html*) and source code.

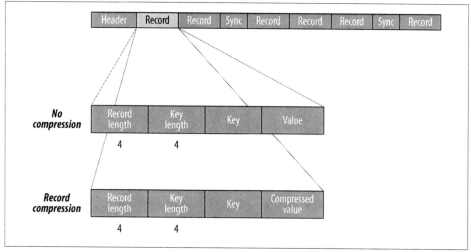

Figure 4-2. The internal structure of a sequence file with no compression and record compression

The internal format of the records depends on whether compression is enabled, and if it is, whether it is record compression or block compression.

If no compression is enabled (the default), then each record is made up of the record length (in bytes), the key length, the key, and then the value. The length fields are written as four-byte integers adhering to the contract of the `writeInt()` method of `java.io.DataOutput`. Keys and values are serialized using the `Serialization` defined for the class being written to the sequence file.

The format for record compression is almost identical to no compression, except the value bytes are compressed using the codec defined in the header. Note that keys are not compressed.

Block compression compresses multiple records at once; it is therefore more compact than and should generally be preferred over record compression because it has the opportunity to take advantage of similarities between records. (See Figure 4-3.) Records are added to a block until it reaches a minimum size in bytes, defined by the `io.seqfile.compress.blocksize` property: the default is 1 million bytes. A sync marker is written before the start of every block. The format of a block is a field indicating the number of records in the block, followed by four compressed fields: the key lengths, the keys, the value lengths, and the values.

MapFile

A `MapFile` is a sorted `SequenceFile` with an index to permit lookups by key. `MapFile` can be thought of as a persistent form of `java.util.Map` (although it doesn't implement this interface), which is able to grow beyond the size of a `Map` that is kept in memory.

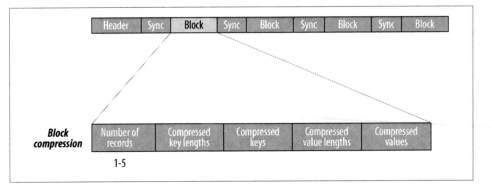

| Block compression | Number of records | Compressed key lengths | Compressed keys | Compressed value lengths | Compressed values |

1-5

Figure 4-3. The internal structure of a sequence file with block compression

Writing a MapFile

Writing a MapFile is similar to writing a SequenceFile: you create an instance of MapFile.Writer, then call the append() method to add entries in order. (Attempting to add entries out of order will result in an IOException.) Keys must be instances of WritableComparable, and values must be Writable—contrast this to SequenceFile, which can use any serialization framework for its entries.

The program in Example 4-14 creates a MapFile, and writes some entries to it. It is very similar to the program in Example 4-12 for creating a SequenceFile.

Example 4-14. Writing a MapFile

```
public class MapFileWriteDemo {

  private static final String[] DATA = {
    "One, two, buckle my shoe",
    "Three, four, shut the door",
    "Five, six, pick up sticks",
    "Seven, eight, lay them straight",
    "Nine, ten, a big fat hen"
  };

  public static void main(String[] args) throws IOException {
    String uri = args[0];
    Configuration conf = new Configuration();
    FileSystem fs = FileSystem.get(URI.create(uri), conf);

    IntWritable key = new IntWritable();
    Text value = new Text();
    MapFile.Writer writer = null;
    try {
      writer = new MapFile.Writer(conf, fs, uri,
          key.getClass(), value.getClass());

      for (int i = 0; i < 1024; i++) {
        key.set(i + 1);
        value.set(DATA[i % DATA.length]);
```

```
      writer.append(key, value);
    }
  } finally {
    IOUtils.closeStream(writer);
  }
 }
}
```

Let's use this program to build a `MapFile`:

```
% hadoop MapFileWriteDemo numbers.map
```

If we look at the `MapFile`, we see it's actually a directory containing two files called *data* and *index*:

```
% ls -l numbers.map
total 104
-rw-r--r--   1 tom  tom  47898 Jul 29 22:06 data
-rw-r--r--   1 tom  tom    251 Jul 29 22:06 index
```

Both files are `SequenceFiles`. The *data* file contains all of the entries, in order:

```
% hadoop fs -text numbers.map/data | head
1       One, two, buckle my shoe
2       Three, four, shut the door
3       Five, six, pick up sticks
4       Seven, eight, lay them straight
5       Nine, ten, a big fat hen
6       One, two, buckle my shoe
7       Three, four, shut the door
8       Five, six, pick up sticks
9       Seven, eight, lay them straight
10      Nine, ten, a big fat hen
```

The *index* file contains a fraction of the keys, and contains a mapping from the key to that key's offset in the *data* file:

```
% hadoop fs -text numbers.map/index
1       128
129     6079
257     12054
385     18030
513     24002
641     29976
769     35947
897     41922
```

As we can see from the output, by default only every 128th key is included in the index, although you can change this value either by setting the io.map.index.interval property or by calling the setIndexInterval() method on the MapFile.Writer instance. A reason to increase the index interval would be to decrease the amount of memory that the MapFile needs to store the index. Conversely, you might decrease the interval to improve the time for random selection (since fewer records need to be skipped on average) at the expense of memory usage.

Since the index is only a partial index of keys, MapFile is not able to provide methods to enumerate, or even count, all the keys it contains. The only way to perform these operations is to read the whole file.

Reading a MapFile

Iterating through the entries in order in a MapFile is similar to the procedure for a SequenceFile: you create a MapFile.Reader, then call the next() method until it returns false, signifying that no entry was read because the end of the file was reached:

```
public boolean next(WritableComparable key, Writable val) throws IOException
```

A random access lookup can be performed by calling the get() method:

```
public Writable get(WritableComparable key, Writable val) throws IOException
```

The return value is used to determine if an entry was found in the MapFile; if it's null, then no value exists for the given key. If key was found, then the value for that key is read into val, as well as being returned from the method call.

It might be helpful to understand how this is implemented. Here is a snippet of code that retrieves an entry for the MapFile we created in the previous section:

```
Text value = new Text();
reader.get(new IntWritable(496), value);
assertThat(value.toString(), is("One, two, buckle my shoe"));
```

For this operation, the MapFile.Reader reads the *index* file into memory (this is cached so that subsequent random access calls will use the same in-memory index). The reader then performs a binary search on the in-memory index to find the key in the index that is less than or equal to the search key, 496. In this example, the index key found is 385, with value 18030, which is the offset in the *data* file. Next the reader seeks to this offset in the *data* file and reads entries until the key is greater than or equal to the search key, 496. In this case, a match is found and the value is read from the *data* file. Overall, a lookup takes a single disk seek and a scan through up to 128 entries on disk. For a random-access read, this is actually very efficient.

The getClosest() method is like get() except it returns the "closest" match to the specified key, rather than returning null on no match. More precisely, if the MapFile contains the specified key, then that is the entry returned; otherwise, the key in the MapFile that is immediately after (or before, according to a boolean argument) the specified key is returned.

A very large MapFile's index can take up a lot of memory. Rather than reindex to change the index interval, it is possible to load only a fraction of the index keys into memory when reading the MapFile by setting the io.map.index.skip property. This property is normally 0, which means no index keys are skipped; a value of 1 means skip one key for every key in the index (so every other key ends up in the index), 2 means skip two keys for every key in the index (so one third of the keys end up in the index), and so on. Larger skip values save memory but at the expense of lookup time, since more entries have to be scanned on disk, on average.

Converting a SequenceFile to a MapFile

One way of looking at a MapFile is as an indexed and sorted SequenceFile. So it's quite natural to want to be able to convert a SequenceFile into a MapFile. We covered how to sort a SequenceFile in "Sorting and merging SequenceFiles" on page 122, so here we look at how to create an index for a SequenceFile. The program in Example 4-15 hinges around the static utility method fix() on MapFile, which re-creates the index for a MapFile.

Example 4-15. Re-creating the index for a MapFile

```
public class MapFileFixer {

  public static void main(String[] args) throws Exception {
    String mapUri = args[0];

    Configuration conf = new Configuration();

    FileSystem fs = FileSystem.get(URI.create(mapUri), conf);
    Path map = new Path(mapUri);
    Path mapData = new Path(map, MapFile.DATA_FILE_NAME);

    // Get key and value types from data sequence file
    SequenceFile.Reader reader = new SequenceFile.Reader(fs, mapData, conf);
    Class keyClass = reader.getKeyClass();
    Class valueClass = reader.getValueClass();
    reader.close();

    // Create the map file index file
    long entries = MapFile.fix(fs, map, keyClass, valueClass, false, conf);
    System.out.printf("Created MapFile %s with %d entries\n", map, entries);
  }
}
```

The fix() method is usually used for re-creating corrupted indexes, but since it creates a new index from scratch, it's exactly what we need here. The recipe is as follows:

1. Sort the sequence file *numbers.seq* into a new directory called *number.map* that will become the MapFile (if the sequence file is already sorted, then you can skip this step. Instead, copy it to a file *number.map/data*, then go to step 3):

   ```
   % hadoop jar $HADOOP_INSTALL/hadoop-*-examples.jar sort -r 1 \
     -inFormat org.apache.hadoop.mapred.SequenceFileInputFormat \
     -outFormat org.apache.hadoop.mapred.SequenceFileOutputFormat \
     -outKey org.apache.hadoop.io.IntWritable \
     -outValue org.apache.hadoop.io.Text \
     numbers.seq numbers.map
   ```

2. Rename the MapReduce output to be the *data* file:

   ```
   % hadoop fs -mv numbers.map/part-00000 numbers.map/data
   ```

3. Create the *index* file:

```
% hadoop MapFileFixer numbers.map
Created MapFile numbers.map with 100 entries
```

The MapFile *numbers.map* now exists and can be used.

## CHAPTER 5

Developing a MapReduce Application

In Chapter 2, we introduced the MapReduce model. In this chapter, we look at the practical aspects of developing a MapReduce application in Hadoop.

Writing a program in MapReduce has a certain flow to it. You start by writing your map and reduce functions, ideally with unit tests to make sure they do what you expect. Then you write a driver program to run a job, which can run from your IDE using a small subset of the data to check that it is working. If it fails, then you can use your IDE's debugger to find the source of the problem. With this information, you can expand your unit tests to cover this case and improve your mapper or reducer as appropriate to handle such input correctly.

When the program runs as expected against the small dataset, you are ready to unleash it on a cluster. Running against the full dataset is likely to expose some more issues, which you can fix as before, by expanding your tests and mapper or reducer to handle the new cases. Debugging failing programs in the cluster is a challenge, but Hadoop provides some tools to help, such as an `IsolationRunner`, which allows you to run a task over the same input on which it failed, with a debugger attached, if necessary.

After the program is working, you may wish to do some tuning, first by running through some standard checks for making MapReduce programs faster and then by doing task profiling. Profiling distributed programs is not trivial, but Hadoop has hooks to aid the process.

Before we start writing a MapReduce program, we need to set up and configure the development environment. And to do that, we need to learn a bit about how Hadoop does configuration.

The Configuration API

Components in Hadoop are configured using Hadoop's own configuration API. An instance of the Configuration class (found in the org.apache.hadoop.conf package) represents a collection of configuration *properties* and their values. Each property is named by a String, and the type of a value may be one of several types, including Java primitives such as boolean, int, long, float, and other useful types such as String, Class, java.io.File, and collections of Strings.

Configurations read their properties from *resources*—XML files with a simple structure for defining name-value pairs. See Example 5-1.

Example 5-1. A simple configuration file, configuration-1.xml

```xml
<?xml version="1.0"?>
<configuration>
  <property>
    <name>color</name>
    <value>yellow</value>
    <description>Color</description>
  </property>

  <property>
    <name>size</name>
    <value>10</value>
    <description>Size</description>
  </property>

  <property>
    <name>weight</name>
    <value>heavy</value>
    <final>true</final>
    <description>Weight</description>
  </property>

  <property>
    <name>size-weight</name>
    <value>${size},${weight}</value>
    <description>Size and weight</description>
  </property>
</configuration>
```

Assuming this configuration file is in a file called *configuration-1.xml*, we can access its properties using a piece of code like this:

```java
Configuration conf = new Configuration();
conf.addResource("configuration-1.xml");
assertThat(conf.get("color"), is("yellow"));
assertThat(conf.getInt("size", 0), is(10));
assertThat(conf.get("breadth", "wide"), is("wide"));
```

There are a couple of things to note: type information is not stored in the XML file; instead, properties can be interpreted as a given type when they are read. Also, the get() methods allow you to specify a default value, which is used if the property is not defined in the XML file, as in the case of breadth here.

Combining Resources

Things get interesting when more than one resource is used to define a configuration. This is used in Hadoop to separate out the default properties for the system, defined internally in a file called *core-default.xml*, from the site-specific overrides, in *core-site.xml*. The file in Example 5-2 defines the size and weight properties.

Example 5-2. A second configuration file, configuration-2.xml

```xml
<?xml version="1.0"?>
<configuration>
  <property>
    <name>size</name>
    <value>12</value>
  </property>

  <property>
    <name>weight</name>
    <value>light</value>
  </property>
</configuration>
```

Resources are added to a Configuration in order:

```
Configuration conf = new Configuration();
conf.addResource("configuration-1.xml");
conf.addResource("configuration-2.xml");
```

Properties defined in resources that are added later override the earlier definitions. So the size property takes its value from the second configuration file, *configuration-2.xml*:

```
assertThat(conf.getInt("size", 0), is(12));
```

However, properties that are marked as final cannot be overridden in later definitions. The weight property is final in the first configuration file, so the attempt to override it in the second fails, and it takes the value from the first:

```
assertThat(conf.get("weight"), is("heavy"));
```

Attempting to override final properties usually indicates a configuration error, so this results in a warning message being logged to aid diagnosis. Administrators mark properties as final in the daemon's site files that they don't want users to change in their client-side configuration files or job submission parameters.

Variable Expansion

Configuration properties can be defined in terms of other properties, or system properties. For example, the property `size-weight` in the first configuration file is defined as `${size},${weight}`, and these properties are expanded using the values found in the configuration:

```
assertThat(conf.get("size-weight"), is("12,heavy"));
```

System properties take priority over properties defined in resource files:

```
System.setProperty("size", "14");
assertThat(conf.get("size-weight"), is("14,heavy"));
```

This feature is useful for overriding properties on the command line by using -D*property=value* JVM arguments.

Note that while configuration properties can be defined in terms of system properties, unless system properties are redefined using configuration properties, they are *not* accessible through the configuration API. Hence:

```
System.setProperty("length", "2");
assertThat(conf.get("length"), is((String) null));
```

Configuring the Development Environment

The first step is to download the version of Hadoop that you plan to use and unpack it on your development machine (this is described in Appendix A). Then, in your favorite IDE, create a new project and add all the JAR files from the top level of the unpacked distribution and from the *lib* directory to the classpath. You will then be able to compile Java Hadoop programs and run them in local (standalone) mode within the IDE.

> For Eclipse users, there is a plug-in available for browsing HDFS and launching MapReduce programs. Instructions are available on the Hadoop wiki at *http://wiki.apache.org/hadoop/EclipsePlugIn*.
>
> Alternatively, Karmasphere (*http://www.karmasphere.com/*) provides Eclipse and NetBeans plug-ins for developing and running MapReduce jobs and browsing Hadoop clusters.

Managing Configuration

When developing Hadoop applications, it is common to switch between running the application locally and running it on a cluster. In fact, you may have several clusters you work with, or you may have a local "pseudo-distributed" cluster that you like to test on (a pseudo-distributed cluster is one whose daemons all run on the local machine; setting up this mode is covered in Appendix A, too).

One way to accommodate these variations is to have Hadoop configuration files containing the connection settings for each cluster you run against, and specify which one you are using when you run Hadoop applications or tools. As a matter of best practice, it's recommended to keep these files outside Hadoop's installation directory tree, as this makes it easy to switch between Hadoop versions without duplicating or losing settings.

For the purposes of this book, we assume the existence of a directory called *conf* that contains three configuration files: *hadoop-local.xml*, *hadoop-localhost.xml*, and *hadoop-cluster.xml* (these are available in the example code for this book). Note that there is nothing special about the names of these files—they are just convenient ways to package up some configuration settings. (Compare this to Table A-1 in Appendix A, which sets out the equivalent server-side configurations.)

The *hadoop-local.xml* file contains the default Hadoop configuration for the default filesystem and the jobtracker:

```xml
<?xml version="1.0"?>
<configuration>

  <property>
    <name>fs.default.name</name>
    <value>file:///</value>
  </property>

  <property>
    <name>mapred.job.tracker</name>
    <value>local</value>
  </property>

</configuration>
```

The settings in *hadoop-localhost.xml* point to a namenode and a jobtracker both running on localhost:

```xml
<?xml version="1.0"?>
<configuration>

  <property>
    <name>fs.default.name</name>
    <value>hdfs://localhost/</value>
  </property>

  <property>
    <name>mapred.job.tracker</name>
    <value>localhost:8021</value>
  </property>

</configuration>
```

Finally, *hadoop-cluster.xml* contains details of the cluster's namenode and jobtracker addresses. In practice, you would name the file after the name of the cluster, rather than "cluster" as we have here:

```xml
<?xml version="1.0"?>
<configuration>

  <property>
    <name>fs.default.name</name>
    <value>hdfs://namenode/</value>
  </property>

  <property>
    <name>mapred.job.tracker</name>
    <value>jobtracker:8021</value>
  </property>

</configuration>
```

You can add other configuration properties to these files as needed. For example, if you wanted to set your Hadoop username for a particular cluster, you could do it in the appropriate file.

Setting User Identity

The user identity that Hadoop uses for permissions in HDFS is determined by running the `whoami` command on the client system. Similarly, the group names are derived from the output of running `groups`.

If, however, your Hadoop user identity is different from the name of your user account on your client machine, then you can explicitly set your Hadoop username and group names by setting the `hadoop.job.ugi` property. The username and group names are specified as a comma-separated list of strings (e.g., `preston,directors,inventors` would set the username to `preston` and the group names to `directors` and `inventors`).

You can set the user identity that the HDFS web interface runs as by setting `dfs.web.ugi` using the same syntax. By default, it is `webuser,webgroup`, which is not a super user, so system files are not accessible through the web interface.

Notice that, by default, there is no authentication with this system. See "Security" on page 281 for how to use Kerberos authentication with Hadoop.

With this setup, it is easy to use any configuration with the `-conf` command-line switch. For example, the following command shows a directory listing on the HDFS server running in pseudo-distributed mode on localhost:

```
% hadoop fs -conf conf/hadoop-localhost.xml -ls .
Found 2 items
drwxr-xr-x   - tom supergroup          0 2009-04-08 10:32 /user/tom/input
drwxr-xr-x   - tom supergroup          0 2009-04-08 13:09 /user/tom/output
```

If you omit the -conf option, then you pick up the Hadoop configuration in the *conf* subdirectory under $HADOOP_INSTALL. Depending on how you set this up, this may be for a standalone setup or a pseudo-distributed cluster.

Tools that come with Hadoop support the -conf option, but it's also straightforward to make your programs (such as programs that run MapReduce jobs) support it, too, using the Tool interface.

GenericOptionsParser, Tool, and ToolRunner

Hadoop comes with a few helper classes for making it easier to run jobs from the command line. GenericOptionsParser is a class that interprets common Hadoop command-line options and sets them on a Configuration object for your application to use as desired. You don't usually use GenericOptionsParser directly, as it's more convenient to implement the Tool interface and run your application with the ToolRunner, which uses GenericOptionsParser internally:

```
public interface Tool extends Configurable {
  int run(String [] args) throws Exception;
}
```

Example 5-3 shows a very simple implementation of Tool, for printing the keys and values of all the properties in the Tool's Configuration object.

Example 5-3. An example Tool implementation for printing the properties in a Configuration

```
public class ConfigurationPrinter extends Configured implements Tool {

  static {
    Configuration.addDefaultResource("hdfs-default.xml");
    Configuration.addDefaultResource("hdfs-site.xml");
    Configuration.addDefaultResource("mapred-default.xml");
    Configuration.addDefaultResource("mapred-site.xml");
  }

  @Override
  public int run(String[] args) throws Exception {
    Configuration conf = getConf();
    for (Entry<String, String> entry: conf) {
      System.out.printf("%s=%s\n", entry.getKey(), entry.getValue());
    }
    return 0;
  }

  public static void main(String[] args) throws Exception {
    int exitCode = ToolRunner.run(new ConfigurationPrinter(), args);
    System.exit(exitCode);
  }
}
```

We make ConfigurationPrinter a subclass of Configured, which is an implementation of the Configurable interface. All implementations of Tool need to implement Configurable (since Tool extends it), and subclassing Configured is often the easiest way to achieve this. The run() method obtains the Configuration using Configurable's getConf() method and then iterates over it, printing each property to standard output.

The static block makes sure that the HDFS and MapReduce configurations are picked up in addition to the core ones (which Configuration knows about already).

ConfigurationPrinter's main() method does not invoke its own run() method directly. Instead, we call ToolRunner's static run() method, which takes care of creating a Configuration object for the Tool, before calling its run() method. ToolRunner also uses a GenericOptionsParser to pick up any standard options specified on the command line and set them on the Configuration instance. We can see the effect of picking up the properties specified in *conf/hadoop-localhost.xml* by running the following command:

```
% hadoop ConfigurationPrinter -conf conf/hadoop-localhost.xml \
  | grep mapred.job.tracker=
mapred.job.tracker=localhost:8021
```

Which Properties Can I Set?

ConfigurationPrinter is a useful tool for telling you what a property is set to in your environment.

You can also see the default settings for all the public properties in Hadoop by looking in the *docs* directory of your Hadoop installation for HTML files called *core-default.html*, *hdfs-default.html* and *mapred-default.html*. Each property has a description that explains what it is for and what values it can be set to.

Be aware that some properties have no effect when set in the client configuration. For example, if in your job submission you set mapred.tasktracker.map.tasks.maximum with the expectation that it would change the number of task slots for the tasktrackers running your job, then you would be disappointed, since this property only is only honored if set in the tasktracker's *mapred-site.xml* file. In general, you can tell the component where a property should be set by its name, so the fact that mapred.task tracker.map.tasks.maximum starts with mapred.tasktracker gives you a clue that it can be set only for the tasktracker daemon. This is not a hard and fast rule, however, so in some cases you may need to resort to trial and error, or even reading the source.

We discuss many of Hadoop's most important configuration properties throughout this book. You can find a configuration property reference on the book's website at *http://www.hadoopbook.com.*

GenericOptionsParser also allows you to set individual properties. For example:

```
% hadoop ConfigurationPrinter -D color=yellow | grep color
color=yellow
```

The -D option is used to set the configuration property with key color to the value yellow. Options specified with -D take priority over properties from the configuration files. This is very useful: you can put defaults into configuration files and then override them with the -D option as needed. A common example of this is setting the number of reducers for a MapReduce job via -D mapred.reduce.tasks=*n*. This will override the number of reducers set on the cluster or set in any client-side configuration files.

The other options that GenericOptionsParser and ToolRunner support are listed in Table 5-1. You can find more on Hadoop's configuration API in "The Configuration API" on page 130.

Do not confuse setting Hadoop properties using the -D *property=value* option to GenericOptionsParser (and ToolRunner) with setting JVM system properties using the -D*property=value* option to the java command. The syntax for JVM system properties does not allow any whitespace between the D and the property name, whereas GenericOptionsParser requires them to be separated by whitespace.

JVM system properties are retrieved from the java.lang.System class, whereas Hadoop properties are accessible only from a Configuration object. So, the following command will print nothing, since the System class is not used by ConfigurationPrinter:

```
% hadoop -Dcolor=yellow ConfigurationPrinter | grep color
```

If you want to be able to set configuration through system properties, then you need to mirror the system properties of interest in the configuration file. See "Variable Expansion" on page 132 for further discussion.

Table 5-1. GenericOptionsParser and ToolRunner options

Option	Description
-D *property=value*	Sets the given Hadoop configuration property to the given value. Overrides any default or site properties in the configuration, and any properties set via the -conf option.
-conf *filename* ...	Adds the given files to the list of resources in the configuration. This is a convenient way to set site properties or to set a number of properties at once.
-fs *uri*	Sets the default filesystem to the given URI. Shortcut for -D fs.default.name=*uri*
-jt *host:port*	Sets the jobtracker to the given host and port. Shortcut for -D mapred.job.tracker=*host:port*
-files *file1,file2,...*	Copies the specified files from the local filesystem (or any filesystem if a scheme is specified) to the shared filesystem used by the jobtracker (usually HDFS) and makes them available to MapReduce programs in the task's working directory. (See "Distributed Cache" on page 253 for more on the distributed cache mechanism for copying files to tasktracker machines.)
-archives *archive1,archive2,...*	Copies the specified archives from the local filesystem (or any filesystem if a scheme is specified) to the shared filesystem used by the jobtracker (usually HDFS), unarchives

Option	Description
	them, and makes them available to MapReduce programs in the task's working directory.
`-libjars jar1,jar2,...`	Copies the specified JAR files from the local filesystem (or any filesystem if a scheme is specified) to the shared filesystem used by the jobtracker (usually HDFS), and adds them to the MapReduce task's classpath. This option is a useful way of shipping JAR files that a job is dependent on.

Writing a Unit Test

The map and reduce functions in MapReduce are easy to test in isolation, which is a consequence of their functional style. For known inputs, they produce known outputs. However, since outputs are written to an OutputCollector, rather than simply being returned from the method call, the OutputCollector needs to be replaced with a mock so that its outputs can be verified. There are several Java mock object frameworks that can help build mocks; here we use Mockito, which is noted for its clean syntax, although any mock framework should work just as well.[*]

All of the tests described here can be run from within an IDE.

Mapper

The test for the mapper is shown in Example 5-4.

Example 5-4. Unit test for MaxTemperatureMapper

```
import static org.mockito.Mockito.*;

import java.io.IOException;
import org.apache.hadoop.io.*;
import org.apache.hadoop.mapred.OutputCollector;
import org.junit.*;

public class MaxTemperatureMapperTest {

  @Test
  public void processesValidRecord() throws IOException {
    MaxTemperatureMapper mapper = new MaxTemperatureMapper();

    Text value = new Text("0043011990999991950051518004+68750+023550FM-12+0382" +
                          // Year ^^^^
        "99999V0203201N00261220001CN9999999N9-00111+99999999999");
                          // Temperature ^^^^^
    OutputCollector<Text, IntWritable> output = mock(OutputCollector.class);

    mapper.map(null, value, output, null);
```

---

[*] See also the MRUnit contrib module, which aims to make unit testing MapReduce programs easier.

```
    verify(output).collect(new Text("1950"), new IntWritable(-11));
  }
}
```

The test is very simple: it passes a weather record as input to the mapper, then checks the output is the year and temperature reading. The input key and Reporter are both ignored by the mapper, so we can pass in anything, including null as we do here. To create a mock OutputCollector, we call Mockito's mock() method (a static import), passing the class of the type we want to mock. Then we invoke the mapper's map() method, which executes the code being tested. Finally, we verify that the mock object was called with the correct method and arguments, using Mockito's verify() method (again, statically imported). Here we verify that OutputCollector's collect() method was called with a Text object representing the year (1950) and an IntWritable representing the temperature (−1.1°C).

Proceeding in a test-driven fashion, we create a Mapper implementation that passes the test (see Example 5-5). Since we will be evolving the classes in this chapter, each is put in a different package indicating its version for ease of exposition. For example, v1.Max TemperatureMapper is version 1 of MaxTemperatureMapper. In reality, of course, you would evolve classes without repackaging them.

Example 5-5. First version of a Mapper that passes MaxTemperatureMapperTest

```
public class MaxTemperatureMapper extends MapReduceBase
  implements Mapper<LongWritable, Text, Text, IntWritable> {

  public void map(LongWritable key, Text value,
      OutputCollector<Text, IntWritable> output, Reporter reporter)
      throws IOException {

    String line = value.toString();
    String year = line.substring(15, 19);
    int airTemperature = Integer.parseInt(line.substring(87, 92));
    output.collect(new Text(year), new IntWritable(airTemperature));
  }
}
```

This is a very simple implementation, which pulls the year and temperature fields from the line and emits them in the OutputCollector. Let's add a test for missing values, which in the raw data are represented by a temperature of +9999:

```
@Test
public void ignoresMissingTemperatureRecord() throws IOException {
  MaxTemperatureMapper mapper = new MaxTemperatureMapper();

  Text value = new Text("0043011990999991950051518004+68750+023550FM-12+0382" +
                        // Year ^^^^
      "99999V0203201N00261220001CN9999999N9+99991+99999999999");
                        // Temperature ^^^^^
  OutputCollector<Text, IntWritable> output = mock(OutputCollector.class);

  mapper.map(null, value, output, null);
```

```
      verify(output, never()).collect(any(Text.class), any(IntWritable.class));
    }
```

Since records with missing temperatures should be filtered out, this test uses Mockito to verify that the collect method on the OutputCollector is *never* called for any Text key or IntWritable value.

The existing test fails with a NumberFormatException, as parseInt() cannot parse integers with a leading plus sign, so we fix up the implementation (version 2) to handle missing values:

```
public void map(LongWritable key, Text value,
    OutputCollector<Text, IntWritable> output, Reporter reporter)
    throws IOException {

  String line = value.toString();
  String year = line.substring(15, 19);
  String temp = line.substring(87, 92);
  if (!missing(temp)) {
      int airTemperature = Integer.parseInt(temp);
      output.collect(new Text(year), new IntWritable(airTemperature));
  }
}

private boolean missing(String temp) {
  return temp.equals("+9999");
}
```

With the test passing, we move on to writing the reducer.

Reducer

The reducer has to find the maximum value for a given key. Here's a simple test for this feature:

```
@Test
public void returnsMaximumIntegerInValues() throws IOException {
  MaxTemperatureReducer reducer = new MaxTemperatureReducer();

  Text key = new Text("1950");
  Iterator<IntWritable> values = Arrays.asList(
      new IntWritable(10), new IntWritable(5)).iterator();
  OutputCollector<Text, IntWritable> output = mock(OutputCollector.class);

  reducer.reduce(key, values, output, null);

  verify(output).collect(key, new IntWritable(10));
}
```

We construct an iterator over some IntWritable values and then verify that MaxTemperatureReducer picks the largest. The code in Example 5-6 is for an implementation of MaxTemperatureReducer that passes the test. Notice that we haven't tested the case of an empty `values` iterator, but arguably we don't need to, since MapReduce would never call the reducer in this case, as every key produced by a mapper has a value.

Example 5-6. Reducer for maximum temperature example

```
public class MaxTemperatureReducer extends MapReduceBase
  implements Reducer<Text, IntWritable, Text, IntWritable> {

  public void reduce(Text key, Iterator<IntWritable> values,
      OutputCollector<Text, IntWritable> output, Reporter reporter)
      throws IOException {

    int maxValue = Integer.MIN_VALUE;
    while (values.hasNext()) {
      maxValue = Math.max(maxValue, values.next().get());
    }
    output.collect(key, new IntWritable(maxValue));
  }
}
```

Running Locally on Test Data

Now that we've got the mapper and reducer working on controlled inputs, the next step is to write a job driver and run it on some test data on a development machine.

Running a Job in a Local Job Runner

Using the `Tool` interface introduced earlier in the chapter, it's easy to write a driver to run our MapReduce job for finding the maximum temperature by year (see `MaxTemperatureDriver` in Example 5-7).

Example 5-7. Application to find the maximum temperature

```
public class MaxTemperatureDriver extends Configured implements Tool {

  @Override
  public int run(String[] args) throws Exception {
    if (args.length != 2) {
      System.err.printf("Usage: %s [generic options] <input> <output>\n",
          getClass().getSimpleName());
      ToolRunner.printGenericCommandUsage(System.err);
      return -1;
    }

    JobConf conf = new JobConf(getConf(), getClass());
    conf.setJobName("Max temperature");

    FileInputFormat.addInputPath(conf, new Path(args[0]));
    FileOutputFormat.setOutputPath(conf, new Path(args[1]));

    conf.setOutputKeyClass(Text.class);
    conf.setOutputValueClass(IntWritable.class);
```

```
    conf.setMapperClass(MaxTemperatureMapper.class);
    conf.setCombinerClass(MaxTemperatureReducer.class);
    conf.setReducerClass(MaxTemperatureReducer.class);

    JobClient.runJob(conf);
    return 0;
  }

  public static void main(String[] args) throws Exception {
    int exitCode = ToolRunner.run(new MaxTemperatureDriver(), args);
    System.exit(exitCode);
  }
}
```

MaxTemperatureDriver implements the Tool interface, so we get the benefit of being able
to set the options that GenericOptionsParser supports. The run() method constructs
and configures a JobConf object, before launching a job described by the JobConf.
Among the possible job configuration parameters, we set the input and output file
paths, the mapper, reducer and combiner classes, and the output types (the input types
are determined by the input format, which defaults to TextInputFormat and has Long
Writable keys and Text values). It's also a good idea to set a name for the job so that
you can pick it out in the job list during execution and after it has completed. By default,
the name is the name of the JAR file, which is normally not particularly descriptive.

Now we can run this application against some local files. Hadoop comes with a local
job runner, a cut-down version of the MapReduce execution engine for running Map-
Reduce jobs in a single JVM. It's designed for testing and is very convenient for use in
an IDE, since you can run it in a debugger to step through the code in your mapper and
reducer.

The local job runner is only designed for simple testing of MapReduce
programs, so inevitably it differs from the full MapReduce implementation. The biggest difference is that it can't run more than one reducer.
(It can support the zero reducer case, too.) This is normally not a problem, as most applications can work with one reducer, although on a
cluster you would choose a larger number to take advantage of parallelism. The thing to watch out for is that even if you set the number of
reducers to a value over one, the local runner will silently ignore the
setting and use a single reducer.

The local job runner also has no support for the DistributedCache feature (described in "Distributed Cache" on page 253).

Neither of these limitations is inherent in the local job runner, and future
versions of Hadoop may relax these restrictions.

The local job runner is enabled by a configuration setting. Normally, `mapred.job.tracker` is a host:port pair to specify the address of the jobtracker, but when it has the special value of `local`, the job is run in-process without accessing an external jobtracker.

From the command line, we can run the driver by typing:

```
% hadoop v2.MaxTemperatureDriver -conf conf/hadoop-local.xml \
  input/ncdc/micro max-temp
```

Equivalently, we could use the `-fs` and `-jt` options provided by `GenericOptionsParser`:

```
% hadoop v2.MaxTemperatureDriver -fs file:/// -jt local input/ncdc/micro max-temp
```

This command executes `MaxTemperatureDriver` using input from the local *input/ncdc/micro* directory, producing output in the local *max-temp* directory. Note that although we've set `-fs` so we use the local filesystem (`file:///`), the local job runner will actually work fine against any filesystem, including HDFS (and it can be handy to do this if you have a few files that are on HDFS).

When we run the program, it fails and prints the following exception:

```
java.lang.NumberFormatException: For input string: "+0000"
```

Fixing the mapper

This exception shows that the map method still can't parse positive temperatures. (If the stack trace hadn't given us enough information to diagnose the fault, we could run the test in a local debugger, since it runs in a single JVM.) Earlier, we made it handle the special case of missing temperature, +9999, but not the general case of any positive temperature. With more logic going into the mapper, it makes sense to factor out a parser class to encapsulate the parsing logic; see Example 5-8 (now on version 3).

Example 5-8. A class for parsing weather records in NCDC format

```
public class NcdcRecordParser {

  private static final int MISSING_TEMPERATURE = 9999;

  private String year;
  private int airTemperature;
  private String quality;

  public void parse(String record) {
    year = record.substring(15, 19);
    String airTemperatureString;
    // Remove leading plus sign as parseInt doesn't like them
    if (record.charAt(87) == '+') {
      airTemperatureString = record.substring(88, 92);
    } else {
      airTemperatureString = record.substring(87, 92);
    }
    airTemperature = Integer.parseInt(airTemperatureString);
    quality = record.substring(92, 93);
```

```
  }

  public void parse(Text record) {
    parse(record.toString());
  }

  public boolean isValidTemperature() {
    return airTemperature != MISSING_TEMPERATURE && quality.matches("[01459]");
  }

  public String getYear() {
    return year;
  }

  public int getAirTemperature() {
    return airTemperature;
  }
}
```

The resulting mapper is much simpler (see Example 5-9). It just calls the parser's parse() method, which parses the fields of interest from a line of input, checks whether a valid temperature was found using the isValidTemperature() query method, and if it was, retrieves the year and the temperature using the getter methods on the parser. Notice that we also check the quality status field as well as missing temperatures in isValidTemperature() to filter out poor temperature readings.

Another benefit of creating a parser class is that it makes it easy to write related mappers for similar jobs without duplicating code. It also gives us the opportunity to write unit tests directly against the parser, for more targeted testing.

Example 5-9. A Mapper that uses a utility class to parse records

```
public class MaxTemperatureMapper extends MapReduceBase
  implements Mapper<LongWritable, Text, Text, IntWritable> {

  private NcdcRecordParser parser = new NcdcRecordParser();

  public void map(LongWritable key, Text value,
      OutputCollector<Text, IntWritable> output, Reporter reporter)
      throws IOException {

    parser.parse(value);
    if (parser.isValidTemperature()) {
      output.collect(new Text(parser.getYear()),
          new IntWritable(parser.getAirTemperature()));
    }
  }
}
```

With these changes, the test passes.

Testing the Driver

Apart from the flexible configuration options offered by making your application implement Tool, you also make it more testable because it allows you to inject an arbitrary Configuration. You can take advantage of this to write a test that uses a local job runner to run a job against known input data, which checks that the output is as expected.

There are two approaches to doing this. The first is to use the local job runner and run the job against a test file on the local filesystem. The code in Example 5-10 gives an idea of how to do this.

Example 5-10. A test for MaxTemperatureDriver that uses a local, in-process job runner

```
@Test
public void test() throws Exception {
  JobConf conf = new JobConf();
  conf.set("fs.default.name", "file:///");
  conf.set("mapred.job.tracker", "local");

  Path input = new Path("input/ncdc/micro");
  Path output = new Path("output");

  FileSystem fs = FileSystem.getLocal(conf);
  fs.delete(output, true); // delete old output

  MaxTemperatureDriver driver = new MaxTemperatureDriver();
  driver.setConf(conf);

  int exitCode = driver.run(new String[] {
      input.toString(), output.toString() });
  assertThat(exitCode, is(0));

  checkOutput(conf, output);
}
```

The test explicitly sets fs.default.name and mapred.job.tracker so it uses the local filesystem and the local job runner. It then runs the MaxTemperatureDriver via its Tool interface against a small amount of known data. At the end of the test, the checkOut put() method is called to compare the actual output with the expected output, line by line.

The second way of testing the driver is to run it using a "mini-" cluster. Hadoop has a pair of testing classes, called MiniDFSCluster and MiniMRCluster, which provide a programmatic way of creating in-process clusters. Unlike the local job runner, these allow testing against the full HDFS and MapReduce machinery. Bear in mind, too, that task-trackers in a mini-cluster launch separate JVMs to run tasks in, which can make debugging more difficult.

Mini-clusters are used extensively in Hadoop's own automated test suite, but they can be used for testing user code, too. Hadoop's ClusterMapReduceTestCase abstract class provides a useful base for writing such a test, handles the details of starting and stopping the in-process HDFS and MapReduce clusters in its `setUp()` and `tearDown()` methods, and generates a suitable `JobConf` object that is configured to work with them. Subclasses need populate only data in HDFS (perhaps by copying from a local file), run a MapReduce job, then confirm the output is as expected. Refer to the `MaxTemperatureDriver MiniTest` class in the example code that comes with this book for the listing.

Tests like this serve as regression tests, and are a useful repository of input edge cases and their expected results. As you encounter more test cases, you can simply add them to the input file and update the file of expected output accordingly.

Running on a Cluster

Now that we are happy with the program running on a small test dataset, we are ready to try it on the full dataset on a Hadoop cluster. Chapter 9 covers how to set up a fully distributed cluster, although you can also work through this section on a pseudo-distributed cluster.

Packaging

We don't need to make any modifications to the program to run on a cluster rather than on a single machine, but we do need to package the program as a JAR file to send to the cluster. This is conveniently achieved using Ant, using a task such as this (you can find the complete build file in the example code):

```
<jar destfile="job.jar" basedir="${classes.dir}"/>
```

If you have a single job per JAR, then you can specify the main class to run in the JAR file's manifest. If the main class is not in the manifest, then it must be specified on the command line (as you will see shortly). Also, any dependent JAR files should be packaged in a *lib* subdirectory in the JAR file. (This is analogous to a Java *Web application archive*, or WAR file, except in that case the JAR files go in a *WEB-INF/lib* subdirectory in the WAR file.)

Launching a Job

To launch the job, we need to run the driver, specifying the cluster that we want to run the job on with the `-conf` option (we could equally have used the `-fs` and `-jt` options):

```
% hadoop jar job.jar v3.MaxTemperatureDriver -conf conf/hadoop-cluster.xml \
    input/ncdc/all max-temp
```

The `runJob()` method on `JobClient` launches the job and polls for progress, writing a line summarizing the map and reduce's progress whenever either changes. Here's the output (some lines have been removed for clarity):

```
09/04/11 08:15:52 INFO mapred.FileInputFormat: Total input paths to process : 101
09/04/11 08:15:53 INFO mapred.JobClient: Running job: job_200904110811_0002
09/04/11 08:15:54 INFO mapred.JobClient:  map 0% reduce 0%
```

```
09/04/11 08:16:06 INFO mapred.JobClient:  map 28% reduce 0%
09/04/11 08:16:07 INFO mapred.JobClient:  map 30% reduce 0%
...
09/04/11 08:21:36 INFO mapred.JobClient:  map 100% reduce 100%
09/04/11 08:21:38 INFO mapred.JobClient: Job complete: job_200904110811_0002
09/04/11 08:21:38 INFO mapred.JobClient: Counters: 19
09/04/11 08:21:38 INFO mapred.JobClient:   Job Counters
09/04/11 08:21:38 INFO mapred.JobClient:     Launched reduce tasks=32
09/04/11 08:21:38 INFO mapred.JobClient:     Rack-local map tasks=82
09/04/11 08:21:38 INFO mapred.JobClient:     Launched map tasks=127
09/04/11 08:21:38 INFO mapred.JobClient:     Data-local map tasks=45
09/04/11 08:21:38 INFO mapred.JobClient:   FileSystemCounters
09/04/11 08:21:38 INFO mapred.JobClient:     FILE_BYTES_READ=12667214
09/04/11 08:21:38 INFO mapred.JobClient:     HDFS_BYTES_READ=33485841275
09/04/11 08:21:38 INFO mapred.JobClient:     FILE_BYTES_WRITTEN=989397
09/04/11 08:21:38 INFO mapred.JobClient:     HDFS_BYTES_WRITTEN=904
09/04/11 08:21:38 INFO mapred.JobClient:   Map-Reduce Framework
09/04/11 08:21:38 INFO mapred.JobClient:     Reduce input groups=100
09/04/11 08:21:38 INFO mapred.JobClient:     Combine output records=4489
09/04/11 08:21:38 INFO mapred.JobClient:     Map input records=1209901509
09/04/11 08:21:38 INFO mapred.JobClient:     Reduce shuffle bytes=19140
09/04/11 08:21:38 INFO mapred.JobClient:     Reduce output records=100
09/04/11 08:21:38 INFO mapred.JobClient:     Spilled Records=9481
09/04/11 08:21:38 INFO mapred.JobClient:     Map output bytes=10282306995
09/04/11 08:21:38 INFO mapred.JobClient:     Map input bytes=274600205558
09/04/11 08:21:38 INFO mapred.JobClient:     Combine input records=1142482941
09/04/11 08:21:38 INFO mapred.JobClient:     Map output records=1142478555
09/04/11 08:21:38 INFO mapred.JobClient:     Reduce input records=103
```

The output includes more useful information. Before the job starts, its ID is printed: this is needed whenever you want to refer to the job, in logfiles for example, or when interrogating it via the hadoop job command. When the job is complete, its statistics (known as counters) are printed out. These are very useful for confirming that the job did what you expected. For example, for this job we can see that around 275 GB of input data was analyzed ("Map input bytes"), read from around 34 GB of compressed files on HDFS ("HDFS_BYTES_READ"). The input was broken into 101 gzipped files of reasonable size, so there was no problem with not being able to split them.

Job, Task, and Task Attempt IDs

The format of a job ID is composed of the time that the jobtracker (not the job) started and an incrementing counter maintained by the jobtracker to uniquely identify the job to that instance of the jobtracker. So the job with this ID:

    job_200904110811_0002

is the second (0002, job IDs are 1-based) job run by the jobtracker which started at 08:11 on April 11, 2009. The counter is formatted with leading zeros to make job IDs sort nicely—in directory listings, for example. However, when the counter reaches 10000 it is *not* reset, resulting in longer job IDs (which don't sort so well).

Tasks belong to a job, and their IDs are formed by replacing the **job** prefix of a job ID with a **task** prefix, and adding a suffix to identify the task within the job. For example:

```
task_200904110811_0002_m_000003
```

is the fourth (000003, task IDs are 0-based) map (m) task of the job with ID **job_200904110811_0002**. The task IDs are created for a job when it is initialized, so they do not necessarily dictate the order that the tasks will be executed in.

Tasks may be executed more than once, due to failure (see "Task Failure" on page 173) or speculative execution (see "Speculative Execution" on page 183), so to identify different instances of a task execution, task attempts are given unique IDs on the jobtracker. For example:

```
attempt_200904110811_0002_m_000003_0
```

is the first (0, attempt IDs are 0-based) attempt at running task **task_200904110811_0002_m_000003**. Task attempts are allocated during the job run as needed, so their ordering represents the order that they were created for tasktrackers to run.

The final count in the task attempt ID is incremented by 1,000 if the job is restarted after the jobtracker is restarted and recovers its running jobs.

The MapReduce Web UI

Hadoop comes with a web UI for viewing information about your jobs. It is useful for following a job's progress while it is running, as well as finding job statistics and logs after the job has completed. You can find the UI at *http://jobtracker-host:50030/*.

The jobtracker page

A screenshot of the home page is shown in Figure 5-1. The first section of the page gives details of the Hadoop installation, such as the version number and when it was compiled, and the current state of the jobtracker (in this case, running), and when it was started.

Next is a summary of the cluster, which has measures of cluster capacity and utilization. This shows the number of maps and reduces currently running on the cluster, the total number of job submissions, the number of tasktracker nodes currently available, and the cluster's capacity: in terms of the number of map and reduce slots available across the cluster ("Map Task Capacity" and "Reduce Task Capacity"), and the number of available slots per node, on average. The number of tasktrackers that have been blacklisted by the jobtracker is listed as well (blacklisting is discussed in "Tasktracker Failure" on page 175).

Below the summary, there is a section about the job scheduler that is running (here the default). You can click through to see job queues.

Further down, we see sections for running, (successfully) completed, and failed jobs. Each of these sections has a table of jobs, with a row per job that shows the job's ID, owner, name (as set using JobConf's `setJobName()` method, which sets the `mapred.job.name` property) and progress information.

Finally, at the foot of the page, there are links to the jobtracker's logs, and the jobtracker's history: information on all the jobs that the jobtracker has run. The main display displays only 100 jobs (configurable via the `mapred.jobtracker.completeuser jobs.maximum` property), before consigning them to the history page. Note also that the job history is persistent, so you can find jobs here from previous runs of the jobtracker.

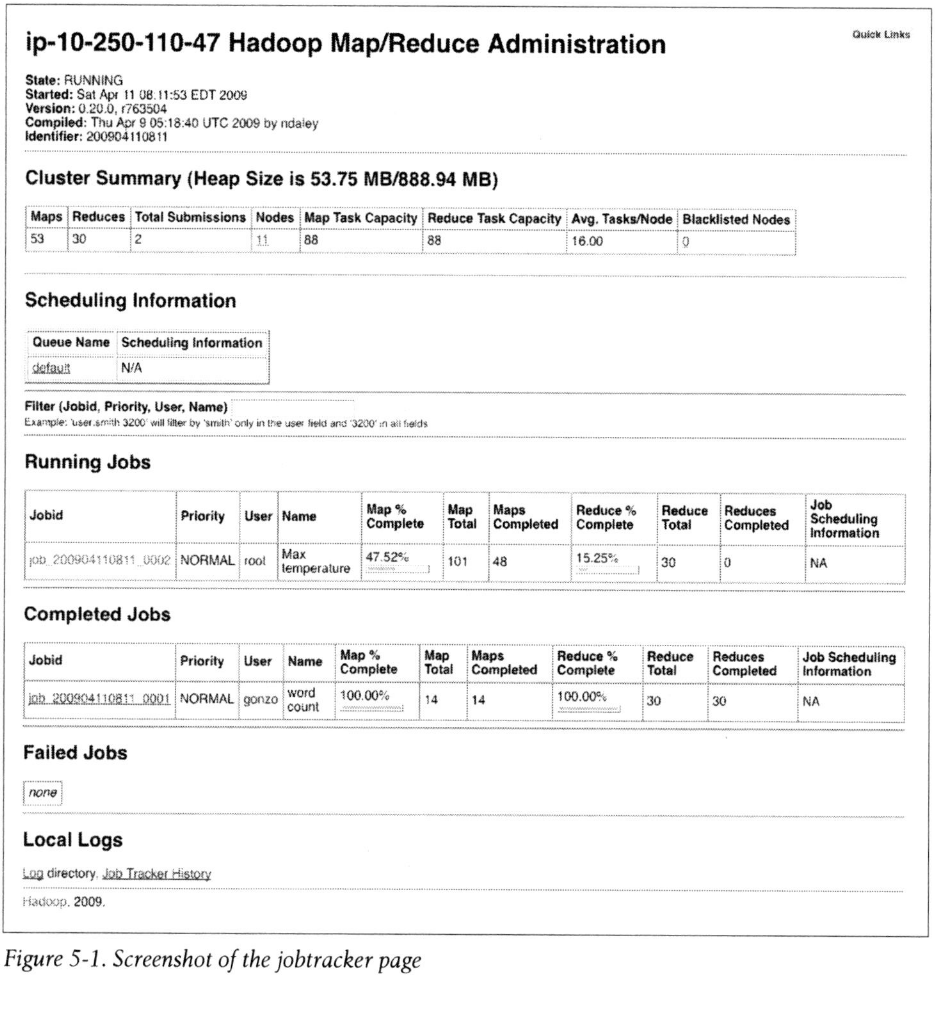

ip-10-250-110-47 Hadoop Map/Reduce Administration

Quick Links

State: RUNNING
Started: Sat Apr 11 08:11:53 EDT 2009
Version: 0.20.0, r763504
Compiled: Thu Apr 9 05:18:40 UTC 2009 by ndaley
Identifier: 200904110811

Cluster Summary (Heap Size is 53.75 MB/888.94 MB)

Maps	Reduces	Total Submissions	Nodes	Map Task Capacity	Reduce Task Capacity	Avg. Tasks/Node	Blacklisted Nodes
53	30	2	11	88	88	16.00	0

Scheduling Information

Queue Name	Scheduling Information
default	N/A

Filter (Jobid, Priority, User, Name)
Example: 'user:smith 3200' will filter by 'smith' only in the user field and '3200' in all fields

Running Jobs

Jobid	Priority	User	Name	Map % Complete	Map Total	Maps Completed	Reduce % Complete	Reduce Total	Reduces Completed	Job Scheduling Information
job_200904110811_0002	NORMAL	root	Max temperature	47.52%	101	48	15.25%	30	0	NA

Completed Jobs

Jobid	Priority	User	Name	Map % Complete	Map Total	Maps Completed	Reduce % Complete	Reduce Total	Reduces Completed	Job Scheduling Information
job_200904110811_0001	NORMAL	gonzo	word count	100.00%	14	14	100.00%	30	30	NA

Failed Jobs

Local Logs

Log directory, Job Tracker History

Hadoop, 2009.

Figure 5-1. Screenshot of the jobtracker page

Job history refers to the events and configuration for a completed job. It is retained whether the job was successful or not. Job history is used to support job recovery after a jobtracker restart (see the `mapred.jobtracker.restart.recover` property), as well as providing interesting information for the user running a job.

Job history files are stored on the local filesystem of the jobtracker in a *history* subdirectory of the logs directory. It is possible to set the location to an arbitrary Hadoop filesystem via the `hadoop.job.history.location` property. The jobtracker's history files are kept for 30 days before being deleted by the system.

A second copy is also stored for the user in the *_logs/history* subdirectory of the job's output directory. This location may be overridden by setting `hadoop.job.history.user.location`. By setting it to the special value `none`, no user job history is saved, although job history is still saved centrally. A user's job history files are never deleted by the system.

The history log includes job, task, and attempt events, all of which are stored in a plaintext file. The history for a particular job may be viewed through the web UI, or via the command line, using `hadoop job -history` (which you point at the job's output directory).

The job page

Clicking on a job ID brings you to a page for the job, illustrated in Figure 5-2. At the top of the page is a summary of the job, with basic information such as job owner and name, and how long the job has been running for. The job file is the consolidated configuration file for the job, containing all the properties and their values that were in effect during the job run. If you are unsure of what a particular property was set to, you can click through to inspect the file.

While the job is running, you can monitor its progress on this page, which periodically updates itself. Below the summary is a table that shows the map progress and the reduce progress. "Num Tasks" shows the total number of map and reduce tasks for this job (a row for each). The other columns then show the state of these tasks: "Pending" (waiting to run), "Running," "Complete" (successfully run), "Killed" (tasks that have failed—this column would be more accurately labeled "Failed"). The final column shows the total number of failed and killed task attempts for all the map or reduce tasks for the job (task attempts may be marked as killed if they are a speculative execution duplicate, if the tasktracker they are running on dies or if they are killed by a user). See "Task Failure" on page 173 for background on task failure.

Further down the page, you can find completion graphs for each task that show their progress graphically. The reduce completion graph is divided into the three phases of the reduce task: copy (when the map outputs are being transferred to the reduce's tasktracker), sort (when the reduce inputs are being merged), and reduce (when the reduce function is being run to produce the final output). The phases are described in more detail in "Shuffle and Sort" on page 177.

In the middle of the page is a table of job counters. These are dynamically updated during the job run, and provide another useful window into the job's progress and general health. There is more information about what these counters mean in "Built-in Counters" on page 225.

Retrieving the Results

Once the job is finished, there are various ways to retrieve the results. Each reducer produces one output file, so there are 30 part files named *part-00000* to *part-00029* in the *max-temp* directory.

As their names suggest, a good way to think of these "part" files is as parts of the *max-temp* "file."

If the output is large (which it isn't in this case), then it is important to have multiple parts so that more than one reducer can work in parallel. Usually, if a file is in this partitioned form, it can still be used easily enough: as the input to another MapReduce job, for example. In some cases, you can exploit the structure of multiple partitions to do a map-side join, for example, ("Map-Side Joins" on page 247) or a MapFile lookup ("An application: Partitioned MapFile lookups" on page 235).

This job produces a very small amount of output, so it is convenient to copy it from HDFS to our development machine. The -getmerge option to the hadoop fs command is useful here, as it gets all the files in the directory specified in the source pattern and merges them into a single file on the local filesystem:

```
% hadoop fs -getmerge max-temp max-temp-local
% sort max-temp-local | tail
1991    607
1992    605
1993    567
1994    568
1995    567
1996    561
1997    565
1998    568
1999    568
2000    558
```

We sorted the output, as the reduce output partitions are unordered (owing to the hash partition function). Doing a bit of postprocessing of data from MapReduce is very common, as is feeding it into analysis tools, such as R, a spreadsheet, or even a relational database.

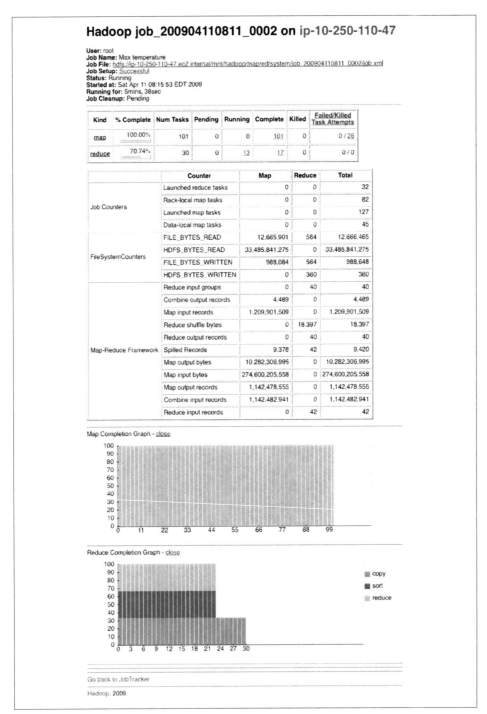

Figure 5-2. Screenshot of the job page

Another way of retrieving the output if it is small is to use the `-cat` option to print the output files to the console:

```
% hadoop fs -cat max-temp/*
```

On closer inspection, we see that some of the results don't look plausible. For instance, the maximum temperature for 1951 (not shown here) is 590°C! How do we find out what's causing this? Is it corrupt input data or a bug in the program?

way of debugging programs is via print statements, and this is cer-
Hadoop. However, there are complications to consider: with pro-
ens, hundreds, or thousands of nodes, how do we find and examine
debug statements, which may be scattered across these nodes? For
e, where we are looking for (what we think is) an unusual case, we
tatement to log to standard error, in conjunction with a message to
status message to prompt us to look in the error log. The web UI
as we will see.

custom counter to count the total number of records with implausible
the whole dataset. This gives us valuable information about how to
ondition—if it turns out to be a common occurrence, then we might
nore about the condition and how to extract the temperature in these
ian simply dropping the record. In fact, when trying to debug a job, you
ask yourself if you can use a counter to get the information you need to
's happening. Even if you need to use logging or a status message, it may
be useful to use a counter to gauge the extent of the problem. (There is more on counters
in "Counters" on page 225.)

If the amount of log data you produce in the course of debugging is large, then you've got a couple of options. The first is to write the information to the map's output, rather than to standard error, for analysis and aggregation by the reduce. This approach usually necessitates structural changes to your program, so start with the other techniques first. Alternatively, you can write a program (in MapReduce of course) to analyze the logs produced by your job.

We add our debugging to the mapper (version 4), as opposed to the reducer, as we want to find out what the source data causing the anomalous output looks like:

```java
public class MaxTemperatureMapper extends MapReduceBase
  implements Mapper<LongWritable, Text, Text, IntWritable> {

  enum Temperature {
    OVER_100
  }

  private NcdcRecordParser parser = new NcdcRecordParser();
```

```
public void map(LongWritable key, Text value,
    OutputCollector<Text, IntWritable> output, Reporter reporter)
    throws IOException {

  parser.parse(value);
  if (parser.isValidTemperature()) {
    int airTemperature = parser.getAirTemperature();
    if (airTemperature > 1000) {
      System.err.println("Temperature over 100 degrees for input: " + value);
      reporter.setStatus("Detected possibly corrupt record: see logs.");
      reporter.incrCounter(Temperature.OVER_100, 1);
    }
    output.collect(new Text(parser.getYear()), new IntWritable(airTemperature));
  }
}
}
```

If the temperature is over 100°C (represented by 1000, since temperatures are in tenths of a degree), we print a line to standard error with the suspect line, as well as updating the map's status message using the setStatus() method on Reporter directing us to look in the log. We also increment a counter, which in Java is represented by a field of an enum type. In this program, we have defined a single field OVER_100 as a way to count the number of records with a temperature of over 100°C.

With this modification, we recompile the code, re-create the JAR file, then rerun the job, and while it's running go to the tasks page.

The tasks page

The job page has a number of links for look at the tasks in a job in more detail. For example, by clicking on the "map" link, you are brought to a page that lists information for all of the map tasks on one page. You can also see just the completed tasks. The screenshot in Figure 5-3 shows a portion of this page for the job run with our debugging statements. Each row in the table is a task, and it provides such information as the start and end times for each task, any errors reported back from the tasktracker, and a link to view the counters for an individual task.

The "Status" column can be helpful for debugging, since it shows a task's latest status message. Before a task starts, it shows its status as "initializing," then once it starts reading records it shows the split information for the split it is reading as a filename with a byte offset and length. You can see the status we set for debugging for task task_200904110811_0003_m_000044, so let's click through to the logs page to find the associated debug message. (Notice, too, that there is an extra counter for this task, since our user counter has a nonzero count for this task.)

The task details page

From the tasks page, you can click on any task to get more information about it. The task details page, shown in Figure 5-4, shows each task attempt. In this case, there was

---

one task attempt, which completed successfully. The table provides further useful data, such as the node the task attempt ran on, and links to task logfiles and counters.

The "Actions" column contains links for killing a task attempt. By default, this is disabled, making the web UI a read-only interface. Set `webinterface.private.actions` to `true` to enable the actions links.

Hadoop map task list for job_200904110811_0003 on ip-10-250-110-47

Completed Tasks

Task	Complete	Status	Start Time	Finish Time	Errors	Counters
task_200904110811_0003_m_000043	100.00%	hdfs://ip-10-250-110-47.ec2.internal /user/root/input/ncdc/all /1949.gz:0+220338475	11-Apr-2009 09:00:06	11-Apr-2009 09:01:25 (1mins, 18sec)		10
task_200904110811_0003_m_000044	100.00%	Detected possibly corrupt record: see logs.	11-Apr-2009 09:00:06	11-Apr-2009 09:01:28 (1mins, 21sec)		11
task_200904110811_0003_m_000045	100.00%	hdfs://ip-10-250-110-47.ec2.internal /user/root/input/ncdc/all /1970.gz:0+208374610	11-Apr-2009 09:00:06	11-Apr-2009 09:01:28 (1mins, 21sec)		10

Figure 5-3. Screenshot of the tasks page

Job job_200904110811_0003

All Task Attempts

Task Attempts	Machine	Status	Progress	Start Time	Finish Time	Errors	Task Logs	Counters	Actions
attempt_200904110811_0003_m_000044_0	/default-rack/ip-10-250-163-143.ec2.internal	SUCCEEDED	100.00%	11-Apr-2009 09:00:06	11-Apr-2009 09:01:25 (1mins, 19sec)		Last 4KB Last 8KB All	11	

Input Split Locations

/default-rack/10.250.202.127
/default-rack/10.250.123.223
/default-rack/10.250.115.79

Go back to the job
Go back to JobTracker

Hadoop, 2009.

Figure 5-4. Screenshot of the task details page

By setting `webinterface.private.actions` to `true`, you also allow anyone with access to the HDFS web interface to delete files. The `dfs.web.ugi` property determines the user that the HDFS web UI runs as, thus controlling which files may be viewed and deleted.

For map tasks, there is also a section showing which nodes the input split was located on.

By following one of the links to the logfiles for the successful task attempt (you can see the last 4 KB or 8 KB of each logfile, or the entire file), we can find the suspect input record that we logged (the line is wrapped and truncated to fit on the page):

```
Temperature over 100 degrees for input:
0335999999433181957042302005+37950+139117SAO   +0004RJSN V02011359003150070356999994
3320195701010005+35317+139650SAO +000899999V02002359002650076249N004000599+0067...
```

This record seems to be in a different format to the others. For one thing, there are spaces in the line, which are not described in the specification.

When the job has finished, we can look at the value of the counter we defined to see how many records over 100°C there are in the whole dataset. Counters are accessible via the web UI or the command line:

```
% hadoop job -counter job_200904110811_0003 'v4.MaxTemperatureMapper$Temperature' \
  OVER_100
3
```

The -counter option takes the job ID, counter group name (which is the fully qualified classname here), and the counter name (the enum name). There are only three malformed records in the entire dataset of over a billion records. Throwing out bad records is standard for many big data problems, although we need to be careful in this case, since we are looking for an extreme value—the maximum temperature rather than an aggregate measure. Still, throwing away three records is probably not going to change the result.

Hadoop User Logs

Hadoop produces logs in various places, for various audiences. These are summarized in Table 5-2.

As you have seen in this section, MapReduce task logs are accessible through the web UI, which is the most convenient way to view them. You can also find the logfiles on the local filesystem of the tasktracker that ran the task attempt, in a directory named by the task attempt. If task JVM reuse is enabled ("Task JVM Reuse" on page 184), then each logfile accumulates the logs for the entire JVM run, so multiple task attempts will be found in each logfile. The web UI hides this by showing only the portion that is relevant for the task attempt being viewed.

It is straightforward to write to these logfiles. Anything written to standard output, or standard error, is directed to the relevant logfile. (Of course, in Streaming, standard output is used for the map or reduce output, so it will not show up in the standard output log.)

In Java, you can write to the task's *syslog* file if you wish by using the Apache Commons Logging API. The actual logging is done by log4j in this case: the relevant log4j appender is called TLA (Task Log Appender) in the *log4j.properties* file in Hadoop's configuration directory.

There are some controls for managing retention and size of task logs. By default, logs are deleted after a minimum of 24 hours (set using the `mapred.userlog.retain.hours` property). You can also set a cap on the maximum size of each logfile using the `mapred.userlog.limit.kb` property, which is 0 by default, meaning there is no cap.

Table 5-2. Hadoop logs

Logs	Primary audience	Description	Further information
System daemon logs	Administrators	Each Hadoop daemon produces a logfile (using log4j) and another file that combines standard out and error. Written in the directory defined by the HADOOP_LOG_DIR environment variable.	"System log-files" on page 271.
HDFS audit logs	Administrators	A log of all HDFS requests, turned off by default. Written to the namenode's log, although this is configurable.	"Audit Logging" on page 300.
MapReduce job history logs	Users	A log of the events (such as task completion) that occur in the course of running a job. Saved centrally on the jobtracker, and in the job's output directory in a *_logs/history* subdirectory.	"Job History" on page 150.
MapReduce task logs	Users	Each tasktracker child process produces a logfile using log4j (called *syslog*), a file for data sent to standard out (*stdout*), and a file for standard error (*stderr*). Written in the *userlogs* subdirectory of the directory defined by the HADOOP_LOG_DIR environment variable.	See next section.

Handling malformed data

Capturing input data that causes a problem is valuable, as we can use it in a test to check that the mapper does the right thing:

```
@Test
public void parsesMalformedTemperature() throws IOException {
    MaxTemperatureMapper mapper = new MaxTemperatureMapper();
    Text value = new Text("0335999999433181957042302005+37950+139117SAO  +0004" +
                                        // Year ^^^^
            "RJSN V02011359003150070356999999433201957010100005+353");
                                        // Temperature ^^^^^
    OutputCollector<Text, IntWritable> output = mock(OutputCollector.class);
    Reporter reporter = mock(Reporter.class);

    mapper.map(null, value, output, reporter);

    verify(output, never()).collect(any(Text.class), any(IntWritable.class));
    verify(reporter).incrCounter(MaxTemperatureMapper.Temperature.MALFORMED, 1);
}
```

The record that was causing the problem is of a different format to the other lines we've seen. Example 5-11 shows a modified program (version 5) using a parser that ignores each line with a temperature field that does not have a leading sign (plus or minus). We've also introduced a counter to measure the number of records that we are ignoring for this reason.

Example 5-11. Mapper for maximum temperature example

```
public class MaxTemperatureMapper extends MapReduceBase
  implements Mapper<LongWritable, Text, Text, IntWritable> {

  enum Temperature {
    MALFORMED
  }

  private NcdcRecordParser parser = new NcdcRecordParser();

  public void map(LongWritable key, Text value,
      OutputCollector<Text, IntWritable> output, Reporter reporter)
      throws IOException {

    parser.parse(value);
    if (parser.isValidTemperature()) {
      int airTemperature = parser.getAirTemperature();
      output.collect(new Text(parser.getYear()), new IntWritable(airTemperature));
    } else if (parser.isMalformedTemperature()) {
      System.err.println("Ignoring possibly corrupt input: " + value);
      reporter.incrCounter(Temperature.MALFORMED, 1);
    }
  }
}
```

Using a Remote Debugger

When a task fails and there is not enough information logged to diagnose the error, you may want to resort to running a debugger for that task. This is hard to arrange when running the job on a cluster, as you don't know which node is going to process which part of the input, so you can't set up your debugger ahead of the failure. Instead, you run the job with a property set that instructs Hadoop to keep all the intermediate data generated during the job run. This data can then be used to rerun the failing task in isolation with a debugger attached. Note that the task is run in situ, on the same node that it failed on, which increases the chances of the error being reproducible.[†]

First, set the configuration property keep.failed.task.files to true, so that when tasks fail, the tasktracker keeps enough information to allow the task to be rerun over the same input data. Then run the job again and note which node the task fails on, and the task attempt ID (it begins with the string attempt_) using the web UI.

---

† This feature is currently broken in Hadoop 0.20.2 but will be fixed in 0.21.0.

Next we need to run a special task runner called `IsolationRunner` with the retained files as input. Log into the node that the task failed on and look for the directory for that task attempt. It will be under one of the local MapReduce directories, as set by the `mapred.local.dir` property (covered in more detail in "Important Hadoop Daemon Properties" on page 273). If this property is a comma-separated list of directories (to spread load across the physical disks on a machine), then you may need to look in all of the directories before you find the directory for that particular task attempt. The task attempt directory is in the following location:

```
mapred.local.dir/taskTracker/jobcache/job-ID/task-attempt-ID
```

This directory contains various files and directories, including *job.xml*, which contains all of the job configuration properties in effect during the task attempt, and which `IsolationRunner` uses to create a `JobConf` instance. For map tasks, this directory also contains a file containing a serialized representation of the input split, so the same input data can be fetched for the task. For reduce tasks, a copy of the map output, which forms the reduce input, is stored in a directory named *output*.

There is also a directory called *work*, which is the working directory for the task attempt. We change into this directory to run the `IsolationRunner`. We need to set some options to allow the remote debugger to connect:‡

```
% export HADOOP_OPTS="-agentlib:jdwp=transport=dt_socket,server=y,suspend=y,\
address=8000"
```

The `suspend=y` option tells the JVM to wait until the debugger has attached before running code. The `IsolationRunner` is launched with the following command:

```
% hadoop org.apache.hadoop.mapred.IsolationRunner ../job.xml
```

Next, set breakpoints, attach your remote debugger (all the major Java IDEs support remote debugging—consult the documentation for instructions), and the task will be run under your control. You can rerun the task any number of times like this. With any luck, you'll be able to find and fix the error.

During the process, you can use other, standard, Java debugging techniques, such as `kill -QUIT pid` or `jstack` to get thread dumps.

More generally, it's worth knowing that this technique isn't only useful for failing tasks. You can keep the intermediate files for successful tasks, too, which may be handy if you want to examine a task that isn't failing. In this case, set the property `keep.task.files.pattern` to a regular expression that matches the IDs of the tasks you want to keep.

---

‡ You can find details about debugging options on the Java Platform Debugger Architecture (*http://java.sun .com/javase/6/docs/technotes/guides/jpda/*) web page.

Tuning a Job

After a job is working, the question many developers ask is, "Can I make it run faster?"

There are a few Hadoop-specific "usual suspects" that are worth checking to see if they are responsible for a performance problem. You should run through the checklist in Table 5-3 before you start trying to profile or optimize at the task level.

Table 5-3. Tuning checklist

Area	Best practice	Further information
Number of mappers	How long are your mappers running for? If they are only running for a few seconds on average, then you should see if there's a way to have fewer mappers and make them all run longer, a minute or so, as a rule of thumb. The extent to which this is possible depends on the input format you are using.	"Small files and CombineFileInputFormat" on page 203
Number of reducers	For maximum performance, the number of reducers should be slightly less than the number of reduce slots in the cluster. This allows the reducers to finish in one wave and fully utilizes the cluster during the reduce phase.	"Choosing the Number of Reducers" on page 195
Combiners	Can your job take advantage of a combiner to reduce the amount of data in passing through the shuffle?	"Combiner Functions" on page 30
Intermediate compression	Job execution time can almost always benefit from enabling map output compression.	"Compressing map output" on page 85
Custom serialization	If you are using your own custom Writable objects, or custom comparators, then make sure you have implemented RawComparator.	"Implementing a RawComparator for speed" on page 99
Shuffle tweaks	The MapReduce shuffle exposes around a dozen tuning parameters for memory management, which may help you eke out the last bit of performance.	"Configuration Tuning" on page 180

Profiling Tasks

Like debugging, profiling a job running on a distributed system like MapReduce presents some challenges. Hadoop allows you to profile a fraction of the tasks in a job, and, as each task completes, pulls down the profile information to your machine for later analysis with standard profiling tools.

Of course, it's possible, and somewhat easier, to profile a job running in the local job runner. And provided you can run with enough input data to exercise the map and reduce tasks, this can be a valuable way of improving the performance of your mappers and reducers. There are a couple of caveats, however. The local job runner is a very different environment from a cluster, and the data flow patterns are very different. Optimizing the CPU performance of your code may be pointless if your MapReduce job is I/O-bound (as many jobs are). To be sure that any tuning is effective, you should compare the new execution time with the old running on a real cluster. Even this is easier said than done, since job execution times can vary due to resource contention with other jobs and the decisions the scheduler makes to do with task placement. To get a good idea of job execution time under these circumstances, perform a series of runs (with and without the change) and check whether any improvement is statistically significant.

It's unfortunately true that some problems (such as excessive memory use) can be reproduced only on the cluster, and in these cases the ability to profile in situ is indispensable.

The HPROF profiler

There are a number of configuration properties to control profiling, which are also exposed via convenience methods on JobConf. The following modification to MaxTemperatureDriver (version 6) will enable remote HPROF profiling. HPROF is a profiling tool that comes with the JDK that, although basic, can give valuable information about a program's CPU and heap usage:[§]

```
conf.setProfileEnabled(true);
conf.setProfileParams("-agentlib:hprof=cpu=samples,heap=sites,depth=6," +
    "force=n,thread=y,verbose=n,file=%s");
conf.setProfileTaskRange(true, "0-2");
```

The first line enables profiling, which by default is turned off. (This is equivalent to setting the configuration property mapred.task.profile to true).

Next we set the profile parameters, which are the extra command-line arguments to pass to the task's JVM. (When profiling is enabled, a new JVM is allocated for each task, even if JVM reuse is turned on; see "Task JVM Reuse" on page 184.) The default parameters specify the HPROF profiler; here we set an extra HPROF option, depth=6, to give more stack trace depth than the HPROF default. The setProfileParams() method on JobConf is equivalent to setting the mapred.task.profile.params.

Finally, we specify which tasks we want to profile. We normally only want profile information from a few tasks, so we use the setProfileTaskRange() method to specify the range of task IDs that we want profile information for. We've set it to 0-2 (which is actually the default), which means tasks with IDs 0, 1, and 2 are profiled. The first argument to the setProfileTaskRange() method dictates whether the range is for map or reduce tasks: true is for maps, false is for reduces. A set of ranges is permitted, using a notation that allows open ranges. For example, 0-1,4,6- would specify all tasks except those with IDs 2, 3, and 5. The tasks to profile can also be controlled using the mapred.task.profile.maps property for map tasks, and mapred.task.profile.reduces for reduce tasks.

When we run a job with the modified driver, the profile output turns up at the end of the job in the directory we launched the job from. Since we are only profiling a few tasks, we can run the job on a subset of the dataset.

[§] HPROF uses byte code insertion to profile your code, so you do not need to recompile your application with special options to use it. For more information on HPROF, see "HPROF: A Heap/CPU Profiling Tool in J2SE 5.0," by Kelly O'Hair at *http://java.sun.com/developer/technicalArticles/Programming/HPROF.html*.

Here's a snippet of one of the mapper's profile files, which shows the CPU sampling information:

```
CPU SAMPLES BEGIN (total = 1002) Sat Apr 11 11:17:52 2009
rank   self  accum    count trace method
   1  3.49%  3.49%       35 307969 java.lang.Object.<init>
   2  3.39%  6.89%       34 307954 java.lang.Object.<init>
   3  3.19% 10.08%       32 307945 java.util.regex.Matcher.<init>
   4  3.19% 13.27%       32 307963 java.lang.Object.<init>
   5  3.19% 16.47%       32 307973 java.lang.Object.<init>
```

Cross-referencing the trace number 307973 gives us the stacktrace from the same file:

```
TRACE 307973: (thread=200001)
        java.lang.Object.<init>(Object.java:20)
        org.apache.hadoop.io.IntWritable.<init>(IntWritable.java:29)
        v5.MaxTemperatureMapper.map(MaxTemperatureMapper.java:30)
        v5.MaxTemperatureMapper.map(MaxTemperatureMapper.java:14)
        org.apache.hadoop.mapred.MapRunner.run(MapRunner.java:50)
        org.apache.hadoop.mapred.MapTask.runOldMapper(MapTask.java:356)
```

So it looks like the mapper is spending 3% of its time constructing IntWritable objects. This observation suggests that it might be worth reusing the Writable instances being output (version 7, see Example 5-12).

Example 5-12. Reusing the Text and IntWritable output objects

```java
public class MaxTemperatureMapper extends MapReduceBase
  implements Mapper<LongWritable, Text, Text, IntWritable> {

  enum Temperature {
    MALFORMED
  }

  private NcdcRecordParser parser = new NcdcRecordParser();
  private Text year = new Text();
  private IntWritable temp = new IntWritable();

  public void map(LongWritable key, Text value,
      OutputCollector<Text, IntWritable> output, Reporter reporter)
      throws IOException {

    parser.parse(value);
    if (parser.isValidTemperature()) {
      year.set(parser.getYear());
      temp.set(parser.getAirTemperature());
      output.collect(year, temp);
    } else if (parser.isMalformedTemperature()) {
      System.err.println("Ignoring possibly corrupt input: " + value);
      reporter.incrCounter(Temperature.MALFORMED, 1);
    }
  }
}
```

However, we know if this is significant only if we can measure an improvement when running the job over the whole dataset. Running each variant five times on an otherwise quiet 11-node cluster showed no statistically significant difference in job execution time. Of course, this result holds only for this particular combination of code, data, and hardware, so you should perform similar benchmarks to see whether such a change is significant for your setup.

Other profilers

At the time of this writing, the mechanism for retrieving profile output is HPROF-specific. Until this is fixed, it should be possible to use Hadoop's profiling settings to trigger profiling using any profiler (see the documentation for the particular profiler), although it may be necessary to manually retrieve the profiler's output from tasktrackers for analysis.

If the profiler is not installed on all the tasktracker machines, consider using the Distributed Cache ("Distributed Cache" on page 253) for making the profiler binary available on the required machines.

MapReduce Workflows

So far in this chapter, you have seen the mechanics of writing a program using Map-Reduce. We haven't yet considered how to turn a data processing problem into the MapReduce model.

The data processing you have seen so far in this book is to solve a fairly simple problem (finding the maximum recorded temperature for given years). When the processing gets more complex, this complexity is generally manifested by having more MapReduce jobs, rather than having more complex map and reduce functions. In other words, as a rule of thumb, think about adding *more* jobs, rather than adding complexity *to* jobs.

For more complex problems, it is worth considering a higher-level language than Map-Reduce, such as Pig, Hive, or Cascading. One immediate benefit is that it frees you up from having to do the translation into MapReduce jobs, allowing you to concentrate on the analysis you are performing.

Finally, the book *Data-Intensive Text Processing with MapReduce* by Jimmy Lin and Chris Dyer (Morgan & Claypool Publishers, 2010, *http://mapreduce.me/*) is a great resource for learning more about MapReduce algorithm design, and is highly recommended.

Decomposing a Problem into MapReduce Jobs

Let's look at an example of a more complex problem that we want to translate into a MapReduce workflow.

Imagine that we want to find the mean maximum recorded temperature for every day of the year and every weather station. In concrete terms, to calculate the mean maximum daily temperature recorded by station 029070-99999, say, on January 1, we take the mean of the maximum daily temperatures for this station for January 1, 1901; January 1, 1902; and so on up to January 1, 2000.

How can we compute this using MapReduce? The computation decomposes most naturally into two stages:

1. Compute the maximum daily temperature for every station-date pair.

   The MapReduce program in this case is a variant of the maximum temperature program, except that the keys in this case are a composite station-date pair, rather than just the year.

2. Compute the mean of the maximum daily temperatures for every station-day-month key.

   The mapper takes the output from the previous job (station-date, maximum temperature) records and projects it into (station-day-month, maximum temperature) records by dropping the year component. The reduce function then takes the mean of the maximum temperatures for each station-day-month key.

The output from first stage looks like this for the station we are interested in (the *mean_max_daily_temp.sh* script in the examples provides an implementation in Hadoop Streaming):

```
029070-99999    19010101    0
029070-99999    19020101    -94
...
```

The first two fields form the key, and the final column is the maximum temperature from all the readings for the given station and date. The second stage averages these daily maxima over years to yield:

```
029070-99999    0101    -68
```

which is interpreted as saying the mean maximum daily temperature on January 1 for station 029070-99999 over the century is –6.8°C.

It's possible to do this computation in one MapReduce stage, but it takes more work on the part of the programmer.[‖]

The arguments for having more (but simpler) MapReduce stages are that doing so leads to more composable and more maintainable mappers and reducers. The case studies in Chapter 16 cover a wide range of real-world problems that were solved using MapReduce, and in each case, the data processing task is implemented using two or more MapReduce jobs. The details in that chapter are invaluable for getting a better idea of how to decompose a processing problem into a MapReduce workflow.

‖ It's an interesting exercise to do this. Hint: use "Secondary Sort" on page 241.

It's possible to make map and reduce functions even more composable than we have done. A mapper commonly performs input format parsing, projection (selecting the relevant fields), and filtering (removing records that are not of interest). In the mappers you have seen so far, we have implemented all of these functions in a single mapper. However, there is a case for splitting these into distinct mappers and chaining them into a single mapper using the ChainMapper library class that comes with Hadoop. Combined with a ChainReducer, you can run a chain of mappers, followed by a reducer and another chain of mappers in a single MapReduce job.

Running Dependent Jobs

When there is more than one job in a MapReduce workflow, the question arises: how do you manage the jobs so they are executed in order? There are several approaches, and the main consideration is whether you have a linear chain of jobs, or a more complex directed acyclic graph (DAG) of jobs.

For a linear chain, the simplest approach is to run each job one after another, waiting until a job completes successfully before running the next:

```
JobClient.runJob(conf1);
JobClient.runJob(conf2);
```

If a job fails, the runJob() method will throw an IOException, so later jobs in the pipeline don't get executed. Depending on your application, you might want to catch the exception and clean up any intermediate data that was produced by any previous jobs.

For anything more complex than a linear chain, there are libraries that can help orchestrate your workflow (although they are suited to linear chains, or even one-off jobs, too). The simplest is in the org.apache.hadoop.mapred.jobcontrol package: the JobControl class. An instance of JobControl represents a graph of jobs to be run. You add the job configurations, then tell the JobControl instance the dependencies between jobs. You run the JobControl in a thread, and it runs the jobs in dependency order. You can poll for progress, and when the jobs have finished, you can query for all the jobs' statuses and the associated errors for any failures. If a job fails, JobControl won't run its dependencies.

Oozie

Unlike JobControl, which runs on the client machine submitting the jobs, *Oozie* (*http://yahoo.github.com/oozie/*) runs as a server, and a client submits a workflow to the server. In Oozie, a workflow is a DAG of *action nodes* and *control-flow nodes*. An action node performs a workflow task, like moving files in HDFS, running a MapReduce job or running a Pig job. A control-flow node governs the workflow execution between actions by allowing such constructs as conditional logic (so different execution branches may be followed depending on the result of an earlier action node) or parallel execution. When the workflow completes, Oozie can make an HTTP callback to the client to inform it of the workflow status. It is also possible to receive callbacks every time the workflow enters or exits an action node.

Oozie allows failed workflows to be re-run from an arbitrary point. This is useful for dealing with transient errors when the early actions in the workflow are time-consuming to execute.

## CHAPTER 6

How MapReduce Works

In this chapter, we look at how MapReduce in Hadoop works in detail. This knowledge provides a good foundation for writing more advanced MapReduce programs, which we will cover in the following two chapters.

Anatomy of a MapReduce Job Run

You can run a MapReduce job with a single line of code: `JobClient.runJob(conf)`. It's very short, but it conceals a great deal of processing behind the scenes. This section uncovers the steps Hadoop takes to run a job.

The whole process is illustrated in Figure 6-1. At the highest level, there are four independent entities:

- The client, which submits the MapReduce job.
- The jobtracker, which coordinates the job run. The jobtracker is a Java application whose main class is `JobTracker`.
- The tasktrackers, which run the tasks that the job has been split into. Tasktrackers are Java applications whose main class is `TaskTracker`.
- The distributed filesystem (normally HDFS, covered in Chapter 3), which is used for sharing job files between the other entities.

Job Submission

The `runJob()` method on `JobClient` is a convenience method that creates a new `JobClient` instance and calls `submitJob()` on it (step 1 in Figure 6-1). Having submitted the job, `runJob()` polls the job's progress once a second and reports the progress to the console if it has changed since the last report. When the job is complete, if it was successful, the job counters are displayed. Otherwise, the error that caused the job to fail is logged to the console.

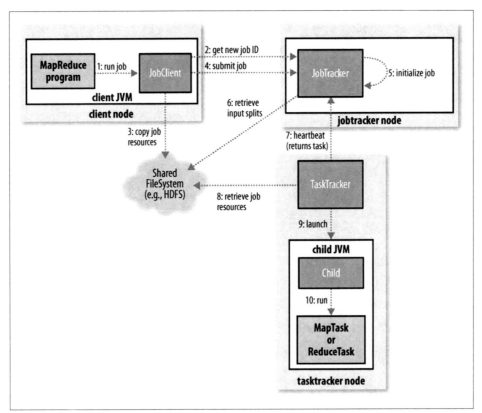

Figure 6-1. How Hadoop runs a MapReduce job

The job submission process implemented by JobClient's submitJob() method does the following:

- Asks the jobtracker for a new job ID (by calling getNewJobId() on JobTracker) (step 2).
- Checks the output specification of the job. For example, if the output directory has not been specified or it already exists, the job is not submitted and an error is thrown to the MapReduce program.
- Computes the input splits for the job. If the splits cannot be computed, because the input paths don't exist, for example, then the job is not submitted and an error is thrown to the MapReduce program.
- Copies the resources needed to run the job, including the job JAR file, the configuration file, and the computed input splits, to the jobtracker's filesystem in a directory named after the job ID. The job JAR is copied with a high replication factor (controlled by the mapred.submit.replication property, which defaults to 10) so that there are lots of copies across the cluster for the tasktrackers to access when they run tasks for the job (step 3).

- Tells the jobtracker that the job is ready for execution (by calling `submitJob()` on `JobTracker`) (step 4).

Job Initialization

When the `JobTracker` receives a call to its `submitJob()` method, it puts it into an internal queue from where the job scheduler will pick it up and initialize it. Initialization involves creating an object to represent the job being run, which encapsulates its tasks, and bookkeeping information to keep track of the tasks' status and progress (step 5).

To create the list of tasks to run, the job scheduler first retrieves the input splits computed by the `JobClient` from the shared filesystem (step 6). It then creates one map task for each split. The number of reduce tasks to create is determined by the `mapred.reduce.tasks` property in the `JobConf`, which is set by the `setNumReduce Tasks()` method, and the scheduler simply creates this number of reduce tasks to be run. Tasks are given IDs at this point.

Task Assignment

Tasktrackers run a simple loop that periodically sends heartbeat method calls to the jobtracker. Heartbeats tell the jobtracker that a tasktracker is alive, but they also double as a channel for messages. As a part of the heartbeat, a tasktracker will indicate whether it is ready to run a new task, and if it is, the jobtracker will allocate it a task, which it communicates to the tasktracker using the heartbeat return value (step 7).

Before it can choose a task for the tasktracker, the jobtracker must choose a job to select the task from. There are various scheduling algorithms as explained later in this chapter (see "Job Scheduling" on page 175), but the default one simply maintains a priority list of jobs. Having chosen a job, the jobtracker now chooses a task for the job.

Tasktrackers have a fixed number of slots for map tasks and for reduce tasks: for example, a tasktracker may be able to run two map tasks and two reduce tasks simultaneously. (The precise number depends on the number of cores and the amount of memory on the tasktracker; see "Memory" on page 269.) The default scheduler fills empty map task slots before reduce task slots, so if the tasktracker has at least one empty map task slot, the jobtracker will select a map task; otherwise, it will select a reduce task.

To choose a reduce task, the jobtracker simply takes the next in its list of yet-to-be-run reduce tasks, since there are no data locality considerations. For a map task, however, it takes account of the tasktracker's network location and picks a task whose input split is as close as possible to the tasktracker. In the optimal case, the task is *data-local*, that is, running on the same node that the split resides on. Alternatively, the task may be *rack-local*: on the same rack, but not the same node, as the split. Some tasks are neither data-local nor rack-local and retrieve their data from a different rack from the one they are running on. You can tell the proportion of each type of task by looking at a job's counters (see "Built-in Counters" on page 225).

Task Execution

Now that the tasktracker has been assigned a task, the next step is for it to run the task. First, it localizes the job JAR by copying it from the shared filesystem to the tasktracker's filesystem. It also copies any files needed from the distributed cache by the application to the local disk; see "Distributed Cache" on page 253 (step 8). Second, it creates a local working directory for the task, and un-jars the contents of the JAR into this directory. Third, it creates an instance of TaskRunner to run the task.

TaskRunner launches a new Java Virtual Machine (step 9) to run each task in (step 10), so that any bugs in the user-defined map and reduce functions don't affect the task-tracker (by causing it to crash or hang, for example). It is, however, possible to reuse the JVM between tasks; see "Task JVM Reuse" on page 184.

The child process communicates with its parent through the *umbilical* interface. This way it informs the parent of the task's progress every few seconds until the task is complete.

Streaming and Pipes

Both Streaming and Pipes run special map and reduce tasks for the purpose of launching the user-supplied executable and communicating with it (Figure 6-2).

In the case of Streaming, the Streaming task communicates with the process (which may be written in any language) using standard input and output streams. The Pipes task, on the other hand, listens on a socket and passes the C++ process a port number in its environment, so that on startup, the C++ process can establish a persistent socket connection back to the parent Java Pipes task.

In both cases, during execution of the task, the Java process passes input key-value pairs to the external process, which runs it through the user-defined map or reduce function and passes the output key-value pairs back to the Java process. From the tasktracker's point of view, it is as if the tasktracker child process ran the map or reduce code itself.

Progress and Status Updates

MapReduce jobs are long-running batch jobs, taking anything from minutes to hours to run. Because this is a significant length of time, it's important for the user to get feedback on how the job is progressing. A job and each of its tasks have a *status*, which includes such things as the state of the job or task (e.g., running, successfully completed, failed), the progress of maps and reduces, the values of the job's counters, and a status message or description (which may be set by user code). These statuses change over the course of the job, so how do they get communicated back to the client?

When a task is running, it keeps track of its *progress*, that is, the proportion of the task completed. For map tasks, this is the proportion of the input that has been processed. For reduce tasks, it's a little more complex, but the system can still estimate the proportion of the reduce input processed. It does this by dividing the total progress into three parts, corresponding to the three phases of the shuffle (see "Shuffle and Sort" on page 177). For example, if the task has run the reducer on half its input, then the task's progress is ⅚, since it has completed the copy and sort phases (⅓ each) and is halfway through the reduce phase (⅙).

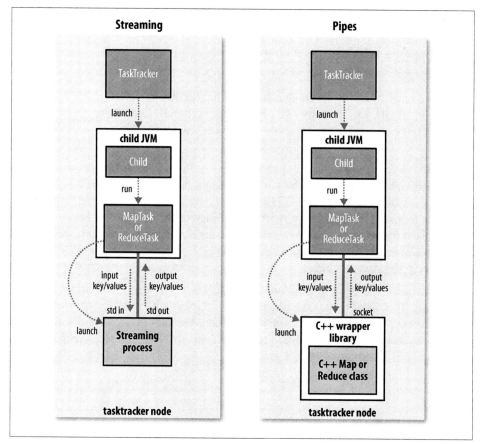

Figure 6-2. The relationship of the Streaming and Pipes executable to the tasktracker and its child

What Constitutes Progress in MapReduce?

Progress is not always measurable, but nevertheless it tells Hadoop that a task is doing something. For example, a task writing output records is making progress, even though it cannot be expressed as a percentage of the total number that will be written, since the latter figure may not be known, even by the task producing the output.

Progress reporting is important, as it means Hadoop will not fail a task that's making progress. All of the following operations constitute progress:

- Reading an input record (in a mapper or reducer)
- Writing an output record (in a mapper or reducer)
- Setting the status description on a reporter (using Reporter's setStatus() method)
- Incrementing a counter (using Reporter's incrCounter() method)
- Calling Reporter's progress() method

Tasks also have a set of counters that count various events as the task runs (we saw an example in "A test run" on page 23), either those built into the framework, such as the number of map output records written, or ones defined by users.

If a task reports progress, it sets a flag to indicate that the status change should be sent to the tasktracker. The flag is checked in a separate thread every three seconds, and if set it notifies the tasktracker of the current task status. Meanwhile, the tasktracker is sending heartbeats to the jobtracker every five seconds (this is a minimum, as the heartbeat interval is actually dependent on the size of the cluster: for larger clusters, the interval is longer), and the status of all the tasks being run by the tasktracker is sent in the call. Counters are sent less frequently than every five seconds, because they can be relatively high-bandwidth.

The jobtracker combines these updates to produce a global view of the status of all the jobs being run and their constituent tasks. Finally, as mentioned earlier, the JobClient receives the latest status by polling the jobtracker every second. Clients can also use JobClient's getJob() method to obtain a RunningJob instance, which contains all of the status information for the job.

The method calls are illustrated in Figure 6-3.

Job Completion

When the jobtracker receives a notification that the last task for a job is complete, it changes the status for the job to "successful." Then, when the JobClient polls for status, it learns that the job has completed successfully, so it prints a message to tell the user and then returns from the runJob() method.

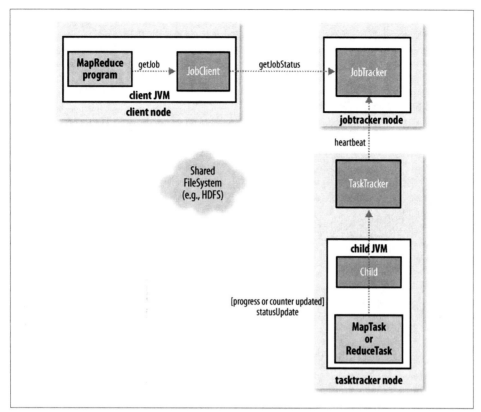

Figure 6-3. How status updates are propagated through the MapReduce system

The jobtracker also sends an HTTP job notification if it is configured to do so. This can be configured by clients wishing to receive callbacks, via the `job.end.notifica tion.url` property.

Last, the jobtracker cleans up its working state for the job and instructs tasktrackers to do the same (so intermediate output is deleted, for example).

Failures

In the real world, user code is buggy, processes crash, and machines fail. One of the major benefits of using Hadoop is its ability to handle such failures and allow your job to complete.

Task Failure

Consider first the case of the child task failing. The most common way that this happens is when user code in the map or reduce task throws a runtime exception. If this happens, the child JVM reports the error back to its parent tasktracker, before it exits. The error ultimately makes it into the user logs. The tasktracker marks the task attempt as *failed*, freeing up a slot to run another task.

For Streaming tasks, if the Streaming process exits with a nonzero exit code, it is marked as failed. This behavior is governed by the `stream.non.zero.exit.is.failure` property (the default is `true`).

Another failure mode is the sudden exit of the child JVM—perhaps there is a JVM bug that causes the JVM to exit for a particular set of circumstances exposed by the MapReduce user code. In this case, the tasktracker notices that the process has exited and marks the attempt as failed.

Hanging tasks are dealt with differently. The tasktracker notices that it hasn't received a progress update for a while and proceeds to mark the task as failed. The child JVM process will be automatically killed after this period.* The timeout period after which tasks are considered failed is normally 10 minutes and can be configured on a per-job basis (or a cluster basis) by setting the `mapred.task.timeout` property to a value in milliseconds.

Setting the timeout to a value of zero disables the timeout, so long-running tasks are never marked as failed. In this case, a hanging task will never free up its slot, and over time there may be cluster slowdown as a result. This approach should therefore be avoided, and making sure that a task is reporting progress periodically will suffice (see "What Constitutes Progress in MapReduce?" on page 172).

When the jobtracker is notified of a task attempt that has failed (by the tasktracker's heartbeat call), it will reschedule execution of the task. The jobtracker will try to avoid rescheduling the task on a tasktracker where it has previously failed. Furthermore, if a task fails four times (or more), it will not be retried further. This value is configurable: the maximum number of attempts to run a task is controlled by the `mapred.map.max.attempts` property for map tasks and `mapred.reduce.max.attempts` for reduce tasks. By default, if any task fails four times (or whatever the maximum number of attempts is configured to), the whole job fails.

For some applications, it is undesirable to abort the job if a few tasks fail, as it may be possible to use the results of the job despite some failures. In this case, the maximum percentage of tasks that are allowed to fail without triggering job failure can be set for the job. Map tasks and reduce tasks are controlled independently, using the `mapred.max.map.failures.percent` and `mapred.max.reduce.failures.percent` properties.

---

* If a Streaming process hangs, the tasktracker does not try to kill it (although the JVM that launched it will be killed), so you should take precautions to monitor for this scenario, and kill orphaned processes by some other means.

A task attempt may also be *killed*, which is different from it failing. A task attempt may be killed because it is a speculative duplicate (for more, see "Speculative Execution" on page 183), or because the tasktracker it was running on failed, and the jobtracker marked all the task attempts running on it as killed. Killed task attempts do not count against the number of attempts to run the task (as set by `mapred.map.max.attempts` and `mapred.reduce.max.attempts`), since it wasn't the task's fault that an attempt was killed.

Users may also kill or fail task attempts using the web UI or the command line (type `hadoop job` to see the options). Jobs may also be killed by the same mechanisms.

Tasktracker Failure

Failure of a tasktracker is another failure mode. If a tasktracker fails by crashing, or running very slowly, it will stop sending heartbeats to the jobtracker (or send them very infrequently). The jobtracker will notice a tasktracker that has stopped sending heartbeats (if it hasn't received one for 10 minutes, configured via the `mapred.task tracker.expiry.interval` property, in milliseconds) and remove it from its pool of tasktrackers to schedule tasks on. The jobtracker arranges for map tasks that were run and completed successfully on that tasktracker to be rerun if they belong to incomplete jobs, since their intermediate output residing on the failed tasktracker's local filesystem may not be accessible to the reduce task. Any tasks in progress are also rescheduled.

A tasktracker can also be *blacklisted* by the jobtracker, even if the tasktracker has not failed. A tasktracker is blacklisted if the number of tasks that have failed on it is significantly higher than the average task failure rate on the cluster. Blacklisted tasktrackers can be restarted to remove them from the jobtracker's blacklist.

Jobtracker Failure

Failure of the jobtracker is the most serious failure mode. Currently, Hadoop has no mechanism for dealing with failure of the jobtracker—it is a single point of failure—so in this case the job fails. However, this failure mode has a low chance of occurring, since the chance of a particular machine failing is low. It is possible that a future release of Hadoop will remove this limitation by running multiple jobtrackers, only one of which is the primary jobtracker at any time (perhaps using ZooKeeper as a coordination mechanism for the jobtrackers to decide who is the primary; see Chapter 14).

Job Scheduling

Early versions of Hadoop had a very simple approach to scheduling users' jobs: they ran in order of submission, using a FIFO scheduler. Typically, each job would use the whole cluster, so jobs had to wait their turn. Although a shared cluster offers great potential for offering large resources to many users, the problem of sharing resources fairly between users requires a better scheduler. Production jobs need to complete in a timely manner, while allowing users who are making smaller ad hoc queries to get results back in a reasonable time.

Later on, the ability to set a job's priority was added, via the `mapred.job.priority` property or the `setJobPriority()` method on `JobClient` (both of which take one of the values `VERY_HIGH`, `HIGH`, `NORMAL`, `LOW`, `VERY_LOW`). When the job scheduler is choosing the next job to run, it selects one with the highest priority. However, with the FIFO scheduler, priorities do not support *preemption*, so a high-priority job can still be blocked by a long-running low priority job that started before the high-priority job was scheduled.

MapReduce in Hadoop comes with a choice of schedulers. The default is the original FIFO queue-based scheduler, and there are also multiuser schedulers called the Fair Scheduler and the Capacity Scheduler.

The Fair Scheduler

The Fair Scheduler aims to give every user a fair share of the cluster capacity over time. If a single job is running, it gets all of the cluster. As more jobs are submitted, free task slots are given to the jobs in such a way as to give each user a fair share of the cluster. A short job belonging to one user will complete in a reasonable time even while another user's long job is running, and the long job will still make progress.

Jobs are placed in pools, and by default, each user gets their own pool. A user who submits more jobs than a second user will not get any more cluster resources than the second, on average. It is also possible to define custom pools with guaranteed minimum capacities defined in terms of the number of map and reduce slots, and to set weightings for each pool.

The Fair Scheduler supports preemption, so if a pool has not received its fair share for a certain period of time, then the scheduler will kill tasks in pools running over capacity in order to give the slots to the pool running under capacity.

The Fair Scheduler is a "contrib" module. To enable it, place its JAR file on Hadoop's classpath, by copying it from Hadoop's *contrib/fairscheduler* directory to the *lib* directory. Then set the `mapred.jobtracker.taskScheduler` property to:

    org.apache.hadoop.mapred.FairScheduler

The Fair Scheduler will work without further configuration, but to take full advantage of its features and how to configure it (including its web interface), refer to README in the *src/contrib/fairscheduler* directory of the distribution.

The Capacity Scheduler

The Capacity Scheduler takes a slightly different approach to multiuser scheduling. A cluster is made up of a number of queues (like the Fair Scheduler's pools), which may be hierarchical (so a queue may be the child of another queue), and each queue has an allocated capacity. This is like the Fair Scheduler, except that within each queue, jobs are scheduled using FIFO scheduling (with priorities). In effect, the Capacity Scheduler allows users or organizations (defined using queues) to simulate a separate MapReduce cluster with FIFO scheduling for each user or organization. The Fair Scheduler, by contrast, (which actually also supports FIFO job scheduling within pools as an option, making it like the Capacity Scheduler) enforces fair sharing within each pool, so running jobs share the pool's resources.

Shuffle and Sort

MapReduce makes the guarantee that the input to every reducer is sorted by key. The process by which the system performs the sort—and transfers the map outputs to the reducers as inputs—is known as the *shuffle*.[†] In this section, we look at how the shuffle works, as a basic understanding would be helpful, should you need to optimize a MapReduce program. The shuffle is an area of the codebase where refinements and improvements are continually being made, so the following description necessarily conceals many details (and may change over time, this is for version 0.20). In many ways, the shuffle is the heart of MapReduce and is where the "magic" happens.

The Map Side

When the map function starts producing output, it is not simply written to disk. The process is more involved, and takes advantage of buffering writes in memory and doing some presorting for efficiency reasons. Figure 6-4 shows what happens.

Each map task has a circular memory buffer that it writes the output to. The buffer is 100 MB by default, a size which can be tuned by changing the `io.sort.mb` property. When the contents of the buffer reaches a certain threshold size (`io.sort.spill.per cent`, default `0.80`, or 80%), a background thread will start to *spill* the contents to disk. Map outputs will continue to be written to the buffer while the spill takes place, but if the buffer fills up during this time, the map will block until the spill is complete.

Spills are written in round-robin fashion to the directories specified by the `mapred.local.dir` property, in a job-specific subdirectory.

---

† The term *shuffle* is actually imprecise, since in some contexts it refers to only the part of the process where map outputs are fetched by reduce tasks. In this section, we take it to mean the whole process from the point where a map produces output to where a reduce consumes input.

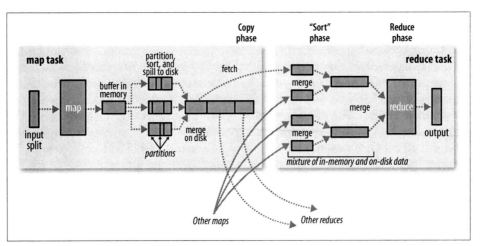

Figure 6-4. Shuffle and sort in MapReduce

Before it writes to disk, the thread first divides the data into partitions corresponding to the reducers that they will ultimately be sent to. Within each partition, the background thread performs an in-memory sort by key, and if there is a combiner function, it is run on the output of the sort.

Each time the memory buffer reaches the spill threshold, a new spill file is created, so after the map task has written its last output record there could be several spill files. Before the task is finished, the spill files are merged into a single partitioned and sorted output file. The configuration property `io.sort.factor` controls the maximum number of streams to merge at once; the default is 10.

If a combiner function has been specified, and the number of spills is at least three (the value of the `min.num.spills.for.combine` property), then the combiner is run before the output file is written. Recall that combiners may be run repeatedly over the input without affecting the final result. The point is that running combiners makes for a more compact map output, so there is less data to write to local disk and to transfer to the reducer.

It is often a good idea to compress the map output as it is written to disk, since doing so makes it faster to write to disk, saves disk space, and reduces the amount of data to transfer to the reducer. By default, the output is not compressed, but it is easy to enable by setting `mapred.compress.map.output` to true. The compression library to use is specified by `mapred.map.output.compression.codec`; see "Compression" on page 77 for more on compression formats.

The output file's partitions are made available to the reducers over HTTP. The number of worker threads used to serve the file partitions is controlled by the `task tracker.http.threads` property—this setting is per tasktracker, not per map task slot. The default of 40 may need increasing for large clusters running large jobs.

The Reduce Side

Let's turn now to the reduce part of the process. The map output file is sitting on the local disk of the tasktracker that ran the map task (note that although map outputs always get written to the local disk of the map tasktracker, reduce outputs may not be), but now it is needed by the tasktracker that is about to run the reduce task for the partition. Furthermore, the reduce task needs the map output for its particular partition from several map tasks across the cluster. The map tasks may finish at different times, so the reduce task starts copying their outputs as soon as each completes. This is known as the *copy phase* of the reduce task. The reduce task has a small number of copier threads so that it can fetch map outputs in parallel. The default is five threads, but this number can be changed by setting the `mapred.reduce.parallel.copies` property.

How do reducers know which tasktrackers to fetch map output from?

As map tasks complete successfully, they notify their parent tasktracker of the status update, which in turn notifies the jobtracker. These notifications are transmitted over the heartbeat communication mechanism described earlier. Therefore, for a given job, the jobtracker knows the mapping between map outputs and tasktrackers. A thread in the reducer periodically asks the jobtracker for map output locations until it has retrieved them all.

Tasktrackers do not delete map outputs from disk as soon as the first reducer has retrieved them, as the reducer may fail. Instead, they wait until they are told to delete them by the jobtracker, which is after the job has completed.

The map outputs are copied to the reduce tasktracker's memory if they are small enough (the buffer's size is controlled by `mapred.job.shuffle.input.buffer.percent`, which specifies the proportion of the heap to use for this purpose); otherwise, they are copied to disk. When the in-memory buffer reaches a threshold size (controlled by `mapred.job.shuffle.merge.percent`), or reaches a threshold number of map outputs (`mapred.inmem.merge.threshold`), it is merged and spilled to disk.

As the copies accumulate on disk, a background thread merges them into larger, sorted files. This saves some time merging later on. Note that any map outputs that were compressed (by the map task) have to be decompressed in memory in order to perform a merge on them.

When all the map outputs have been copied, the reduce task moves into the *sort phase* (which should properly be called the *merge* phase, as the sorting was carried out on the map side), which merges the map outputs, maintaining their sort ordering. This is done in rounds. For example, if there were 50 map outputs, and the *merge factor* was 10 (the default, controlled by the `io.sort.factor` property, just like in the map's merge), then there would be 5 rounds. Each round would merge 10 files into one, so at the end there would be five intermediate files.

Rather than have a final round that merges these five files into a single sorted file, the merge saves a trip to disk by directly feeding the reduce function in what is the last phase: the *reduce phase*. This final merge can come from a mixture of in-memory and on-disk segments.

> The number of files merged in each round is actually more subtle than this example suggests. The goal is to merge the minimum number of files to get to the merge factor for the final round. So if there were 40 files, the merge would not merge 10 files in each of the four rounds to get 4 files. Instead, the first round would merge only 4 files, and the subsequent three rounds would merge the full 10 files. The 4 merged files, and the 6 (as yet unmerged) files make a total of 10 files for the final round.
>
> Note that this does not change the number of rounds, it's just an optimization to minimize the amount of data that is written to disk, since the final round always merges directly into the reduce.

During the reduce phase, the reduce function is invoked for each key in the sorted output. The output of this phase is written directly to the output filesystem, typically HDFS. In the case of HDFS, since the tasktracker node is also running a datanode, the first block replica will be written to the local disk.

Configuration Tuning

We are now in a better position to understand how to tune the shuffle to improve MapReduce performance. The relevant settings, which can be used on a per-job basis (except where noted), are summarized in Tables 6-1 and 6-2, along with the defaults, which are good for general-purpose jobs.

The general principle is to give the shuffle as much memory as possible. However, there is a trade-off, in that you need to make sure that your map and reduce functions get enough memory to operate. This is why it is best to write your map and reduce functions to use as little memory as possible—certainly they should not use an unbounded amount of memory (by avoiding accumulating values in a map, for example).

The amount of memory given to the JVMs in which the map and reduce tasks run is set by the `mapred.child.java.opts` property. You should try to make this as large as possible for the amount of memory on your task nodes; the discussion in "Memory" on page 269 goes through the constraints to consider.

On the map side, the best performance can be obtained by avoiding multiple spills to disk; one is optimal. If you can estimate the size of your map outputs, then you can set the `io.sort.*` properties appropriately to minimize the number of spills. In particular, you should increase `io.sort.mb` if you can. There is a MapReduce counter ("Spilled records"; see "Counters" on page 225) that counts the total number of records that were spilled to disk over the course of a job, which can be useful for tuning. Note that the counter includes both map and reduce side spills.

On the reduce side, the best performance is obtained when the intermediate data can reside entirely in memory. By default, this does not happen, since for the general case all the memory is reserved for the reduce function. But if your reduce function has light memory requirements, then setting `mapred.inmem.merge.threshold` to 0 and `mapred.job.reduce.input.buffer.percent` to 1.0 (or a lower value; see Table 6-2) may bring a performance boost.

More generally, Hadoop uses a buffer size of 4 KB by default, which is low, so you should increase this across the cluster (by setting `io.file.buffer.size`, see also "Other Hadoop Properties" on page 279).

In April 2008, Hadoop won the general-purpose terabyte sort benchmark (described in "TeraByte Sort on Apache Hadoop" on page 553), and one of the optimizations used was this one of keeping the intermediate data in memory on the reduce side.

Table 6-1. Map-side tuning properties

Property name	Type	Default value	Description
`io.sort.mb`	int	100	The size, in megabytes, of the memory buffer to use while sorting map output.
`io.sort.record.percent`	float	0.05	The proportion of `io.sort.mb` reserved for storing record boundaries of the map outputs. The remaining space is used for the map output records themselves.
`io.sort.spill.percent`	float	0.80	The threshold usage proportion for both the map output memory buffer and the record boundaries index to start the process of spilling to disk.
`io.sort.factor`	int	10	The maximum number of streams to merge at once when sorting files. This property is also used in the reduce. It's fairly common to increase this to 100.
`min.num.spills.for.combine`	int	3	The minimum number of spill files needed for the combiner to run (if a combiner is specified).
`mapred.compress.map.output`	boolean	false	Compress map outputs.
`mapred.map.output.compression.codec`	Class name	org.apache.hadoop.io.compress.DefaultCodec	The compression codec to use for map outputs.

Property name	Type	Default value	Description
task tracker.http.threads	int	40	The number of worker threads per tasktracker for serving the map outputs to reducers. This is a cluster-wide setting and cannot be set by individual jobs.

Table 6-2. Reduce-side tuning properties

Property name	Type	Default value	Description
mapred.reduce.parallel. copies	int	5	The number of threads used to copy map outputs to the reducer.
mapred.reduce.copy.backoff	int	300	The maximum amount of time, in seconds, to spend retrieving one map output for a reducer before declaring it as failed. The reducer may repeatedly reattempt a transfer within this time if it fails (using exponential backoff).
io.sort.factor	int	10	The maximum number of streams to merge at once when sorting files. This property is also used in the map.
mapred.job.shuffle.input. buffer.percent	float	0.70	The proportion of total heap size to be allocated to the map outputs buffer during the copy phase of the shuffle.
mapred.job.shuffle.merge. percent	float	0.66	The threshold usage proportion for the map outputs buffer (defined by `mapred.job.shuf fle.input.buffer.percent`) for starting the process of merging the outputs and spilling to disk.
mapred.inmem.merge.threshold	int	1000	The threshold number of map outputs for starting the process of merging the outputs and spilling to disk. A value of 0 or less means there is no threshold, and the spill behavior is governed solely by `mapred.job.shuffle.merge.percent`.
mapred.job.reduce.input. buffer.percent	float	0.0	The proportion of total heap size to be used for retaining map outputs in memory during the reduce. For the reduce phase to begin, the size of map outputs in memory must be no more than this size. By default, all map outputs are merged to disk before the reduce begins, to give the reducers as much memory as possible. However, if your reducers require less memory, this value may be increased to minimize the number of trips to disk.

Task Execution

We saw how the MapReduce system executes tasks in the context of the overall job at the beginning of the chapter in "Anatomy of a MapReduce Job Run" on page 167. In this section, we'll look at some more controls that MapReduce users have over task execution.

Speculative Execution

The MapReduce model is to break jobs into tasks and run the tasks in parallel to make the overall job execution time smaller than it would otherwise be if the tasks ran sequentially. This makes job execution time sensitive to slow-running tasks, as it takes only one slow task to make the whole job take significantly longer than it would have done otherwise. When a job consists of hundreds or thousands of tasks, the possibility of a few straggling tasks is very real.

Tasks may be slow for various reasons, including hardware degradation or software mis-configuration, but the causes may be hard to detect since the tasks still complete successfully, albeit after a longer time than expected. Hadoop doesn't try to diagnose and fix slow-running tasks; instead, it tries to detect when a task is running slower than expected and launches another, equivalent, task as a backup. This is termed *speculative execution* of tasks.

It's important to understand that speculative execution does not work by launching two duplicate tasks at about the same time so they can race each other. This would be wasteful of cluster resources. Rather, a speculative task is launched only after all the tasks for a job have been launched, and then only for tasks that have been running for some time (at least a minute) and have failed to make as much progress, on average, as the other tasks from the job. When a task completes successfully, any duplicate tasks that are running are killed since they are no longer needed. So if the original task completes before the speculative task, then the speculative task is killed; on the other hand, if the speculative task finishes first, then the original is killed.

Speculative execution is an optimization, not a feature to make jobs run more reliably. If there are bugs that sometimes cause a task to hang or slow down, then relying on speculative execution to avoid these problems is unwise, and won't work reliably, since the same bugs are likely to affect the speculative task. You should fix the bug so that the task doesn't hang or slow down.

Speculative execution is turned on by default. It can be enabled or disabled independently for map tasks and reduce tasks, on a cluster-wide basis, or on a per-job basis. The relevant properties are shown in Table 6-3.

Table 6-3. *Speculative execution properties*

Property name	Type	Default value	Description
mapred.map.tasks.speculative.execution	boolean	true	Whether extra instances of map tasks may be launched if a task is making slow progress.
mapred.reduce.tasks.speculative.execution	boolean	true	Whether extra instances of reduce tasks may be launched if a task is making slow progress.

Why would you ever want to turn off speculative execution? The goal of speculative execution is reducing job execution time, but this comes at the cost of cluster efficiency. On a busy cluster, speculative execution can reduce overall throughput, since redundant tasks are being executed in an attempt to bring down the execution time for a single job. For this reason, some cluster administrators prefer to turn it off on the cluster and have users explicitly turn it on for individual jobs. This was especially relevant for older versions of Hadoop, when speculative execution could be overly aggressive in scheduling speculative tasks.

Task JVM Reuse

Hadoop runs tasks in their own Java Virtual Machine to isolate them from other running tasks. The overhead of starting a new JVM for each task can take around a second, which for jobs that run for a minute or so is insignificant. However, jobs that have a large number of very short-lived tasks (these are usually map tasks), or that have lengthy initialization, can see performance gains when the JVM is reused for subsequent tasks.

With task JVM reuse enabled, tasks do *not* run concurrently in a single JVM. The JVM runs tasks sequentially. Tasktrackers can, however, run more than one task at a time, but this is always done in separate JVMs. The properties for controlling the tasktrackers number of map task slots and reduce task slots are discussed in "Memory" on page 269.

The property for controlling task JVM reuse is mapred.job.reuse.jvm.num.tasks: it specifies the maximum number of tasks to run for a given job for each JVM launched; the default is 1 (see Table 6-4). Tasks from different jobs are always run in separate JVMs. If the property is set to −1, there is no limit to the number of tasks from the same job that may share a JVM. The method setNumTasksToExecutePerJvm() on JobConf can also be used to configure this property.

Table 6-4. Task JVM Reuse properties

Property name	Type	Default value	Description
mapred.job.reuse.jvm.num.tasks	int	1	The maximum number of tasks to run for a given job for each JVM on a tasktracker. A value of -1 indicates no limit: the same JVM may be used for all tasks for a job.

Tasks that are CPU-bound may also benefit from task JVM reuse by taking advantage of runtime optimizations applied by the HotSpot JVM. After running for a while, the HotSpot JVM builds up enough information to detect performance-critical sections in the code and dynamically translates the Java byte codes of these hot spots into native machine code. This works well for long-running processes, but JVMs that run for seconds or a few minutes may not gain the full benefit of HotSpot. In these cases, it is worth enabling task JVM reuse.

Another place where a shared JVM is useful is for sharing state between the tasks of a job. By storing reference data in a static field, tasks get rapid access to the shared data.

Skipping Bad Records

Large datasets are messy. They often have corrupt records. They often have records that are in a different format. They often have missing fields. In an ideal world, your code would cope gracefully with all of these conditions. In practice, it is often expedient to ignore the offending records. Depending on the analysis being performed, if only a small percentage of records are affected, then skipping them may not significantly affect the result. However, if a task trips up when it encounters a bad record—by throwing a runtime exception—then the task fails. Failing tasks are retried (since the failure may be due to hardware failure or some other reason outside the task's control), but if a task fails four times, then the whole job is marked as failed (see "Task Failure" on page 173). If it is the data that is causing the task to throw an exception, rerunning the task won't help, since it will fail in exactly the same way each time.

 If you are using TextInputFormat ("TextInputFormat" on page 209), then you can set a maximum expected line length to safeguard against corrupted files. Corruption in a file can manifest itself as a very long line, which can cause out of memory errors and then task failure. By setting mapred.linerecordreader.maxlength to a value in bytes that fits in memory (and is comfortably greater than the length of lines in your input data), the record reader will skip the (long) corrupt lines without the task failing.

The best way to handle corrupt records is in your mapper or reducer code. You can detect the bad record and ignore it, or you can abort the job by throwing an exception. You can also count the total number of bad records in the job using counters to see how widespread the problem is.

In rare cases, though, you can't handle the problem because there is a bug in a third-party library that you can't work around in your mapper or reducer. In these cases, you can use Hadoop's optional *skipping mode* for automatically skipping bad records.

When skipping mode is enabled, tasks report the records being processed back to the tasktracker. When the task fails, the tasktracker retries the task, skipping the records that caused the failure. Because of the extra network traffic and bookkeeping to maintain the failed record ranges, skipping mode is turned on for a task only after it has failed twice.

Thus, for a task consistently failing on a bad record, the tasktracker runs the following task attempts with these outcomes:

1. Task fails.
2. Task fails.
3. Skipping mode is enabled. Task fails, but failed record is stored by the tasktracker.
4. Skipping mode is still enabled. Task succeeds by skipping the bad record that failed in the previous attempt.

Skipping mode is off by default; you enable it independently for map and reduce tasks using the SkipBadRecords class. It's important to note that skipping mode can detect only one bad record per task attempt, so this mechanism is appropriate only for detecting occasional bad records (a few per task, say). You may need to increase the maximum number of task attempts (via mapred.map.max.attempts and mapred.reduce.max.attempts) to give skipping mode enough attempts to detect and skip all the bad records in an input split.

Bad records that have been detected by Hadoop are saved as sequence files in the job's output directory under the *_logs/skip* subdirectory. These can be inspected for diagnostic purposes after the job has completed (using hadoop fs -text, for example).

The Task Execution Environment

Hadoop provides information to a map or reduce task about the environment in which it is running. For example, a map task can discover the name of the file it is processing (see "File information in the mapper" on page 205), and a map or reduce task can find out the attempt number of the task. The properties in Table 6-5 can be accessed from the job's configuration, obtained by providing an implementation of the configure() method for Mapper or Reducer, where the configuration is passed in as an argument.

Table 6-5. Task environment properties

Property name	Type	Description	Example
mapred.job.id	String	The job ID. (See "Job, Task, and Task Attempt IDs" on page 147 for a description of the format.)	job_200811201130_0004
mapred.tip.id	String	The task ID.	task_200811201130_0004_m_000003
mapred.task.id	String	The task attempt ID. (*Not* the task ID.)	attempt_200811201130_0004_m_000003_0
mapred.task. partition	int	The ID of the task within the job.	3
mapred.task.is.map	boolean	Whether this task is a map task.	true

Streaming environment variables

Hadoop sets job configuration parameters as environment variables for Streaming programs. However, it replaces nonalphanumeric characters with underscores to make sure they are valid names. The following Python expression illustrates how you can retrieve the value of the mapred.job.id property from within a Python Streaming script:

```
os.environ["mapred_job_id"]
```

You can also set environment variables for the Streaming processes launched by Map-Reduce by supplying the -cmdenv option to the Streaming launcher program (once for each variable you wish to set). For example, the following sets the MAGIC_PARAMETER environment variable:

```
-cmdenv MAGIC_PARAMETER=abracadabra
```

Task side-effect files

The usual way of writing output from map and reduce tasks is by using the OutputCollector to collect key-value pairs. Some applications need more flexibility than a single key-value pair model, so these applications write output files directly from the map or reduce task to a distributed filesystem, like HDFS. (There are other ways to produce multiple outputs, too, as described in "Multiple Outputs" on page 217.)

Care needs to be taken to ensure that multiple instances of the same task don't try to write to the same file. There are two problems to avoid: if a task failed and was retried, then the old partial output would still be present when the second task ran, and it would have to delete the old file first. Second, with speculative execution enabled, two instances of the same task could try to write to the same file simultaneously.

Hadoop solves this problem for the regular outputs from a task by writing outputs to a temporary directory that is specific to that task attempt. The directory is ${mapred.out put.dir}/_temporary/${mapred.task.id}. On successful completion of the task, the contents of the directory are copied to the job's output directory (${mapred.out put.dir}). Thus, if the task fails and is retried, the first attempt's partial output will just be cleaned up. A task and another speculative instance of the same task will get separate working directories, and only the first to finish will have the content of its working directory promoted to the output directory—the other will be discarded.

The way that a task's output is committed on completion is implemented by an OutputCommitter, which is associated with the OutputFormat. The OutputCommitter for FileOutputFormat is a FileOutputCommitter, which implements the commit protocol described earlier. The getOut putCommitter() method on OutputFormat may be overridden to return a custom OutputCommitter, in case you want to implement the commit process in a different way.

Hadoop provides a mechanism for application writers to use this feature, too. A task may find its working directory by retrieving the value of the mapred.work.output.dir property from its configuration file. Alternatively, a MapReduce program using the Java API may call the getWorkOutputPath() static method on FileOutputFormat to get the Path object representing the working directory. The framework creates the working directory before executing the task, so you don't need to create it.

To take a simple example, imagine a program for converting image files from one format to another. One way to do this is to have a map-only job, where each map is given a set of images to convert (perhaps using NLineInputFormat; see "NLineInputFor-mat" on page 211). If a map task writes the converted images into its working directory, then they will be promoted to the output directory when the task successfully finishes.

## CHAPTER 7

MapReduce Types and Formats

MapReduce has a simple model of data processing: inputs and outputs for the map and reduce functions are key-value pairs. This chapter looks at the MapReduce model in detail and, in particular, how data in various formats, from simple text to structured binary objects, can be used with this model.

MapReduce Types

The map and reduce functions in Hadoop MapReduce have the following general form:

```
map: (K1, V1) → list(K2, V2)
reduce: (K2, list(V2)) → list(K3, V3)
```

In general, the map input key and value types (K1 and V1) are different from the map output types (K2 and V2). However, the reduce input must have the same types as the map output, although the reduce output types may be different again (K3 and V3). The Java interfaces mirror this form:

```
public interface Mapper<K1, V1, K2, V2> extends JobConfigurable, Closeable {

  void map(K1 key, V1 value, OutputCollector<K2, V2> output, Reporter reporter)
    throws IOException;
}

public interface Reducer<K2, V2, K3, V3> extends JobConfigurable, Closeable {

  void reduce(K2 key, Iterator<V2> values,
    OutputCollector<K3, V3> output, Reporter reporter) throws IOException;
}
```

Recall that the OutputCollector is purely for emitting key-value pairs (and is hence parameterized with their types), while the Reporter is for updating counters and status. (In the new MapReduce API in release 0.20.0 and later, these two functions are combined in a single context object.)

If a combine function is used, then it is the same form as the reduce function (and is an implementation of Reducer), except its output types are the intermediate key and value types (K2 and V2), so they can feed the reduce function:

```
map:     (K1, V1)      → list(K2, V2)
combine: (K2, list(V2)) → list(K2, V2)
reduce:  (K2, list(V2)) → list(K3, V3)
```

Often the combine and reduce functions are the same, in which case, K3 is the same as K2, and V3 is the same as V2.

The partition function operates on the intermediate key and value types (K2 and V2), and returns the partition index. In practice, the partition is determined solely by the key (the value is ignored):

```
partition: (K2, V2) → integer
```

Or in Java:

```
public interface Partitioner<K2, V2> extends JobConfigurable {

    int getPartition(K2 key, V2 value, int numPartitions);
}
```

So much for the theory, how does this help configure MapReduce jobs? Table 7-1 summarizes the configuration options. It is divided into the properties that determine the types and those that have to be compatible with the configured types.

Input types are set by the input format. So, for instance, a TextInputFormat generates keys of type LongWritable and values of type Text. The other types are set explicitly by calling the methods on the JobConf. If not set explicitly, the intermediate types default to the (final) output types, which default to LongWritable and Text. So if K2 and K3 are the same, you don't need to call setMapOutputKeyClass(), since it falls back to the type set by calling setOutputKeyClass(). Similarly, if V2 and V3 are the same, you only need to use setOutputValueClass().

It may seem strange that these methods for setting the intermediate and final output types exist at all. After all, why can't the types be determined from a combination of the mapper and the reducer? The answer is that it's to do with a limitation in Java generics: type erasure means that the type information isn't always present at runtime, so Hadoop has to be given it explicitly. This also means that it's possible to configure a MapReduce job with incompatible types, because the configuration isn't checked at compile time. The settings that have to be compatible with the MapReduce types are listed in the lower part of Table 7-1. Type conflicts are detected at runtime during job execution, and for this reason, it is wise to run a test job using a small amount of data to flush out and fix any type incompatibilities.

Table 7-1. *Configuration of MapReduce types*

Property	JobConf setter method	Input types K1	Input types V1	Intermediate types K2	Intermediate types V2	Output types K3	Output types V3
Properties for configuring types:							
mapred.input.format.class	setInputFormat()	•	•				
mapred.mapoutput.key.class	setMapOutputKeyClass()			•			
mapred.mapoutput.value.class	setMapOutputValueClass()				•		
mapred.output.key.class	setOutputKeyClass()					•	
mapred.output.value.class	setOutputValueClass()						•
Properties that must be consistent with the types:							
mapred.mapper.class	setMapperClass()	•	•	•	•		
mapred.map.runner.class	setMapRunnerClass()	•	•	•	•		
mapred.combiner.class	setCombinerClass()			•	•		
mapred.partitioner.class	setPartitionerClass()			•	•		
mapred.output.key.comparator.class	setOutputKeyComparatorClass()			•			
mapred.output.value.groupfn.class	setOutputValueGroupingComparator()			•			
mapred.reducer.class	setReducerClass()			•	•	•	•
mapred.output.format.class	setOutputFormat()					•	•

The Default MapReduce Job

What happens when you run MapReduce without setting a mapper or a reducer? Let's try it by running this minimal MapReduce program:

```
public class MinimalMapReduce extends Configured implements Tool {

  @Override
  public int run(String[] args) throws Exception {
    if (args.length != 2) {
      System.err.printf("Usage: %s [generic options] <input> <output>\n",
          getClass().getSimpleName());
      ToolRunner.printGenericCommandUsage(System.err);
      return -1;
    }

    JobConf conf = new JobConf(getConf(), getClass());
    FileInputFormat.addInputPath(conf, new Path(args[0]));
    FileOutputFormat.setOutputPath(conf, new Path(args[1]));
    JobClient.runJob(conf);
    return 0;
  }

  public static void main(String[] args) throws Exception {
    int exitCode = ToolRunner.run(new MinimalMapReduce(), args);
    System.exit(exitCode);
  }
}
```

The only configuration that we set is an input path and an output path. We run it over a subset of our weather data with the following:

```
% hadoop MinimalMapReduce "input/ncdc/all/190{1,2}.gz" output
```

We do get some output: one file named *part-00000* in the output directory. Here's what the first few lines look like (truncated to fit the page):

```
0→0029029070999991901010106004+64333+023450FM-12+000599999V0202701N01591...
0→0035029070999991902010106004+64333+023450FM-12+000599999V0201401N01181...
135→0029029070999991901010113004+64333+023450FM-12+000599999V0202901N00821...
141→0035029070999991902010113004+64333+023450FM-12+000599999V0201401N01181...
270→0029029070999991901010120004+64333+023450FM-12+000599999V0209991C00001...
282→0035029070999991902010120004+64333+023450FM-12+000599999V0201401N01391...
```

Each line is an integer followed by a tab character, followed by the original weather data record. Admittedly, it's not a very useful program, but understanding how it produces its output does provide some insight into the defaults that Hadoop uses when running MapReduce jobs. Example 7-1 shows a program that has exactly the same effect as MinimalMapReduce, but explicitly sets the job settings to their defaults.

Example 7-1. A minimal MapReduce driver, with the defaults explicitly set

```java
public class MinimalMapReduceWithDefaults extends Configured implements Tool {

  @Override
  public int run(String[] args) throws IOException {
    JobConf conf = JobBuilder.parseInputAndOutput(this, getConf(), args);
    if (conf == null) {
      return -1;
    }

    conf.setInputFormat(TextInputFormat.class);

    conf.setNumMapTasks(1);
    conf.setMapperClass(IdentityMapper.class);
    conf.setMapRunnerClass(MapRunner.class);

    conf.setMapOutputKeyClass(LongWritable.class);
    conf.setMapOutputValueClass(Text.class);

    conf.setPartitionerClass(HashPartitioner.class);

    conf.setNumReduceTasks(1);
    conf.setReducerClass(IdentityReducer.class);

    conf.setOutputKeyClass(LongWritable.class);
    conf.setOutputValueClass(Text.class);

    conf.setOutputFormat(TextOutputFormat.class);

    JobClient.runJob(conf);
    return 0;
  }
  public static void main(String[] args) throws Exception {
    int exitCode = ToolRunner.run(new MinimalMapReduceWithDefaults(), args);
    System.exit(exitCode);
  }
}
```

We've simplified the first few lines of the run() method, by extracting the logic for printing usage and setting the input and output paths into a helper method. Almost all MapReduce drivers take these two arguments (input and output), so reducing the boilerplate code here is a good thing. Here are the relevant methods in the JobBuilder class for reference:

```java
public static JobConf parseInputAndOutput(Tool tool, Configuration conf,
    String[] args) {

  if (args.length != 2) {
    printUsage(tool, "<input> <output>");
    return null;
  }
  JobConf jobConf = new JobConf(conf, tool.getClass());
  FileInputFormat.addInputPath(jobConf, new Path(args[0]));
  FileOutputFormat.setOutputPath(jobConf, new Path(args[1]));
```

```
        return jobConf;
    }

    public static void printUsage(Tool tool, String extraArgsUsage) {
        System.err.printf("Usage: %s [genericOptions] %s\n\n",
            tool.getClass().getSimpleName(), extraArgsUsage);
        GenericOptionsParser.printGenericCommandUsage(System.err);
    }
```

Going back to MinimalMapReduceWithDefaults in Example 7-1, although there are many other default job settings, the ones highlighted are those most central to running a job. Let's go through them in turn.

The default input format is TextInputFormat, which produces keys of type LongWrita ble (the offset of the beginning of the line in the file) and values of type Text (the line of text). This explains where the integers in the final output come from: they are the line offsets.

Despite appearances, the setNumMapTasks() call does not necessarily set the number of map tasks to one, in fact. It is a hint, and the actual number of map tasks depends on the size of the input, and the file's block size (if the file is in HDFS). This is discussed further in "FileInputFormat input splits" on page 202.

The default mapper is IdentityMapper, which writes the input key and value unchanged to the output:

```
public class IdentityMapper<K, V>
        extends MapReduceBase implements Mapper<K, V, K, V> {

    public void map(K key, V val,
                    OutputCollector<K, V> output, Reporter reporter)
        throws IOException {
        output.collect(key, val);
    }
}
```

IdentityMapper is a generic type, which allows it to work with any key or value types, with the restriction that the map input and output keys are of the same type, and the map input and output values are of the same type. In this case, the map output key is LongWritable and the map output value is Text.

Map tasks are run by MapRunner, the default implementation of MapRunnable that calls the Mapper's map() method sequentially with each record.

The default partitioner is HashPartitioner, which hashes a record's key to determine which partition the record belongs in. Each partition is processed by a reduce task, so the number of partitions is equal to the number of reduce tasks for the job:

```
public class HashPartitioner<K2, V2> implements Partitioner<K2, V2> {

    public void configure(JobConf job) {}

    public int getPartition(K2 key, V2 value,
```

```
                         int numPartitions) {
      return (key.hashCode() & Integer.MAX_VALUE) % numPartitions;
    }

  }
```

The key's hash code is turned into a nonnegative integer by bitwise ANDing it with the largest integer value. It is then reduced modulo the number of partitions to find the index of the partition that the record belongs in.

By default, there is a single reducer, and therefore a single partition, so the action of the partitioner is irrelevant in this case since everything goes into one partition. However, it is important to understand the behavior of HashPartitioner when you have more than one reduce task. Assuming the key's hash function is a good one, the records will be evenly allocated across reduce tasks, with all records sharing the same key being processed by the same reduce task.

Choosing the Number of Reducers

The single reducer default is something of a gotcha for new users to Hadoop. Almost all real-world jobs should set this to a larger number; otherwise, the job will be very slow since all the intermediate data flows through a single reduce task. (Note that when running under the local job runner, only zero or one reducers are supported.)

The optimal number of reducers is related to the total number of available reducer slots in your cluster. The total number of slots is found by multiplying the number of nodes in the cluster and the number of slots per node (which is determined by the value of the mapred.tasktracker.reduce.tasks.maximum property, described in "Environment Settings" on page 269).

One common setting is to have slightly fewer reducers than total slots, which gives one wave of reduce tasks (and tolerates a few failures, without extending job execution time). If your reduce tasks are very big, then it makes sense to have a larger number of reducers (resulting in two waves, for example) so that the tasks are more fine-grained, and failure doesn't affect job execution time significantly.

The default reducer is IdentityReducer, again a generic type, which simply writes all its input to its output:

```
public class IdentityReducer<K, V>
    extends MapReduceBase implements Reducer<K, V, K, V> {

  public void reduce(K key, Iterator<V> values,
                     OutputCollector<K, V> output, Reporter reporter)
    throws IOException {
    while (values.hasNext()) {
      output.collect(key, values.next());
    }
  }
}
```

For this job, the output key is LongWritable, and the output value is Text. In fact, all the keys for this MapReduce program are LongWritable, and all the values are Text, since these are the input keys and values, and the map and reduce functions are both identity functions which by definition preserve type. Most MapReduce programs, however, don't use the same key or value types throughout, so you need to configure the job to declare the types you are using, as described in the previous section.

Records are sorted by the MapReduce system before being presented to the reducer. In this case, the keys are sorted numerically, which has the effect of interleaving the lines from the input files into one combined output file.

The default output format is TextOutputFormat, which writes out records, one per line, by converting keys and values to strings and separating them with a tab character. This is why the output is tab-separated: it is a feature of TextOutputFormat.

The default Streaming job

In Streaming, the default job is similar, but not identical, to the Java equivalent. The minimal form is:

```
% hadoop jar $HADOOP_INSTALL/contrib/streaming/hadoop-*-streaming.jar \
  -input input/ncdc/sample.txt \
  -output output \
  -mapper /bin/cat
```

Notice that you have to supply a mapper: the default identity mapper will not work. The reason has to do with the default input format, TextInputFormat, which generates LongWritable keys and Text values. However, Streaming output keys and values (including the map keys and values) are always both of type Text.* The identity mapper cannot change LongWritable keys to Text keys, so it fails.

When we specify a non-Java mapper, and the input format is TextInputFormat, Streaming does something special. It doesn't pass the key to the mapper process, it just passes the value. This is actually very useful, since the key is just the line offset in the file, and the value is the line, which is all most applications are interested in. The overall effect of this job is to perform a sort of the input.

With more of the defaults spelled out, the command looks like this:

```
% hadoop jar $HADOOP_INSTALL/contrib/streaming/hadoop-*-streaming.jar \
  -input input/ncdc/sample.txt \
  -output output \
  -inputformat org.apache.hadoop.mapred.TextInputFormat \
  -mapper /bin/cat \
  -partitioner org.apache.hadoop.mapred.lib.HashPartitioner \
  -numReduceTasks 1 \
  -reducer org.apache.hadoop.mapred.lib.IdentityReducer \
  -outputformat org.apache.hadoop.mapred.TextOutputFormat
```

---

* Except when used in binary mode, from version 0.21.0 onward, via the -io rawbytes or -io typedbytes options. Text mode (-io text) is the default.

The mapper and reducer arguments take a command or a Java class. A combiner may optionally be specified, using the -combiner argument.

Keys and values in Streaming

A Streaming application can control the separator that is used when a key-value pair is turned into a series of bytes and sent to the map or reduce process over standard input. The default is a tab character, but it is useful to be able to change it in the case that the keys or values themselves contain tab characters.

Similarly, when the map or reduce writes out key-value pairs, they may be separated by a configurable separator. Furthermore, the key from the output can be composed of more than the first field: it can be made up of the first n fields (defined by stream.num.map.output.key.fields or stream.num.reduce.output.key.fields), with the value being the remaining fields. For example, if the output from a Streaming process was a,b,c (and the separator is a comma), and n is two, then the key would be parsed as a,b and the value as c.

Separators may be configured independently for maps and reduces. The properties are listed in Table 7-2 and shown in a diagram of the data flow path in Figure 7-1.

These settings do not have any bearing on the input and output formats. For example, if stream.reduce.output.field.separator were set to be a colon, say, and the reduce stream process wrote the line a:b to standard out, then the Streaming reducer would know to extract the key as a and the value as b. With the standard TextOutputFormat, this record would be written to the output file with a tab separating a and b. You can change the separator that TextOutputFormat uses by setting mapred.textoutputformat.separator.

Table 7-2. Streaming separator properties

Property name	Type	Default value	Description
stream.map.input.field.separator	String	\t	The separator to use when passing the input key and value strings to the stream map process as a stream of bytes.
stream.map.output.field.separator	String	\t	The separator to use when splitting the output from the stream map process into key and value strings for the map output.
stream.num.map.output.key.fields	int	1	The number of fields separated by stream.map.output.field.separator to treat as the map output key.
stream.reduce.input.field.separator	String	\t	The separator to use when passing the input key and value strings to the stream reduce process as a stream of bytes.
stream.reduce.output.field.separator	String	\t	The separator to use when splitting the output from the stream reduce process into key and value strings for the final reduce output.

Property name	Type	Default value	Description
`stream.num.reduce.` `output.key.fields`	int	1	The number of fields separated by `stream.reduce.output.field.separator` to treat as the reduce output key.

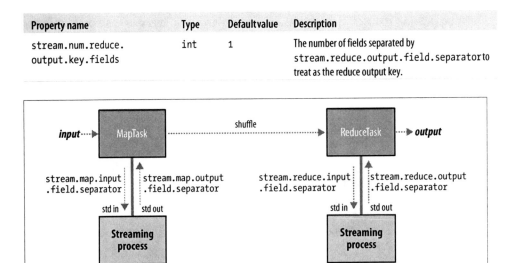

Figure 7-1. Where separators are used in a Streaming MapReduce job

Input Formats

Hadoop can process many different types of data formats, from flat text files to databases. In this section, we explore the different formats available.

Input Splits and Records

As we saw in Chapter 2, an input split is a chunk of the input that is processed by a single map. Each map processes a single split. Each split is divided into records, and the map processes each record—a key-value pair—in turn. Splits and records are logical: there is nothing that requires them to be tied to files, for example, although in their most common incarnations, they are. In a database context, a split might correspond to a range of rows from a table and a record to a row in that range (this is precisely what `DBInputFormat` does, an input format for reading data from a relational database).

Input splits are represented by the Java interface, `InputSplit` (which, like all of the classes mentioned in this section, is in the `org.apache.hadoop.mapred` package[†]):

```
public interface InputSplit extends Writable {

    long getLength() throws IOException;

    String[] getLocations() throws IOException;
```

---

† But see the new MapReduce classes in `org.apache.hadoop.mapreduce`, described in "The new Java MapReduce API" on page 25.

```
}
```

An InputSplit has a length in bytes and a set of storage locations, which are just host-name strings. Notice that a split doesn't contain the input data; it is just a reference to the data. The storage locations are used by the MapReduce system to place map tasks as close to the split's data as possible, and the size is used to order the splits so that the largest get processed first, in an attempt to minimize the job runtime (this is an instance of a greedy approximation algorithm).

As a MapReduce application writer, you don't need to deal with InputSplits directly, as they are created by an InputFormat. An InputFormat is responsible for creating the input splits and dividing them into records. Before we see some concrete examples of InputFormat, let's briefly examine how it is used in MapReduce. Here's the interface:

```
public interface InputFormat<K, V> {

  InputSplit[] getSplits(JobConf job, int numSplits) throws IOException;

  RecordReader<K, V> getRecordReader(InputSplit split,
                                     JobConf job,
                                     Reporter reporter) throws IOException;
}
```

The JobClient calls the getSplits() method, passing the desired number of map tasks as the numSplits argument. This number is treated as a hint, as InputFormat implementations are free to return a different number of splits to the number specified in numSplits. Having calculated the splits, the client sends them to the jobtracker, which uses their storage locations to schedule map tasks to process them on the tasktrackers. On a tasktracker, the map task passes the split to the getRecordReader() method on InputFormat to obtain a RecordReader for that split. A RecordReader is little more than an iterator over records, and the map task uses one to generate record key-value pairs, which it passes to the map function. A code snippet (based on the code in MapRunner) illustrates the idea:

```
K key = reader.createKey();
V value = reader.createValue();
while (reader.next(key, value)) {
  mapper.map(key, value, output, reporter);
}
```

Here the RecordReader's next() method is called repeatedly to populate the key and value objects for the mapper. When the reader gets to the end of the stream, the next() method returns false, and the map task completes.

This code snippet makes it clear that the *same* key and value objects are used on each invocation of the map() method—only their contents are changed (by the reader's next() method). This can be a surprise to users, who might expect keys and values to be immutable. This causes problems when a reference to a key or value object is retained outside the map() method, as its value can change without warning. If you need to do this, make a copy of the object you want to hold on to. For example, for a Text object, you can use its copy constructor: new Text(value).

The situation is similar with reducers. In this case, the value objects in the reducer's iterator are reused, so you need to copy any that you need to retain between calls to the iterator (see Example 8-14).

Finally, note that MapRunner is only one way of running mappers. MultithreadedMapRunner is another implementation of the MapRunnable interface that runs mappers concurrently in a configurable number of threads (set by mapred.map.multithreadedrunner.threads). For most data processing tasks, it confers no advantage over MapRunner. However, for mappers that spend a long time processing each record, because they contact external servers, for example, it allows multiple mappers to run in one JVM with little contention. See "Fetcher: A multithreaded MapRunner in action" on page 527 for an example of an application that uses MultithreadedMapRunner.

FileInputFormat

FileInputFormat is the base class for all implementations of InputFormat that use files as their data source (see Figure 7-2). It provides two things: a place to define which files are included as the input to a job, and an implementation for generating splits for the input files. The job of dividing splits into records is performed by subclasses.

FileInputFormat input paths

The input to a job is specified as a collection of paths, which offers great flexibility in constraining the input to a job. FileInputFormat offers four static convenience methods for setting a JobConf's input paths:

```
public static void addInputPath(JobConf conf, Path path)
public static void addInputPaths(JobConf conf, String commaSeparatedPaths)
public static void setInputPaths(JobConf conf, Path... inputPaths)
public static void setInputPaths(JobConf conf, String commaSeparatedPaths)
```

The addInputPath() and addInputPaths() methods add a path or paths to the list of inputs. You can call these methods repeatedly to build the list of paths. The setInputPaths() methods set the entire list of paths in one go (replacing any paths set on the JobConf in previous calls).

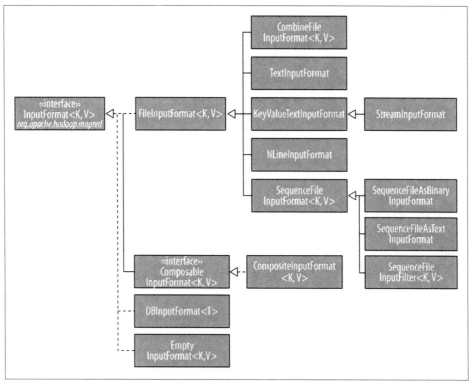

Figure 7-2. InputFormat class hierarchy

A path may represent a file, a directory, or, by using a glob, a collection of files and directories. A path representing a directory includes all the files in the directory as input to the job. See "File patterns" on page 60 for more on using globs.

 The contents of a directory specified as an input path are not processed recursively. In fact, the directory should only contain files: if the directory contains a subdirectory, it will be interpreted as a file, which will cause an error. The way to handle this case is to use a file glob or a filter to select only the files in the directory based on a name pattern.

The add and set methods allow files to be specified by inclusion only. To exclude certain files from the input, you can set a filter using the `setInputPathFilter()` method on `FileInputFormat`:

```
public static void setInputPathFilter(JobConf conf,
                               Class<? extends PathFilter> filter)
```

Filters are discussed in more detail in "PathFilter" on page 61.

Even if you don't set a filter, `FileInputFormat` uses a default filter that excludes hidden files (those whose names begin with a dot or an underscore). If you set a filter by calling `setInputPathFilter()`, it acts in addition to the default filter. In other words, only non-hidden files that are accepted by your filter get through.

Paths and filters can be set through configuration properties, too (Table 7-3), which can be handy for Streaming and Pipes. Setting paths is done with the `-input` option for both Streaming and Pipes interfaces, so setting paths directly is not usually needed.

Table 7-3. Input path and filter properties

Property name	Type	Default value	Description
`mapred.input.dir`	comma-separated paths	none	The input files for a job. Paths that contain commas should have those commas escaped by a backslash character. For example, the glob `{a,b}` would be escaped as `{a\,b}`.
`mapred.input.path Filter.class`	`PathFilter` classname	none	The filter to apply to the input files for a job.

FileInputFormat input splits

Given a set of files, how does `FileInputFormat` turn them into splits? `FileInputFormat` splits only large files. Here "large" means larger than an HDFS block. The split size is normally the size of an HDFS block, which is appropriate for most applications; however, it is possible to control this value by setting various Hadoop properties, as shown in Table 7-4.

Table 7-4. Properties for controlling split size

Property name	Type	Default value	Description
`mapred.min.split.size`	int	1	The smallest valid size in bytes for a file split.
`mapred.max.split.size`[a]	long	`Long.MAX_VALUE`, that is 9223372036854775807	The largest valid size in bytes for a file split.
`dfs.block.size`	long	64 MB, that is 67108864	The size of a block in HDFS in bytes.

[a] This property is not present in the old MapReduce API (with the exception of `CombineFileInputFormat`). Instead, it is calculated indirectly as the size of the total input for the job, divided by the guide number of map tasks specified by `mapred.map.tasks` (or the `setNumMapTasks()` method on `JobConf`). Because `mapred.map.tasks` defaults to 1, this makes the maximum split size the size of the input.

The minimum split size is usually 1 byte, although some formats have a lower bound on the split size. (For example, sequence files insert sync entries every so often in the stream, so the minimum split size has to be large enough to ensure that every split has a sync point to allow the reader to resynchronize with a record boundary.)

Applications may impose a minimum split size: by setting this to a value larger than the block size, they can force splits to be larger than a block. There is no good reason for doing this when using HDFS, since doing so will increase the number of blocks that are not local to a map task.

The maximum split size defaults to the maximum value that can be represented by a Java long type. It has an effect only when it is less than the block size, forcing splits to be smaller than a block.

The split size is calculated by the formula (see the computeSplitSize() method in FileInputFormat):

    max(minimumSize, min(maximumSize, blockSize))

by default:

    minimumSize < blockSize < maximumSize

so the split size is blockSize. Various settings for these parameters and how they affect the final split size are illustrated in Table 7-5.

Table 7-5. Examples of how to control the split size

Minimum split size	Maximum split size	Block size	Split size	Comment
1 (default)	Long.MAX_VALUE (default)	64 MB (default)	64 MB	By default, split size is the same as the default block size.
1 (default)	Long.MAX_VALUE (default)	128 MB	128 MB	The most natural way to increase the split size is to have larger blocks in HDFS, by setting dfs.block.size, or on a per-file basis at file construction time.
128 MB	Long.MAX_VALUE (default)	64 MB (default)	128 MB	Making the minimum split size greater than the block size increases the split size, but at the cost of locality.
1 (default)	32 MB	64 MB (default)	32 MB	Making the maximum split size less than the block size decreases the split size.

Small files and CombineFileInputFormat

Hadoop works better with a small number of large files than a large number of small files. One reason for this is that FileInputFormat generates splits in such a way that each split is all or part of a single file. If the file is very small ("small" means significantly smaller than an HDFS block) and there are a lot of them, then each map task will process very little input, and there will be a lot of them (one per file), each of which imposes extra bookkeeping overhead. Compare a 1 GB file broken into sixteen 64 MB blocks, and 10,000 or so 100 KB files. The 10,000 files use one map each, and the job time can be tens or hundreds of times slower than the equivalent one with a single input file and 16 map tasks.

The situation is alleviated somewhat by CombineFileInputFormat, which was designed to work well with small files. Where FileInputFormat creates a split per file, CombineFileInputFormat packs many files into each split so that each mapper has more to process. Crucially, CombineFileInputFormat takes node and rack locality into account when deciding which blocks to place in the same split, so it does not compromise the speed at which it can process the input in a typical MapReduce job.

Of course, if possible, it is still a good idea to avoid the many small files case since MapReduce works best when it can operate at the transfer rate of the disks in the cluster, and processing many small files increases the number of seeks that are needed to run a job. Also, storing large numbers of small files in HDFS is wasteful of the namenode's memory. One technique for avoiding the many small files case is to merge small files into larger files by using a SequenceFile: the keys can act as filenames (or a constant such as NullWritable, if not needed) and the values as file contents. See Example 7-4. But if you already have a large number of small files in HDFS, then CombineFileInput Format is worth trying.

CombineFileInputFormat isn't just good for small files—it can bring benefits when processing large files, too. Essentially, CombineFileInputFor mat decouples the amount of data that a mapper consumes from the block size of the files in HDFS.

If your mappers can process each block in a matter of seconds, then you could use CombineFileInputFormat with the maximum split size set to a small multiple of the number of blocks (by setting the mapred.max.split.size property in bytes) so that each mapper processes more than one block. In return, the overall processing time falls, since proportionally fewer mappers run, which reduces the overhead in task bookkeeping and startup time associated with a large number of short-lived mappers.

Since CombineFileInputFormat is an abstract class without any concrete classes (unlike FileInputFormat), you need to do a bit more work to use it. (Hopefully, common implementations will be added to the library over time.) For example, to have the CombineFileInputFormat equivalent of TextInputFormat, you would create a concrete subclass of CombineFileInputFormat and implement the getRecordReader() method.

Preventing splitting

Some applications don't want files to be split so that a single mapper can process each input file in its entirety. For example, a simple way to check if all the records in a file are sorted is to go through the records in order, checking whether each record is not less than the preceding one. Implemented as a map task, this algorithm will work only if one map processes the whole file.[‡]

There are a couple of ways to ensure that an existing file is not split. The first (quick and dirty) way is to increase the minimum split size to be larger than the largest file in your system. Setting it to its maximum value, Long.MAX_VALUE, has this effect. The second is to subclass the concrete subclass of FileInputFormat that you want to use, to override the isSplitable() method[§] to return false. For example, here's a nonsplittable TextInputFormat:

```
import org.apache.hadoop.fs.*;
import org.apache.hadoop.mapred.TextInputFormat;

public class NonSplittableTextInputFormat extends TextInputFormat {
  @Override
  protected boolean isSplitable(FileSystem fs, Path file) {
    return false;
  }
}
```

File information in the mapper

A mapper processing a file input split can find information about the split by reading some special properties from its job configuration object, which may be obtained by implementing configure() in your Mapper implementation to get access to the JobConf object. Table 7-6 lists the properties available. These are in addition to the ones available to all mappers and reducers, listed in "The Task Execution Environment" on page 186.

Table 7-6. File split properties

Property name	Type	Description
map.input.file	String	The path of the input file being processed
map.input.start	long	The byte offset of the start of the split
map.input.length	long	The length of the split in bytes

In the next section, you shall see how to use this when we need to access the split's filename.

[‡] This is how the mapper in SortValidator.RecordStatsChecker is implemented.

[§] In the method name isSplitable(), "splitable" has a single "t." It is usually spelled "splittable," which is the spelling I have used in this book.

Processing a whole file as a record

A related requirement that sometimes crops up is for mappers to have access to the full contents of a file. Not splitting the file gets you part of the way there, but you also need to have a RecordReader that delivers the file contents as the value of the record. The listing for WholeFileInputFormat in Example 7-2 shows a way of doing this.

Example 7-2. An InputFormat for reading a whole file as a record

```
public class WholeFileInputFormat
    extends FileInputFormat<NullWritable, BytesWritable> {

  @Override
  protected boolean isSplitable(FileSystem fs, Path filename) {
    return false;
  }

  @Override
  public RecordReader<NullWritable, BytesWritable> getRecordReader(
      InputSplit split, JobConf job, Reporter reporter) throws IOException {

    return new WholeFileRecordReader((FileSplit) split, job);
  }
}
```

WholeFileInputFormat defines a format where the keys are not used, represented by NullWritable, and the values are the file contents, represented by BytesWritable instances. It defines two methods. First, the format is careful to specify that input files should never be split, by overriding isSplitable() to return false. Second, we implement getRecordReader() to return a custom implementation of RecordReader, which appears in Example 7-3.

Example 7-3. The RecordReader used by WholeFileInputFormat for reading a whole file as a record

```
class WholeFileRecordReader implements RecordReader<NullWritable, BytesWritable> {

  private FileSplit fileSplit;
  private Configuration conf;
  private boolean processed = false;

  public WholeFileRecordReader(FileSplit fileSplit, Configuration conf)
      throws IOException {
    this.fileSplit = fileSplit;
    this.conf = conf;
  }

  @Override
  public NullWritable createKey() {
    return NullWritable.get();
  }

  @Override
  public BytesWritable createValue() {
    return new BytesWritable();
```

```
  }

  @Override
  public long getPos() throws IOException {
    return processed ? fileSplit.getLength() : 0;
  }

  @Override
  public float getProgress() throws IOException {
    return processed ? 1.0f : 0.0f;
  }

  @Override
  public boolean next(NullWritable key, BytesWritable value) throws IOException {
    if (!processed) {
      byte[] contents = new byte[(int) fileSplit.getLength()];
      Path file = fileSplit.getPath();
      FileSystem fs = file.getFileSystem(conf);
      FSDataInputStream in = null;
      try {
        in = fs.open(file);
        IOUtils.readFully(in, contents, 0, contents.length);
        value.set(contents, 0, contents.length);
      } finally {
        IOUtils.closeStream(in);
      }
      processed = true;
      return true;
    }
    return false;
  }

  @Override
  public void close() throws IOException {
    // do nothing
  }
}
```

WholeFileRecordReader is responsible for taking a FileSplit and converting it into a
single record, with a null key and a value containing the bytes of the file. Because there
is only a single record, WholeFileRecordReader has either processed it or not, so it maintains a boolean called processed. If, when the next() method is called, the file has not
been processed, then we open the file, create a byte array whose length is the length of
the file, and use the Hadoop IOUtils class to slurp the file into the byte array. Then we
set the array on the BytesWritable instance that was passed into the next() method,
and return true to signal that a record has been read.

The other methods are straightforward bookkeeping methods for creating the correct
key and value types, getting the position and progress of the reader, and a close()
method, which is invoked by the MapReduce framework when the reader is done with.

To demonstrate how WholeFileInputFormat can be used, consider a MapReduce job for packaging small files into sequence files, where the key is the original filename, and the value is the content of the file. The listing is in Example 7-4.

Example 7-4. A MapReduce program for packaging a collection of small files as a single SequenceFile

```java
public class SmallFilesToSequenceFileConverter extends Configured
  implements Tool {

  static class SequenceFileMapper extends MapReduceBase
      implements Mapper<NullWritable, BytesWritable, Text, BytesWritable> {

    private JobConf conf;

    @Override
    public void configure(JobConf conf) {
      this.conf = conf;
    }

    @Override
    public void map(NullWritable key, BytesWritable value,
        OutputCollector<Text, BytesWritable> output, Reporter reporter)
        throws IOException {

      String filename = conf.get("map.input.file");
      output.collect(new Text(filename), value);
    }

  }

  @Override
  public int run(String[] args) throws IOException {
    JobConf conf = JobBuilder.parseInputAndOutput(this, getConf(), args);
    if (conf == null) {
      return -1;
    }

    conf.setInputFormat(WholeFileInputFormat.class);
    conf.setOutputFormat(SequenceFileOutputFormat.class);

    conf.setOutputKeyClass(Text.class);
    conf.setOutputValueClass(BytesWritable.class);

    conf.setMapperClass(SequenceFileMapper.class);
    conf.setReducerClass(IdentityReducer.class);

    JobClient.runJob(conf);
    return 0;
  }
  public static void main(String[] args) throws Exception {
    int exitCode = ToolRunner.run(new SmallFilesToSequenceFileConverter(), args);
    System.exit(exitCode);
  }
}
```

Since the input format is a `WholeFileInputFormat`, the mapper has to find only the filename for the input file split. It does this by retrieving the `map.input.file` property from the `JobConf`, which is set to the split's filename by the MapReduce framework, but only for splits that are `FileSplit` instances (this includes most subclasses of `FileInputFormat`). The reducer is the `IdentityReducer`, and the output format is a `SequenceFileOutputFormat`.

Here's a run on a few small files. We've chosen to use two reducers, so we get two output sequence files:

```
% hadoop jar job.jar SmallFilesToSequenceFileConverter \
  -conf conf/hadoop-localhost.xml -D mapred.reduce.tasks=2 input/smallfiles output
```

Two part files are created, each of which is a sequence file, which we can inspect with the -text option to the filesystem shell:

```
% hadoop fs -conf conf/hadoop-localhost.xml -text output/part-00000
hdfs://localhost/user/tom/input/smallfiles/a    61 61 61 61 61 61 61 61 61 61
hdfs://localhost/user/tom/input/smallfiles/c    63 63 63 63 63 63 63 63 63 63
hdfs://localhost/user/tom/input/smallfiles/e
% hadoop fs -conf conf/hadoop-localhost.xml -text output/part-00001
hdfs://localhost/user/tom/input/smallfiles/b    62 62 62 62 62 62 62 62 62 62
hdfs://localhost/user/tom/input/smallfiles/d    64 64 64 64 64 64 64 64 64 64
hdfs://localhost/user/tom/input/smallfiles/f    66 66 66 66 66 66 66 66 66 66
```

The input files were named *a*, *b*, *c*, *d*, *e*, and *f*, and each contained 10 characters of the corresponding letter (so, for example, *a* contained 10 "a" characters), except *e*, which was empty. We can see this in the textual rendering of the sequence files, which prints the filename followed by the hex representation of the file.

There's at least one way we could improve this program. As mentioned earlier, having one mapper per file is inefficient, so subclassing `CombineFileInputFormat` instead of `FileInputFormat` would be a better approach. Also, for a related technique of packing files into a Hadoop Archive, rather than a sequence file, see the section "Hadoop Archives" on page 71.

Text Input

Hadoop excels at processing unstructured text. In this section, we discuss the different `InputFormats` that Hadoop provides to process text.

TextInputFormat

`TextInputFormat` is the default `InputFormat`. Each record is a line of input. The key, a `LongWritable`, is the byte offset within the file of the beginning of the line. The value is the contents of the line, excluding any line terminators (newline, carriage return), and is packaged as a `Text` object. So a file containing the following text:

```
On the top of the Crumpetty Tree
The Quangle Wangle sat,
```

```
But his face you could not see,
On account of his Beaver Hat.
```

is divided into one split of four records. The records are interpreted as the following key-value pairs:

```
(0, On the top of the Crumpetty Tree)
(33, The Quangle Wangle sat,)
(57, But his face you could not see,)
(89, On account of his Beaver Hat.)
```

Clearly, the keys are *not* line numbers. This would be impossible to implement in general, in that a file is broken into splits, at byte, not line, boundaries. Splits are processed independently. Line numbers are really a sequential notion: you have to keep a count of lines as you consume them, so knowing the line number within a split would be possible, but not within the file.

However, the offset within the file of each line is known by each split independently of the other splits, since each split knows the size of the preceding splits and just adds this on to the offsets within the split to produce a global file offset. The offset is usually sufficient for applications that need a unique identifier for each line. Combined with the file's name, it is unique within the filesystem. Of course, if all the lines are a fixed width, then calculating the line number is simply a matter of dividing the offset by the width.

The Relationship Between Input Splits and HDFS Blocks

The logical records that `FileInputFormat`s define do not usually fit neatly into HDFS blocks. For example, a `TextInputFormat`'s logical records are lines, which will cross HDFS boundaries more often than not. This has no bearing on the functioning of your program—lines are not missed or broken, for example—but it's worth knowing about, as it does mean that data-local maps (that is, maps that are running on the same host as their input data) will perform some remote reads. The slight overhead this causes is not normally significant.

Figure 7-3 shows an example. A single file is broken into lines, and the line boundaries do not correspond with the HDFS block boundaries. Splits honor logical record boundaries, in this case lines, so we see that the first split contains line 5, even though it spans the first and second block. The second split starts at line 6.

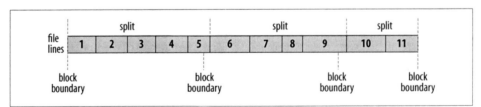

Figure 7-3. Logical records and HDFS blocks for TextInputFormat

KeyValueTextInputFormat

TextInputFormat's keys, being simply the offset within the file, are not normally very useful. It is common for each line in a file to be a key-value pair, separated by a delimiter such as a tab character. For example, this is the output produced by TextOutputFormat, Hadoop's default OutputFormat. To interpret such files correctly, KeyValueTextInputFormat is appropriate.

You can specify the separator via the key.value.separator.in.input.line property. It is a tab character by default. Consider the following input file, where → represents a (horizontal) tab character:

```
line1→On the top of the Crumpetty Tree
line2→The Quangle Wangle sat,
line3→But his face you could not see,
line4→On account of his Beaver Hat.
```

Like in the TextInputFormat case, the input is in a single split comprising four records, although this time the keys are the Text sequences before the tab in each line:

```
(line1, On the top of the Crumpetty Tree)
(line2, The Quangle Wangle sat,)
(line3, But his face you could not see,)
(line4, On account of his Beaver Hat.)
```

NLineInputFormat

With TextInputFormat and KeyValueTextInputFormat, each mapper receives a variable number of lines of input. The number depends on the size of the split and the length of the lines. If you want your mappers to receive a fixed number of lines of input, then NLineInputFormat is the InputFormat to use. Like TextInputFormat, the keys are the byte offsets within the file and the values are the lines themselves.

N refers to the number of lines of input that each mapper receives. With N set to one (the default), each mapper receives exactly one line of input. The mapred.line.input.format.linespermap property controls the value of N. By way of example, consider these four lines again:

```
On the top of the Crumpetty Tree
The Quangle Wangle sat,
But his face you could not see,
On account of his Beaver Hat.
```

If, for example, N is two, then each split contains two lines. One mapper will receive the first two key-value pairs:

```
(0, On the top of the Crumpetty Tree)
(33, The Quangle Wangle sat,)
```

And another mapper will receive the second two key-value pairs:

```
(57, But his face you could not see,)
(89, On account of his Beaver Hat.)
```

The keys and values are the same as `TextInputFormat` produces. What is different is the way the splits are constructed.

Usually, having a map task for a small number of lines of input is inefficient (due to the overhead in task setup), but there are applications that take a small amount of input data and run an extensive (that is, CPU-intensive) computation for it, then emit their output. Simulations are a good example. By creating an input file that specifies input parameters, one per line, you can perform a *parameter sweep*: run a set of simulations in parallel to find how a model varies as the parameter changes.

 If you have long-running simulations, you may fall afoul of task time-outs. When a task doesn't report progress for more than 10 minutes, then the tasktracker assumes it has failed and aborts the process (see "Task Failure" on page 173).

The best way to guard against this is to report progress periodically, by writing a status message, or incrementing a counter, for example. See "What Constitutes Progress in MapReduce?" on page 172.

Another example is using Hadoop to bootstrap data loading from multiple data sources, such as databases. You create a "seed" input file that lists the data sources, one per line. Then each mapper is allocated a single data source, and it loads the data from that source into HDFS. The job doesn't need the reduce phase, so the number of reducers should be set to zero (by calling `setNumReduceTasks()` on `Job`). Furthermore, MapReduce jobs can be run to process the data loaded into HDFS. See Appendix C for an example.

XML

Most XML parsers operate on whole XML documents, so if a large XML document is made up of multiple input splits, then it is a challenge to parse these individually. Of course, you can process the entire XML document in one mapper (if it is not too large) using the technique in "Processing a whole file as a record" on page 206.

Large XML documents that are composed of a series of "records" (XML document fragments) can be broken into these records using simple string or regular-expression matching to find start and end tags of records. This alleviates the problem when the document is split by the framework, since the next start tag of a record is easy to find by simply scanning from the start of the split, just like `TextInputFormat` finds newline boundaries.

Hadoop comes with a class for this purpose called StreamXmlRecordReader (which is in the org.apache.hadoop.streaming package, although it can be used outside of Streaming). You can use it by setting your input format to StreamInputFormat and setting the stream.recordreader.class property to org.apache.hadoop.streaming.StreamXmlRecordReader. The reader is configured by setting job configuration properties to tell it the patterns for the start and end tags (see the class documentation for details).‖

To take an example, Wikipedia provides dumps of its content in XML form, which are appropriate for processing in parallel using MapReduce using this approach. The data is contained in one large XML wrapper document, which contains a series of elements, such as page elements that contain a page's content and associated metadata. Using StreamXmlRecordReader, the page elements can be interpreted as records for processing by a mapper.

Binary Input

Hadoop MapReduce is not just restricted to processing textual data—it has support for binary formats, too.

SequenceFileInputFormat

Hadoop's sequence file format stores sequences of binary key-value pairs. They are well suited as a format for MapReduce data since they are splittable (they have sync points so that readers can synchronize with record boundaries from an arbitrary point in the file, such as the start of a split), they support compression as a part of the format, and they can store arbitrary types using a variety of serialization frameworks. (These topics are covered in "SequenceFile" on page 116.)

To use data from sequence files as the input to MapReduce, you use SequenceFileInputFormat. The keys and values are determined by the sequence file, and you need to make sure that your map input types correspond. For example, if your sequence file has IntWritable keys and Text values, like the one created in Chapter 4, then the map signature would be Mapper<IntWritable, Text, K, V>, where K and V are the types of the map's output keys and values.

 Although its name doesn't give it away, SequenceFileInputFormat can read MapFiles as well as sequence files. If it finds a directory where it was expecting a sequence file, SequenceFileInputFormat assumes that it is reading a MapFile and uses its data file. This is why there is no MapFileInputFormat class.

‖ See Mahout's XmlInputFormat (available from *http://mahout.apache.org/*) for an improved XML input format.

SequenceFileAsTextInputFormat

SequenceFileAsTextInputFormat is a variant of SequenceFileInputFormat that converts the sequence file's keys and values to Text objects. The conversion is performed by calling toString() on the keys and values. This format makes sequence files suitable input for Streaming.

SequenceFileAsBinaryInputFormat

SequenceFileAsBinaryInputFormat is a variant of SequenceFileInputFormat that retrieves the sequence file's keys and values as opaque binary objects. They are encapsulated as BytesWritable objects, and the application is free to interpret the underlying byte array as it pleases. Combined with SequenceFile.Reader's appendRaw() method, this provides a way to use any binary data types with MapReduce (packaged as a sequence file), although plugging into Hadoop's serialization mechanism is normally a cleaner alternative (see "Serialization Frameworks" on page 101).

Multiple Inputs

Although the input to a MapReduce job may consist of multiple input files (constructed by a combination of file globs, filters, and plain paths), all of the input is interpreted by a single InputFormat and a single Mapper. What often happens, however, is that over time, the data format evolves, so you have to write your mapper to cope with all of your legacy formats. Or, you have data sources that provide the same type of data but in different formats. This arises in the case of performing joins of different datasets; see "Reduce-Side Joins" on page 249. For instance, one might be tab-separated plain text, the other a binary sequence file. Even if they are in the same format, they may have different representations and, therefore, need to be parsed differently.

These cases are handled elegantly by using the MultipleInputs class, which allows you to specify the InputFormat and Mapper to use on a per-path basis. For example, if we had weather data from the UK Met Office[#] that we wanted to combine with the NCDC data for our maximum temperature analysis, then we might set up the input as follows:

```
MultipleInputs.addInputPath(conf, ncdcInputPath,
    TextInputFormat.class, MaxTemperatureMapper.class)
MultipleInputs.addInputPath(conf, metOfficeInputPath,
    TextInputFormat.class, MetOfficeMaxTemperatureMapper.class);
```

[#]Met Office data is generally available only to the research and academic community. However, there is a small amount of monthly weather station data available at *http://www.metoffice.gov.uk/climate/uk/stationdata/*.

This code replaces the usual calls to `FileInputFormat.addInputPath()` and `conf.setMap` `perClass()`. Both Met Office and NCDC data is text-based, so we use `TextInputFor` `mat` for each. But the line format of the two data sources is different, so we use two different mappers. The `MaxTemperatureMapper` reads NCDC input data and extracts the year and temperature fields. The `MetOfficeMaxTemperatureMapper` reads Met Office input data and extracts the year and temperature fields. The important thing is that the map outputs have the same types, since the reducers (which are all of the same type) see the aggregated map outputs and are not aware of the different mappers used to produce them.

The `MultipleInputs` class has an overloaded version of `addInputPath()` that doesn't take a mapper:

```
public static void addInputPath(JobConf conf, Path path,
                        Class<? extends InputFormat> inputFormatClass)
```

This is useful when you only have one mapper (set using the JobConf's `setMapper` `Class()` method) but multiple input formats.

Database Input (and Output)

`DBInputFormat` is an input format for reading data from a relational database, using JDBC. Because it doesn't have any sharding capabilities, you need to be careful not to overwhelm the database you are reading from by running too many mappers. For this reason, it is best used for loading relatively small datasets, perhaps for joining with larger datasets from HDFS, using `MultipleInputs`. The corresponding output format is `DBOutputFormat`, which is useful for dumping job outputs (of modest size) into a database.[*]

For an alternative way of moving data between relational databases and HDFS, consider using Sqoop, which is described in Chapter 15.

HBase's `TableInputFormat` is designed to allow a MapReduce program to operate on data stored in an HBase table. `TableOutputFormat` is for writing MapReduce outputs into an HBase table.

Output Formats

Hadoop has output data formats that correspond to the input formats covered in the previous section. The `OutputFormat` class hierarchy appears in Figure 7-4.

---

[*] Instructions for how to use these formats are provided in "Database Access with Hadoop," *http://www .cloudera.com/blog/2009/03/06/database-access-with-hadoop/*, by Aaron Kimball.

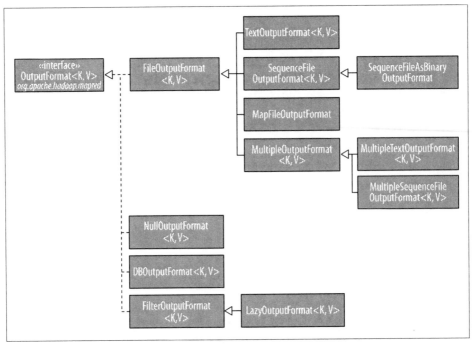

Figure 7-4. OutputFormat class hierarchy

Text Output

The default output format, TextOutputFormat, writes records as lines of text. Its keys and values may be of any type, since TextOutputFormat turns them to strings by calling toString() on them. Each key-value pair is separated by a tab character, although that may be changed using the mapred.textoutputformat.separator property. The counterpart to TextOutputFormat for reading in this case is KeyValueTextInputFormat, since it breaks lines into key-value pairs based on a configurable separator (see "KeyValue-TextInputFormat" on page 211).

You can suppress the key or the value (or both, making this output format equivalent to NullOutputFormat, which emits nothing) from the output using a NullWritable type. This also causes no separator to be written, which makes the output suitable for reading in using TextInputFormat.

Binary Output

SequenceFileOutputFormat

As the name indicates, SequenceFileOutputFormat writes sequence files for its output. This is a good choice of output if it forms the input to a further MapReduce job, since it is compact and is readily compressed. Compression is controlled via the static methods on SequenceFileOutputFormat, as described in "Using Compression in Map-Reduce" on page 84. For an example of how to use SequenceFileOutputFormat, see "Sorting" on page 232.

SequenceFileAsBinaryOutputFormat

SequenceFileAsBinaryOutputFormat is the counterpart to SequenceFileAsBinaryInput Format, and it writes keys and values in raw binary format into a SequenceFile container.

MapFileOutputFormat

MapFileOutputFormat writes MapFiles as output. The keys in a MapFile must be added in order, so you need to ensure that your reducers emit keys in sorted order.

 The reduce *input* keys are guaranteed to be sorted, but the output keys are under the control of the reduce function, and there is nothing in the general MapReduce contract that states that the reduce *output* keys have to be ordered in any way. The extra constraint of sorted reduce output keys is just needed for MapFileOutputFormat.

Multiple Outputs

FileOutputFormat and its subclasses generate a set of files in the output directory. There is one file per reducer, and files are named by the partition number: *part-00000*, *part-00001*, etc. There is sometimes a need to have more control over the naming of the files or to produce multiple files per reducer. MapReduce comes with two libraries to help you do this: MultipleOutputFormat and MultipleOutputs.

An example: Partitioning data

Consider the problem of partitioning the weather dataset by weather station. We would like to run a job whose output is a file per station, with each file containing all the records for that station.

One way of doing this is to have a reducer for each weather station. To arrange this, we need to do two things. First, write a partitioner that puts records from the same weather station into the same partition. Second, set the number of reducers on the job to be the number of weather stations. The partitioner would look like this:

```
public class StationPartitioner implements Partitioner<LongWritable, Text> {

  private NcdcRecordParser parser = new NcdcRecordParser();

  @Override
  public int getPartition(LongWritable key, Text value, int numPartitions) {
    parser.parse(value);
    return getPartition(parser.getStationId());
```

```
    }

    private int getPartition(String stationId) {
      ...
    }

    @Override
    public void configure(JobConf conf) { }
}
```

The getPartition(String) method, whose implementation is not shown, turns the station ID into a partition index. To do this, it needs a list of all the station IDs and then just returns the index of the station ID in the list.

There are two drawbacks to this approach. The first is that since the number of partitions needs to be known before the job is run, so does the number of weather stations. Although the NCDC provides metadata about its stations, there is no guarantee that the IDs encountered in the data match those in the metadata. A station that appears in the metadata but not in the data wastes a reducer slot. Worse, a station that appears in the data but not in the metadata doesn't get a reducer slot—it has to be thrown away. One way of mitigating this problem would be to write a job to extract the unique station IDs, but it's a shame that we need an extra job to do this.

The second drawback is more subtle. It is generally a bad idea to allow the number of partitions to be rigidly fixed by the application, since it can lead to small or uneven-sized partitions. Having many reducers doing a small amount of work isn't an efficient way of organizing a job: it's much better to get reducers to do more work and have fewer of them, as the overhead in running a task is then reduced. Uneven-sized partitions can be difficult to avoid, too. Different weather stations will have gathered a widely varying amount of data: compare a station that opened one year ago to one that has been gathering data for one century. If a few reduce tasks take significantly longer than the others, they will dominate the job execution time and cause it to be longer than it needs to be.

 There are two special cases when it does make sense to allow the application to set the number of partitions (or equivalently, the number of reducers):

Zero reducers
> This is a vacuous case: there are no partitions, as the application needs to run only map tasks.

One reducer
> It can be convenient to run small jobs to combine the output of previous jobs into a single file. This should only be attempted when the amount of data is small enough to be processed comfortably by one reducer.

It is much better to let the cluster drive the number of partitions for a job—the idea being that the more cluster reduce slots are available the faster the job can complete. This is why the default HashPartitioner works so well, as it works with any number of partitions and ensures each partition has a good mix of keys leading to more even-sized partitions.

If we go back to using HashPartitioner, each partition will contain multiple stations, so to create a file per station, we need to arrange for each reducer to write multiple files, which is where MultipleOutputFormat comes in.

MultipleOutputFormat

MultipleOutputFormat allows you to write data to multiple files whose names are derived from the output keys and values. MultipleOutputFormat is an abstract class with two concrete subclasses, MultipleTextOutputFormat and MultipleSequenceFileOutput Format, which are the multiple file equivalents of TextOutputFormat and SequenceFileOutputFormat. MultipleOutputFormat provides a few protected methods that subclasses can override to control the output filename. In Example 7-5, we create a subclass of MultipleTextOutputFormat to override the generateFileNameForKey Value() method to return the station ID, which we extracted from the record value.

Example 7-5. Partitioning whole dataset into files named by the station ID using MultipleOutputFormat

```
public class PartitionByStationUsingMultipleOutputFormat extends Configured
  implements Tool {

  static class StationMapper extends MapReduceBase
    implements Mapper<LongWritable, Text, Text, Text> {

    private NcdcRecordParser parser = new NcdcRecordParser();

    public void map(LongWritable key, Text value,
        OutputCollector<Text, Text> output, Reporter reporter)
        throws IOException {

      parser.parse(value);
      output.collect(new Text(parser.getStationId()), value);
    }
  }

  static class StationReducer extends MapReduceBase
    implements Reducer<Text, Text, NullWritable, Text> {

    @Override
    public void reduce(Text key, Iterator<Text> values,
        OutputCollector<NullWritable, Text> output, Reporter reporter)
        throws IOException {
      while (values.hasNext()) {
        output.collect(NullWritable.get(), values.next());
      }
```

```
    }
  }

  static class StationNameMultipleTextOutputFormat
    extends MultipleTextOutputFormat<NullWritable, Text> {

    private NcdcRecordParser parser = new NcdcRecordParser();

    protected String generateFileNameForKeyValue(NullWritable key, Text value,
        String name) {
      parser.parse(value);
      return parser.getStationId();
    }
  }

  @Override
  public int run(String[] args) throws IOException {
    JobConf conf = JobBuilder.parseInputAndOutput(this, getConf(), args);
    if (conf == null) {
      return -1;
    }

    conf.setMapperClass(StationMapper.class);
    conf.setMapOutputKeyClass(Text.class);
    conf.setReducerClass(StationReducer.class);
    conf.setOutputKeyClass(NullWritable.class);
    conf.setOutputFormat(StationNameMultipleTextOutputFormat.class);

    JobClient.runJob(conf);
    return 0;
  }

  public static void main(String[] args) throws Exception {
    int exitCode = ToolRunner.run(
        new PartitionByStationUsingMultipleOutputFormat(), args);
    System.exit(exitCode);
  }
}
```

StationMapper pulls the station ID from the record and uses it as the key. This causes
records from the same station to go into the same partition. StationReducer replaces
the key with a NullWritable so that when the final output is written using StationName
MultipleTextOutputFormat (which like TextOutputFormat drops NullWritable keys), it
consists solely of weather records (and not the station ID key).

The overall effect is to place all the records for one station in a file named by the station
ID. Here are a few lines of output after running the program over a subset of the total
dataset:

```
-rw-r--r--   3 root supergroup   2887145 2009-04-17 10:34 /output/010010-99999
-rw-r--r--   3 root supergroup   1395129 2009-04-17 10:33 /output/010050-99999
-rw-r--r--   3 root supergroup   2054455 2009-04-17 10:33 /output/010100-99999
-rw-r--r--   3 root supergroup   1422448 2009-04-17 10:34 /output/010280-99999
-rw-r--r--   3 root supergroup   1419378 2009-04-17 10:34 /output/010550-99999
```

```
-rw-r--r--   3 root supergroup   1384421 2009-04-17 10:33 /output/010980-99999
-rw-r--r--   3 root supergroup   1480077 2009-04-17 10:33 /output/011060-99999
-rw-r--r--   3 root supergroup   1400448 2009-04-17 10:33 /output/012030-99999
-rw-r--r--   3 root supergroup    307141 2009-04-17 10:34 /output/012350-99999
-rw-r--r--   3 root supergroup   1433994 2009-04-17 10:33 /output/012620-99999
```

The filename returned by generateFileNameForKeyValue() is actually a path that is interpreted relative to the output directory. It's possible to create subdirectories of arbitrary depth. For example, the following modification partitions the data by station and year so that each year's data is contained in a directory named by the station ID:

```
protected String generateFileNameForKeyValue(NullWritable key, Text value,
    String name) {
  parser.parse(value);
  return parser.getStationId() + "/" + parser.getYear();
}
```

MultipleOutputFormat has more features that are not discussed here, such as the ability to copy the input directory structure and file naming for a map-only job. Please consult the Java documentation for details.

MultipleOutputs

There's a second library in Hadoop for generating multiple outputs, provided by the MultipleOutputs class. Unlike MultipleOutputFormat, MultipleOutputs can emit different types for each output. On the other hand, there is less control over the naming of outputs. The program in Example 7-6 shows how to use MultipleOutputs to partition the dataset by station.

Example 7-6. Partitioning whole dataset into files named by the station ID using MultipleOutputs

```
public class PartitionByStationUsingMultipleOutputs extends Configured
  implements Tool {

  static class StationMapper extends MapReduceBase
    implements Mapper<LongWritable, Text, Text, Text> {

    private NcdcRecordParser parser = new NcdcRecordParser();

    public void map(LongWritable key, Text value,
        OutputCollector<Text, Text> output, Reporter reporter)
        throws IOException {

      parser.parse(value);
      output.collect(new Text(parser.getStationId()), value);
    }
  }

  static class MultipleOutputsReducer extends MapReduceBase
    implements Reducer<Text, Text, NullWritable, Text> {

    private MultipleOutputs multipleOutputs;
```

```java
  @Override
  public void configure(JobConf conf) {
    multipleOutputs = new MultipleOutputs(conf);
  }

  public void reduce(Text key, Iterator<Text> values,
      OutputCollector<NullWritable, Text> output, Reporter reporter)
      throws IOException {

    OutputCollector collector = multipleOutputs.getCollector("station",
        key.toString().replace("-", ""), reporter);
    while (values.hasNext()) {
      collector.collect(NullWritable.get(), values.next());
    }
  }

  @Override
  public void close() throws IOException {
    multipleOutputs.close();
  }
}

@Override
public int run(String[] args) throws IOException {
  JobConf conf = JobBuilder.parseInputAndOutput(this, getConf(), args);
  if (conf == null) {
    return -1;
  }

  conf.setMapperClass(StationMapper.class);
  conf.setMapOutputKeyClass(Text.class);
  conf.setReducerClass(MultipleOutputsReducer.class);
  conf.setOutputKeyClass(NullWritable.class);
  conf.setOutputFormat(NullOutputFormat.class); // suppress empty part file

  MultipleOutputs.addMultiNamedOutput(conf, "station", TextOutputFormat.class,
      NullWritable.class, Text.class);

  JobClient.runJob(conf);
  return 0;
}
  public static void main(String[] args) throws Exception {
    int exitCode = ToolRunner.run(new PartitionByStationUsingMultipleOutputs(),
        args);
    System.exit(exitCode);
  }
}
```

The `MultipleOutputs` class is used to generate additional outputs to the usual output. Outputs are given names and may be written to a single file (called *single named output*) or to multiple files (called *multinamed output*). In this case, we want multiple files, one for each station, so we use a multi named output, which we initialize in the driver by calling the `addMultiNamedOutput()` method of `MultipleOutputs` to specify the name of the output (here `"station"`), the output format, and the output types. In addition, we set the regular output format to be `NullOutputFormat` in order to suppress the usual output.

In the reducer, where we generate the output, we construct an instance of `MultipleOut puts` in the `configure()` method and assign it to an instance variable. We use the `MultipleOutputs` instance in the `reduce()` method to retrieve an `OutputCollector` for the multinamed output. The `getCollector()` method takes the name of the output (`"station"` again) as well as a string identifying the part within the multinamed output. Here we use the station identifier, with the "-" separator in the key removed, since only alphanumeric characters are allowed by `MultipleOutputs`.

The overall effect is to produce output files with the naming scheme `station_<station identifier>-r-<part_number>`. The `r` appears in the name because the output is produced by the reducer, and the part number is appended to be sure that there are no collisions resulting from different partitions (reducers) writing output for the same station. Since we partition by station, it cannot happen in this case (but it can in the general case).

In one run, the first few output files were named as follows (other columns from the directory listing have been dropped):

```
/output/station_01001099999-r-00027
/output/station_01005099999-r-00013
/output/station_01010099999-r-00015
/output/station_01028099999-r-00014
/output/station_01055099999-r-00000
/output/station_01098099999-r-00011
/output/station_01106099999-r-00025
/output/station_01203099999-r-00029
/output/station_01235099999-r-00018
/output/station_01262099999-r-00004
```

What's the Difference Between MultipleOutputFormat and MultipleOutputs?

It's unfortunate (although not necessarily unusual in an open source project) to have two libraries that do almost the same thing, since it is confusing for users. To help you choose which to use, here is a brief comparison:

Feature	MultipleOutputFormat	MultipleOutputs
Complete control over names of files and directories	Yes	No
Different key and value types for different outputs	No	Yes
Use from map and reduce in the same job	No	Yes
Multiple outputs per record	No	Yes
Use with any OutputFormat	No, need to subclass	Yes

So in summary, MultipleOutputs is more fully featured, but MultipleOutputFormat has more control over the output directory structure and file naming.

In the new MapReduce API, the situation is improved, since there is only MultipleOutputs, which supports all the features of the two multiple output classes in the old API.

Lazy Output

FileOutputFormat subclasses will create output (*part-nnnnn*) files, even if they are empty. Some applications prefer that empty files not be created, which is where LazyOutputFormat helps.[†] It is a wrapper output format that ensures that the output file is created only when the first record is emitted for a given partition. To use it, call its setOutputFormatClass() method with the JobConf and the underlying output format.

Streaming and Pipes support a -lazyOutput option to enable LazyOutputFormat.

Database Output

The output formats for writing to relational databases and to HBase are mentioned in "Database Input (and Output)" on page 215.

---

† LazyOutputFormat is available from release 0.21.0 of Hadoop.

## CHAPTER 8

MapReduce Features

This chapter looks at some of the more advanced features of MapReduce, including counters and sorting and joining datasets.

Counters

There are often things you would like to know about the data you are analyzing but that are peripheral to the analysis you are performing. For example, if you were counting invalid records and discovered that the proportion of invalid records in the whole dataset was very high, you might be prompted to check why so many records were being marked as invalid—perhaps there is a bug in the part of the program that detects invalid records? Or if the data were of poor quality and genuinely did have very many invalid records, after discovering this, you might decide to increase the size of the dataset so that the number of good records was large enough for meaningful analysis.

Counters are a useful channel for gathering statistics about the job: for quality control or for application level-statistics. They are also useful for problem diagnosis. If you are tempted to put a log message into your map or reduce task, then it is often better to see whether you can use a counter instead to record that a particular condition occurred. In addition to counter values being much easier to retrieve than log output for large distributed jobs, you get a record of the number of times that condition occurred, which is more work to obtain from a set of logfiles.

Built-in Counters

Hadoop maintains some built-in counters for every job (Table 8-1), which report various metrics for your job. For example, there are counters for the number of bytes and records processed, which allows you to confirm that the expected amount of input was consumed and the expected amount of output was produced.

Table 8-1. Built-in counters

Group	Counter	Description
Map-Reduce Framework	Map input records	The number of input records consumed by all the maps in the job. Incremented every time a record is read from a RecordReader and passed to the map's map() method by the framework.
	Map skipped records	The number of input records skipped by all the maps in the job. See "Skipping Bad Records" on page 185.
	Map input bytes	The number of bytes of uncompressed input consumed by all the maps in the job. Incremented every time a record is read from a RecordReader and passed to the map's map() method by the framework.
	Map output records	The number of map output records produced by all the maps in the job. Incremented every time the collect() method is called on a map's OutputCollector.
	Map output bytes	The number of bytes of uncompressed output produced by all the maps in the job. Incremented every time the collect() method is called on a map's OutputCollector.
	Combine input records	The number of input records consumed by all the combiners (if any) in the job. Incremented every time a value is read from the combiner's iterator over values. Note that this count is the number of values consumed by the combiner, not the number of distinct key groups (which would not be a useful metric, since there is not necessarily one group per key for a combiner; see "Combiner Functions" on page 30, and also "Shuffle and Sort" on page 177).
	Combine output records	The number of output records produced by all the combiners (if any) in the job. Incremented every time the collect() method is called on a combiner's OutputCollector.
	Reduce input groups	The number of distinct key groups consumed by all the reducers in the job. Incremented every time the reducer's reduce() method is called by the framework.
	Reduce input records	The number of input records consumed by all the reducers in the job. Incremented every time a value is read from the reducer's iterator over values. If reducers consume all of their inputs, this count should be the same as the count for Map output records.
	Reduce output records	The number of reduce output records produced by all the maps in the job. Incremented every time the collect() method is called on a reducer's OutputCollector.
	Reduce skipped groups	The number of distinct key groups skipped by all the reducers in the job. See "Skipping Bad Records" on page 185.
	Reduce skipped records	The number of input records skipped by all the reducers in the job.
	Spilled records	The number of records spilled to disk in all map and reduce tasks in the job.
File Systems	*Filesystem* bytes read	The number of bytes read by each filesystem by map and reduce tasks. There is a counter for each filesystem: *Filesystem* may be Local, HDFS, S3, KFS, etc.
	Filesystem bytes written	The number of bytes written by each filesystem by map and reduce tasks.

Group	Counter	Description
Job Counters	Launched map tasks	The number of map tasks that were launched. Includes tasks that were started speculatively.
	Launched reduce tasks	The number of reduce tasks that were launched. Includes tasks that were started speculatively.
	Failed map tasks	The number of map tasks that failed. See "Task Failure" on page 173 for potential causes.
	Failed reduce tasks	The number of reduce tasks that failed.
	Data-local map tasks	The number of map tasks that ran on the same node as their input data.
	Rack-local map tasks	The number of map tasks that ran on a node in the same rack as their input data.
	Other local map tasks	The number of map tasks that ran on a node in a different rack to their input data. Inter-rack bandwidth is scarce, and Hadoop tries to place map tasks close to their input data, so this count should be low.

Counters are maintained by the task with which they are associated, and periodically sent to the tasktracker and then to the jobtracker, so they can be globally aggregated. (This is described in "Progress and Status Updates" on page 170.) The built-in Job Counters are actually maintained by the jobtracker, so they don't need to be sent across the network, unlike all other counters, including user-defined ones.

A task's counters are sent in full every time, rather than sending the counts since the last transmission, since this guards against errors due to lost messages. Furthermore, during a job run, counters may go down if a task fails. Counter values are definitive only once a job has successfully completed.

User-Defined Java Counters

MapReduce allows user code to define a set of counters, which are then incremented as desired in the mapper or reducer. Counters are defined by a Java enum, which serves to group related counters. A job may define an arbitrary number of enums, each with an arbitrary number of fields. The name of the enum is the group name, and the enum's fields are the counter names. Counters are global: the MapReduce framework aggregates them across all maps and reduces to produce a grand total at the end of the job.

We created some counters in Chapter 5 for counting malformed records in the weather dataset. The program in Example 8-1 extends that example to count the number of missing records and the distribution of temperature quality codes.

Example 8-1. Application to run the maximum temperature job, including counting missing and malformed fields and quality codes

```
public class MaxTemperatureWithCounters extends Configured implements Tool {

  enum Temperature {
    MISSING,
    MALFORMED
  }

  static class MaxTemperatureMapperWithCounters extends MapReduceBase
    implements Mapper<LongWritable, Text, Text, IntWritable> {

    private NcdcRecordParser parser = new NcdcRecordParser();

    public void map(LongWritable key, Text value,
        OutputCollector<Text, IntWritable> output, Reporter reporter)
        throws IOException {

      parser.parse(value);
      if (parser.isValidTemperature()) {
        int airTemperature = parser.getAirTemperature();
        output.collect(new Text(parser.getYear()),
            new IntWritable(airTemperature));
      } else if (parser.isMalformedTemperature()) {
        System.err.println("Ignoring possibly corrupt input: " + value);
        reporter.incrCounter(Temperature.MALFORMED, 1);
      } else if (parser.isMissingTemperature()) {
        reporter.incrCounter(Temperature.MISSING, 1);
      }

      // dynamic counter
      reporter.incrCounter("TemperatureQuality", parser.getQuality(), 1);

    }
  }

  @Override
  public int run(String[] args) throws IOException {
    JobConf conf = JobBuilder.parseInputAndOutput(this, getConf(), args);
    if (conf == null) {
      return -1;
    }

    conf.setOutputKeyClass(Text.class);
    conf.setOutputValueClass(IntWritable.class);

    conf.setMapperClass(MaxTemperatureMapperWithCounters.class);
    conf.setCombinerClass(MaxTemperatureReducer.class);
    conf.setReducerClass(MaxTemperatureReducer.class);

    JobClient.runJob(conf);
    return 0;
  }
```

```
public static void main(String[] args) throws Exception {
    int exitCode = ToolRunner.run(new MaxTemperatureWithCounters(), args);
    System.exit(exitCode);
  }
}
```

The best way to see what this program does is run it over the complete dataset:

```
% hadoop jar job.jar MaxTemperatureWithCounters input/ncdc/all output-counters
```

When the job has successfully completed, it prints out the counters at the end (this is done by JobClient's runJob() method). Here are the ones we are interested in:

```
09/04/20 06:33:36 INFO mapred.JobClient:     TemperatureQuality
09/04/20 06:33:36 INFO mapred.JobClient:       2=1246032
09/04/20 06:33:36 INFO mapred.JobClient:       1=973422173
09/04/20 06:33:36 INFO mapred.JobClient:       0=1
09/04/20 06:33:36 INFO mapred.JobClient:       6=40066
09/04/20 06:33:36 INFO mapred.JobClient:       5=158291879
09/04/20 06:33:36 INFO mapred.JobClient:       4=10764500
09/04/20 06:33:36 INFO mapred.JobClient:       9=66136858
09/04/20 06:33:36 INFO mapred.JobClient:     Air Temperature Records
09/04/20 06:33:36 INFO mapred.JobClient:       Malformed=3
09/04/20 06:33:36 INFO mapred.JobClient:       Missing=66136856
```

Dynamic counters

The code makes use of a dynamic counter—one that isn't defined by a Java enum. Since a Java enum's fields are defined at compile time, you can't create new counters on the fly using enums. Here we want to count the distribution of temperature quality codes, and though the format specification defines the values that it can take, it is more convenient to use a dynamic counter to emit the values that it actually takes. The method we use on the Reporter object takes a group and counter name using String names:

```
public void incrCounter(String group, String counter, long amount)
```

The two ways of creating and accessing counters—using enums and using Strings—are actually equivalent since Hadoop turns enums into Strings to send counters over RPC. Enums are slightly easier to work with, provide type safety, and are suitable for most jobs. For the odd occasion when you need to create counters dynamically, you can use the String interface.

Readable counter names

By default, a counter's name is the enum's fully qualified Java classname. These names are not very readable when they appear on the web UI, or in the console, so Hadoop provides a way to change the display names using resource bundles. We've done this here, so we see "Air Temperature Records" instead of "Temperature$MISSING." For dynamic counters, the group and counter names are used for the display names, so this is not normally an issue.

The recipe to provide readable names is as follows. Create a properties file named after the enum, using an underscore as a separator for nested classes. The properties file should be in the same directory as the top-level class containing the enum. The file is named *MaxTemperatureWithCounters_Temperature.properties* for the counters in Example 8-1.

The properties file should contain a single property named CounterGroupName, whose value is the display name for the whole group. Then each field in the enum should have a corresponding property defined for it, whose name is the name of the field suffixed with .name, and whose value is the display name for the counter. Here are the contents of *MaxTemperatureWithCounters_Temperature.properties*:

```
CounterGroupName=Air Temperature Records
MISSING.name=Missing
MALFORMED.name=Malformed
```

Hadoop uses the standard Java localization mechanisms to load the correct properties for the locale you are running in, so, for example, you can create a Chinese version of the properties in a file named *MaxTemperatureWithCounters_Temperature_zh_CN.properties*, and they will be used when running in the zh_CN locale. Refer to the documentation for java.util.PropertyResourceBundle for more information.

Retrieving counters

In addition to being available via the web UI and the command line (using hadoop job -counter), you can retrieve counter values using the Java API. You can do this while the job is running, although it is more usual to get counters at the end of a job run, when they are stable. Example 8-2 shows a program that calculates the proportion of records that have missing temperature fields.

Example 8-2. Application to calculate the proportion of records with missing temperature fields

```
import org.apache.hadoop.conf.Configured;
import org.apache.hadoop.mapred.*;
import org.apache.hadoop.util.*;

public class MissingTemperatureFields extends Configured implements Tool {

  @Override
  public int run(String[] args) throws Exception {
    if (args.length != 1) {
      JobBuilder.printUsage(this, "<job ID>");
      return -1;
    }
    JobClient jobClient = new JobClient(new JobConf(getConf()));
    String jobID = args[0];
    RunningJob job = jobClient.getJob(JobID.forName(jobID));
    if (job == null) {
      System.err.printf("No job with ID %s found.\n", jobID);
      return -1;
    }
```

```
  if (!job.isComplete()) {
    System.err.printf("Job %s is not complete.\n", jobID);
    return -1;
  }

  Counters counters = job.getCounters();
  long missing = counters.getCounter(
      MaxTemperatureWithCounters.Temperature.MISSING);

  long total = counters.findCounter("org.apache.hadoop.mapred.Task$Counter",
      "MAP_INPUT_RECORDS").getCounter();

  System.out.printf("Records with missing temperature fields: %.2f%%\n",
      100.0 * missing / total);
  return 0;
  }
  public static void main(String[] args) throws Exception {
    int exitCode = ToolRunner.run(new MissingTemperatureFields(), args);
    System.exit(exitCode);
  }
}
```

First we retrieve a RunningJob object from a JobClient, by calling the getJob() method with the job ID. We check whether there is actually a job with the given ID. There may not be, either because the ID was incorrectly specified or because the jobtracker no longer has a reference to the job (only the last 100 jobs are kept in memory, controlled by mapred.jobtracker.completeuserjobs.maximum, and all are cleared out if the jobtracker is restarted).

After confirming that the job has completed, we call the RunningJob's getCounters() method, which returns a Counters object, encapsulating all the counters for a job. The Counters class provides various methods for finding the names and values of counters. We use the getCounter() method, which takes an enum to find the number of records that had a missing temperature field.

There are also findCounter() methods, all of which return a Counter object. We use this form to retrieve the built-in counter for map input records. To do this, we refer to the counter by its group name—the fully qualified Java classname for the enum—and counter name (both strings).[*]

Finally, we print the proportion of records that had a missing temperature field. Here's what we get for the whole weather dataset:

```
% hadoop jar job.jar MissingTemperatureFields job_200904200610_0003
Records with missing temperature fields: 5.47%
```

---

[*] The built-in counter's enums are not currently a part of the public API, so this is the only way to retrieve them. From release 0.21.0, counters are available via the JobCounter and TaskCounter enums in the org.apache.hadoop.mapreduce package.

User-Defined Streaming Counters

A Streaming MapReduce program can increment counters by sending a specially formatted line to the standard error stream, which is co-opted as a control channel in this case. The line must have the following format:

```
reporter:counter:group,counter,amount
```

This snippet in Python shows how to increment the "Missing" counter in the "Temperature" group by one:

```
sys.stderr.write("reporter:counter:Temperature,Missing,1\n")
```

In a similar way, a status message may be sent with a line formatted like this:

```
reporter:status:message
```

Sorting

The ability to sort data is at the heart of MapReduce. Even if your application isn't concerned with sorting per se, it may be able to use the sorting stage that MapReduce provides to organize its data. In this section, we will examine different ways of sorting datasets and how you can control the sort order in MapReduce.

Preparation

We are going to sort the weather dataset by temperature. Storing temperatures as Text objects doesn't work for sorting purposes, since signed integers don't sort lexicographically.[†] Instead, we are going to store the data using sequence files whose IntWritable keys represent the temperature (and sort correctly), and whose Text values are the lines of data.

The MapReduce job in Example 8-3 is a map-only job that also filters the input to remove records that don't have a valid temperature reading. Each map creates a single block-compressed sequence file as output. It is invoked with the following command:

```
% hadoop jar job.jar SortDataPreprocessor input/ncdc/all input/ncdc/all-seq
```

Example 8-3. A MapReduce program for transforming the weather data into SequenceFile format

```
public class SortDataPreprocessor extends Configured implements Tool {

  static class CleanerMapper extends MapReduceBase
    implements Mapper<LongWritable, Text, IntWritable, Text> {

    private NcdcRecordParser parser = new NcdcRecordParser();
```

---

† One commonly used workaround for this problem—particularly in text-based Streaming applications—is to add an offset to eliminate all negative numbers, and left pad with zeros, so all numbers are the same number of characters. However, see "Streaming" on page 245 for another approach.

```
    public void map(LongWritable key, Text value,
        OutputCollector<IntWritable, Text> output, Reporter reporter)
        throws IOException {

      parser.parse(value);
      if (parser.isValidTemperature()) {
        output.collect(new IntWritable(parser.getAirTemperature()), value);
      }
    }
  }

  @Override
  public int run(String[] args) throws IOException {
    JobConf conf = JobBuilder.parseInputAndOutput(this, getConf(), args);
    if (conf == null) {
      return -1;
    }

    conf.setMapperClass(CleanerMapper.class);
    conf.setOutputKeyClass(IntWritable.class);
    conf.setOutputValueClass(Text.class);
    conf.setNumReduceTasks(0);
    conf.setOutputFormat(SequenceFileOutputFormat.class);
    SequenceFileOutputFormat.setCompressOutput(conf, true);
    SequenceFileOutputFormat.setOutputCompressorClass(conf, GzipCodec.class);
    SequenceFileOutputFormat.setOutputCompressionType(conf,
        CompressionType.BLOCK);

    JobClient.runJob(conf);
    return 0;
  }
  public static void main(String[] args) throws Exception {
    int exitCode = ToolRunner.run(new SortDataPreprocessor(), args);
    System.exit(exitCode);
  }
}
```

Partial Sort

In "The Default MapReduce Job" on page 192, we saw that, by default, MapReduce
will sort input records by their keys. Example 8-4 is a variation for sorting sequence
files with IntWritable keys.

*Example 8-4. A MapReduce program for sorting a SequenceFile with IntWritable keys using the
default HashPartitioner*

```
public class SortByTemperatureUsingHashPartitioner extends Configured
  implements Tool {

  @Override
  public int run(String[] args) throws IOException {
    JobConf conf = JobBuilder.parseInputAndOutput(this, getConf(), args);
    if (conf == null) {
      return -1;
```

```
    }

    conf.setInputFormat(SequenceFileInputFormat.class);
    conf.setOutputKeyClass(IntWritable.class);
    conf.setOutputFormat(SequenceFileOutputFormat.class);
    SequenceFileOutputFormat.setCompressOutput(conf, true);
    SequenceFileOutputFormat.setOutputCompressorClass(conf, GzipCodec.class);
    SequenceFileOutputFormat.setOutputCompressionType(conf,
        CompressionType.BLOCK);

    JobClient.runJob(conf);
    return 0;
  }

  public static void main(String[] args) throws Exception {
    int exitCode = ToolRunner.run(new SortByTemperatureUsingHashPartitioner(),
        args);
    System.exit(exitCode);
  }
}
```

Controlling Sort Order

The sort order for keys is controlled by a `RawComparator`, which is found as follows:

1. If the property `mapred.output.key.comparator.class` is set, an instance of that class is used. (The `setOutputKeyComparatorClass()` method on `JobConf` is a convenient way to set this property.)

2. Otherwise, keys must be a subclass of `WritableComparable`, and the registered comparator for the key class is used.

3. If there is no registered comparator, then a `RawComparator` is used that deserializes the byte streams being compared into objects and delegates to the `WritableCompar able`'s `compareTo()` method.

These rules reinforce why it's important to register optimized versions of `RawCompara tors` for your own custom `Writable` classes (which is covered in "Implementing a Raw-Comparator for speed" on page 99), and also that it's straightforward to override the sort order by setting your own comparator (we do this in "Secondary Sort" on page 241).

Suppose we run this program using 30 reducers:[‡]

```
% hadoop jar job.jar SortByTemperatureUsingHashPartitioner \
    -D mapred.reduce.tasks=30 input/ncdc/all-seq output-hashsort
```

[‡] See "Sorting and merging SequenceFiles" on page 122 for how to do the same thing using the sort program example that comes with Hadoop.

This command produces 30 output files, each of which is sorted. However, there is no easy way to combine the files (by concatenation, for example, in the case of plain-text files) to produce a globally sorted file. For many applications, this doesn't matter. For example, having a partially sorted set of files is fine if you want to do lookups.

An application: Partitioned MapFile lookups

To perform lookups by key, for instance, having multiple files works well. If we change the output format to be a `MapFileOutputFormat`, as shown in Example 8-5, then the output is 30 map files, which we can perform lookups against.

Example 8-5. A MapReduce program for sorting a SequenceFile and producing MapFiles as output

```
public class SortByTemperatureToMapFile extends Configured implements Tool {

  @Override
  public int run(String[] args) throws IOException {
    JobConf conf = JobBuilder.parseInputAndOutput(this, getConf(), args);
    if (conf == null) {
      return -1;
    }

    conf.setInputFormat(SequenceFileInputFormat.class);
    conf.setOutputKeyClass(IntWritable.class);
    conf.setOutputFormat(MapFileOutputFormat.class);
    SequenceFileOutputFormat.setCompressOutput(conf, true);
    SequenceFileOutputFormat.setOutputCompressorClass(conf, GzipCodec.class);
    SequenceFileOutputFormat.setOutputCompressionType(conf,
        CompressionType.BLOCK);

    JobClient.runJob(conf);
    return 0;
  }

  public static void main(String[] args) throws Exception {
    int exitCode = ToolRunner.run(new SortByTemperatureToMapFile(), args);
    System.exit(exitCode);
  }
}
```

`MapFileOutputFormat` provides a pair of convenience static methods for performing lookups against MapReduce output; their use is shown in Example 8-6.

Example 8-6. Retrieve the first entry with a given key from a collection of MapFiles

```
public class LookupRecordByTemperature extends Configured implements Tool {

  @Override
  public int run(String[] args) throws Exception {
    if (args.length != 2) {
      JobBuilder.printUsage(this, "<path> <key>");
      return -1;
    }
```

```
    Path path = new Path(args[0]);
    IntWritable key = new IntWritable(Integer.parseInt(args[1]));
    FileSystem fs = path.getFileSystem(getConf());

    Reader[] readers = MapFileOutputFormat.getReaders(fs, path, getConf());
    Partitioner<IntWritable, Text> partitioner =
      new HashPartitioner<IntWritable, Text>();
    Text val = new Text();
    Writable entry =
      MapFileOutputFormat.getEntry(readers, partitioner, key, val);
    if (entry == null) {
      System.err.println("Key not found: " + key);
      return -1;
    }
    NcdcRecordParser parser = new NcdcRecordParser();
    parser.parse(val.toString());
    System.out.printf("%s\t%s\n", parser.getStationId(), parser.getYear());
    return 0;
  }

  public static void main(String[] args) throws Exception {
    int exitCode = ToolRunner.run(new LookupRecordByTemperature(), args);
    System.exit(exitCode);
  }
}
```

The getReaders() method opens a MapFile.Reader for each of the output files created by the MapReduce job. The getEntry() method then uses the partitioner to choose the reader for the key and finds the value for that key by calling Reader's get() method. If getEntry() returns null, it means no matching key was found. Otherwise, it returns the value, which we translate into a station ID and year.

To see this in action, let's find the first entry for a temperature of −10°C (remember that temperatures are stored as integers representing tenths of a degree, which is why we ask for a temperature of -100):

```
% hadoop jar job.jar LookupRecordByTemperature output-hashmapsort -100
357460-99999    1956
```

We can also use the readers directly, in order to get all the records for a given key. The array of readers that is returned is ordered by partition, so that the reader for a given key may be found using the same partitioner that was used in the MapReduce job:

```
Reader reader = readers[partitioner.getPartition(key, val, readers.length)];
```

Then once we have the reader, we get the first key using MapFile's get() method, then repeatedly call next() to retrieve the next key and value, until the key changes. A program to do this is shown in Example 8-7.

Example 8-7. Retrieve all entries with a given key from a collection of MapFiles

```
public class LookupRecordsByTemperature extends Configured implements Tool {

  @Override
```

```
public int run(String[] args) throws Exception {
  if (args.length != 2) {
    JobBuilder.printUsage(this, "<path> <key>");
    return -1;
  }
  Path path = new Path(args[0]);
  IntWritable key = new IntWritable(Integer.parseInt(args[1]));
  FileSystem fs = path.getFileSystem(getConf());

  Reader[] readers = MapFileOutputFormat.getReaders(fs, path, getConf());
  Partitioner<IntWritable, Text> partitioner =
    new HashPartitioner<IntWritable, Text>();
  Text val = new Text();

  Reader reader = readers[partitioner.getPartition(key, val, readers.length)];
  Writable entry = reader.get(key, val);
  if (entry == null) {
    System.err.println("Key not found: " + key);
    return -1;
  }
  NcdcRecordParser parser = new NcdcRecordParser();
  IntWritable nextKey = new IntWritable();
  do {
    parser.parse(val.toString());
    System.out.printf("%s\t%s\n", parser.getStationId(), parser.getYear());
  } while(reader.next(nextKey, val) && key.equals(nextKey));
  return 0;
}

public static void main(String[] args) throws Exception {
  int exitCode = ToolRunner.run(new LookupRecordsByTemperature(), args);
  System.exit(exitCode);
}
}
```

And here is a sample run to retrieve all readings of −10°C and count them:

```
% hadoop jar job.jar LookupRecordsByTemperature output-hashmapsort -100 \
  2> /dev/null | wc -l
1489272
```

Total Sort

How can you produce a globally sorted file using Hadoop? The naive answer is to use a single partition.§ But this is incredibly inefficient for large files, since one machine has to process all of the output, so you are throwing away the benefits of the parallel architecture that MapReduce provides.

---

§ A better answer is to use Pig ("Sorting Data" on page 359) or Hive ("Sorting and Aggregating" on page 395), both of which can sort with a single command.

Instead, it is possible to produce a set of sorted files that, if concatenated, would form a globally sorted file. The secret to doing this is to use a partitioner that respects the total order of the output. For example, if we had four partitions, we could put keys for temperatures less than −10°C in the first partition, those between −10°C and 0°C in the second, those between 0°C and 10°C in the third, and those over 10°C in the fourth.

Although this approach works, you have to choose your partition sizes carefully to ensure that they are fairly even so that job times aren't dominated by a single reducer. For the partitioning scheme just described, the relative sizes of the partitions are as follows:

Temperature range	< −10°C	[−10°C, 0°C)	[0°C, 10°C)	>= 10°C
Proportion of records	11%	13%	17%	59%

These partitions are not very even. To construct more even partitions, we need to have a better understanding of the temperature distribution for the whole dataset. It's fairly easy to write a MapReduce job to count the number of records that fall into a collection of temperature buckets. For example, Figure 8-1 shows the distribution for buckets of size 1°C, where each point on the plot corresponds to one bucket.

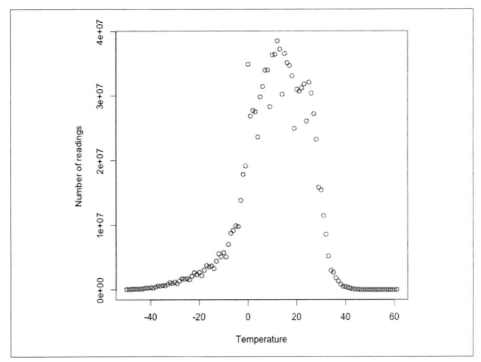

Figure 8-1. Temperature distribution for the weather dataset

While we could use this information to construct a very even set of partitions, the fact that we needed to run a job that used the entire dataset to construct them is not ideal. It's possible to get a fairly even set of partitions, by *sampling* the key space. The idea behind sampling is that you look at a small subset of the keys to approximate the key distribution, which is then used to construct partitions. Luckily, we don't have to write the code to do this ourselves, as Hadoop comes with a selection of samplers.

The InputSampler class defines a nested Sampler interface whose implementations return a sample of keys given an InputFormat and JobConf:

```
public interface Sampler<K,V> {
  K[] getSample(InputFormat<K,V> inf, JobConf job) throws IOException;
}
```

This interface is not usually called directly by clients. Instead, the writePartition File() static method on InputSampler is used, which creates a sequence file to store the keys that define the partitions:

```
public static <K,V> void writePartitionFile(JobConf job,
        Sampler<K,V> sampler) throws IOException
```

The sequence file is used by TotalOrderPartitioner to create partitions for the sort job. Example 8-8 puts it all together.

Example 8-8. A MapReduce program for sorting a SequenceFile with IntWritable keys using the TotalOrderPartitioner to globally sort the data

```
public class SortByTemperatureUsingTotalOrderPartitioner extends Configured
  implements Tool {

  @Override
  public int run(String[] args) throws Exception {
    JobConf conf = JobBuilder.parseInputAndOutput(this, getConf(), args);
    if (conf == null) {
      return -1;
    }

    conf.setInputFormat(SequenceFileInputFormat.class);
    conf.setOutputKeyClass(IntWritable.class);
    conf.setOutputFormat(SequenceFileOutputFormat.class);
    SequenceFileOutputFormat.setCompressOutput(conf, true);
    SequenceFileOutputFormat.setOutputCompressorClass(conf, GzipCodec.class);
    SequenceFileOutputFormat.setOutputCompressionType(conf,
        CompressionType.BLOCK);

    conf.setPartitionerClass(TotalOrderPartitioner.class);

    InputSampler.Sampler<IntWritable, Text> sampler =
      new InputSampler.RandomSampler<IntWritable, Text>(0.1, 10000, 10);

    Path input = FileInputFormat.getInputPaths(conf)[0];
    input = input.makeQualified(input.getFileSystem(conf));

    Path partitionFile = new Path(input, "_partitions");
```

```
      TotalOrderPartitioner.setPartitionFile(conf, partitionFile);
      InputSampler.writePartitionFile(conf, sampler);

      // Add to DistributedCache
      URI partitionUri = new URI(partitionFile.toString() + "#_partitions");
      DistributedCache.addCacheFile(partitionUri, conf);
      DistributedCache.createSymlink(conf);

      JobClient.runJob(conf);
      return 0;
    }

  public static void main(String[] args) throws Exception {
    int exitCode = ToolRunner.run(
        new SortByTemperatureUsingTotalOrderPartitioner(), args);
    System.exit(exitCode);
  }
}
```

We use a RandomSampler, which chooses keys with a uniform probability—here, 0.1.
There are also parameters for the maximum number of samples to take and the maximum number of splits to sample (here, 10,000 and 10, respectively; these settings are
the defaults when InputSampler is run as an application), and the sampler stops when
the first of these limits is met. Samplers run on the client, making it important to limit
the number of splits that are downloaded, so the sampler runs quickly. In practice, the
time taken to run the sampler is a small fraction of the overall job time.

The partition file that InputSampler writes is called _partitions, which we have set to be
in the input directory (it will not be picked up as an input file since it starts with an
underscore). To share the partition file with the tasks running on the cluster, we add
it to the distributed cache (see "Distributed Cache" on page 253).

On one run, the sampler chose −5.6°C, 13.9°C, and 22.0°C as partition boundaries (for
four partitions), which translates into more even partition sizes than the earlier choice
of partitions:

Temperature range	< −5.6°C	[−5.6°C, 13.9°C)	[13.9°C, 22.0°C)	>= 22.0°C
Proportion of records	29%	24%	23%	24%

Your input data determines the best sampler for you to use. For example, SplitSam
pler, which samples only the first n records in a split, is not so good for sorted data[||]
because it doesn't select keys from throughout the split.

[||] In some applications, it's common for some of the input to already be sorted, or at least partially sorted. For
example, the weather dataset is ordered by time, which may introduce certain biases, making the
RandomSampler a safer choice.

On the other hand, `IntervalSampler` chooses keys at regular intervals through the split and makes a better choice for sorted data. `RandomSampler` is a good general-purpose sampler. If none of these suits your application (and remember that the point of sampling is to produce partitions that are *approximately* equal in size), you can write your own implementation of the `Sampler` interface.

One of the nice properties of `InputSampler` and `TotalOrderPartitioner` is that you are free to choose the number of partitions. This choice is normally driven by the number of reducer slots in your cluster (choose a number slightly fewer than the total, to allow for failures). However, `TotalOrderPartitioner` will work only if the partition boundaries are distinct: one problem with choosing a high number is that you may get collisions if you have a small key space.

Here's how we run it:

```
% hadoop jar job.jar SortByTemperatureUsingTotalOrderPartitioner \
    -D mapred.reduce.tasks=30 input/ncdc/all-seq output-totalsort
```

The program produces 30 output partitions, each of which is internally sorted; in addition, for these partitions, all the keys in partition *i* are less than the keys in partition *i* + 1.

Secondary Sort

The MapReduce framework sorts the records by key before they reach the reducers. For any particular key, however, the values are *not* sorted. The order that the values appear is not even stable from one run to the next, since they come from different map tasks, which may finish at different times from run to run. Generally speaking, most MapReduce programs are written so as not to depend on the order that the values appear to the reduce function. However, it is possible to impose an order on the values by sorting and grouping the keys in a particular way.

To illustrate the idea, consider the MapReduce program for calculating the maximum temperature for each year. If we arranged for the values (temperatures) to be sorted in descending order, we wouldn't have to iterate through them to find the maximum— we could take the first for each year and ignore the rest. (This approach isn't the most efficient way to solve this particular problem, but it illustrates how secondary sort works in general.)

To achieve this, we change our keys to be composite: a combination of year and temperature. We want the sort order for keys to be by year (ascending) and then by temperature (descending):

```
1900 35°C
1900 34°C
1900 34°C
...
1901 36°C
1901 35°C
```

If all we did was change the key, then this wouldn't help since now records for the same year would not (in general) go to the same reducer since they have different keys. For example, (1900, 35°C) and (1900, 34°C) could go to different reducers. By setting a partitioner to partition by the year part of the key, we can guarantee that records for the same year go to the same reducer. This still isn't enough to achieve our goal, however. A partitioner ensures only that one reducer receives all the records for a year; it doesn't change the fact that the reducer groups by key within the partition:

```
       Partition  Group
1900 35°C  |       |
1900 34°C  |       |
1900 34°C  |       |
    ...
1901 36°C  |       |
1901 35°C  |       |
```

The final piece of the puzzle is the setting to control the grouping. If we group values in the reducer by the year part of the key, then we will see all the records for the same year in one reduce group. And since they are sorted by temperature in descending order, the first is the maximum temperature:

```
       Partition  Group
1900 35°C  |       |
1900 34°C  |       |
1900 34°C  |       |
    ...
1901 36°C  |       |
1901 35°C  |       |
```

To summarize, there is a recipe here to get the effect of sorting by value:

- Make the key a composite of the natural key and the natural value.
- The key comparator should order by the composite key, that is, the natural key *and* natural value.
- The partitioner and grouping comparator for the composite key should consider only the natural key for partitioning and grouping.

Java code

Putting this all together results in the code in Example 8-9. This program uses the plaintext input again.

Example 8-9. Application to find the maximum temperature by sorting temperatures in the key

```java
public class MaxTemperatureUsingSecondarySort
  extends Configured implements Tool {

  static class MaxTemperatureMapper extends MapReduceBase
```

```
      implements Mapper<LongWritable, Text, IntPair, NullWritable> {

    private NcdcRecordParser parser = new NcdcRecordParser();

    public void map(LongWritable key, Text value,
        OutputCollector<IntPair, NullWritable> output, Reporter reporter)
        throws IOException {

      parser.parse(value);
      if (parser.isValidTemperature()) {
        output.collect(new IntPair(parser.getYearInt(),
            + parser.getAirTemperature()), NullWritable.get());
      }
    }
  }

  static class MaxTemperatureReducer extends MapReduceBase
    implements Reducer<IntPair, NullWritable, IntPair, NullWritable> {

    public void reduce(IntPair key, Iterator<NullWritable> values,
        OutputCollector<IntPair, NullWritable> output, Reporter reporter)
        throws IOException {

      output.collect(key, NullWritable.get());
    }
  }

  public static class FirstPartitioner
    implements Partitioner<IntPair, NullWritable> {

    @Override
    public void configure(JobConf job) {}

    @Override
    public int getPartition(IntPair key, NullWritable value, int numPartitions) {
      return Math.abs(key.getFirst() * 127) % numPartitions;
    }
  }

  public static class KeyComparator extends WritableComparator {
    protected KeyComparator() {
      super(IntPair.class, true);
    }
    @Override
    public int compare(WritableComparable w1, WritableComparable w2) {
      IntPair ip1 = (IntPair) w1;
      IntPair ip2 = (IntPair) w2;
      int cmp = IntPair.compare(ip1.getFirst(), ip2.getFirst());
      if (cmp != 0) {
        return cmp;
      }
      return -IntPair.compare(ip1.getSecond(), ip2.getSecond()); //reverse
    }
  }
```

```
public static class GroupComparator extends WritableComparator {
  protected GroupComparator() {
    super(IntPair.class, true);
  }
  @Override
  public int compare(WritableComparable w1, WritableComparable w2) {
    IntPair ip1 = (IntPair) w1;
    IntPair ip2 = (IntPair) w2;
    return IntPair.compare(ip1.getFirst(), ip2.getFirst());
  }
}

@Override
public int run(String[] args) throws IOException {
  JobConf conf = JobBuilder.parseInputAndOutput(this, getConf(), args);
  if (conf == null) {
    return -1;
  }

  conf.setMapperClass(MaxTemperatureMapper.class);
  conf.setPartitionerClass(FirstPartitioner.class);
  conf.setOutputKeyComparatorClass(KeyComparator.class);
  conf.setOutputValueGroupingComparator(GroupComparator.class);
  conf.setReducerClass(MaxTemperatureReducer.class);
  conf.setOutputKeyClass(IntPair.class);
  conf.setOutputValueClass(NullWritable.class);

  JobClient.runJob(conf);
  return 0;
}

public static void main(String[] args) throws Exception {
  int exitCode = ToolRunner.run(new MaxTemperatureUsingSecondarySort(), args);
  System.exit(exitCode);
}
}
```

In the mapper, we create a key representing the year and temperature, using an IntPair Writable implementation. (IntPair is like the TextPair class we developed in "Implementing a Custom Writable" on page 96.) We don't need to carry any information in the value, since we can get the first (maximum) temperature in the reducer from the key, so we use a NullWritable. The reducer emits the first key, which due to the secondary sorting, is an IntPair for the year and its maximum temperature. IntPair's toString() method creates a tab-separated string, so the output is a set of tab-separated year-temperature pairs.

 Many applications need to access all the sorted values, not just the first value as we have provided here. To do this, you need to populate the value fields since in the reducer you can retrieve only the first key. This necessitates some unavoidable duplication of information between key and value.

We set the partitioner to partition by the first field of the key (the year), using a custom partitioner. To sort keys by year (ascending) and temperature (descending), we use a custom key comparator that extracts the fields and performs the appropriate comparisons. Similarly, to group keys by year, we set a custom comparator, using setOutput ValueGroupingComparator(), to extract the first field of the key for comparison.#

Running this program gives the maximum temperatures for each year:

```
% hadoop jar job.jar MaxTemperatureUsingSecondarySort input/ncdc/all \
> output-secondarysort
% hadoop fs -cat output-secondarysort/part-* | sort | head
1901    317
1902    244
1903    289
1904    256
1905    283
1906    294
1907    283
1908    289
1909    278
1910    294
```

Streaming

To do a secondary sort in Streaming, we can take advantage of a couple of library classes that Hadoop provides. Here's the driver that we can use to do a secondary sort:

```
hadoop jar $HADOOP_INSTALL/contrib/streaming/hadoop-*-streaming.jar \
    -D stream.num.map.output.key.fields=2 \
    -D mapred.text.key.partitioner.options=-k1,1 \
    -D mapred.output.key.comparator.class=\
org.apache.hadoop.mapred.lib.KeyFieldBasedComparator \
    -D mapred.text.key.comparator.options="-k1n -k2nr" \
    -input input/ncdc/all \
    -output output_secondarysort_streaming \
    -mapper ch08/src/main/python/secondary_sort_map.py \
    -partitioner org.apache.hadoop.mapred.lib.KeyFieldBasedPartitioner \
    -reducer ch08/src/main/python/secondary_sort_reduce.py \
    -file ch08/src/main/python/secondary_sort_map.py \
    -file ch08/src/main/python/secondary_sort_reduce.py
```

Our map function (Example 8-10) emits records with year and temperature fields. We want to treat the combination of both of these fields as the key, so we set stream.num.map.output.key.fields to 2. This means that values will be empty, just like in the Java case.

\# For simplicity, these custom comparators as shown are not optimized; see "Implementing a RawComparator for speed" on page 99 for the steps we would need to take to make them faster.

Example 8-10. Map function for secondary sort in Python

```
#!/usr/bin/env python

import re
import sys

for line in sys.stdin:
  val = line.strip()
  (year, temp, q) = (val[15:19], int(val[87:92]), val[92:93])
  if temp == 9999:
    sys.stderr.write("reporter:counter:Temperature,Missing,1\n")
  elif re.match("[01459]", q):
    print "%s\t%s" % (year, temp)
```

However, we don't want to partition by the entire key, so we use the `KeyFieldBased` `Partitioner` partitioner, which allows us to partition by a part of the key. The specification `mapred.text.key.partitioner.options` configures the partitioner. The value `-k1,1` instructs the partitioner to use only the first field of the key, where fields are assumed to be separated by a string defined by the `map.output.key.field.separator` property (a tab character by default).

Next, we want a comparator that sorts the year field in ascending order and the temperature field in descending order, so that the reduce function can simply return the first record in each group. Hadoop provides `KeyFieldBasedComparator`, which is ideal for this purpose. The comparison order is defined by a specification that is like the one used for GNU *sort*. It is set using the `mapred.text.key.comparator.options` property. The value `-k1n -k2nr` used in this example means "sort by the first field in numerical order, then by the second field in reverse numerical order." Like its partitioner cousin, `KeyFieldBasedPartitioner`, it uses the separator defined by the `map.out` `put.key.field.separator` to split a key into fields.

In the Java version, we had to set the grouping comparator; however, in Streaming, groups are not demarcated in any way, so in the reduce function we have to detect the group boundaries ourselves by looking for when the year changes (Example 8-11).

Example 8-11. Reducer function for secondary sort in Python

```
#!/usr/bin/env python

import sys

last_group = None
for line in sys.stdin:
  val = line.strip()
  (year, temp) = val.split("\t")
  group = year
  if last_group != group:
    print val
    last_group = group
```

When we run the streaming program, we get the same output as the Java version.

Finally, note that `KeyFieldBasedPartitioner` and `KeyFieldBasedComparator` are not confined to use in Streaming programs—they are applicable to Java MapReduce programs, too.

Joins

MapReduce can perform joins between large datasets, but writing the code to do joins from scratch is fairly involved. Rather than writing MapReduce programs, you might consider using a higher-level framework such as Pig, Hive, or Cascading, in which join operations are a core part of the implementation.

Let's briefly consider the problem we are trying to solve. We have two datasets; for example, the weather stations database and the weather records—and we want to reconcile the two. For example, we want to see each station's history, with the station's metadata inlined in each output row. This is illustrated in Figure 8-2.

How we implement the join depends on how large the datasets are and how they are partitioned. If one dataset is large (the weather records) but the other one is small enough to be distributed to each node in the cluster (as the station metadata is), then the join can be effected by a MapReduce job that brings the records for each station together (a partial sort on station ID, for example). The mapper or reducer uses the smaller dataset to look up the station metadata for a station ID, so it can be written out with each record. See "Side Data Distribution" on page 252 for a discussion of this approach, where we focus on the mechanics of distributing the data to tasktrackers.

If the join is performed by the mapper, it is called a *map-side join*, whereas if it is performed by the reducer it is called a *reduce-side join*.

If both datasets are too large for either to be copied to each node in the cluster, then we can still join them using MapReduce with a map-side or reduce-side join, depending on how the data is structured. One common example of this case is a user database and a log of some user activity (such as access logs). For a popular service, it is not feasible to distribute the user database (or the logs) to all the MapReduce nodes.

Map-Side Joins

A map-side join between large inputs works by performing the join before the data reaches the map function. For this to work, though, the inputs to each map must be partitioned and sorted in a particular way. Each input dataset must be divided into the same number of partitions, and it must be sorted by the same key (the join key) in each source. All the records for a particular key must reside in the same partition. This may sound like a strict requirement (and it is), but it actually fits the description of the output of a MapReduce job.

Stations

Station ID	Station Name
011990-99999	SIHCCAJAVRI
012650-99999	TYNSET-HANSMOEN

Records

Station ID	Timestamp	Temperature
012650-99999	194903241200	111
012650-99999	194903241800	78
011990-99999	195005150700	0
011990-99999	195005151200	22
011990-99999	195005151800	-11

Join

Station ID	Station Name	Timestamp	Temperature
011990-99999	SIHCCAJAVRI	195005150700	0
011990-99999	SIHCCAJAVRI	195005151200	22
011990-99999	SIHCCAJAVRI	195005151800	-11
012650-99999	TYNSET-HANSMOEN	194903241200	111
012650-99999	TYNSET-HANSMOEN	194903241800	78

Figure 8-2. Inner join of two datasets

A map-side join can be used to join the outputs of several jobs that had the same number of reducers, the same keys, and output files that are not splittable (by being smaller than an HDFS block, or by virtue of being gzip compressed, for example). In the context of the weather example, if we ran a partial sort on the stations file by station ID, and another, identical sort on the records, again by station ID, and with the same number of reducers, then the two outputs would satisfy the conditions for running a map-side join.

Use a `CompositeInputFormat` from the `org.apache.hadoop.mapred.join` package to run a map-side join. The input sources and join type (inner or outer) for `CompositeInput Format` are configured through a join expression that is written according to a simple grammar. The package documentation has details and examples.

The `org.apache.hadoop.examples.Join` example is a general-purpose command-line program for running a map-side join, since it allows you to run a MapReduce job for any specified mapper and reducer over multiple inputs that are joined with a given join operation.

Reduce-Side Joins

A reduce-side join is more general than a map-side join, in that the input datasets don't have to be structured in any particular way, but it is less efficient as both datasets have to go through the MapReduce shuffle. The basic idea is that the mapper tags each record with its source and uses the join key as the map output key, so that the records with the same key are brought together in the reducer. We use several ingredients to make this work in practice:

Multiple inputs

>   The input sources for the datasets have different formats, in general, so it is very convenient to use the `MultipleInputs` class (see "Multiple Inputs" on page 214) to separate the logic for parsing and tagging each source.

Secondary sort

>   As described, the reducer will see the records from both sources that have same key, but they are not guaranteed to be in any particular order. However, to perform the join, it is important to have the data from one source before another. For the weather data join, the station record must be the first of the values seen for each key, so the reducer can fill in the weather records with the station name and emit them straightaway. Of course, it would be possible to receive the records in any order if we buffered them in memory, but this should be avoided, since the number of records in any group may be very large and exceed the amount of memory available to the reducer.[*]

>   We saw in "Secondary Sort" on page 241 how to impose an order on the values for each key that the reducers see, so we use this technique here.

To tag each record, we use `TextPair` from Chapter 4 for the keys, to store the station ID, and the tag. The only requirement for the tag values is that they sort in such a way that the station records come before the weather records. This can be achieved by tagging station records as 0 and weather records as 1. The mapper classes to do this are shown in Examples 8-12 and 8-13.

Example 8-12. Mapper for tagging station records for a reduce-side join

```
public class JoinStationMapper extends MapReduceBase
    implements Mapper<LongWritable, Text, TextPair, Text> {
  private NcdcStationMetadataParser parser = new NcdcStationMetadataParser();
```

---

[*] The `data_join` package in the *contrib* directory implements reduce-side joins by buffering records in memory, so it suffers from this limitation.

```
  public void map(LongWritable key, Text value,
      OutputCollector<TextPair, Text> output, Reporter reporter)
      throws IOException {

    if (parser.parse(value)) {
      output.collect(new TextPair(parser.getStationId(), "0"),
        new Text(parser.getStationName()));
    }
  }
}
```

Example 8-13. Mapper for tagging weather records for a reduce-side join

```
public class JoinRecordMapper extends MapReduceBase
    implements Mapper<LongWritable, Text, TextPair, Text> {
  private NcdcRecordParser parser = new NcdcRecordParser();

  public void map(LongWritable key, Text value,
      OutputCollector<TextPair, Text> output, Reporter reporter)
      throws IOException {

    parser.parse(value);
    output.collect(new TextPair(parser.getStationId(), "1"), value);
  }
}
```

The reducer knows that it will receive the station record first, so it extracts its name from the value and writes it out as a part of every output record (Example 8-14).

Example 8-14. Reducer for joining tagged station records with tagged weather records

```
public class JoinReducer extends MapReduceBase implements
    Reducer<TextPair, Text, Text, Text> {

  public void reduce(TextPair key, Iterator<Text> values,
      OutputCollector<Text, Text> output, Reporter reporter)
      throws IOException {

    Text stationName = new Text(values.next());
    while (values.hasNext()) {
      Text record = values.next();
      Text outValue = new Text(stationName.toString() + "\t" + record.toString());
      output.collect(key.getFirst(), outValue);
    }
  }
}
```

The code assumes that every station ID in the weather records has exactly one matching record in the station dataset. If this were not the case, we would need to generalize the code to put the tag into the value objects, by using another TextPair. The reduce() method would then be able to tell which entries were station names and detect (and handle) missing or duplicate entries, before processing the weather records.

Because objects in the reducer's values iterator are re-used (for efficiency purposes), it is vital that the code makes a copy of the first Text object from the values iterator:

```
Text stationName = new Text(values.next());
```

If the copy is not made, then the stationName reference will refer to the value just read when it is turned into a string, which is a bug.

Tying the job together is the driver class, shown in Example 8-15. The essential point is that we partition and group on the first part of the key, the station ID, which we do with a custom Partitioner (KeyPartitioner) and a custom comparator, FirstCompara tor (from TextPair).

Example 8-15. Application to join weather records with station names

```
public class JoinRecordWithStationName extends Configured implements Tool {

  public static class KeyPartitioner implements Partitioner<TextPair, Text> {
    @Override
    public void configure(JobConf job) {}

    @Override
    public int getPartition(TextPair key, Text value, int numPartitions) {
      return (key.getFirst().hashCode() & Integer.MAX_VALUE) % numPartitions;
    }
  }

  @Override
  public int run(String[] args) throws Exception {
    if (args.length != 3) {
      JobBuilder.printUsage(this, "<ncdc input> <station input> <output>");
      return -1;
    }

    JobConf conf = new JobConf(getConf(), getClass());
    conf.setJobName("Join record with station name");

    Path ncdcInputPath = new Path(args[0]);
    Path stationInputPath = new Path(args[1]);
    Path outputPath = new Path(args[2]);

    MultipleInputs.addInputPath(conf, ncdcInputPath,
        TextInputFormat.class, JoinRecordMapper.class);
    MultipleInputs.addInputPath(conf, stationInputPath,
        TextInputFormat.class, JoinStationMapper.class);
    FileOutputFormat.setOutputPath(conf, outputPath);

    conf.setPartitionerClass(KeyPartitioner.class);
    conf.setOutputValueGroupingComparator(TextPair.FirstComparator.class);

    conf.setMapOutputKeyClass(TextPair.class);

    conf.setReducerClass(JoinReducer.class);
```

```
    conf.setOutputKeyClass(Text.class);

    JobClient.runJob(conf);
    return 0;
  }

  public static void main(String[] args) throws Exception {
    int exitCode = ToolRunner.run(new JoinRecordWithStationName(), args);
    System.exit(exitCode);
  }
}
```

Running the program on the sample data yields the following output:

```
011990-99999    SIHCCAJAVRI         0067011990999991950051507004+68750...
011990-99999    SIHCCAJAVRI         0043011990999991950051512004+68750...
011990-99999    SIHCCAJAVRI         0043011990999991950051518004+68750...
012650-99999    TYNSET-HANSMOEN     0043012650999991949032412004+62300...
012650-99999    TYNSET-HANSMOEN     0043012650999991949032418004+62300...
```

Side Data Distribution

Side data can be defined as extra read-only data needed by a job to process the main dataset. The challenge is to make side data available to all the map or reduce tasks (which are spread across the cluster) in a convenient and efficient fashion.

In addition to the distribution mechanisms described in this section, it is possible to cache side-data in memory in a static field, so that tasks of the same job that run in succession on the same tasktracker can share the data. "Task JVM Reuse" on page 184 describes how to enable this feature. If you take this approach, be aware of the amount of memory that you are using, as it might affect the memory needed by the shuffle (see "Shuffle and Sort" on page 177).

Using the Job Configuration

You can set arbitrary key-value pairs in the job configuration using the various setter methods on JobConf (inherited from Configuration). This is very useful if you need to pass a small piece of metadata to your tasks. To retrieve the values in the task, override the configure() method in the Mapper or Reducer and use a getter method on the JobConf object passed in.

Usually, a primitive type is sufficient to encode your metadata, but for arbitrary objects you can either handle the serialization yourself (if you have an existing mechanism for turning objects to strings and back), or you can use Hadoop's Stringifier class. DefaultStringifier uses Hadoop's serialization framework to serialize objects (see "Serialization" on page 86).

You shouldn't use this mechanism for transferring more than a few kilobytes of data because it can put pressure on the memory usage in the Hadoop daemons, particularly in a system running hundreds of jobs. The job configuration is read by the jobtracker, the tasktracker, and the child JVM, and each time the configuration is read, all of its entries are read into memory, even if they are not used. User properties are not read on the jobtracker or the tasktracker, so they just waste time and memory.

Distributed Cache

Rather than serializing side data in the job configuration, it is preferable to distribute datasets using Hadoop's distributed cache mechanism. This provides a service for copying files and archives to the task nodes in time for the tasks to use them when they run. To save network bandwidth, files are normally copied to any particular node once per job.

Usage

For tools that use `GenericOptionsParser` (this includes many of the programs in this book—see "GenericOptionsParser, Tool, and ToolRunner" on page 135), you can specify the files to be distributed as a comma-separated list of URIs as the argument to the `-files` option. Files can be on the local filesystem, on HDFS, or on another Hadoop readable filesystem (such as S3). If no scheme is supplied, then the files are assumed to be local. (This is true even if the default filesystem is not the local filesystem.)

You can also copy archive files (JAR files, ZIP files, tar files, and gzipped tar files) to your tasks, using the `-archives` option; these are unarchived on the task node. The `-libjars` option will add JAR files to the classpath of the mapper and reducer tasks. This is useful if you haven't bundled library JAR files in your job JAR file.

> Streaming doesn't use the distributed cache for copying the streaming scripts across the cluster. You specify a file to be copied using the `-file` option (note the singular), which should be repeated for each file to be copied. Furthermore, files specified using the `-file` option must be file paths only, not URIs, so they must be accessible from the local filesystem of the client launching the Streaming job.
>
> Streaming also accepts the `-files` and `-archives` options for copying files into the distributed cache for use by your Streaming scripts.

Let's see how to use the distributed cache to share a metadata file for station names. The command we will run is:

```
% hadoop jar job.jar MaxTemperatureByStationNameUsingDistributedCacheFile \
  -files input/ncdc/metadata/stations-fixed-width.txt input/ncdc/all output
```

This command will copy the local file *stations-fixed-width.txt* (no scheme is supplied, so the path is automatically interpreted as a local file) to the task nodes, so we can use it to look up station names. The listing for `MaxTemperatureByStationNameUsingDistributedCacheFile` appears in Example 8-16.

Example 8-16. Application to find the maximum temperature by station, showing station names from a lookup table passed as a distributed cache file

```
public class MaxTemperatureByStationNameUsingDistributedCacheFile
  extends Configured implements Tool {

  static class StationTemperatureMapper extends MapReduceBase
    implements Mapper<LongWritable, Text, Text, IntWritable> {

    private NcdcRecordParser parser = new NcdcRecordParser();

    public void map(LongWritable key, Text value,
        OutputCollector<Text, IntWritable> output, Reporter reporter)
        throws IOException {

      parser.parse(value);
      if (parser.isValidTemperature()) {
        output.collect(new Text(parser.getStationId()),
            new IntWritable(parser.getAirTemperature()));
      }
    }
  }

  static class MaxTemperatureReducerWithStationLookup extends MapReduceBase
    implements Reducer<Text, IntWritable, Text, IntWritable> {

    private NcdcStationMetadata metadata;

    @Override
    public void configure(JobConf conf) {
      metadata = new NcdcStationMetadata();
      try {
        metadata.initialize(new File("stations-fixed-width.txt"));
      } catch (IOException e) {
        throw new RuntimeException(e);
      }
    }

    public void reduce(Text key, Iterator<IntWritable> values,
        OutputCollector<Text, IntWritable> output, Reporter reporter)
        throws IOException {

      String stationName = metadata.getStationName(key.toString());

      int maxValue = Integer.MIN_VALUE;
      while (values.hasNext()) {
        maxValue = Math.max(maxValue, values.next().get());
      }
      output.collect(new Text(stationName), new IntWritable(maxValue));
```

```
    }
  }

  @Override
  public int run(String[] args) throws IOException {
    JobConf conf = JobBuilder.parseInputAndOutput(this, getConf(), args);
    if (conf == null) {
      return -1;
    }

    conf.setOutputKeyClass(Text.class);
    conf.setOutputValueClass(IntWritable.class);

    conf.setMapperClass(StationTemperatureMapper.class);
    conf.setCombinerClass(MaxTemperatureReducer.class);
    conf.setReducerClass(MaxTemperatureReducerWithStationLookup.class);

    JobClient.runJob(conf);
    return 0;
  }

  public static void main(String[] args) throws Exception {
    int exitCode = ToolRunner.run(
        new MaxTemperatureByStationNameUsingDistributedCacheFile(), args);
    System.exit(exitCode);
  }
}
```

The program finds the maximum temperature by weather station, so the mapper (StationTemperatureMapper) simply emits (station ID, temperature) pairs. For the combiner, we reuse MaxTemperatureReducer (from Chapters 2 and 5) to pick the maximum temperature for any given group of map outputs on the map side. The reducer (MaxTemperatureReducerWithStationLookup) is different from the combiner, since in addition to finding the maximum temperature, it uses the cache file to look up the station name.

We use the reducer's configure() method to retrieve the cache file using its original name, relative to the working directory of the task.

You can use the distributed cache for copying files that do not fit in memory. MapFiles are very useful in this regard, since they serve as an on-disk lookup format (see "MapFile" on page 123). Because MapFiles are a collection of files with a defined directory structure, you should put them into an archive format (JAR, ZIP, tar, or gzipped tar) and add them to the cache using the -archives option.

Here's a snippet of the output, showing some maximum temperatures for a few weather stations:

```
PEATS RIDGE WARATAH          372
STRATHALBYN RACECOU          410
SHEOAKS AWS                  399
WANGARATTA AERO              409
MOOGARA                      334
MACKAY AERO                  331
```

How it works

When you launch a job, Hadoop copies the files specified by the `-files` and `-archives` options to the jobtracker's filesystem (normally HDFS). Then, before a task is run, the tasktracker copies the files from the jobtracker's filesystem to a local disk—the cache—so the task can access the files. From the task's point of view, the files are just there (and it doesn't care that they came from HDFS).

The tasktracker also maintains a reference count for the number of tasks using each file in the cache. Before the task has run, the file's reference count is incremented by one; then after the task has run, the count is decreased by one. Only when the count reaches zero it is eligible for deletion, since no tasks are using it. Files are deleted to make room for a new file when the cache exceeds a certain size—10 GB by default. The cache size may be changed by setting the configuration property `local.cache.size`, which is measured in bytes.

Although this design doesn't guarantee that subsequent tasks from the same job running on the same tasktracker will find the file in the cache, it is very likely that they will, since tasks from a job are usually scheduled to run at around the same time, so there isn't the opportunity for enough other jobs to run and cause the original task's file to be deleted from the cache.

Files are localized under the `${mapred.local.dir}/taskTracker/archive` directory on the tasktrackers. Applications don't have to know this, however, since the files are symbolically linked from the task's working directory.

The DistributedCache API

Most applications don't need to use the `DistributedCache` API because they can use the distributed cache indirectly via `GenericOptionsParser`. `GenericOptionsParser` makes it much more convenient to use the distributed cache: for example, it copies local files into HDFS and then the `JobClient` informs the `DistributedCache` of their locations in HDFS using the `addCacheFile()` and `addCacheArchive()` methods. The `JobClient` also gets `DistributedCache` to create symbolic links when the files are localized, by adding fragment identifiers to the files' URIs. For example, the file specified by the URI *hdfs://namenode/foo/bar#myfile* is symlinked as *myfile* in the task's working directory. There's an example of using this API in Example 8-8.

On the task node, it is most convenient to access the localized file directly; however, sometimes you may need to get a list of all the available cache files. JobConf has two methods for this purpose: getLocalCacheFiles() and getLocalCacheArchives(), which both return an array of Path objects pointing to local files.

MapReduce Library Classes

Hadoop comes with a library of mappers and reducers for commonly used functions. They are listed with brief descriptions in Table 8-2. For further information on how to use them, please consult their Java documentation.

Table 8-2. MapReduce library classes

Classes	Description
ChainMapper, ChainReducer	Run a chain of mappers in a single mapper, and a reducer followed by a chain of mappers in a single reducer. (Symbolically: M+RM*, where M is a mapper and R is a reducer.) This can substantially reduce the amount of disk I/O incurred compared to running multiple MapReduce jobs.
FieldSelectionMapReduce	A mapper and a reducer that can select fields (like the Unix cut command) from the input keys and values and emit them as output keys and values.
IntSumReducer, LongSumReducer	Reducers that sum integer values to produce a total for every key.
InverseMapper	A mapper that swaps keys and values.
TokenCounterMapper	A mapper that tokenizes the input value into words (using Java's StringTokenizer) and emits each word along with a count of one.
RegexMapper	A mapper that finds matches of a regular expression in the input value and emits the matches along with a count of one.

## CHAPTER 9

Setting Up a Hadoop Cluster

This chapter explains how to set up Hadoop to run on a cluster of machines. Running HDFS and MapReduce on a single machine is great for learning about these systems, but to do useful work they need to run on multiple nodes.

There are a few options when it comes to getting a Hadoop cluster, from building your own to running on rented hardware, or using an offering that provides Hadoop as a service in the cloud. This chapter and the next give you enough information to set up and operate your own cluster, but even if you are using a Hadoop service in which a lot of the routine maintenance is done for you, these chapters still offer valuable information about how Hadoop works from an operations point of view.

Cluster Specification

Hadoop is designed to run on commodity hardware. That means that you are not tied to expensive, proprietary offerings from a single vendor; rather, you can choose standardized, commonly available hardware from any of a large range of vendors to build your cluster.

"Commodity" does not mean "low-end." Low-end machines often have cheap components, which have higher failure rates than more expensive (but still commodity-class) machines. When you are operating tens, hundreds, or thousands of machines, cheap components turn out to be a false economy, as the higher failure rate incurs a greater maintenance cost. On the other hand, large database class machines are not recommended either, since they don't score well on the price/performance curve. And even though you would need fewer of them to build a cluster of comparable performance to one built of mid-range commodity hardware, when one did fail it would have a bigger impact on the cluster, since a larger proportion of the cluster hardware would be unavailable.

Hardware specifications rapidly become obsolete, but for the sake of illustration, a typical choice of machine for running a Hadoop datanode and tasktracker in mid-2010 would have the following specifications:

Processor
    2 quad-core 2-2.5GHz CPUs

Memory
    16-24 GB ECC RAM*

Storage
    4 × 1TB SATA disks

Network
    Gigabit Ethernet

While the hardware specification for your cluster will assuredly be different, Hadoop is designed to use multiple cores and disks, so it will be able to take full advantage of more powerful hardware.

Why Not Use RAID?

HDFS clusters do not benefit from using RAID (Redundant Array of Independent Disks) for datanode storage (although RAID is recommended for the namenode's disks, to protect against corruption of its metadata). The redundancy that RAID provides is not needed, since HDFS handles it by replication between nodes.

Furthermore, RAID striping (RAID 0), which is commonly used to increase performance, turns out to be *slower* than the JBOD (Just a Bunch Of Disks) configuration used by HDFS, which round-robins HDFS blocks between all disks. The reason for this is that RAID 0 read and write operations are limited by the speed of the slowest disk in the RAID array. In JBOD, disk operations are independent, so the average speed of operations is greater than that of the slowest disk. Disk performance often shows considerable variation in practice, even for disks of the same model. In some benchmarking carried out on a Yahoo! cluster (*http://markmail.org/message/xmzc45zi25htr7ry*), JBOD performed 10% faster than RAID 0 in one test (Gridmix), and 30% better in another (HDFS write throughput).

Finally, if a disk fails in a JBOD configuration, HDFS can continue to operate without the failed disk, whereas with RAID, failure of a single disk causes the whole array (and hence the node) to become unavailable.

The bulk of Hadoop is written in Java, and can therefore run on any platform with a JVM, although there are enough parts that harbor Unix assumptions (the control scripts, for example) to make it unwise to run on a non-Unix platform in production.

---

* ECC memory is strongly recommended, as several Hadoop users have reported seeing many checksum errors when using non-ECC memory on Hadoop clusters.

In fact, Windows operating systems are not supported production platforms (although they can be used with Cygwin as a development platform; see Appendix A).

How large should your cluster be? There isn't an exact answer to this question, but the beauty of Hadoop is that you can start with a small cluster (say, 10 nodes) and grow it as your storage and computational needs grow. In many ways, a better question is this: how fast does my cluster need to grow? You can get a good feel for this by considering storage capacity.

For example, if your data grows by 1 TB a week, and you have three-way HDFS replication, then you need an additional 3 TB of raw storage per week. Allow some room for intermediate files and logfiles (around 30%, say), and this works out at about one machine (2010 vintage) per week, on average. In practice, you wouldn't buy a new machine each week and add it to the cluster. The value of doing a back-of-the-envelope calculation like this is that it gives you a feel for how big your cluster should be: in this example, a cluster that holds two years of data needs 100 machines.

For a small cluster (on the order of 10 nodes), it is usually acceptable to run the namenode and the jobtracker on a single master machine (as long as at least one copy of the namenode's metadata is stored on a remote filesystem). As the cluster and the number of files stored in HDFS grow, the namenode needs more memory, so the namenode and jobtracker should be moved onto separate machines.

The secondary namenode can be run on the same machine as the namenode, but again for reasons of memory usage (the secondary has the same memory requirements as the primary), it is best to run it on a separate piece of hardware, especially for larger clusters. (This topic is discussed in more detail in "Master node scenarios" on page 268.) Machines running the namenodes should typically run on 64-bit hardware to avoid the 3 GB limit on Java heap size in 32-bit architectures.[†]

Network Topology

A common Hadoop cluster architecture consists of a two-level network topology, as illustrated in Figure 9-1. Typically there are 30 to 40 servers per rack, with a 1 GB switch for the rack (only three are shown in the diagram), and an uplink to a core switch or router (which is normally 1 GB or better). The salient point is that the aggregate bandwidth between nodes on the same rack is much greater than that between nodes on different racks.

---

† The traditional advice says other machines in the cluster (jobtracker, datanodes/tasktrackers) should be 32-bit to avoid the memory overhead of larger pointers. Sun's Java 6 update 14 features "compressed ordinary object pointers," which eliminates much of this overhead, so there's now no real downside to running on 64-bit hardware.

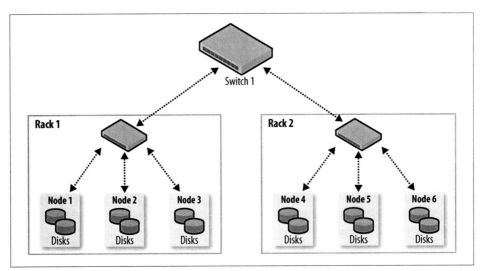

Figure 9-1. Typical two-level network architecture for a Hadoop cluster

Rack awareness

To get maximum performance out of Hadoop, it is important to configure Hadoop so that it knows the topology of your network. If your cluster runs on a single rack, then there is nothing more to do, since this is the default. However, for multirack clusters, you need to map nodes to racks. By doing this, Hadoop will prefer within-rack transfers (where there is more bandwidth available) to off-rack transfers when placing MapReduce tasks on nodes. HDFS will be able to place replicas more intelligently to trade-off performance and resilience.

Network locations such as nodes and racks are represented in a tree, which reflects the network "distance" between locations. The namenode uses the network location when determining where to place block replicas (see "Network Topology and Hadoop" on page 64); the jobtracker uses network location to determine where the closest replica is as input for a map task that is scheduled to run on a tasktracker.

For the network in Figure 9-1, the rack topology is described by two network locations, say, */switch1/rack1* and */switch1/rack2*. Since there is only one top-level switch in this cluster, the locations can be simplified to */rack1* and */rack2*.

The Hadoop configuration must specify a map between node addresses and network locations. The map is described by a Java interface, `DNSToSwitchMapping`, whose signature is:

```
public interface DNSToSwitchMapping {
  public List<String> resolve(List<String> names);
}
```

The `names` parameter is a list of IP addresses, and the return value is a list of corresponding network location strings. The `topology.node.switch.mapping.impl` configuration property defines an implementation of the `DNSToSwitchMapping` interface that the namenode and the jobtracker use to resolve worker node network locations.

For the network in our example, we would map *node1*, *node2*, and *node3* to */rack1*, and *node4*, *node5*, and *node6* to */rack2*.

Most installations don't need to implement the interface themselves, however, since the default implementation is `ScriptBasedMapping`, which runs a user-defined script to determine the mapping. The script's location is controlled by the property `topology.script.file.name`. The script must accept a variable number of arguments that are the hostnames or IP addresses to be mapped, and it must emit the corresponding network locations to standard output, separated by whitespace. The Hadoop wiki has an example at *http://wiki.apache.org/hadoop/topology_rack_awareness_scripts*.

If no script location is specified, the default behavior is to map all nodes to a single network location, called */default-rack*.

Cluster Setup and Installation

Your hardware has arrived. The next steps are to get it racked up and install the software needed to run Hadoop.

There are various ways to install and configure Hadoop. This chapter describes how to do it from scratch using the Apache Hadoop distribution, and will give you the background to cover the things you need to think about when setting up Hadoop. Alternatively, if you would like to use RPMs or Debian packages for managing your Hadoop installation, then you might want to start with Cloudera's Distribution, described in Appendix B.

To ease the burden of installing and maintaining the same software on each node, it is normal to use an automated installation method like Red Hat Linux's Kickstart or Debian's Fully Automatic Installation. These tools allow you to automate the operating system installation by recording the answers to questions that are asked during the installation process (such as the disk partition layout), as well as which packages to install. Crucially, they also provide hooks to run scripts at the end of the process, which are invaluable for doing final system tweaks and customization that is not covered by the standard installer.

The following sections describe the customizations that are needed to run Hadoop. These should all be added to the installation script.

Installing Java

Java 6 or later is required to run Hadoop. The latest stable Sun JDK is the preferred option, although Java distributions from other vendors may work, too. The following command confirms that Java was installed correctly:

```
% java -version
java version "1.6.0_12"
Java(TM) SE Runtime Environment (build 1.6.0_12-b04)
Java HotSpot(TM) 64-Bit Server VM (build 11.2-b01, mixed mode)
```

Creating a Hadoop User

It's good practice to create a dedicated Hadoop user account to separate the Hadoop installation from other services running on the same machine.

Some cluster administrators choose to make this user's home directory an NFS-mounted drive, to aid with SSH key distribution (see the following discussion). The NFS server is typically outside the Hadoop cluster. If you use NFS, it is worth considering autofs, which allows you to mount the NFS filesystem on demand, when the system accesses it. Autofs provides some protection against the NFS server failing and allows you to use replicated filesystems for failover. There are other NFS gotchas to watch out for, such as synchronizing UIDs and GIDs. For help setting up NFS on Linux, refer to the HOWTO at *http://nfs.sourceforge.net/nfs-howto/index.html*.

Installing Hadoop

Download Hadoop from the Apache Hadoop releases page (*http://hadoop.apache.org/core/releases.html*), and unpack the contents of the distribution in a sensible location, such as */usr/local* (*/opt* is another standard choice). Note that Hadoop is *not* installed in the hadoop user's home directory, as that may be an NFS-mounted directory:

```
% cd /usr/local
% sudo tar xzf hadoop-x.y.z.tar.gz
```

We also need to change the owner of the Hadoop files to be the hadoop user and group:

```
% sudo chown -R hadoop:hadoop hadoop-x.y.z
```

Some administrators like to install HDFS and MapReduce in separate locations on the same system. At the time of this writing, only HDFS and MapReduce from the same Hadoop release are compatible with one another; however, in future releases, the compatibility requirements will be loosened. When this happens, having independent installations makes sense, as it gives more upgrade options (for more, see "Upgrades" on page 316). For example, it is convenient to be able to upgrade MapReduce—perhaps to patch a bug—while leaving HDFS running.

Note that separate installations of HDFS and MapReduce can still share configuration by using the --config option (when starting daemons) to refer to a common configuration directory. They can also log to the same directory, as the logfiles they produce are named in such a way as to avoid clashes.

Testing the Installation

Once you've created the installation file, you are ready to test it by installing it on the machines in your cluster. This will probably take a few iterations as you discover kinks in the install. When it's working, you can proceed to configure Hadoop and give it a test run. This process is documented in the following sections.

SSH Configuration

The Hadoop control scripts rely on SSH to perform cluster-wide operations. For example, there is a script for stopping and starting all the daemons in the cluster. Note that the control scripts are optional—cluster-wide operations can be performed by other mechanisms, too (such as a distributed shell).

To work seamlessly, SSH needs to be set up to allow password-less login for the hadoop user from machines in the cluster. The simplest way to achieve this is to generate a public/private key pair, and it will be shared across the cluster using NFS.

First, generate an RSA key pair by typing the following in the hadoop user account:

```
% ssh-keygen -t rsa -f ~/.ssh/id_rsa
```

Even though we want password-less logins, keys without passphrases are not considered good practice (it's OK to have an empty passphrase when running a local pseudo-distributed cluster, as described in Appendix A), so we specify a passphrase when prompted for one. We shall use *ssh-agent* to avoid the need to enter a password for each connection.

The private key is in the file specified by the -f option, *~/.ssh/id_rsa*, and the public key is stored in a file with the same name with *.pub* appended, *~/.ssh/id_rsa.pub*.

Next we need to make sure that the public key is in the ~/.ssh/authorized_keys file on all the machines in the cluster that we want to connect to. If the hadoop user's home directory is an NFS filesystem, as described earlier, then the keys can be shared across the cluster by typing:

```
% cat ~/.ssh/id_rsa.pub >> ~/.ssh/authorized_keys
```

If the home directory is not shared using NFS, then the public keys will need to be shared by some other means.

Test that you can SSH from the master to a worker machine by making sure *ssh-agent* is running,‡ and then run *ssh-add* to store your passphrase. You should be able to *ssh* to a worker without entering the passphrase again.

Hadoop Configuration

There are a handful of files for controlling the configuration of a Hadoop installation; the most important ones are listed in Table 9-1.

Table 9-1. Hadoop configuration files

Filename	Format	Description
hadoop-env.sh	Bash script	Environment variables that are used in the scripts to run Hadoop.
core-site.xml	Hadoop configuration XML	Configuration settings for Hadoop Core, such as I/O settings that are common to HDFS and MapReduce.
hdfs-site.xml	Hadoop configuration XML	Configuration settings for HDFS daemons: the namenode, the secondary namenode, and the datanodes.
mapred-site.xml	Hadoop configuration XML	Configuration settings for MapReduce daemons: the jobtracker, and the tasktrackers.
masters	Plain text	A list of machines (one per line) that each run a secondary namenode.
slaves	Plain text	A list of machines (one per line) that each run a datanode and a tasktracker.
hadoop-metrics.properties	Java Properties	Properties for controlling how metrics are published in Hadoop (see "Metrics" on page 306).
log4j.properties	Java Properties	Properties for system logfiles, the namenode audit log, and the task log for the tasktracker child process ("Hadoop User Logs" on page 156).

These files are all found in the *conf* directory of the Hadoop distribution. The configuration directory can be relocated to another part of the filesystem (outside the Hadoop installation, which makes upgrades marginally easier) as long as daemons are started with the --config option specifying the location of this directory on the local filesystem.

---

‡ See its main page for instructions on how to start *ssh-agent*.

Configuration Management

Hadoop does not have a single, global location for configuration information. Instead, each Hadoop node in the cluster has its own set of configuration files, and it is up to administrators to ensure that they are kept in sync across the system. Hadoop provides a rudimentary facility for synchronizing configuration using *rsync* (see upcoming discussion); alternatively, there are parallel shell tools that can help do this, like *dsh* or *pdsh*.

Hadoop is designed so that it is possible to have a single set of configuration files that are used for all master and worker machines. The great advantage of this is simplicity, both conceptually (since there is only one configuration to deal with) and operationally (as the Hadoop scripts are sufficient to manage a single configuration setup).

For some clusters, the one-size-fits-all configuration model breaks down. For example, if you expand the cluster with new machines that have a different hardware specification to the existing ones, then you need a different configuration for the new machines to take advantage of their extra resources.

In these cases, you need to have the concept of a *class* of machine, and maintain a separate configuration for each class. Hadoop doesn't provide tools to do this, but there are several excellent tools for doing precisely this type of configuration management, such as Chef, Puppet, cfengine, and bcfg2.

For a cluster of any size, it can be a challenge to keep all of the machines in sync: consider what happens if the machine is unavailable when you push out an update—who ensures it gets the update when it becomes available? This is a big problem and can lead to divergent installations, so even if you use the Hadoop control scripts for managing Hadoop, it may be a good idea to use configuration management tools for maintaining the cluster. These tools are also excellent for doing regular maintenance, such as patching security holes and updating system packages.

Control scripts

Hadoop comes with scripts for running commands, and starting and stopping daemons across the whole cluster. To use these scripts (which can be found in the *bin* directory), you need to tell Hadoop which machines are in the cluster. There are two files for this purpose, called *masters* and *slaves*, each of which contains a list of the machine hostnames or IP addresses, one per line. The *masters* file is actually a misleading name, in that it determines which machine or machines should run a secondary namenode. The *slaves* file lists the machines that the datanodes and tasktrackers should run on. Both *masters* and *slaves* files reside in the configuration directory, although the *slaves* file may be placed elsewhere (and given another name) by changing the HADOOP_SLAVES setting in *hadoop-env.sh*. Also, these files do not need to be distributed to worker nodes, since they are used only by the control scripts running on the namenode or jobtracker.

You don't need to specify which machine (or machines) the namenode and jobtracker runs on in the *masters* file, as this is determined by the machine the scripts are run on. (In fact, specifying these in the *masters* file would cause a secondary namenode to run there, which isn't always what you want.) For example, the *start-dfs.sh* script, which starts all the HDFS daemons in the cluster, runs the namenode on the machine the script is run on. In slightly more detail, it:

1. Starts a namenode on the local machine (the machine that the script is run on)
2. Starts a datanode on each machine listed in the *slaves* file
3. Starts a secondary namenode on each machine listed in the *masters* file

There is a similar script called *start-mapred.sh*, which starts all the MapReduce daemons in the cluster. More specifically, it:

1. Starts a jobtracker on the local machine
2. Starts a tasktracker on each machine listed in the *slaves* file

Note that *masters* is not used by the MapReduce control scripts.

Also provided are *stop-dfs.sh* and *stop-mapred.sh* scripts to stop the daemons started by the corresponding start script.

These scripts start and stop Hadoop daemons using the *hadoop-daemon.sh* script. If you use the aforementioned scripts, you shouldn't call *hadoop-daemon.sh* directly. But if you need to control Hadoop daemons from another system or from your own scripts, then the *hadoop-daemon.sh* script is a good integration point. Likewise, *hadoop-daemons.sh* (with an "s") is handy for starting the same daemon on a set of hosts.

Master node scenarios

Depending on the size of the cluster, there are various configurations for running the master daemons: the namenode, secondary namenode, and jobtracker. On a small cluster (a few tens of nodes), it is convenient to put them on a single machine; however, as the cluster gets larger, there are good reasons to separate them.

The namenode has high memory requirements, as it holds file and block metadata for the entire namespace in memory. The secondary namenode, while idle most of the time, has a comparable memory footprint to the primary when it creates a checkpoint. (This is explained in detail in "The filesystem image and edit log" on page 294.) For filesystems with a large number of files, there may not be enough physical memory on one machine to run both the primary and secondary namenode.

The secondary namenode keeps a copy of the latest checkpoint of the filesystem metadata that it creates. Keeping this (stale) backup on a different node to the namenode allows recovery in the event of loss (or corruption) of all the namenode's metadata files. (This is discussed further in Chapter 10.)

On a busy cluster running lots of MapReduce jobs, the jobtracker uses considerable memory and CPU resources, so it should run on a dedicated node.

Whether the master daemons run on one or more nodes, the following instructions apply:

- Run the HDFS control scripts from the namenode machine. The masters file should contain the address of the secondary namenode.
- Run the MapReduce control scripts from the jobtracker machine.

When the namenode and jobtracker are on separate nodes, their *slaves* files need to be kept in sync, since each node in the cluster should run a datanode and a tasktracker.

Environment Settings

In this section, we consider how to set the variables in *hadoop-env.sh*.

Memory

By default, Hadoop allocates 1000 MB (1 GB) of memory to each daemon it runs. This is controlled by the HADOOP_HEAPSIZE setting in *hadoop-env.sh*. In addition, the task tracker launches separate child JVMs to run map and reduce tasks in, so we need to factor these into the total memory footprint of a worker machine.

The maximum number of map tasks that will be run on a tasktracker at one time is controlled by the mapred.tasktracker.map.tasks.maximum property, which defaults to two tasks. There is a corresponding property for reduce tasks, mapred.task tracker.reduce.tasks.maximum, which also defaults to two tasks. The memory given to each of these child JVMs can be changed by setting the mapred.child.java.opts property. The default setting is -Xmx200m, which gives each task 200 MB of memory. (Incidentally, you can provide extra JVM options here, too. For example, you might enable verbose GC logging to debug GC.) The default configuration therefore uses 2,800 MB of memory for a worker machine (see Table 9-2).

Table 9-2. Worker node memory calculation

JVM	Default memory used (MB)	Memory used for 8 processors, 400 MB per child (MB)
Datanode	1,000	1,000
Tasktracker	1,000	1,000
Tasktracker child map task	2 × 200	7 × 400
Tasktracker child reduce task	2 × 200	7 × 400
Total	2,800	7,600

The number of tasks that can be run simultaneously on a tasktracker is governed by the number of processors available on the machine. Because MapReduce jobs are normally I/O-bound, it makes sense to have more tasks than processors to get better utilization. The amount of oversubscription depends on the CPU utilization of jobs you run, but a good rule of thumb is to have a factor of between one and two more tasks (counting both map and reduce tasks) than processors.

For example, if you had 8 processors and you wanted to run 2 processes on each processor, then you could set each of `mapred.tasktracker.map.tasks.maximum` and `mapred.tasktracker.reduce.tasks.maximum` to 7 (not 8, since the datanode and the tasktracker each take one slot). If you also increased the memory available to each child task to 400 MB, then the total memory usage would be 7,600 MB (see Table 9-2).

Whether this Java memory allocation will fit into 8 GB of physical memory depends on the other processes that are running on the machine. If you are running Streaming or Pipes programs, this allocation will probably be inappropriate (and the memory allocated to the child should be dialed down), since it doesn't allow enough memory for users' (Streaming or Pipes) processes to run. The thing to avoid is processes being swapped out, as this it leads to severe performance degradation. The precise memory settings are necessarily very cluster-dependent and can be optimized over time with experience gained from monitoring the memory usage across the cluster. Tools like Ganglia ("GangliaContext" on page 308) are good for gathering this information.

Hadoop also provides settings to control how much memory is used for MapReduce operations. These can be set on a per-job basis and are covered in the section on "Shuffle and Sort" on page 177.

For the master node, each of the namenode, secondary namenode, and jobtracker daemons uses 1,000 MB by default, a total of 3,000 MB.

A namenode can eat up memory, since a reference to every block of every file is maintained in memory. For example, 1,000 MB is enough for a few million files. You can increase the namenode's memory without changing the memory allocated to other Hadoop daemons by setting `HADOOP_NAMENODE_OPTS` in *hadoop-env.sh* to include a JVM option for setting the memory size. `HADOOP_NAMENODE_OPTS` allows you to pass extra options to the namenode's JVM. So, for example, if using a Sun JVM, `-Xmx2000m` would specify that 2000 MB of memory should be allocated to the namenode.

If you change the namenode's memory allocation, don't forget to do the same for the secondary namenode (using the `HADOOP_SECONDARYNAME NODE_OPTS` variable), since its memory requirements are comparable to the primary namenode's. You will probably also want to run the secondary namenode on a different machine, in this case.

There are corresponding environment variables for the other Hadoop daemons, so you can customize their memory allocations, if desired. See *hadoop-env.sh* for details.

Java

The location of the Java implementation to use is determined by the `JAVA_HOME` setting in *hadoop-env.sh* or from the `JAVA_HOME` shell environment variable, if not set in *hadoop-env.sh*. It's a good idea to set the value in *hadoop-env.sh*, so that it is clearly defined in one place and to ensure that the whole cluster is using the same version of Java.

System logfiles

System logfiles produced by Hadoop are stored in `$HADOOP_INSTALL/logs` by default. This can be changed using the `HADOOP_LOG_DIR` setting in *hadoop-env.sh*. It's a good idea to change this so that logfiles are kept out of the directory that Hadoop is installed in, since this keeps logfiles in one place even after the installation directory changes after an upgrade. A common choice is */var/log/hadoop*, set by including the following line in *hadoop-env.sh*:

```
export HADOOP_LOG_DIR=/var/log/hadoop
```

The log directory will be created if it doesn't already exist (if not, confirm that the Hadoop user has permission to create it). Each Hadoop daemon running on a machine produces two logfiles. The first is the log output written via log4j. This file, which ends in *.log*, should be the first port of call when diagnosing problems, since most application log messages are written here. The standard Hadoop log4j configuration uses a Daily Rolling File Appender to rotate logfiles. Old logfiles are never deleted, so you should arrange for them to be periodically deleted or archived, so as to not run out of disk space on the local node.

The second logfile is the combined standard output and standard error log. This logfile, which ends in *.out*, usually contains little or no output, since Hadoop uses log4j for logging. It is only rotated when the daemon is restarted, and only the last five logs are retained. Old logfiles are suffixed with a number between 1 and 5, with 5 being the oldest file.

Logfile names (of both types) are a combination of the name of the user running the daemon, the daemon name, and the machine hostname. For example, *hadoop-tom-datanode-sturges.local.log.2008-07-04* is the name of a logfile after it has been rotated. This naming structure makes it possible to archive logs from all machines in the cluster in a single directory, if needed, since the filenames are unique.

The username in the logfile name is actually the default for the `HADOOP_IDENT_STRING` setting in *hadoop-env.sh*. If you wish to give the Hadoop instance a different identity for the purposes of naming the logfiles, change `HADOOP_IDENT_STRING` to be the identifier you want.

SSH settings

The control scripts allow you to run commands on (remote) worker nodes from the master node using SSH. It can be useful to customize the SSH settings, for various reasons. For example, you may want to reduce the connection timeout (using the ConnectTimeout option) so the control scripts don't hang around waiting to see whether a dead node is going to respond. Obviously, this can be taken too far. If the timeout is too low, then busy nodes will be skipped, which is bad.

Another useful SSH setting is StrictHostKeyChecking, which can be set to no to automatically add new host keys to the known hosts files. The default, ask, is to prompt the user to confirm they have verified the key fingerprint, which is not a suitable setting in a large cluster environment.§

To pass extra options to SSH, define the HADOOP_SSH_OPTS environment variable in *hadoop-env.sh*. See the ssh and ssh_config manual pages for more SSH settings.

The Hadoop control scripts can distribute configuration files to all nodes of the cluster using rsync. This is not enabled by default, but by defining the HADOOP_MASTER setting in *hadoop-env.sh*, worker daemons will rsync the tree rooted at HADOOP_MASTER to the local node's HADOOP_INSTALL whenever the daemon starts up.

What if you have two masters—a namenode and a jobtracker on separate machines? You can pick one as the source and the other can rsync from it, along with all the workers. In fact, you could use any machine, even one outside the Hadoop cluster, to rsync from.

Because HADOOP_MASTER is unset by default, there is a bootstrapping problem: how do we make sure *hadoop-env.sh* with HADOOP_MASTER set is present on worker nodes? For small clusters, it is easy to write a small script to copy *hadoop-env.sh* from the master to all of the worker nodes. For larger clusters, tools like *dsh* can do the copies in parallel. Alternatively, a suitable *hadoop-env.sh* can be created as a part of the automated installation script (such as Kickstart).

When starting a large cluster with rsyncing enabled, the worker nodes can overwhelm the master node with rsync requests since the workers start at around the same time. To avoid this, set the HADOOP_SLAVE_SLEEP setting to a small number of seconds, such as 0.1, for one-tenth of a second. When running commands on all nodes of the cluster, the master will sleep for this period between invoking the command on each worker machine in turn.

---

§ For more discussion on the security implications of SSH Host Keys, consult the article "SSH Host Key Protection" by Brian Hatch at *http://www.securityfocus.com/infocus/1806*.

Important Hadoop Daemon Properties

Hadoop has a bewildering number of configuration properties. In this section, we address the ones that you need to define (or at least understand why the default is appropriate) for any real-world working cluster. These properties are set in the Hadoop site files: *core-site.xml*, *hdfs-site.xml*, and *mapred-site.xml*. Example 9-1 shows a typical example set of files. Notice that most are marked as final, in order to prevent them from being overridden by job configurations. You can learn more about how to write Hadoop's configuration files in "The Configuration API" on page 130.

Example 9-1. A typical set of site configuration files

```xml
<?xml version="1.0"?>
<!-- core-site.xml -->
<configuration>
  <property>
    <name>fs.default.name</name>
    <value>hdfs://namenode/</value>
    <final>true</final>
  </property>
</configuration>

<?xml version="1.0"?>
<!-- hdfs-site.xml -->
<configuration>
  <property>
    <name>dfs.name.dir</name>
    <value>/disk1/hdfs/name,/remote/hdfs/name</value>
    <final>true</final>
  </property>

  <property>
    <name>dfs.data.dir</name>
    <value>/disk1/hdfs/data,/disk2/hdfs/data</value>
    <final>true</final>
  </property>

  <property>
    <name>fs.checkpoint.dir</name>
    <value>/disk1/hdfs/namesecondary,/disk2/hdfs/namesecondary</value>
    <final>true</final>
  </property>
</configuration>

<?xml version="1.0"?>
<!-- mapred-site.xml -->
<configuration>
  <property>
    <name>mapred.job.tracker</name>
    <value>jobtracker:8021</value>
    <final>true</final>
  </property>

  <property>
```

```
    <name>mapred.local.dir</name>
    <value>/disk1/mapred/local,/disk2/mapred/local</value>
    <final>true</final>
  </property>

  <property>
    <name>mapred.system.dir</name>
    <value>/tmp/hadoop/mapred/system</value>
    <final>true</final>
  </property>

  <property>
    <name>mapred.tasktracker.map.tasks.maximum</name>
    <value>7</value>
    <final>true</final>
  </property>

  <property>
    <name>mapred.tasktracker.reduce.tasks.maximum</name>
    <value>7</value>
    <final>true</final>
  </property>

  <property>
    <name>mapred.child.java.opts</name>
    <value>-Xmx400m</value>
    <!-- Not marked as final so jobs can include JVM debugging options -->
  </property>
</configuration>
```

HDFS

To run HDFS, you need to designate one machine as a namenode. In this case, the property fs.default.name is an HDFS filesystem URI, whose host is the namenode's hostname or IP address, and port is the port that the namenode will listen on for RPCs. If no port is specified, the default of 8020 is used.

> The *masters* file that is used by the control scripts is not used by the HDFS (or MapReduce) daemons to determine hostnames. In fact, because the *masters* file is only used by the scripts, you can ignore it if you don't use them.

The fs.default.name property also doubles as specifying the default filesystem. The default filesystem is used to resolve relative paths, which are handy to use since they save typing (and avoid hardcoding knowledge of a particular namenode's address). For example, with the default filesystem defined in Example 9-1, the relative URI */a/b* is resolved to *hdfs://namenode/a/b*.

If you are running HDFS, the fact that `fs.default.name` is used to specify both the HDFS namenode *and* the default filesystem means HDFS has to be the default filesystem in the server configuration. Bear in mind, however, that it is possible to specify a different filesystem as the default in the client configuration, for convenience.

For example, if you use both HDFS and S3 filesystems, then you have a choice of specifying either as the default in the client configuration, which allows you to refer to the default with a relative URI and the other with an absolute URI.

There are a few other configuration properties you should set for HDFS: those that set the storage directories for the namenode and for datanodes. The property `dfs.name.dir` specifies a list of directories where the namenode stores persistent filesystem metadata (the edit log and the filesystem image). A copy of each of the metadata files is stored in each directory for redundancy. It's common to configure `dfs.name.dir` so that the namenode metadata is written to one or two local disks, and a remote disk, such as an NFS-mounted directory. Such a setup guards against failure of a local disk and failure of the entire namenode, since in both cases the files can be recovered and used to start a new namenode. (The secondary namenode takes only periodic checkpoints of the namenode, so it does not provide an up-to-date backup of the namenode.)

You should also set the `dfs.data.dir` property, which specifies a list of directories for a datanode to store its blocks. Unlike the namenode, which uses multiple directories for redundancy, a datanode round-robins writes between its storage directories, so for performance you should specify a storage directory for each local disk. Read performance also benefits from having multiple disks for storage, because blocks will be spread across them, and concurrent reads for distinct blocks will be correspondingly spread across disks.

For maximum performance, you should mount storage disks with the `noatime` option. This setting means that last accessed time information is not written on file reads, which gives significant performance gains.

Finally, you should configure where the secondary namenode stores its checkpoints of the filesystem. The `fs.checkpoint.dir` property specifies a list of directories where the checkpoints are kept. Like the storage directories for the namenode, which keep redundant copies of the namenode metadata, the checkpointed filesystem image is stored in each checkpoint directory for redundancy.

Table 9-3 summarizes the important configuration properties for HDFS.

Table 9-3. Important HDFS daemon properties

Property name	Type	Default value	Description
fs.default.name	URI	file:///	The default filesystem. The URI defines the hostname and port that the namenode's RPC server runs on. The default port is 8020. This property should be set in *core-site.xml*.
dfs.name.dir	comma-separated directory names	${hadoop.tmp.dir}/ dfs/name	The list of directories where the namenode stores its persistent metadata. The namenode stores a copy of the metadata in each directory in the list.
dfs.data.dir	comma-separated directory names	${hadoop.tmp.dir}/ dfs/data	A list of directories where the datanode stores blocks. Each block is stored in only one of these directories.
fs.checkpoint.dir	comma-separated directory names	${hadoop.tmp.dir}/ dfs/namesecondary	A list of directories where the secondary namenode stores checkpoints. It stores a copy of the checkpoint in each directory in the list.

 Note that the storage directories for HDFS are under Hadoop's temporary directory by default (the hadoop.tmp.dir property, whose default is /tmp/hadoop-${user.name}). Therefore, it is critical that these properties are set so that data is not lost by the system clearing out temporary directories.

MapReduce

To run MapReduce, you need to designate one machine as a jobtracker, which on small clusters may be the same machine as the namenode. To do this, set the mapred.job.tracker property to the hostname or IP address and port that the jobtracker will listen on. Note that this property is not a URI, but a host-port pair, separated by a colon. The port number 8021 is a common choice.

During a MapReduce job, intermediate data and working files are written to temporary local files. Since this data includes the potentially very large output of map tasks, you need to ensure that the mapred.local.dir property, which controls the location of local temporary storage, is configured to use disk partitions that are large enough. The mapred.local.dir property takes a comma-separated list of directory names, and you should use all available local disks to spread disk I/O. Typically, you will use the same disks and partitions (but different directories) for MapReduce temporary data as you use for datanode block storage, as governed by the dfs.data.dir property, discussed earlier.

MapReduce uses a distributed filesystem to share files (such as the job JAR file) with the tasktrackers that run the MapReduce tasks. The `mapred.system.dir` property is used to specify a directory where these files can be stored. This directory is resolved relative to the default filesystem (configured in `fs.default.name`), which is usually HDFS.

Finally, you should set the `mapred.tasktracker.map.tasks.maximum` and `mapred.task tracker.reduce.tasks.maximum` properties to reflect the number of available cores on the tasktracker machines and `mapred.child.java.opts` to reflect the amount of memory available for the tasktracker child JVMs. See the discussion in "Memory" on page 269.

Table 9-4 summarizes the important configuration properties for HDFS.

Table 9-4. Important MapReduce daemon properties

Property name	Type	Default value	Description
mapred.job.tracker	hostname and port	local	The hostname and port that the job-tracker's RPC server runs on. If set to the default value of `local`, then the jobtracker is run in-process on demand when you run a MapReduce job (you don't need to start the jobtracker in this case, and in fact you will get an error if you try to start it in this mode).
mapred.local.dir	comma-separated directory names	$ {hadoop.tmp.dir} /mapred/local	A list of directories where the Map-Reduce stores intermediate data for jobs. The data is cleared out when the job ends.
mapred.system.dir	URI	$ {hadoop.tmp.dir} /mapred/system	The directory relative to `fs.default.name` where shared files are stored, during a job run.
mapred.task tracker.map.tasks. maximum	int	2	The number of map tasks that may be run on a tasktracker at any one time.
mapred.task tracker.reduce.tasks. maximum	int	2	The number of reduce tasks that may be run on a tasktracker at any one time.
mapred.child.java.opts	String	-Xmx200m	The JVM options used to launch the tasktracker child process that runs map and reduce tasks. This property can be set on a per-job basis, which can be useful for setting JVM properties for debugging, for example.

Hadoop Daemon Addresses and Ports

Hadoop daemons generally run both an RPC server (Table 9-5) for communication between daemons and an HTTP server to provide web pages for human consumption (Table 9-6). Each server is configured by setting the network address and port number to listen on. By specifying the network address as 0.0.0.0, Hadoop will bind to all addresses on the machine. Alternatively, you can specify a single address to bind to. A port number of 0 instructs the server to start on a free port: this is generally discouraged, since it is incompatible with setting cluster-wide firewall policies.

Table 9-5. RPC server properties

Property name	Default value	Description
fs.default.name	file:///	When set to an HDFS URI, this property determines the namenode's RPC server address and port. The default port is 8020 if not specified.
dfs.datanode.ipc.address	0.0.0.0:50020	The datanode's RPC server address and port.
mapred.job.tracker	local	When set to a hostname and port, this property specifies the jobtracker's RPC server address and port. A commonly used port is 8021.
mapred.task.tracker.report.address	127.0.0.1:0	The tasktracker's RPC server address and port. This is used by the tasktracker's child JVM to communicate with the tasktracker. Using any free port is acceptable in this case, as the server only binds to the loopback address. You should change this setting only if the machine has no loopback address.

In addition to an RPC server, datanodes run a TCP/IP server for block transfers. The server address and port is set by the dfs.datanode.address property, and has a default value of 0.0.0.0:50010.

Table 9-6. HTTP server properties

Property name	Default value	Description
mapred.job.tracker.http.address	0.0.0.0:50030	The jobtracker's HTTP server address and port.
mapred.task.tracker.http.address	0.0.0.0:50060	The tasktracker's HTTP server address and port.
dfs.http.address	0.0.0.0:50070	The namenode's HTTP server address and port.
dfs.datanode.http.address	0.0.0.0:50075	The datanode's HTTP server address and port.
dfs.secondary.http.address	0.0.0.0:50090	The secondary namenode's HTTP server address and port.

There are also settings for controlling which network interfaces the datanodes and tasktrackers report as their IP addresses (for HTTP and RPC servers). The relevant properties are `dfs.datanode.dns.interface` and `mapred.tasktracker.dns.interface`, both of which are set to `default`, which will use the default network interface. You can set this explicitly to report the address of a particular interface (`eth0`, for example).

Other Hadoop Properties

This section discusses some other properties that you might consider setting.

Cluster membership

To aid the addition and removal of nodes in the future, you can specify a file containing a list of authorized machines that may join the cluster as datanodes or tasktrackers. The file is specified using the `dfs.hosts` (for datanodes) and `mapred.hosts` (for tasktrackers) properties, as well as the corresponding `dfs.hosts.exclude` and `mapred.hosts.exclude` files used for decommissioning. See "Commissioning and Decommissioning Nodes" on page 313 for further discussion.

Buffer size

Hadoop uses a buffer size of 4 KB (4,096 bytes) for its I/O operations. This is a conservative setting, and with modern hardware and operating systems, you will likely see performance benefits by increasing it; 64 KB (65,536 bytes) or 128 KB (131,072 bytes) are common choices. Set this using the `io.file.buffer.size` property in *core-site.xml*.

HDFS block size

The HDFS block size is 64 MB by default, but many clusters use 128 MB (134,217,728 bytes) or even 256 MB (268,435,456 bytes) to ease memory pressure on the namenode and to give mappers more data to work on. Set this using the `dfs.block.size` property in *hdfs-site.xml*.

Reserved storage space

By default, datanodes will try to use all of the space available in their storage directories. If you want to reserve some space on the storage volumes for non-HDFS use, then you can set `dfs.datanode.du.reserved` to the amount, in bytes, of space to reserve.

Trash

Hadoop filesystems have a trash facility, in which deleted files are not actually deleted, but rather are moved to a trash folder, where they remain for a minimum period before being permanently deleted by the system. The minimum period in minutes that a file will remain in the trash is set using the `fs.trash.interval` configuration property in *core-site.xml*. By default, the trash interval is zero, which disables trash.

Like in many operating systems, Hadoop's trash facility is a user-level feature, meaning that only files that are deleted using the filesystem shell are put in the trash. Files deleted programmatically are deleted immediately. It is possible to use the trash programmatically, however, by constructing a Trash instance, then calling its moveToTrash() method with the Path of the file intended for deletion. The method returns a value indicating success; a value of false means either that trash is not enabled or that the file is already in the trash.

When trash is enabled, each user has her own trash directory called *.Trash* in her home directory. File recovery is simple: you look for the file in a subdirectory of *.Trash* and move it out of the trash subtree.

HDFS will automatically delete files in trash folders, but other filesystems will not, so you have to arrange for this to be done periodically. You can *expunge* the trash, which will delete files that have been in the trash longer than their minimum period, using the filesystem shell:

```
% hadoop fs -expunge
```

The Trash class exposes an expunge() method that has the same effect.

Task memory limits

On a shared cluster, it shouldn't be possible for one user's errant MapReduce program to bring down nodes in the cluster. This can happen if the map or reduce task has a memory leak, for example, because the machine on which the tasktracker is running will run out of memory and may affect the other running processes. To prevent this situation, you can set mapred.child.ulimit, which sets a maximum limit on the virtual memory of the child process launched by the tasktracker. It is set in kilobytes, and should be comfortably larger than the memory of the JVM set by mapred.child.java.opts; otherwise, the child JVM might not start.

As an alternative, you can use *limits.conf* to set process limits at the operating system level.

Job scheduler

Particularly in a multiuser MapReduce setting, consider changing the default FIFO job scheduler to one of the more fully featured alternatives. See "Job Scheduling" on page 175.

User Account Creation

Once you have a Hadoop cluster up and running, you need to give users access to it. This involves creating a home directory for each user and setting ownership permissions on it:

```
% hadoop fs -mkdir /user/username
% hadoop fs -chown username:username /user/username
```

This is a good time to set space limits on the directory. The following sets a 1 TB limit on the given user directory:

```
% hadoop dfsadmin -setSpaceQuota 1t /user/username
```

Security

Early versions of Hadoop assumed that HDFS and MapReduce clusters would be used by a group of cooperating users within a secure environment. The measures for restricting access were designed to prevent accidental data loss, rather than to prevent unauthorized access to data. For example, the file permissions system in HDFS prevents one user from accidentally wiping out the whole filesystem from a bug in a program, or by mistakenly typing hadoop fs -rmr /, but it doesn't prevent a malicious user from assuming root's identity (see "Setting User Identity" on page 134) to access or delete any data in the cluster.

In security parlance, what was missing was a secure *authentication* mechanism to assure Hadoop that the user seeking to perform an operation on the cluster is who they claim to be and therefore trusted. HDFS file permissions provide only a mechanism for *authorization*, which controls what a particular user can do to a particular file. For example, a file may only be readable by a group of users, so anyone not in that group is not authorized to read it. However, authorization is not enough by itself, since the system is still open to abuse via spoofing by a malicious user who can gain network access to the cluster.

It's common to restrict access to data that contains personally identifiable information (such as an end user's full name or IP address) to a small set of users (of the cluster) within the organization, who are authorized to access such information. Less sensitive (or anonymized) data may be made available to a larger set of users. It is convenient to host a mix of datasets with different security levels on the same cluster (not least because it means the datasets with lower security levels can be shared). However, to meet regulatory requirements for data protection, secure authentication must be in place for shared clusters.

This is the situation that Yahoo! faced in 2009, which led a team of engineers there to implement secure authentication for Hadoop. In their design, Hadoop itself does not manage user credentials, since it relies on Kerberos, a mature open-source network authentication protocol, to authenticate the user. In turn, Kerberos doesn't manage permissions. Kerberos says that a user is who they say they are; it's Hadoop's job to determine whether that user has permission to perform a given action. There's a lot to Kerberos, so here we only cover enough to use it in the context of Hadoop, referring readers who want more background to *Kerberos: The Definitive Guide (http://oreilly .com/catalog/9780596004033/)* by Jason Garman (O'Reilly, 2003).

Which Versions of Hadoop Support Kerberos Authentication?

Kerberos for authentication was added after the 0.20 series of releases of Apache Hadoop. However, it was not complete at the time of the first 0.21 release, so it will not be generally available and stable until the 0.22 release series. Alternatively, you can find it in the 0.20.S Yahoo! Distribution of Hadoop. The same security support will also be available in Cloudera's first stable CDH3 release.

Kerberos and Hadoop

At a high level, there are three steps that a client must take to access a service when using Kerberos, each of which involves a message exchange with a server:

1. *Authentication.* The client authenticates itself to the Authentication Server and receives a timestamped Ticket-Granting Ticket (TGT).

2. *Authorization.* The client uses the TGT to request a service ticket from the Ticket Granting Server.

3. *Service Request.* The client uses the service ticket to authenticate itself to the server that is providing the service the client is using. In the case of Hadoop, this might be the namenode or the jobtracker.

Together, the Authentication Server and the Ticket Granting Server form the *Key Distribution Center* (KDC). The process is shown graphically in Figure 9-2.

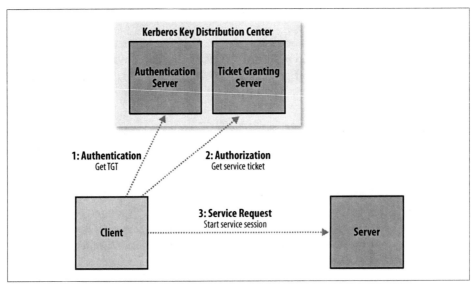

Figure 9-2. The three-step Kerberos ticket exchange protocol

The authorization and service request steps are not user-level actions: the client performs these steps on the user's behalf. The authentication step, however, is normally carried out explicitly by the user using the kinit command, which will prompt for a password. However, this doesn't mean you need to enter your password every time you run a job or access HDFS, since TGTs last for 10 hours by default (and can be renewed for up to a week). It's common to automate authentication at operating system login time, thereby providing *single sign-on* to Hadoop.

In cases where you don't want to be prompted for a password (for running an unattended MapReduce job, for example), you can create a Kerberos *keytab* file using the ktutil command. A keytab is a file that stores passwords and may be supplied to kinit with the -t option.

An example

Let's look at an example of the process in action. The first step is to enable Kerberos authentication by setting the hadoop.security.authentication property in *core-site.xml* to kerberos.[‖] The default setting is simple, which signifies that the old backwards-compatible (but insecure) behavior of using the operating system user name to determine identity should be employed.

We also need to enable service-level authorization by setting hadoop.security.author ization to true in the same file. You may configure Access Control Lists (ACLs) in the *hadoop-policy.xml* configuration file to control which users and groups have permission to connect to each Hadoop service. Services are defined at the protocol level, so there are ones for MapReduce job submission, namenode communication, and so on. By default, all ACLs are set to *, which means that all users have permission to access each service, but on a real cluster you should lock the ACLs down to only those users and groups that should have access.

The format for an ACL is a comma-separated list of usernames, followed by whitespace, followed by a comma-separated list of group names. For example, the ACL preston,howard directors,inventors would authorize access to users named preston or howard, or in groups directors or inventors.

With Kerberos authentication turned on, let's see what happens when we try to copy a local file to HDFS:

```
% hadoop fs -put quangle.txt .
10/07/03 15:44:58 WARN ipc.Client: Exception encountered while connecting to the
server: javax.security.sasl.SaslException: GSS initiate failed [Caused by GSSEx
ception: No valid credentials provided (Mechanism level: Failed to find any Ker
```

‖ To use Kerberos authentication with Hadoop, you need to install, configure, and run a KDC (Hadoop does not come with one). Your organization may already have a KDC you can use (an Active Directory installation, for example); if not, you can set up an MIT Kerberos 5 KDC using the instructions in the *Linux Security Cookbook* (*http://oreilly.com/catalog/9780596003913/*) (O'Reilly, 2003). For getting started with Hadoop security, consider using Yahoo!'s Hadoop 0.20.S Virtual Machine Appliance, which includes a local KDC as well as a pseudo-distributed Hadoop cluster.

```
beros tgt)]
Bad connection to FS. command aborted. exception: Call to localhost/127.0.0.1:80
20 failed on local exception: java.io.IOException: javax.security.sasl.SaslExcep
tion: GSS initiate failed [Caused by GSSException: No valid credentials provided
(Mechanism level: Failed to find any Kerberos tgt)]
```

The operation fails, since we don't have a Kerberos ticket. We can get one by authenticating to the KDC, using `kinit`:

```
% kinit
Password for hadoop-user@LOCALDOMAIN: password
% hadoop fs -put quangle.txt .
% hadoop fs -stat %n quangle.txt
quangle.txt
```

And we see that the file is successfully written to HDFS. Notice that even though we carried out two filesystem commands, we only needed to call `kinit` once, since the Kerberos ticket is valid for 10 hours (use the `klist` command to see the expiry time of your tickets and `kdestroy` to invalidate your tickets). After we get a ticket, everything works just as normal.

Delegation Tokens

In a distributed system like HDFS or MapReduce, there are many client-server interactions, each of which must be authenticated. For example, an HDFS read operation will involve multiple calls to the namenode and calls to one or more datanodes. Instead of using the three-step Kerberos ticket exchange protocol to authenticate each call, which would present a high load on the KDC on a busy cluster, Hadoop uses *delegation tokens* to allow later authenticated access without having to contact the KDC again. Delegation tokens are created and used transparently by Hadoop on behalf of users, so there's no action you need to take as a user over using `kinit` to sign in, however it's useful to have a basic idea of how they are used.

A delegation token is generated by the server (the namenode in this case), and can be thought of as a shared secret between the client and the server. On the first RPC call to the namenode, the client has no delegation token, so it uses Kerberos to authenticate, and as a part of the response it gets a delegation token from the namenode. In subsequent calls, it presents the delegation token, which the namenode can verify (since it generated it using a secret key), and hence the client is authenticated to the server.

When it wants to perform operations on HDFS blocks, the client uses a special kind of delegation token, called a *block access token*, that the namenode passes to the client in response to a metadata request. The client uses the block access token to authenticate itself to datanodes. This is possible only because the namenode shares its secret key used to generate the block access token with datanodes (which it sends in heartbeat messages), so that they can verify block access tokens. Thus, an HDFS block may only be accessed by a client with a valid block access token from a namenode. This closes the security hole in unsecured Hadoop where only the block ID was needed to gain access to a block. This property is enabled by setting `dfs.block.access.token.enable` to `true`.

In MapReduce, job resources and metadata (such as JAR files, input splits, configuration files) are shared in HDFS for the jobtracker to access, and user code runs on the tasktrackers and accesses files on HDFS (the process is explained in "Anatomy of a MapReduce Job Run" on page 167). Delegation tokens are used by the jobtracker and tasktrackers to access HDFS during the course of the job. When the job has finished, the delegation tokens are invalidated.

Delegation tokens are automatically obtained for the default HDFS instance, but if your job needs to access other HDFS clusters, then you can have the delegation tokens for these loaded by setting the `mapreduce.job.hdfs-servers` job property to a comma-separated list of HDFS URIs.

Other Security Enhancements

Security has been tightened throughout HDFS and MapReduce to protect against unauthorized access to resources.# The more notable changes are listed here:

- Tasks can be run using the operating system account for the user who submitted the job, rather than the user running the tasktracker. This means that the operating system is used to isolate running tasks, so they can't send signals to each other (to kill another user's tasks, for example), and so local information, such as task data, is kept private via local file system permissions.

  This feature is enabled by setting `mapred.task.tracker.task-controller` to `org.apache.hadoop.mapred.LinuxTaskController`.* In addition, administrators need to ensure that each user is given an account on every node in the cluster (typically using LDAP).

- When tasks are run as the user who submitted the job, the distributed cache ("Distributed Cache" on page 253) is secure: files that are world-readable are put in a shared cache (the insecure default), otherwise they go in a private cache, only readable by the owner.

- Users can view and modify only their own jobs, not others. This is enabled by setting `mapred.acls.enabled` to `true`. There are two job configuration properties, `mapreduce.job.acl-view-job` and `mapreduce.job.acl-modify-job`, which may be set to a comma-separated list of users to control who may view or modify a particular job.

- The shuffle is secure, preventing a malicious user from requesting another user's map outputs.

#At the time of writing, other projects like HBase and Hive had not been integrated with this security model.

* `LinuxTaskController` uses a setuid executable called *task-controller* found in the *bin* directory. You should ensure that this binary is owned by root and has the setuid bit set (with `chmod +s`).

- When appropriately configured, it's no longer possible for a malicious user to run a rogue secondary namenode, datanode, or tasktracker that can join the cluster and potentially compromise data stored in the cluster. This is enforced by requiring daemons to authenticate with the master node they are connecting to.

  To enable this feature, you first need to configure Hadoop to use a keytab previously generated with the `ktutil` command. For a datanode, for example, you would set the `dfs.datanode.keytab.file` property to the keytab filename and `dfs.data node.kerberos.principal` to the username to use for the datanode. Finally, the ACL for the `DataNodeProtocol` (which is used by datanodes to communicate with the namenode) must be set in *hadoop-policy.xml*, by restricting `security.datanode.pro tocol.acl` to the datanode's username.

- A datanode may be run on a privileged port (one lower than 1024), so a client may be reasonably sure that it was started securely.

- A task may only communicate with its parent tasktracker, thus preventing an attacker from obtaining MapReduce data from another user's job.

One area that hasn't yet been addressed in the security work is encryption: neither RPC nor block transfers are encrypted. HDFS blocks are not stored in an encrypted form either. These features are planned for a future release, and in fact, encrypting the data stored in HDFS could be carried out in existing versions of Hadoop by the application itself (by writing an encryption `CompressionCodec`, for example).

Benchmarking a Hadoop Cluster

Is the cluster set up correctly? The best way to answer this question is empirically: run some jobs and confirm that you get the expected results. Benchmarks make good tests, as you also get numbers that you can compare with other clusters as a sanity check on whether your new cluster is performing roughly as expected. And you can tune a cluster using benchmark results to squeeze the best performance out of it. This is often done with monitoring systems in place ("Monitoring" on page 305), so you can see how resources are being used across the cluster.

To get the best results, you should run benchmarks on a cluster that is not being used by others. In practice, this is just before it is put into service and users start relying on it. Once users have periodically scheduled jobs on a cluster, it is generally impossible to find a time when the cluster is not being used (unless you arrange downtime with users), so you should run benchmarks to your satisfaction before this happens.

Experience has shown that most hardware failures for new systems are hard drive failures. By running I/O intensive benchmarks—such as the ones described next—you can "burn in" the cluster before it goes live.

Hadoop Benchmarks

Hadoop comes with several benchmarks that you can run very easily with minimal setup cost. Benchmarks are packaged in the test JAR file, and you can get a list of them, with descriptions, by invoking the JAR file with no arguments:

```
% hadoop jar $HADOOP_INSTALL/hadoop-*-test.jar
```

Most of the benchmarks show usage instructions when invoked with no arguments. For example:

```
% hadoop jar $HADOOP_INSTALL/hadoop-*-test.jar TestDFSIO
TestFDSIO.0.0.4
Usage: TestFDSIO -read | -write | -clean [-nrFiles N] [-fileSize MB] [-resFile
resultFileName] [-bufferSize Bytes]
```

Benchmarking HDFS with TestDFSIO

TestDFSIO tests the I/O performance of HDFS. It does this by using a MapReduce job as a convenient way to read or write files in parallel. Each file is read or written in a separate map task, and the output of the map is used for collecting statistics relating to the file just processed. The statistics are accumulated in the reduce to produce a summary.

The following command writes 10 files of 1,000 MB each:

```
% hadoop jar $HADOOP_INSTALL/hadoop-*-test.jar TestDFSIO -write -nrFiles 10
-fileSize 1000
```

At the end of the run, the results are written to the console and also recorded in a local file (which is appended to, so you can rerun the benchmark and not lose old results):

```
% cat TestDFSIO_results.log
----- TestDFSIO ----- : write
           Date & time: Sun Apr 12 07:14:09 EDT 2009
       Number of files: 10
Total MBytes processed: 10000
     Throughput mb/sec: 7.796340865378244
Average IO rate mb/sec: 7.8862199783325195
 IO rate std deviation: 0.9101254683525547
     Test exec time sec: 163.387
```

The files are written under the */benchmarks/TestDFSIO* directory by default (this can be changed by setting the `test.build.data` system property), in a directory called *io_data*.

To run a read benchmark, use the `-read` argument. Note that these files must already exist (having been written by TestDFSIO -write):

```
% hadoop jar $HADOOP_INSTALL/hadoop-*-test.jar TestDFSIO -read -nrFiles 10
-fileSize 1000
```

Here are the results for a real run:

```
----- TestDFSIO ----- : read
           Date & time: Sun Apr 12 07:24:28 EDT 2009
       Number of files: 10
 Total MBytes processed: 10000
     Throughput mb/sec: 80.25553361904304
 Average IO rate mb/sec: 98.6801528930664
 IO rate std deviation: 36.63507598174921
     Test exec time sec: 47.624
```

When you've finished benchmarking, you can delete all the generated files from HDFS using the -clean argument:

```
% hadoop jar $HADOOP_INSTALL/hadoop-*-test.jar TestDFSIO -clean
```

Benchmarking MapReduce with Sort

Hadoop comes with a MapReduce program that does a partial sort of its input. It is very useful for benchmarking the whole MapReduce system, as the full input dataset is transferred through the shuffle. The three steps are: generate some random data, perform the sort, then validate the results.

First we generate some random data using RandomWriter. It runs a MapReduce job with 10 maps per node, and each map generates (approximately) 10 GB of random binary data, with key and values of various sizes. You can change these values if you like by setting the properties test.randomwriter.maps_per_host and test.randomwrite.bytes_per_map. There are also settings for the size ranges of the keys and values; see RandomWriter for details.

Here's how to invoke RandomWriter (found in the example JAR file, not the test one) to write its output to a directory called *random-data*:

```
% hadoop jar $HADOOP_INSTALL/hadoop-*-examples.jar randomwriter random-data
```

Next we can run the Sort program:

```
% hadoop jar $HADOOP_INSTALL/hadoop-*-examples.jar sort random-data sorted-data
```

The overall execution time of the sort is the metric we are interested in, but it's instructive to watch the job's progress via the web UI (*http://jobtracker-host:50030/*), where you can get a feel for how long each phase of the job takes. Adjusting the parameters mentioned in "Tuning a Job" on page 160 is a useful exercise, too.

As a final sanity check, we validate that the data in *sorted-data* is, in fact, correctly sorted:

```
% hadoop jar $HADOOP_INSTALL/hadoop-*-test.jar testmapredsort -sortInput random-data \
    -sortOutput sorted-data
```

This command runs the SortValidator program, which performs a series of checks on the unsorted and sorted data to check whether the sort is accurate. It reports the outcome to the console at the end of its run:

```
SUCCESS! Validated the MapReduce framework's 'sort' successfully.
```

Other benchmarks

There are many more Hadoop benchmarks, but the following are widely used:

- MRBench (invoked with mrbench) runs a small job a number of times. It acts as a good counterpoint to sort, as it checks whether small job runs are responsive.
- NNBench (invoked with nnbench) is useful for load testing namenode hardware.
- *Gridmix* is a suite of benchmarks designed to model a realistic cluster workload, by mimicking a variety of data-access patterns seen in practice. See *src/benchmarks/ gridmix2* in the distribution for further details. For release 0.21.0 onward, there is a new version of Gridmix in the *src/contrib/gridmix* MapReduce directory, described further at *http://developer.yahoo.net/blogs/hadoop/2010/04/gridmix3 _emulating_production.html*.[†]

User Jobs

For tuning, it is best to include a few jobs that are representative of the jobs that your users run, so your cluster is tuned for these and not just for the standard benchmarks. If this is your first Hadoop cluster and you don't have any user jobs yet, then Gridmix is a good substitute.

When running your own jobs as benchmarks, you should select a dataset for your user jobs that you use each time you run the benchmarks to allow comparisons between runs. When you set up a new cluster, or upgrade a cluster, you will be able to use the same dataset to compare the performance with previous runs.

Hadoop in the Cloud

Although many organizations choose to run Hadoop in-house, it is also popular to run Hadoop in the cloud on rented hardware or as a service. For instance, Cloudera offers tools for running Hadoop (see Appendix B) in a public or private cloud, and Amazon has a Hadoop cloud service called Elastic MapReduce.

In this section, we look at running Hadoop on Amazon EC2, which is a great way to try out your own Hadoop cluster on a low-commitment, trial basis.

---

† In a similar vein, *PigMix* is a set of benchmarks for Pig available at *http://wiki.apache.org/pig/PigMix*.

Hadoop on Amazon EC2

Amazon Elastic Compute Cloud (EC2) is a computing service that allows customers to rent computers (*instances*) on which they can run their own applications. A customer can launch and terminate instances on demand, paying by the hour for active instances.

The Apache Whirr project (*http://incubator.apache.org/whirr*) provides a set of scripts that make it easy to run Hadoop on EC2 and other cloud providers.[‡] The scripts allow you to perform such operations as launching or terminating a cluster, or adding instances to an existing cluster.

Running Hadoop on EC2 is especially appropriate for certain workflows. For example, if you store data on Amazon S3, then you can run a cluster on EC2 and run MapReduce jobs that read the S3 data and write output back to S3, before shutting down the cluster. If you're working with longer-lived clusters, you might copy S3 data onto HDFS running on EC2 for more efficient processing, as HDFS can take advantage of data locality, but S3 cannot (since S3 storage is not collocated with EC2 nodes).

Setup

Before you can run Hadoop on EC2, you need to work through Amazon's Getting Started Guide (linked from the EC2 website *http://aws.amazon.com/ec2/*), which goes through setting up an account, installing the EC2 command-line tools, and launching an instance.

Next, install Whirr, then configure the scripts to set your Amazon Web Service credentials, security key details, and the type and size of server instances to use. Detailed instructions for doing this may be found in Whirr's README file.

Launching a cluster

We are now ready to launch a cluster. To launch a cluster named *test-hadoop-cluster* with one master node (running the namenode and jobtracker) and five worker nodes (running the datanodes and tasktrackers), type:

```
% hadoop-ec2 launch-cluster test-hadoop-cluster 5
```

This will create EC2 security groups for the cluster, if they don't already exist, and give the master and worker nodes unfettered access to one another. It will also enable SSH access from anywhere. Once the security groups have been set up, the master instance will be launched; then, once it has started, the five worker instances will be launched. The reason that the worker nodes are launched separately is so that the master's hostname can be passed to the worker instances, and allow the datanodes and tasktrackers to connect to the master when they start up.

[‡] There are also bash scripts in the *src/contrib/ec2* subdirectory of the Hadoop distribution, but these are deprecated in favor of Whirr. In this section, we use Whirr's Python scripts (found in *contrib/python*), but note that Whirr also has Java libraries that implement similar functionality.

To use the cluster, network traffic from the client needs to be proxied through the master node of the cluster using an SSH tunnel, which we can set up using the following command:

```
% eval 'hadoop-ec2 proxy test-hadoop-cluster'
Proxy pid 27134
```

Running a MapReduce job

You can run MapReduce jobs either from within the cluster or from an external machine. Here we show how to run a job from the machine we launched the cluster on. Note that this requires that the same version of Hadoop has been installed locally as is running on the cluster.

When we launched the cluster, a *hadoop-site.xml* file was created in the directory *~/.hadoop-cloud/test-hadoop-cluster*. We can use this to connect to the cluster by setting the HADOOP_CONF_DIR environment variable as follows:

```
% export HADOOP_CONF_DIR=~/.hadoop-cloud/test-hadoop-cluster
```

The cluster's filesystem is empty, so before we run a job, we need to populate it with data. Doing a parallel copy from S3 (see "Hadoop Filesystems" on page 47 for more on the S3 filesystems in Hadoop) using Hadoop's *distcp* tool is an efficient way to transfer data into HDFS:

```
% hadoop distcp s3n://hadoopbook/ncdc/all input/ncdc/all
```

After the data has been copied, we can run a job in the usual way:

```
% hadoop jar job.jar MaxTemperatureWithCombiner input/ncdc/all output
```

Alternatively, we could have specified the input to be S3, which would have the same effect. When running multiple jobs over the same input data, it's best to copy the data to HDFS first to save bandwidth:

```
% hadoop jar job.jar MaxTemperatureWithCombiner s3n://hadoopbook/ncdc/all output
```

You can track the progress of the job using the jobtracker's web UI, found at *http://master_host:50030/*. To access web pages running on worker nodes, you need set up a proxy auto-config (PAC) file in your browser. See the Whirr documentation for details on how to do this.

Terminating a cluster

To shut down the cluster, issue the terminate-cluster command:

```
% hadoop-ec2 terminate-cluster test-hadoop-cluster
```

You will be asked to confirm that you want to terminate all the instances in the cluster.

Finally, stop the proxy process (the HADOOP_CLOUD_PROXY_PID environment variable was set when we started the proxy):

```
% kill $HADOOP_CLOUD_PROXY_PID
```

## CHAPTER 10

Administering Hadoop

The previous chapter was devoted to setting up a Hadoop cluster. In this chapter, we look at the procedures to keep a cluster running smoothly.

HDFS

Persistent Data Structures

As an administrator, it is invaluable to have a basic understanding of how the components of HDFS—the namenode, the secondary namenode, and the datanodes—organize their persistent data on disk. Knowing which files are which can help you diagnose problems or spot that something is awry.

Namenode directory structure

A newly formatted namenode creates the following directory structure:

```
${dfs.name.dir}/current/VERSION
                      /edits
                      /fsimage
                      /fstime
```

Recall from Chapter 9 that the `dfs.name.dir` property is a list of directories, with the same contents mirrored in each directory. This mechanism provides resilience, particularly if one of the directories is an NFS mount, as is recommended.

The *VERSION* file is a Java properties file that contains information about the version of HDFS that is running. Here are the contents of a typical file:

```
#Tue Mar 10 19:21:36 GMT 2009
namespaceID=134368441
cTime=0
storageType=NAME_NODE
layoutVersion=-18
```

The `layoutVersion` is a negative integer that defines the version of HDFS's persistent data structures. This version number has no relation to the release number of the Hadoop distribution. Whenever the layout changes, the version number is decremented (for example, the version after –18 is –19). When this happens, HDFS needs to be upgraded, since a newer namenode (or datanode) will not operate if its storage layout is an older version. Upgrading HDFS is covered in "Upgrades" on page 316.

The `namespaceID` is a unique identifier for the filesystem, which is created when the filesystem is first formatted. The namenode uses it to identify new datanodes, since they will not know the `namespaceID` until they have registered with the namenode.

The `cTime` property marks the creation time of the namenode's storage. For newly formatted storage, the value is always zero, but it is updated to a timestamp whenever the filesystem is upgraded.

The `storageType` indicates that this storage directory contains data structures for a namenode.

The other files in the namenode's storage directory are *edits*, *fsimage*, and *fstime*. These are all binary files, which use Hadoop `Writable` objects as their serialization format (see "Serialization" on page 86). To understand what these files are for, we need to dig into the workings of the namenode a little more.

The filesystem image and edit log

When a filesystem client performs a write operation (such as creating or moving a file), it is first recorded in the edit log. The namenode also has an in-memory representation of the filesystem metadata, which it updates after the edit log has been modified. The in-memory metadata is used to serve read requests.

The edit log is flushed and synced after every write before a success code is returned to the client. For namenodes that write to multiple directories, the write must be flushed and synced to every copy before returning successfully. This ensures that no operation is lost due to machine failure.

The *fsimage* file is a persistent checkpoint of the filesystem metadata. However, it is *not* updated for every filesystem write operation, since writing out the *fsimage* file, which can grow to be gigabytes in size, would be very slow. This does not compromise resilience, however, because if the namenode fails, then the latest state of its metadata can be reconstructed by loading the *fsimage* from disk into memory, then applying each of the operations in the edit log. In fact, this is precisely what the namenode does when it starts up (see "Safe Mode" on page 298).

The *fsimage* file contains a serialized form of all the directory and file inodes in the filesystem. Each inode is an internal representation of a file or directory's metadata and contains such information as the file's replication level, modification and access times, access permissions, block size, and the blocks a file is made up of. For directories, the modification time, permissions, and quota metadata is stored.

The *fsimage* file does *not* record the datanodes on which the blocks are stored. Instead the namenode keeps this mapping in memory, which it constructs by asking the datanodes for their block lists when they join the cluster and periodically afterward to ensure the namenode's block mapping is up-to-date.

As described, the *edits* file would grow without bound. Though this state of affairs would have no impact on the system while the namenode is running, if the namenode were restarted, it would take a long time to apply each of the operations in its (very long) edit log. During this time, the filesystem would be offline, which is generally undesirable.

The solution is to run the secondary namenode, whose purpose is to produce checkpoints of the primary's in-memory filesystem metadata.* The checkpointing process proceeds as follows (and is shown schematically in Figure 10-1):

1. The secondary asks the primary to roll its *edits* file, so new edits go to a new file.

2. The secondary retrieves *fsimage* and *edits* from the primary (using HTTP GET).

3. The secondary loads *fsimage* into memory, applies each operation from *edits*, then creates a new consolidated *fsimage* file.

4. The secondary sends the new *fsimage* back to the primary (using HTTP POST).

5. The primary replaces the old *fsimage* with the new one from the secondary, and the old *edits* file with the new one it started in step 1. It also updates the *fstime* file to record the time that the checkpoint was taken.

At the end of the process, the primary has an up-to-date *fsimage* file and a shorter *edits* file (it is not necessarily empty, as it may have received some edits while the checkpoint was being taken). It is possible for an administrator to run this process manually while the namenode is in safe mode, using the `hadoop dfsadmin -saveNamespace` command.

This procedure makes it clear why the secondary has similar memory requirements to the primary (since it loads the *fsimage* into memory), which is the reason that the secondary needs a dedicated machine on large clusters.

---

* From Hadoop version 0.21.0 onward, the secondary namenode will be deprecated and replaced by a *checkpoint node*, which has the same functionality. At the same time, a new type of namenode, called a *backup node*, will be introduced, whose purpose is to maintain an up-to-date copy of the namenode metadata and to act as a replacement for storing a copy of the metadata on NFS.

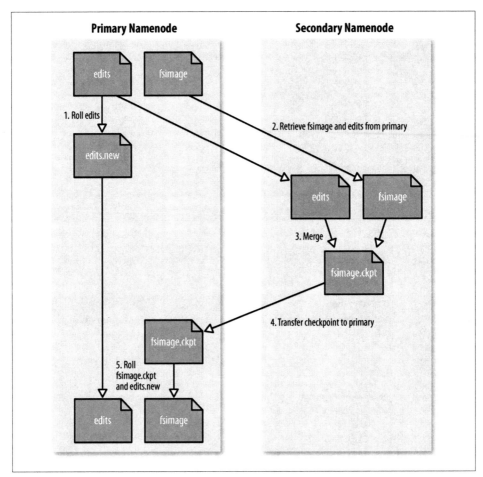

Figure 10-1. The checkpointing process

The schedule for checkpointing is controlled by two configuration parameters. The secondary namenode checkpoints every hour (`fs.checkpoint.period` in seconds) or sooner if the edit log has reached 64 MB (`fs.checkpoint.size` in bytes), which it checks every five minutes.

Secondary namenode directory structure

A useful side effect of the checkpointing process is that the secondary has a checkpoint at the end of the process, which can be found in a subdirectory called *previous.checkpoint*. This can be used as a source for making (stale) backups of the namenode's metadata:

```
${fs.checkpoint.dir}/current/VERSION
                    /edits
                    /fsimage
```

```
                    /fstime
      /previous.checkpoint/VERSION
                    /edits
                    /fsimage
                    /fstime
```

The layout of this directory and of the secondary's *current* directory is identical to the namenode's. This is by design, since in the event of total namenode failure (when there are no recoverable backups, even from NFS), it allows recovery from a secondary namenode. This can be achieved either by copying the relevant storage directory to a new namenode, or, if the secondary is taking over as the new primary namenode, by using the -importCheckpoint option when starting the namenode daemon. The -importCheckpoint option will load the namenode metadata from the latest checkpoint in the directory defined by the fs.checkpoint.dir property, but only if there is no metadata in the dfs.name.dir directory, so there is no risk of overwriting precious metadata.

Datanode directory structure

Unlike namenodes, datanodes do not need to be explicitly formatted, since they create their storage directories automatically on startup. Here are the key files and directories:

```
${dfs.data.dir}/current/VERSION
                       /blk_<id_1>
                       /blk_<id_1>.meta
                       /blk_<id_2>
                       /blk_<id_2>.meta
                       /...
                       /blk_<id_64>
                       /blk_<id_64>.meta
                       /subdir0/
                       /subdir1/
                       /...
                       /subdir63/
```

A datanode's *VERSION* file is very similar to the namenode's:

```
#Tue Mar 10 21:32:31 GMT 2009
namespaceID=134368441
storageID=DS-547717739-172.16.85.1-50010-1236720751627
cTime=0
storageType=DATA_NODE
layoutVersion=-18
```

The namespaceID, cTime, and layoutVersion are all the same as the values in the namenode (in fact, the namespaceID is retrieved from the namenode when the datanode first connects). The storageID is unique to the datanode (it is the same across all storage directories) and is used by the namenode to uniquely identify the datanode. The storageType identifies this directory as a datanode storage directory.

The other files in the datanode's *current* storage directory are the files with the *blk_* prefix. There are two types: the HDFS blocks themselves (which just consist of the file's raw bytes) and the metadata for a block (with a *.meta* suffix). A block file just consists of the raw bytes of a portion of the file being stored; the metadata file is made up of a header with version and type information, followed by a series of checksums for sections of the block.

When the number of blocks in a directory grows to a certain size, the datanode creates a new subdirectory in which to place new blocks and their accompanying metadata. It creates a new subdirectory every time the number of blocks in a directory reaches 64 (set by the dfs.datanode.numblocks configuration property). The effect is to have a tree with high fan-out, so even for systems with a very large number of blocks, the directories will only be a few levels deep. By taking this measure, the datanode ensures that there is a manageable number of files per directory, which avoids the problems that most operating systems encounter when there are a large number of files (tens or hundreds of thousands) in a single directory.

If the configuration property dfs.data.dir specifies multiple directories (on different drives), blocks are written to each in a round-robin fashion. Note that blocks are *not* replicated on each drive on a single datanode: block replication is across distinct datanodes.

Safe Mode

When the namenode starts, the first thing it does is load its image file (*fsimage*) into memory and apply the edits from the edit log (*edits*). Once it has reconstructed a consistent in-memory image of the filesystem metadata, it creates a new *fsimage* file (effectively doing the checkpoint itself, without recourse to the secondary namenode) and an empty edit log. Only at this point does the namenode start listening for RPC and HTTP requests. However, the namenode is running in *safe mode*, which means that it offers only a read-only view of the filesystem to clients.

 Strictly speaking, in safe mode, only filesystem operations that access the filesystem metadata (like producing a directory listing) are guaranteed to work. Reading a file will work only if the blocks are available on the current set of datanodes in the cluster; and file modifications (writes, deletes, or renames) will always fail.

Recall that the locations of blocks in the system are not persisted by the namenode—this information resides with the datanodes, in the form of a list of the blocks it is storing. During normal operation of the system, the namenode has a map of block locations stored in memory. Safe mode is needed to give the datanodes time to check in to the namenode with their block lists, so the namenode can be informed of enough block locations to run the filesystem effectively. If the namenode didn't wait for enough datanodes to check in, then it would start the process of replicating blocks to new datanodes, which would be unnecessary in most cases (since it only needed to wait for the extra datanodes to check in), and would put a great strain on the cluster's resources. Indeed, while in safe mode, the namenode does not issue any block replication or deletion instructions to datanodes.

Safe mode is exited when the *minimal replication condition* is reached, plus an extension time of 30 seconds. The minimal replication condition is when 99.9% of the blocks in the whole filesystem meet their minimum replication level (which defaults to one, and is set by dfs.replication.min, see Table 10-1).

When you are starting a newly formatted HDFS cluster, the namenode does not go into safe mode since there are no blocks in the system.

Table 10-1. Safe mode properties

Property name	Type	Default value	Description
dfs.replication.min	int	1	The minimum number of replicas that have to be written for a write to be successful.
dfs.safemode.threshold.pct	float	0.999	The proportion of blocks in the system that must meet the minimum replication level defined by dfs.replication.min before the namenode will exit safe mode. Setting this value to 0 or less forces the namenode not to start in safe mode. Setting this value to more than 1 means the namenode never exits safe mode.
dfs.safemode.extension	int	30,000	The time, in milliseconds, to extend safe mode by after the minimum replication condition defined by dfs.safemode.threshold.pct has been satisfied. For small clusters (tens of nodes), it can be set to 0.

Entering and leaving safe mode

To see whether the namenode is in safe mode, you can use the dfsadmin command:

```
% hadoop dfsadmin -safemode get
Safe mode is ON
```

The front page of the HDFS web UI provides another indication of whether the namenode is in safe mode.

Sometimes you want to wait for the namenode to exit safe mode before carrying out a command, particularly in scripts. The wait option achieves this:

```
hadoop dfsadmin -safemode wait
# command to read or write a file
```

An administrator has the ability to make the namenode enter or leave safe mode at any time. It is sometimes necessary to do this when carrying out maintenance on the cluster or after upgrading a cluster to confirm that data is still readable. To enter safe mode, use the following command:

```
% hadoop dfsadmin -safemode enter
Safe mode is ON
```

You can use this command when the namenode is still in safe mode while starting up to ensure that it never leaves safe mode. Another way of making sure that the namenode stays in safe mode indefinitely is to set the property `dfs.safemode.threshold.pct` to a value over one.

You can make the namenode leave safe mode by using:

```
% hadoop dfsadmin -safemode leave
Safe mode is OFF
```

Audit Logging

HDFS has the ability to log all filesystem access requests, a feature that some organizations require for auditing purposes. Audit logging is implemented using log4j logging at the `INFO` level, and in the default configuration it is disabled, as the log threshold is set to `WARN` in *log4j.properties*:

```
log4j.logger.org.apache.hadoop.hdfs.server.namenode.FSNamesystem.audit=WARN
```

You can enable audit logging by replacing `WARN` with `INFO`, and the result will be a log line written to the namenode's log for every HDFS event. Here's an example for a list status request on */user/tom*:

```
2009-03-13 07:11:22,982 INFO org.apache.hadoop.hdfs.server.namenode.FSNamesystem.
audit: ugi=tom,staff,admin  ip=/127.0.0.1  cmd=listStatus  src=/user/tom  dst=null
perm=null
```

It is a good idea to configure log4j so that the audit log is written to a separate file and isn't mixed up with the namenode's other log entries. An example of how to do this can be found on the Hadoop wiki at *http://wiki.apache.org/hadoop/HowToConfigure*.

Tools

dfsadmin

The *dfsadmin* tool is a multipurpose tool for finding information about the state of HDFS, as well as performing administration operations on HDFS. It is invoked as `hadoop dfsadmin`. Commands that alter HDFS state typically require superuser privileges.

The available commands to *dfsadmin* are described in Table 10-2.

Table 10-2. dfsadmin commands

Command	Description
-help	Shows help for a given command, or all commands if no command is specified.
-report	Shows filesystem statistics (similar to those shown in the web UI) and information on connected datanodes.
-metasave	Dumps information to a file in Hadoop's log directory about blocks that are being replicated or deleted, and a list of connected datanodes.
-safemode	Changes or query the state of safe mode. See "Safe Mode" on page 298.
-saveNamespace	Saves the current in-memory filesystem image to a new *fsimage* file and resets the *edits* file. This operation may be performed only in safe mode.
-refreshNodes	Updates the set of datanodes that are permitted to connect to the namenode. See "Commissioning and Decommissioning Nodes" on page 313.
-upgradeProgress	Gets information on the progress of an HDFS upgrade or forces an upgrade to proceed. See "Upgrades" on page 316.
-finalizeUpgrade	Removes the previous version of the datanodes' and namenode's storage directories. Used after an upgrade has been applied and the cluster is running successfully on the new version. See "Upgrades" on page 316.
-setQuota	Sets directory quotas. Directory quotas set a limit on the number of names (files or directories) in the directory tree. Directory quotas are useful for preventing users from creating large numbers of small files, a measure that helps preserve the namenode's memory (recall that accounting information for every file, directory, and block in the filesystem is stored in memory).
-clrQuota	Clears specified directory quotas.
-setSpaceQuota	Sets space quotas on directories. Space quotas set a limit on the size of files that may be stored in a directory tree. They are useful for giving users a limited amount of storage.
-clrSpaceQuota	Clears specified space quotas.
-refreshServiceAcl	Refreshes the namenode's service-level authorization policy file.

Filesystem check (fsck)

Hadoop provides an *fsck* utility for checking the health of files in HDFS. The tool looks for blocks that are missing from all datanodes, as well as under- or over-replicated blocks. Here is an example of checking the whole filesystem for a small cluster:

```
% hadoop fsck /
.....................Status: HEALTHY
 Total size:    511799225 B
 Total dirs:    10
 Total files:   22
 Total blocks (validated):    22 (avg. block size 23263601 B)
 Minimally replicated blocks:    22 (100.0 %)
 Over-replicated blocks:    0 (0.0 %)
 Under-replicated blocks:    0 (0.0 %)
 Mis-replicated blocks:    0 (0.0 %)
 Default replication factor:    3
 Average block replication:    3.0
```

```
Corrupt blocks:          0
Missing replicas:        0 (0.0 %)
Number of data-nodes:       4
Number of racks:         1
```

```
The filesystem under path '/' is HEALTHY
```

fsck recursively walks the filesystem namespace, starting at the given path (here the filesystem root), and checks the files it finds. It prints a dot for every file it checks. To check a file, *fsck* retrieves the metadata for the file's blocks and looks for problems or inconsistencies. Note that *fsck* retrieves all of its information from the namenode; it does not communicate with any datanodes to actually retrieve any block data.

Most of the output from *fsck* is self-explanatory, but here are some of the conditions it looks for:

Over-replicated blocks

> These are blocks that exceed their target replication for the file they belong to. Over-replication is not normally a problem, and HDFS will automatically delete excess replicas.

Under-replicated blocks

> These are blocks that do not meet their target replication for the file they belong to. HDFS will automatically create new replicas of under-replicated blocks until they meet the target replication. You can get information about the blocks being replicated (or waiting to be replicated) using `hadoop dfsadmin -metasave`.

Misreplicated blocks

> These are blocks that do not satisfy the block replica placement policy (see "Replica Placement" on page 67). For example, for a replication level of three in a multirack cluster, if all three replicas of a block are on the same rack, then the block is mis-replicated since the replicas should be spread across at least two racks for resilience.
>
> A misreplicated block is not fixed automatically by HDFS (at the time of this writing). As a workaround, you can fix the problem manually by increasing the replication of the file the block belongs to (using `hadoop fs -setrep`), waiting until the block gets replicated, then decreasing the replication of the file back to its original value.

Corrupt blocks

> These are blocks whose replicas are all corrupt. Blocks with at least one noncorrupt replica are not reported as corrupt; the namenode will replicate the noncorrupt replica until the target replication is met.

Missing replicas

> These are blocks with no replicas anywhere in the cluster.

Corrupt or missing blocks are the biggest cause for concern, as it means data has been lost. By default, *fsck* leaves files with corrupt or missing blocks, but you can tell it to perform one of the following actions on them:

- *Move* the affected files to the */lost+found* directory in HDFS, using the -move option. Files are broken into chains of contiguous blocks to aid any salvaging efforts you may attempt.

- *Delete* the affected files, using the -delete option. Files cannot be recovered after being deleted.

Finding the blocks for a file. The *fsck* tool provides an easy way to find out which blocks are in any particular file. For example:

```
% hadoop fsck /user/tom/part-00007 -files -blocks -racks
/user/tom/part-00007 25582428 bytes, 1 block(s):  OK
0. blk_-3724870485760122836_1035 len=25582428 repl=3 [/default-rack/10.251.43.2:50010,
/default-rack/10.251.27.178:50010, /default-rack/10.251.123.163:50010]
```

This says that the file */user/tom/part-00007* is made up of one block and shows the datanodes where the blocks are located. The *fsck* options used are as follows:

- The -files option shows the line with the filename, size, number of blocks, and its health (whether there are any missing blocks).

- The -blocks option shows information about each block in the file, one line per block.

- The -racks option displays the rack location and the datanode addresses for each block.

Running hadoop fsck without any arguments displays full usage instructions.

Datanode block scanner

Every datanode runs a block scanner, which periodically verifies all the blocks stored on the datanode. This allows bad blocks to be detected and fixed before they are read by clients. The DataBlockScanner maintains a list of blocks to verify and scans them one by one for checksum errors. The scanner employs a throttling mechanism to preserve disk bandwidth on the datanode.

Blocks are periodically verified every three weeks to guard against disk errors over time (this is controlled by the dfs.datanode.scan.period.hours property, which defaults to 504 hours). Corrupt blocks are reported to the namenode to be fixed.

You can get a block verification report for a datanode by visiting the datanode's web interface at *http://datanode:50075/blockScannerReport*. Here's an example of a report, which should be self-explanatory:

```
Total Blocks                 :  21131
Verified in last hour        :     70
Verified in last day         :   1767
Verified in last week        :   7360
```

```
Verified in last four weeks    :  20057
Verified in SCAN_PERIOD        :  20057
Not yet verified               :   1074
Verified since restart         :  35912
Scans since restart            :   6541
Scan errors since restart      :      0
Transient scan errors          :      0
Current scan rate limit KBps   :   1024
Progress this period           :    109%
Time left in cur period        : 53.08%
```

By specifying the `listblocks` parameter, *http://datanode:50075/blockScannerReport ?listblocks*, the report is preceded by a list of all the blocks on the datanode along with their latest verification status. Here is a snippet of the block list (lines are split to fit the page):

```
blk_6035596358209321442    : status : ok    type : none   scan time : 0
    not yet verified
blk_3065580480714947643    : status : ok    type : remote scan time : 1215755306400
    2008-07-11 05:48:26,400
blk_8729669677359108508    : status : ok    type : local  scan time : 1215755727345
    2008-07-11 05:55:27,345
```

The first column is the block ID, followed by some key-value pairs. The status can be one of failed or ok according to whether the last scan of the block detected a checksum error. The type of scan is local if it was performed by the background thread, remote if it was performed by a client or a remote datanode, or none if a scan of this block has yet to be made. The last piece of information is the scan time, which is displayed as the number of milliseconds since midnight 1 January 1970, and also as a more readable value.

balancer

Over time, the distribution of blocks across datanodes can become unbalanced. An unbalanced cluster can affect locality for MapReduce, and it puts a greater strain on the highly utilized datanodes, so it's best avoided.

The *balancer* program is a Hadoop daemon that re-distributes blocks by moving them from over-utilized datanodes to under-utilized datanodes, while adhering to the block replica placement policy that makes data loss unlikely by placing block replicas on different racks (see "Replica Placement" on page 67). It moves blocks until the cluster is deemed to be balanced, which means that the utilization of every datanode (ratio of used space on the node to total capacity of the node) differs from the utilization of the cluster (ratio of used space on the cluster to total capacity of the cluster) by no more than a given threshold percentage. You can start the balancer with:

```
% start-balancer.sh
```

The -threshold argument specifies the threshold percentage that defines what it means for the cluster to be balanced. The flag is optional, in which case the threshold is 10%. At any one time, only one balancer may be running on the cluster.

The balancer runs until the cluster is balanced; it cannot move any more blocks, or it loses contact with the namenode. It produces a logfile in the standard log directory, where it writes a line for every iteration of redistribution that it carries out. Here is the output from a short run on a small cluster:

```
Time Stamp       Iteration# Bytes Already Moved Bytes Left To Move Bytes Being Moved
Mar 18, 2009 5:23:42 PM  0                 0 KB           219.21 MB         150.29 MB
Mar 18, 2009 5:27:14 PM  1            195.24 MB            22.45 MB         150.29 MB
The cluster is balanced. Exiting...
Balancing took 6.072933333333333 minutes
```

The balancer is designed to run in the background without unduly taxing the cluster or interfering with other clients using the cluster. It limits the bandwidth that it uses to copy a block from one node to another. The default is a modest 1 MB/s, but this can be changed by setting the `dfs.balance.bandwidthPerSec` property in *hdfs-site.xml*, specified in bytes.

Monitoring

Monitoring is an important part of system administration. In this section, we look at the monitoring facilities in Hadoop and how they can hook into external monitoring systems.

The purpose of monitoring is to detect when the cluster is not providing the expected level of service. The master daemons are the most important to monitor: the namenodes (primary and secondary) and the jobtracker. Failure of datanodes and tasktrackers is to be expected, particularly on larger clusters, so you should provide extra capacity so that the cluster can tolerate having a small percentage of dead nodes at any time.

In addition to the facilities described next, some administrators run test jobs on a periodic basis as a test of the cluster's health.

There is lot of work going on to add more monitoring capabilities to Hadoop, which is not covered here. For example, Chukwa[†] is a data collection and monitoring system built on HDFS and MapReduce, and excels at mining log data for finding large-scale trends.

Logging

All Hadoop daemons produce logfiles that can be very useful for finding out what is happening in the system. "System logfiles" on page 271 explains how to configure these files.

---

† *http://hadoop.apache.org/chukwa*

Setting log levels

When debugging a problem, it is very convenient to be able to change the log level temporarily for a particular component in the system.

Hadoop daemons have a web page for changing the log level for any log4j log name, which can be found at */logLevel* in the daemon's web UI. By convention, log names in Hadoop correspond to the classname doing the logging, although there are exceptions to this rule, so you should consult the source code to find log names.

For example, to enable debug logging for the `JobTracker` class, we would visit the job-tracker's web UI at *http://jobtracker-host:50030/logLevel* and set the log name `org.apache.hadoop.mapred.JobTracker` to level `DEBUG`.

The same thing can be achieved from the command line as follows:

```
% hadoop daemonlog -setlevel jobtracker-host:50030 \
    org.apache.hadoop.mapred.JobTracker DEBUG
```

Log levels changed in this way are reset when the daemon restarts, which is usually what you want. However, to make a persistent change to a log level, simply change the *log4j.properties* file in the configuration directory. In this case, the line to add is:

```
log4j.logger.org.apache.hadoop.mapred.JobTracker=DEBUG
```

Getting stack traces

Hadoop daemons expose a web page (*/stacks* in the web UI) that produces a thread dump for all running threads in the daemon's JVM. For example, you can get a thread dump for a jobtracker from *http://jobtracker-host:50030/stacks*.

Metrics

The HDFS and MapReduce daemons collect information about events and measurements that are collectively known as *metrics*. For example, datanodes collect the following metrics (and many more): the number of bytes written, the number of blocks replicated, and the number of read requests from clients (both local and remote).

Metrics belong to a *context*, and Hadoop currently uses "dfs", "mapred", "rpc", and "jvm" contexts. Hadoop daemons usually collect metrics under several contexts. For example, datanodes collect metrics for the "dfs", "rpc", and "jvm" contexts.

How Do Metrics Differ from Counters?

The main difference is their scope: metrics are collected by Hadoop daemons, whereas counters (see "Counters" on page 225) are collected for MapReduce tasks and aggregated for the whole job. They have different audiences, too: broadly speaking, metrics are for administrators, and counters are for MapReduce users.

The way they are collected and aggregated is also different. Counters are a MapReduce feature, and the MapReduce system ensures that counter values are propagated from the tasktrackers where they are produced, back to the jobtracker, and finally back to the client running the MapReduce job. (Counters are propagated via RPC heartbeats; see "Progress and Status Updates" on page 170.) Both the tasktrackers and the jobtracker perform aggregation.

The collection mechanism for metrics is decoupled from the component that receives the updates, and there are various pluggable outputs, including local files, Ganglia, and JMX. The daemon collecting the metrics performs aggregation on them before they are sent to the output.

A context defines the unit of publication; you can choose to publish the "dfs" context, but not the "jvm" context, for instance. Metrics are configured in the *conf/hadoop-metrics.properties* file, and, by default, all contexts are configured so they do not publish their metrics. This is the contents of the default configuration file (minus the comments):

```
dfs.class=org.apache.hadoop.metrics.spi.NullContext
mapred.class=org.apache.hadoop.metrics.spi.NullContext
jvm.class=org.apache.hadoop.metrics.spi.NullContext
rpc.class=org.apache.hadoop.metrics.spi.NullContext
```

Each line in this file configures a different context and specifies the class that handles the metrics for that context. The class must be an implementation of the MetricsCon text interface; and, as the name suggests, the NullContext class neither publishes nor updates metrics.[‡]

The other implementations of MetricsContext are covered in the following sections.

FileContext

FileContext writes metrics to a local file. It exposes two configuration properties: fileName, which specifies the absolute name of the file to write to, and period, for the time interval (in seconds) between file updates. Both properties are optional; if not set, the metrics will be written to standard output every five seconds.

[‡] The term "context" is (perhaps unfortunately) overloaded here, since it can refer to either a collection of metrics (the "dfs" context, for example) or the class that publishes metrics (the NullContext, for example).

Configuration properties apply to a context name and are specified by appending the property name to the context name (separated by a dot). For example, to dump the "jvm" context to a file, we alter its configuration to be the following:

```
jvm.class=org.apache.hadoop.metrics.file.FileContext
jvm.fileName=/tmp/jvm_metrics.log
```

In the first line, we have changed the "jvm" context to use a `FileContext`, and in the second, we have set the "jvm" context's `fileName` property to be a temporary file. Here are two lines of output from the logfile, split over several lines to fit the page:

```
jvm.metrics: hostName=ip-10-250-59-159, processName=NameNode, sessionId=, ↵
gcCount=46, gcTimeMillis=394, logError=0, logFatal=0, logInfo=59, logWarn=1, ↵
memHeapCommittedM=4.9375, memHeapUsedM=2.5322647, memNonHeapCommittedM=18.25, ↵
memNonHeapUsedM=11.330269, threadsBlocked=0, threadsNew=0, threadsRunnable=6, ↵
threadsTerminated=0, threadsTimedWaiting=8, threadsWaiting=13
jvm.metrics: hostName=ip-10-250-59-159, processName=SecondaryNameNode, sessionId=, ↵
gcCount=36, gcTimeMillis=261, logError=0, logFatal=0, logInfo=18, logWarn=4, ↵
memHeapCommittedM=5.4414062, memHeapUsedM=4.46756, memNonHeapCommittedM=18.25, ↵
memNonHeapUsedM=10.624519, threadsBlocked=0, threadsNew=0, threadsRunnable=5, ↵
threadsTerminated=0, threadsTimedWaiting=4, threadsWaiting=2
```

`FileContext` can be useful on a local system for debugging purposes, but is unsuitable on a larger cluster since the output files are spread across the cluster, which makes analyzing them difficult.

GangliaContext

Ganglia (*http://ganglia.info/*) is an open source distributed monitoring system for very large clusters. It is designed to impose very low resource overheads on each node in the cluster. Ganglia itself collects metrics, such as CPU and memory usage; by using `GangliaContext`, you can inject Hadoop metrics into Ganglia.

`GangliaContext` has one required property, `servers`, which takes a space- and/or comma-separated list of Ganglia server host-port pairs. Further details on configuring this context can be found on the Hadoop wiki (*http://wiki.apache.org/hadoop/Ganglia Metrics*).

For a flavor of the kind of information you can get out of Ganglia, see Figure 10-2, which shows how the number of tasks in the jobtracker's queue varies over time.

NullContextWithUpdateThread

Both `FileContext` and a `GangliaContext` push metrics to an external system. However, some monitoring systems—notably JMX—need to pull metrics from Hadoop. `Null ContextWithUpdateThread` is designed for this. Like `NullContext`, it doesn't publish any metrics, but in addition it runs a timer that periodically updates the metrics stored in memory. This ensures that the metrics are up-to-date when they are fetched by another system.

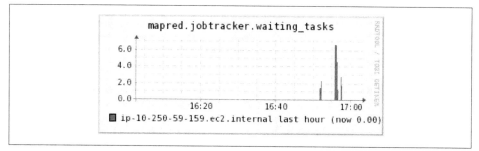

Figure 10-2. Ganglia plot of number of tasks in the jobtracker queue

All implementations of `MetricsContext`, except `NullContext`, perform this updating function (and they all expose a `period` property that defaults to five seconds), so you need to use `NullContextWithUpdateThread` only if you are not collecting metrics using another output. If you were using `GangliaContext`, for example, then it would ensure the metrics are updated, so you would be able to use JMX in addition with no further configuration of the metrics system. JMX is discussed in more detail shortly.

CompositeContext

`CompositeContext` allows you to output the same set of metrics to multiple contexts, such as a `FileContext` and a `GangliaContext`. The configuration is slightly tricky and is best shown by an example:

```
jvm.class=org.apache.hadoop.metrics.spi.CompositeContext
jvm.arity=2
jvm.sub1.class=org.apache.hadoop.metrics.file.FileContext
jvm.fileName=/tmp/jvm_metrics.log
jvm.sub2.class=org.apache.hadoop.metrics.ganglia.GangliaContext
jvm.servers=ip-10-250-59-159.ec2.internal:8649
```

The `arity` property is used to specify the number of subcontexts; in this case, there are two. The property names for each subcontext are modified to have a part specifying the subcontext number, hence `jvm.sub1.class` and `jvm.sub2.class`.

Java Management Extensions

Java Management Extensions (JMX) is a standard Java API for monitoring and managing applications. Hadoop includes several managed beans (MBeans), which expose Hadoop metrics to JMX-aware applications. There are MBeans that expose the metrics in the "dfs" and "rpc" contexts, but none for the "mapred" context (at the time of this writing) or the "jvm" context (as the JVM itself exposes a richer set of JVM metrics). These MBeans are listed in Table 10-3.

Table 10-3. Hadoop MBeans

MBean class	Daemons	Metrics
NameNodeActivityMBean	Namenode	Namenode activity metrics, such as the number of create file operations
FSNamesystemMBean	Namenode	Namenode status metrics, such as the number of connected datanodes
DataNodeActivityMBean	Datanode	Datanode activity metrics, such as number of bytes read
FSDatasetMBean	Datanode	Datanode storage metrics, such as capacity and free storage space
RpcActivityMBean	All daemons that use RPC: namenode, datanode, jobtracker, tasktracker	RPC statistics, such as average processing time

The JDK comes with a tool called JConsole for viewing MBeans in a running JVM. It's useful for browsing Hadoop metrics, as demonstrated in Figure 10-3.

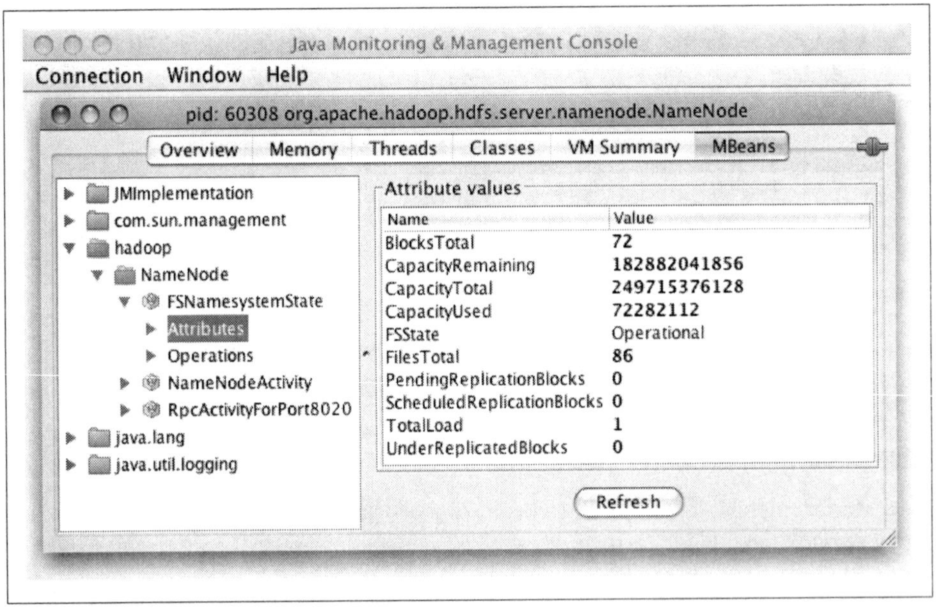

Figure 10-3. JConsole view of a locally running namenode, showing metrics for the filesystem state

Although you can see Hadoop metrics via JMX using the default metrics configuration, they will not be updated unless you change the MetricsContext implementation to something other than NullContext. For example, NullContextWithUpdateThread is appropriate if JMX is the only way you will be monitoring metrics.

Many third-party monitoring and alerting systems (such as Nagios or Hyperic) can query MBeans, making JMX the natural way to monitor your Hadoop cluster from an existing monitoring system. You will need to enable remote access to JMX, however, and choose a level of security that is appropriate for your cluster. The options here include password authentication, SSL connections, and SSL client-authentication. See the official Java documentation[§] for an in-depth guide on configuring these options.

All the options for enabling remote access to JMX involve setting Java system properties, which we do for Hadoop by editing the *conf/hadoop-env.sh* file. The following configuration settings show how to enable password-authenticated remote access to JMX on the namenode (with SSL disabled). The process is very similar for other Hadoop daemons:

```
export HADOOP_NAMENODE_OPTS="-Dcom.sun.management.jmxremote
 -Dcom.sun.management.jmxremote.ssl=false
 -Dcom.sun.management.jmxremote.password.file=$HADOOP_CONF_DIR/jmxremote.password
 -Dcom.sun.management.jmxremote.port=8004 $HADOOP_NAMENODE_OPTS"
```

The *jmxremote.password* file lists the usernames and their passwords in plain text; the JMX documentation has further details on the format of this file.

With this configuration, we can use JConsole to browse MBeans on a remote namenode. Alternatively, we can use one of the many JMX tools to retrieve MBean attribute values. Here is an example of using the "jmxquery" command-line tool (and Nagios plug-in, available from *http://code.google.com/p/jmxquery/*) to retrieve the number of under-replicated blocks:

```
% ./check_jmx -U service:jmx:rmi:///jndi/rmi://namenode-host:8004/jmxrmi -O \
hadoop:service=NameNode,name=FSNamesystemState -A UnderReplicatedBlocks \
-w 100 -c 1000 -username monitorRole -password secret
JMX OK - UnderReplicatedBlocks is 0
```

This command establishes a JMX RMI connection to the host *namenode-host* on port 8004 and authenticates using the given username and password. It reads the attribute UnderReplicatedBlocks of the object named hadoop:service=NameNode,name=FSNamesystemState and prints out its value on the console.[‖] The -w and -c options specify warning and critical levels for the value: the appropriate values of these are normally determined after operating a cluster for a while.

It's common to use Ganglia in conjunction with an alerting system like Nagios for monitoring a Hadoop cluster. Ganglia is good for efficiently collecting a large number of metrics and graphing them, whereas Nagios and similar systems are good at sending alerts when a critical threshold is reached in any of a smaller set of metrics.

---

§ *http://java.sun.com/javase/6/docs/technotes/guides/management/agent.html*

‖ It's convenient to use JConsole to find the object names of the MBeans that you want to monitor. Note that MBeans for datanode metrics contain a random identifier in Hadoop 0.20, which makes it difficult to monitor them in anything but an ad hoc way. This was fixed in Hadoop 0.21.0.

Maintenance

Routine Administration Procedures

Metadata backups

If the namenode's persistent metadata is lost or damaged, the entire filesystem is rendered unusable, so it is critical that backups are made of these files. You should keep multiple copies of different ages (one hour, one day, one week, and one month, say) to protect against corruption, either in the copies themselves or in the live files running on the namenode.

A straightforward way to make backups is to write a script to periodically archive the secondary namenode's *previous.checkpoint* subdirectory (under the directory defined by the `fs.checkpoint.dir` property) to an offsite location. The script should additionally test the integrity of the copy. This can be done by starting a local namenode daemon and verifying that it has successfully read the *fsimage* and *edits* files into memory (by scanning the namenode log for the appropriate success message, for example).#

Data backups

Although HDFS is designed to store data reliably, data loss can occur, just like in any storage system, and thus a backup strategy is essential. With the large data volumes that Hadoop can store, deciding what data to back up and where to store it is a challenge. The key here is to prioritize your data. The highest priority is the data that cannot be regenerated and that is critical to the business; however, data that is straightforward to regenerate, or essentially disposable because it is of limited business value, is the lowest priority, and you may choose not to make backups of this category of data.

> Do not make the mistake of thinking that HDFS replication is a substitute for making backups. Bugs in HDFS can cause replicas to be lost, and so can hardware failures. Although Hadoop is expressly designed so that hardware failure is very unlikely to result in data loss, the possibility can never be completely ruled out, particularly when combined with software bugs or human error.
>
> When it comes to backups, think of HDFS in the same way as you would RAID. Although the data will survive the loss of an individual RAID disk, it may not if the RAID controller fails, or is buggy (perhaps overwriting some data), or the entire array is damaged.

#Hadoop 0.21.0 comes with an Offline Image Viewer, which can be used to check the integrity of the image files.

It's common to have a policy for user directories in HDFS. For example, they may have space quotas and be backed up nightly. Whatever the policy, make sure your users know what it is, so they know what to expect.

The *distcp* tool is ideal for making backups to other HDFS clusters (preferably running on a different version of the software, to guard against loss due to bugs in HDFS) or other Hadoop filesystems (such as S3 or KFS), since it can copy files in parallel. Alternatively, you can employ an entirely different storage system for backups, using one of the ways to export data from HDFS described in "Hadoop Filesystems" on page 47.

Filesystem check (fsck)

It is advisable to run HDFS's *fsck* tool regularly (for example, daily) on the whole filesystem to proactively look for missing or corrupt blocks. See "Filesystem check (fsck)" on page 301.

Filesystem balancer

Run the balancer tool (see "balancer" on page 304) regularly to keep the filesystem datanodes evenly balanced.

Commissioning and Decommissioning Nodes

As an administrator of a Hadoop cluster, you will need to add or remove nodes from time to time. For example, to grow the storage available to a cluster, you commission new nodes. Conversely, sometimes you may wish to shrink a cluster, and to do so, you decommission nodes. It can sometimes be necessary to decommission a node if it is misbehaving, perhaps because it is failing more often than it should or its performance is noticeably slow.

Nodes normally run both a datanode and a tasktracker, and both are typically commissioned or decommissioned in tandem.

Commissioning new nodes

Although commissioning a new node can be as simple as configuring the *hdfs-site.xml* file to point to the namenode and the *mapred-site.xml* file to point to the job-tracker, and starting the datanode and jobtracker daemons, it is generally best to have a list of authorized nodes.

It is a potential security risk to allow any machine to connect to the namenode and act as a datanode, since the machine may gain access to data that it is not authorized to see. Furthermore, since such a machine is not a real datanode, it is not under your control, and may stop at any time, causing potential data loss. (Imagine what would happen if a number of such nodes were connected, and a block of data was present only on the "alien" nodes?) This scenario is a risk even inside a firewall, through misconfiguration, so datanodes (and tasktrackers) should be explicitly managed on all production clusters.

Datanodes that are permitted to connect to the namenode are specified in a file whose name is specified by the `dfs.hosts` property. The file resides on the namenode's local filesystem, and it contains a line for each datanode, specified by network address (as reported by the datanode—you can see what this is by looking at the namenode's web UI). If you need to specify multiple network addresses for a datanode, put them on one line, separated by whitespace.

Similarly, tasktrackers that may connect to the jobtracker are specified in a file whose name is specified by the `mapred.hosts` property. In most cases, there is one shared file, referred to as the *include file*, that both `dfs.hosts` and `mapred.hosts` refer to, since nodes in the cluster run both datanode and tasktracker daemons.

> The file (or files) specified by the `dfs.hosts` and `mapred.hosts` properties is different from the *slaves* file. The former is used by the namenode and jobtracker to determine which worker nodes may connect. The *slaves* file is used by the Hadoop control scripts to perform cluster-wide operations, such as cluster restarts. It is never used by the Hadoop daemons.

To add new nodes to the cluster:

1. Add the network addresses of the new nodes to the include file.
2. Update the namenode with the new set of permitted datanodes using this command:

   ```
   % hadoop dfsadmin -refreshNodes
   ```
3. Update the *slaves* file with the new nodes, so that they are included in future operations performed by the Hadoop control scripts.
4. Start the new datanodes.
5. Restart the MapReduce cluster.[*]
6. Check that the new datanodes and tasktrackers appear in the web UI.

---

[*] At the time of this writing, there is no command to refresh the set of permitted nodes in the jobtracker. Consider setting the `mapred.jobtracker.restart.recover` property to `true` to make the jobtracker recover running jobs after a restart.

HDFS will not move blocks from old datanodes to new datanodes to balance the cluster. To do this, you should run the balancer described in "balancer" on page 304.

Decommissioning old nodes

Although HDFS is designed to tolerate datanode failures, this does not mean you can just terminate datanodes en masse with no ill effect. With a replication level of three, for example, the chances are very high that you will lose data by simultaneously shutting down three datanodes if they are on different racks. The way to decommission datanodes is to inform the namenode of the nodes that you wish to take out of circulation, so that it can replicate the blocks to other datanodes before the datanodes are shut down.

With tasktrackers, Hadoop is more forgiving. If you shut down a tasktracker that is running tasks, the jobtracker will notice the failure and reschedule the tasks on other tasktrackers.

The decommissioning process is controlled by an *exclude file*, which for HDFS is set by the `dfs.hosts.exclude` property and for MapReduce by the `mapred.hosts.exclude` property. It is often the case that these properties refer to the same file. The exclude file lists the nodes that are not permitted to connect to the cluster.

The rules for whether a tasktracker may connect to the jobtracker are simple: a tasktracker may connect only if it appears in the include file and does *not* appear in the exclude file. An unspecified or empty include file is taken to mean that all nodes are in the include file.

For HDFS, the rules are slightly different. If a datanode appears in both the include and the exclude file, then it may connect, but only to be decommissioned. Table 10-4 summarizes the different combinations for datanodes. As for tasktrackers, an unspecified or empty include file means all nodes are included.

Table 10-4. HDFS include and exclude file precedence

Node appears in include file	Node appears in exclude file	Interpretation
No	No	Node may not connect.
No	Yes	Node may not connect.
Yes	No	Node may connect.
Yes	Yes	Node may connect and will be decommissioned.

To remove nodes from the cluster:

1. Add the network addresses of the nodes to be decommissioned to the exclude file. Do not update the include file at this point.
2. Restart the MapReduce cluster to stop the tasktrackers on the nodes being decommissioned.

3. Update the namenode with the new set of permitted datanodes, with this command:

```
% hadoop dfsadmin -refreshNodes
```

4. Go to the web UI and check whether the admin state has changed to "Decommission In Progress" for the datanodes being decommissioned. They will start copying their blocks to other datanodes in the cluster.

5. When all the datanodes report their state as "Decommissioned," then all the blocks have been replicated. Shut down the decommissioned nodes.

6. Remove the nodes from the include file, and run:

```
% hadoop dfsadmin -refreshNodes
```

7. Remove the nodes from the *slaves* file.

Upgrades

Upgrading an HDFS and MapReduce cluster requires careful planning. The most important consideration is the HDFS upgrade. If the layout version of the filesystem has changed, then the upgrade will automatically migrate the filesystem data and metadata to a format that is compatible with the new version. As with any procedure that involves data migration, there is a risk of data loss, so you should be sure that both your data and metadata is backed up (see "Routine Administration Procedures" on page 312).

Part of the planning process should include a trial run on a small test cluster with a copy of data that you can afford to lose. A trial run will allow you to familiarize yourself with the process, customize it to your particular cluster configuration and toolset, and iron out any snags before running the upgrade procedure on a production cluster. A test cluster also has the benefit of being available to test client upgrades on.

Version Compatibility

All pre-1.0 Hadoop components have very rigid version compatibility requirements. Only components from the same release are guaranteed to be compatible with each other, which means the whole system—from daemons to clients—has to be upgraded simultaneously, in lockstep. This necessitates a period of cluster downtime.

Version 1.0 of Hadoop promises to loosen these requirements so that, for example, older clients can talk to newer servers (within the same major release number). In later releases, rolling upgrades may be supported, which would allow cluster daemons to be upgraded in phases, so that the cluster would still be available to clients during the upgrade.

Upgrading a cluster when the filesystem layout has not changed is fairly straightforward: install the new versions of HDFS and MapReduce on the cluster (and on clients at the same time), shut down the old daemons, update configuration files, then start up the new daemons and switch clients to use the new libraries. This process is reversible, so rolling back an upgrade is also straightforward.

After every successful upgrade, you should perform a couple of final cleanup steps:

- Remove the old installation and configuration files from the cluster.
- Fix any deprecation warnings in your code and configuration.

HDFS data and metadata upgrades

If you use the procedure just described to upgrade to a new version of HDFS and it expects a different layout version, then the namenode will refuse to run. A message like the following will appear in its log:

```
File system image contains an old layout version -16.
An upgrade to version -18 is required.
Please restart NameNode with -upgrade option.
```

The most reliable way of finding out whether you need to upgrade the filesystem is by performing a trial on a test cluster.

An upgrade of HDFS makes a copy of the previous version's metadata and data. Doing an upgrade does not double the storage requirements of the cluster, as the datanodes use hard links to keep two references (for the current and previous version) to the same block of data. This design makes it straightforward to roll back to the previous version of the filesystem, should you need to. You should understand that any changes made to the data on the upgraded system will be lost after the rollback completes.

You can keep only the previous version of the filesystem: you can't roll back several versions. Therefore, to carry out another upgrade to HDFS data and metadata, you will need to delete the previous version, a process called *finalizing the upgrade*. Once an upgrade is finalized, there is no procedure for rolling back to a previous version.

In general, you can skip releases when upgrading (for example, you can upgrade from release 0.18.3 to 0.20.0 without having to upgrade to a 0.19.x release first), but in some cases, you may have to go through intermediate releases. The release notes make it clear when this is required.

You should only attempt to upgrade a healthy filesystem. Before running the upgrade, do a full *fsck* (see "Filesystem check (fsck)" on page 301). As an extra precaution, you can keep a copy of the *fsck* output that lists all the files and blocks in the system, so you can compare it with the output of running *fsck* after the upgrade.

It's also worth clearing out temporary files before doing the upgrade, both from the MapReduce system directory on HDFS and local temporary files.

With these preliminaries out of the way, here is the high-level procedure for upgrading a cluster when the filesystem layout needs to be migrated:

1. Make sure that any previous upgrade is finalized before proceeding with another upgrade.

2. Shut down MapReduce and kill any orphaned task processes on the tasktrackers.

3. Shut down HDFS and backup the namenode directories.

4. Install new versions of Hadoop HDFS and MapReduce on the cluster and on clients.

5. Start HDFS with the -upgrade option.

6. Wait until the upgrade is complete.

7. Perform some sanity checks on HDFS.

8. Start MapReduce.

9. Roll back or finalize the upgrade (optional).

While running the upgrade procedure, it is a good idea to remove the Hadoop scripts from your PATH environment variable. This forces you to be explicit about which version of the scripts you are running. It can be convenient to define two environment variables for the new installation directories; in the following instructions, we have defined OLD_HADOOP_INSTALL and NEW_HADOOP_INSTALL.

Start the upgrade. To perform the upgrade, run the following command (this is step 5 in the high-level upgrade procedure):

```
% $NEW_HADOOP_INSTALL/bin/start-dfs.sh -upgrade
```

This causes the namenode to upgrade its metadata, placing the previous version in a new directory called *previous*:

```
${dfs.name.dir}/current/VERSION
                       /edits
                       /fsimage
                       /fstime
              /previous/VERSION
                       /edits
                       /fsimage
                       /fstime
```

Similarly, datanodes upgrade their storage directories, preserving the old copy in a directory called *previous*.

Wait until the upgrade is complete. The upgrade process is not instantaneous, but you can check the progress of an upgrade using *dfsadmin* (upgrade events also appear in the daemons' logfiles, step 6):

```
% $NEW_HADOOP_INSTALL/bin/hadoop dfsadmin -upgradeProgress status
Upgrade for version -18 has been completed.
Upgrade is not finalized.
```

Check the upgrade. This shows that the upgrade is complete. At this stage, you should run some sanity checks (step 7) on the filesystem (check files and blocks using *fsck*, basic file operations). You might choose to put HDFS into safe mode while you are running some of these checks (the ones that are read-only) to prevent others from making changes.

Roll back the upgrade (optional). If you find that the new version is not working correctly, you may choose to roll back to the previous version (step 9). This is only possible if you have not finalized the upgrade.

 A rollback reverts the filesystem state to before the upgrade was performed, so any changes made in the meantime will be lost. In other words, it rolls back to the previous state of the filesystem, rather than downgrading the current state of the filesystem to a former version.

First, shut down the new daemons:

```
% $NEW_HADOOP_INSTALL/bin/stop-dfs.sh
```

Then start up the old version of HDFS with the -rollback option:

```
% $OLD_HADOOP_INSTALL/bin/start-dfs.sh -rollback
```

This command gets the namenode and datanodes to replace their current storage directories with their previous copies. The filesystem will be returned to its previous state.

Finalize the upgrade (optional). When you are happy with the new version of HDFS, you can finalize the upgrade (step 9) to remove the previous storage directories.

 After an upgrade has been finalized, there is no way to roll back to the previous version.

This step is required before performing another upgrade:

```
% $NEW_HADOOP_INSTALL/bin/hadoop dfsadmin -finalizeUpgrade
% $NEW_HADOOP_INSTALL/bin/hadoop dfsadmin -upgradeProgress status
There are no upgrades in progress.
```

HDFS is now fully upgraded to the new version.

## CHAPTER 11

Pig

Pig raises the level of abstraction for processing large datasets. MapReduce allows you the programmer to specify a map function followed by a reduce function, but working out how to fit your data processing into this pattern, which often requires multiple MapReduce stages, can be a challenge. With Pig, the data structures are much richer, typically being multivalued and nested; and the set of transformations you can apply to the data are much more powerful—they include joins, for example, which are not for the faint of heart in MapReduce.

Pig is made up of two pieces:

- The language used to express data flows, called *Pig Latin*.
- The execution environment to run Pig Latin programs. There are currently two environments: local execution in a single JVM and distributed execution on a Hadoop cluster.

A Pig Latin program is made up of a series of operations, or transformations, that are applied to the input data to produce output. Taken as a whole, the operations describe a data flow, which the Pig execution environment translates into an executable representation and then runs. Under the covers, Pig turns the transformations into a series of MapReduce jobs, but as a programmer you are mostly unaware of this, which allows you to focus on the data rather than the nature of the execution.

Pig is a scripting language for exploring large datasets. One criticism of MapReduce is that the development cycle is very long. Writing the mappers and reducers, compiling and packaging the code, submitting the job(s), and retrieving the results is a time-consuming business, and even with Streaming, which removes the compile and package step, the experience is still involved. Pig's sweet spot is its ability to process terabytes of data simply by issuing a half-dozen lines of Pig Latin from the console. Indeed, it was created at Yahoo! to make it easier for researchers and engineers to mine the huge datasets there. Pig is very supportive of a programmer writing a query, since it provides several commands for introspecting the data structures in your program, as it is written. Even more useful, it can perform a sample run on a representative subset of your input data, so you can see whether there are errors in the processing before unleashing it on the full dataset.

Pig was designed to be extensible. Virtually all parts of the processing path are customizable: loading, storing, filtering, grouping, and joining can all be altered by user-defined functions (UDFs). These functions operate on Pig's nested data model, so they can integrate very deeply with Pig's operators. As another benefit, UDFs tend to be more reusable than the libraries developed for writing MapReduce programs.

Pig isn't suitable for all data processing tasks, however. Like MapReduce, it is designed for batch processing of data. If you want to perform a query that touches only a small amount of data in a large dataset, then Pig will not perform well, since it is set up to scan the whole dataset, or at least large portions of it.

In some cases, Pig doesn't perform as well as programs written in MapReduce. However, the gap is narrowing with each release, as the Pig team implements sophisticated algorithms for implementing Pig's relational operators. It's fair to say that unless you are willing to invest a lot of effort optimizing Java MapReduce code, writing queries in Pig Latin will save you time.

Installing and Running Pig

Pig runs as a client-side application. Even if you want to run Pig on a Hadoop cluster, there is nothing extra to install on the cluster: Pig launches jobs and interacts with HDFS (or other Hadoop filesystems) from your workstation.

Installation is straightforward. Java 6 is a prerequisite (and on Windows, you will need Cygwin). Download a stable release from *http://hadoop.apache.org/pig/releases.html*, and unpack the tarball in a suitable place on your workstation:

```
% tar xzf pig-x.y.z.tar.gz
```

It's convenient to add Pig's binary directory to your command-line path. For example:

```
% export PIG_INSTALL=/home/tom/pig-x.y.z
% export PATH=$PATH:$PIG_INSTALL/bin
```

You also need to set the JAVA_HOME environment variable to point to a suitable Java installation.

Try typing pig -help to get usage instructions.

Execution Types

Pig has two execution types or modes: local mode and MapReduce mode.

Local mode

In local mode, Pig runs in a single JVM and accesses the local filesystem. This mode is suitable only for small datasets and when trying out Pig.

The execution type is set using the -x or -exectype option. To run in local mode, set the option to local:

```
% pig -x local
grunt>
```

This starts Grunt, the Pig interactive shell, which is discussed in more detail shortly.

MapReduce mode

In MapReduce mode, Pig translates queries into MapReduce jobs and runs them on a Hadoop cluster. The cluster may be a pseudo- or fully distributed cluster. MapReduce mode (with a fully distributed cluster) is what you use when you want to run Pig on large datasets.

To use MapReduce mode, you first need to check that the version of Pig you downloaded is compatible with the version of Hadoop you are using. Pig releases will only work against particular versions of Hadoop; this is documented on the releases page. For example, Pig 0.3 and 0.4 run against a Hadoop 0.18.x release, while Pig 0.5 to 0.7 work with Hadoop 0.20.x.

If a Pig release supports multiple versions of Hadoop, you can use the environment variable PIG_HADOOP_VERSION to tell Pig the version of Hadoop it is connecting to. For example, the following makes Pig use any 0.18.x version of Hadoop:

```
% export PIG_HADOOP_VERSION=18
```

Next, you need to point Pig at the cluster's namenode and jobtracker. If you already have a Hadoop site file (or files) that define fs.default.name and mapred.job.tracker, you can simply add Hadoop's configuration directory to Pig's classpath:

```
% export PIG_CLASSPATH=$HADOOP_INSTALL/conf/
```

Alternatively, you can set these two properties in the *pig.properties* file in Pig's *conf* directory. Here's an example for a pseudo-distributed setup:

```
fs.default.name=hdfs://localhost/
mapred.job.tracker=localhost:8021
```

Once you have configured Pig to connect to a Hadoop cluster, you can launch Pig, setting the -x option to mapreduce, or omitting it entirely, as MapReduce mode is the default:

```
% pig
10/07/16 16:27:37 INFO pig.Main: Logging error messages to: /Users/tom/dev/pig-0
.7.0/pig_1279294057867.log
2010-07-16 16:27:38,243 [main] INFO  org.apache.pig.backend.hadoop.executionengi
ne.HExecutionEngine - Connecting to hadoop file system at: hdfs://localhost/
2010-07-16 16:27:38,741 [main] INFO  org.apache.pig.backend.hadoop.executionengi
```

```
ne.HExecutionEngine - Connecting to map-reduce job tracker at: localhost:8021
grunt>
```

As you can see from the output, Pig reports the filesystem and jobtracker that it has connected to.

Running Pig Programs

There are three ways of executing Pig programs, all of which work in both local and MapReduce mode:

Script
> Pig can run a script file that contains Pig commands. For example, `pig script.pig` runs the commands in the local file *script.pig*. Alternatively, for very short scripts, you can use the -e option to run a script specified as a string on the command line.

Grunt
> Grunt is an interactive shell for running Pig commands. Grunt is started when no file is specified for Pig to run, and the -e option is not used. It is also possible to run Pig scripts from within Grunt using `run` and `exec`.

Embedded
> You can run Pig programs from Java, much like you can use JDBC to run SQL programs from Java. There are more details on the Pig wiki at *http://wiki.apache .org/pig/EmbeddedPig*.

Grunt

Grunt has line-editing facilities like those found in GNU Readline (used in the bash shell and many other command-line applications). For instance, the Ctrl-E key combination will move the cursor to the end of the line. Grunt remembers command history, too,* and you can recall lines in the history buffer using Ctrl-P or Ctrl-N (for previous and next) or, equivalently, the up or down cursor keys.

Another handy feature is Grunt's completion mechanism, which will try to complete Pig Latin keywords and functions when you press the Tab key. For example, consider the following incomplete line:

```
grunt> a = foreach b ge
```

If you press the Tab key at this point, ge will expand to generate, a Pig Latin keyword:

```
grunt> a = foreach b generate
```

You can customize the completion tokens by creating a file named *autocomplete* and placing it on Pig's classpath (such as in the *conf* directory in Pig's install directory), or

---

* History is stored in a file called *.pig_history* in your home directory.

in the directory you invoked Grunt from. The file should have one token per line, and tokens must not contain any whitespace. Matching is case-sensitive. It can be very handy to add commonly used file paths (especially because Pig does not perform file-name completion) or the names of any user-defined functions you have created.

You can get a list of commands using the `help` command. When you've finished your Grunt session, you can exit with the `quit` command.

Pig Latin Editors

PigPen is an Eclipse plug-in that provides an environment for developing Pig programs. It includes a Pig script text editor, an example generator (equivalent to the ILLUS-TRATE command), and a button for running the script on a Hadoop cluster. There is also an operator graph window, which shows a script in graph form, for visualizing the data flow. For full installation and usage instructions, please refer to the Pig wiki at *http://wiki.apache.org/pig/PigPen*.

There are also Pig Latin syntax highlighters for other editors, including Vim and Text-Mate. Details are available on the Pig wiki.

An Example

Let's look at a simple example by writing the program to calculate the maximum recorded temperature by year for the weather dataset in Pig Latin (just like we did using MapReduce in Chapter 2). The complete program is only a few lines long:

```
-- max_temp.pig: Finds the maximum temperature by year
records = LOAD 'input/ncdc/micro-tab/sample.txt'
  AS (year:chararray, temperature:int, quality:int);
filtered_records = FILTER records BY temperature != 9999 AND
  (quality == 0 OR quality == 1 OR quality == 4 OR quality == 5 OR quality == 9);
grouped_records = GROUP filtered_records BY year;
max_temp = FOREACH grouped_records GENERATE group,
  MAX(filtered_records.temperature);
DUMP max_temp;
```

To explore what's going on, we'll use Pig's Grunt interpreter, which allows us to enter lines and interact with the program to understand what it's doing. Start up Grunt in local mode, then enter the first line of the Pig script:

```
grunt> records = LOAD 'input/ncdc/micro-tab/sample.txt'
>>    AS (year:chararray, temperature:int, quality:int);
```

For simplicity, the program assumes that the input is tab-delimited text, with each line having just year, temperature, and quality fields. (Pig actually has more flexibility than this with regard to the input formats it accepts, as you'll see later.) This line describes the input data we want to process. The `year:chararray` notation describes the field's name and type; a `chararray` is like a Java string, and an `int` is like a Java `int`. The LOAD operator takes a URI argument; here we are just using a local file, but we could refer to an HDFS URI. The AS clause (which is optional) gives the fields names to make it convenient to refer to them in subsequent statements.

The result of the LOAD operator, indeed any operator in Pig Latin, is a *relation*, which is just a set of tuples. A *tuple* is just like a row of data in a database table, with multiple fields in a particular order. In this example, the LOAD function produces a set of (year, temperature, quality) tuples that are present in the input file. We write a relation with one tuple per line, where tuples are represented as comma-separated items in parentheses:

```
(1950,0,1)
(1950,22,1)
(1950,-11,1)
(1949,111,1)
```

Relations are given names, or *aliases*, so they can be referred to. This relation is given the records alias. We can examine the contents of an alias using the DUMP operator:

```
grunt> DUMP records;
(1950,0,1)
(1950,22,1)
(1950,-11,1)
(1949,111,1)
(1949,78,1)
```

We can also see the structure of a relation—the relation's *schema*—using the DESCRIBE operator on the relation's alias:

```
grunt> DESCRIBE records;
records: {year: chararray,temperature: int,quality: int}
```

This tells us that records has three fields, with aliases year, temperature, and quality, which are the names we gave them in the AS clause. The fields have the types given to them in the AS clause, too. We shall examine types in Pig in more detail later.

The second statement removes records that have a missing temperature (indicated by a value of 9999) or an unsatisfactory quality reading. For this small dataset, no records are filtered out:

```
grunt> filtered_records = FILTER records BY temperature != 9999 AND
>>    (quality == 0 OR quality == 1 OR quality == 4 OR quality == 5 OR quality == 9);
grunt> DUMP filtered_records;
(1950,0,1)
(1950,22,1)
(1950,-11,1)
(1949,111,1)
(1949,78,1)
```

The third statement uses the GROUP function to group the records relation by the year field. Let's use DUMP to see what it produces:

```
grunt> grouped_records = GROUP filtered_records BY year;
grunt> DUMP grouped_records;
(1949,{(1949,111,1),(1949,78,1)})
(1950,{(1950,0,1),(1950,22,1),(1950,-11,1)})
```

We now have two rows, or tuples, one for each year in the input data. The first field in each tuple is the field being grouped by (the year), and the second field is a bag of tuples for that year. A *bag* is just an unordered collection of tuples, which in Pig Latin is represented using curly braces.

By grouping the data in this way, we have created a row per year, so now all that remains is to find the maximum temperature for the tuples in each bag. Before we do this, let's understand the structure of the grouped_records relation:

```
grunt> DESCRIBE grouped_records;
grouped_records: {group: chararray,filtered_records: {year: chararray,
temperature: int,quality: int}}
```

This tells us that the grouping field is given the alias group by Pig, and the second field is the same structure as the filtered_records relation that was being grouped. With this information, we can try the fourth transformation:

```
grunt> max_temp = FOREACH grouped_records GENERATE group,
>>    MAX(filtered_records.temperature);
```

FOREACH processes every row to generate a derived set of rows, using a GENERATE clause to define the fields in each derived row. In this example, the first field is group, which is just the year. The second field is a little more complex. The filtered_records.temperature reference is to the temperature field of the filtered_records bag in the grouped_records relation. MAX is a built-in function for calculating the maximum value of fields in a bag. In this case, it calculates the maximum temperature for the fields in each filtered_records bag. Let's check the result:

```
grunt> DUMP max_temp;
(1949,111)
(1950,22)
```

So we've successfully calculated the maximum temperature for each year.

Generating Examples

In this example, we've used a small sample dataset with just a handful of rows to make it easier to follow the data flow and aid debugging. Creating a cut-down dataset is an art, as ideally it should be rich enough to cover all the cases to exercise your queries (the *completeness* property), yet be small enough to reason about by the programmer (the *conciseness* property). Using a random sample doesn't work well in general, since join and filter operations tend to remove all random data, leaving an empty result, which is not illustrative of the general flow.

With the ILLUSTRATE operator, Pig provides a tool for generating a reasonably complete and concise dataset. Although it can't generate examples for all queries (it doesn't support LIMIT, SPLIT, or nested FOREACH statements, for example), it can generate useful examples for many queries. ILLUSTRATE works only if the relation has a schema.

Here is the output from running ILLUSTRATE (slightly reformatted to fit the page):

```
grunt> ILLUSTRATE max_temp;
-------------------------------------------------------------------------
| records    | year: bytearray | temperature: bytearray | quality: bytearray |
-------------------------------------------------------------------------
|            | 1949            | 9999                   | 1                  |
|            | 1949            | 111                    | 1                  |
|            | 1949            | 78                     | 1                  |
-------------------------------------------------------------------------


-------------------------------------------------------------------------
| records    | year: chararray | temperature: int | quality: int |
-------------------------------------------------------------------------
|            | 1949            | 9999             | 1            |
|            | 1949            | 111              | 1            |
|            | 1949            | 78               | 1            |
-------------------------------------------------------------------------


-------------------------------------------------------------------------
| filtered_records     | year: chararray | temperature: int | quality: int |
-------------------------------------------------------------------------
|                      | 1949            | 111              | 1            |
|                      | 1949            | 78               | 1            |
-------------------------------------------------------------------------


-------------------------------------------------------------------------
| grouped_records    | group: chararray | filtered_records: bag({year: chararray, |
|                    |                  |               temperature: int,quality: int}) |
-------------------------------------------------------------------------
|                    | 1949             | {(1949, 111, 1), (1949, 78, 1)}           |
-------------------------------------------------------------------------


----------------------------------------------------
| max_temp    | group: chararray | int  |
----------------------------------------------------
|             | 1949             | 111  |
----------------------------------------------------
```

Notice that Pig used some of the original data (this is important to keep the generated dataset realistic), as well as creating some new data. It noticed the special value 9999 in the query and created a tuple containing this value to exercise the FILTER statement.

In summary, the output of the ILLUSTRATE is easy to follow and can help you understand what your query is doing.

Comparison with Databases

Having seen Pig in action, it might seem that Pig Latin is similar to SQL. The presence of such operators as GROUP BY and DESCRIBE reinforces this impression. However, there are several differences between the two languages, and between Pig and RDBMSs in general.

The most significant difference is that Pig Latin is a data flow programming language, whereas SQL is a declarative programming language. In other words, a Pig Latin program is a step-by-step set of operations on an input relation, in which each step is a single transformation. By contrast, SQL statements are a set of constraints that, taken together, define the output. In many ways, programming in Pig Latin is like working at the level of an RDBMS query planner, which figures out how to turn a declarative statement into a system of steps.

RDBMSs store data in tables, with tightly predefined schemas. Pig is more relaxed about the data that it processes: you can define a schema at runtime, but it's optional. Essentially, it will operate on any source of tuples (although the source should support being read in parallel, by being in multiple files, for example), where a UDF is used to read the tuples from their raw representation.[†] The most common representation is a text file with tab-separated fields, and Pig provides a built-in load function for this format. Unlike with a traditional database, there is no data import process to load the data into the RDBMS. The data is loaded from the filesystem (usually HDFS) as the first step in the processing.

Pig's support for complex, nested data structures differentiates it from SQL, which operates on flatter data structures. Also, Pig's ability to use UDFs and streaming operators that are tightly integrated with the language and Pig's nested data structures makes Pig Latin more customizable than most SQL dialects.

There are several features to support online, low-latency queries that RDBMSs have that are absent in Pig, such as transactions and indexes. As mentioned earlier, Pig does not support random reads or queries in the order of tens of milliseconds. Nor does it support random writes to update small portions of data; all writes are bulk, streaming writes, just like MapReduce.

Hive (covered in Chapter 12) sits between Pig and conventional RDBMSs. Like Pig, Hive is designed to use HDFS for storage, but otherwise there are some significant differences. Its query language, HiveQL, is based on SQL, and anyone who is familiar with SQL would have little trouble writing queries in HiveQL. Like RDBMSs, Hive mandates that all data be stored in tables, with a schema under its management; however, it can associate a schema with preexisting data in HDFS, so the load step is optional. Hive does not support low-latency queries, a characteristic it shares with Pig.

[†] Or as the Pig Philosophy (*http://hadoop.apache.org/pig/philosophy.html*) has it, "Pigs eat anything."

Pig Latin

This section gives an informal description of the syntax and semantics of the Pig Latin programming language.[‡] It is not meant to offer a complete reference to the language,[§] but there should be enough here for you to get a good understanding of Pig Latin's constructs.

Structure

A Pig Latin program consists of a collection of statements. A statement can be thought of as an operation, or a command.[‖] For example, a GROUP operation is a type of statement:

```
grouped_records = GROUP records BY year;
```

The command to list the files in a Hadoop filesystem is another example of a statement:

```
ls /
```

Statements are usually terminated with a semicolon, as in the example of the GROUP statement. In fact, this is an example of a statement that must be terminated with a semicolon: it is a syntax error to omit it. The ls command, on the other hand, does not have to be terminated with a semicolon. As a general guideline, statements or commands for interactive use in Grunt do not need the terminating semicolon. This group includes the interactive Hadoop commands, as well as the diagnostic operators like DESCRIBE. It's never an error to add a terminating semicolon, so if in doubt, it's simplest to add one.

Statements that have to be terminated with a semicolon can be split across multiple lines for readability:

```
records = LOAD 'input/ncdc/micro-tab/sample.txt'
   AS (year:chararray, temperature:int, quality:int);
```

Pig Latin has two forms of comments. Double hyphens are single-line comments. Everything from the first hyphen to the end of the line is ignored by the Pig Latin interpreter:

```
-- My program
DUMP A; -- What's in A?
```

---

‡ Not to be confused with Pig Latin, the language game. English words are translated into Pig Latin by moving the initial consonant sound to the end of the word and adding an "ay" sound. For example, "pig" becomes "ig-pay," and "Hadoop" becomes "Adoop-hay."

§ Pig Latin does not have a formal language definition as such, but there is a comprehensive guide to the language that can be found linked to from the Pig wiki at *http://wiki.apache.org/pig/*.

‖ You sometimes see these terms being used interchangeably in documentation on Pig Latin. For example, "GROUP command, " "GROUP operation," "GROUP statement."

C-style comments are more flexible since they delimit the beginning and end of the comment block with /* and */ markers. They can span lines or be embedded in a single line:

```
/*
 * Description of my program spanning
 * multiple lines.
 */
A = LOAD 'input/pig/join/A';
B = LOAD 'input/pig/join/B';
C = JOIN A BY $0, /* ignored */ B BY $1;
DUMP C;
```

Pig Latin has a list of keywords that have a special meaning in the language and cannot be used as identifiers. These include the operators (LOAD, ILLUSTRATE), commands (cat, ls), expressions (matches, FLATTEN), and functions (DIFF, MAX)—all of which are covered in the following sections.

Pig Latin has mixed rules on case sensitivity. Operators and commands are not case-sensitive (to make interactive use more forgiving); however, aliases and function names are case-sensitive.

Statements

As a Pig Latin program is executed, each statement is parsed in turn. If there are syntax errors, or other (semantic) problems such as undefined aliases, the interpreter will halt and display an error message. The interpreter builds a *logical plan* for every relational operation, which forms the core of a Pig Latin program. The logical plan for the statement is added to the logical plan for the program so far, then the interpreter moves on to the next statement.

It's important to note that no data processing takes place while the logical plan of the program is being constructed. For example, consider again the Pig Latin program from the first example:

```
-- max_temp.pig: Finds the maximum temperature by year
records = LOAD 'input/ncdc/micro-tab/sample.txt'
  AS (year:chararray, temperature:int, quality:int);
filtered_records = FILTER records BY temperature != 9999 AND
  (quality == 0 OR quality == 1 OR quality == 4 OR quality == 5 OR quality == 9);
grouped_records = GROUP filtered_records BY year;
max_temp = FOREACH grouped_records GENERATE group,
  MAX(filtered_records.temperature);
DUMP max_temp;
```

When the Pig Latin interpreter sees the first line containing the LOAD statement, it confirms that it is syntactically and semantically correct, and adds it to the logical plan, but it does *not* load the data from the file (or even check whether the file exists). Indeed, where would it load it? Into memory? Even if it did fit into memory, what would it do with the data? Perhaps not all the input data is needed (since later statements filter it, for example), so it would be pointless to load it. The point is that it makes no sense to start any processing until the whole flow is defined. Similarly, Pig validates the GROUP and FOREACH...GENERATE statements, and adds them to the logical plan without executing them. The trigger for Pig to start execution is the DUMP statement. At that point, the logical plan is compiled into a physical plan and executed.

Multiquery execution

Since DUMP is a diagnostic tool, it will always trigger execution. However, the STORE command is different. In interactive mode, STORE acts like DUMP and will always trigger execution (this includes the `run` command), but in batch mode it will not (this includes the `exec` command). The reason for this is efficiency. In batch mode, Pig will parse the whole script to see if there are any optimizations that could be made to limit the amount of data to be written to or read from disk. Consider the following simple example:

```
A = LOAD 'input/pig/multiquery/A';
B = FILTER A BY $1 == 'banana';
C = FILTER A BY $1 != 'banana';
STORE B INTO 'output/b';
STORE C INTO 'output/c';
```

Relations B and C are both derived from A, so to save reading A twice, Pig can run this script as a single MapReduce job by reading A once and writing two output files from the job, one for each of B and C. This feature is called *multiquery execution*.

In previous versions of Pig that did not have multiquery execution, each STORE statement in a script run in batch mode triggered execution, resulting in a job for each STORE statement. It is possible to restore the old behavior by disabling multiquery execution with the `-M` or `-no_multiquery` option to `pig`.

The physical plan that Pig prepares is a series of MapReduce jobs, which in local mode Pig runs in the local JVM, and in MapReduce mode Pig runs on a Hadoop cluster.

You can see the logical and physical plans created by Pig using the EXPLAIN command on a relation (`EXPLAIN max_temp;` for example).

EXPLAIN will also show the MapReduce plan, which shows how the physical operators are grouped into MapReduce jobs. This is a good way to find out how many MapReduce jobs Pig will run for your query.

The relational operators that can be a part of a logical plan in Pig are summarized in Table 11-1. We shall go through the operators in more detail in "Data Processing Operators" on page 351.

Table 11-1. Pig Latin relational operators

Category	Operator	Description
Loading and storing	LOAD	Loads data from the filesystem or other storage into a relation
	STORE	Saves a relation to the filesystem or other storage
	DUMP	Prints a relation to the console
Filtering	FILTER	Removes unwanted rows from a relation
	DISTINCT	Removes duplicate rows from a relation
	FOREACH...GENERATE	Adds or removes fields from a relation
	STREAM	Transforms a relation using an external program
	SAMPLE	Selects a random sample of a relation
Grouping and joining	JOIN	Joins two or more relations
	COGROUP	Groups the data in two or more relations
	GROUP	Groups the data in a single relation
	CROSS	Creates the cross-product of two or more relations
Sorting	ORDER	Sorts a relation by one or more fields
	LIMIT	Limits the size of a relation to a maximum number of tuples
Combining and splitting	UNION	Combines two or more relations into one
	SPLIT	Splits a relation into two or more relations

There are other types of statements that are not added to the logical plan. For example, the diagnostic operators, DESCRIBE, EXPLAIN, and ILLUSTRATE are provided to allow the user to interact with the logical plan, for debugging purposes (see Table 11-2). DUMP is a sort of diagnostic operator, too, since it is used only to allow interactive debugging of small result sets or in combination with LIMIT to retrieve a few rows from a larger relation. The STORE statement should be used when the size of the output is more than a few lines, as it writes to a file, rather than to the console.

Table 11-2. Pig Latin diagnostic operators

Operator	Description
DESCRIBE	Prints a relation's schema
EXPLAIN	Prints the logical and physical plans
ILLUSTRATE	Shows a sample execution of the logical plan, using a generated subset of the input

Pig Latin provides two statements, REGISTER and DEFINE, to make it possible to incorporate user-defined functions into Pig scripts (see Table 11-3).

Table 11-3. Pig Latin UDF statements

Statement	Description
REGISTER	Registers a JAR file with the Pig runtime
DEFINE	Creates an alias for a UDF, streaming script, or a command specification

Since they do not process relations, commands are not added to the logical plan; instead, they are executed immediately. Pig provides commands to interact with Hadoop filesystems (which are very handy for moving data around before or after processing with Pig) and MapReduce, as well as a few utility commands (described in Table 11-4).

Table 11-4. Pig Latin commands

Category	Command	Description
Hadoop Filesystem	cat	Prints the contents of one or more files
	cd	Changes the current directory
	copyFromLocal	Copies a local file or directory to a Hadoop filesystem
	copyToLocal	Copies a file or directory on a Hadoop filesystem to the local filesystem
	cp	Copies a file or directory to another directory
	fs	Accesses Hadoop's filesystem shell
	ls	Lists files
	mkdir	Creates a new directory
	mv	Moves a file or directory to another directory
	pwd	Prints the path of the current working directory
	rm	Deletes a file or directory
	rmf	Forcibly deletes a file or directory (does not fail if the file or directory does not exist)
Hadoop MapReduce	kill	Kills a MapReduce job
Utility	exec	Runs a script in a new Grunt shell in batch mode
	help	Shows the available commands and options
	quit	Exits the interpreter
	run	Runs a script within the existing Grunt shell
	set	Sets Pig options

The filesystem commands can operate on files or directories in any Hadoop filesystem, and they are very similar to the hadoop fs commands (which is not surprising, as both are simple wrappers around the Hadoop FileSystem interface). You can access all of the Hadoop filesystem shell commands using Pig's fs command. For example, fs -ls will show a file listing, and fs -help will show help on all the available commands.

Precisely which Hadoop filesystem is used is determined by the `fs.default.name` property in the site file for Hadoop Core. See "The Command-Line Interface" on page 45 for more details on how to configure this property.

These commands are mostly self-explanatory, except `set`, which is used to set options that control Pig's behavior. The `debug` option is used to turn debug logging on or off from within a script (you can also control the log level when launching Pig, using the `-d` or `-debug` option):

```
grunt> set debug on
```

Another useful option is the `job.name` option, which gives a Pig job a meaningful name, making it easier to pick out your Pig MapReduce jobs when running on a shared Hadoop cluster. If Pig is running a script (rather than being an interactive query from Grunt), its job name defaults to a value based on the script name.

There are two commands in Table 11-4 for running a Pig script, `exec` and `run`. The difference is that `exec` runs the script in batch mode in a new Grunt shell, so any aliases defined in the script are not accessible to the shell after the script has completed. On the other hand, when running a script with `run`, it is as if the contents of the script had been entered manually, so the command history of the invoking shell contains all the statements from the script. Multiquery execution, where Pig executes a batch of statements in one go (see "Multiquery execution" on page 332), is only used by `exec`, not `run`.

Expressions

An expression is something that is evaluated to yield a value. Expressions can be used in Pig as a part of a statement containing a relational operator. Pig has a rich variety of expressions, many of which will be familiar from other programming languages. They are listed in Table 11-5, with brief descriptions and examples. We shall see examples of many of these expressions throughout the chapter.

Table 11-5. Pig Latin expressions

Category	Expressions	Description	Examples
Constant	Literal	Constant value (see also literals in Table 11-6)	`1.0`, `'a'`
Field (by position)	$n	Field in position *n* (zero-based)	`$0`
Field (by name)	*f*	Field named *f*	`year`
Projection	`c.$n, c.f`	Field in container *c* (relation, bag, or tuple) by position, by name	`records.$0`, `records.year`
Map lookup	*m#k*	Value associated with key *k* in map *m*	`items#'Coat'`
Cast	`(t) f`	Cast of field *f* to type *t*	`(int) year`
Arithmetic	`x + y, x - y`	Addition, subtraction	`$1 + $2, $1 - $2`

Category	Expressions	Description	Examples
	x * y, x / y	Multiplication, division	$1 * $2, $1 / $2
	x % y	Modulo, the remainder of x divided by y	$1 % $2
	+x, -x	Unary positive, negation	+1, -1
Conditional	x ? y : z	Bincond/ternary, y if x evaluates to true, z otherwise	quality == 0 ? 0 : 1
Comparison	x == y, x != y	Equals, not equals	quality == 0, tempera ture != 9999
	x > y, x < y	Greater than, less than	quality > 0, quality < 10
	x >= y, x <= y	Greater than or equal to, less than or equal to	quality >= 1, quality <= 9
	x matches y	Pattern matching with regular expression	quality matches '[01459]'
	x is null	Is null	temperature is null
	x is not null	Is not null	temperature is not null
Boolean	x or y	Logical or	q == 0 or q == 1
	x and y	Logical and	q == 0 and r == 0
	not x	Logical negation	not q matches '[01459]'
Functional	fn(f1,f2,…)	Invocation of function fn on fields f1, f2, etc.	isGood(quality)
Flatten	FLATTEN(f)	Removal of nesting from bags and tuples	FLATTEN(group)

Types

So far you have seen some of the simple types in Pig, such as int and chararray. Here
we will discuss Pig's built-in types in more detail.

Pig has four numeric types: int, long, float, and double, which are identical to their
Java counterparts. There is also a bytearray type, like Java's byte array type for representing a blob of binary data, and chararray, which, like java.lang.String, represents
textual data in UTF-16 format, although it can be loaded or stored in UTF-8 format.
Pig does not have types corresponding to Java's boolean,[#] byte, short, or char primitive
types. These are all easily represented using Pig's int type, or chararray for char.

The numeric, textual, and binary types are simple atomic types. Pig Latin also has three
complex types for representing nested structures: tuple, bag, and map. All of Pig Latin's
types are listed in Table 11-6.

[#] Although there is no boolean type for data, Pig has the concept of an expression evaluating to true or false,
for testing conditions (such as in a FILTER statement). However, Pig does not allow a boolean expression to
be stored in a field.

Table 11-6. Pig Latin types

Category	Type	Description	Literal example
Numeric	int	32-bit signed integer	1
	long	64-bit signed integer	1L
	float	32-bit floating-point number	1.0F
	double	64-bit floating-point number	1.0
Text	chararray	Character array in UTF-16 format	'a'
Binary	bytearray	Byte array	Not supported
Complex	tuple	Sequence of fields of any type	(1,'pomegranate')
	bag	An unordered collection of tuples, possibly with duplicates	{(1,'pomegranate'),(2)}
	map	A set of key-value pairs. Keys must be character arrays; values may be any type	['a'#'pomegranate']

The complex types are usually loaded from files or constructed using relational operators. Be aware, however, that the literal form in Table 11-6 is used when a constant value is created from within a Pig Latin program. The raw form in a file is usually different when using the standard PigStorage loader. For example, the representation in a file of the bag in Table 11-6 would be {(1,pomegranate),(2)} (note the lack of quotes), and with a suitable schema, this would be loaded as a relation with a single field and row, whose value was the bag.

Maps are always loaded from files, since there is no relational operator in Pig that produces a map. It's possible to write a UDF to generate maps, if desired.

Although relations and bags are conceptually the same (an unordered collection of tuples), in practice Pig treats them slightly differently. A relation is a top-level construct, whereas a bag has to be contained in a relation. Normally, you don't have to worry about this, but there are a few restrictions that can trip up the uninitiated. For example, it's not possible to create a relation from a bag literal. So the following statement fails:

```
A = {(1,2),(3,4)}; -- Error
```

The simplest workaround in this case is to load the data from a file using the LOAD statement.

As another example, you can't treat a relation like a bag and project a field into a new relation ($0 refers to the first field of A, using the positional notation):

```
B = A.$0;
```

Instead, you have to use a relational operator to turn the relation A into relation B:

```
B = FOREACH A GENERATE $0;
```

It's possible that a future version of Pig Latin will remove these inconsistencies and treat relations and bags in the same way.

Schemas

A relation in Pig may have an associated schema, which gives the fields in the relation names and types. We've seen how an AS clause in a LOAD statement is used to attach a schema to a relation:

```
grunt> records = LOAD 'input/ncdc/micro-tab/sample.txt'
>>    AS (year:int, temperature:int, quality:int);
grunt> DESCRIBE records;
records: {year: int,temperature: int,quality: int}
```

This time we've declared the year to be an integer, rather than a chararray, even though the file it is being loaded from is the same. An integer may be more appropriate if we needed to manipulate the year arithmetically (to turn it into a timestamp, for example), whereas the chararray representation might be more appropriate when it's being used as a simple identifier. Pig's flexibility in the degree to which schemas are declared contrasts with schemas in traditional SQL databases, which are declared before the data is loaded into to the system. Pig is designed for analyzing plain input files with no associated type information, so it is quite natural to choose types for fields later than you would with an RDBMS.

It's possible to omit type declarations completely, too:

```
grunt> records = LOAD 'input/ncdc/micro-tab/sample.txt'
>>    AS (year, temperature, quality);
grunt> DESCRIBE records;
records: {year: bytearray,temperature: bytearray,quality: bytearray}
```

In this case, we have specified only the names of the fields in the schema, year, temperature, and quality. The types default to bytearray, the most general type, representing a binary string.

You don't need to specify types for every field; you can leave some to default to byte array, as we have done for year in this declaration:

```
grunt> records = LOAD 'input/ncdc/micro-tab/sample.txt'
>>    AS (year, temperature:int, quality:int);
grunt> DESCRIBE records;
records: {year: bytearray,temperature: int,quality: int}
```

However, if you specify a schema in this way, you do need to specify every field. Also, there's no way to specify the type of a field without specifying the name. On the other hand, the schema is entirely optional and can be omitted by not specifying an AS clause:

```
grunt> records = LOAD 'input/ncdc/micro-tab/sample.txt';
grunt> DESCRIBE records;
Schema for records unknown.
```

Fields in a relation with no schema can be referenced only using positional notation: $0 refers to the first field in a relation, $1 to the second, and so on. Their types default to bytearray:

```
grunt> projected_records = FOREACH records GENERATE $0, $1, $2;
grunt> DUMP projected_records;
(1950,0,1)
(1950,22,1)
(1950,-11,1)
(1949,111,1)
(1949,78,1)
grunt> DESCRIBE projected_records;
projected_records: {bytearray,bytearray,bytearray}
```

Although it can be convenient not to have to assign types to fields (particularly in the first stages of writing a query), doing so can improve the clarity and efficiency of Pig Latin programs, and is generally recommended.

 Declaring a schema as a part of the query is flexible, but doesn't lend itself to schema reuse. A set of Pig queries over the same input data will often have the same schema repeated in each query. If the query processes a large number of fields, this repetition can become hard to maintain, since Pig (unlike Hive) doesn't have a way to associate a schema with data outside of a query. One way to solve this problem is to write your own load function, which encapsulates the schema. This is described in more detail in "A Load UDF" on page 348.

Validation and nulls

An SQL database will enforce the constraints in a table's schema at load time: for example, trying to load a string into a column that is declared to be a numeric type will fail. In Pig, if the value cannot be cast to the type declared in the schema, then it will substitute a null value. Let's see how this works if we have the following input for the weather data, which has an "e" character in place of an integer:

```
1950    0    1
1950    22   1
1950    e    1
1949    111  1
1949    78   1
```

Pig handles the corrupt line by producing a null for the offending value, which is displayed as the absence of a value when dumped to screen (and also when saved using STORE):

```
grunt> records = LOAD 'input/ncdc/micro-tab/sample_corrupt.txt'
>>    AS (year:chararray, temperature:int, quality:int);
grunt> DUMP records;
(1950,0,1)
(1950,22,1)
(1950,,1)
```

```
(1949,111,1)
(1949,78,1)
```

Pig produces a warning for the invalid field (not shown here), but does not halt its processing. For large datasets, it is very common to have corrupt, invalid, or merely unexpected data, and it is generally infeasible to incrementally fix every unparsable record. Instead, we can pull out all of the invalid records in one go, so we can take action on them, perhaps by fixing our program (because they indicate we have made a mistake) or by filtering them out (because the data is genuinely unusable):

```
grunt> corrupt_records = FILTER records BY temperature is null;
grunt> DUMP corrupt_records;
(1950,,1)
```

Note the use of the is null operator, which is analogous to SQL. In practice, we would include more information from the original record, such as an identifier and the value that could not be parsed, to help our analysis of the bad data.

We can find the number of corrupt records using the following idiom for counting the number of rows in a relation:

```
grunt> grouped = GROUP corrupt_records ALL;
grunt> all_grouped = FOREACH grouped GENERATE group, COUNT(corrupt_records);
grunt> DUMP all_grouped;
(all,1L)
```

Another useful technique is to use the SPLIT operator to partition the data into "good" and "bad" relations, which can then be analyzed separately:

```
grunt> SPLIT records INTO good_records IF temperature is not null,
>>    bad_records IF temperature is null;
grunt> DUMP good_records;
(1950,0,1)
(1950,22,1)
(1949,111,1)
(1949,78,1)
grunt> DUMP bad_records;
(1950,,1)
```

Going back to the case in which temperature's type was left undeclared, the corrupt data cannot be easily detected, since it doesn't surface as a null:

```
grunt> records = LOAD 'input/ncdc/micro-tab/sample_corrupt.txt'
>>    AS (year:chararray, temperature, quality:int);
grunt> DUMP records;
(1950,0,1)
(1950,22,1)
(1950,e,1)
(1949,111,1)
(1949,78,1)
grunt> filtered_records = FILTER records BY temperature != 9999 AND
>>    (quality == 0 OR quality == 1 OR quality == 4 OR quality == 5 OR quality == 9);
grunt> grouped_records = GROUP filtered_records BY year;
grunt> max_temp = FOREACH grouped_records GENERATE group,
>>    MAX(filtered_records.temperature);
```

```
grunt> DUMP max_temp;
(1949,111.0)
(1950,22.0)
```

What happens in this case is that the temperature field is interpreted as a bytearray, so the corrupt field is not detected when the input is loaded. When passed to the MAX function, the temperature field is cast to a double, since MAX works only with numeric types. The corrupt field can not be represented as a double, so it becomes a null, which MAX silently ignores. The best approach is generally to declare types for your data on loading, and look for missing or corrupt values in the relations themselves before you do your main processing.

Sometimes corrupt data shows up as smaller tuples since fields are simply missing. You can filter these out by using the SIZE function as follows:

```
grunt> A = LOAD 'input/pig/corrupt/missing_fields';
grunt> DUMP A;
(2,Tie)
(4,Coat)
(3)
(1,Scarf)
grunt> B = FILTER A BY SIZE(*) > 1;
grunt> DUMP B;
(2,Tie)
(4,Coat)
(1,Scarf)
```

Schema merging

In Pig, you don't declare the schema for every new relation in the data flow. In most cases, Pig can figure out the resulting schema for the output of a relational operation by considering the schema of the input relation.

How are schemas propagated to new relations? Some relational operators don't change the schema, so the relation produced by the LIMIT operator (which restricts a relation to a maximum number of tuples), for example, has the same schema as the relation it operates on. For other operators, the situation is more complicated. UNION, for example, combines two or more relations into one, and tries to merge the input relations schemas. If the schemas are incompatible, due to different types or number of fields, then the schema of the result of the UNION is unknown.

You can find out the schema for any relation in the data flow using the DESCRIBE operator. If you want to redefine the schema for a relation, you can use the FOREACH...GENERATE operator with AS clauses to define the schema for some or all of the fields of the input relation.

See "User-Defined Functions" on page 343 for further discussion of schemas.

Functions

Functions in Pig come in four types:

Eval function

A function that takes one or more expressions and returns another expression. An example of a built-in eval function is MAX, which returns the maximum value of the entries in a bag. Some eval functions are *aggregate functions*, which means they operate on a bag of data to produce a scalar value; MAX is an example of an aggregate function. Furthermore, many aggregate functions are *algebraic*, which means that the result of the function may be calculated incrementally. In MapReduce terms, algebraic functions make use of the combiner and are much more efficient to calculate (see "Combiner Functions" on page 30). MAX is an algebraic function, whereas a function to calculate the median of a collection of values is an example of a function that is not algebraic.

Filter function

A special type of eval function that returns a logical boolean result. As the name suggests, filter functions are used in the FILTER operator to remove unwanted rows. They can also be used in other relational operators that take boolean conditions and, in general, expressions using boolean or conditional expressions. An example of a built-in filter function is IsEmpty, which tests whether a bag or a map contains any items.

Load function

A function that specifies how to load data into a relation from external storage.

Store function

A function that specifies how to save the contents of a relation to external storage. Often, load and store functions are implemented by the same type. For example, PigStorage, which loads data from delimited text files, can store data in the same format.

Pig has a small collection of built-in functions, which are listed in Table 11-7.

Table 11-7. Pig built-in functions

Category	Function	Description
Eval	AVG	Calculates the average (mean) value of entries in a bag.
	CONCAT	Concatenates two byte arrays or two character arrays together.
	COUNT	Calculates the number of non-null entries in a bag.
	COUNT_STAR	Calculates the number of entries in a bag, including those that are null.
	DIFF	Calculates the set difference of two bags. If the two arguments are not bags, then returns a bag containing both if they are equal; otherwise, returns an empty bag.
	MAX	Calculates the maximum value of entries in a bag.
	MIN	Calculates the minimum value of entries in a bag.

Category	Function	Description
	SIZE	Calculates the size of a type. The size of numeric types is always one; for character arrays, it is the number of characters; for byte arrays, the number of bytes; and for containers (tuple, bag, map), it is the number of entries.
	SUM	Calculates the sum of the values of entries in a bag.
	TOKENIZE	Tokenizes a character array into a bag of its constituent words.
Filter	IsEmpty	Tests if a bag or map is empty.
Load/Store	PigStorage	Loads or stores relations using a field-delimited text format. Each line is broken into fields using a configurable field delimiter (defaults to a tab character) to be stored in the tuple's fields. It is the default storage when none is specified.
	BinStorage	Loads or stores relations from or to binary files. An internal Pig format is used that uses Hadoop Writable objects.
	BinaryStorage	Loads or stores relations containing only single-field tuples with a value of type byte array from or to binary files. The bytes of the bytearray values are stored verbatim. Used with Pig streaming.
	TextLoader	Loads relations from a plain-text format. Each line corresponds to a tuple whose single field is the line of text.
	PigDump	Stores relations by writing the toString() representation of tuples, one per line. Useful for debugging.

If the function you need is not available, you can write your own. Before you do that, however, have a look in the *Piggy Bank*, a repository of Pig functions shared by the Pig community. There are details on the Pig wiki at *http://wiki.apache.org/pig/PiggyBank* on how to browse and obtain the Piggy Bank functions. If the Piggy Bank doesn't have what you need, you can write your own function (and if it is sufficiently general, you might consider contributing it to the Piggy Bank so that others can benefit from it, too). These are known as *user-defined functions*, or UDFs.

User-Defined Functions

Pig's designers realized that the ability to plug-in custom code is crucial for all but the most trivial data processing jobs. For this reason, they made it easy to define and use user-defined functions.

A Filter UDF

Let's demonstrate by writing a filter function for filtering out weather records that do not have a temperature quality reading of satisfactory (or better). The idea is to change this line:

```
filtered_records = FILTER records BY temperature != 9999 AND
  (quality == 0 OR quality == 1 OR quality == 4 OR quality == 5 OR quality == 9);
```

to:

```
filtered_records = FILTER records BY temperature != 9999 AND isGood(quality);
```

This achieves two things: it makes the Pig script more concise, and it encapsulates the logic in one place so that it can be easily reused in other scripts. If we were just writing an ad hoc query, then we probably wouldn't bother to write a UDF. It's when you start doing the same kind of processing over and over again that you see opportunities for reusable UDFs.

UDFs are written in Java, and filter functions are all subclasses of FilterFunc, which itself is a subclass of EvalFunc. We'll look at EvalFunc in more detail later, but for the moment just note that, in essence, EvalFunc looks like the following class:

```
public abstract class EvalFunc<T> {
  public abstract T exec(Tuple input) throws IOException;
}
```

EvalFunc's only abstract method, exec(), takes a tuple and returns a single value, the (parameterized) type T. The fields in the input tuple consist of the expressions passed to the function—in this case, a single integer. For FilterFunc, T is Boolean, so the method should return true only for those tuples that should not be filtered out.

For the quality filter, we write a class, IsGoodQuality, that extends FilterFunc and implements the exec() method. See Example 11-1. The Tuple class is essentially a list of objects with associated types. Here we are concerned only with the first field (since the function only has a single argument), which we extract by index using the get() method on Tuple. The field is an integer, so if it's not null, we cast it and check whether the value is one that signifies the temperature was a good reading, returning the appropriate value, true or false.

Example 11-1. A FilterFunc UDF to remove records with unsatisfactory temperature quality readings

```
package com.hadoopbook.pig;

import java.io.IOException;
import java.util.ArrayList;
import java.util.List;

import org.apache.pig.FilterFunc;

import org.apache.pig.backend.executionengine.ExecException;
import org.apache.pig.data.DataType;
import org.apache.pig.data.Tuple;
import org.apache.pig.impl.logicalLayer.FrontendException;

public class IsGoodQuality extends FilterFunc {

  @Override
  public Boolean exec(Tuple tuple) throws IOException {
    if (tuple == null || tuple.size() == 0) {
      return false;
    }
```

```
    try {
      Object object = tuple.get(0);
      if (object == null) {
        return false;
      }
      int i = (Integer) object;
      return i == 0 || i == 1 || i == 4 || i == 5 || i == 9;
    } catch (ExecException e) {
      throw new IOException(e);
    }
  }

}
```

To use the new function, we first compile it and package it in a JAR file (in the example code that accompanies this book, we can do this by typing ant pig). Then we tell Pig about the JAR file with the REGISTER operator, which is given the local path to the filename (and is *not* enclosed in quotes):

```
grunt> REGISTER pig-examples.jar;
```

Finally, we can invoke the function:

```
grunt> filtered_records = FILTER records BY temperature != 9999 AND
>>    com.hadoopbook.pig.IsGoodQuality(quality);
```

Pig resolves function calls by treating the function's name as a Java classname and attempting to load a class of that name. (This, incidentally, is why function names are case-sensitive: because Java classnames are.) When searching for classes, Pig uses a classloader that includes the JAR files that have been registered. When running in distributed mode, Pig will ensure that your JAR files get shipped to the cluster.

For the UDF in this example, Pig looks for a class with the name com.hadoop book.pig.IsGoodQuality, which it finds in the JAR file we registered.

Resolution of built-in functions proceeds in the same way, except for one difference: Pig has a set of built-in package names that it searches, so the function call does not have to be a fully qualified name. For example, the function MAX is actually implemented by a class MAX in the package org.apache.pig.builtin. This is one of the packages that Pig looks in, so we can write MAX rather than org.apache.pig.builtin.MAX in our Pig programs.

We can't register our package with Pig, but we can shorten the function name by defining an alias, using the DEFINE operator:

```
grunt> DEFINE isGood com.hadoopbook.pig.IsGoodQuality();
grunt> filtered_records = FILTER records BY temperature != 9999 AND isGood(quality);
```

Defining an alias is a good idea if you want to use the function several times in the same script. It's also necessary if you want to pass arguments to the constructor of the UDF's implementation class.

Leveraging types

The filter works when the quality field is declared to be of type int, but if the type information is absent, then the UDF fails! This happens because the field is the default type, bytearray, represented by the DataByteArray class. Because DataByteArray is not an Integer, the cast fails.

The obvious way to fix this is to convert the field to an integer in the exec() method. However, there is a better way, which is to tell Pig the types of the fields that the function expects. The getArgToFuncMapping() method on EvalFunc is provided for precisely this reason. We can override it to tell Pig that the first field should be an integer:

```
@Override
public List<FuncSpec> getArgToFuncMapping() throws FrontendException {
  List<FuncSpec> funcSpecs = new ArrayList<FuncSpec>();
  funcSpecs.add(new FuncSpec(this.getClass().getName(),
      new Schema(new Schema.FieldSchema(null, DataType.INTEGER))));

  return funcSpecs;
}
```

This method returns a FuncSpec object corresponding to each of the fields of the tuple that are passed to the exec() method. Here there is a single field, and we construct an anonymous FieldSchema (the name is passed as null, since Pig ignores the name when doing type conversion). The type is specified using the INTEGER constant on Pig's DataType class.

With the amended function, Pig will attempt to convert the argument passed to the function to an integer. If the field cannot be converted, then a null is passed for the field. The exec() method always returns false if the field is null. For this application, this behavior is appropriate, as we want to filter out records whose quality field is unintelligible.

Here's the final program using the new function:

```
-- max_temp_filter_udf.pig
REGISTER pig-examples.jar;
DEFINE isGood com.hadoopbook.pig.IsGoodQuality();
records = LOAD 'input/ncdc/micro-tab/sample.txt'
  AS (year:chararray, temperature:int, quality:int);
filtered_records = FILTER records BY temperature != 9999 AND isGood(quality);
grouped_records = GROUP filtered_records BY year;
max_temp = FOREACH grouped_records GENERATE group,
  MAX(filtered_records.temperature);
DUMP max_temp;
```

An Eval UDF

Writing an eval function is a small step up from writing a filter function. Consider a UDF (see Example 11-2) for trimming the leading and trailing whitespace from chararray values, just like the trim() method on java.lang.String. We will use this UDF later in the chapter.

Example 11-2. An EvalFunc UDF to trim leading and trailing whitespace from chararray values

```
public class Trim extends EvalFunc<String> {

  @Override
  public String exec(Tuple input) throws IOException {
    if (input == null || input.size() == 0) {
      return null;
    }
    try {
      Object object = input.get(0);
      if (object == null) {
        return null;
      }
      return ((String) object).trim();
    } catch (ExecException e) {
      throw new IOException(e);
    }
  }

  @Override
  public List<FuncSpec> getArgToFuncMapping() throws FrontendException {
    List<FuncSpec> funcList = new ArrayList<FuncSpec>();
    funcList.add(new FuncSpec(this.getClass().getName(), new Schema(
        new Schema.FieldSchema(null, DataType.CHARARRAY))));

    return funcList;
  }
}
```

An eval function extends the EvalFunc class, parameterized by the type of the return value (which is String for the Trim UDF).[*] The exec() and getArgToFuncMapping() methods are straightforward, like the ones in the IsGoodQuality UDF.

When you write an eval function, you need to consider what the output's schema looks like. In the following statement, the schema of B is determined by the function udf:

```
B = FOREACH A GENERATE udf($0);
```

If udf creates tuples with scalar fields, then Pig can determine B's schema through reflection. For complex types such as bags, tuples, or maps, Pig needs more help, and

---

[*] Although not relevant for this example, eval functions that operate on a bag may additionally implement Pig's Algebraic or Accumulator interfaces for more efficient processing of the bag in chunks.

you should implement the outputSchema() method to give Pig the information about the output schema.

The Trim UDF returns a string, which Pig translates as a chararray, as can be seen from the following session:

```
grunt> DUMP A;
( pomegranate)
(banana   )
(apple)
(   lychee )
grunt> DESCRIBE A;
A: {fruit: chararray}
grunt> B = FOREACH A GENERATE com.hadoopbook.pig.Trim(fruit);
grunt> DUMP B;
(pomegranate)
(banana)
(apple)
(lychee)
grunt> DESCRIBE B;
B: {chararray}
```

A has chararray fields that have leading and trailing spaces. We create B from A by applying the Trim function to the first field in A (named fruit). B's fields are correctly inferred to be of type chararray.

A Load UDF

We'll demonstrate a custom load function that can read plain-text column ranges as fields, very much like the Unix cut command. It is used as follows:

```
grunt> records = LOAD 'input/ncdc/micro/sample.txt'
>>    USING com.hadoopbook.pig.CutLoadFunc('16-19,88-92,93-93')
>>    AS (year:int, temperature:int, quality:int);
grunt> DUMP records;
(1950,0,1)
(1950,22,1)
(1950,-11,1)
(1949,111,1)
(1949,78,1)
```

The string passed to CutLoadFunc is the column specification; each comma-separated range defines a field, which is assigned a name and type in the AS clause. Let's examine the implementation of CutLoadFunc shown in Example 11-3.

Example 11-3. A LoadFunc UDF to load tuple fields as column ranges

```
public class CutLoadFunc extends LoadFunc {

  private static final Log LOG = LogFactory.getLog(CutLoadFunc.class);

  private final List<Range> ranges;
  private final TupleFactory tupleFactory = TupleFactory.getInstance();
  private RecordReader reader;
```

```
  public CutLoadFunc(String cutPattern) {
    ranges = Range.parse(cutPattern);
  }

  @Override
  public void setLocation(String location, Job job)
      throws IOException {
    FileInputFormat.setInputPaths(job, location);
  }

  @Override
  public InputFormat getInputFormat() {
    return new TextInputFormat();
  }

  @Override
  public void prepareToRead(RecordReader reader, PigSplit split) {
    this.reader = reader;
  }

  @Override
  public Tuple getNext() throws IOException {
    try {
      if (!reader.nextKeyValue()) {
        return null;
      }
      Text value = (Text) reader.getCurrentValue();
      String line = value.toString();
      Tuple tuple = tupleFactory.newTuple(ranges.size());
      for (int i = 0; i < ranges.size(); i++) {
        Range range = ranges.get(i);
        if (range.getEnd() > line.length()) {
          LOG.warn(String.format(
              "Range end (%s) is longer than line length (%s)",
              range.getEnd(), line.length()));
          continue;
        }
        tuple.set(i, new DataByteArray(range.getSubstring(line)));
      }
      return tuple;
    } catch (InterruptedException e) {
      throw new ExecException(e);
    }
  }
}
```

In Pig, like in Hadoop, data loading takes place before the mapper runs, so it is important that the input can be split into portions that are independently handled by each mapper (see "Input Splits and Records" on page 198 for background).

From Pig 0.7.0 (which is the version used here), the load and store function interfaces have been overhauled to be more closely aligned with Hadoop's InputFormat and OutputFormat classes. Functions written for previous versions of Pig will need rewriting (guidelines for doing so are provided at *http://wiki.apache.org/pig/LoadStore MigrationGuide*). A LoadFunc will typically use an existing underlying InputFormat to create records, with the LoadFunc providing the logic for turning the records into Pig tuples.

CutLoadFunc is constructed with a string that specifies the column ranges to use for each field. The logic for parsing this string and creating a list of internal Range objects that encapsulates these ranges is contained in the Range class, and is not shown here (it is available in the example code that accompanies this book).

Pig calls setLocation() on a LoadFunc to pass the input location to the loader. Since CutLoadFunc uses a TextInputFormat to break the input into lines, we just pass the location to set the input path using a static method on FileInputFormat.

 Pig uses the new MapReduce API, so we use the input and output formats and associated classes from the org.apache.hadoop.mapreduce package.

Next, Pig calls the getInputFormat() method to create a RecordReader for each split, just like in MapReduce. Pig passes each RecordReader to the prepareToRead() method of CutLoadFunc, which we store a reference to, so we can use it in the getNext() method for iterating through the records.

The Pig runtime calls getNext() repeatedly, and the load function reads tuples from the reader until the reader reaches the last record in its split. At this point, it returns null to signal that there are no more tuples to be read.

It is the responsibility of the getNext() implementation to turn lines of the input file into Tuple objects. It does this by means of a TupleFactory, a Pig class for creating Tuple instances. The newTuple() method creates a new tuple with the required number of fields, which is just the number of Range classes, and the fields are populated using substrings of the line, which are determined by the Range objects.

We need to think about what to do if the line is shorter than the range asked for. One option is to throw an exception and stop further processing. This is appropriate if your application cannot tolerate incomplete or corrupt records. In many cases, it is better to return a tuple with null fields and let the Pig script handle the incomplete data as it sees fit. This is the approach we take here; by exiting the for loop if the range end is past the end of the line, we leave the current field and any subsequent fields in the tuple with their default value of null.

Using a schema

Let's now consider the type of the fields being loaded. If the user has specified a schema, then the fields need converting to the relevant types. However, this is performed lazily by Pig, and so the loader should always construct tuples of type bytearray, using the

DataByteArray type. The loader function still has the opportunity to do the conversion, however, by overriding getLoadCaster() to return a custom implementation of the LoadCaster interface, which provides a collection of conversion methods for this purpose:

```
public interface LoadCaster {
  public Integer bytesToInteger(byte[] b) throws IOException;
  public Long bytesToLong(byte[] b) throws IOException;
  public Float bytesToFloat(byte[] b) throws IOException;
  public Double bytesToDouble(byte[] b) throws IOException;
  public String bytesToCharArray(byte[] b) throws IOException;
  public Map<String, Object> bytesToMap(byte[] b) throws IOException;
  public Tuple bytesToTuple(byte[] b) throws IOException;
  public DataBag bytesToBag(byte[] b) throws IOException;
}
```

CutLoadFunc doesn't override getLoadCaster() since the default implementation returns Utf8StorageConverter, which provides standard conversions between UTF-8 encoded data and Pig data types.

In some cases, the load function itself can determine the schema. For example, if we were loading self-describing data like XML or JSON, we could create a schema for Pig by looking at the data. Alternatively, the load function may determine the schema in another way, such as an external file, or by being passed information in its constructor. To support such cases, the load function should implement the LoadMetadata interface (in addition to the LoadFunc interface), so it can supply a schema to the Pig runtime. Note, however, that if a user supplies a schema in the AS clause of LOAD, then it takes precedence over the schema one specified by the LoadMetadata interface.

A load function may additionally implement the LoadPushDown interface as a means for finding out which columns the query is asking for. This can be a useful optimization for column-oriented storage, so that the loader only loads the columns that are needed by the query. There is no obvious way for CutLoadFunc to load only a subset of columns, since it reads the whole line for each tuple, so we don't use this optimization.

Data Processing Operators

Loading and Storing Data

Throughout this chapter, we have seen how to load data from external storage for processing in Pig. Storing the results is straightforward, too. Here's an example of using PigStorage to store tuples as plain-text values separated by a colon character:

```
grunt> STORE A INTO 'out' USING PigStorage(':');
grunt> cat out
Joe:cherry:2
Ali:apple:3
Joe:banana:2
Eve:apple:7
```

Other built-in storage functions were described in Table 11-7.

Filtering Data

Once you have some data loaded into a relation, the next step is often to filter it to remove the data that you are not interested in. By filtering early in the processing pipeline, you minimize the amount of data flowing through the system, which can improve efficiency.

FOREACH...GENERATE

We have already seen how to remove rows from a relation using the FILTER operator with simple expressions and a UDF. The FOREACH...GENERATE operator is used to act on every row in a relation. It can be used to remove fields or to generate new ones. In this example, we do both:

```
grunt> DUMP A;
(Joe,cherry,2)
(Ali,apple,3)
(Joe,banana,2)
(Eve,apple,7)
grunt> B = FOREACH A GENERATE $0, $2+1, 'Constant';
grunt> DUMP B;
(Joe,3,Constant)
(Ali,4,Constant)
(Joe,3,Constant)
(Eve,8,Constant)
```

Here we have created a new relation B with three fields. Its first field is a projection of the first field ($0) of A. B's second field is the third field of A ($2) with one added to it. B's third field is a constant field (every row in B has the same third field) with the chararray value Constant.

The FOREACH...GENERATE operator has a nested form to support more complex processing. In the following example, we compute various statistics for the weather dataset:

```
-- year_stats.pig
REGISTER pig-examples.jar;
DEFINE isGood com.hadoopbook.pig.IsGoodQuality();
records = LOAD 'input/ncdc/all/19{1,2,3,4,5}0*'
  USING com.hadoopbook.pig.CutLoadFunc('5-10,11-15,16-19,88-92,93-93')
  AS (usaf:chararray, wban:chararray, year:int, temperature:int, quality:int);

grouped_records = GROUP records BY year PARALLEL 30;

year_stats = FOREACH grouped_records {
  uniq_stations = DISTINCT records.usaf;
  good_records = FILTER records BY isGood(quality);
  GENERATE FLATTEN(group), COUNT(uniq_stations) AS station_count,
    COUNT(good_records) AS good_record_count, COUNT(records) AS record_count;
}
```

```
DUMP year_stats;
```

Using the cut UDF we developed earlier, we load various fields from the input dataset into the **records** relation. Next we group **records** by year. Notice the PARALLEL keyword for setting the number of reducers to use; this is vital when running on a cluster. Then we process each group using a nested FOREACH...GENERATE operator. The first nested statement creates a relation for the distinct USAF identifiers for stations using the DISTINCT operator. The second nested statement creates a relation for the records with "good" readings using the FILTER operator and a UDF. The final nested statement is a GENERATE statement (a nested FOREACH...GENERATE must always have a GENERATE statement as the last nested statement) that generates the summary fields of interest using the grouped records, as well as the relations created in the nested block.

Running it on a few years of data, we get the following:

```
(1920,8L,8595L,8595L)
(1950,1988L,8635452L,8641353L)
(1930,121L,89245L,89262L)
(1910,7L,7650L,7650L)
(1940,732L,1052333L,1052976L)
```

The fields are year, number of unique stations, total number of good readings, and total number of readings. We can see how the number of weather stations and readings grew over time.

STREAM

The STREAM operator allows you to transform data in a relation using an external program or script. It is named by analogy with Hadoop Streaming, which provides a similar capability for MapReduce (see "Hadoop Streaming" on page 33).

STREAM can use built-in commands with arguments. Here is an example that uses the Unix cut command to extract the second field of each tuple in A. Note that the command and its arguments are enclosed in backticks:

```
grunt> C = STREAM A THROUGH `cut -f 2`;
grunt> DUMP C;
(cherry)
(apple)
(banana)
(apple)
```

The STREAM operator uses PigStorage to serialize and deserialize relations to and from the program's standard input and output streams. Tuples in A are converted to tab-delimited lines that are passed to the script. The output of the script is read one line at a time and split on tabs to create new tuples for the output relation C. You can provide a custom serializer and deserializer, which implement `PigToStream` and `StreamToPig` respectively (both in the `org.apache.pig` package), using the DEFINE command.

Pig streaming is most powerful when you write custom processing scripts. The following Python script filters out bad weather records:

```
#!/usr/bin/env python

import re
import sys

for line in sys.stdin:
  (year, temp, q) = line.strip().split()
  if (temp != "9999" and re.match("[01459]", q)):
    print "%s\t%s" % (year, temp)
```

To use the script, you need to ship it to the cluster. This is achieved via a DEFINE clause, which also creates an alias for the STREAM command. The STREAM statement can then refer to the alias, as the following Pig script shows:

```
-- max_temp_filter_stream.pig
DEFINE is_good_quality `is_good_quality.py`
  SHIP ('ch11/src/main/python/is_good_quality.py');
records = LOAD 'input/ncdc/micro-tab/sample.txt'
  AS (year:chararray, temperature:int, quality:int);
filtered_records = STREAM records THROUGH is_good_quality
  AS (year:chararray, temperature:int);
grouped_records = GROUP filtered_records BY year;
max_temp = FOREACH grouped_records GENERATE group,
  MAX(filtered_records.temperature);
DUMP max_temp;
```

Grouping and Joining Data

Joining datasets in MapReduce takes some work on the part of the programmer (see "Joins" on page 247), whereas Pig has very good built-in support for join operations, making it much more approachable. Since the large datasets that are suitable for analysis by Pig (and MapReduce in general) are not normalized, joins are used more infrequently in Pig than they are in SQL.

JOIN

Let's look at an example of an inner join. Consider the relations A and B:

```
grunt> DUMP A;
(2,Tie)
(4,Coat)
(3,Hat)
(1,Scarf)
grunt> DUMP B;
(Joe,2)
(Hank,4)
(Ali,0)
(Eve,3)
(Hank,2)
```

We can join the two relations on the numerical (identity) field in each:

```
grunt> C = JOIN A BY $0, B BY $1;
grunt> DUMP C;
(2,Tie,Joe,2)
(2,Tie,Hank,2)
(3,Hat,Eve,3)
(4,Coat,Hank,4)
```

This is a classic inner join, where each match between the two relations corresponds to a row in the result. (It's actually an equijoin since the join predicate is equality.) The result's fields are made up of all the fields of all the input relations.

You should use the general join operator if all the relations being joined are too large to fit in memory. If one of the relations is small enough to fit in memory, there is a special type of join called a *fragment replicate join*, which is implemented by distributing the small input to all the mappers and performing a map-side join using an in-memory lookup table against the (fragmented) larger relation. There is a special syntax for telling Pig to use a fragment replicate join:[†]

```
grunt> C = JOIN A BY $0, B BY $1 USING "replicated";
```

The first relation must be the large one, followed by one or more small ones (all of which must fit in memory).

Pig also supports outer joins using a syntax that is similar to SQL's (this is covered for Hive in "Outer joins" on page 398). For example:

```
grunt> C = JOIN A BY $0 LEFT OUTER, B BY $1;
grunt> DUMP C;
(1,Scarf,,)
(2,Tie,Joe,2)
(2,Tie,Hank,2)
(3,Hat,Eve,3)
(4,Coat,Hank,4)
```

COGROUP

JOIN always gives a flat structure: a set of tuples. The COGROUP statement is similar to JOIN, but creates a nested set of output tuples. This can be useful if you want to exploit the structure in subsequent statements:

```
grunt> D = COGROUP A BY $0, B BY $1;
grunt> DUMP D;
(0,{},{(Ali,0)})
(1,{(1,Scarf)},{})
(2,{(2,Tie)},{(Joe,2),(Hank,2)})
(3,{(3,Hat)},{(Eve,3)})
(4,{(4,Coat)},{(Hank,4)})
```

† There are more keywords that may be used in the USING clause, including "skewed" (for large datasets with a skewed keyspace) and "merge" (to effect a merge join for inputs that are already sorted on the join key). See Pig's documentation for details on how to use these specialized joins.

COGROUP generates a tuple for each unique grouping key. The first field of each tuple is the key, and the remaining fields are bags of tuples from the relations with a matching key. The first bag contains the matching tuples from relation A with the same key. Similarly, the second bag contains the matching tuples from relation B with the same key.

If for a particular key a relation has no matching key, then the bag for that relation is empty. For example, since no one has bought a scarf (with ID 1), the second bag in the tuple for that row is empty. This is an example of an outer join, which is the default type for COGROUP. It can be made explicit using the OUTER keyword, making this COGROUP statement the same as the previous one:

```
D = COGROUP A BY $0 OUTER, B BY $1 OUTER;
```

You can suppress rows with empty bags by using the INNER keyword, which gives the COGROUP inner join semantics. The INNER keyword is applied per relation, so the following only suppresses rows when relation A has no match (dropping the unknown product 0 here):

```
grunt> E = COGROUP A BY $0 INNER, B BY $1;
grunt> DUMP E;
(1,{(1,Scarf)},{})
(2,{(2,Tie)},{(Joe,2),(Hank,2)})
(3,{(3,Hat)},{(Eve,3)})
(4,{(4,Coat)},{(Hank,4)})
```

We can flatten this structure to discover who bought each of the items in relation A:

```
grunt> F = FOREACH E GENERATE FLATTEN(A), B.$0;
grunt> DUMP F;
(1,Scarf,{})
(2,Tie,{(Joe),(Hank)})
(3,Hat,{(Eve)})
(4,Coat,{(Hank)})
```

Using a combination of COGROUP, INNER, and FLATTEN (which removes nesting) it's possible to simulate an (inner) JOIN:

```
grunt> G = COGROUP A BY $0 INNER, B BY $1 INNER;
grunt> H = FOREACH G GENERATE FLATTEN($1), FLATTEN($2);
grunt> DUMP H;
(2,Tie,Joe,2)
(2,Tie,Hank,2)
(3,Hat,Eve,3)
(4,Coat,Hank,4)
```

This gives the same result as JOIN A BY $0, B BY $1.

If the join key is composed of several fields, you can specify them all in the BY clauses of the JOIN or COGROUP statement. Make sure that the number of fields in each BY clause is the same.

Here's another example of a join in Pig, in a script for calculating the maximum temperature for every station over a time period controlled by the input:

```
-- max_temp_station_name.pig
REGISTER pig-examples.jar;
DEFINE isGood com.hadoopbook.pig.IsGoodQuality();

stations = LOAD 'input/ncdc/metadata/stations-fixed-width.txt'
  USING com.hadoopbook.pig.CutLoadFunc('1-6,8-12,14-42')
  AS (usaf:chararray, wban:chararray, name:chararray);

trimmed_stations = FOREACH stations GENERATE usaf, wban,
  com.hadoopbook.pig.Trim(name);

records = LOAD 'input/ncdc/all/191*'
  USING com.hadoopbook.pig.CutLoadFunc('5-10,11-15,88-92,93-93')
  AS (usaf:chararray, wban:chararray, temperature:int, quality:int);

filtered_records = FILTER records BY temperature != 9999 AND isGood(quality);
grouped_records = GROUP filtered_records BY (usaf, wban) PARALLEL 30;
max_temp = FOREACH grouped_records GENERATE FLATTEN(group),
  MAX(filtered_records.temperature);
max_temp_named = JOIN max_temp BY (usaf, wban), trimmed_stations BY (usaf, wban)
  PARALLEL 30;
max_temp_result = FOREACH max_temp_named GENERATE $0, $1, $5, $2;

STORE max_temp_result INTO 'max_temp_by_station';
```

We use the cut UDF we developed earlier to load one relation holding the station IDs (USAF and WBAN identifiers) and names, and one relation holding all the weather records, keyed by station ID. We group the filtered weather records by station ID and aggregate by maximum temperature, before joining with the stations. Finally, we project out the fields we want in the final result: USAF, WBAN, station name, maximum temperature.

Here are a few results for the 1910s:

```
228020      99999      SORTAVALA       322
029110      99999      VAASA AIRPORT   300
040650      99999      GRIMSEY         378
```

This query could be made more efficient by using a fragment replicate join, as the station metadata is small.

CROSS

Pig Latin includes the cross-product operator (also known as the cartesian product), which joins every tuple in a relation with every tuple in a second relation (and with every tuple in further relations if supplied). The size of the output is the product of the size of the inputs, potentially making the output very large:

```
grunt> I = CROSS A, B;
grunt> DUMP I;
(2,Tie,Joe,2)
(2,Tie,Hank,4)
(2,Tie,Ali,0)
(2,Tie,Eve,3)
(2,Tie,Hank,2)
(4,Coat,Joe,2)
(4,Coat,Hank,4)
(4,Coat,Ali,0)
(4,Coat,Eve,3)
(4,Coat,Hank,2)
(3,Hat,Joe,2)
(3,Hat,Hank,4)
(3,Hat,Ali,0)
(3,Hat,Eve,3)
(3,Hat,Hank,2)
(1,Scarf,Joe,2)
(1,Scarf,Hank,4)
(1,Scarf,Ali,0)
(1,Scarf,Eve,3)
(1,Scarf,Hank,2)
```

When dealing with large datasets, you should try to avoid operations that generate intermediate representations that are quadratic (or worse) in size. Computing the cross-product of the whole input dataset is rarely needed, if ever.

For example, at first blush one might expect that calculating pairwise document similarity in a corpus of documents would require every document pair to be generated before calculating their similarity. However, if one starts with the insight that most document pairs have a similarity score of zero (that is, they are unrelated), then we can find a way to a better algorithm.

In this case, the key idea is to focus on the entities that we are using to calculate similarity (terms in a document, for example) and make them the center of the algorithm. In practice, we also remove terms that don't help discriminate between documents (stopwords), and this reduces the problem space still further. Using this technique to analyze a set of roughly one million (10^6) documents generates in the order of one billion (10^9) intermediate pairs,[‡] rather than the one trillion (10^{12}) produced by the naive approach (generating the cross-product of the input) or the approach with no stopword removal.

[‡] "Pairwise Document Similarity in Large Collections with MapReduce," Elsayed, Lin, and Oard (2008, College Park, MD: University of Maryland).

GROUP

Although COGROUP groups the data in two or more relations, the GROUP statement groups the data in a single relation. GROUP supports grouping by more than equality of keys: you can use an expression or user-defined function as the group key. For example, consider the following relation A:

```
grunt> DUMP A;
(Joe,cherry)
(Ali,apple)
(Joe,banana)
(Eve,apple)
```

Let's group by the number of characters in the second field:

```
grunt> B = GROUP A BY SIZE($1);
grunt> DUMP B;
(5L,{(Ali,apple),(Eve,apple)})
(6L,{(Joe,cherry),(Joe,banana)})
```

GROUP creates a relation whose first field is the grouping field, which is given the alias group. The second field is a bag containing the grouped fields with the same schema as the original relation (in this case, A).

There are also two special grouping operations: ALL and ANY. ALL groups all the tuples in a relation in a single group, as if the GROUP function was a constant:

```
grunt> C = GROUP A ALL;
grunt> DUMP C;
(all,{(Joe,cherry),(Ali,apple),(Joe,banana),(Eve,apple)})
```

Note that there is no BY in this form of the GROUP statement. The ALL grouping is commonly used to count the number of tuples in a relation, as shown in "Validation and nulls" on page 339.

The ANY keyword is used to group the tuples in a relation randomly, which can be useful for sampling.

Sorting Data

Relations are unordered in Pig. Consider a relation A:

```
grunt> DUMP A;
(2,3)
(1,2)
(2,4)
```

There is no guarantee which order the rows will be processed in. In particular, when retrieving the contents of A using DUMP or STORE, the rows may be written in any order. If you want to impose an order on the output, you can use the ORDER operator to sort a relation by one or more fields. The default sort order compares fields of the same type using the natural ordering, and different types are given an arbitrary, but deterministic, ordering (a tuple is always "less than" a bag, for example).

The following example sorts A by the first field in ascending order and by the second field in descending order:

```
grunt> B = ORDER A BY $0, $1 DESC;
grunt> DUMP B;
(1,2)
(2,4)
(2,3)
```

Any further processing on a sorted relation is not guaranteed to retain its order. For example:

```
grunt> C = FOREACH B GENERATE *;
```

Even though relation C has the same contents as relation B, its tuples may be emitted in any order by a DUMP or a STORE. It is for this reason that it is usual to perform the ORDER operation just before retrieving the output.

The LIMIT statement is useful for limiting the number of results, as a quick and dirty way to get a sample of a relation; prototyping (the ILLUSTRATE command) should be preferred for generating more representative samples of the data. It can be used immediately after the ORDER statement to retrieve the first *n* tuples. Usually, LIMIT will select any *n* tuples from a relation, but when used immediately after an ORDER statement, the order is retained (in an exception to the rule that processing a relation does not retain its order):

```
grunt> D = LIMIT B 2;
grunt> DUMP D;
(1,2)
(2,4)
```

If the limit is greater than the number of tuples in the relation, all tuples are returned (so LIMIT has no effect).

Using LIMIT can improve the performance of a query because Pig tries to apply the limit as early as possible in the processing pipeline, to minimize the amount of data that needs to be processed. For this reason, you should always use LIMIT if you are not interested in the entire output.

Combining and Splitting Data

Sometimes you have several relations that you would like to combine into one. For this, the UNION statement is used. For example:

```
grunt> DUMP A;
(2,3)
(1,2)
(2,4)
grunt> DUMP B;
(z,x,8)
(w,y,1)
grunt> C = UNION A, B;
grunt> DUMP C;
```

```
(z,x,8)
(w,y,1)
(2,3)
(1,2)
(2,4)
```

C is the union of relations A and B, and since relations are unordered, the order of the tuples in C is undefined. Also, it's possible to form the union of two relations with different schemas or with different numbers of fields, as we have done here. Pig attempts to merge the schemas from the relations that UNION is operating on. In this case, they are incompatible, so C has no schema:

```
grunt> DESCRIBE A;
A: {f0: int,f1: int}
grunt> DESCRIBE B;
B: {f0: chararray,f1: chararray,f2: int}
grunt> DESCRIBE C;
Schema for C unknown.
```

If the output relation has no schema, your script needs to be able to handle tuples that vary in the number of fields and/or types.

The SPLIT operator is the opposite of UNION; it partitions a relation into two or more relations. See "Validation and nulls" on page 339 for an example of how to use it.

Pig in Practice

There are some practical techniques that are worth knowing about when you are developing and running Pig programs. This section covers some of them.

Parallelism

When running in MapReduce mode, you need to tell Pig how many reducers you want for each job. You do this using a PARALLEL clause for operators that run in the reduce phase, which includes all the grouping and joining operators (GROUP, COGROUP, JOIN, CROSS), as well as DISTINCT and ORDER. By default, the number of reducers is one (just like for MapReduce), so it is important to set the degree of parallelism when running on a large dataset. The following line sets the number of reducers to 30 for the GROUP:

```
grouped_records = GROUP records BY year PARALLEL 30;
```

A good setting for the number of reduce tasks is slightly fewer than the number of reduce slots in the cluster. See "Choosing the Number of Reducers" on page 195 for further discussion.

The number of map tasks is set by the size of the input (with one map per HDFS block) and is not affected by the PARALLEL clause.

Parameter Substitution

If you have a Pig script that you run on a regular basis, then it's quite common to want to be able to run the same script with different parameters. For example, a script that runs daily may use the date to determine which input files it runs over. Pig supports *parameter substitution*, where parameters in the script are substituted with values supplied at runtime. Parameters are denoted by identifiers prefixed with a $ character; for example, $input and $output are used in the following script to specify the input and output paths:

```
-- max_temp_param.pig
records = LOAD '$input' AS (year:chararray, temperature:int, quality:int);
filtered_records = FILTER records BY temperature != 9999 AND
  (quality == 0 OR quality == 1 OR quality == 4 OR quality == 5 OR quality == 9);
grouped_records = GROUP filtered_records BY year;
max_temp = FOREACH grouped_records GENERATE group,
  MAX(filtered_records.temperature);
STORE max_temp into '$output';
```

Parameters can be specified when launching Pig, using the -param option, one for each parameter:

```
% pig -param input=/user/tom/input/ncdc/micro-tab/sample.txt \
>     -param output=/tmp/out \
>     ch11/src/main/pig/max_temp_param.pig
```

You can also put parameters in a file and pass them to Pig using the -param_file option. For example, we can achieve the same result as the previous command by placing the parameter definitions in a file:

```
# Input file
input=/user/tom/input/ncdc/micro-tab/sample.txt
# Output file
output=/tmp/out
```

The *pig* invocation then becomes:

```
% pig -param_file ch11/src/main/pig/max_temp_param.param \
>     ch11/src/main/pig/max_temp_param.pig
```

You can specify multiple parameter files using -param_file repeatedly. You can also use a combination of -param and -param_file options, and if any parameter is defined in both a parameter file and on the command line, the last value on the command line takes precedence.

Dynamic parameters

For parameters that are supplied using the `-param` option, it is easy to make the value dynamic by running a command or script. Many Unix shells support command substitution for a command enclosed in backticks, and we can use this to make the output directory date-based:

```
% pig -param input=/user/tom/input/ncdc/micro-tab/sample.txt \
>     -param output=/tmp/`date "+%Y-%m-%d"`/out \
>     ch11/src/main/pig/max_temp_param.pig
```

Pig also supports backticks in parameter files, by executing the enclosed command in a shell and using the shell output as the substituted value. If the command or scripts exits with a nonzero exit status, then the error message is reported and execution halts. Backtick support in parameter files is a useful feature; it means that parameters can be defined in the same way if they are defined in a file or on the command line.

Parameter substitution processing

Parameter substitution occurs as a preprocessing step before the script is run. You can see the substitutions that the preprocessor made by executing Pig with the `-dryrun` option. In dry run mode, Pig performs parameter substitution and generates a copy of the original script with substituted values, but does not execute the script. You can inspect the generated script and check that the substitutions look sane (because they are dynamically generated, for example) before running it in normal mode.

At the time of this writing, Grunt does not support parameter substitution.

## CHAPTER 12

Hive

In "Information Platforms and the Rise of the Data Scientist,"[*] Jeff Hammerbacher describes Information Platforms as "the locus of their organization's efforts to ingest, process, and generate information," and how they "serve to accelerate the process of learning from empirical data."

One of the biggest ingredients in the Information Platform built by Jeff's team at Facebook was Hive, a framework for data warehousing on top of Hadoop. Hive grew from a need to manage and learn from the huge volumes of data that Facebook was producing every day from its burgeoning social network. After trying a few different systems, the team chose Hadoop for storage and processing, since it was cost-effective and met their scalability needs.[†]

Hive was created to make it possible for analysts with strong SQL skills (but meager Java programming skills) to run queries on the huge volumes of data that Facebook stored in HDFS. Today, Hive is a successful Apache project used by many organizations as a general-purpose, scalable data processing platform.

Of course, SQL isn't ideal for every big data problem—it's not a good fit for building complex machine learning algorithms, for example—but it's great for many analyses, and it has the huge advantage of being very well known in the industry. What's more, SQL is the *lingua franca* in business intelligence tools (ODBC is a common bridge, for example), so Hive is well placed to integrate with these products.

This chapter is an introduction to using Hive. It assumes that you have working knowledge of SQL and general database architecture; as we go through Hive's features, we'll often compare them to the equivalent in a traditional RDBMS.

---

[*] *Beautiful Data: The Stories Behind Elegant Data Solutions (http://oreilly.com/catalog/9780596157128/)*, by Toby Segaran and Jeff Hammerbacher (O'Reilly, 2009)

[†] You can read more about the history of Hadoop at Facebook in "Hadoop and Hive at Facebook" on page 506.

Installing Hive

In normal use, Hive runs on your workstation and converts your SQL query into a series of MapReduce jobs for execution on a Hadoop cluster. Hive organizes data into tables, which provide a means for attaching structure to data stored in HDFS. Metadata—such as table schemas—is stored in a database called the *metastore*.

When starting out with Hive, it is convenient to run the metastore on your local machine. In this configuration, which is the default, the Hive table definitions that you create will be local to your machine, so you can't share them with other users. We'll see how to configure a shared remote metastore, which is the norm in production environments, later in "The Metastore" on page 373.

Installation of Hive is straightforward. Java 6 is a prerequisite; and on Windows, you will need Cygwin, too. You also need to have the same version of Hadoop installed locally that your cluster is running.[‡] Of course, you may choose to run Hadoop locally, either in standalone or pseudo-distributed mode, while getting started with Hive. These options are all covered in Appendix A.

Which Versions of Hadoop Does Hive Work With?

Any given release of Hive is designed to work with multiple versions of Hadoop. Generally, Hive works with the latest release of Hadoop, as well as supporting a number of older versions. For example, Hive 0.5.0 is compatible with versions of Hadoop between 0.17.x and 0.20.x (inclusive). You don't need to do anything special to tell Hive which version of Hadoop you are using, beyond making sure that the *hadoop* executable is on the path or setting the `HADOOP_HOME` environment variable.

Download a release at *http://hadoop.apache.org/hive/releases.html*, and unpack the tarball in a suitable place on your workstation:

```
% tar xzf hive-x.y.z-dev.tar.gz
```

It's handy to put Hive on your path to make it easy to launch:

```
% export HIVE_INSTALL=/home/tom/hive-x.y.z-dev
% export PATH=$PATH:$HIVE_INSTALL/bin
```

Now type hive to launch the Hive shell:

```
% hive
hive>
```

[‡] It is assumed that you have network connectivity from your workstation to the Hadoop cluster. You can test this before running Hive by installing Hadoop locally and performing some HDFS operations with the `hadoop fs` command.

The Hive Shell

The shell is the primary way that we will interact with Hive, by issuing commands in *HiveQL*. HiveQL is Hive's query language, a dialect of SQL. It is heavily influenced by MySQL, so if you are familiar with MySQL you should feel at home using Hive.

When starting Hive for the first time, we can check that it is working by listing its tables: there should be none. The command must be terminated with a semicolon to tell Hive to execute it:

```
hive> SHOW TABLES;
OK
Time taken: 10.425 seconds
```

Like SQL, HiveQL is generally case insensitive (except for string comparisons), so `show tables;` works equally well here.

For a fresh install, the command takes a few seconds to run since it is lazily creating the metastore database on your machine. (The database stores its files in a directory called *metastore_db*, which is relative to where you ran the `hive` command from.)

You can also run the Hive shell in non-interactive mode. The `-f` option runs the commands in the specified file, *script.q*, in this example:

```
% hive -f script.q
```

For short scripts, you can use the `-e` option to specify the commands inline, in which case the final semicolon is not required:

```
% hive -e 'SELECT * FROM dummy'
Hive history file=/tmp/tom/hive_job_log_tom_201005042112_1906486281.txt
OK
X
Time taken: 4.734 seconds
```

 It's useful to have a small table of data to test queries against, such as trying out functions in `SELECT` expressions using literal data (see "Operators and Functions" on page 380). Here's one way of populating a single row table:

```
% echo 'X' > /tmp/dummy.txt
% hive -e "CREATE TABLE dummy (value STRING); \
LOAD DATA LOCAL INPATH '/tmp/dummy.txt' \
OVERWRITE INTO TABLE dummy"
```

In both interactive and non-interactive mode, Hive will print information to standard error—such as the time taken to run a query—during the course of operation. You can suppress these messages using the `-S` option at launch time, which has the effect of only showing the output result for queries:

```
% hive -S -e 'SELECT * FROM dummy'
X
```

Other useful Hive shell features include the ability to run commands on the host operating system by using a ! prefix to the command and the ability to access Hadoop filesystems using the dfs command.

An Example

Let's see how to use Hive to run a query on the weather dataset we explored in earlier chapters. The first step is to load the data into Hive's managed storage. Here we'll have Hive use the local filesystem for storage; later we'll see how to store tables in HDFS.

Just like an RDBMS, Hive organizes its data into tables. We create a table to hold the weather data using the CREATE TABLE statement:

```
CREATE TABLE records (year STRING, temperature INT, quality INT)
ROW FORMAT DELIMITED
  FIELDS TERMINATED BY '\t';
```

The first line declares a records table with three columns: year, temperature, and quality. The type of each column must be specified, too: here the year is a string, while the other two columns are integers.

So far, the SQL is familiar. The ROW FORMAT clause, however, is particular to HiveQL. What this declaration is saying is that each row in the data file is tab-delimited text. Hive expects there to be three fields in each row, corresponding to the table columns, with fields separated by tabs, and rows by newlines.

Next we can populate Hive with the data. This is just a small sample, for exploratory purposes:

```
LOAD DATA LOCAL INPATH 'input/ncdc/micro-tab/sample.txt'
OVERWRITE INTO TABLE records;
```

Running this command tells Hive to put the specified local file in its warehouse directory. This is a simple filesystem operation. There is no attempt, for example, to parse the file and store it in an internal database format, since Hive does not mandate any particular file format. Files are stored verbatim: they are not modified by Hive.

In this example, we are storing Hive tables on the local filesystem (fs.default.name is set to its default value of file:///). Tables are stored as directories under Hive's warehouse directory, which is controlled by the hive.metastore.warehouse.dir, and defaults to /user/hive/warehouse.

Thus, the files for the records table are found in the /user/hive/warehouse/records directory on the local filesystem:

```
% ls /user/hive/warehouse/records/
sample.txt
```

In this case, there is only one file, *sample.txt*, but in general there can be more, and Hive will read all of them when querying the table.

The OVERWRITE keyword in the LOAD DATA statement tells Hive to delete any existing files in the directory for the table. If it is omitted, then the new files are simply added to the table's directory (unless they have the same names, in which case they replace the old files).

Now that the data is in Hive, we can run a query against it:

```
hive> SELECT year, MAX(temperature)
    > FROM records
    > WHERE temperature != 9999
    >   AND (quality = 0 OR quality = 1 OR quality = 4 OR quality = 5 OR quality = 9)
    > GROUP BY year;
1949   111
1950   22
```

This SQL query is unremarkable. It is a SELECT statement with a GROUP BY clause for grouping rows into years, which uses the MAX() aggregate function to find the maximum temperature for each year group. But the remarkable thing is that Hive transforms this query into a MapReduce job, which it executes on our behalf, then prints the results to the console. There are some nuances such as the SQL constructs that Hive supports and the format of the data that we can query—and we shall explore some of these in this chapter—but it is the ability to execute SQL queries against our raw data that gives Hive its power.

Running Hive

In this section, we look at some more practical aspects of running Hive, including how to set up Hive to run against a Hadoop cluster and a shared metastore. In doing so, we'll see Hive's architecture in some detail.

Configuring Hive

Hive is configured using an XML configuration file like Hadoop's. The file is called *hive-site.xml* and is located in Hive's *conf* directory. This file is where you can set properties that you want to set every time you run Hive. The same directory contains *hive-default.xml*, which documents the properties that Hive exposes and their default values.

You can override the configuration directory that Hive looks for in *hive-site.xml* by passing the --config option to the *hive* command:

```
% hive --config /Users/tom/dev/hive-conf
```

Note that this option specifies the containing directory, not *hive-site.xml* itself. It can be useful if you have multiple site files—for different clusters, say—that you switch between on a regular basis. Alternatively, you can set the HIVE_CONF_DIR environment variable to the configuration directory, for the same effect.

The *hive-site.xml* is a natural place to put the cluster connection details: you can specify the filesystem and jobtracker using the usual Hadoop properties, `fs.default.name` and `mapred.job.tracker` (see Appendix A for more details on configuring Hadoop). If not set, they default to the local filesystem and the local (in-process) job runner—just like they do in Hadoop—which is very handy when trying out Hive on small trial datasets. Metastore configuration settings (covered in "The Metastore" on page 373) are commonly found in *hive-site.xml*, too.

Hive also permits you to set properties on a per-session basis, by passing the `-hiveconf` option to the *hive* command. For example, the following command sets the cluster (to a pseudo-distributed cluster) for the duration of the session:

```
% hive -hiveconf fs.default.name=localhost -hiveconf mapred.job.tracker=localhost:8021
```

> If you plan to have more than one Hive user sharing a Hadoop cluster, then you need to make the directories that Hive uses writable by all users. The following commands will create the directories and set their permissions appropriately:
>
> ```
> % hadoop fs -mkdir /tmp
> % hadoop fs -chmod a+w /tmp
> % hadoop fs -mkdir /user/hive/warehouse
> % hadoop fs -chmod a+w /user/hive/warehouse
> ```
>
> If all users are in the same group, then permissions g+w are sufficient on the warehouse directory.

You can change settings from within a session, too, using the SET command. This is useful for changing Hive or MapReduce job settings for a particular query. For example, the following command ensures buckets are populated according to the table definition (see "Buckets" on page 384):

```
hive> SET hive.enforce.bucketing=true;
```

To see the current value of any property, use SET with just the property name:

```
hive> SET hive.enforce.bucketing;
hive.enforce.bucketing=true
```

By itself, SET will list all the properties (and their values) set by Hive. Note that the list will not include Hadoop defaults, unless they have been explicitly overridden in one of the ways covered in this section. Use SET -v to list all the properties in the system, including Hadoop defaults.

There is a precedence hierarchy to setting properties. In the following list, lower numbers take precedence over higher numbers:

1. The Hive SET command
2. The command line -hiveconf option
3. *hive-site.xml*
4. *hive-default.xml*

5. *hadoop-site.xml* (or, equivalently, *core-site.xml*, *hdfs-site.xml*, and *mapred-site.xml*)

6. *hadoop-default.xml* (or, equivalently, *core-default.xml*, *hdfs-default.xml*, and *mapred-default.xml*)

Logging

You can find Hive's error log on the local file system at */tmp/$USER/hive.log*. It can be very useful when trying to diagnose configuration problems or other types of error. Hadoop's MapReduce task logs are also a useful source for troubleshooting; see "Hadoop User Logs" on page 156 for where to find them.

The logging configuration is in *conf/hive-log4j.properties*, and you can edit this file to change log levels and other logging-related settings. Often though, it's more convenient to set logging configuration for the session. For example, the following handy invocation will send debug messages to the console:

```
% hive -hiveconf hive.root.logger=DEBUG,console
```

Hive Services

The Hive shell is only one of several services that you can run using the hive command. You can specify the service to run using the --service option. Type hive --service help to get a list of available service names; the most useful are described below.

cli
> The command line interface to Hive (the shell). This is the default service.

hiveserver
> Runs Hive as a server exposing a Thrift service, enabling access from a range of clients written in different languages. Applications using the Thrift, JDBC, and ODBC connectors need to run a Hive server to communicate with Hive. Set the HIVE_PORT environment variable to specify the port the server will listen on (defaults to 10,000).

hwi
> The Hive Web Interface. See "The Hive Web Interface (HWI)" on page 372.

jar
> The Hive equivalent to hadoop jar, a convenient way to run Java applications that includes both Hadoop and Hive classes on the classpath.

metastore
> By default, the metastore is run in the same process as the Hive service. Using this service, it is possible to run the metastore as a standalone (remote) process. Set the METASTORE_PORT environment variable to specify the port the server will listen on.

Hive clients

If you run Hive as a server (hive --service hiveserver), then there are a number of different mechanisms for connecting to it from applications. The relationship between Hive clients and Hive services is illustrated in Figure 12-1.

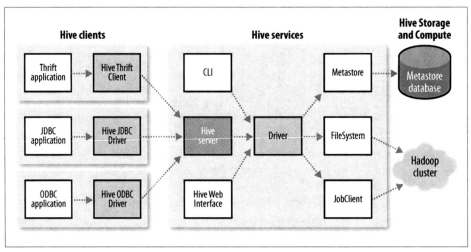

Figure 12-1. Hive architecture

Thrift Client

The Hive Thrift Client makes it easy to run Hive commands from a wide range of programming languages. Thrift bindings for Hive are available for C++, Java, PHP, Python, and Ruby. They can be found in the *src/service/src* subdirectory in the Hive distribution.

JDBC Driver

Hive provides a Type 4 (pure Java) JDBC driver, defined in the class `org.apache.hadoop.hive.jdbc.HiveDriver`. When configured with a JDBC URI of the form `jdbc:hive://host:port/dbname`, a Java application will connect to a Hive server running in a separate process at the given host and port. (The driver makes calls to an interface implemented by the Hive Thrift Client using the Java Thrift bindings.) At the time of writing, `default` is the only database name supported.

You may alternatively choose to connect to Hive via JDBC in *embedded mode* using the URI `jdbc:hive://`. In this mode, Hive runs in the same JVM as the application invoking it, so there is no need to launch it as a standalone server since it does not use the Thrift service or the Hive Thrift Client.

The JDBC driver is still in development, and in particular it does not support the full JDBC API.

ODBC Driver

The Hive ODBC Driver allows applications that support the ODBC protocol to connect to Hive. (Like the JDBC driver, the ODBC driver uses Thrift to communicate with the Hive server.) The ODBC driver is still in development, so you should refer to the latest instructions on the Hive wiki for how to build and run it.

There are more details on using these clients on the Hive wiki at *http://wiki.apache.org/ hadoop/Hive/HiveClient*.

The Metastore

The *metastore* is the central repository of Hive metadata. The metastore is divided into two pieces: a service and the backing store for the data. By default, the metastore service runs in the same JVM as the Hive service and contains an embedded Derby database instance backed by the local disk. This is called the *embedded metastore* configuration (see Figure 12-2).

Using an embedded metastore is a simple way to get started with Hive; however, only one embedded Derby database can access the database files on disk at any one time, which means you can only have one Hive session open at a time that shares the same metastore. Trying to start a second session gives the error:

```
Failed to start database 'metastore_db'
```

when it attempts to open a connection to the metastore.

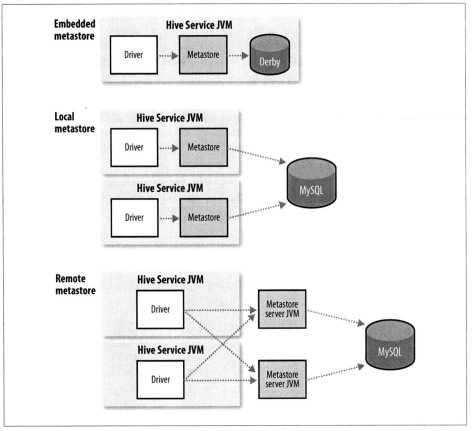

Figure 12-2. Metastore configurations

The solution to supporting multiple sessions (and therefore multiple users) is to use a standalone database. This configuration is referred to as a *local metastore*, since the metastore service still runs in the same process as the Hive service, but connects to a database running in a separate process, either on the same machine or on a remote machine. Any JDBC-compliant database may be used by setting the `javax.jdo.option.*` configuration properties listed in Table 12-1.[§]

MySQL is a popular choice for the standalone metastore. In this case, `javax.jdo.option.ConnectionURL` is set to `jdbc:mysql://host/dbname?createDatabaseIf NotExist=true`, and `javax.jdo.option.ConnectionDriverName` is set to `com.mysql.jdbc.Driver`. (The user name and password should be set, too, of course.) The JDBC driver JAR file for MySQL (Connector/J) must be on Hive's classpath, which is simply achieved by placing it in Hive's *lib* directory.

[§] The properties have the `javax.jdo` prefix since the metastore implementation uses the Java Data Objects (JDO) API for persisting Java objects. It uses the DataNucleus implementation of JDO.

Going a step further, there's another metastore configuration called a *remote meta-store*, where one or more metastore servers run in separate processes to the Hive service. This brings better manageability and security, since the database tier can be completely firewalled off, and the clients no longer need the database credentials.

A Hive service is configured to use a remote metastore by setting `hive.meta store.local` to `false`, and `hive.metastore.uris` to the metastore server URIs, separated by commas if there is more than one. Metastore server URIs are of the form `thrift://host:port`, where the port corresponds to the one set by `METASTORE_PORT` when starting the metastore server (see "Hive Services" on page 371).

Table 12-1. Important metastore configuration properties

Property name	Type	Default value	Description
hive.metastore. warehouse.dir	URI	/user/hive/ warehouse	The directory relative to fs.default.name where managed tables are stored.
hive.metastore. local	boolean	true	Whether to use an embedded metastore server (true), or connect to a remote instance (false). If false, then hive.metastore.uris must be set.
hive.metastore.uris	comma-separated URIs	Not set	The URIs specifying the remote metastore servers to connect to. Clients connect in a round-robin fashion if there are multiple remote servers.
javax.jdo.option. ConnectionURL	URI	jdbc:derby:;database Name=metastore_db; create=true	The JDBC URL of the metastore database.
javax.jdo.option. ConnectionDriverName	String	org.apache.derby. jdbc.EmbeddedDriver	The JDBC driver classname.
javax.jdo.option. ConnectionUserName	String	APP	The JDBC user name.
javax.jdo.option. ConnectionPassword	String	mine	The JDBC password.

Comparison with Traditional Databases

While Hive resembles a traditional database in many ways (such as supporting an SQL interface), its HDFS and MapReduce underpinnings mean that there are a number of architectural differences that directly influence the features that Hive supports, which in turn affects the uses that Hive can be put to.

Schema on Read Versus Schema on Write

In a traditional database, a table's schema is enforced at data load time. If the data being loaded doesn't conform to the schema, then it is rejected. This design is sometimes called *schema on write*, since the data is checked against the schema when it is written into the database.

Hive, on the other hand, doesn't verify the data when it is loaded, but rather when a query is issued. This is called *schema on read*.

There are trade-offs between the two approaches. Schema on read makes for a very fast initial load, since the data does not have to be read, parsed, and serialized to disk in the database's internal format. The load operation is just a file copy or move. It is more flexible, too: consider having two schemas for the same underlying data, depending on the analysis being performed. (This is possible in Hive using external tables, see "Managed Tables and External Tables" on page 381.)

Schema on write makes query time performance faster, since the database can index columns and perform compression on the data. The trade-off, however, is that it takes longer to load data into the database. Furthermore, there are many scenarios where the schema is not known at load time, so there are no indexes to apply, since the queries have not been formulated yet. These scenarios are where Hive shines.

Updates, Transactions, and Indexes

Updates, transactions, and indexes are mainstays of traditional databases. Yet, until recently, these features have not been considered a part of Hive's feature set. This is because Hive was built to operate over HDFS data using MapReduce, where full-table scans are the norm and a table update is achieved by transforming the data into a new table. For a data warehousing application that runs over large portions of the dataset, this works well.

However, there are workloads where updates (or insert appends, at least) are needed, or where indexes would yield significant performance gains. On the transactions front, Hive doesn't define clear semantics for concurrent access to tables, which means applications need to build their own application-level concurrency or locking mechanism. The Hive team is actively working on improvements in all these areas.[||]

Change is also coming from another direction: HBase integration. HBase (Chapter 13) has different storage characteristics to HDFS, such as the ability to do row updates and column indexing, so we can expect to see these features used by Hive in future releases. HBase integration with Hive is still in the early stages of development; you can find out more at *http://wiki.apache.org/hadoop/Hive/HBaseIntegration*.

[||] See, for example, *https://issues.apache.org/jira/browse/HIVE-306*, *https://issues.apache.org/jira/browse/HIVE -417*, and *https://issues.apache.org/jira/browse/HIVE-1293*.

HiveQL

Hive's SQL dialect, called HiveQL, does not support the full SQL-92 specification. There are a number of reasons for this. Being a fairly young project, it has not had time to provide the full repertoire of SQL-92 language constructs. More fundamentally, SQL-92 compliance has never been an explicit project goal; rather, as an open source project, features were added by developers to meet their users' needs. Furthermore, Hive has some extensions that are not in SQL-92, which have been inspired by syntax from other database systems, notably MySQL. In fact, to a first-order approximation, HiveQL most closely resembles MySQL's SQL dialect.

Some of Hive's extensions to SQL-92 were inspired by MapReduce, such as multitable inserts (see "Multitable insert" on page 393) and the TRANSFORM, MAP, and REDUCE clauses (see "MapReduce Scripts" on page 396).

It turns out that some SQL-92 constructs that are missing from HiveQL are easy to work around using other language features, so there has not been much pressure to implement them. For example, SELECT statements do not (at the time of writing) support a HAVING clause in HiveQL, but the same result can be achieved by adding a subquery in the FROM clause (see "Subqueries" on page 400).

This chapter does not provide a complete reference to HiveQL; for that, see the Hive documentation at *http://wiki.apache.org/hadoop/Hive/LanguageManual*. Instead, we focus on commonly used features and pay particular attention to features that diverge from SQL-92, or popular databases like MySQL. Table 12-2 provides a high-level comparison of SQL and HiveQL.

Table 12-2. A high-level comparison of SQL and HiveQL

Feature	SQL	HiveQL	References
Updates	UPDATE, INSERT, DELETE	INSERT OVERWRITE TABLE (populates whole table or partition)	"INSERT OVERWRITE TABLE" on page 392, "Updates, Transactions, and Indexes" on page 376
Transactions	Supported	Not supported	
Indexes	Supported	Not supported	
Latency	Sub-second	Minutes	
Data types	Integral, floating point, fixed point, text and binary strings, temporal	Integral, floating point, boolean, string, array, map, struct	"Data Types" on page 378
Functions	Hundreds of built-in functions	Dozens of built-in functions	"Operators and Functions" on page 380
Multitable inserts	Not supported	Supported	"Multitable insert" on page 393
Create table as select	Not valid SQL-92, but found in some databases	Supported	"CREATE TABLE...AS SELECT" on page 394

Feature	SQL	HiveQL	References
Select	SQL-92	Single table or view in the FROM clause. SORT BY for partial ordering. LIMIT to limit number of rows returned. HAVING not supported.	"Querying Data" on page 395
Joins	SQL-92 or variants (join tables in the FROM clause, join condition in the WHERE clause)	Inner joins, outer joins, semi joins, map joins. SQL-92 syntax, with hinting.	"Joins" on page 397
Subqueries	In any clause. Correlated or noncorrelated.	Only in the FROM clause. Correlated subqueries not supported	"Subqueries" on page 400
Views	Updatable. Materialized or nonmaterialized.	Read-only. Materialized views not supported	"Views" on page 401
Extension points	User-defined functions. Stored procedures.	User-defined functions. Map-Reduce scripts.	"User-Defined Functions" on page 402, "MapReduce Scripts" on page 396

Data Types

Hive supports both primitive and complex data types. Primitives include numeric, boolean, and string types. The complex data types include arrays, maps, and structs. Hive's data types are listed in Table 12-3. Note that the literals shown are those used from within HiveQL; they are not the serialized form used in the table's storage format (see "Storage Formats" on page 387).

Table 12-3. Hive data types

Category	Type	Description	Literal examples
Primitive	TINYINT	1-byte (8-bit) signed integer, from -128 to 127	1
	SMALLINT	2-byte (16-bit) signed integer, from -32,768 to 32,767	1
	INT	4-byte (32-bit) signed integer, from -2,147,483,648 to 2,147,483,647	1
	BIGINT	8-byte (64-bit) signed integer, from -9,223,372,036,854,775,808 to 9,223,372,036,854,775,807	1
	FLOAT	4-byte (32-bit) single-precision floating-point number	1.0
	DOUBLE	8-byte (64-bit) double-precision floating-point number	1.0
	BOOLEAN	true/false value	TRUE
	STRING	Character string	'a', "a"
Complex	ARRAY	An ordered collection of fields. The fields must all be of the same type.	array(1, 2) [a]

Category	Type	Description	Literal examples
	MAP	An unordered collection of key-value pairs. Keys must be primitives; values may be any type. For a particular map, the keys must be the same type, and the values must be the same type.	map('a', 1, 'b', 2)
	STRUCT	A collection of named fields. The fields may be of different types.	struct('a', 1, 1.0) [b]

[a] The literal forms for arrays, maps, and structs are provided as functions. That is, array(), map(), and struct() are built-in Hive functions.

[b] From Hive 0.6.0. The columns are named col1, col2, col3, etc.

Primitive types

Compared to traditional databases, Hive supports only a small set of primitive data types. There is currently no support for temporal types (dates and times), although there are functions for converting Unix timestamps (stored as integers) to strings, which makes most common date operations tractable using Hive.

Hive's primitive types correspond roughly to Java's, although some names are influenced by MySQL's type names (some of which, in turn, overlap with SQL-92). There are four signed integral types: TINYINT, SMALLINT, INT, and BIGINT, which are equivalent to Java's byte, short, int, and long primitive types, respectively; they are 1-byte, 2-byte, 4-byte, and 8-byte signed integers.

Hive's floating-point types, FLOAT and DOUBLE, correspond to Java's float and double, which are 32-bit and 64-bit floating point numbers. Unlike some databases, there is no option to control the number of significant digits or decimal places stored for floating point values.

Hive supports a BOOLEAN type for storing true and false values.

There is a single Hive data type for storing text, STRING, which is a variable-length character string. Hive's STRING type is like VARCHAR in other databases, although there is no declaration of the maximum number of characters to store with STRING. (The theoretical maximum size STRING that may be stored is 2GB, although in practice it may be inefficient to materialize such large values. Sqoop has large object support, see "Importing Large Objects" on page 489.)

Conversions

Primitive types form a hierarchy, which dictates the implicit type conversions that Hive will perform. For example, a TINYINT will be converted to an INT, if an expression expects an INT; however, the reverse conversion will not occur and Hive will return an error unless the CAST operator is used.

The implicit conversion rules can be summarized as follows. Any integral numeric type can be implicitly converted to a wider type. All the integral numeric types, FLOAT, and (perhaps surprisingly) STRING can be implicitly converted to DOUBLE. TINYINT, SMALL INT, and INT can all be converted to FLOAT. BOOLEAN types cannot be converted to any other type.

You can perform explicit type conversion using CAST. For example, CAST('1' AS INT) will convert the string '1' to the integer value 1. If the cast fails—as it does in CAST('X' AS INT), for example—then the expression returns NULL.

Complex types

Hive has three complex types: ARRAY, MAP, and STRUCT. ARRAY and MAP are like their namesakes in Java, while a STRUCT is a record type which encapsulates a set of named fields. Complex types permit an arbitrary level of nesting. Complex type declarations must specify the type of the fields in the collection, using an angled bracket notation, as illustrated in this table definition which has three columns, one for each complex type:

```
CREATE TABLE complex (
  col1 ARRAY<INT>,
  col2 MAP<STRING, INT>,
  col3 STRUCT<a:STRING, b:INT, c:DOUBLE>
);
```

If we load the table with one row of data for ARRAY, MAP, and STRUCT shown in the "Literal examples" column in Table 12-3 (we'll see the file format needed to do this in "Storage Formats" on page 387), then the following query demonstrates the field accessor operators for each type:

```
hive> SELECT col1[0], col2['b'], col3.c FROM complex;
1     2    1.0
```

Operators and Functions

The usual set of SQL operators is provided by Hive: relational operators (such as x = 'a' for testing equality, x IS NULL for testing nullity, x LIKE 'a%' for pattern matching), arithmetic operators (such as x + 1 for addition), and logical operators (such as x OR y for logical OR). The operators match those in MySQL, which deviates from SQL-92 since || is logical OR, not string concatenation. Use the concat function for the latter in both MySQL and Hive.

Hive comes with a large number of built-in functions—too many to list here—divided into categories including mathematical and statistical functions, string functions, date functions (for operating on string representations of dates), conditional functions, aggregate functions, and functions for working with XML (using the xpath function) and JSON.

You can retrieve a list of functions from the Hive shell by typing SHOW FUNCTIONS.[#] To get brief usage instructions for a particular function, use the DESCRIBE command:

```
hive> DESCRIBE FUNCTION length;
length(str) - Returns the length of str
```

[#] Or see the Hive function reference at *http://wiki.apache.org/hadoop/Hive/LanguageManual/UDF*.

In the case when there is no built-in function that does what you want, you can write your own; see "User-Defined Functions" on page 402.

Tables

A Hive table is logically made up of the data being stored and the associated metadata describing the layout of the data in the table. The data typically resides in HDFS, although it may reside in any Hadoop filesystem, including the local filesystem or S3. Hive stores the metadata in a relational database—and not in HDFS, say (see "The Metastore" on page 373).

In this section, we shall look in more detail at how to create tables, the different physical storage formats that Hive offers, and how to import data into them.

Multiple Database/Schema Support

Many relational databases have a facility for multiple namespaces, which allow users and applications to be segregated into different databases or schemas. At the time of writing, all tables in Hive live in a single default namespace; however, Hive 0.6.0 plans to support multiple databases, providing commands such as CREATE DATABASE *dbname*, USE *dbname*, and DROP DATABASE *dbname*.

Managed Tables and External Tables

When you create a table in Hive, by default Hive will manage the data, which means that Hive moves the data into its warehouse directory. Alternatively, you may create an *external table*, which tells Hive to refer to the data that is at an existing location outside the warehouse directory.

The difference between the two types of table is seen in the LOAD and DROP semantics. Let's consider a managed table first.

When you load data into a managed table, it is moved into Hive's warehouse directory. For example:

```
CREATE TABLE managed_table (dummy STRING);
LOAD DATA INPATH '/user/tom/data.txt' INTO table managed_table;
```

will *move* the file *hdfs://user/tom/data.txt* into Hive's warehouse directory for the managed_table table, which is *hdfs://user/hive/warehouse/managed_table.*[*]

---

[*] The move will only succeed if the source and target filesystems are the same. Also, there is a special case if the LOCAL keyword is used, where Hive will *copy* the data from the local filesystem into Hive's warehouse directory (even if it, too, is on the same local filesystem). In all other cases though, LOAD is a move operation and is best thought of as such.

The load operation is very fast, since it is just a filesystem move. However, bear in mind that Hive does not check that the files in the table directory conform to the schema declared for the table, even for managed tables. If there is a mismatch, then this will become apparent at query time, often by the query returning NULL for a missing field. You can check that the data is being parsed correctly by issuing a simple SELECT statement to retrieve a few rows directly from the table.

If the table is later dropped, using:

```
DROP TABLE managed_table;
```

then the table, including its metadata *and its data*, is deleted. It bears repeating that since the initial LOAD performed a move operation, and the DROP performed a delete operation, the data no longer exists anywhere. This is what it means for Hive to manage the data.

An external table behaves differently. You control the creation and deletion of the data. The location of the external data is specified at table creation time:

```
CREATE EXTERNAL TABLE external_table (dummy STRING)
  LOCATION '/user/tom/external_table';
LOAD DATA INPATH '/user/tom/data.txt' INTO TABLE external_table;
```

With the EXTERNAL keyword, Hive knows that it is not managing the data, so it doesn't move it to its warehouse directory. Indeed, it doesn't even check if the external location exists at the time it is defined. This is a useful feature, since it means you can create the data lazily after creating the table.

When you drop an external table, Hive will leave the data untouched and only delete the metadata.

So how do you choose which type of table to use? In most cases, there is not much difference between the two (except of course for the difference in DROP semantics), so it is a just a matter of preference. As a rule of thumb, if you are doing all your processing with Hive, then use managed tables, but if you wish to use Hive and other tools on the same dataset, then use external tables. A common pattern is to use an external table to access an initial dataset stored in HDFS (created by another process), then use a Hive transform to move the data into a managed Hive table. This works the other way around, too—an external table (not necessarily on HDFS) can be used to export data from Hive for other applications to use.[†]

---

† You can also use INSERT OVERWRITE DIRECTORY to export data to a Hadoop filesystem, but unlike external tables you cannot control the output format, which is Control-A separated text files. Complex data types are serialized using a JSON representation.

Another reason for using external tables is when you wish to associate multiple schemas with the same dataset.

Partitions and Buckets

Hive organizes tables into *partitions*, a way of dividing a table into coarse-grained parts based on the value of a *partition column*, such as date. Using partitions can make it faster to do queries on slices of the data.

Tables or partitions may further be subdivided into *buckets*, to give extra structure to the data that may be used for more efficient queries. For example, bucketing by user ID means we can quickly evaluate a user-based query by running it on a randomized sample of the total set of users.

Partitions

To take an example where partitions are commonly used, imagine log files where each record includes a timestamp. If we partitioned by date, then records for the same date would be stored in the same partition. The advantage to this scheme is that queries that are restricted to a particular date or set of dates can be answered much more efficiently since they only need to scan the files in the partitions that the query pertains to. Notice that partitioning doesn't preclude more wide-ranging queries: it is still feasible to query the entire dataset across many partitions.

A table may be partitioned in multiple dimensions. For example, in addition to partitioning logs by date, we might also *subpartition* each date partition by country to permit efficient queries by location.

Partitions are defined at table creation time‡ using the PARTITIONED BY clause, which takes a list of column definitions. For the hypothetical log files example, we might define a table with records comprising a timestamp and the log line itself:

```
CREATE TABLE logs (ts BIGINT, line STRING)
PARTITIONED BY (dt STRING, country STRING);
```

When we load data into a partitioned table, the partition values are specified explicitly:

```
LOAD DATA LOCAL INPATH 'input/hive/partitions/file1'
INTO TABLE logs
PARTITION (dt='2001-01-01', country='GB');
```

---

‡ However, partitions may be added to or removed from a table after creation using an ALTER TABLE statement.

At the filesystem level, partitions are simply nested subdirectories of the table directory. After loading a few more files into the logs table, the directory structure might look like this:

```
/user/hive/warehouse/logs/dt=2010-01-01/country=GB/file1
                                               /file2
                                 /country=US/file3
                    /dt=2010-01-02/country=GB/file4
                                 /country=US/file5
                                               /file6
```

The logs table has two date partitions, 2010-01-01 and 2010-01-02, corresponding to subdirectories called *dt=2010-01-01* and *dt=2010-01-02*; and two country subpartitions, GB and US, corresponding to nested subdirectories called *country=GB* and *country=US*. The data files reside in the leaf directories.

We can ask Hive for the partitions in a table using SHOW PARTITIONS:

```
hive> SHOW PARTITIONS logs;
dt=2001-01-01/country=GB
dt=2001-01-01/country=US
dt=2001-01-02/country=GB
dt=2001-01-02/country=US
```

One thing to bear in mind is that the column definitions in the PARTITIONED BY clause are full-fledged table columns, called partition columns; however, the data files do not contain values for these columns since they are derived from the directory names.

You can use partition columns in SELECT statements in the usual way. Hive performs *input pruning* to scan only the relevant partitions. For example:

```
SELECT ts, dt, line
FROM logs
WHERE country='GB';
```

will only scan *file1*, *file2*, and *file4*. Notice, too, that the query returns the values of the dt partition column, which Hive reads from the directory names since they are not in the data files.

Buckets

There are two reasons why you might want to organize your tables (or partitions) into buckets. The first is to enable more efficient queries. Bucketing imposes extra structure on the table, which Hive can take advantage of when performing certain queries. In particular, a join of two tables that are bucketed on the same columns—which include the join columns—can be efficiently implemented as a map-side join.

The second reason to bucket a table is to make sampling more efficient. When working with large datasets, it is very convenient to try out queries on a fraction of your dataset while you are in the process of developing or refining them. We shall see how to do efficient sampling at this end of this section.

First, let's see how to tell Hive that a table should be bucketed. We use the CLUSTERED BY clause to specify the columns to bucket on and the number of buckets:

```
CREATE TABLE bucketed_users (id INT, name STRING)
CLUSTERED BY (id) INTO 4 BUCKETS;
```

Here we are using the user ID to determine the bucket (which Hive does by hashing the value and reducing modulo the number of buckets), so any particular bucket will effectively have a random set of users in it.

In the map-side join case, where the two tables are bucketed in the same way, a mapper processing a bucket of the left table knows that the matching rows in the right table are in its corresponding bucket, so it need only retrieve that bucket (which is a small fraction of all the data stored in the right table) to effect the join. This optimization works, too, if the number of buckets in the two tables are multiples of each other—they do not have to have exactly the same number of buckets. The HiveQL for joining two bucketed tables is shown in "Map joins" on page 400.

The data within a bucket may additionally be sorted by one or more columns. This allows even more efficient map-side joins, since the join of each bucket becomes an efficient merge-sort. The syntax for declaring that a table has sorted buckets is:

```
CREATE TABLE bucketed_users (id INT, name STRING)
CLUSTERED BY (id) SORTED BY (id ASC) INTO 4 BUCKETS;
```

How can we make sure the data in our table is bucketed? While it's possible to load data generated outside Hive into a bucketed table, it's often easier to get Hive to do the bucketing, usually from an existing table.

 Hive does not check that the buckets in the data files on disk are consistent with the buckets in the table definition (either in number, or on the basis of bucketing columns). If there is a mismatch, then you may get an error or undefined behavior at query time. For this reason, it is advisable to get Hive to perform the bucketing.

Take an unbucketed users table:

```
hive> SELECT * FROM users;
0    Nat
2    Joe
3    Kay
4    Ann
```

To populate the bucketed table, we need to set the `hive.enforce.bucketing` property to **true**§, so that Hive knows to create the number of buckets declared in the table definition. Then it is a matter of just using the INSERT command:

```
INSERT OVERWRITE TABLE bucketed_users
SELECT * FROM users;
```

Physically, each bucket is just a file in the table (or partition) directory. The file name is not important, but bucket n is the nth file, when arranged in lexicographic order. In fact, buckets correspond to MapReduce output file partitions: a job will produce as many buckets (output files) as reduce tasks. We can see this by looking at the layout of the `bucketed_users` table we just created. Running this command:

```
hive> dfs -ls /user/hive/warehouse/bucketed_users;
```

shows that four files were created, with the following names (the name is generated by Hive and incorporates a timestamp, so it will change from run to run):

```
attempt_201005221636_0016_r_000000_0
attempt_201005221636_0016_r_000001_0
attempt_201005221636_0016_r_000002_0
attempt_201005221636_0016_r_000003_0
```

The first bucket contains the users with IDs 0 and 4, since for an INT the hash is the integer itself, and the value is reduced modulo the number of buckets—4 in this case:‖

```
hive> dfs -cat /user/hive/warehouse/bucketed_users/*0_0;
0Nat
4Ann
```

We can see the same thing by sampling the table using the TABLESAMPLE clause, which restricts the query to a fraction of the buckets in the table rather than the whole table:

```
hive> SELECT * FROM bucketed_users
    > TABLESAMPLE(BUCKET 1 OUT OF 4 ON id);
0       Nat
4       Ann
```

Bucket numbering is 1-based, so this query retrieves all the users from the first of four buckets. For a large, evenly distributed dataset, approximately one quarter of the table's rows would be returned. It's possible to sample a number of buckets by specifying a different proportion (which need not be an exact multiple of the number of buckets, since sampling is not intended to be a precise operation). For example, this query returns half of the buckets:

```
hive> SELECT * FROM bucketed_users
    > TABLESAMPLE(BUCKET 1 OUT OF 2 ON id);
```

§ From Hive 0.6.0. In previous versions, it was instead necessary to set `mapred.reduce.tasks` to the number of buckets in the table being populated. If the buckets are sorted, you also need to set `hive.enforce.sorting` to **true**.

‖ The fields appear run together when displaying the raw file since the separator character in the output is a nonprinting control character. The control characters used are explained in the next section.

```
0    Nat
4    Ann
2    Joe
```

Sampling a bucketed table is very efficient, since the query only has to read the buckets that match the TABLESAMPLE clause. Contrast this with sampling a non-bucketed table, using the rand() function, where the whole input dataset is scanned, even if a very small sample is needed:

```
hive> SELECT * FROM users
    > TABLESAMPLE(BUCKET 1 OUT OF 4 ON rand());
2    Joe
```

Storage Formats

There are two dimensions that govern table storage in Hive: the *row format* and the *file format*. The row format dictates how rows, and the fields in a particular row, are stored. In Hive parlance, the row format is defined by a *SerDe*, a portmanteau word for a *Serializer-Deserializer*.

When acting as a deserializer, which is the case when querying a table, a SerDe will deserialize a row of data from the bytes in the file to objects used internally by Hive to operate on that row of data. When used as a serializer, which is the case when performing an INSERT or CTAS (see "Importing Data" on page 392), the table's SerDe will serialize Hive's internal representation of a row of data into the bytes that are written to the output file.

The file format dictates the container format for fields in a row. The simplest format is a plain text file, but there are row-oriented and column-oriented binary formats available, too.

The default storage format: Delimited text

When you create a table with no ROW FORMAT or STORED AS clauses, the default format is delimited text, with a row per line.

The default row delimiter is not a tab character, but the Control-A character from the set of ASCII control codes (it has ASCII code 1). The choice of Control-A, sometimes written as ^A in documentation, came about since it is less likely to be a part of the field text than a tab character. There is no means for escaping delimiter characters in Hive, so it is important to choose ones that don't occur in data fields.

The default collection item delimiter is a Control-B character, used to delimit items in an ARRAY or STRUCT, or key-value pairs in a MAP. The default map key delimiter is a Control-C character, used to delimit the key and value in a MAP. Rows in a table are delimited by a newline character.

The preceding description of delimiters is correct for the usual case of flat data structures, where the complex types only contain primitive types. For nested types, however, this isn't the whole story, and in fact the *level* of the nesting determines the delimiter.

For an array of arrays, for example, the delimiters for the outer array are Control-B characters, as expected, but for the inner array they are Control-C characters, the next delimiter in the list. If you are unsure which delimiters Hive uses for a particular nested structure, you can run a command like:

```
CREATE TABLE nested
AS
SELECT array(array(1, 2), array(3, 4))
FROM dummy;
```

then use hexdump, or similar, to examine the delimiters in the output file.

Hive actually supports eight levels of delimiters, corresponding to ASCII codes 1, 2, ... 8, but you can only override the first three.

Thus, the statement:

```
CREATE TABLE ...;
```

is identical to the more explicit:

```
CREATE TABLE ...
ROW FORMAT DELIMITED
  FIELDS TERMINATED BY '\001'
  COLLECTION ITEMS TERMINATED BY '\002'
  MAP KEYS TERMINATED BY '\003'
  LINES TERMINATED BY '\n'
STORED AS TEXTFILE;
```

Notice that the octal form of the delimiter characters can be used—001 for Control-A, for instance.

Internally, Hive uses a SerDe called LazySimpleSerDe for this delimited format, along with the line-oriented MapReduce text input and output formats we saw in Chapter 7. The "lazy" prefix comes about since it deserializes fields lazily—only as they are accessed. However, it is not a compact format since fields are stored in a verbose textual format, so a boolean value, for instance, is written as the literal string true or false.

The simplicity of the format has a lot going for it, such as making it easy to process with other tools, including MapReduce programs or Streaming, but there are more compact and performant binary SerDe's that you might consider using. Some are listed in Table 12-4.

Binary SerDe's should not be used with the default TEXTFILE format (or explicitly using a STORED AS TEXTFILE clause). There is always the possibility that a binary row will contain a newline character, which would cause Hive to truncate the row and fail at deserialization time.

Table 12-4. Hive SerDe's

SerDe name	Java package	Description
LazySimpleSerDe	org.apache.hadoop.hive.serde2.lazy	The default SerDe. Delimited textual format, with lazy field access.
LazyBinarySerDe	org.apache.hadoop.hive.serde2.lazybinary	A more efficient version of LazySimpleSerDe. Binary format with lazy field access. Used internally for such things as temporary tables.
BinarySortableSerDe	org.apache.hadoop.hive.serde2.binarysortable	A binary SerDe like LazyBinarySerDe, but optimized for sorting at the expense of compactness (although it is still significantly more compact than LazySimpleSerDe).
ColumnarSerDe	org.apache.hadoop.hive.serde2.columnar	A variant of LazySimpleSerDe for column-based storage with RCFile.
RegexSerDe	org.apache.hadoop.hive.contrib.serde2	A SerDe for reading textual data where columns are specified by a regular expression. Also writes data using a formatting expression. Useful for reading log files, but inefficient, so not suitable for general-purpose storage.
ThriftByteStreamTypedSerDe	org.apache.hadoop.hive.serde2.thrift	A SerDe for reading Thrift-encoded binary data. There is ongoing work to add write capability (*https://issues.apache.org/jira/browse/HIVE-706*).
HBaseSerDe	org.apache.hadoop.hive.hbase	A SerDe for storing data in an HBase table. HBase storage uses a Hive storage handler, which unifies (and generalizes) the roles of row format and file format. Storage handlers are specified using a STORED BY clause, which replaces the ROW FORMAT and STORED AS clauses. See *http://wiki.apache.org/hadoop/Hive/HBaseIntegration*.

Binary storage formats: Sequence files and RCFiles

Hadoop's sequence file format ("SequenceFile" on page 116) is a general purpose binary format for sequences of records (key-value pairs). You can use sequence files in Hive by using the declaration STORED AS SEQUENCEFILE in the CREATE TABLE statement.

One of the main benefits of using sequence files is their support for splittable compression. If you have a collection of sequence files that were created outside Hive, then Hive will read them with no extra configuration. If, on the other hand, you want tables populated from Hive to use compressed sequence files for their storage, you need to set a few properties to enable compression (see "Using Compression in MapReduce" on page 84):

```
hive> SET hive.exec.compress.output=true;
hive> SET mapred.output.compress=true;
hive> SET mapred.output.compression.codec=org.apache.hadoop.io.compress.GzipCodec;
hive> INSERT OVERWRITE TABLE ...;
```

Sequence files are row-oriented. What this means is that the fields in each row are stored together, as the contents of a single sequence file record.

Hive provides another binary storage format called *RCFile*, short for *Record Columnar File*. RCFiles are similar to sequence files, except that they store data in a column-oriented fashion. RCFile breaks up the table into row splits, then within each split stores the values for each row in the first column, followed by the values for each row in the second column, and so on. This is shown diagrammatically in Figure 12-3.

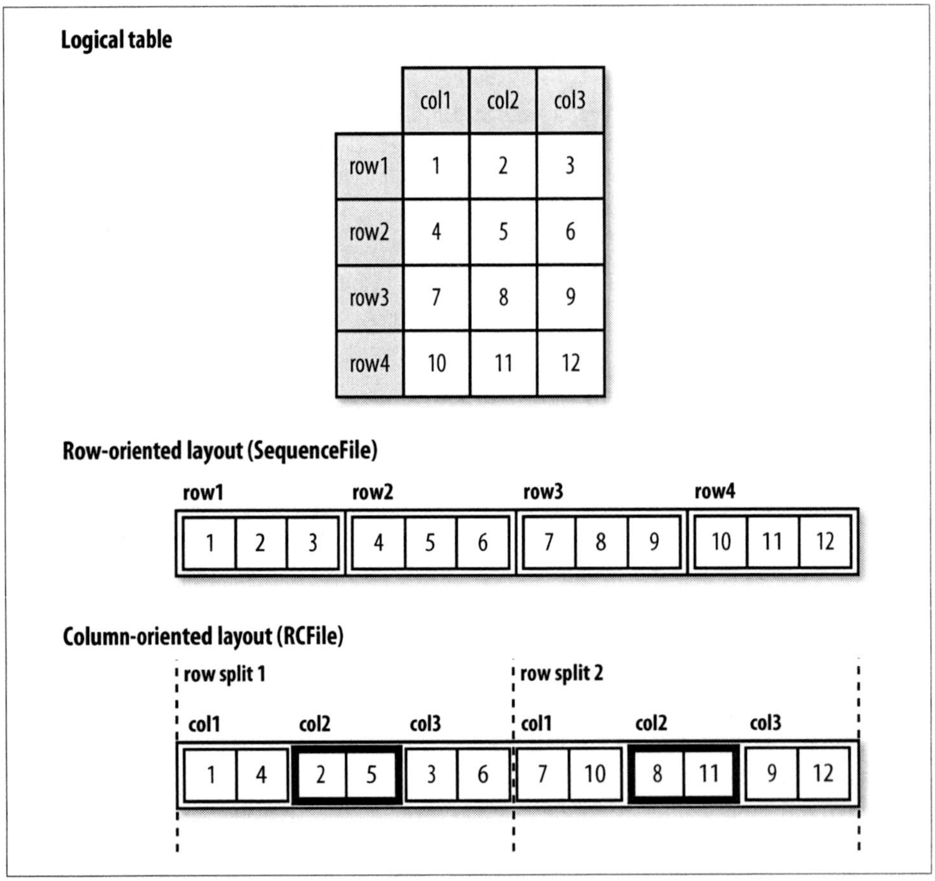

Figure 12-3. Row-oriented versus column-oriented storage

A column-oriented layout permits columns that are not accessed in a query to be skipped. Consider a query of the table in Figure 12-3 that processes only column 2. With row-oriented storage, like a sequence file, the whole row (stored in a sequence file record) is loaded into memory, even though only the second column is actually read. Lazy deserialization goes some way to save processing cycles by only deserializing the columns fields that are accessed, but it can't avoid the cost of reading each row's bytes from disk.

With column-oriented storage, only the column 2 parts of the file (shaded in the figure) need to be read into memory.

In general, column-oriented formats work well when queries access only a small number of columns in the table. Conversely, row-oriented formats are appropriate when a large number of columns of a single row are needed for processing at the same time. Space permitting, it is relatively straightforward to measure the performance difference between the two formats for your particular workload, since you can create a copy of a table with a different storage format for comparison, using "CREATE TABLE...AS SELECT" on page 394.

Use the following CREATE TABLE clauses to enable column-oriented storage in Hive:

```
CREATE TABLE ...
ROW FORMAT SERDE 'org.apache.hadoop.hive.serde2.columnar.ColumnarSerDe'
STORED AS RCFILE;
```

An example: RegexSerDe

Let's see how to use another SerDe for storage. We'll use a contrib SerDe that uses a regular expression for reading the fixed-width station metadata from a text file:

```
CREATE TABLE stations (usaf STRING, wban STRING, name STRING)
ROW FORMAT SERDE 'org.apache.hadoop.hive.contrib.serde2.RegexSerDe'
WITH SERDEPROPERTIES (
  "input.regex" = "(\\d{6}) (\\d{5}) (.{29}) .*"
);
```

In previous examples, we have used the DELIMITED keyword to refer to delimited text in the ROW FORMAT clause. In this example, we instead specify a SerDe with the SERDE keyword and the fully qualified classname of the Java class that implements the SerDe, org.apache.hadoop.hive.contrib.serde2.RegexSerDe.

SerDe's can be configured with extra properties using the WITH SERDEPROPERTIES clause. Here we set the input.regex property, which is specific to RegexSerDe.

input.regex is the regular expression pattern to be used during deserialization to turn the line of text forming the row into a set of columns. Java regular expression syntax is used for the matching (see *http://java.sun.com/javase/6/docs/api/java/util/regex/Pat tern.html*), and columns are formed from capturing groups of parentheses.# In this

---

#Sometimes you need to use parentheses for regular expression constructs that you don't want to count as a capturing group. For example, the pattern (ab)+ for matching a string of one or more ab characters. The solution is to use a noncapturing group, which has a ? character after the first parenthesis. There are various noncapturing group constructs (see the Java documentation), but in this example we could use (?:ab)+ to avoid capturing the group as a Hive column.

example, there are three capturing groups for usaf (a six-digit identifier), wban (a five-digit identifier), and name (a fixed-width column of 29 characters).

To populate the table, we use a LOAD DATA statement as before:

```
LOAD DATA LOCAL INPATH "input/ncdc/metadata/stations-fixed-width.txt"
INTO TABLE stations;
```

Recall that LOAD DATA copies or moves the files to Hive's warehouse directory (in this case, it's a copy since the source is the local filesystem). The table's SerDe is not used for the load operation.

When we retrieve data from the table, the SerDe is invoked for deserialization, as we can see from this simple query, which correctly parses the fields for each row:

```
hive> SELECT * FROM stations LIMIT 4;
010000    99999    BOGUS NORWAY
010003    99999    BOGUS NORWAY
010010    99999    JAN MAYEN
010013    99999    ROST
```

Importing Data

We've already seen how to use the LOAD DATA operation to import data into a Hive table (or partition) by copying or moving files to the table's directory. You can also populate a table with data from another Hive table using an INSERT statement, or at creation time using the *CTAS* construct, which is an abbreviation used to refer to CREATE TABLE...AS SELECT.

If you want to import data from a relational database directly into Hive, have a look at Sqoop, which is covered in "Imported Data and Hive" on page 487.

INSERT OVERWRITE TABLE

Here's an example of an INSERT statement:

```
INSERT OVERWRITE TABLE target
SELECT col1, col2
  FROM source;
```

For partitioned tables, you can specify the partition to insert into by supplying a PARTITION clause:

```
INSERT OVERWRITE TABLE target
PARTITION (dt='2010-01-01')
SELECT col1, col2
  FROM source;
```

The OVERWRITE keyword is actually mandatory in both cases, and means that the contents of the target table (for the first example) or the 2010-01-01 partition (for the second example) are replaced by the results of the SELECT statement. At the time of writing, Hive does not support adding records to an already-populated nonpartitioned table or partition using an INSERT statement. Instead, you can achieve the same effect using a LOAD DATA operation without the OVERWRITE keyword.

From Hive 0.6.0 onward, you can specify the partition dynamically, by determining the partition value from the SELECT statement:

```
INSERT OVERWRITE TABLE target
PARTITION (dt)
SELECT col1, col2, dt
  FROM source;
```

This is known as a *dynamic-partition insert*. This feature is off by default, so you need to enable it by setting `hive.exec.dynamic.partition` to true first.

 Unlike other databases, Hive does not (currently) support a form of the INSERT statement for inserting a collection of records specified in the query, in literal form. That is, statements of the form INSERT INTO...VALUES... are not allowed.

Multitable insert

In HiveQL, you can turn the INSERT statement around and start with the FROM clause, for the same effect:

```
FROM source
INSERT OVERWRITE TABLE target
  SELECT col1, col2;
```

The reason for this syntax becomes clear when you see that it's possible to have multiple INSERT clauses in the same query. This so-called *multitable insert* is more efficient than multiple INSERT statements, since the source table need only be scanned once to produce the multiple, disjoint outputs.

Here's an example that computes various statistics over the weather dataset:

```
FROM records2
INSERT OVERWRITE TABLE stations_by_year
  SELECT year, COUNT(DISTINCT station)
  GROUP BY year
INSERT OVERWRITE TABLE records_by_year
  SELECT year, COUNT(1)
  GROUP BY year
INSERT OVERWRITE TABLE good_records_by_year
  SELECT year, COUNT(1)
  WHERE temperature != 9999
    AND (quality = 0 OR quality = 1 OR quality = 4 OR quality = 5 OR quality = 9)
  GROUP BY year;
```

There is a single source table (records2), but three tables to hold the results from three different queries over the source.

CREATE TABLE...AS SELECT

It's often very convenient to store the output of a Hive query in a new table, perhaps because it is too large to be dumped to the console or because there are further processing steps to carry out on the result.

The new table's column definitions are derived from the columns retrieved by the SELECT clause. In the following query, the target table has two columns named col1 and col2 whose types are the same as the ones in the source table:

```
CREATE TABLE target
AS
SELECT col1, col2
FROM source;
```

A CTAS operation is atomic, so if the SELECT query fails for some reason, then the table is not created.

Altering Tables

Since Hive uses the schema on read approach, it's flexible in permitting a table's definition to change after the table has been created. The general caveat, however, is that it is up to you, in many cases, to ensure that the data is changed to reflect the new structure.

You can rename a table using the ALTER TABLE statement:

```
ALTER TABLE source RENAME TO target;
```

In addition to updating the table metadata, ALTER TABLE moves the underlying table directory so that it reflects the new name. In the current example, */user/hive/warehouse/source* is renamed to */user/hive/warehouse/target*. (An external table's underlying directory is not moved; only the metadata is updated.)

Hive allows you to change the definition for columns, add new columns, or even replace all existing columns in a table with a new set.

For example, consider adding a new column:

```
ALTER TABLE target ADD COLUMNS (col3 STRING);
```

The new column col3 is added after the existing (nonpartition) columns. The data files are not updated, so queries will return null for all values of col3 (unless of course there were extra fields already present in the files). Since Hive does not permit updating existing records, you will need to arrange for the underlying files to be updated by another mechanism. For this reason, it is more common to create a new table that defines new columns and populates them using a SELECT statement.

Changing a column's metadata, such as a column's name or data type, is more straightforward, assuming that the new data type can be interpreted as the new data type.

To learn more about how to alter a table's structure, including adding and dropping partitions, changing and replacing columns, and changing table and SerDe properties, see the Hive wiki at *http://wiki.apache.org/hadoop/Hive/LanguageManual/DDL*.

Dropping Tables

The DROP TABLE statement deletes the data and metadata for a table. In the case of external tables, only the metadata is deleted—the data is left untouched.

If you want to delete all the data in a table, but keep the table definition (like DELETE or TRUNCATE in MySQL), then you can simply delete the data files. For example:

```
hive> dfs -rmr /user/hive/warehouse/my_table;
```

Hive treats a lack of files (or indeed no directory for the table) as an empty table.

Another possibility, which achieves a similar effect, is to create a new, empty table that has the same schema as the first, using the LIKE keyword:

```
CREATE TABLE new_table LIKE existing_table;
```

Querying Data

This section discusses how to use various forms of the SELECT statement to retrieve data from Hive.

Sorting and Aggregating

Sorting data in Hive can be achieved by use of a standard ORDER BY clause, but there is a catch. ORDER BY produces a result that is totally sorted, as expected, but to do so it sets the number of reducers to one, making it very inefficient for large datasets. (Hopefully, a future release of Hive will employ the techniques described in "Total Sort" on page 237 to support efficient parallel sorting.)

When a globally sorted result is not required—and in many cases it isn't—then you can use Hive's nonstandard extension, SORT BY instead. SORT BY produces a sorted file per reducer.

In some cases, you want to control which reducer a particular row goes to, typically so you can perform some subsequent aggregation. This is what Hive's DISTRIBUTE BY clause does. Here's an example to sort the weather dataset by year and temperature, in such a way to ensure that all the rows for a given year end up in the same reducer partition:[*]

```
hive> FROM records2
    > SELECT year, temperature
    > DISTRIBUTE BY year
```

---

[*] This is a reworking in Hive of the discussion in "Secondary Sort" on page 241.

```
    > SORT BY year ASC, temperature DESC;
1949    111
1949    78
1950    22
1950    0
1950    -11
```

A follow-on query (or a query that nested this query as a subquery, see "Subqueries" on page 400) would be able to use the fact that each year's temperatures were grouped and sorted (in descending order) in the same file.

If the columns for SORT BY and DISTRIBUTE BY are the same, you can use CLUSTER BY as a shorthand for specifying both.

MapReduce Scripts

Using an approach like Hadoop Streaming, the TRANSFORM, MAP, and REDUCE clauses make it possible to invoke an external script or program from Hive. Suppose we want to use a script to filter out rows that don't meet some condition, such as the script in Example 12-1, which removes poor quality readings.

Example 12-1. Python script to filter out poor quality weather records

```python
#!/usr/bin/env python

import re
import sys

for line in sys.stdin:
  (year, temp, q) = line.strip().split()
  if (temp != "9999" and re.match("[01459]", q)):
    print "%s\t%s" % (year, temp)
```

We can use the script as follows:

```
hive> ADD FILE /path/to/is_good_quality.py;
hive> FROM records2
    > SELECT TRANSFORM(year, temperature, quality)
    > USING 'is_good_quality.py'
    > AS year, temperature;
1949    111
1949    78
1950    0
1950    22
1950    -11
```

Before running the query, we need to register the script with Hive. This is so Hive knows to ship the file to the Hadoop cluster (see "Distributed Cache" on page 253).

The query itself streams the year, temperature, and quality fields as a tab-separated line to the *is_good_quality.py* script, and parses the tab-separated output into year and temperature fields to form the output of the query.

This example has no reducers. If we use a nested form for the query, we can specify a map and a reduce function. This time we use the MAP and REDUCE keywords, but SELECT TRANSFORM in both cases would have the same result. The source for the *max_tempera-ture_reduce.py* script is shown in Example 2-11:

```
FROM (
  FROM records2
  MAP year, temperature, quality
  USING 'is_good_quality.py'
  AS year, temperature) map_output
REDUCE year, temperature
USING 'max_temperature_reduce.py'
AS year, temperature;
```

Joins

One of the nice things about using Hive, rather than raw MapReduce, is that it makes performing commonly used operations very simple. Join operations are a case in point, given how involved they are to implement in MapReduce ("Joins" on page 247).

Inner joins

The simplest kind of join is the inner join, where each match in the input tables results in a row in the output. Consider two small demonstration tables: sales, which lists the names of people and the ID of the item they bought; and things, which lists the item ID and its name:

```
hive> SELECT * FROM sales;
Joe     2
Hank    4
Ali     0
Eve     3
Hank    2
hive> SELECT * FROM things;
2       Tie
4       Coat
3       Hat
1       Scarf
```

We can perform an inner join on the two tables as follows:

```
hive> SELECT sales.*, things.*
    > FROM sales JOIN things ON (sales.id = things.id);
Joe     2   2   Tie
Hank    2   2   Tie
Eve     3   3   Hat
Hank    4   4   Coat
```

The table in the FROM clause (sales) is joined with the table in the JOIN clause (things), using the predicate in the ON clause. Hive only supports equijoins, which means that only equality can be used in the join predicate, which here matches on the id column in both tables.

Some databases, such as MySQL and Oracle, allow you to list the join tables in the FROM clause and specify the join condition in the WHERE clause of a SELECT statement. However, this syntax is *not* supported in Hive, so the following fails with a parse error:

```
SELECT sales.*, things.*
FROM sales, things
WHERE sales.id = things.id;
```

Hive only allows a single table in the FROM clause, and joins must follow the SQL-92 JOIN clause syntax.

In Hive, you can join on multiple columns in the join predicate by specifying a series of expressions, separated by AND keywords. You can also join more than two tables by supplying additional JOIN...ON... clauses in the query. Hive is intelligent about trying to minimize the number of MapReduce jobs to perform the joins.

A single join is implemented as a single MapReduce job, but multiple joins can be performed in less than one MapReduce job per join if the same column is used in the join condition.[†] You can see how many MapReduce jobs Hive will use for any particular query by prefixing it with the EXPLAIN keyword:

```
EXPLAIN
SELECT sales.*, things.*
FROM sales JOIN things ON (sales.id = things.id);
```

The EXPLAIN output includes many details about the execution plan for the query, including the abstract syntax tree, the dependency graph for the stages that Hive will execute, and information about each stage. Stages may be MapReduce jobs or operations such as file moves. For even more detail, prefix the query with EXPLAIN EXTENDED.

Hive currently uses a rule-based query optimizer for determining how to execute a query, but it's likely that in the future a cost-based optimizer will be added.

Outer joins

Outer joins allow you to find nonmatches in the tables being joined. In the current example, when we performed an inner join, the row for Ali did not appear in the output, since the ID of the item she purchased was not present in the things table. If we change the join type to LEFT OUTER JOIN, then the query will return a row for every row in the left table (sales), even if there is no corresponding row in the table it is being joined to (things):

```
hive> SELECT sales.*, things.*
    > FROM sales LEFT OUTER JOIN things ON (sales.id = things.id);
Ali     0    NULL NULL
```

[†] The order of the tables in the JOIN clauses is significant: it's generally best to have the largest table last, but see *http://wiki.apache.org/hadoop/Hive/LanguageManual/Joins* for more details, including how to give hints to the Hive planner.

```
Joe      2   2   Tie
Hank     2   2   Tie
Eve      3   3   Hat
Hank     4   4   Coat
```

Notice that the row for Ali is now returned, and the columns from the things table are NULL, since there is no match.

Hive supports right outer joins, which reverses the roles of the tables relative to the left join. In this case, all items from the things table are included, even those that weren't purchased by anyone (a scarf):

```
hive> SELECT sales.*, things.*
    > FROM sales RIGHT OUTER JOIN things ON (sales.id = things.id);
NULL    NULL 1   Scarf
Joe      2   2   Tie
Hank     2   2   Tie
Eve      3   3   Hat
Hank     4   4   Coat
```

Finally, there is a full outer join, where the output has a row for each row from both tables in the join:

```
hive> SELECT sales.*, things.*
    > FROM sales FULL OUTER JOIN things ON (sales.id = things.id);
Ali      0   NULL NULL
NULL    NULL 1   Scarf
Joe      2   2   Tie
Hank     2   2   Tie
Eve      3   3   Hat
Hank     4   4   Coat
```

Semi joins

Hive doesn't support IN subqueries (at the time of writing), but you can use a LEFT SEMI JOIN to do the same thing.

Consider this IN subquery, which finds all the items in the things table that are in the sales table:

```
SELECT *
FROM things
WHERE things.id IN (SELECT id from sales);
```

We can rewrite it as follows:

```
hive> SELECT *
    > FROM things LEFT SEMI JOIN sales ON (sales.id = things.id);
2    Tie
3    Hat
4    Coat
```

There is a restriction that we must observe for LEFT SEMI JOIN queries: the right table (sales) may only appear in the ON clause. It cannot be referenced in a SELECT expression, for example.

Map joins

If one table is small enough to fit in memory, then Hive can load the smaller table into memory to perform the join in each of the mappers. The syntax for specifying a map join is a hint embedded in an SQL C-style comment:

```
SELECT /*+ MAPJOIN(things) */ sales.*, things.*
FROM sales JOIN things ON (sales.id = things.id);
```

The job to execute this query has no reducers, so this query would not work for a RIGHT or FULL OUTER JOIN, since absence of matching can only be detected in an aggregating (reduce) step across all the inputs.

Map joins can take advantage of bucketed tables ("Buckets" on page 384), since a mapper working on a bucket of the left table only needs to load the corresponding buckets of the right table to perform the join. The syntax for the join is the same as for the in-memory case above; however, you also need to enable the optimization with:

```
SET hive.optimize.bucketmapjoin=true;
```

Subqueries

A subquery is a SELECT statement that is embedded in another SQL statement. Hive has limited support for subqueries, only permitting a subquery in the FROM clause of a SELECT statement.

> Other databases allow subqueries almost anywhere that an expression is valid, such as in the list of values to retrieve from a SELECT statement or in the WHERE clause. Many uses of subqueries can be rewritten as joins, so if you find yourself writing a subquery where Hive does not support it, then see if it can be expressed as a join. For example, an IN subquery can be written as a semi join, or an inner join (see "Joins" on page 397).

The following query finds the mean maximum temperature for every year and weather station:

```
SELECT station, year, AVG(max_temperature)
FROM (
  SELECT station, year, MAX(temperature) AS max_temperature
  FROM records2
  WHERE temperature != 9999
    AND (quality = 0 OR quality = 1 OR quality = 4 OR quality = 5 OR quality = 9)
  GROUP BY station, year
) mt
GROUP BY station, year;
```

The subquery is used to find the maximum temperature for each station/date combination, then the outer query uses the AVG aggregate function to find the average of the maximum temperature readings for each station/date combination.

The outer query accesses the results of the subquery like it does a table, which is why the subquery must be given an alias (mt). The columns of the subquery have to be given unique names so that the outer query can refer to them.

Views

A view is a sort of "virtual table" that is defined by a SELECT statement. Views can be used to present data to users in a different way to the way it is actually stored on disk. Often, the data from existing tables is simplified or aggregated in a particular way that makes it convenient for further processing. Views may also be used to restrict users' access to particular subsets of tables that they are authorized to see.

In Hive, a view is not materialized to disk when it is created; rather, the view's SELECT statement is executed when the statement that refers to the view is run. If a view performs extensive transformations on the base tables, or is used frequently, then you may choose to manually materialize it by creating a new table that stores the contents of the view (see "CREATE TABLE...AS SELECT" on page 394).

We can use views to rework the query from the previous section for finding the mean maximum temperature for every year and weather station. First, let's create a view for valid records, that is, records that have a particular quality value:

```
CREATE VIEW valid_records
AS
SELECT *
FROM records2
WHERE temperature != 9999
  AND (quality = 0 OR quality = 1 OR quality = 4 OR quality = 5 OR quality = 9);
```

When we create a view, the query is not run; it is simply stored in the metastore. Views are included in the output of the SHOW TABLES command, and you can see more details about a particular view, including the query used to define it, by issuing the DESCRIBE EXTENDED view_name command.

Next, let's create a second view of maximum temperatures for each station and year. It is based on the valid_records view:

```
CREATE VIEW max_temperatures (station, year, max_temperature)
AS
SELECT station, year, MAX(temperature)
FROM valid_records
GROUP BY station, year;
```

In this view definition, we list the column names explicitly. We do this since the maximum temperature column is an aggregate expression, and otherwise Hive would create a column alias for us (such as _c2). We could equally well have used an AS clause in the SELECT to name the column.

With the views in place, we can now use them by running a query:

```
SELECT station, year, AVG(max_temperature)
FROM max_temperatures
GROUP BY station, year;
```

The result of the query is the same as running the one that uses a subquery, and, in particular, the number of MapReduce jobs that Hive creates is the same for both: two in each case, one for each GROUP BY. This example shows that Hive can combine a query on a view into a sequence of jobs that is equivalent to writing the query without using a view. In other words, Hive won't needlessly materialize a view even at execution time.

Views in Hive are read-only, so there is no way to load or insert data into an underlying base table via a view.

User-Defined Functions

Sometimes the query you want to write can't be expressed easily (or at all) using the built-in functions that Hive provides. By writing a *user-defined function* (UDF), Hive makes it easy to plug in your own processing code and invoke it from a Hive query.

UDFs have to be written in Java, the language that Hive itself is written in. For other languages, consider using a SELECT TRANSFORM query, which allows you to stream data through a user-defined script ("MapReduce Scripts" on page 396).

There are three types of UDF in Hive: (regular) UDFs, UDAFs (user-defined aggregate functions), and UDTFs (user-defined table-generating functions). They differ in the numbers of rows that they accept as input and produce as output:

- A UDF operates on a single row and produces a single row as its output. Most functions, such as mathematical functions and string functions, are of this type.
- A UDAF works on multiple input rows and creates a single output row. Aggregate functions include such functions as COUNT and MAX.
- A UDTF operates on a single row and produces multiple rows—a table—as output.

Table-generating functions are less well known than the other two types, so let's look at an example. Consider a table with a single column, x, which contains arrays of strings. It's instructive to take a slight detour to see how the table is defined and populated:

```
CREATE TABLE arrays (x ARRAY<STRING>)
ROW FORMAT DELIMITED
  FIELDS TERMINATED BY '\001'
  COLLECTION ITEMS TERMINATED BY '\002';
```

Notice that the ROW FORMAT clause specifies that the entries in the array are delimited by Control-B characters. The example file that we are going to load has the following contents, where ^B is a representation of the Control-B character to make it suitable for printing:

```
a^Bb
c^Bd^Be
```

After running a LOAD DATA command, the following query confirms that the data was loaded correctly:

```
hive > SELECT * FROM arrays;
["a","b"]
["c","d","e"]
```

Next, we can use the explode UDTF to transform this table. This function emits a row for each entry in the array, so in this case the type of the output column y is STRING. The result is that the table is flattened into five rows:

```
hive > SELECT explode(x) AS y FROM arrays;
a
b
c
d
e
```

SELECT statements using UDTFs have some restrictions (such as not being able to retrieve additional column expressions), which make them less useful in practice. For this reason, Hive supports LATERAL VIEW queries, which are more powerful. LATERAL VIEW queries not covered here, but you may find out more about them at *http://wiki .apache.org/hadoop/Hive/LanguageManual/LateralView*.

Writing a UDF

To illustrate the process of writing and using a UDF, we'll write a simple UDF to trim characters from the ends of strings. Hive already has a built-in function called trim, so we'll call ours strip. The code for the Strip Java class is shown in Example 12-2.

Example 12-2. A UDF for stripping characters from the ends of strings

```java
package com.hadoopbook.hive;

import org.apache.commons.lang.StringUtils;
import org.apache.hadoop.hive.ql.exec.UDF;
import org.apache.hadoop.io.Text;

public class Strip extends UDF {
  private Text result = new Text();

  public Text evaluate(Text str) {
    if (str == null) {
      return null;
    }
```

```
    result.set(StringUtils.strip(str.toString()));
    return result;
  }

  public Text evaluate(Text str, String stripChars) {
    if (str == null) {
      return null;
    }
    result.set(StringUtils.strip(str.toString(), stripChars));
    return result;
  }
}
```

A UDF must satisfy the following two properties:

1. A UDF must be a subclass of `org.apache.hadoop.hive.ql.exec.UDF`.
2. A UDF must implement at least one `evaluate()` method.

The `evaluate()` method is not defined by an interface since it may take an arbitrary number of arguments, of arbitrary types, and it may return a value of arbitrary type. Hive introspects the UDF to find the `evaluate()` method that matches the Hive function that was invoked.

The `Strip` class has two `evaluate()` methods. The first strips leading and trailing whitespace from the input, while the second can strip any of a set of supplied characters from the ends of the string. The actual string processing is delegated to the `StringUtils` class from the Apache Commons project, which makes the only noteworthy part of the code the use of `Text` from the Hadoop Writable library. Hive actually supports Java primitives in UDFs (and a few other types like `java.util.List` and `java.util.Map`), so a signature like:

```
public String evaluate(String str)
```

would work equally well. However, by using `Text`, we can take advantage of object reuse, which can bring efficiency savings, and so is to be preferred in general.

To use the UDF in Hive, we need to package the compiled Java class in a JAR file (you can do this by typing `ant hive` with the book's example code) and register the file with Hive:

```
ADD JAR /path/to/hive-examples.jar;
```

We also need to create an alias for the Java classname:

```
CREATE TEMPORARY FUNCTION strip AS 'com.hadoopbook.hive.Strip';
```

The `TEMPORARY` keyword here highlights the fact that UDFs are only defined for the duration of the Hive session (they are not persisted in the metastore). In practice, this means you need to add the JAR file, and define the function at the beginning of each script or session.

As an alternative to calling `ADD JAR`, you can specify—at launch time—a path where Hive looks for auxiliary JAR files to put on its classpath (including the MapReduce classpath). This technique is useful for automatically adding your own library of UDFs every time you run Hive.

There are two ways of specifying the path, either passing the `--auxpath` option to the *hive* command:

```
% hive --auxpath /path/to/hive-examples.jar
```

or by setting the `HIVE_AUX_JARS_PATH` environment variable before invoking Hive. The auxiliary path may be a comma-separated list of JAR file paths or a directory containing JAR files.

The UDF is now ready to be used, just like a built-in function:

```
hive> SELECT strip('  bee  ') FROM dummy;
bee
hive> SELECT strip('banana', 'ab') FROM dummy;
nan
```

Notice that the UDF's name is not case-sensitive:

```
hive> SELECT STRIP('  bee  ') FROM dummy;
bee
```

Writing a UDAF

An aggregate function is more difficult to write than a regular UDF, since values are aggregated in chunks (potentially across many Map or Reduce tasks), so the implementation has to be capable of combining partial aggregations into a final result. The code to achieve this is best explained by example, so let's look at the implementation of a simple UDAF for calculating the maximum of a collection of integers (Example 12-3).

Example 12-3. A UDAF for calculating the maximum of a collection of integers

```
package com.hadoopbook.hive;

import org.apache.hadoop.hive.ql.exec.UDAF;
import org.apache.hadoop.hive.ql.exec.UDAFEvaluator;
import org.apache.hadoop.io.IntWritable;

public class Maximum extends UDAF {

  public static class MaximumIntUDAFEvaluator implements UDAFEvaluator {

    private IntWritable result;

    public void init() {
      result = null;
    }
```

```
public boolean iterate(IntWritable value) {
  if (value == null) {
    return true;
  }
  if (result == null) {
    result = new IntWritable(value.get());
  } else {
    result.set(Math.max(result.get(), value.get()));
  }
  return true;
}

public IntWritable terminatePartial() {
  return result;
}

public boolean merge(IntWritable other) {
  return iterate(other);
}

public IntWritable terminate() {
  return result;
}
  }
}
```

The class structure is slightly different to the one for UDFs. A UDAF must be a subclass of org.apache.hadoop.hive.ql.exec.UDAF (note the "A" in UDAF) and contain one or more nested static classes implementing org.apache.hadoop.hive.ql.exec.UDAFEvalua tor. In this example, there is a single nested class, MaximumIntUDAFEvaluator, but we could add more evaluators such as MaximumLongUDAFEvaluator, MaximumFloatUDAFEva luator, and so on, to provide overloaded forms of the UDAF for finding the maximum of a collection of longs, floats, and so on.

An evaluator must implement five methods, described in turn below (the flow is illustrated in Figure 12-4):

init()

> The init() method initializes the evaluator and resets its internal state. In MaximumIntUDAFEvaluator, we set the IntWritable object holding the final result to null. We use null to indicate that no values have been aggregated yet, which has the desirable effect of making the maximum value of an empty set NULL.

iterate()

> The iterate() method is called every time there is a new value to be aggregated. The evaluator should update its internal state with the result of performing the aggregation. The arguments that iterate() takes correspond to those in the Hive function from which it was called. In this example, there is only one argument. The value is first checked to see if it is null, and if it is, it is ignored. Otherwise, the result instance variable is set to value's integer value (if this is the first value that has been seen), or set to the larger of the current result and value (if one or

more values have already been seen). We return `true` to indicate that the input value was valid.

terminatePartial()

The `terminatePartial()` method is called when Hive wants a result for the partial aggregation. The method must return an object that encapsulates the state of the aggregation. In this case, an `IntWritable` suffices, since it encapsulates either the maximum value seen or `null` if no values have been processed.

merge()

The `merge()` method is called when Hive decides to combine one partial aggregation with another. The method takes a single object whose type must correspond to the return type of the `terminatePartial()` method. In this example, the `merge()` method can simply delegate to the `iterate()` method, because the partial aggregation is represented in the same way as a value being aggregated. This is not generally the case (and we'll see a more general example later), and the method should implement the logic to combine the evaluator's state with the state of the partial aggregation.

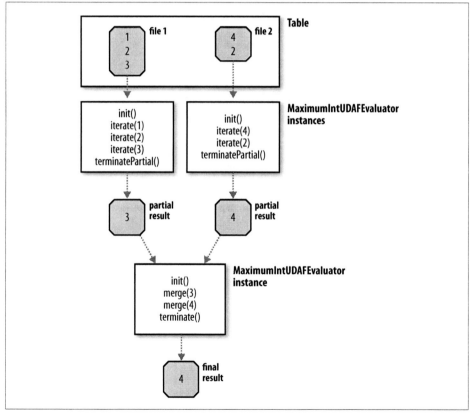

Figure 12-4. Data flow with partial results for a UDAF

terminate()

The terminate() method is called when the final result of the aggregation is needed. The evaluator should return its state as a value. In this case, we return the result instance variable.

Let's exercise our new function:

```
hive> CREATE TEMPORARY FUNCTION maximum AS 'com.hadoopbook.hive.Maximum';
hive> SELECT maximum(temperature) FROM records;
110
```

A more complex UDAF

The previous example is unusual in that a partial aggregation can be represented using the same type (IntWritable) as the final result. This is not generally the case for more complex aggregate functions, as can be seen by considering a UDAF for calculating the mean (average) of a collection of double values. It's not mathematically possible to combine partial means into a final mean value (see "Combiner Functions" on page 30). Instead, we can represent the partial aggregation as a pair of numbers: the cumulative sum of the double values processed so far, and the number of values.

This idea is implemented in the UDAF shown in Example 12-4. Notice that the partial aggregation is implemented as a "struct" nested static class, called PartialResult, which Hive is intelligent enough to serialize and deserialize, since we are using field types that Hive can handle (Java primitives in this case).

In this example, the merge() method is different to iterate(), since it combines the partial sums and partial counts, by pairwise addition. Also, the return type of terminatePartial() is PartialResult—which of course is never seen by the user calling the function—while the return type of terminate() is DoubleWritable, the final result seen by the user.

Example 12-4. A UDAF for calculating the mean of a collection of doubles

```
package com.hadoopbook.hive;

import org.apache.hadoop.hive.ql.exec.UDAF;
import org.apache.hadoop.hive.ql.exec.UDAFEvaluator;
import org.apache.hadoop.hive.serde2.io.DoubleWritable;

public class Mean extends UDAF {

  public static class MeanDoubleUDAFEvaluator implements UDAFEvaluator {
    public static class PartialResult {
      double sum;
      long count;
    }

    private PartialResult partial;
```

```java
  public void init() {
    partial = null;
  }

  public boolean iterate(DoubleWritable value) {
    if (value == null) {
      return true;
    }
    if (partial == null) {
      partial = new PartialResult();
    }
    partial.sum += value.get();
    partial.count++;
    return true;
  }

  public PartialResult terminatePartial() {
    return partial;
  }

  public boolean merge(PartialResult other) {
    if (other == null) {
      return true;
    }
    if (partial == null) {
      partial = new PartialResult();
    }
    partial.sum += other.sum;
    partial.count += other.count;
    return true;
  }

  public DoubleWritable terminate() {
    if (partial == null) {
      return null;
    }
    return new DoubleWritable(partial.sum / partial.count);
  }
  }
}
```

## CHAPTER 13

HBase

Jonathan Gray and Michael Stack

HBasics

HBase is a distributed column-oriented database built on top of HDFS. HBase is the Hadoop application to use when you require real-time read/write random-access to very large datasets.

Although there are countless strategies and implementations for database storage and retrieval, most solutions—especially those of the relational variety—are not built with very large scale and distribution in mind. Many vendors offer replication and partitioning solutions to grow the database beyond the confines of a single node, but these add-ons are generally an afterthought and are complicated to install and maintain. They also come at some severe compromise to the RDBMS feature set. Joins, complex queries, triggers, views, and foreign-key constraints become prohibitively expensive to run on a scaled RDBMS or do not work at all.

HBase comes at the scaling problem from the opposite direction. It is built from the ground-up to scale linearly just by adding nodes. HBase is not relational and does not support SQL, but given the proper problem space, it is able to do what an RDBMS cannot: host very large, sparsely populated tables on clusters made from commodity hardware.

The canonical HBase use case is the *webtable*, a table of crawled web pages and their attributes (such as language and MIME type) keyed by the web page URL. The webtable is large, with row counts that run into the billions. Batch analytic and parsing MapReduce jobs are continuously run against the webtable deriving statistics and adding new columns of verified MIME type and parsed text content for later indexing by a search engine. Concurrently, the table is randomly accessed by crawlers running at various rates updating random rows while random web pages are served in real time as users click on a website's cached-page feature.

Backdrop

The HBase project was started toward the end of 2006 by Chad Walters and Jim Kellerman at Powerset. It was modeled after Google's "Bigtable: A Distributed Storage System for Structured Data" by Chang et al. (*http://labs.google.com/papers/bigtable .html*), which had just been published. In February 2007, Mike Cafarella made a code drop of a mostly working system that Jim Kellerman then carried forward.

The first HBase release was bundled as part of Hadoop 0.15.0 in October 2007. In May 2010, HBase graduated from a Hadoop subproject to become an Apache Top Level Project. Production users of HBase include Adobe, StumbleUpon, Twitter, and groups at Yahoo!.

Concepts

In this section, we provide a quick overview of core HBase concepts. At a minimum, a passing familiarity will ease the digestion of all that follows.*

Whirlwind Tour of the Data Model

Applications store data into labeled tables. Tables are made of rows and columns. Table cells—the intersection of row and column coordinates—are versioned. By default, their version is a timestamp auto-assigned by HBase at the time of cell insertion. A cell's content is an uninterpreted array of bytes.

Table row keys are also byte arrays, so theoretically anything can serve as a row key from strings to binary representations of long or even serialized data structures. Table rows are sorted by row key, the table's primary key. The sort is byte-ordered. All table accesses are via the table primary key.†

Row columns are grouped into *column families*. All column family members have a common prefix, so, for example, the columns *temperature:air* and *tempera-ture:dew_point* are both members of the *temperature* column family, whereas *station:identifier* belongs to the *station* family.‡ The column family prefix must be composed of *printable* characters. The qualifying tail, the column family *qualifier*, can be made of any arbitrary bytes.

---

* For more detail than is provided here, see the HBase Architecture page (*http://wiki.apache.org/hadoop/Hbase/ HbaseArchitecture*) on the HBase wiki.

† As of this writing, there are at least two projects up on github that add secondary indices to HBase.

‡ In HBase, by convention, the colon character (:) delimits the column family from the column family *qualifier*. It is hardcoded.

A table's column families must be specified up front as part of the table schema definition, but new column family members can be added on demand. For example, a new column *station:address* can be offered by a client as part of an update, and its value persisted, as long as the column family *station* is already in existence on the targeted table.

Physically, all column family members are stored together on the filesystem. So, though earlier we described HBase as a column-oriented store, it would be more accurate if it were described as a column-*family*-oriented store. Because tunings and storage specifications are done at the column family level, it is advised that all column family members have the same general access pattern and size characteristics.

In synopsis, HBase tables are like those in an RDBMS, only cells are versioned, rows are sorted, and columns can be added on the fly by the client as long as the column family they belong to preexists.

Regions

Tables are automatically partitioned horizontally by HBase into *regions*. Each region comprises a subset of a table's rows. A region is denoted by the table it belongs to, its first row, inclusive, and last row, exclusive. Initially, a table comprises a single region, but as the size of the region grows, after it crosses a configurable size threshold, it splits at a row boundary into two new regions of approximately equal size. Until this first split happens, all loading will be against the single server hosting the original region. As the table grows, the number of its regions grows. Regions are the units that get distributed over an HBase cluster. In this way, a table that is too big for any one server can be carried by a cluster of servers with each node hosting a subset of the table's total regions. This is also the means by which the loading on a table gets distributed. The online set of sorted regions comprises the table's total content.

Locking

Row updates are atomic, no matter how many row columns constitute the row-level transaction. This keeps the locking model simple.

Implementation

Just as HDFS and MapReduce are built of clients, slaves, and a coordinating master—*namenode* and *datanodes* in HDFS and *jobtracker* and *tasktrackers* in MapReduce—so is HBase modeled with an HBase *master* node orchestrating a cluster of one or more *regionserver* slaves (see Figure 13-1). The HBase master is responsible for bootstrapping a virgin install, for assigning regions to registered regionservers, and for recovering regionserver failures. The master node is lightly loaded. The regionservers carry zero or more regions and field client read/write requests. They also manage region splits informing the HBase master about the new daughter regions for it to manage the off-lining of parent region and assignment of the replacement daughters.

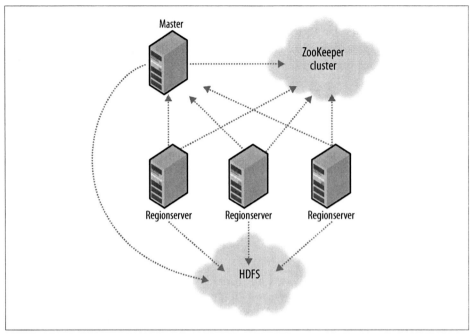

Figure 13-1. HBase cluster members

HBase depends on ZooKeeper (Chapter 14) and by default it manages a ZooKeeper instance as the authority on cluster state. HBase hosts vitals such as the location of the root catalog table and the address of the current cluster Master. Assignment of regions is mediated via ZooKeeper in case participating servers crash mid-assignment. Hosting the assignment transaction state in ZooKeeper makes it so recovery can pick up on the assignment at where the crashed server left off. At a minimum, bootstrapping a client connection to an HBase cluster, the client must be passed the location of the ZooKeeper ensemble. Thereafter, the client navigates the ZooKeeper hierarchy to learn cluster attributes such as server locations.[§]

Regionserver slave nodes are listed in the HBase *conf/regionservers* file as you would list datanodes and tasktrackers in the Hadoop *conf/slaves* file. Start and stop scripts are like those in Hadoop using the same SSH-based running of remote commands mechanism. Cluster site-specific configuration is made in the HBase *conf/hbase-site.xml* and *conf/hbase-env.sh* files, which have the same format as that of their equivalents up in the Hadoop parent project (see Chapter 9).

[§] HBase can be configured to use an existing ZooKeeper cluster instead.

Where there is commonality to be found, HBase directly uses or sub-classes the parent Hadoop implementation, whether a service or type. When this is not possible, HBase will follow the Hadoop model where it can. For example, HBase uses the Hadoop Configuration system so configuration files have the same format. What this means for you, the user, is that you can leverage any Hadoop familiarity in your exploration of HBase. HBase deviates from this rule only when adding its specializations.

HBase persists data via the Hadoop filesystem API. Since there are multiple implementations of the filesystem interface—one for the local filesystem, one for the KFS filesystem, Amazon's S3, and HDFS (the Hadoop Distributed Filesystem)—HBase can persist to any of these implementations. Most experience though has been had using HDFS, though by default, unless told otherwise, HBase writes the local filesystem. The local filesystem is fine for experimenting with your initial HBase install, but thereafter, usually the first configuration made in an HBase cluster involves pointing HBase at the HDFS cluster to use.

HBase in operation

HBase, internally, keeps special catalog tables named *-ROOT-* and *.META.* within which it maintains the current list, state, and location of all regions afloat on the cluster. The -ROOT- table holds the list of .META. table regions. The .META. table holds the list of all user-space regions. Entries in these tables are keyed using by region name where a region name is made of the table name the region belongs to, the region's start row, its time of creation, and finally, an MD5 hash of all of the former (i.e., a hash of tablename, start row, and creation timestamp.)[||] Row keys, as noted previously, are sorted so finding the region that hosts a particular row is a matter of a lookup to find the first entry whose key is greater than or equal to that of the requested row key. As regions transition—are split, disabled/enabled, deleted, redeployed by the region load balancer, or redeployed due to a regionserver crash—the catalog tables are updated so the state of all regions on the cluster is kept current.

Fresh clients connect to the ZooKeeper cluster first to learn the location of -ROOT-. Clients consult -ROOT- to elicit the location of the .META. region whose scope covers that of the requested row. The client then does a lookup against the found .META. region to figure the hosting user-space region and its location. Thereafter, the client interacts directly with the hosting regionserver.

To save on having to make three round-trips per row operation, clients cache all they learn traversing -ROOT- and .META. caching locations as well as user-space region start

---

[||] Here is an example region name from the table `TestTable` whose start row is `xyz`: `TestTable,xyz, 1279729913622.1b6e176fb8d8aa88fd4ab6bc80247ece`. A comma delimits table name, start row, and timestamp. The name always ends in a period.

and stop rows so they can figure hosting regions themselves without having to go back to the .META. table. Clients continue to use the cached entry as they work until there is a fault. When this happens—the region has moved—the client consults the .META. again to learn the new location. If, in turn, the consulted .META. region has moved, then -ROOT- is reconsulted.

Writes arriving at a regionserver are first appended to a commit log and then are added to an in-memory *memstore*. When a memstore fills, its content is flushed to the filesystem.

The commit log is hosted on HDFS, so it remains available through a regionserver crash. When the master notices that a regionserver is no longer reachable, usually because the servers's znode has expired in ZooKeeper, it splits the dead regionserver's commit log by region. On reassignment, regions that were on the dead regionserver, before they open for business, will pick up their just-split file of not yet persisted edits and replay them to bring themselves up-to-date with the state they had just before the failure.

Reading, the region's memstore is consulted first. If sufficient versions are found reading memstore alone, we return. Otherwise, flush files are consulted in order, from newest to oldest until versions sufficient to satisfy the query are found, or until we run out of flush files.

A background process compacts flush files once their number has broached a threshold, rewriting many files as one, because the fewer files a read consults, the more performant it will be. On compaction, versions beyond the schema configured maximum, deletes and expired cells are cleaned out. A separate process running in the regionserver monitors flush file sizes splitting the region when they grow in excess of the configured maximum.

Installation

Download a stable release from an Apache Download Mirror (*http://www.apache.org/ dyn/closer.cgi/hbase/*) and unpack it on your local filesystem. For example:

```
% tar xzf hbase-x.y.z.tar.gz
```

As with Hadoop, you first need to tell HBase where Java is located on your system. If you have the JAVA_HOME environment variable set to point to a suitable Java installation, then that will be used, and you don't have to configure anything further. Otherwise, you can set the Java installation that HBase uses by editing HBase's *conf/hbase-env.sh*, and specifying the JAVA_HOME variable (see Appendix A for some examples) to point to version 1.6.0 of Java.

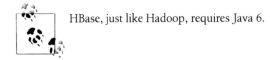 HBase, just like Hadoop, requires Java 6.

For convenience, add the HBase binary directory to your command-line path. For example:

```
% export HBASE_HOME=/home/hbase/hbase-x.y.z
% export PATH=$PATH:$HBASE_HOME/bin
```

To get the list of HBase options, type:

```
% hbase
Usage: hbase <command>
where <command> is one of:
  shell            run the HBase shell
  master           run an HBase HMaster node
  regionserver     run an HBase HRegionServer node
  zookeeper        run a Zookeeper server
  rest             run an HBase REST server
  thrift           run an HBase Thrift server
  avro             run an HBase Avro server
  migrate          upgrade an hbase.rootdir
  hbck             run the hbase 'fsck' tool
 or
  CLASSNAME        run the class named CLASSNAME
Most commands print help when invoked w/o parameters.
```

Test Drive

To start a temporary instance of HBase that uses the */tmp* directory on the local filesystem for persistence, type:

```
% start-hbase.sh
```

This will launch a standalone HBase instance that persists to the local filesystem; by default, HBase will write to */tmp/hbase-${USERID}.#*

To administer your HBase instance, launch the HBase shell by typing:

```
% hbase shell
HBase Shell; enter 'help<RETURN>' for list of supported commands.
Type "exit<RETURN>" to leave the HBase Shell
Version: 0.89.0-SNAPSHOT, ra4ea1a9a7b074a2e5b7b24f761302d4ea28ed1b2, Sun Jul 18
15:01:50 PDT 2010 hbase(main):001:0>
```

This will bring up a JRuby IRB interpreter that has had some HBase-specific commands added to it. Type help and then RETURN to see the list of shell commands grouped into categories. Type help *COMMAND_GROUP* for help by category or help *COMMAND* for help on a specific command and example usage. Commands use Ruby formatting to specify lists and dictionaries. See the end of the main help screen for a quick tutorial.

Now let us create a simple table, add some data, and then clean up.

To create a table, you must name your table and define its schema. A table's schema comprises table attributes and the list of table column families. Column families

---

#In standalone mode, HBase master, regionserver, and a ZooKeeper instance are all run in the same JVM.

themselves have attributes that you in turn set at schema definition time. Examples of column family attributes include whether the family content should be compressed on the filesystem and how many versions of a cell to keep. Schemas can be later edited by offlining the table using the shell `disable` command, making the necessary alterations using `alter`, then putting the table back online with `enable`.

To create a table named *test* with a single column family name *data* using defaults for table and column family attributes, enter:

```
hbase(main):007:0> create 'test', 'data'
0 row(s) in 1.3066 seconds
```

 If the previous command does not complete successfully, and the shell displays an error and a stack trace, your install was not successful. Check the master logs under the HBase *logs* directory—the default location for the logs directory is *${HBASE_HOME}/logs*—for a clue as to where things went awry.

See the `help` output for examples adding table and column family attributes when specifying a schema.

To prove the new table was created successfully, run the `list` command. This will output all tables in user space:

```
hbase(main):019:0> list
test
1 row(s) in 0.1485 seconds
```

To insert data into three different rows and columns in the *data* column family, and then list the table content, do the following:

```
hbase(main):021:0> put 'test', 'row1', 'data:1', 'value1'
0 row(s) in 0.0454 seconds
hbase(main):022:0> put 'test', 'row2', 'data:2', 'value2'
0 row(s) in 0.0035 seconds
hbase(main):023:0> put 'test', 'row3', 'data:3', 'value3'
0 row(s) in 0.0090 seconds
hbase(main):024:0> scan 'test'
ROW                      COLUMN+CELL
 row1                    column=data:1, timestamp=1240148026198, value=value1
 row2                    column=data:2, timestamp=1240148040035, value=value2
 row3                    column=data:3, timestamp=1240148047497, value=value3
3 row(s) in 0.0825 seconds
```

Notice how we added three new columns without changing the schema.

To remove the table, you must first disable it before dropping it:

```
hbase(main):025:0> disable 'test'
09/04/19 06:40:13 INFO client.HBaseAdmin: Disabled test
0 row(s) in 6.0426 seconds
hbase(main):026:0> drop 'test'
09/04/19 06:40:17 INFO client.HBaseAdmin: Deleted test
```

```
0 row(s) in 0.0210 seconds
hbase(main):027:0> list
0 row(s) in 2.0645 seconds
```

Shut down your HBase instance by running:

```
% stop-hbase.sh
```

To learn how to set up a distributed HBase and point it at a running HDFS, see the
Getting Started (*http://hadoop.apache.org/hbase/docs/current/api/overview-summary
.html#overview_description*) section of the HBase documentation.

Clients

There are a number of client options for interacting with an HBase cluster.

Java

HBase, like Hadoop, is written in Java. Example 13-1 shows how you would do in Java
the shell operations listed previously at "Test Drive" on page 417.

Example 13-1. Basic table administration and access

```
public class ExampleClient {
  public static void main(String[] args) throws IOException {
    Configuration config = HBaseConfiguration.create();

    // Create table
    HBaseAdmin admin = new HBaseAdmin(config);
    HTableDescriptor htd = new HTableDescriptor("test");
    HColumnDescriptor hcd = new HColumnDescriptor("data");
    htd.addFamily(hcd);
    admin.createTable(htd);
    byte [] tablename = htd.getName();
    HTableDescriptor [] tables = admin.listTables();
    if (tables.length != 1 && Bytes.equals(tablename, tables[0].getName())) {
      throw new IOException("Failed create of table");
    }

    // Run some operations -- a put, a get, and a scan -- against the table.
    HTable table = new HTable(config, tablename);
    byte [] row1 = Bytes.toBytes("row1");
    Put p1 = new Put(row1);
    byte [] databytes = Bytes.toBytes("data");
    p1.add(databytes, Bytes.toBytes("1"), Bytes.toBytes("value1"));
    table.put(p1);
    Get g = new Get(row1);
    Result result = table.get(g);
    System.out.println("Get: " + result);
    Scan scan = new Scan();
    ResultScanner scanner = table.getScanner(scan);
    try {
      for (Result scannerResult: scanner) {
```

```
      System.out.println("Scan: " + scannerResult);
    }
  } finally {
    scanner.close();
  }

  // Drop the table
  admin.disableTable(tablename);
  admin.deleteTable(tablename);
  }
}
```

This class has a main method only. For the sake of brevity, we do not include package name nor imports. In this class, we first create an instance of org.apache.hadoop.conf.Configuration. We ask the org.apache.hadoop.hbase.HBase Configuration class to create the instance. It will return a Configuration that has read HBase configuration from *hbase-site.xml* and *hbase-default.xml* files found on the program's classpath. This Configuration is subsequently used to create instances of HBaseAdmin and HTable, two classes found in the org.apache.hadoop.hbase.client Java package. HBaseAdmin is used for administering your HBase cluster, for adding and dropping tables. HTable is used to access a specific table. The Configuration instance points these classes at the cluster the code is to work against.

To create a table, we need to first create an instance of HBaseAdmin and then ask it to create the table named test with a single column family named data. In our example, our table schema is the default. Use methods on org.apache.hadoop.hbase.HTableDe scriptor and org.apache.hadoop.hbase.HColumnDescriptor to change the table schema. The code next asserts the table was actually created and then it moves to run operations against the just-created table.

Operating on a table, we will need an instance of org.apache.hadoop.hbase.cli ent.HTable passing it our Configuration instance and the name of the table we want to operate on. After creating an HTable, we then create an instance of org.apache.hadoop.hbase.client.Put to put a single cell value of value1 into a row named row1 on the column named data:1 (The column name is specified in two parts; the column family name as bytes—databytes in the code above—and then the column family qualifier specified as Bytes.toBytes("1")). Next we create an org.apache.hadoop.hbase.client.Get, do a get of the just-added cell, and then use an org.apache.hadoop.hbase.client.Scan to scan over the table against the just-created table printing out what we find.

Finally, we clean up by first disabling the table and then deleting it. A table must be disabled before it can be dropped.

MapReduce

HBase classes and utilities in the org.apache.hadoop.hbase.mapreduce package facilitate using HBase as a source and/or sink in MapReduce jobs. The TableInputFormat class makes splits on region boundaries so maps are handed a single region to work on. The TableOutputFormat will write the result of reduce into HBase. The RowCounter class in Example 13-2 can be found in the HBase mapreduce package. It runs a map task to count rows using TableInputFormat.

Example 13-2. A MapReduce application to count the number of rows in an HBase table

```
public class RowCounter {
  /** Name of this 'program'. */
  static final String NAME = "rowcounter";

  static class RowCounterMapper
  extends TableMapper<ImmutableBytesWritable, Result> {
    /** Counter enumeration to count the actual rows. */
    public static enum Counters {ROWS}

    @Override
    public void map(ImmutableBytesWritable row, Result values,
      Context context)
    throws IOException {
      for (KeyValue value: values.list()) {
        if (value.getValue().length > 0) {
          context.getCounter(Counters.ROWS).increment(1);
          break;
        }
      }
    }
  }

  public static Job createSubmittableJob(Configuration conf, String[] args)
  throws IOException {
    String tableName = args[0];
    Job job = new Job(conf, NAME + "_" + tableName);
    job.setJarByClass(RowCounter.class);
    // Columns are space delimited
    StringBuilder sb = new StringBuilder();
    final int columnoffset = 1;
    for (int i = columnoffset; i < args.length; i++) {
      if (i > columnoffset) {
        sb.append(" ");
      }
      sb.append(args[i]);
    }
    Scan scan = new Scan();
    scan.setFilter(new FirstKeyOnlyFilter());
    if (sb.length() > 0) {
      for (String columnName :sb.toString().split(" ")) {
        String [] fields = columnName.split(":");
        if(fields.length == 1) {
          scan.addFamily(Bytes.toBytes(fields[0]));
        } else {
          scan.addColumn(Bytes.toBytes(fields[0]), Bytes.toBytes(fields[1]));
        }
      }
    }
```

```
      // Second argument is the table name.
      job.setOutputFormatClass(NullOutputFormat.class);
      TableMapReduceUtil.initTableMapperJob(tableName, scan,
        RowCounterMapper.class, ImmutableBytesWritable.class, Result.class, job);
      job.setNumReduceTasks(0);
      return job;
  }

  public static void main(String[] args) throws Exception {
      Configuration conf = HBaseConfiguration.create();
      String[] otherArgs = new GenericOptionsParser(conf, args).getRemainingArgs();
      if (otherArgs.length < 1) {
        System.err.println("ERROR: Wrong number of parameters: " + args.length);
        System.err.println("Usage: RowCounter <tablename> [<column1> <column2>...]");
        System.exit(-1);
      }
      Job job = createSubmittableJob(conf, otherArgs);
      System.exit(job.waitForCompletion(true) ? 0 : 1);
  }
}
```

This class uses GenericOptionsParser, which is discussed in "GenericOptionsParser,
Tool, and ToolRunner" on page 135, for parsing command line arguments. The Row
CounterMapper inner class implements the HBase TableMapper abstract, a specialization
of org.apache.hadoop.mapreduce.Mapper that sets the map inputs types passed by
TableInputFormat. The createSubmittableJob() method parses arguments added to the
configuration that were passed on the command line figuring the table and columns
we are to run RowCounter against. The resultant parse is used configuring an instance
of org.apache.hadoop.hbase.client.Scan, a scan object that will be passed through to
TableInputFormat and used constraining what our Mapper sees. Notice how we set a
filter, an instance of org.apache.hadoop.hbase.filter.FirstKeyOnlyFilter, on the
scan. This filter instructs the server short-circuit when running server-side doing no
more than verify a row has an entry before returning. This speeds the row count. The
createSubmittableJob() method also invokes the TableMapReduceUtil.initTableMap
Job() utility method, which among other things such as setting the map class to use,
sets the input format to TableInputFormat. The map is simple. It checks for empty
values. If empty, it doesn't count the row. Otherwise, it increments Counters.ROWS by
one.

Avro, REST, and Thrift

HBase ships with Avro, REST, and Thrift interfaces. These are useful when the interacting application is written in a language other than Java. In all cases, a Java server
hosts an instance of the HBase client brokering application Avro, REST, and Thrift
requests in and out of the HBase cluster. This extra work proxying requests and responses means these interfaces are slower than using the Java client directly.

REST

To put up a *stargate* instance (stargate is the name for the HBase REST service), start it using the following command:

```
% hbase-daemon.sh start rest
```

This will start a server instance, by default on port 8080, background it, and catch any emissions by the server in logfiles under the HBase *logs* directory.

Clients can ask for the response to be formatted as JSON, Google's protobufs, or as XML, depending on how the client *HTTP Accept* header is set. See the REST wiki page (*http://wiki.apache.org/hadoop/Hbase/Stargate*) for documentation and examples of making REST client requests.

To stop the REST server, type:

```
% hbase-daemon.sh stop rest
```

Thrift

Similarly, start a Thrift service by putting up a server to field Thrift clients by running the following:

```
% hbase-daemon.sh start thrift
```

This will start the server instance, by default on port 9090, background it, and catch any emissions by the server in logfiles under the HBase *logs* directory. The HBase Thrift documentation[*] notes the Thrift version used generating classes. The HBase Thrift IDL can be found at *src/main/resources/org/apache/hadoop/hbase/thrift/Hbase.thrift* in the HBase source code.

To stop the Thrift server, type:

```
% hbase-daemon.sh stop thrift
```

Avro

The Avro server is started and stopped in the same manner as you'd start and stop the Thrift or REST services. The Avro server by default uses port 9090.

Example

Although HDFS and MapReduce are powerful tools for processing batch operations over large datasets, they do not provide ways to read or write individual records efficiently. In this example, we'll explore using HBase as the tool to fill this gap.

The existing weather dataset described in previous chapters contains observations for tens of thousands of stations over 100 years and this data is growing without bound.

---

[*] *http://hbase.apache.org/docs/current/api/org/apache/hadoop/hbase/thrift/package-summary.html*

Example | 423

In this example, we will build a simple web interface that allows a user to navigate the different stations and page through their historical temperature observations in time order. For the sake of this example, let us allow that the dataset is massive, that the observations run to the billions, and that the rate at which temperature updates arrive is significant—say hundreds to thousands of updates a second from around the world across the whole range of weather stations. Also, let us allow that it is a requirement that the web application must display the most up-to-date observation within a second or so of receipt.

The first size requirement should preclude our use of a simple RDBMS instance and make HBase a candidate store. The second latency requirement rules out plain HDFS. A MapReduce job could build initial indices that allowed random-access over all of the observation data, but keeping up this index as the updates arrived is not what HDFS and MapReduce are good at.

Schemas

In our example, there will be two tables:

Stations
> This table holds station data. Let the row key be the `stationid`. Let this table have a column family *info* that acts as a key/val dictionary for station information. Let the dictionary keys be the column names `info:name`, `info:location`, and `info:description`. This table is static and the *info* family, in this case, closely mirrors a typical RDBMS table design.

Observations
> This table holds temperature observations. Let the row key be a composite key of `stationid` + reverse order timestamp. Give this table a column family `data` that will contain one column `airtemp` with the observed temperature as the column value.

Our choice of schema is derived from how we want to most efficiently read from HBase. Rows and columns are stored in increasing lexicographical order. Though there are facilities for secondary indexing and regular expression matching, they come at a performance penalty. It is vital that you understand how you want to most efficiently query your data in order to most effectively store and access it.

For the `stations` table, the choice of `stationid` as key is obvious because we will always access information for a particular station by its id. The `observations` table, however, uses a composite key that adds the observation timestamp at the end. This will group all observations for a particular station together, and by using a reverse order timestamp (`Long.MAX_VALUE - epoch`) and storing it as binary, observations for each station will be ordered with most recent observation first.

In the shell, you would define your tables as follows:

```
hbase(main):036:0> create 'stations', {NAME => 'info', VERSIONS => 1}
0 row(s) in 0.1304 seconds
hbase(main):037:0> create 'observations', {NAME => 'data', VERSIONS => 1}
0 row(s) in 0.1332 seconds
```

In both cases, we are interested only in the latest version of a table cell, so set VERSIONS to 1. The default is 3.

Loading Data

There are a relatively small number of stations, so their static data is easily inserted using any of the available interfaces.

However, let's assume that there are billions of individual observations to be loaded. This kind of import is normally an extremely complex and long-running database operation, but MapReduce and HBase's distribution model allow us to make full use of the cluster. Copy the raw input data onto HDFS and then run a MapReduce job that can read the input and write to HBase.

Example 13-3 shows an example MapReduce job that imports observations to HBase from the same input file used in the previous chapters' examples.

Example 13-3. A MapReduce application to import temperature data from HDFS into an HBase table

```
public class HBaseTemperatureImporter extends Configured implements Tool {

  // Inner-class for map
  static class HBaseTemperatureMapper<K, V> extends MapReduceBase implements
      Mapper<LongWritable, Text, K, V> {
    private NcdcRecordParser parser = new NcdcRecordParser();
    private HTable table;

    public void map(LongWritable key, Text value,
      OutputCollector<K, V> output, Reporter reporter)
    throws IOException {
      parser.parse(value.toString());
      if (parser.isValidTemperature()) {
        byte[] rowKey = RowKeyConverter.makeObservationRowKey(parser.getStationId(),
          parser.getObservationDate().getTime());
        Put p = new Put(rowKey);
        p.add(HBaseTemperatureCli.DATA_COLUMNFAMILY,
          HBaseTemperatureCli.AIRTEMP_QUALIFIER,
          Bytes.toBytes(parser.getAirTemperature()));
        table.put(p);
      }
    }
  }

  public void configure(JobConf jc) {
    super.configure(jc);
    // Create the HBase table client once up-front and keep it around
    // rather than create on each map invocation.
```

Example | 425

```
    try {
      this.table = new HTable(new HBaseConfiguration(jc), "observations");
    } catch (IOException e) {
      throw new RuntimeException("Failed HTable construction", e);
    }
  }

  @Override
  public void close() throws IOException {
    super.close();
    table.close();
  }
}

public int run(String[] args) throws IOException {
  if (args.length != 1) {
    System.err.println("Usage: HBaseTemperatureImporter <input>");
    return -1;
  }
  JobConf jc = new JobConf(getConf(), getClass());
  FileInputFormat.addInputPath(jc, new Path(args[0]));
  jc.setMapperClass(HBaseTemperatureMapper.class);
  jc.setNumReduceTasks(0);
  jc.setOutputFormat(NullOutputFormat.class);
  JobClient.runJob(jc);
  return 0;
}

public static void main(String[] args) throws Exception {
  int exitCode = ToolRunner.run(new HBaseConfiguration(),
      new HBaseTemperatureImporter(), args);
  System.exit(exitCode);
}
}
```

HBaseTemperatureImporter has an inner class named HBaseTemperatureMapper that is like the MaxTemperatureMapper class from Chapter 5. The outer class implements Tool and does the setup to launch the HBaseTemperatureMapper inner class. HBaseTemperatureMapper takes the same input as MaxTemperatureMapper and does the same parse—using the NcdcRecordParser introduced in Chapter 5—to check for valid temperatures, but rather than add valid temperatures to the output collector as MaxTemperatureMapper does, instead it adds valid temperatures to the observations HBase table into the *data:airtemp* column. (We are using static defines for data and airtemp imported from HBase TemperatureCli class described later below.) In the configure() method, we create an HTable instance once against the observations table and use it afterward in map invocations talking to HBase. Finally, we call close on our HTable instance to flush out any write buffers not yet cleared.

The row key used is created in the makeObservationRowKey() method on RowKey Converter from the station ID and observation time:

```
public class RowKeyConverter {

    private static final int STATION_ID_LENGTH = 12;

    /**
     * @return A row key whose format is: <station_id> <reverse_order_epoch>
     */
    public static byte[] makeObservationRowKey(String stationId,
        long observationTime) {
      byte[] row = new byte[STATION_ID_LENGTH + Bytes.SIZEOF_LONG];
      Bytes.putBytes(row, 0, Bytes.toBytes(stationId), 0, STATION_ID_LENGTH);
      long reverseOrderEpoch = Long.MAX_VALUE - observationTime;
      Bytes.putLong(row, STATION_ID_LENGTH, reverseOrderEpoch);
      return row;
    }

}
```

The conversion takes advantage of the fact that the station ID is a fixed-length string. The Bytes class used in makeObservationRowKey() is from the HBase utility package. It includes methods for converting between byte arrays and common Java and Hadoop types. In makeObservationRowKey(), the Bytes.putLong() method is used to fill the key byte array. The Bytes.SIZEOF_LONG constant is used for sizing and positioning in the row key array.

We can run the program with the following:

```
% hbase HBaseTemperatureImporter input/ncdc/all
```

Optimization notes

- Watch for the phenomenon where an import walks in lock-step through the table with all clients in concert pounding one of the table's regions (and thus, a single node), then moving on to the next, and so on, rather than evenly distributing the load over all regions. This is usually brought on by some interaction between sorted input and how the splitter works. Randomizing the ordering of your row keys prior to insertion may help. In our example, given the distribution of stationid values and how TextInputFormat makes splits, the upload should be sufficiently distributed.[†]

- Only obtain one HTable instance per task. There is a cost to instantiating an HTable, so if you do this for each insert, you may have a negative impact on performance, hence our setup of HTable in the configure() step.

---

† If a table is new, it will have only one region and initially all updates will be to this single region until it splits. This will happen even if row keys are randomly distributed. This startup phenomenon means uploads run slow at first until there are sufficient regions distributed so all cluster members are able to participate in the upload. Do not confuse this phenomenon with that noted here.

Example | 427

- By default, each `HTable.put(put)` actually performs the insert without any buffering. You can disable the `HTable` auto-flush feature using `HTable.setAutoFlush(false)` and then set the size of configurable write buffer. When the inserts committed fill the write buffer, it is then flushed. Remember though, you must call a manual `HTable.flushCommits()`, or `HTable.close()`, which will call through to `HTable.flushCommits()` at the end of each task to ensure that nothing is left unflushed in the buffer. You could do this in an override of the mapper's `close()` method.

- HBase includes `TableInputFormat` and `TableOutputFormat` to help with MapReduce jobs that source and sink HBase (see Example 13-2). One way to write the previous example would have been to use `MaxTemperatureMapper` from Chapter 5 as is but add a reducer task that takes the output of the `MaxTemperatureMapper` and feeds it to HBase via `TableOutputFormat`.

Web Queries

To implement the web application, we will use the HBase Java API directly. Here it becomes clear how important your choice of schema and storage format is.

The simplest query will be to get the static station information. This type of query is simple in a traditional database, but HBase gives you additional control and flexibility. Using the info family as a key/value dictionary (column names as keys, column values as values), the code would look like this:

```
public Map<String, String> getStationInfo(HTable table, String stationId)
    throws IOException {
  Get get = new Get(Bytes.toBytes(stationId));
  get.addColumn(INFO_COLUMNFAMILY);
  Result res = table.get(get);
  if (res == null) {
    return null;
  }
  Map<String, String> resultMap = new HashMap<String, String>();
  resultMap.put("name", getValue(res, INFO_COLUMNFAMILY, NAME_QUALIFIER));
  resultMap.put("location", getValue(res, INFO_COLUMNFAMILY, LOCATION_QUALIFIER));
  resultMap.put("description", getValue(res, INFO_COLUMNFAMILY,
    DESCRIPTION_QUALIFIER));
  return resultMap;
}

private static String getValue(Result res, byte [] cf, byte [] qualifier) {
  byte [] value = res.getValue(cf, qualifier);
  return value == null? "": Bytes.toString(value);
}
```

In this example, getStationInfo() takes an HTable instance and a station ID. To get the station info, we use HTable.get() passing a Get instance configured to get all in the defined column family INFO_COLUMNFAMILY.

The get() results are returned in Result. It contains the row and you can fetch cell values by stipulating the column cell wanted. The getStationInfo() method converts the Result Map into a more friendly Map of String keys and values.

We can already see how there is a need for utility functions when using HBase. There are an increasing number of abstractions being built atop HBase to deal with this low-level interaction, but it's important to understand how this works and how storage choices make a difference.

One of the strengths of HBase over a relational database is that you don't have to prespecify the columns. So, in the future, if each station now has at least these three attributes but there are hundreds of optional ones, we can just insert them without modifying the schema. Your applications reading and writing code would of course need to be changed. The example code might change in this case to looping through Result rather than explicitly grabbing each value explicitly.

We will make use of HBase scanners for retrieval of observations in our web application.

Here we are after a Map<ObservationTime, ObservedTemp> result. We will use a NavigableMap<Long, Integer> because it is sorted and has a descendingMap() method, so we can access observations in both ascending or descending order. The code is in Example 13-4.

Example 13-4. Methods for retrieving a range of rows of weather station observations from an HBase table

```
public NavigableMap<Long, Integer> getStationObservations(HTable table,
    String stationId, long maxStamp, int maxCount) throws IOException {
  byte[] startRow = RowKeyConverter.makeObservationRowKey(stationId, maxStamp);
  NavigableMap<Long, Integer> resultMap = new TreeMap<Long, Integer>();
  Scan scan = new Scan(startRow);
  scan.addColumn(DATA_COLUMNFAMILY, AIRTEMP_QUALIFIER);
  ResultScanner scanner = table.getScanner(scan);
  Result res = null;
  int count = 0;
  try {
    while ((res = scanner.next()) != null && count++ < maxCount) {
      byte[] row = res.getRow();
      byte[] value = res.getValue(DATA_COLUMNFAMILY, AIRTEMP_QUALIFIER);
      Long stamp = Long.MAX_VALUE -
        Bytes.toLong(row, row.length - Bytes.SIZEOF_LONG, Bytes.SIZEOF_LONG);
      Integer temp = Bytes.toInt(value);
      resultMap.put(stamp, temp);
    }
  } finally {
    scanner.close();
  }
  return resultMap;
}
```

Example | 429

```
/**
 * Return the last ten observations.
 */
public NavigableMap<Long, Integer> getStationObservations(HTable table,
    String stationId) throws IOException {
  return getStationObservations(table, stationId, Long.MAX_VALUE, 10);
```

The getStationObservations() method takes a station ID and a range defined by max
Stamp and a maximum number of rows (maxCount). Note that the NavigableMap that is
returned is actually now in descending time order. If you want to read through it in
ascending order, you would make use of NavigableMap.descendingMap().

Scanners

HBase scanners are like cursors in a traditional database or Java iterators, except—
unlike the latter—they have to be closed after use. Scanners return rows in order. Users
obtain a scanner on an HBase table by calling HTable.getScanner(scan) where the
scan parameter is a configured instance of a Scan object. In the Scan instance, you can
pass the row at which to start and stop the scan, which columns in a row to return in
the row result, and optionally, a filter to run on the server side.[‡] The ResultScanner
Interface, the Interface returned when you call HTable.getScanner() absent Javadoc, is
as follows:

```
public interface ResultScanner extends Closeable, Iterable<Result> {
  public Result next() throws IOException;
  public Result [] next(int nbRows) throws IOException;
  public void close();
}
```

You can ask for the next row's results or a number of rows. Each invocation of
next() involves a trip back to the regionserver, so grabbing a bunch of rows at once can
make for significant performance savings.[§]

[‡] To learn more about the server-side filtering mechanism in HBase, see *http://hadoop.apache.org/hbase/docs/current/api/org/apache/hadoop/hbase/filter/package-summary.html*.

[§] The hbase.client.scanner.caching configuration option is set to 1 by default. You can also set how much to cache/prefetch on the Scan instance itself. Scanners will, under the covers, fetch this many results at a time, bringing them client side, and returning to the server to fetch the next batch only after the current batch has been exhausted. Higher caching values will enable faster scanning but will eat up more memory in the client. Also, avoid setting the caching so high that the time spent processing the batch client-side exceeds the scanner lease period. If a client fails to check back with the server before the scanner lease expires, the server will go ahead and garbage collect resources consumed by the scanner server-side. The default scanner lease is 60 seconds, the default value for hbase.regionserver.lease.period. Clients will see a *UnknownScannerException* if the scanner lease has expired.

The advantage of storing things as `Long.MAX_VALUE - stamp` may not be clear in the previous example. It has more use when you want to get the newest observations for a given offset and limit, which is often the case in web applications. If the observations were stored with the actual stamps, we would be able to get only the oldest observations for a given offset and limit efficiently. Getting the newest would mean getting all of them and then grabbing them off the end. One of the prime reasons for moving from RDBMS to HBase is to allow for these types of "early-out" scenarios.

HBase Versus RDBMS

HBase and other column-oriented databases are often compared to more traditional and popular relational databases or RDBMSs. Although they differ dramatically in their implementations and in what they set out to accomplish, the fact that they are potential solutions to the same problems means that despite their enormous differences, the comparison is a fair one to make.

As described previously, HBase is a distributed, column-oriented data storage system. It picks up where Hadoop left off by providing random reads and writes on top of HDFS. It has been designed from the ground up with a focus on scale in every direction: tall in numbers of rows (billions), wide in numbers of columns (millions), and to be horizontally partitioned and replicated across thousands of commodity nodes automatically. The table schemas mirror the physical storage, creating a system for efficient data structure serialization, storage, and retrieval. The burden is on the application developer to make use of this storage and retrieval in the right way.

Strictly speaking, an RDBMS is a database that follows Codd's 12 Rules (*http://en.wikipedia.org/wiki/Codd%27s_12_rules*). Typical RDBMSs are fixed-schema, row-oriented databases with ACID properties and a sophisticated SQL query engine. The emphasis is on strong consistency, referential integrity, abstraction from the physical layer, and complex queries through the SQL language. You can easily create secondary indexes, perform complex inner and outer joins, count, sum, sort, group, and page your data across a number of tables, rows, and columns.

For a majority of small- to medium-volume applications, there is no substitute for the ease of use, flexibility, maturity, and powerful feature set of available open source RDBMS solutions like MySQL and PostgreSQL. However, if you need to scale up in terms of dataset size, read/write concurrency, or both, you'll soon find that the conveniences of an RDBMS come at an enormous performance penalty and make distribution inherently difficult. The scaling of an RDBMS usually involves breaking Codd's rules, loosening ACID restrictions, forgetting conventional DBA wisdom, and on the way losing most of the desirable properties that made relational databases so convenient in the first place.

Successful Service

Here is a synopsis of how the typical RDBMS scaling story runs. The following list presumes a successful growing service:

Initial public launch
Move from local workstation to shared, remote hosted MySQL instance with a well-defined schema.

Service becomes more popular; too many reads hitting the database
Add memcached to cache common queries. Reads are now no longer strictly ACID; cached data must expire.

Service continues to grow in popularity; too many writes hitting the database
Scale MySQL vertically by buying a beefed up server with 16 cores, 128 GB of RAM, and banks of 15 k RPM hard drives. Costly.

New features increases query complexity; now we have too many joins
Denormalize your data to reduce joins. (That's not what they taught me in DBA school!)

Rising popularity swamps the server; things are too slow
Stop doing any server-side computations.

Some queries are still too slow
Periodically prematerialize the most complex queries, try to stop joining in most cases.

Reads are OK, but writes are getting slower and slower
Drop secondary indexes and triggers (no indexes?).

At this point, there are no clear solutions for how to solve your scaling problems. In any case, you'll need to begin to scale horizontally. You can attempt to build some type of partitioning on your largest tables, or look into some of the commercial solutions that provide multiple master capabilities.

Countless applications, businesses, and websites have successfully achieved scalable, fault-tolerant, and distributed data systems built on top of RDBMSs and are likely using many of the previous strategies. But what you end up with is something that is no longer a true RDBMS, sacrificing features and conveniences for compromises and complexities. Any form of slave replication or external caching introduces weak consistency into your now denormalized data. The inefficiency of joins and secondary indexes means almost all queries become primary key lookups. A multiwriter setup likely means no real joins at all and distributed transactions are a nightmare. There's now an incredibly complex network topology to manage with an entirely separate cluster for caching. Even with this system and the compromises made, you will still worry about your primary master crashing and the daunting possibility of having 10 times the data and 10 times the load in a few months.

HBase

Enter HBase, which has the following characteristics:

No real indexes
Rows are stored sequentially, as are the columns within each row. Therefore, no issues with index bloat, and insert performance is independent of table size.

Automatic partitioning
As your tables grow, they will automatically be split into regions and distributed across all available nodes.

Scale linearly and automatically with new nodes
Add a node, point it to the existing cluster, and run the regionserver. Regions will automatically rebalance and load will spread evenly.

Commodity hardware
Clusters are built on $1,000–$5,000 nodes rather than $50,000 nodes. RDBMSs are I/O hungry, requiring more costly hardware.

Fault tolerance
Lots of nodes means each is relatively insignificant. No need to worry about individual node downtime.

Batch processing
MapReduce integration allows fully parallel, distributed jobs against your data with locality awareness.

If you stay up at night worrying about your database (uptime, scale, or speed), then you should seriously consider making a jump from the RDBMS world to HBase. Utilize a solution that was intended to scale rather than a solution based on stripping down and throwing money at what used to work. With HBase, the software is free, the hardware is cheap, and the distribution is intrinsic.

Use Case: HBase at Streamy.com

Streamy.com is a real-time news aggregator and social sharing platform. With a broad feature set, we started out with a complex implementation on top of PostgreSQL. It's a terrific product with a great community and a beautiful codebase. We tried every trick in the book to keep things fast as we scaled, going so far as to modify the code directly to suit our needs. Originally taking advantage of all RDBMS goodies, we found that eventually, one by one, we had to let them all go. Along the way, our entire team became the DBA.

We did manage to solve many of the issues that we ran into, but there were two that eventually led to the decision to find another solution from outside the world of RDBMS.

Streamy crawls thousands of RSS feeds and aggregates hundreds of millions of items from them. In addition to having to store these items, one of our more complex queries reads a time-ordered list of all items from a set of sources. At the high end, this can run to several thousand sources and all of their items all in a single query.

Very large items tables

At first, this was a single items table, but the high number of secondary indexes made inserts and updates very slow. We started to divide items up into several one-to-one link tables to store other information, separating static fields from dynamic ones, grouping fields based on how they were queried, and denormalizing everything along the way. Even with these changes, single updates required rewriting the entire record, so tracking statistics on items was difficult to scale. The rewriting of records and having to update indexes along the way are intrinsic properties of the RDBMS we were using. They could not be decoupled. We partitioned our tables, which was not too difficult because of the natural partition of time, but the complexity got out of hand fast. We needed another solution!

Very large sort merges

Performing sorted merges of time-ordered lists is common in many Web 2.0 applications. An example SQL query might look like this:

```
SELECT id, stamp, type FROM streams
    WHERE type IN ('type1','type2','type3','type4',...,'typeN')
    ORDER BY stamp DESC LIMIT 10 OFFSET 0;
```

Assuming id is a primary key on streams, and that stamp and type have secondary indexes, an RDBMS query planner treats this query as follows:

```
MERGE (
    SELECT id, stamp, type FROM streams
      WHERE type = 'type1' ORDER BY stamp DESC,
    ...,
    SELECT id, stamp, type FROM streams
      WHERE type = 'typeN' ORDER BY stamp DESC
) ORDER BY stamp DESC LIMIT 10 OFFSET 0;
```

The problem here is that we are after only the top 10 IDs, but the query planner actually materializes an entire merge and then limits at the end. A simple heapsort across each of the types would allow you to "early out" once you have the top 10. In our case, each type could have tens of thousands of IDs in it, so materializing the entire list and sorting it was extremely slow and unnecessary. We actually went so far as to write a custom PL/Python script that performed a heapsort using a series of queries like the following:

```
SELECT id, stamp, type FROM streams
    WHERE type = 'typeN'
    ORDER BY stamp DESC LIMIT 1 OFFSET 0;
```

If we ended up taking from typeN (it was the next most recent in the heap), we would run another query:

```
SELECT id, stamp, type FROM streams
  WHERE type = 'typeN'
  ORDER BY stamp DESC LIMIT 1 OFFSET 1;
```

In nearly all cases, this outperformed the native SQL implementation and the query planner's strategy. In the worst cases for SQL, we were more than an order of magnitude faster using the Python procedure. We found ourselves continually trying to outsmart the query planner.

Again, at this point, we really needed another solution.

Life with HBase

Our RDBMS-based system was always capable of correctly implementing our requirements; the issue was scaling. When you start to focus on scale and performance rather than correctness, you end up short-cutting and optimizing for your domain-specific use cases everywhere possible. Once you start implementing your own solutions to your data problems, the overhead and complexity of an RDBMS gets in your way. The abstraction from the storage layer and ACID requirements are an enormous barrier and luxury that you cannot always afford when building for scale. HBase is a distributed, column-oriented, sorted map store and not much else. The only major part that is abstracted from the user is the distribution, and that's exactly what we don't want to deal with. Business logic, on the other hand, is very specialized and optimized. With HBase not trying to solve all of our problems, we've been able to solve them better ourselves and rely on HBase for scaling our storage, not our logic. It was an extremely liberating experience to be able to focus on our applications and logic rather than the scaling of the data itself.

We currently have tables with hundreds of millions of rows and tens of thousands of columns; the thought of storing billions of rows and millions of columns is exciting, not scary.

Praxis

In this section, we discuss some of the common issues users run into when running an HBase cluster under load.

Versions

Up until HBase 0.20, HBase aligned its versioning with that of Hadoop. A particular HBase version would run on any Hadoop that had a matching minor version, where minor version in this context is considered the number between the periods (e.g., 20 is the minor version of an HBase 0.20.5). HBase 0.20.5 would run on an Hadoop 0.20.2, but HBase 0.19.5 would not run on Hadoop 0.20.0.

With HBase 0.90,[||] the version relationship was broken. The Hadoop release cycle has slowed and no longer aligns with that of HBase developments. Also, the intent is that now a particular HBase version can run on multiple versions of Hadoop. For example, HBase 0.90.x will work with both Hadoop 0.20.x and 0.21.x.

This said, ensure you are running compatible versions of Hadoop and HBase. Check the requirements section of your download. Incompatible versions will throw an exception complaining about the version mismatch, if you are lucky. If they cannot talk to each sufficiently to pass versions, you may see your HBase cluster hang indefinitely, soon after startup. The mismatch exception or HBase hang can also happen on upgrade if older versions of either HBase or Hadoop can still be found on the classpath because of imperfect cleanup of the old software.

HDFS

HBase's use of HDFS is very different from how it's used by MapReduce. In MapReduce, generally, HDFS files are opened, with their content streamed through a map task and then closed. In HBase, data files are opened on cluster startup and kept open so that we avoid paying the file open costs on each access. Because of this, HBase tends to see issues not normally encountered by MapReduce clients:

Running out of file descriptors
Because we keep files open, on a loaded cluster, it doesn't take long before we run into system- and Hadoop-imposed limits. For instance, say we have a cluster that has three nodes each running an instance of a datanode and a regionserver and we're running an upload into a table that is currently at 100 regions and 10 column families. Allow that each column family has on average two flush files. Doing the math, we can have 100 × 10 × 2, or 2,000, files open at any one time. Add to this total miscellaneous other descriptors consumed by outstanding scanners and Java libraries. Each open file consumes at least one descriptor over on the remote datanode. The default limit on the number of file descriptors per process is 1,024. When we exceed the filesystem *ulimit*, we'll see the complaint about *Too many open files* in logs, but often you'll first see indeterminate behavior in HBase. The fix requires increasing the file descriptor *ulimit* count.[#] You can verify that the HBase process is running with sufficient file descriptors by looking at the first few lines of a regionservers log. It emits vitals such as the JVM being used and environment settings such as the file descriptor *ulimit*.

|| Why 0.90? We wanted there to be no confusion that a break had been made, so we put a large gap between our new versioning and that of Hadoop's.

#See the HBase FAQ (*http://wiki.apache.org/hadoop/Hbase/FAQ*) for how to up the *ulimit* on your cluster.

Running out of datanode threads

Similarly, the Hadoop datanode has an upper bound of 256 on the number of threads it can run at any one time. Given the same table statistics quoted in the preceding bullet, it's easy to see how we can exceed this upper bound relatively early, given that in the datanode as of this writing each open connection to a file block consumes a thread. If you look in the datanode log, you'll see a complaint like *xceiverCount 258 exceeds the limit of concurrent xcievers 256* but again, you'll likely see HBase act erratically before you encounter this log entry. Increase the `dfs.datanode.max.xcievers` (note that the property name is misspelled) count in HDFS and restart your cluster.[*]

Sync

You must run HBase on an HDFS that has a working sync. Otherwise, you will lose data. This means running HBase on Hadoop 0.21.x or on a Hadoop that has been built from the `branch-0.20-append`[†] branch, which adds a working sync/append to Hadoop 0.20.[‡]

UI

HBase runs a web server on the master to present a view on the state of your running cluster. By default, it listens on port 60010. The master UI displays a list of basic attributes such as software versions, cluster load, request rates, lists of cluster tables, and participating regionservers. Click on a regionserver in the master UI and you are taken to the web server running on the individual regionserver. It lists the regions this server is carrying and basic metrics such as resources consumed and request rates.

Metrics

Hadoop has a metrics system that can be used to emit vitals over a period to a *context* (this is covered in "Metrics" on page 306). Enabling Hadoop metrics, and in particular tying them to Ganglia or emitting them via JMX, will give you views on what is happening on your cluster currently and in the recent past. HBase also adds metrics of its own—request rates, counts of vitals, resources used—that can be caught by a Hadoop context. See the file *hadoop-metrics.properties* under the HBase *conf* directory.[§]

---

[*] See the HBase troubleshooting guide (*http://wiki.apache.org/hadoop/Hbase/Troubleshooting*) for more detail on this issue.

[†] You can find the `branch-0.20-append` branch at *http://svn.apache.org/repos/asf/hadoop/common/branches/branch-0.20-append/*

[‡] On regionserver crash, before Hadoop 0.21 or 0.20-append, edits written to the commit log kept in HDFS were not recoverable as files that had not been properly closed lost all edits no matter how much had been written them at crash time.

[§] Yes, this file is named for Hadoop, though it's for setting up HBase metrics.

Schema Design

HBase tables are like those in an RDBMS, except that cells are versioned, rows are sorted, and columns can be added on the fly by the client as long as the column family they belong to preexists. These factors should be considered when designing schemas for HBase, but far and away the most important concern designing schemas is consideration of how the data will be accessed. All access is via primary key so the key design should lend itself to how the data is going to be queried. The other property to keep in mind when designing schemas is that a defining attribute of column(-family)-oriented stores (*http://en.wikipedia.org/wiki/Column-oriented_DBMS*), like HBase, is that it can host wide and sparsely populated tables at no incurred cost.‖

Joins

There is no native database join facility in HBase, but wide tables can make it so that there is no need for database joins pulling from secondary or tertiary tables. A wide row can sometimes be made to hold all data that pertains to a particular primary key.

Row keys

Take time designing your row key. In the weather data example in this chapter, the compound row key has a station prefix that served to group temperatures by station. The reversed timestamp suffix made it so temperatures could be scanned ordered from most recent to oldest. A smart compound key can be used to cluster data in ways amenable to how it will be accessed.

Designing compound keys, you may have to zero-pad number components so row keys sort properly. Otherwise, you will run into the issue where 10 sorts before 2 when only byte-order is considered (02 sorts before 10).

If your keys are integers, use a binary representation rather than persist the string version of a number—it consumes less space.

Counters

At StumbleUpon, the first production feature deployed on HBase was keeping counters for `stumbleupon.com` frontend. Counters used to be kept in MySQL, but the rate of change was such that drops were frequent and the load imposed by the counter writes was such that web designers self-imposed limits on what was counted. Using the `incrementColumnValue()` method on `org.apache.hadoop.hbase.HTable`, counters can be incremented many thousands of times a second.

‖ "Column-Stores for Wide and Sparse Data" (*http://db.csail.mit.edu/projects/cstore/abadicidr07.pdf*) by Daniel J. Abadi.

Bulk Load

HBase has an efficient facility for bulk loading HBase by writing its internal data format directly into the filesystem from MapReduce. Going this route, it's possible to load an HBase instance at rates that are an order of magnitude or more beyond those attainable by writing via the HBase client API. The facility is described at *http://hbase.apache.org/docs/current/bulk-loads.html*. It's also possible to bulk load into a live table.

ZooKeeper

So far in this book, we have been studying large-scale data processing. This chapter is different: it is about building general distributed applications using Hadoop's distributed coordination service, called ZooKeeper.

Writing distributed applications is hard. It's hard primarily because of partial failure. When a message is sent across the network between two nodes and the network fails, the sender does not know whether the receiver got the message. It may have gotten through before the network failed, or it may not have. Or perhaps the receiver's process died. The only way that the sender can find out what happened is to reconnect to the receiver and ask it. This is partial failure: when we don't even know if an operation failed.

ZooKeeper can't make partial failures go away, since they are intrinsic to distributed systems. It certainly does not hide partial failures, either.* But what ZooKeeper does do is give you a set of tools to build distributed applications that can safely handle partial failures.

ZooKeeper also has the following characteristics:

ZooKeeper is simple
> ZooKeeper is, at its core, a stripped-down filesystem that exposes a few simple operations, and some extra abstractions such as ordering and notifications.

ZooKeeper is expressive
> The ZooKeeper primitives are a rich set of building blocks that can be used to build a large class of coordination data structures and protocols. Examples include: distributed queues, distributed locks, and leader election among a group of peers.

---

* This is the message of J. Waldo et al., "A Note on Distributed Computing," (1994), *http://research.sun.com/ techrep/1994/smli_tr-94-29.pdf*. That is, distributed programming is fundamentally different from local programming, and the differences cannot simply be papered over.

ZooKeeper is highly available

ZooKeeper runs on a collection of machines and is designed to be highly available, so applications can depend on it. ZooKeeper can help you avoid introducing single points of failure into your system, so you can build a reliable application.

ZooKeeper facilitates loosely coupled interactions

ZooKeeper interactions support participants that do not need to know about one another. For example, ZooKeeper can be used as a rendezvous mechanism so that processes that otherwise don't know of each other's existence (or network details) can discover and interact with each other. Coordinating parties may not even be contemporaneous, since one process may leave a message in ZooKeeper that is read by another after the first has shut down.

ZooKeeper is a library

ZooKeeper provides an open source, shared repository of implementations and recipes of common coordination patterns. Individual programmers are spared the burden of writing common protocols themselves (which are often difficult to get right). Over time, the community can add to and improve the libraries, which is to everyone's benefit.

ZooKeeper is highly performant, too. At Yahoo!, where it was created, ZooKeeper's throughput has been benchmarked at over 10,000 operations per second for write-dominant workloads. For workloads where reads dominate, which is the norm, the throughput is several times higher.[†]

Installing and Running ZooKeeper

When trying out ZooKeeper for the first time, it's simplest to run it in standalone mode with a single ZooKeeper server. You can do this on a development machine, for example. ZooKeeper requires Java 6 to run, so make sure you have it installed first. You don't need Cygwin to run ZooKeeper on Windows, since there are Windows versions of the ZooKeeper scripts. (Windows is supported only as a development platform, not as a production platform.)

Download a stable release of ZooKeeper from the Apache ZooKeeper releases page at *http://hadoop.apache.org/zookeeper/releases.html*, and unpack the tarball in a suitable location:

```
% tar xzf zookeeper-x.y.z.tar.gz
```

ZooKeeper provides a few binaries to run and interact with the service, and it's convenient to put the directory containing the binaries on your command-line path:

[†] Detailed benchmarks are available in the excellent paper "ZooKeeper: Wait-free coordination for Internet-scale systems," by Patrick Hunt, Mahadev Konar, Flavio P. Junqueira, and Benjamin Reed (USENIX Annual Technology Conference, 2010).

```
% export ZOOKEEPER_INSTALL=/home/tom/zookeeper-x.y.z
% export PATH=$PATH:$ZOOKEEPER_INSTALL/bin
```

Before running the ZooKeeper service, we need to set up a configuration file. The configuration file is conventionally called *zoo.cfg* and placed in the *conf* subdirectory (although you can also place it in */etc/zookeeper*, or in the directory defined by the ZOOCFGDIR environment variable, if set). Here's an example:

```
tickTime=2000
dataDir=/Users/tom/zookeeper
clientPort=2181
```

This is a standard Java properties file, and the three properties defined in this example are the minimum required for running ZooKeeper in standalone mode. Briefly, tickTime is the basic time unit in ZooKeeper (specified in milliseconds), dataDir is the local filesystem location where ZooKeeper stores persistent data, and clientPort is the port the ZooKeeper listens on for client connections (2181 is a common choice). You should change dataDir to an appropriate setting for your system.

With a suitable configuration defined, we are now ready to start a local ZooKeeper server:

```
% zkServer.sh start
```

To check whether ZooKeeper is running, send the ruok command ("Are you OK?") to the client port using nc (telnet works, too):

```
% echo ruok | nc localhost 2181
imok
```

That's ZooKeeper saying, "I'm OK." There are other commands, known as the "four-letter words," for interacting with ZooKeeper. Most are queries: dump lists sessions and ephemeral znodes, envi lists server properties, reqs lists outstanding requests, and stat lists service statistics and connected clients. However, you can also update Zoo-Keeper's state: srst resets the service statistics, and kill shuts down ZooKeeper if issued from the host running the ZooKeeper server.

For more extensive ZooKeeper monitoring (including more four-letter words), have a look at its JMX support, which is covered in the ZooKeeper documentation (linked from *http://hadoop.apache.org/zookeeper/*).

An Example

Imagine a group of servers that provide some service to clients. We want clients to be able to locate one of the servers, so they can use the service. One of the challenges is maintaining the list of servers in the group.

The membership list clearly cannot be stored on a single node in the network, as the failure of that node would mean the failure of the whole system (we would like the list to be highly available). Suppose for a moment that we had a robust way of storing the list. We would still have the problem of how to remove a server from the list if it failed. Some process needs to be responsible for removing failed servers, but note that it can't be the servers themselves, since they are no longer running!

What we are describing is not a passive distributed data structure, but an active one, and one that can change the state of an entry when some external event occurs. Zoo-Keeper provides this service, so let's see how to build this group membership application (as it is known) with it.

Group Membership in ZooKeeper

One way of understanding ZooKeeper is to think of it as providing a high-availability filesystem. It doesn't have files and directories, but a unified concept of a node, called a *znode*, which acts both as a container of data (like a file) and a container of other znodes (like a directory). Znodes form a hierarchical namespace, and a natural way to build a membership list is to create a parent znode with the name of the group and child znodes with the name of the group members (servers). This is shown in Figure 14-1.

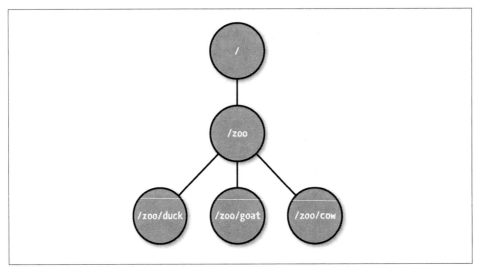

Figure 14-1. ZooKeeper znodes

In this example, we won't store data in any of the znodes, but in a real application, you could imagine storing data about the members in their znodes, such as hostname.

Creating the Group

Let's introduce ZooKeeper's Java API by writing a program to create a znode for the group, */zoo* in this example. See Example 14-1.

Example 14-1. A program to create a znode representing a group in ZooKeeper

```
public class CreateGroup implements Watcher {

  private static final int SESSION_TIMEOUT = 5000;

  private ZooKeeper zk;
  private CountDownLatch connectedSignal = new CountDownLatch(1);

  public void connect(String hosts) throws IOException, InterruptedException {
    zk = new ZooKeeper(hosts, SESSION_TIMEOUT, this);
    connectedSignal.await();
  }

  @Override
  public void process(WatchedEvent event) { // Watcher interface
    if (event.getState() == KeeperState.SyncConnected) {
      connectedSignal.countDown();
    }
  }

  public void create(String groupName) throws KeeperException,
      InterruptedException {
    String path = "/" + groupName;
    String createdPath = zk.create(path, null/*data*/, Ids.OPEN_ACL_UNSAFE,
        CreateMode.PERSISTENT);
    System.out.println("Created " + createdPath);
  }

  public void close() throws InterruptedException {
    zk.close();
  }

  public static void main(String[] args) throws Exception {
    CreateGroup createGroup = new CreateGroup();
    createGroup.connect(args[0]);
    createGroup.create(args[1]);
    createGroup.close();
  }
}
```

When the `main()` method is run, it creates a `CreateGroup` instance and then calls its `connect()` method. This method instantiates a new `ZooKeeper` object, the main class of the client API and the one that maintains the connection between the client and the ZooKeeper service. The constructor takes three arguments: the first is the host address (and optional port, which defaults to 2181) of the ZooKeeper service;[‡] the second is the session timeout in milliseconds (which we set to 5 seconds), explained in more detail later; and the third is an instance of a `Watcher` object. The `Watcher` object receives

---

[‡] For a replicated ZooKeeper service, this parameter is the comma-separated list of servers (host and optional port) in the ensemble.

callbacks from ZooKeeper to inform it of various events. In this case, CreateGroup is a Watcher, so we pass this to the ZooKeeper constructor.

When a ZooKeeper instance is created, it starts a thread to connect to the ZooKeeper service. The call to the constructor returns immediately, so it is important to wait for the connection to be established before using the ZooKeeper object. We make use of Java's CountDownLatch class (in the java.util.concurrent package) to block until the ZooKeeper instance is ready. This is where the Watcher comes in. The Watcher interface has a single method:

```
public void process(WatchedEvent event);
```

When the client has connected to ZooKeeper, the Watcher receives a call to its process() method with an event indicating that it has connected. On receiving a connection event (represented by the Watcher.Event.KeeperState enum, with value SyncConnected), we decrement the counter in the CountDownLatch, using its count Down() method. The latch was created with a count of one, representing the number of events that need to occur before it releases all waiting threads. After calling count Down() once, the counter reaches zero and the await() method returns.

The connect() method has now returned, and the next method to be invoked on the CreateGroup is the create() method. In this method, we create a new ZooKeeper znode using the create() method on the ZooKeeper instance. The arguments it takes are the path (represented by a string), the contents of the znode (a byte array, null here), an access control list (or ACL for short, which here is a completely open ACL, allowing any client to read or write the znode), and the nature of the znode to be created.

Znodes may be ephemeral or persistent. An ephemeral znode will be deleted by the ZooKeeper service when the client that created it disconnects, either by explicitly disconnecting or if the client terminates for whatever reason. A persistent znode, on the other hand, is not deleted when the client disconnects. We want the znode representing a group to live longer than the lifetime of the program that creates it, so we create a persistent znode.

The return value of the create() method is the path that was created by ZooKeeper. We use it to print a message that the path was successfully created. We will see how the path returned by create() may differ from the one passed into the method when we look at sequential znodes.

To see the program in action, we need to have ZooKeeper running on the local machine, and then we can type:

```
% export CLASSPATH=build/classes:$ZOOKEEPER_INSTALL/*:$ZOOKEEPER_INSTALL/lib/*:\
$ZOOKEEPER_INSTALL/conf
% java CreateGroup localhost zoo
Created /zoo
```

Joining a Group

The next part of the application is a program to register a member in a group. Each member will run as a program and join a group. When the program exits, it should be removed from the group, which we can do by creating an ephemeral znode that represents it in the ZooKeeper namespace.

The JoinGroup program implements this idea, and its listing is in Example 14-2. The logic for creating and connecting to a ZooKeeper instance has been refactored into a base class, ConnectionWatcher, and appears in Example 14-3.

Example 14-2. A program that joins a group

```
public class JoinGroup extends ConnectionWatcher {

  public void join(String groupName, String memberName) throws KeeperException,
      InterruptedException {
    String path = "/" + groupName + "/" + memberName;
    String createdPath = zk.create(path, null/*data*/, Ids.OPEN_ACL_UNSAFE,
      CreateMode.EPHEMERAL);
    System.out.println("Created " + createdPath);
  }

  public static void main(String[] args) throws Exception {
    JoinGroup joinGroup = new JoinGroup();
    joinGroup.connect(args[0]);
    joinGroup.join(args[1], args[2]);

    // stay alive until process is killed or thread is interrupted
    Thread.sleep(Long.MAX_VALUE);
  }
}
```

Example 14-3. A helper class that waits for the connection to ZooKeeper to be established

```
public class ConnectionWatcher implements Watcher {

  private static final int SESSION_TIMEOUT = 5000;

  protected ZooKeeper zk;
  private CountDownLatch connectedSignal = new CountDownLatch(1);

  public void connect(String hosts) throws IOException, InterruptedException {
    zk = new ZooKeeper(hosts, SESSION_TIMEOUT, this);
    connectedSignal.await();
  }

  @Override
  public void process(WatchedEvent event) {
    if (event.getState() == KeeperState.SyncConnected) {
      connectedSignal.countDown();
    }
  }

  public void close() throws InterruptedException {
```

```
      zk.close();
  }
}
```

The code for JoinGroup is very similar to CreateGroup. It creates an ephemeral znode as a child of the group znode in its join() method, then simulates doing work of some kind by sleeping until the process is forcibly terminated. Later, you will see that upon termination, the ephemeral znode is removed by ZooKeeper.

Listing Members in a Group

Now we need a program to find the members in a group (see Example 14-4).

Example 14-4. A program to list the members in a group

```
public class ListGroup extends ConnectionWatcher {

  public void list(String groupName) throws KeeperException,
      InterruptedException {
    String path = "/" + groupName;

    try {
      List<String> children = zk.getChildren(path, false);
      if (children.isEmpty()) {
        System.out.printf("No members in group %s\n", groupName);
        System.exit(1);
      }
      for (String child : children) {
        System.out.println(child);
      }
    } catch (KeeperException.NoNodeException e) {
      System.out.printf("Group %s does not exist\n", groupName);
      System.exit(1);
    }
  }

  public static void main(String[] args) throws Exception {
    ListGroup listGroup = new ListGroup();
    listGroup.connect(args[0]);
    listGroup.list(args[1]);
    listGroup.close();
  }
}
```

In the list() method, we call getChildren() with a znode path and a watch flag to retrieve a list of child paths for the znode, which we print out. Placing a watch on a znode causes the registered Watcher to be triggered if the znode changes state. Although we're not using it here, watching a znode's children would permit a program to get notifications of members joining or leaving the group, or of the group being deleted.

We catch KeeperException.NoNodeException, which is thrown in the case when the group's znode does not exist.

Let's see `ListGroup` in action. As expected, the zoo group is empty, since we haven't added any members yet:

```
% java ListGroup localhost zoo
No members in group zoo
```

We can use `JoinGroup` to add some members. We launch them as background processes, since they don't terminate on their own (due to the sleep statement):

```
% java JoinGroup localhost zoo duck &
% java JoinGroup localhost zoo cow &
% java JoinGroup localhost zoo goat &
% goat_pid=$!
```

The last line saves the process ID of the Java process running the program that adds goat as a member. We need to remember the ID so that we can kill the process in a moment, after checking the members:

```
% java ListGroup localhost zoo
goat
duck
cow
```

To remove a member, we kill its process:

```
%
kill $goat_pid
```

And a few seconds later, it has disappeared from the group because the process's Zoo-Keeper session has terminated (the timeout was set to 5 seconds) and its associated ephemeral node has been removed:

```
% java ListGroup localhost zoo
duck
cow
```

Let's stand back and see what we've built here. We have a way of building up a list of a group of nodes that are participating in a distributed system. The nodes may have no knowledge of each other. A client that wants to use the nodes in the list to perform some work, for example, can discover the nodes without them being aware of the client's existence.

Finally, note that group membership is not a substitution for handling network errors when communicating with a node. Even if a node is a group member, communications with it may fail, and such failures must be handled in the usual ways (retrying, trying a different member of the group, and so on).

ZooKeeper command-line tools

ZooKeeper comes with a command-line tool for interacting with the ZooKeeper namespace. We can use it to list the znodes under the */zoo* znode as follows:

```
% zkCli.sh localhost ls /zoo
Processing ls
```

```
WatchedEvent: Server state change. New state: SyncConnected
[duck, cow]
```

You can run the command without arguments to display usage instructions.

Deleting a Group

To round off the example, let's see how to delete a group. The ZooKeeper class provides a delete() method that takes a path and a version number. ZooKeeper will delete a znode only if the version number specified is the same as the version number of the znode it is trying to delete, an optimistic locking mechanism that allows clients to detect conflicts over znode modification. You can bypass the version check, however, by using a version number of -1 to delete the znode regardless of its version number.

There is no recursive delete operation in ZooKeeper, so you have to delete child znodes before parents. This is what we do in the DeleteGroup class, which will remove a group and all its members (Example 14-5).

Example 14-5. A program to delete a group and its members

```
public class DeleteGroup extends ConnectionWatcher {

  public void delete(String groupName) throws KeeperException,
      InterruptedException {
    String path = "/" + groupName;

    try {
      List<String> children = zk.getChildren(path, false);
      for (String child : children) {
        zk.delete(path + "/" + child, -1);
      }
      zk.delete(path, -1);
    } catch (KeeperException.NoNodeException e) {
      System.out.printf("Group %s does not exist\n", groupName);
      System.exit(1);
    }
  }

  public static void main(String[] args) throws Exception {
    DeleteGroup deleteGroup = new DeleteGroup();
    deleteGroup.connect(args[0]);
    deleteGroup.delete(args[1]);
    deleteGroup.close();
  }
}
```

Finally, we can delete the zoo group that we created earlier:

```
% java DeleteGroup localhost zoo
% java ListGroup localhost zoo
Group zoo does not exist
```

The ZooKeeper Service

ZooKeeper is a highly available, high-performance coordination service. In this section, we look at the nature of the service it provides: its model, operations, and implementation.

Data Model

ZooKeeper maintains a hierarchical tree of nodes called znodes. A znode stores data and has an associated ACL. ZooKeeper is designed for coordination (which typically uses small data files), not high-volume data storage, so there is a limit of 1 MB on the amount of data that may be stored in any znode.

Data access is atomic. A client reading the data stored at a znode will never receive only some of the data; either the data will be delivered in its entirety, or the read will fail. Similarly, a write will replace all the data associated with a znode. ZooKeeper guarantees that the write will either succeed or fail; there is no such thing as a partial write, where only some of the data written by the client is stored. ZooKeeper does not support an append operation. These characteristics contrast with HDFS, which is designed for high-volume data storage, with streaming data access, and provides an append operation.

Znodes are referenced by paths, which in ZooKeeper are represented as slash-delimited Unicode character strings, like filesystem paths in Unix. Paths must be absolute, so they must begin with a slash character. Furthermore, they are canonical, which means that each path has a single representation, and so paths do not undergo resolution. For example, in Unix, a file with the path /a/b can equivalently be referred to by the path /a/./b, since "." refers to the current directory at the point it is encountered in the path. In ZooKeeper, "." does not have this special meaning and is actually illegal as a path component (as is ".." for the parent of the current directory).

Path components are composed of Unicode characters, with a few restrictions (these are spelled out in the ZooKeeper reference documentation). The string "zookeeper" is a reserved word and may not be used as a path component. In particular, ZooKeeper uses the /zookeeper subtree to store management information, such as information on quotas.

Note that paths are not URIs, and they are represented in the Java API by a `java.lang.String`, rather than the Hadoop `Path` class (or by the `java.net.URI` class, for that matter).

Znodes have some properties that are very useful for building distributed applications, which we discuss in the following sections.

Ephemeral znodes

Znodes can be one of two types: ephemeral or persistent. A znode's type is set at creation time and may not be changed later. An ephemeral znode is deleted by ZooKeeper when the creating client's session ends. By contrast, a persistent znode is not tied to the client's session and is deleted only when explicitly deleted by a client (not necessarily the one that created it). An ephemeral znode may not have children, not even ephemeral ones.

Even though ephemeral nodes are tied to a client session, they are visible to all clients (subject to their ACL policy, of course).

Ephemeral znodes are ideal for building applications that need to know when certain distributed resources are available. The example earlier in this chapter uses ephemeral znodes to implement a group membership service, so any process can discover the members of the group at any particular time.

Sequence numbers

A *sequential* znode is given a sequence number by ZooKeeper as a part of its name. If a znode is created with the sequential flag set, then the value of a monotonically increasing counter (maintained by the parent znode) is appended to its name.

If a client asks to create a sequential znode with the name */a/b-*, for example, then the znode created may actually have the name */a/b-3*.[§] If, later on, another sequential znode with the name */a/b-* is created, then it will be given a unique name with a larger value of the counter—for example, */a/b-5*. In the Java API, the actual path given to sequential znodes is communicated back to the client as the return value of the `create()` call.

Sequence numbers can be used to impose a global ordering on events in a distributed system, and may be used by the client to infer the ordering. In "A Lock Service" on page 470, you will learn how to use sequential znodes to build a shared lock.

Watches

Watches allow clients to get notifications when a znode changes in some way. Watches are set by operations on the ZooKeeper service, and are triggered by other operations on the service. For example, a client might call the `exists` operation on a znode, placing a watch on it at the same time. If the znode doesn't exist, then the `exists` operation will return false. If, some time later, the znode is created by a second client, then the watch is triggered, notifying the first client of the znode's creation. You will see precisely which operations trigger others in the next section.

Watchers are triggered only once.[||] To receive multiple notifications, a client needs to reregister the watch. If the client in the previous example wishes to receive further

---

[§] It is conventional (but not required) to have a trailing dash on path names for sequential nodes, to make their sequence numbers easy to read and parse (by the application).

[||] Except for callbacks for connection events, which do not need reregistration.

notifications for the znode's existence (to be notified when it is deleted, for example), it needs to call the `exists` operation again to set a new watch.

There is an example in "A Configuration Service" on page 463 demonstrating how to use watches to update configuration across a cluster.

Operations

There are nine basic operations in ZooKeeper, listed in Table 14-1.

Table 14-1. Operations in the ZooKeeper service

Operation	Description
create	Creates a znode (the parent znode must already exist)
delete	Deletes a znode (the znode must not have any children)
exists	Tests whether a znode exists and retrieves its metadata
getACL, setACL	Gets/sets the ACL for a znode
getChildren	Gets a list of the children of a znode
getData, setData	Gets/sets the data associated with a znode
sync	Synchronizes a client's view of a znode with ZooKeeper

Update operations in ZooKeeper are conditional. A `delete` or `setData` operation has to specify the version number of the znode that is being updated (which is found from a previous `exists` call). If the version number does not match, the update will fail. Updates are a nonblocking operation, so a client that loses an update (because another process updated the znode in the meantime) can decide whether to try again or take some other action, and it can do so without blocking the progress of any other process.

Although ZooKeeper can be viewed as a filesystem, there are some filesystem primitives that it does away with in the name of simplicity. Because files are small and are written and read in their entirety, there is no need to provide open, close, or seek operations.

 The `sync` operation is not like `fsync()` in POSIX filesystems. As mentioned earlier, writes in ZooKeeper are atomic, and a successful write operation is guaranteed to have been written to persistent storage on a majority of ZooKeeper servers. However, it is permissible for reads to lag the latest state of ZooKeeper service, and the `sync` operation exists to allow a client to bring itself up-to-date. This topic is covered in more detail in the section on "Consistency" on page 458.

APIs

There are two core language bindings for ZooKeeper clients, one for Java and one for C; there are also `contrib` bindings for Perl, Python, and REST clients. For each binding, there is a choice between performing operations synchronously or asynchronously.

We've already seen the synchronous Java API. Here's the signature for the `exists` operation, which returns a `Stat` object encapsulating the znode's metadata, or `null` if the znode doesn't exist:

```
public Stat exists(String path, Watcher watcher) throws KeeperException,
        InterruptedException
```

The asynchronous equivalent, which is also found in the `ZooKeeper` class, looks like this:

```
public void exists(String path, Watcher watcher, StatCallback cb, Object ctx)
```

In the Java API, all the asynchronous methods have `void` return types, since the result of the operation is conveyed via a callback. The caller passes a callback implementation, whose method is invoked when a response is received from ZooKeeper. In this case, the callback is the `StatCallback` interface, which has the following method:

```
public void processResult(int rc, String path, Object ctx, Stat stat);
```

The `rc` argument is the return code, corresponding to the codes defined by `KeeperException`. A nonzero code represents an exception, in which case the `stat` parameter will be `null`. The `path` and `ctx` arguments correspond to the equivalent arguments passed by the client to the `exists()` method, and can be used to identify the request for which this callback is a response. The `ctx` parameter can be an arbitrary object that may be used by the client when the path does not give enough context to disambiguate the request. If not needed, it may be set to `null`.

There are actually two C shared libraries. The single-threaded library, `zookeeper_st`, supports only the asynchronous API and is intended for platforms where the `pthread` library is not available or stable. Most developers will use the multithreaded library, `zookeeper_mt`, as it supports both the synchronous and asynchronous APIs. For details on how to build and use the C API, please refer to the *README* file in the *src/c* directory of the ZooKeeper distribution.

Should I Use the Synchronous or Asynchronous API?

Both APIs offer the same functionality, so the one you use is largely a matter of style. The asynchronous API is appropriate if you have an event-driven programming model, for example.

The asynchronous API allows you to pipeline requests, which in some scenarios can offer better throughput. Imagine that you want to read a large batch of znodes and process them independently. Using the synchronous API, each read would block until it returned, whereas with the asynchronous API, you can fire off all the asynchronous reads very quickly and process the responses in a separate thread as they come back.

Watch triggers

The read operations `exists`, `getChildren`, and `getData` may have watches set on them, and the watches are triggered by write operations: `create`, `delete`, and `setData`. ACL operations do not participate in watches. When a watch is triggered, a watch event is generated, and the watch event's type depends both on the watch and the operation that triggered it:

- A watch set on an `exists` operation will be triggered when the znode being watched is created, deleted, or has its data updated.

- A watch set on a `getData` operation will be triggered when the znode being watched is deleted or has its data updated. No trigger can occur on creation, since the znode must already exist for the `getData` operation to succeed.

- A watch set on a `getChildren` operation will be triggered when a child of the znode being watched is created or deleted, or when the znode itself is deleted. You can tell whether the znode or its child was deleted by looking at the watch event type: `NodeDeleted` shows the znode was deleted, and `NodeChildrenChanged` indicates that it was a child that was deleted.

The combinations are summarized in Table 14-2.

Table 14-2. Watch creation operations and their corresponding triggers

Watch creation	Watch trigger				
	create		delete		setData
	znode	child	znode	child	
exists	NodeCreated		NodeDeleted		NodeData Changed
getData			NodeDeleted		NodeData Changed
getChildren		NodeChildren Changed	NodeDeleted	NodeChildren Changed	

A watch event includes the path of the znode that was involved in the event, so for `NodeCreated` and `NodeDeleted` events, you can tell which node was created or deleted simply by inspecting the path. To discover which children have changed after a `Node ChildrenChanged` event, you need to call `getChildren` again to retrieve the new list of children. Similarly, to discover the new data for a `NodeDataChanged` event, you need to call `getData`. In both of these cases, the state of the znodes may have changed between receiving the watch event and performing the read operation, so you should bear this in mind when writing applications.

ACLs

A znode is created with a list of ACLs, which determines who can perform certain operations on it.

ACLs depend on authentication, the process by which the client identifies itself to ZooKeeper. There are a few authentication schemes that ZooKeeper provides:

digest
> The client is identified by a username and password.

host
> The client is identified by his hostname.

ip
> The client is identified by his IP address.

Clients may authenticate themselves after establishing a ZooKeeper session. Authentication is optional, although a znode's ACL may require an authenticated client, in which case the client must authenticate itself to access the znode. Here is an example of using the *digest* scheme to authenticate with a username and password:

```
zk.addAuthInfo("digest", "tom:secret".getBytes());
```

An ACL is the combination of an authentication scheme, an identity for that scheme, and a set of permissions. For example, if we wanted to give clients in the domain *example.com* read access to a znode, we would set an ACL on the znode with the host scheme, an ID of example.com, and READ permission. In Java, we would create the ACL object as follows:

```
new ACL(Perms.READ, new Id("host", "example.com"));
```

The full set of permissions are listed in Table 14-3. Note that the exists operation is not governed by an ACL permission, so any client may call exists to find the Stat for a znode or to discover that a znode does not in fact exist.

Table 14-3. ACL permissions

ACL permission	Permitted operations
CREATE	create (a child znode)
READ	getChildren
	getData
WRITE	setData
DELETE	delete (a child znode)
ADMIN	setACL

There are a number of predefined ACLs defined in the `ZooDefs.Ids` class, including `OPEN_ACL_UNSAFE`, which gives all permissions (except `ADMIN` permission) to everyone.

In addition, ZooKeeper has a pluggable authentication mechanism, which makes it possible to integrate third-party authentication systems if needed.

Implementation

The ZooKeeper service can run in two modes. In *standalone mode*, there is a single ZooKeeper server, which is useful for testing due to its simplicity (it can even be embedded in unit tests), but provides no guarantees of high-availability or resilience. In production, ZooKeeper runs in *replicated mode*, on a cluster of machines called an *ensemble*. ZooKeeper achieves high-availability through replication, and can provide a service as long as a majority of the machines in the ensemble are up. For example, in a five-node ensemble, any two machines can fail and the service will still work because a majority of three remain. Note that a six-node ensemble can also tolerate only two machines failing, since with three failures the remaining three do not constitute a majority of the six. For this reason, it is usual to have an odd number of machines in an ensemble.

Conceptually, ZooKeeper is very simple: all it has to do is ensure that every modification to the tree of znodes is replicated to a majority of the ensemble. If a minority of the machines fail, then a minimum of one machine will survive with the latest state. The other remaining replicas will eventually catch up with this state.

The implementation of this simple idea, however, is nontrivial. ZooKeeper uses a protocol called Zab that runs in two phases, which may be repeated indefinitely:

Phase 1: Leader election
> The machines in an ensemble go through a process of electing a distinguished member, called the *leader*. The other machines are termed *followers*. This phase is finished once a majority (or *quorum*) of followers have synchronized their state with the leader.

Phase 2: Atomic broadcast
> All write requests are forwarded to the leader, which broadcasts the update to the followers. When a majority have persisted the change, the leader commits the update, and the client gets a response saying the update succeeded. The protocol for achieving consensus is designed to be atomic, so a change either succeeds or fails. It resembles a two-phase commit.

If the leader fails, the remaining machines hold another leader election and continue as before with the new leader. If the old leader later recovers, it then starts as a follower. Leader election is very fast, around 200 ms according to one published result,[#] so performance does not noticeably degrade during an election.

All machines in the ensemble write updates to disk before updating their in-memory copy of the znode tree. Read requests may be serviced from any machine, and since they involve only a lookup from memory, they are very fast.

Consistency

Understanding the basis of ZooKeeper's implementation helps in understanding the consistency guarantees that the service makes. The terms "leader" and "follower" for the machines in an ensemble are apt, for they make the point that a follower may lag the leader by a number of updates. This is a consequence of the fact that only a majority and not all of the ensemble needs to have persisted a change before it is committed. A good mental model for ZooKeeper is of clients connected to ZooKeeper servers that are following the leader. A client may actually be connected to the leader, but it has no control over this, and cannot even know if this is the case.[*] See Figure 14-2.

Every update made to the znode tree is given a globally unique identifier, called a *zxid* (which stands for "ZooKeeper transaction ID"). Updates are ordered, so if *zxid* z_1 is less than z_2, then z_1 happened before z_2, according to ZooKeeper, which is the single authority on ordering in the distributed system.

[#] Reported by Yahoo! at *http://hadoop.apache.org/zookeeper/docs/current/zookeeperOver.html*.

[*] It is possible to configure ZooKeeper so that the leader does not accept client connections. In this case, its only job is to coordinate updates. Do this by setting the leaderServes property to no. This is recommended for ensembles of more than three servers.

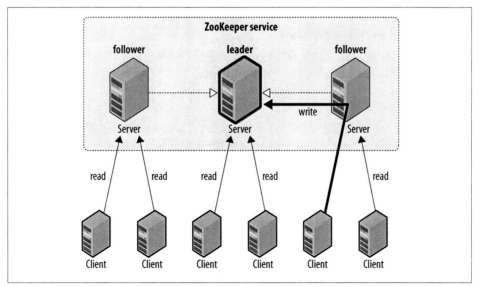

Figure 14-2. *Reads are satisfied by followers, while writes are committed by the leader*

The following guarantees for data consistency flow from ZooKeeper's design:

Sequential consistency

Updates from any particular client are applied in the order that they are sent. This means that if a client updates the znode z to the value a, and in a later operation, it updates z to the value b, then no client will ever see z with value a after it has seen it with value b (if no other updates are made to z).

Atomicity

Updates either succeed or fail. This means that if an update fails, no client will ever see it.

Single system image

A client will see the same view of the system regardless of the server it connects to. This means that if a client connects to a new server during the same session, it will not see an older state of the system than the one it saw with the previous server. When a server fails and a client tries to connect to another in the ensemble, a server that is behind the one that failed will not accept connections from the client until it has caught up with the failed server.

Durability

Once an update has succeeded, it will persist and will not be undone. This means updates will survive server failures.

Timeliness

The lag in any client's view of the system is bounded, so it will not be out of date by more than some multiple of tens of seconds. This means that rather than allow a client to see data that is very stale, a server will shut down, forcing the client to switch to a more up-to-date server.

For performance reasons, reads are satisfied from a ZooKeeper's server's memory and do not participate in the global ordering of writes. This property can lead to the appearance of inconsistent ZooKeeper states from clients that communicate through a mechanism outside ZooKeeper.

For example, client A updates znode z from a to a', A tells B to read z, B reads the value of z as a, not a'. This is perfectly compatible with the guarantees that ZooKeeper makes (this condition that it does *not* promise is called "Simultaneously Consistent Cross-Client Views"). To prevent this condition from happening, B should call sync on z, before reading z's value. The sync operation forces the ZooKeeper server to which B is connected to "catch up" with the leader, so that when B reads z's value it will be the one that A set (or a later value).

 Slightly confusingly, the sync operation is only available as an *asynchronous* call. The reason for this is that you don't need to wait for it to return, since ZooKeeper guarantees that any subsequent operation will happen after the sync completes on the server, even if the operation is issued before the sync completes.

Sessions

A ZooKeeper client is configured with the list of servers in the ensemble. On startup, it tries to connect to one of the servers in the list. If the connection fails, it tries another server in the list, and so on, until it either successfully connects to one of them or fails if all ZooKeeper servers are unavailable.

Once a connection has been made with a ZooKeeper server, the server creates a new session for the client. A session has a timeout period that is decided on by the application that creates it. If the server hasn't received a request within the timeout period, it may expire the session. Once a session has expired, it may not be reopened, and any ephemeral nodes associated with the session will be lost. Although session expiry is a comparatively rare event, since sessions are long-lived, it is important for applications to handle it (we will see how in "The Resilient ZooKeeper Application" on page 466).

Sessions are kept alive by the client sending ping requests (also known as heartbeats) whenever the session is idle for longer than a certain period. (Pings are automatically sent by the ZooKeeper client library, so your code doesn't need to worry about maintaining the session.) The period is chosen to be low enough to detect server failure (manifested by a read timeout) and reconnect to another server within the session timeout period.

Failover to another ZooKeeper server is handled automatically by the ZooKeeper client, and, crucially, sessions (and associated ephemeral znodes) are still valid after another server takes over from the failed one.

During failover, the application will receive notifications of disconnections and connections to the service. Watch notifications will not be delivered while the client is disconnected, but they will be delivered when the client successfully reconnects. Also, if the application tries to perform an operation while the client is reconnecting to another server, the operation will fail. This underlines the importance of handling connection loss exceptions in real-world ZooKeeper applications (described in "The Resilient ZooKeeper Application" on page 466).

Time

There are several time parameters in ZooKeeper. The *tick time* is the fundamental period of time in ZooKeeper and is used by servers in the ensemble to define the schedule on which their interactions run. Other settings are defined in terms of tick time, or are at least constrained by it. The session timeout, for example, may not be less than 2 ticks or more than 20. If you attempt to set a session timeout outside this range, it will be modified to fall within the range.

A common tick time setting is 2 seconds (2,000 milliseconds). This translates to an allowable session timeout of between 4 and 40 seconds. There are a few considerations in selecting a session timeout.

A low session timeout leads to faster detection of machine failure. In the group membership example, the session timeout is the time it takes for a failed machine to be removed from the group. Beware of setting the session timeout too low, however, since a busy network can cause packets to be delayed and may cause inadvertent session expiry. In such an event, a machine would appear to "flap": leaving and then rejoining the group repeatedly in a short space of time.

Applications that create more complex ephemeral state should favor longer session timeouts, as the cost of reconstruction is higher. In some cases, it is possible to design the application so it can restart within the session timeout period and avoid session expiry. (This might be desirable to perform maintenance or upgrades.) Every session is given a unique identity and password by the server, and if these are passed to Zoo-Keeper while a connection is being made, it is possible to recover a session (as long as it hasn't expired). An application can therefore arrange a graceful shutdown, whereby it stores the session identity and password to stable storage before restarting the process, retrieving the stored session identity and password and recovering the session.

You should view this feature as an optimization, which can help avoid expire sessions. It does not remove the need to handle session expiry, which can still occur if a machine fails unexpectedly, or even if an application is shut down gracefully but does not restart before its session expires—for whatever reason.

As a general rule, the larger the ZooKeeper ensemble, the larger the session timeout should be. Connection timeouts, read timeouts, and ping periods are all defined internally as a function of the number of servers in the ensemble, so as the ensemble grows, these periods decrease. Consider increasing the timeout if you experience frequent connection loss. You can monitor ZooKeeper metrics—such as request latency statistics—using JMX.

States

The ZooKeeper object transitions through different states in its lifecycle (see Figure 14-3). You can query its state at any time by using the getState() method:

```
public States getState()
```

States is an enum representing the different states that a ZooKeeper object may be in. (Despite the enum's name, an instance of ZooKeeper may only be in one state at a time.) A newly constructed ZooKeeper instance is in the CONNECTING state, while it tries to establish a connection with the ZooKeeper service. Once a connection is established, it goes into the CONNECTED state.

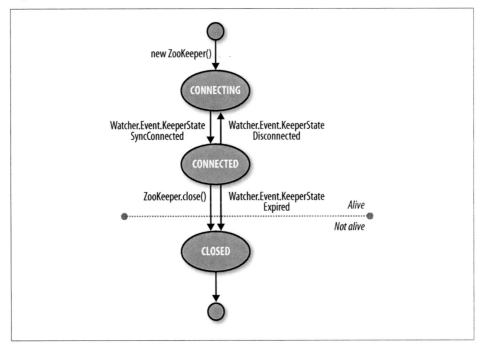

Figure 14-3. ZooKeeper state transitions

A client using the ZooKeeper object can receive notifications of the state transitions by registering a Watcher object. On entering the CONNECTED state, the watcher receives a WatchedEvent whose KeeperState value is SyncConnected.

A ZooKeeper `Watcher` object serves double duty: it can be used to be notified of changes in the ZooKeeper state (as described in this section), and it can be used to be notified of changes in znodes (described in "Watch triggers" on page 455). The (default) watcher passed into the `ZooKeeper` object constructor is used for state changes, but znode changes may either use a dedicated instance of `Watcher` (by passing one in to the appropriate read operation), or they may share the default one if using the form of the read operation that takes a boolean flag to specify whether to use a watcher.

The `ZooKeeper` instance may disconnect and reconnect to the ZooKeeper service, moving between the `CONNECTED` and `CONNECTING` states. If it disconnects, the watcher receives a `Disconnected` event. Note that these state transitions are initiated by the `ZooKeeper` instance itself, and it will automatically try to reconnect if the connection is lost.

The `ZooKeeper` instance may transition to a third state, `CLOSED`, if either the `close()` method is called or the session times out as indicated by a `KeeperState` of type `Expired`. Once in the `CLOSED` state, the `ZooKeeper` object is no longer considered to be alive (this can be tested using the `isAlive()` method on `States`) and cannot be reused. To reconnect to the ZooKeeper service, the client must construct a new `ZooKeeper` instance.

Building Applications with ZooKeeper

Having covered ZooKeeper in some depth, let's turn back to writing some useful applications with it.

A Configuration Service

One of the most basic services that a distributed application needs is a configuration service so that common pieces of configuration information can be shared by machines in a cluster. At the simplest level, ZooKeeper can act as a highly available store for configuration, allowing application participants to retrieve or update configuration files. Using ZooKeeper watches, it is possible to create an active configuration service, where interested clients are notified of changes in configuration.

Let's write such a service. We make a couple of assumptions that simplify the implementation (they could be removed with a little more work). First, the only configuration values we need to store are strings, and keys are just znode paths, so we use a znode to store each key-value pair. Second, there is a single client that performs updates at any one time. Among other things, this model fits with the idea of a master (such as the namenode in HDFS) that wishes to update information that its workers need to follow.

We wrap the code up in a class called ActiveKeyValueStore:

```
public class ActiveKeyValueStore extends ConnectionWatcher {

  private static final Charset CHARSET = Charset.forName("UTF-8");

  public void write(String path, String value) throws InterruptedException,
      KeeperException {
    Stat stat = zk.exists(path, false);
    if (stat == null) {
      zk.create(path, value.getBytes(CHARSET), Ids.OPEN_ACL_UNSAFE,
          CreateMode.PERSISTENT);
    } else {
      zk.setData(path, value.getBytes(CHARSET), -1);
    }
  }
}
```

The contract of the write() method is that a key with the given value is written to ZooKeeper. It hides the difference between creating a new znode and updating an existing znode with a new value, by testing first for the znode using the exists operation and then performing the appropriate operation. The other detail worth mentioning is the need to convert the string value to a byte array, for which we just use the getBytes() method with a UTF-8 encoding.

To illustrate the use of the ActiveKeyValueStore, consider a ConfigUpdater class that updates a configuration property with a value. The listing appears in Example 14-6.

Example 14-6. An application that updates a property in ZooKeeper at random times

```
public class ConfigUpdater {

  public static final String PATH = "/config";

  private ActiveKeyValueStore store;
  private Random random = new Random();

  public ConfigUpdater(String hosts) throws IOException, InterruptedException {
    store = new ActiveKeyValueStore();
    store.connect(hosts);
  }

  public void run() throws InterruptedException, KeeperException {
    while (true) {
      String value = random.nextInt(100) + "";
      store.write(PATH, value);
      System.out.printf("Set %s to %s\n", PATH, value);
      TimeUnit.SECONDS.sleep(random.nextInt(10));
    }
  }
}
```

```
  public static void main(String[] args) throws Exception {
    ConfigUpdater configUpdater = new ConfigUpdater(args[0]);
    configUpdater.run();
  }
}
```

The program is simple. A `ConfigUpdater` has an `ActiveKeyValueStore` that connects to ZooKeeper in `ConfigUpdater`'s constructor. The `run()` method loops forever, updating the *lconfig* znode at random times with random values.

Next, let's look at how to read the *lconfig* configuration property. First, we add a read method to `ActiveKeyValueStore`:

```
public String read(String path, Watcher watcher) throws InterruptedException,
    KeeperException {
  byte[] data = zk.getData(path, watcher, null/*stat*/);
  return new String(data, CHARSET);
}
```

The `getData()` method of ZooKeeper takes the path, a `Watcher`, and a `Stat` object. The `Stat` object is filled in with values by `getData()`, and is used to pass information back to the caller. In this way, the caller can get both the data and the metadata for a znode, although in this case, we pass a null `Stat` because we are not interested in the metadata.

As a consumer of the service, `ConfigWatcher` (see Example 14-7) creates an `ActiveKeyValueStore`, and after starting, calls the store's `read()` method (in its `displayConfig()` method) to pass a reference to itself as the watcher. It displays the initial value of the configuration that it reads.

Example 14-7. An application that watches for updates of a property in ZooKeeper and prints them to the console

```
public class ConfigWatcher implements Watcher {

  private ActiveKeyValueStore store;

  public ConfigWatcher(String hosts) throws IOException, InterruptedException {
    store = new ActiveKeyValueStore();
    store.connect(hosts);
  }

  public void displayConfig() throws InterruptedException, KeeperException {
    String value = store.read(ConfigUpdater.PATH, this);
    System.out.printf("Read %s as %s\n", ConfigUpdater.PATH, value);
  }

  @Override
  public void process(WatchedEvent event) {
    if (event.getType() == EventType.NodeDataChanged) {
      try {
        displayConfig();
      } catch (InterruptedException e) {
        System.err.println("Interrupted. Exiting.");
        Thread.currentThread().interrupt();
```

```
      } catch (KeeperException e) {
        System.err.printf("KeeperException: %s. Exiting.\n", e);
      }
    }
  }

  public static void main(String[] args) throws Exception {
    ConfigWatcher configWatcher = new ConfigWatcher(args[0]);
    configWatcher.displayConfig();

    // stay alive until process is killed or thread is interrupted
    Thread.sleep(Long.MAX_VALUE);
  }
}
```

When the `ConfigUpdater` updates the znode, ZooKeeper causes the watcher to fire with an event type of `EventType.NodeDataChanged`. `ConfigWatcher` acts on this event in its `process()` method by reading and displaying the latest version of the config.

Because watches are one-time signals, we tell ZooKeeper of the new watch each time we call `read()` on `ActiveKeyValueStore`—this ensures we see future updates. Furthermore, we are not guaranteed to receive every update, since between the receipt of the watch event and the next read, the znode may have been updated, possibly many times, and as the client has no watch registered during that period, it is not notified. For the configuration service, this is not a problem because clients care only about the latest value of a property, as it takes precedence over previous values, but in general you should be aware of this potential limitation.

Let's see the code in action. Launch the `ConfigUpdater` in one terminal window:

```
% java ConfigUpdater localhost
Set /config to 79
Set /config to 14
Set /config to 78
```

Then launch the `ConfigWatcher` in another window immediately afterward:

```
% java ConfigWatcher localhost
Read /config as 79
Read /config as 14
Read /config as 78
```

The Resilient ZooKeeper Application

The first of the Fallacies of Distributed Computing[†] states that "The network is reliable." As they stand, the programs so far have been assuming a reliable network, so when they run on a real network, they can fail in several ways. Let's examine possible failure modes and what we can do to correct them so that our programs are resilient in the face of failure.

---

† See *http://en.wikipedia.org/wiki/Fallacies_of_Distributed_Computing*.

Every ZooKeeper operation in the Java API declares two types of exception in its throws clause: `InterruptedException` and `KeeperException`.

InterruptedException

An `InterruptedException` is thrown if the operation is interrupted. There is a standard Java mechanism for canceling blocking methods, which is to call `interrupt()` on the thread from which the blocking method was called. A successful cancellation will result in an `InterruptedException`. ZooKeeper adheres to this standard, so you can cancel a ZooKeeper operation in this way. Classes or libraries that use ZooKeeper should usually propagate the `InterruptedException` so that their clients can cancel their operations.[‡]

An `InterruptedException` does not indicate a failure, but rather that the operation has been canceled, so in the configuration application example, it is appropriate to propagate the exception, causing the application to terminate.

KeeperException

A `KeeperException` is thrown if the ZooKeeper server signals an error or if there is a communication problem with the server. There are various subclasses of `KeeperException` for different error cases. For example, `KeeperException.NoNodeException` is a subclass of `KeeperException` that is thrown if you try to perform an operation on a znode that doesn't exist.

Every subclass of `KeeperException` has a corresponding code with information about the type of error. For example, for `KeeperException.NoNodeException` the code is `KeeperException.Code.NONODE` (an enum value).

There are two ways then to handle `KeeperException`: either catch `KeeperException` and test its code to determine what remedying action to take, or catch the equivalent `KeeperException` subclasses and perform the appropriate action in each catch block.

`KeeperExceptions` fall into three broad categories.

State exceptions. A state exception occurs when the operation fails because it cannot be applied to the znode tree. State exceptions usually happen because another process is mutating a znode at the same time. For example, a `setData` operation with a version number will fail with a `KeeperException.BadVersionException` if the znode is updated by another process first, since the version number does not match. The programmer is usually aware that this kind of conflict is possible and will code to deal with it.

Some state exceptions indicate an error in the program, such as `KeeperException.NoChildrenForEphemeralsException`, which is thrown when trying to create a child znode of an ephemeral znode.

[‡] For more detail, see the excellent article "Dealing with InterruptedException" (*http://www.ibm.com/developerworks/java/library/j-jtp05236.html*) by Brian Goetz.

Recoverable exceptions. Recoverable exceptions are those from which the application can recover within the same ZooKeeper session. A recoverable exception is manifested by `KeeperException.ConnectionLossException`, which means that the connection to ZooKeeper has been lost. ZooKeeper will try to reconnect, and in most cases the reconnection will succeed and ensure that the session is intact.

However, ZooKeeper cannot tell whether the operation that failed with `KeeperException.ConnectionLossException` was applied. This is an example of partial failure (which we introduced at the beginning of the chapter). The onus is therefore on the programmer to deal with the uncertainty, and the action that should be taken depends on the application.

At this point, it is useful to make a distinction between *idempotent* and *nonidempotent* operations. An idempotent operation is one that may be applied one or more times with the same result, such as a read request or an unconditional `setData`. These can simply be retried.

A nonidempotent operation cannot be indiscriminately retried, as the effect of applying it multiple times is not the same as applying it once. The program needs a way of detecting whether its update was applied by encoding information in the znode's path name or its data. We shall discuss how to deal with failed nonidempotent operations in "Recoverable exceptions" on page 471, when we look at the implementation of a lock service.

Unrecoverable exceptions. In some cases, the ZooKeeper session becomes invalid—perhaps because of a timeout or because the session was closed (both get a `KeeperException.SessionExpiredException`), or perhaps because authentication failed (`KeeperException.AuthFailedException`). In any case, all ephemeral nodes associated with the session will be lost, so the application needs to rebuild its state before reconnecting to ZooKeeper.

A reliable configuration service

Going back to the `write()` method in `ActiveKeyValueStore`, recall that it is composed of an `exists` operation followed by either a `create` or a `setData`:

```
public void write(String path, String value) throws InterruptedException,
    KeeperException {
  Stat stat = zk.exists(path, false);
  if (stat == null) {
    zk.create(path, value.getBytes(CHARSET), Ids.OPEN_ACL_UNSAFE,
        CreateMode.PERSISTENT);
  } else {
    zk.setData(path, value.getBytes(CHARSET), -1);
  }
}
```

Taken as a whole, the `write()` method is idempotent, so we can afford to unconditionally retry it. Here's a modified version of the `write()` method that retries in a loop.

It is set to try a maximum number of retries (MAX_RETRIES) and sleeps for RETRY_PERIOD_SECONDS between each attempt:

```java
public void write(String path, String value) throws InterruptedException,
    KeeperException {
  int retries = 0;
  while (true) {
    try {
      Stat stat = zk.exists(path, false);
      if (stat == null) {
        zk.create(path, value.getBytes(CHARSET), Ids.OPEN_ACL_UNSAFE,
            CreateMode.PERSISTENT);
      } else {
        zk.setData(path, value.getBytes(CHARSET), stat.getVersion());
      }
    } catch (KeeperException.SessionExpiredException e) {
      throw e;
    } catch (KeeperException e) {
      if (retries++ == MAX_RETRIES) {
        throw e;
      }
      // sleep then retry
      TimeUnit.SECONDS.sleep(RETRY_PERIOD_SECONDS);
    }
  }
}
```

The code is careful not to retry KeeperException.SessionExpiredException, since when a session expires, the ZooKeeper object enters the CLOSED state, from which it can never reconnect (refer to Figure 14-3). We simply rethrow the exception[§] and let the caller create a new ZooKeeper instance, so that the whole write() method can be retried. A simple way to create a new instance is to create a new ConfigUpdater (which we've actually renamed ResilientConfigUpdater) to recover from an expired session:

```java
public static void main(String[] args) throws Exception {
  while (true) {
    try {
      ResilientConfigUpdater configUpdater =
        new ResilientConfigUpdater(args[0]);
      configUpdater.run();
    } catch (KeeperException.SessionExpiredException e) {
      // start a new session
    } catch (KeeperException e) {
      // already retried, so exit
      e.printStackTrace();
      break;
    }
  }
}
```

[§] Another way of writing the code would be to have a single catch block, just for KeeperException, and a test to see whether its code has the value KeeperException.Code.SESSIONEXPIRED. Which method you use is a matter of style, since they both behave in the same way.

An alternative way of dealing with session expiry would be to look for a `KeeperState` of type `Expired` in the watcher (that would be the `ConnectionWatcher` in the example here), and create a new connection when this is detected. This way, we would just keep retrying in the `write()` method, even if we got a `KeeperException.SessionExpiredExcep tion`, since the connection should eventually be reestablished. Regardless of the precise mechanics of how we recover from an expired session, the important point is that it is a different kind of failure from connection loss and needs to be handled differently.

There's actually another failure mode that we've ignored here. When the `ZooKeeper` object is created, it tries to connect to a ZooKeeper server. If the connection fails or times out, then it tries another server in the ensemble. If, after trying all of the servers in the ensemble, it can't connect, then it throws an `IOException`. The likelihood of all ZooKeeper servers being unavailable is low; nevertheless, some applications may choose to retry the operation in a loop until ZooKeeper is available.

This is just one strategy for retry handling—there are many others, such as using exponential backoff where the period between retries is multiplied by a constant each time. The `org.apache.hadoop.io.retry` package in Hadoop Core is a set of utilities for adding retry logic into your code in a reusable way, and it may be helpful for building ZooKeeper applications.

A Lock Service

A distributed lock is a mechanism for providing mutual exclusion between a collection of processes. At any one time, only a single process may hold the lock. Distributed locks can be used for leader election in a large distributed system, where the leader is the process that holds the lock at any point in time.

Do not confuse ZooKeeper's own leader election with a general leader election service, which can be built using ZooKeeper primitives. Zoo-Keeper's own leader election is not exposed publicly, unlike the type of general leader election service we are describing here, which is designed to be used by distributed systems that need to agree upon a master process.

To implement a distributed lock using ZooKeeper, we use sequential znodes to impose an order on the processes vying for the lock. The idea is simple: first designate a lock znode, typically describing the entity being locked on, say */leader*; then clients that want to acquire the lock create sequential ephemeral znodes as children of the lock znode. At any point in time, the client with the lowest sequence number holds the lock. For example, if two clients create znodes at around the same time, */leader/lock-1* and */leader/lock-2*, then the client that created */leader/lock-1* holds the lock, since its znode has the lowest sequence number. The ZooKeeper service is the arbiter of order, since it assigns the sequence numbers.

The lock may be released simply by deleting the znode */leader/lock-1*; alternatively, if the client process dies, it will be deleted by virtue of it being an ephemeral znode. The client that created */leader/lock-2* will then hold the lock, since it has the next lowest sequence number. It will be notified that it has the lock by creating a watch that fires when znodes go away.

The pseudocode for lock acquisition is as follows:

1. Create an ephemeral sequential znode named *lock-* under the lock znode and re-member its actual path name (the return value of the create operation).
2. Get the children of the lock znode and set a watch.
3. If the path name of the znode created in 1 has the lowest number of the children returned in 2, then the lock has been acquired. Exit.
4. Wait for the notification from the watch set in 2 and go to step 2.

The herd effect

Although this algorithm is correct, there are some problems with it. The first problem is that this implementation suffers from the *herd effect*. Consider hundreds or thousands of clients, all trying to acquire the lock. Each client places a watch on the lock znode for changes in its set of children. Every time the lock is released, or another process starts the lock acquisition process, the watch fires and every client receives a notification. The "herd effect" refers to a large number of clients being notified of the same event, when only a small number of them can actually proceed. In this case, only one client will successfully acquire the lock, and the process of maintaining and sending watch events to all clients causes traffic spikes, which put pressure on the ZooKeeper servers.

To avoid the herd effect, we need to refine the condition for notification. The key observation for implementing locks is that a client needs to be notified only when the child znode with the *previous* sequence number goes away, not when any child znode is deleted (or created). In our example, if clients have created the znodes */leader/lock-1*, */leader/lock-2*, and */leader/lock-3*, then the client holding */leader/lock-3* only needs to be notified when */leader/lock-2* disappears. It does not need to be notified when */leader/lock-1* disappears or when a new znode */leader/lock-4* is added.

Recoverable exceptions

Another problem with the lock algorithm as it stands is that it doesn't handle the case when the create operation fails due to connection loss. Recall that in this case we do not know if the operation succeeded or failed. Creating a sequential znode is a nonidempotent operation, so we can't simply retry, since if the first create had succeeded, we would have an orphaned znode that would never be deleted (until the client session ended, at least). Deadlock would be the unfortunate result.

The problem is that after reconnecting, the client can't tell whether it created any of the child znodes. By embedding an identifier in the znode name, if it suffers a connection loss, it can check to see whether any of the children of the lock node have its identifier in their name. If a child contains its identifier, it knows that the create operation succeeded, and it shouldn't create another child znode. If no child has the identifier in its name, then the client can safely create a new sequential child znode.

The client's session identifier is a long integer that is unique for the ZooKeeper service and therefore ideal for the purpose of identifying a client across connection loss events. The session identifier can be obtained by calling the getSessionId() method on the ZooKeeper Java class.

The ephemeral sequential znode should be created with a name of the form *lock-<sessionId>-*, so that when the sequence number is appended by ZooKeeper, the name becomes *lock-<sessionId>-<sequenceNumber>*. The sequence numbers are unique to the parent, not to the name of the child, so this technique allows the child znodes to identify their creators as well as impose an order of creation.

Unrecoverable exceptions

If a client's ZooKeeper session expires, the ephemeral znode created by the client will be deleted, effectively relinquishing the lock or at least forfeiting the client's turn to acquire the lock. The application using the lock should realize that it no longer holds the lock, clean up its state, and then start again by creating a new lock object and trying to acquire it. Notice that it is the application that controls this process, not the lock implementation, since it cannot second-guess how the application needs to clean up its state.

Implementation

Implementing a distributed lock correctly is a delicate matter, since accounting for all of the failure modes is nontrivial. ZooKeeper comes with a production-quality lock implementation in Java called WriteLock that is very easy for clients to use.

More Distributed Data Structures and Protocols

There are many distributed data structures and protocols that can be built with ZooKeeper, such as barriers, queues, and two-phase commit. One interesting thing to note is that these are synchronous protocols, even though we use asynchronous ZooKeeper primitives (such as notifications) to build them.

The ZooKeeper website (*http://hadoop.apache.org/zookeeper/*) describes several such data structures and protocols in pseudocode. ZooKeeper comes with implementations of some of these standard recipes; they can be found in the *recipes* directory of the distribution.

BookKeeper

BookKeeper is a highly available and reliable logging service. It can be used to provide write-ahead logging, which is a common technique for ensuring data integrity in storage systems. In a system using write-ahead logging, every write operation is written to the transaction log before it is applied. Using this procedure, we don't have to write the data to permanent storage after every write operation because in the event of a system failure, the latest state may be recovered by replaying the transaction log for any writes that had not been applied.

BookKeeper clients create logs called *ledgers*, and each record appended to a ledger is called a *ledger entry*, which is simply a byte array. Ledgers are managed by *bookies*, which are servers that replicate the ledger data. Note that ledger data is not stored in ZooKeeper, only metadata is.

Traditionally, the challenge has been to make systems that use write-ahead logging robust in the face of failure of the node writing the transaction log. This is usually done by replicating the transaction log in some manner. Hadoop's HDFS namenode, for instance, writes its edit log to multiple disks, one of which is typically an NFS mounted disk. However, in the event of failure of the primary, failover is still manual. By providing logging as a highly available service, BookKeeper promises to make failover transparent, since it can tolerate the loss of bookie servers.

BookKeeper is provided in the *contrib* directory of the ZooKeeper distribution, where you can find more information on how to use it.

ZooKeeper in Production

In production, you should run ZooKeeper in replicated mode. Here we will cover some of the considerations for running an ensemble of ZooKeeper servers. However, this section is not exhaustive, so you should consult the ZooKeeper Administrator's Guide (*http://hadoop.apache.org/zookeeper/docs/current/*) for detailed up-to-date instructions, including supported platforms, recommended hardware, maintenance procedures, and configuration properties.

Resilience and Performance

ZooKeeper machines should be located to minimize the impact of machine and network failure. In practice, this means that servers should be spread across racks, power supplies, and switches, so that the failure of any one of these does not cause the ensemble to lose a majority of its servers. ZooKeeper relies on having low-latency connections between all of the servers in the ensemble, so for that reason an ensemble should be confined to a single data center.

 ZooKeeper has the concept of an *observer node*, which is like a non-voting follower. Since they do not participate in the vote for consensus during write requests, observers allow a ZooKeeper cluster to improve read performance without hurting write performance.[‖] In addition, a ZooKeeper cluster can span data centers by placing the voting members in one data center and observers in the other.

ZooKeeper is a highly available system, and it is critical that it can perform its functions in a timely manner. Therefore, ZooKeeper should run on machines that are dedicated to ZooKeeper alone. Having other applications contend for resources can cause ZooKeeper's performance to degrade significantly.

Configure ZooKeeper to keep its transaction log on a different disk drive from its snapshots. By default, both go in the directory specified by the `dataDir` property, but by specifying a location for `dataLogDir`, the transaction log will be written there. By having its own dedicated device (not just a partition), a ZooKeeper server can maximize the rate at which it writes log entries to disk, which is does sequentially, without seeking. Since all writes go through the leader, write throughput does not scale by adding servers, so it is crucial that writes are as fast as possible.

If the process swaps to disk, performance will suffer adversely. This can be avoided by setting the Java heap size to less than the amount of physical memory available on the machine. The ZooKeeper scripts will source a file called *java.env* from its configuration directory, and this can be used to set the `JVMFLAGS` environment variable to set the heap size (and any other desired JVM arguments).

Configuration

Each server in the ensemble of ZooKeeper servers has a numeric identifier that is unique within the ensemble, and must fall between 1 and 255. The server number is specified in plain text in a file named *myid* in the directory specified by the `dataDir` property.

Setting each server number is only half of the job. We also need to give all the servers all the identities and network locations of the others in the ensemble. The ZooKeeper configuration file must include a line for each server, of the form:

```
server.n=hostname:port:port
```

‖ This is discussed in more detail in "Observers: Making ZooKeeper Scale Even Further" (*http://www.cloudera.com/blog/2009/12/observers-making-zookeeper-scale-even-further/*) by Henry Robinson.

The value of *n* is replaced by the server number. There are two port settings: the first is the port that followers use to connect to the leader, and the second is used for leader election. Here is a sample configuration for a three-machine replicated ZooKeeper ensemble:

```
tickTime=2000
dataDir=/disk1/zookeeper
dataLogDir=/disk2/zookeeper
clientPort=2181
initLimit=5
syncLimit=2
server.1=zookeeper1:2888:3888
server.2=zookeeper2:2888:3888
server.3=zookeeper3:2888:3888
```

Servers listen on three ports: 2181 for client connections; 2888 for follower connections, if they are the leader; and 3888 for other server connections during the leader election phase. When a ZooKeeper server starts up, it reads the *myid* file to determine which server it is, then reads the configuration file to determine the ports it should listen on, as well as the network addresses of the other servers in the ensemble.

Clients connecting to this ZooKeeper ensemble should use `zookeeper1:2181,zookeeper2:2181,zookeeper3:2181` as the host string in the constructor for the `ZooKeeper` object.

In replicated mode, there are two extra mandatory properties: `initLimit` and `syncLimit`, both measured in multiples of `tickTime`.

`initLimit` is the amount of time to allow for followers to connect to and sync with the leader. If a majority of followers fail to sync within this period, then the leader renounces its leadership status and another leader election takes place. If this happens often (and you can discover if this is the case because it is logged), it is a sign that the setting is too low.

`syncLimit` is the amount of time to allow a follower to sync with the leader. If a follower fails to sync within this period, it will restart itself. Clients that were attached to this follower will connect to another one.

These are the minimum settings needed to get up and running with a cluster of ZooKeeper servers. There are, however, more configuration options, particularly for tuning performance, documented in the ZooKeeper Administrator's Guide.

Sqoop

Aaron Kimball

A great strength of the Hadoop platform is its ability to work with data in several different forms. HDFS can reliably store logs and other data from a plethora of sources, and MapReduce programs can parse diverse ad hoc data formats, extracting relevant information and combining multiple data sets into powerful results.

But to interact with data in storage repositories outside of HDFS, MapReduce programs need to use external APIs to get to this data. Often, valuable data in an organization is stored in relational database systems (RDBMS). *Sqoop* is an open-source tool that allows users to extract data from a relational database into Hadoop for further processing. This processing can be done with MapReduce programs or other higher-level tools such as Hive. When the final results of an analytic pipeline are available, Sqoop can export these results back to the database for consumption by other clients.

In this chapter, we'll take a look at how Sqoop works and how you can use it in your data processing pipeline.

Getting Sqoop

Sqoop is available in a few places. The primary home of the project is *http://github.com/cloudera/sqoop*. This repository contains all the Sqoop source code and documentation. Official releases are available at this site, as well as the source code for the version currently under development. The repository itself contains instructions for compiling the project. Alternatively, Cloudera's Distribution for Hadoop contains an installation package for Sqoop alongside compatible editions of Hadoop and other tools like Hive.

If you download a release from github, it will be placed in a directory such as */home/yourname/sqoop-x.y.z/*. We'll call this directory `$SQOOP_HOME`. You can run Sqoop by running the executable script `$SQOOP_HOME/bin/sqoop`.

If you've installed a release from Cloudera, the package will have placed Sqoop's scripts in standard locations like */usr/bin/sqoop*. You can run Sqoop by simply typing `sqoop` at the command line.

(Regardless of how you install Sqoop, we'll refer to this script as just `sqoop` from here on.)

Running Sqoop with no arguments does not do much of interest:

```
% sqoop
Try sqoop help for usage.
```

Sqoop is organized as a set of tools or commands. Without selecting a tool, Sqoop does not know what to do. `help` is the name of one such tool; it can print out the list of available tools, like this:

```
% sqoop help
usage: sqoop COMMAND [ARGS]

Available commands:
  codegen            Generate code to interact with database records
  create-hive-table  Import a table definition into Hive
  eval               Evaluate a SQL statement and display the results
  export             Export an HDFS directory to a database table
  help               List available commands
  import             Import a table from a database to HDFS
  import-all-tables  Import tables from a database to HDFS
  list-databases     List available databases on a server
  list-tables        List available tables in a database
  version            Display version information

See 'sqoop help COMMAND' for information on a specific command.
```

As it explains, the `help` tool can also provide specific usage instructions on a particular tool, by providing that tool's name as an argument:

```
% sqoop help import
usage: sqoop import [GENERIC-ARGS] [TOOL-ARGS]

Common arguments:
   --connect <jdbc-uri>     Specify JDBC connect string
   --driver <class-name>    Manually specify JDBC driver class to use
   --hadoop-home <dir>      Override $HADOOP_HOME
   --help                   Print usage instructions
-P                          Read password from console
   --password <password>    Set authentication password
   --username <username>    Set authentication username
   --verbose                Print more information while working
...
```

An alternate way of running a Sqoop tool is to use a tool-specific script. This script will be named `sqoop-toolname`. For example, `sqoop-help`, `sqoop-import`, etc. These commands are identical to running `sqoop help` or `sqoop import`.

A Sample Import

After you install Sqoop, you can use it to import data to Hadoop.

Sqoop imports from databases; if you don't already have a database server installed, you'll need to choose one. MySQL is an easy-to-use database available for a large number of platforms.

To install and configure MySQL, follow the documentation at *http://dev.mysql.com/ doc/refman/5.1/en/*. Chapter 2 ("Installing and Upgrading MySQL") in particular should help. Users of Debian-based Linux systems (e.g., Ubuntu) can type `sudo apt-get install mysql-client mysql-server`. RedHat users can type `sudo yum install mysql mysql-server`.

Now that MySQL is installed, let's log in and create a database (Example 15-1).

Example 15-1. Creating a new MySQL database schema

```
% mysql -u root -p
Enter password:
Welcome to the MySQL monitor.  Commands end with ; or \g.
Your MySQL connection id is 349
Server version: 5.1.37-1ubuntu5.4 (Ubuntu)

Type 'help;' or '\h' for help. Type '\c' to clear the current input
statement.

mysql> CREATE DATABASE hadoopguide;
Query OK, 1 row affected (0.02 sec)

mysql> GRANT ALL PRIVILEGES ON hadoopguide.* TO '%'@'localhost';
Query OK, 0 rows affected (0.00 sec)

mysql> GRANT ALL PRIVILEGES ON hadoopguide.* TO ''@'localhost';
Query OK, 0 rows affected (0.00 sec)

mysql> quit;
Bye
```

The password prompt above asks for your root user password. This is likely the same as the password for the root shell login. If you are running Ubuntu or another variant of Linux where root cannot directly log in, then enter the password you picked at MySQL installation time.

In this session, we created a new database schema called hadoopguide, which we'll use throughout this appendix. We then allowed any local user to view and modify the contents of the hadoopguide schema, and closed our session.[*]

---

[*] Of course, in a production deployment, we'd need to be much more careful about access control, but this serves for demonstration purposes. The above privilege grant also assumes you're running a pseudo-distributed Hadoop instance. If you're working with a distributed Hadoop cluster, you'd need to enable remote access by at least one user, whose account will be used to perform imports and exports via Sqoop.

Now let's log back into the database (not as root, but as yourself this time), and create a table to import into HDFS (Example 15-2).

Example 15-2. Populating the database

```
% mysql hadoopguide
Welcome to the MySQL monitor.  Commands end with ; or \g.
Your MySQL connection id is 352
Server version: 5.1.37-1ubuntu5.4 (Ubuntu)

Type 'help;' or '\h' for help. Type '\c' to clear the current input statement.

mysql> CREATE TABLE widgets(id INT NOT NULL PRIMARY KEY AUTO_INCREMENT,
    -> widget_name VARCHAR(64) NOT NULL,
    -> price DECIMAL(10,2),
    -> design_date DATE,
    -> version INT,
    -> design_comment VARCHAR(100));
Query OK, 0 rows affected (0.00 sec)

mysql> INSERT INTO widgets VALUES (NULL, 'sprocket', 0.25, '2010-02-10',
    -> 1, 'Connects two gizmos');
Query OK, 1 row affected (0.00 sec)

mysql> INSERT INTO widgets VALUES (NULL, 'gizmo', 4.00, '2009-11-30', 4,
    -> NULL);
Query OK, 1 row affected (0.00 sec)

mysql> INSERT INTO widgets VALUES (NULL, 'gadget', 99.99, '1983-08-13',
    -> 13, 'Our flagship product');
Query OK, 1 row affected (0.00 sec)

mysql> quit;
```

In the above listing, we created a new table called widgets. We'll be using this fictional product database in further examples in this chapter. The widgets table contains several fields representing a variety of data types.

Now let's use Sqoop to import this table into HDFS:

```
% sqoop import --connect jdbc:mysql://localhost/hadoopguide \
> --table widgets -m 1
10/06/23 14:44:18 INFO tool.CodeGenTool: Beginning code generation
...
10/06/23 14:44:20 INFO mapred.JobClient: Running job: job_201006231439_0002
10/06/23 14:44:21 INFO mapred.JobClient:  map 0% reduce 0%
10/06/23 14:44:32 INFO mapred.JobClient:  map 100% reduce 0%
10/06/23 14:44:34 INFO mapred.JobClient: Job complete:
job_201006231439_0002
...
10/06/23 14:44:34 INFO mapreduce.ImportJobBase: Retrieved 3 records.
```

Sqoop's `import` tool will run a MapReduce job that connects to the MySQL database and reads the table. By default, this will use four map tasks in parallel to speed up the import process. Each task will write its imported results to a different file, but all in a common directory. Since we knew that we had only three rows to import in this example, we specified that Sqoop should use a single map task (`-m 1`) so we get a single file in HDFS.

We can inspect this file's contents like so:

```
% hadoop fs -cat widgets/part-m-00000
1,sprocket,0.25,2010-02-10,1,Connects two gizmos
2,gizmo,4.00,2009-11-30,4,null
3,gadget,99.99,1983-08-13,13,Our flagship product
```

 The connect string (*jdbc:mysql://localhost/hadoopguide*) shown in the example will read from a database on the local machine. If a distributed Hadoop cluster is being used, then `localhost` should not be specified in the connect string; map tasks not running on the same machine as the database will fail to connect. Even if Sqoop is run from the same host as the database sever, the full hostname should be specified.

By default, Sqoop will generate comma-delimited text files for our imported data. Delimiters can be explicitly specified, as well as field enclosing and escape characters to allow the presence of delimiters in the field contents. The command-line arguments that specify delimiter characters, file formats, compression, and more fine-grained control of the import process are described in the *Sqoop User Guide* distributed with Sqoop,[†] as well as in the online help (`sqoop help import`, or `man sqoop-import` in CDH).

 Text and binary file formats

Sqoop is capable of importing into a few different file formats. Text files (the default) offer a human-readable representation of data, platform independence, and the simplest structure. However, they cannot hold binary fields (such as database columns of type `VARBINARY`) and cannot distinguish between `null` values and String-based fields containing the value `"null"`. To handle these conditions, you should use Sqoop's SequenceFile-based format. The disadvantages of SequenceFiles is that they are Java-specific, and current versions of Sqoop cannot load them into Hive. But SequenceFiles provide the most precise representation of the imported data possible. SequenceFiles also allow data to be compressed while retaining MapReduce's ability to process different sections of the same file in parallel.

† Available at *http://archive.cloudera.com/cdh/3/sqoop/*.

Generated Code

In addition to writing the contents of the database table to HDFS, Sqoop has also provided you with a generated Java source file (*widgets.java*) written to the current local directory. (After running the `sqoop import` command above, you can see this file by running `ls widgets.java`.)

Code generation is a necessary part of Sqoop's import process; as you'll learn in "Database Imports: A Deeper Look" on page 483, Sqoop uses generated code to handle the deserialization of table-specific data from the database source before writing it to HDFS.

The generated class (`widgets`) is capable of holding a single record retrieved from the imported table. It can manipulate such a record in MapReduce or store it in a SequenceFile in HDFS. (SequenceFiles written by Sqoop during the import process will store each imported row in the "value" element of the SequenceFile's key-value pair format, using the generated class.)

It is likely that you don't want to name your generated class `widgets` since each instance of the class refers to only a single record. We can use a different Sqoop tool to generate source code without performing an import; this generated code will still examine the database table to determine the appropriate data types for each field:

```
% sqoop codegen --connect jdbc:mysql://localhost/hadoopguide \
> --table widgets --class-name Widget
```

The codegen tool simply generates code; it does not perform the full import. We specified that we'd like it to generate a class named `Widget`; this will be written to *Widget.java*. We also could have specified `--class-name` and other code-generation arguments during the import process we performed earlier. This tool can be used to regenerate code, if you accidentally remove the source file, or generate code with different settings than were used during the import.

If you're working with records imported to SequenceFiles, it is inevitable that you'll need to use the generated classes (to deserialize data from the SequenceFile storage). You can work with text file-based records without using generated code, but as we'll see in "Working with Imported Data" on page 486, Sqoop's generated code can handle some tedious aspects of data processing for you.

Additional Serialization Systems

As Sqoop continues to develop, the number of ways Sqoop can serialize and interact with your data is expected to grow. The current implementation of Sqoop at the time of this writing requires generated code that implements the `Writable` interface. Future versions of Sqoop should support Avro-based serialization and schema generation as well (see "Avro" on page 103), allowing you to use Sqoop in your project without integrating with generated code.

Database Imports: A Deeper Look

As mentioned earlier, Sqoop imports a table from a database by running a MapReduce job that extracts rows from the table, and writes the records to HDFS. How does MapReduce read the rows? This section explains how Sqoop works under the hood.

At a high level, Figure 15-1 demonstrates how Sqoop interacts with both the database source and Hadoop. Like Hadoop itself, Sqoop is written in Java. Java provides an API called Java Database Connectivity, or JDBC, that allows applications to access data stored in an RDBMS as well as inspect the nature of this data. Most database vendors provide a JDBC *driver* that implements the JDBC API and contains the necessary code to connect to their database server.

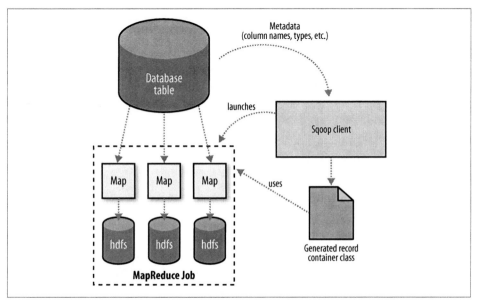

Figure 15-1. Sqoop's import process

 Based on the URL in the connect string used to access the database, Sqoop attempts to predict which driver it should load. You may still need to download the JDBC driver itself and install it on your Sqoop client. For cases where Sqoop does not know which JDBC driver is appropriate, users can specify exactly how to load the JDBC driver into Sqoop. This capability allows Sqoop to work with a wide variety of database platforms.

Before the import can start, Sqoop uses JDBC to examine the table it is to import. It retrieves a list of all the columns and their SQL data types. These SQL types (VARCHAR, INTEGER, and so on) can then be mapped to Java data types (String, Integer, etc.), which will hold the field values in MapReduce applications. Sqoop's code generator will use this information to create a table-specific class to hold a record extracted from the table.

The Widget class from earlier, for example, contains the following methods that retrieve each column from an extracted record:

```
public Integer get_id();
public String get_widget_name();
public java.math.BigDecimal get_price();
public java.sql.Date get_design_date();
public Integer get_version();
public String get_design_comment();
```

More critical to the import system's operation, though, are the serialization methods that form the DBWritable interface, which allow the Widget class to interact with JDBC:

```
public void readFields(ResultSet __dbResults) throws SQLException;
public void write(PreparedStatement __dbStmt) throws SQLException;
```

JDBC's ResultSet interface provides a cursor that retrieves records from a query; the readFields() method here will populate the fields of the Widget object with the columns from one row of the ResultSet's data. The write() method shown above allows Sqoop to insert new Widget rows into a table, a process called *exporting*. Exports are discussed in "Performing an Export" on page 491.

The MapReduce job launched by Sqoop uses an InputFormat that can read sections of a table from a database via JDBC. The DataDrivenDBInputFormat provided with Hadoop partitions a query's results over several map tasks.

Reading a table is typically done with a simple query such as:

```
SELECT col1,col2,col3,... FROM tableName
```

But often, better import performance can be gained by dividing this query across multiple nodes. This is done using a *splitting column*. Using metadata about the table, Sqoop will guess a good column to use for splitting the table (typically the primary key for the table, if one exists). The minimum and maximum values for the primary key column are retrieved, and then these are used in conjunction with a target number of tasks to determine the queries that each map task should issue.

For example, suppose the widgets table had 100,000 entries, with the id column containing values 0 through 99,999. When importing this table, Sqoop would determine that id is the primary key column for the table. When starting the MapReduce job, the DataDrivenDBInputFormat used to perform the import would then issue a statement such as SELECT MIN(id), MAX(id) FROM widgets. These values would then be used to interpolate over the entire range of data. Assuming we specified that 5 map tasks should run in parallel (with -m 5), this would result in each map task executing queries such as: SELECT id, widget_name, ... FROM widgets WHERE id >= 0 AND id < 20000, SELECT id, widget_name, ... FROM widgets WHERE id >= 20000 AND id < 40000, and so on.

The choice of splitting column is essential to efficiently parallelizing work. If the id column were not uniformly distributed (perhaps there are no widgets with IDs between 50,000 and 75,000), then some map tasks may have little or no work to perform, whereas others have a great deal. Users can specify a particular splitting column when running an import job, to tune the job to the data's actual distribution. If an import job is run as a single (sequential) task with -m 1, then this split process is not performed.

After generating the deserialization code and configuring the InputFormat, Sqoop sends the job to the MapReduce cluster. Map tasks execute the queries and deserialize rows from the ResultSet into instances of the generated class, which are either stored directly in SequenceFiles or transformed into delimited text before being written to HDFS.

Controlling the Import

Sqoop does not need to import an entire table at a time. For example, a subset of the table's columns can be specified for import. Users can also specify a WHERE clause to include in queries, which bound the rows of the table to import. For example, if widgets 0 through 99,999 were imported last month, but this month our vendor catalog included 1,000 new types of widget, an import could be configured with the clause WHERE id >= 100000; this will start an import job retrieving all the new rows added to the source database since the previous import run. User-supplied WHERE clauses are applied before task splitting is performed, and are pushed down into the queries executed by each task.

Imports and Consistency

When importing data to HDFS, it is important that you ensure access to a consistent snapshot of the source data. Map tasks reading from a database in parallel are running in separate processes. Thus, they cannot share a single database transaction. The best way to do this is to ensure that any processes that update existing rows of a table are disabled during the import.

Direct-mode Imports

Sqoop's architecture allows it to choose from multiple available strategies for performing an import. Most databases will use the DataDrivenDBInputFormat-based approach described above. Some databases offer specific tools designed to extract data quickly. For example, MySQL's mysqldump application can read from a table with greater throughput than a JDBC channel. The use of these external tools is referred to as *direct mode* in Sqoop's documentation. Direct mode must be specifically enabled by the user (via the --direct argument), as it is not as general-purpose as the JDBC approach. (For example, MySQL's direct mode cannot handle large objects—CLOB or BLOB columns, as Sqoop needs to use a JDBC-specific API to load these columns into HDFS.)

For databases that provide such tools, Sqoop can use these to great effect. A direct-mode import from MySQL is usually much more efficient (in terms of map tasks and time required) than a comparable JDBC-based import. Sqoop will still launch multiple map tasks in parallel. These tasks will then spawn instances of the mysqldump program and read its output. The effect is similar to a distributed implementation of mk-parallel-dump from the Maatkit (*http://www.maatkit.org*) tool set.

Even when direct mode is used to access the contents of a database, the metadata is still queried through JDBC.

Working with Imported Data

Once data has been imported to HDFS, it is now ready for processing by custom MapReduce programs. Text-based imports can be easily used in scripts run with Hadoop Streaming or in MapReduce jobs run with the default TextInputFormat.

To use individual fields of an imported record, though, the field delimiters (and any escape/enclosing characters) must be parsed and the field values extracted and converted to the appropriate data types. For example, the id of the "sprocket" widget is represented as the string "1" in the text file, but should be parsed into an Integer or int variable in Java. The generated table class provided by Sqoop can automate this process, allowing you to focus on the actual MapReduce job to run. Each auto-generated class has several overloaded methods named parse() that operate on the data represented as Text, CharSequence, char[], or other common types.

The MapReduce application called MaxWidgetId (available in the example code) will find the widget with the highest ID.

The class can be compiled into a JAR file along with *Widget.java*. Both Hadoop (*hadoop-core-version.jar*) and Sqoop (*sqoop-version.jar*) will need to be on the classpath for compilation. The class files can then be combined into a JAR file and executed like so:

```
% jar cvvf widgets.jar *.class
% HADOOP_CLASSPATH=/usr/lib/sqoop/sqoop-version.jar hadoop jar \
> widgets.jar MaxWidgetId -libjars /usr/lib/sqoop/sqoop-version.jar
```

This command line ensures that Sqoop is on the classpath locally (via $HADOOP_CLASS PATH), when running the MaxWidgetId.run() method, as well as when map tasks are running on the cluster (via the -libjars argument).

When run, the *maxwidgets* path in HDFS will contain a file named *part-r-00000* with the following expected result:

```
3,gadget,99.99,1983-08-13,13,Our flagship product
```

It is worth noting that in this example MapReduce program, a `Widget` object was emitted from the mapper to the reducer; the auto-generated `Widget` class implements the `Writable` interface provided by Hadoop, which allows the object to be sent via Hadoop's serialization mechanism, as well as written to and read from SequenceFiles.

The `MaxWidgetId` example is built on the new MapReduce API. MapReduce applications that rely on Sqoop-generated code can be built on the new or old APIs, though some advanced features (such as working with large objects) are more convenient to use in the new API.

Imported Data and Hive

As noted in Chapter 12, for many types of analysis, using a system like Hive to handle relational operations can dramatically ease the development of the analytic pipeline. Especially for data originally from a relational data source, using Hive makes a lot of sense. Hive and Sqoop together form a powerful toolchain for performing analysis.

Suppose we had another log of data in our system, coming from a web-based widget purchasing system. This may return log files containing a widget id, a quantity, a shipping address, and an order date.

Here is a snippet from an example log of this type:

```
1,15,120 Any St.,Los Angeles,CA,90210,2010-08-01
3,4,120 Any St.,Los Angeles,CA,90210,2010-08-01
2,5,400 Some Pl.,Cupertino,CA,95014,2010-07-30
2,7,88 Mile Rd.,Manhattan,NY,10005,2010-07-18
```

By using Hadoop to analyze this purchase log, we can gain insight into our sales operation. By combining this data with the data extracted from our relational data source (the `widgets` table), we can do better. In this example session, we will compute which zip code is responsible for the most sales dollars, so we can better focus our sales team's operations. Doing this requires data from both the sales log and the `widgets` table.

The above table should be in a local file named *sales.log* for this to work.

First, let's load the sales data into Hive:

```
hive> CREATE TABLE sales(widget_id INT, qty INT,
    > street STRING, city STRING, state STRING,
    > zip INT, sale_date STRING)
    > ROW FORMAT DELIMITED FIELDS TERMINATED BY ',';
OK
Time taken: 5.248 seconds
hive> LOAD DATA LOCAL INPATH "sales.log" INTO TABLE sales;
Copying data from file:/home/sales.log
Loading data to table sales
OK
Time taken: 0.188 seconds
```

Sqoop can generate a Hive table based on a table from an existing relational data source. Since we've already imported the widgets data to HDFS, we can generate the Hive table definition and then load in the HDFS-resident data:

```
% sqoop create-hive-table --connect jdbc:mysql://localhost/hadoopguide \
> --table widgets --fields-terminated-by ','
...
10/06/23 18:05:34 INFO hive.HiveImport: OK
10/06/23 18:05:34 INFO hive.HiveImport: Time taken: 3.22 seconds
10/06/23 18:05:35 INFO hive.HiveImport: Hive import complete.
% hive
hive> LOAD DATA INPATH "widgets" INTO TABLE widgets;
Loading data to table widgets
OK
Time taken: 3.265 seconds
```

When creating a Hive table definition with a specific already-imported dataset in mind, we need to specify the delimiters used in that dataset. Otherwise, Sqoop will allow Hive to use its default delimiters (which are different from Sqoop's default delimiters).

Hive's type system is less rich than that of most SQL systems. Many SQL types do not have direct analogues in Hive. When Sqoop generates a Hive table definition for an import, it uses the best Hive type available to hold a column's values. This may result in a decrease in precision. When this occurs, Sqoop will provide you with a warning message, such as this one:

```
10/06/23 18:09:36 WARN hive.TableDefWriter:
Column design_date had to be
cast to a less precise type in Hive
```

This three-step process of importing data to HDFS, creating the Hive table, and then loading the HDFS-resident data into Hive can be shortened to one step if you know that you want to import straight from a database directly into Hive. During an import, Sqoop can generate the Hive table definition and then load in the data. Had we not already performed the import, we could have executed this command, which re-creates the widgets table in Hive, based on the copy in MySQL:

```
% sqoop import --connect jdbc:mysql://localhost/hadoopguide \
> --table widgets -m 1 --hive-import
```

The sqoop import tool run with the --hive-import argument will load the data directly from the source database into Hive; it infers a Hive schema automatically based on the schema for the table in the source database. Using this, you can get started working with your data in Hive with only one command.

Regardless of which data import route we chose, we can now use the `widgets` data set and the `sales` data set together to calculate the most profitable zip code. Let's do so, and also save the result of this query in another table for later:

```
hive> CREATE TABLE zip_profits (sales_vol DOUBLE, zip INT);
OK

hive> INSERT OVERWRITE TABLE zip_profits
    > SELECT SUM(w.price * s.qty) AS sales_vol, s.zip  FROM SALES s
    > JOIN widgets w ON (s.widget_id = w.id) GROUP BY s.zip;
...
3 Rows loaded to zip_profits
OK

hive> SELECT * FROM zip_profits ORDER BY sales_vol DESC;
...
OK
403.71  90210
28.0    10005
20.0    95014
```

Importing Large Objects

Most databases provide the capability to store large amounts of data in a single field. Depending on whether this data is textual or binary in nature, it is usually represented as a `CLOB` or `BLOB` column in the table. These "large objects" are often handled specially by the database itself. In particular, most tables are physically laid out on disk as in Figure 15-2. When scanning through rows to determine which rows match the criteria for a particular query, this typically involves reading all columns of each row from disk. If large objects were stored "inline" in this fashion, they would adversely affect the performance of such scans. Therefore, large objects are often stored externally from their rows, as in Figure 15-3. Accessing a large object often requires "opening" it through the reference contained in the row.

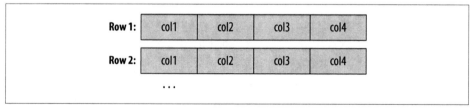

Figure 15-2. Database tables are typically physically represented as an array of rows, with all the columns in a row stored adjacent to one another

The difficulty of working with large objects in a database suggests that a system such as Hadoop, which is much better suited to storing and processing large, complex data objects, is an ideal repository for such information. Sqoop can extract large objects from tables and store them in HDFS for further processing.

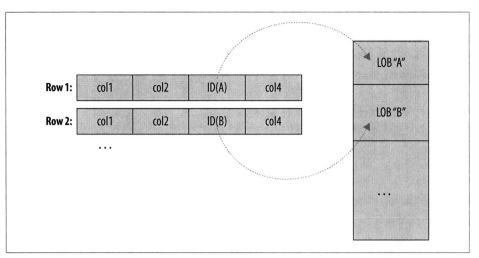

Figure 15-3. Large objects are usually held in a separate area of storage; the main row storage contains indirect references to the large objects

As in a database, MapReduce typically *materializes* every record before passing it along to the mapper. If individual records are truly large, this can be very inefficient.

As shown earlier, records imported by Sqoop are laid out on disk in a fashion very similar to a database's internal structure: an array of records with all fields of a record concatenated together. When running a MapReduce program over imported records, each map task must fully materialize all fields of each record in its input split. If the contents of a large object field are only relevant for a small subset of the total number of records used as input to a MapReduce program, it would be inefficient to fully materialize all these records. Furthermore, depending on the size of the large object, full materialization in memory may be impossible.

To overcome these difficulties, Sqoop will store imported large objects in a separate file called a LobFile. The LobFile format can store individual records of very large size (a 64-bit address space is used). Each record in a LobFile holds a single large object. The LobFile format allows clients to hold a reference to a record without accessing the record contents. When records are accessed, this is done through a `java.io.Input Stream` (for binary objects) or `java.io.Reader` (for character-based objects).

When a record is imported, the "normal" fields will be materialized together in a text file, along with a reference to the LobFile where a CLOB or BLOB column is stored. For example, suppose our `widgets` table contained a BLOB field named `schematic` holding the actual schematic diagram for each widget.

An imported record might then look like:

```
2,gizmo,4.00,2009-11-30,4,null,externalLob(lf,lobfile0,100,5011714)
```

The externalLob(...) text is a reference to an externally stored large object, stored in LobFile format (lf) in a file named *lobfile0*, with the specified byte offset and length inside that file.

When working with this record, the Widget.get_schematic() method would return an object of type BlobRef referencing the schematic column, but not actually containing its contents. The BlobRef.getDataStream() method actually opens the LobFile and returns an InputStream allowing you to access the schematic field's contents.

When running a MapReduce job processing many Widget records, you might need to access the schematic field of only a handful of records. This system allows you to incur the I/O costs of accessing only the required large object entries, as individual schematics may be several megabytes or more of data.

The BlobRef and ClobRef classes cache references to underlying LobFiles within a map task. If you do access the schematic field of several sequentially ordered records, they will take advantage of the existing file pointer's alignment on the next record body.

Performing an Export

In Sqoop, an *import* refers to the movement of data from a database system into HDFS. By contrast, an *export* uses HDFS as the source of data and a remote database as the destination. In the previous sections, we imported some data and then performed some analysis using Hive. We can export the results of this analysis to a database for consumption by other tools.

Before exporting a table from HDFS to a database, we must prepare the database to receive the data by creating the target table. While Sqoop can infer which Java types are appropriate to hold SQL data types, this translation does not work in both directions (for example, there are several possible SQL column definitions that can hold data in a Java String; this could be CHAR(64), VARCHAR(200), or something else entirely). Consequently, you must determine which types are most appropriate.

We are going to export the zip_profits table from Hive. We need to create a table in MySQL that has target columns in the same order, with the appropriate SQL types:

```
% mysql hadoopguide
mysql> CREATE TABLE sales_by_zip (volume DECIMAL(8,2), zip INTEGER);
Query OK, 0 rows affected (0.01 sec)
```

Then we run the export command:

```
% sqoop export --connect jdbc:mysql://localhost/hadoopguide -m 1 \
> --table sales_by_zip --export-dir /user/hive/warehouse/zip_profits \
> --input-fields-terminated-by '\0001'
...
10/07/02 16:16:50 INFO mapreduce.ExportJobBase: Transferred 41 bytes in 10.8947
seconds (3.7633 bytes/sec)
10/07/02 16:16:50 INFO mapreduce.ExportJobBase: Exported 3 records.
```

Finally, we can verify that the export worked by checking MySQL:

```
% mysql hadoopguide -e 'SELECT * FROM sales_by_zip'
+--------+-------+
| volume | zip   |
+--------+-------+
|  28.00 | 10005 |
| 403.71 | 90210 |
|  20.00 | 95014 |
+--------+-------+
```

When we created the `zip_profits` table in Hive, we did not specify any delimiters. So Hive used its default delimiters: a Ctrl-A character (Unicode `0x0001`) between fields, and a newline at the end of each record. When we used Hive to access the contents of this table (in a `SELECT` statement), Hive converted this to a tab-delimited representation for display on the console. But when reading the tables directly from files, we need to tell Sqoop which delimiters to use. Sqoop assumes records are newline-delimited by default, but needs to be told about the Ctrl-A field delimiters. The `--input-fields-terminated-by` argument to `sqoop export` specified this information. Sqoop supports several escape sequences (which start with a `'\'` character) when specifying delimiters. In the example syntax above, the escape sequence is enclosed in `'single quotes'` to ensure that the shell processes it literally. Without the quotes, the leading backslash itself may need to be escaped (for example, `--input-fields-terminated-by \\0001`). The escape sequences supported by Sqoop are listed in Table 15-1.

Table 15-1. Escape sequences can be used to specify nonprintable characters as field and record delimiters in Sqoop

Escape	Description
\b	backspace
\n	newline
\r	carriage return
\t	tab
\'	single-quote
\"	double-quote
\\	backslash
\0	NUL. This will insert NUL characters between fields or lines, or will disable enclosing/escaping if used for one of the `--enclosed-by`, `--optionally-enclosed-by`, or `--escaped-by` arguments.
\0*ooo*	The octal representation of a Unicode character's code point. The actual character is specified by the octal value *ooo*.
\0x*hhh*	The hexadecimal representation of a Unicode character's code point. This should be of the form \0x*hhh*, where *hhh* is the hex value. For example, `--fields-terminated-by '\0x10'` specifies the carriage return character.

Exports: A Deeper Look

The architecture of Sqoop's export capability is very similar in nature to how Sqoop performs imports. (See Figure 15-4.) Before performing the export, Sqoop picks a strategy based on the database connect string. For most systems, Sqoop uses JDBC. Sqoop then generates a Java class based on the target table definition. This generated class has the ability to parse records from text files and insert values of the appropriate types into a table (in addition to the ability to read the columns from a ResultSet). A MapReduce job is then launched that reads the source data files from HDFS, parses the records using the generated class, and executes the chosen export strategy.

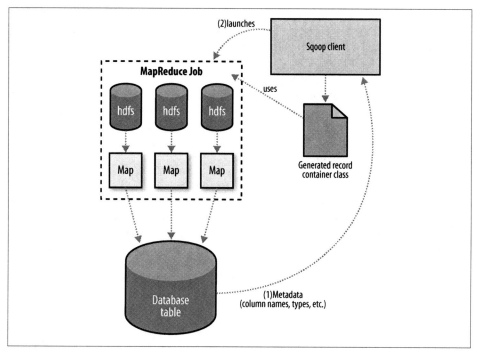

Figure 15-4. Exports are performed in parallel using MapReduce

The JDBC-based export strategy builds up batch INSERT statements that will each add multiple records to the target table. Inserting many records per statement performs much better than executing many single-row INSERT statements on most database systems. Separate threads are used to read from HDFS and communicate with the database, to ensure that I/O operations involving different systems are overlapped as much as possible.

For MySQL, Sqoop can employ a direct-mode strategy using mysqlimport. Each map task spawns a mysqlimport process that it communicates with via a named FIFO on the local filesystem. Data is then streamed into `mysqlimport` via the FIFO channel, and from there into the database.

While most MapReduce jobs reading from HDFS pick the degree of parallelism (number of map tasks) based on the number and size of the files to process, Sqoop's export system allows users explicit control over the number of tasks. The performance of the export can be affected by the number of parallel writers to the database, so Sqoop uses the `CombineFileInputFormat` class to group up the input files into a smaller number of map tasks.

Exports and Transactionality

Due to the parallel nature of the process, an export is often not an atomic operation. Sqoop will spawn multiple tasks to export slices of the data in parallel. These tasks can complete at different times, meaning that even though transactions are used inside tasks, results from one task may be visible before the results of another task. Moreover, databases often use fixed-size buffers to store transactions. As a result, one transaction cannot necessarily contain the entire set of operations performed by a task. Sqoop commits results every few thousand rows, to ensure that it does not run out of memory. These intermediate results are visible while the export continues. Applications that will use the results of an export should not be started until the export process is complete, or they may see partial results.

More problematically, if tasks fail (due to network problems or other issues), they may attempt to restart their slice of the export operation from the beginning, inserting duplicate records. At the time of this writing, Sqoop does not guard against this potentiality. Before launching an export job, constraints should be placed on the database table (for example, by designating a column as the primary key) to ensure uniqueness of rows. While future versions of Sqoop may use better recovery logic, this is not currently available.

Exports and SequenceFiles

The example export read source data from a Hive table, which is stored in HDFS as a delimited text file. Sqoop can also export delimited text files that were not Hive tables. For example, it can export text files that are the output of a MapReduce job.

Sqoop can also export records stored in SequenceFiles to an output table, although some restrictions apply. A SequenceFile can contain arbitrary record types. Sqoop's export tool will read objects from SequenceFiles and send them directly to the `Output` `Collector`, which passes the objects to the database export `OutputFormat`. To work with Sqoop, the record must be stored in the "value" portion of the SequenceFile's key-value pair format and must subclass the `com.cloudera.sqoop.lib.SqoopRecord` abstract class (as is done by all classes generated by Sqoop).

If you use the codegen tool (`sqoop-codegen`) to generate a `SqoopRecord` implementation for a record based on your export target table, you can then write a MapReduce program, which populates instances of this class and writes them to SequenceFiles. `sqoop-export` can then export these SequenceFiles to the table. Another means by which data may be in `SqoopRecord` instances in SequenceFiles is if data is imported from a database table to HDFS, modified in some fashion, and the results stored in SequenceFiles holding records of the same data type.

In this case, Sqoop should reuse the existing class definition to read data from SequenceFiles, rather than generate a new (temporary) record container class to perform the export, as is done when converting text-based records to database rows. You can suppress code generation and instead use an existing record class and jar by providing the `--class-name` and `--jar-file` arguments to Sqoop. Sqoop will use the specified class, loaded from the specified jar, when exporting records.

In the following example, we will re-import the `widgets` table as SequenceFiles, and then export it back to the database in a different table:

```
% sqoop import --connect jdbc:mysql://localhost/hadoopguide \
> --table widgets -m 1 --class-name WidgetHolder --as-sequencefile \
> --target-dir widget_sequence_files --bindir .
...
10/07/05 17:09:13 INFO mapreduce.ImportJobBase: Retrieved 3 records.

% mysql hadoopguide
mysql> CREATE TABLE widgets2(id INT, widget_name VARCHAR(100),
    -> price DOUBLE, designed DATE, version INT, notes VARCHAR(200));
Query OK, 0 rows affected (0.03 sec)

mysql> exit;

% sqoop export --connect jdbc:mysql://localhost/hadoopguide \
> --table widgets2 -m 1 --class-name WidgetHolder \
> --jar-file widgets.jar --export-dir widget_sequence_files
...
10/07/05 17:26:44 INFO mapreduce.ExportJobBase: Exported 3 records.
```

During the import, we specified the SequenceFile format, and that we wanted the jar file to be placed in the current directory (with `--bindir`), so we can reuse it. Otherwise, it would be placed in a temporary directory. We then created a destination table for the export, which had a slightly different schema, albeit one that is compatible with the original data. We then ran an export that used the existing generated code to read the records from the SequenceFile and write them to the database.

CHAPTER 16

Case Studies

Hadoop Usage at Last.fm

Last.fm: The Social Music Revolution

Founded in 2002, Last.fm is an Internet radio and music community website that offers many services to its users, such as free music streams and downloads, music and event recommendations, personalized charts, and much more. There are about 25 million people who use Last.fm every month, generating huge amounts of data that need to be processed. One example of this is users transmitting information indicating which songs they are listening to (this is known as "scrobbling"). This data is processed and stored by Last.fm, so the user can access it directly (in the form of charts), and it is also used to make decisions about users' musical tastes and compatibility, and artist and track similarity.

Hadoop at Last.fm

As Last.fm's service developed and the number of users grew from thousands to millions, storing, processing, and managing all the incoming data became increasingly challenging. Fortunately, Hadoop was quickly becoming stable enough and was enthusiastically adopted as it became clear how many problems it solved. It was first used at Last.fm in early 2006 and was put into production a few months later. There were several reasons for adopting Hadoop at Last.fm:

- The distributed filesystem provided redundant backups for the data stored on it (e.g., web logs, user listening data) at no extra cost.
- Scalability was simplified through the ability to add cheap, commodity hardware when required.
- The cost was right (free) at a time when Last.fm had limited financial resources.

- The open source code and active community meant that Last.fm could freely modify Hadoop to add custom features and patches.
- Hadoop provided a flexible framework for running distributed computing algorithms with a relatively easy learning curve.

Hadoop has now become a crucial part of Last.fm's infrastructure, currently consisting of two Hadoop clusters spanning over 50 machines, 300 cores, and 100 TB of disk space. Hundreds of daily jobs are run on the clusters performing operations, such as logfile analysis, evaluation of A/B tests, ad hoc processing, and charts generation. This case study will focus on the process of generating charts, as this was the first usage of Hadoop at Last.fm and illustrates the power and flexibility that Hadoop provides over other approaches when working with very large datasets.

Generating Charts with Hadoop

Last.fm uses user-generated track listening data to produce many different types of charts, such as weekly charts for tracks, per country and per user. A number of Hadoop programs are used to process the listening data and generate these charts, and these run on a daily, weekly, or monthly basis. Figure 16-1 shows an example of how this data is displayed on the site; in this case, the weekly top tracks.

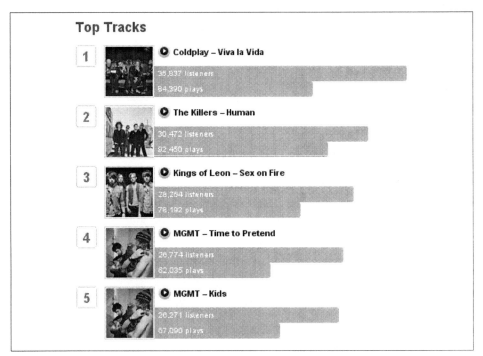

Figure 16-1. Last.fm top tracks chart

Listening data typically arrives at Last.fm from one of two sources:

- A user plays a track of her own (e.g., listening to an MP3 file on a PC or other device), and this information is sent to Last.fm using either the official Last.fm client application or one of many hundreds of third-party applications.
- A user tunes into one of Last.fm's Internet radio stations and streams a song to her computer. The Last.fm player or website can be used to access these streams and extra functionality is made available to the user, allowing her to love, skip, or ban each track that she listens to.

When processing the received data, we distinguish between a track listen submitted by a user (the first source above, referred to as a *scrobble* from here on) and a track listened to on the Last.fm radio (the second source, mentioned earlier, referred to as a *radio listen* from here on). This distinction is very important in order to prevent a feedback loop in the Last.fm recommendation system, which is based only on scrobbles. One of the most fundamental Hadoop jobs at Last.fm takes the incoming listening data and summarizes it into a format that can be used for display purposes on the Last.fm website as well as input to other Hadoop programs. This is achieved by the Track Statistics program, which is the example described in the following sections.

The Track Statistics Program

When track listening data is submitted to Last.fm, it undergoes a validation and conversion phase, the end result of which is a number of space-delimited text files containing the user ID, the track ID, the number of times the track was scrobbled, the number of times the track was listened to on the radio, and the number of times it was skipped. Table 16-1 contains sample listening data, which is used in the following examples as input to the Track Statistics program (the real data is gigabytes in size and includes many more fields that have been omitted here for simplicity's sake).

Table 16-1. Listening data

UserId	TrackId	Scrobble	Radio	Skip
111115	222	0	1	0
111113	225	1	0	0
111117	223	0	1	1
111115	225	1	0	0

These text files are the initial input provided to the Track Statistics program, which consists of two jobs that calculate various values from this data and a third job that merges the results (see Figure 16-2).

The Unique Listeners job calculates the total number of unique listeners for a track by counting the first listen by a user and ignoring all other listens by the same user. The Sum job accumulates the total listens, scrobbles, radio listens, and skips for each track

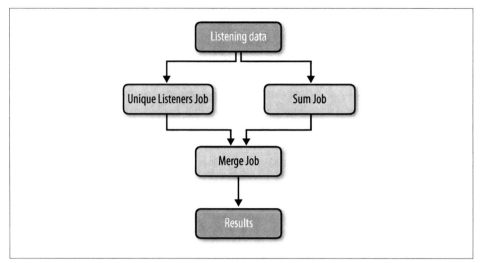

Figure 16-2. TrackStats jobs

by counting these values for all listens by all users. Although the input format of these two jobs is identical, two separate jobs are needed, as the Unique Listeners job is responsible for emitting values per track per user, and the Sum job emits values per track. The final "Merge" job is responsible for merging the intermediate output of the two other jobs into the final result. The end results of running the program are the following values per track:

- Number of unique listeners
- Number of times the track was scrobbled
- Number of times the track was listened to on the radio
- Number of times the track was listened to in total
- Number of times the track was skipped on the radio

Each job and its MapReduce phases are described in more detail next. Please note that the provided code snippets have been simplified due to space constraints; for download details for the full code listings, refer to the preface.

Calculating the number of unique listeners

The Unique Listeners job calculates, per track, the number of unique listeners.

UniqueListenerMapper. The UniqueListenersMapper processes the space-delimited raw listening data and emits the user ID associated with each track ID:

```
public void map(LongWritable position, Text rawLine, OutputCollector<IntWritable,
    IntWritable> output, Reporter reporter) throws IOException {

    String[] parts = (rawLine.toString()).split(" ");
```

```
    int scrobbles = Integer.parseInt(parts[TrackStatisticsProgram.COL_SCROBBLES]);
    int radioListens = Integer.parseInt(parts[TrackStatisticsProgram.COL_RADIO]);
    // if track somehow is marked with zero plays - ignore
    if (scrobbles <= 0 && radioListens <= 0) {
      return;
    }
    // if we get to here then user has listened to track,
    // so output user id against track id
    IntWritable trackId = new IntWritable(
      Integer.parseInt(parts[TrackStatisticsProgram.COL_TRACKID]));
    IntWritable userId = new IntWritable(
      Integer.parseInt(parts[TrackStatisticsProgram.COL_USERID]));
    output.collect(trackId, userId);
  }
```

UniqueListenersReducer. The UniqueListenersReducers receives a list of user IDs per track ID and puts these IDs into a Set to remove any duplicates. The size of this set is then emitted (i.e., the number of unique listeners) for each track ID. Storing all the reduce values in a Set runs the risk of running out of memory if there are many values for a certain key. This hasn't happened in practice, but to overcome this, an extra MapReduce step could be introduced to remove all the duplicate values or a secondary sort could be used (for more details, see "Secondary Sort" on page 241):

```
public void reduce(IntWritable trackId, Iterator<IntWritable> values,
    OutputCollector<IntWritable, IntWritable> output, Reporter reporter)
    throws IOException {

  Set<Integer> userIds = new HashSet<Integer>();
  // add all userIds to the set, duplicates automatically removed (set contract)
  while (values.hasNext()) {
    IntWritable userId = values.next();
    userIds.add(Integer.valueOf(userId.get()));
  }
  // output trackId -> number of unique listeners per track
  output.collect(trackId, new IntWritable(userIds.size()));
}
```

Table 16-2 shows the sample input data for the job. The map output appears in Table 16-3 and the reduce output in Table 16-4.

Table 16-2. Job input

Line of file	UserId	TrackId	Scrobbled	Radio play	Skip
LongWritable	IntWritable	IntWritable	Boolean	Boolean	Boolean
0	11115	222	0	1	0
1	11113	225	1	0	0
2	11117	223	0	1	1
3	11115	225	1	0	0

Table 16-3. Mapper output

TrackId	UserId
IntWritable	IntWritable
222	11115
225	11113
223	11117
225	11115

Table 16-4. Reducer output

TrackId	#listeners
IntWritable	IntWritable
222	1
225	2
223	1

Summing the track totals

The Sum job is relatively simple; it just adds up the values we are interested in for each track.

SumMapper. The input data is again the raw text files, but in this case, it is handled quite differently. The desired end result is a number of totals (unique listener count, play count, scrobble count, radio listen count, skip count) associated with each track. To simplify things, we use an intermediate TrackStats object generated using Hadoop Record I/O, which implements WritableComparable (so it can be used as output) to hold these values. The mapper creates a TrackStats object and sets the values on it for each line in the file, except for the unique listener count, which is left empty (it will be filled in by the final merge job):

```
public void map(LongWritable position, Text rawLine,
        OutputCollector<IntWritable, TrackStats> output, Reporter reporter)
        throws IOException {

    String[] parts = (rawLine.toString()).split(" ");
    int trackId = Integer.parseInt(parts[TrackStatisticsProgram.COL_TRACKID]);
    int scrobbles = Integer.parseInt(parts[TrackStatisticsProgram.COL_SCROBBLES]);
    int radio = Integer.parseInt(parts[TrackStatisticsProgram.COL_RADIO]);
    int skip = Integer.parseInt(parts[TrackStatisticsProgram.COL_SKIP]);
    // set number of listeners to 0 (this is calculated later)
    // and other values as provided in text file
    TrackStats trackstat = new TrackStats(0, scrobbles + radio, scrobbles, radio, skip);
    output.collect(new IntWritable(trackId), trackstat);
}
```

SumReducer. In this case, the reducer performs a very similar function to the mapper—it sums the statistics per track and returns an overall total:

```
public void reduce(IntWritable trackId, Iterator<TrackStats> values,
    OutputCollector<IntWritable, TrackStats> output, Reporter reporter)
    throws IOException {

  TrackStats sum = new TrackStats(); // holds the totals for this track
  while (values.hasNext()) {
    TrackStats trackStats = (TrackStats) values.next();
    sum.setListeners(sum.getListeners() + trackStats.getListeners());
    sum.setPlays(sum.getPlays() + trackStats.getPlays());
    sum.setSkips(sum.getSkips() + trackStats.getSkips());
    sum.setScrobbles(sum.getScrobbles() + trackStats.getScrobbles());
    sum.setRadioPlays(sum.getRadioPlays() + trackStats.getRadioPlays());
  }
  output.collect(trackId, sum);
}
```

Table 16-5 shows the input data for the job (the same as for the Unique Listeners job). The map output appears in Table 16-6 and the reduce output in Table 16-7.

Table 16-5. Job input

Line	UserId	TrackId	Scrobbled	Radio play	Skip
LongWritable	IntWritable	IntWritable	Boolean	Boolean	Boolean
0	11115	222	0	1	0
1	11113	225	1	0	0
2	11117	223	0	1	1
3	11115	225	1	0	0

Table 16-6. Map output

TrackId	#listeners	#plays	#scrobbles	#radio plays	#skips
IntWritable	IntWritable	IntWritable	IntWritable	IntWritable	IntWritable
222	0	1	0	1	0
225	0	1	1	0	0
223	0	1	0	1	1
225	0	1	1	0	0

Table 16-7. Reduce output

TrackId	#listeners	#plays	#scrobbles	#radio plays	#skips
IntWritable	IntWritable	IntWritable	IntWritable	IntWritable	IntWritable
222	0	1	0	1	0
225	0	2	2	0	0
223	0	1	0	1	1

Merging the results

The final job needs to merge the output from the two previous jobs: the number of unique listeners per track and the statistics per track. In order to be able to merge these different inputs, two different mappers (one for each type of input) are used. The two intermediate jobs are configured to write their results to different paths, and the MultipleInputs class is used to specify which mapper will process which files. The following code shows how the JobConf for the job is set up to do this:

```
MultipleInputs.addInputPath(conf, sumInputDir,
    SequenceFileInputFormat.class, IdentityMapper.class);

MultipleInputs.addInputPath(conf, listenersInputDir,
    SequenceFileInputFormat.class, MergeListenersMapper.class);
```

It is possible to use a single mapper to handle different inputs, but the example solution is more convenient and elegant.

MergeListenersMapper. This mapper is used to process the UniqueListenerJob's output of unique listeners per track. It creates a TrackStats object in a similar manner to the SumMapper, but this time, it fills in only the unique listener count per track and leaves the other values empty:

```
public void map(IntWritable trackId, IntWritable uniqueListenerCount,
    OutputCollector<IntWritable, TrackStats> output, Reporter reporter)
    throws IOException {
  TrackStats trackStats = new TrackStats();
  trackStats.setListeners(uniqueListenerCount.get());
  output.collect(trackId, trackStats);
}
```

Table 16-8 shows some input for the mapper; the corresponding output is shown in Table 16-9.

Table 16-8. MergeListenersMapper input

TrackId	#listeners
IntWritable	IntWritable
222	1
225	2
223	1

Table 16-9. MergeListenersMapper output

TrackId	#listeners	#plays	#scrobbles	#radio	#skips
222	1	0	0	0	0
225	2	0	0	0	0
223	1	0	0	0	0

IdentityMapper. The `IdentityMapper` is configured to process the `SumJob`'s output of `TrackStats` objects and, as no additional processing is required, it directly emits the input data (see Table 16-10).

Table 16-10. IdentityMapper input and output

TrackId	#listeners	#plays	#scrobbles	#radio	#skips
IntWritable	IntWritable	IntWritable	IntWritable	IntWritable	IntWritable
222	0	1	0	1	0
225	0	2	2	0	0
223	0	1	0	1	1

SumReducer. The two mappers above emit values of the same type: a `TrackStats` object per track, with different values filled in. The final reduce phase can reuse the `SumReducer` described earlier to create a `TrackStats` object per track, sum up all the values, and emit it (see Table 16-11).

Table 16-11. Final SumReducer output

TrackId	#listeners	#plays	#scrobbles	#radio	#skips
IntWritable	IntWritable	IntWritable	IntWritable	IntWritable	IntWritable
222	1	1	0	1	0
225	2	2	2	0	0
223	1	1	0	1	1

The final output files are then accumulated and copied to a server where a web service makes the data available to the Last.fm website for display. An example of this is shown in Figure 16-3, where the total number of listeners and plays are displayed for a track.

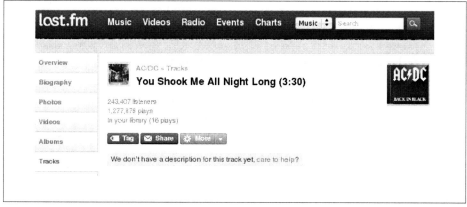

Figure 16-3. TrackStats result

Summary

Hadoop has become an essential part of Last.fm's infrastructure and is used to generate and process a wide variety of datasets ranging from web logs to user listening data. The example covered here has been simplified considerably in order to get the key concepts across; in real-world usage the input data has a more complicated structure and the code that processes it is more complex. Hadoop itself, while mature enough for production use, is still in active development, and new features and improvements are added by the Hadoop community every week. We at Last.fm are happy to be part of this community as a contributor of code and ideas, and as end users of a great piece of open source technology.

—Adrian Woodhead and Marc de Palol

Hadoop and Hive at Facebook

Introduction

Hadoop can be used to form core backend batch and near real-time computing infrastructures. It can also be used to store and archive massive datasets. In this case study, we will explore backend data architectures and the role Hadoop can play in them. We will describe hypothetical Hadoop configurations, potential uses of Hive—an open source data warehousing and SQL infrastructure built on top of Hadoop—and the different kinds of business and product applications that have been built using this infrastructure.

Hadoop at Facebook

History

The amount of log and dimension data in Facebook that needs to be processed and stored has exploded as the usage of the site has increased. A key requirement for any data processing platform for this environment is the ability to be able to scale rapidly in tandem. Further, engineering resources being limited, the system should be very reliable and easy to use and maintain.

Initially, data warehousing at Facebook was performed entirely on an Oracle instance. After we started hitting scalability and performance problems, we investigated whether there were open source technologies that could be used in our environment. As part of this investigation, we deployed a relatively small Hadoop instance and started publishing some of our core datasets into this instance. Hadoop was attractive because Yahoo! was using it internally for its batch processing needs and because we were familiar with the simplicity and scalability of the MapReduce model as popularized by Google.

Our initial prototype was very successful: the engineers loved the ability to process massive amounts of data in reasonable timeframes, an ability that we just did not have before. They also loved being able to use their favorite programming language for processing (using Hadoop streaming). Having our core datasets published in one centralized data store was also very convenient. At around the same time, we started developing Hive. This made it even easier for users to process data in the Hadoop cluster by being able to express common computations in the form of SQL, a language with which most engineers and analysts are familiar.

As a result, the cluster size and usage grew leaps and bounds, and today Facebook is running the second largest Hadoop cluster in the world. As of this writing, we hold more than 2 PB of data in Hadoop and load more than 10 TB of data into it every day. Our Hadoop instance has 2,400 cores and about 9 TB of memory and runs at 100% utilization at many points during the day. We are able to scale out this cluster rapidly in response to our growth, and we have been able to take advantage of open source by modifying Hadoop where required to suit our needs. We have contributed back to open source, both in the form of contributions to some core components of Hadoop as well as by open-sourcing Hive, which is now a Hadoop subproject.

Use cases

There are at least four interrelated but distinct classes of uses for Hadoop at Facebook:

- Producing daily and hourly summaries over large amounts of data. These summaries are used for a number of different purposes within the company:
    - Reports based on these summaries are used by engineering and nonengineering functional teams to drive product decisions. These summaries include reports on growth of the users, page views, and average time spent on the site by the users.
    - Providing performance numbers about advertisement campaigns that are run on Facebook.
    - Backend processing for site features such as people you may like and applications you may like.
- Running ad hoc jobs over historical data. These analyses help answer questions from our product groups and executive team.
- As a de facto long-term archival store for our log datasets.
- To look up log events by specific attributes (where logs are indexed by such attributes), which is used to maintain the integrity of the site and protect users against spambots.

Data architecture

Figure 16-4 shows the basic components of our architecture and the data flow within these components.

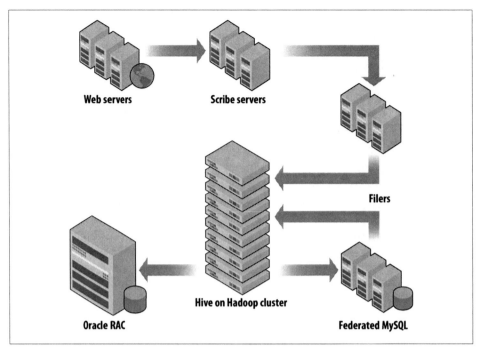

Figure 16-4. Data warehousing architecture at Facebook

As shown in Figure 16-4, the following components are used in processing data:

Scribe

Log data is generated by web servers as well as internal services such as the Search backend. We use Scribe, an open source log collection service developed in Facebook that deposits hundreds of log datasets with daily volume in tens of terabytes into a handful of NFS servers.

HDFS

A large fraction of this log data is copied into one central HDFS instance. Dimension data is also scraped from our internal MySQL databases and copied over into HDFS daily.

Hive/Hadoop

We use Hive, a Hadoop subproject developed in Facebook, to build a data warehouse over all the data collected in HDFS. Files in HDFS, including log data from Scribe and dimension data from the MySQL tier, are made available as tables with logical partitions. A SQL-like query language provided by Hive is used in conjunction with MapReduce to create/publish a variety of summaries and reports, as well as to perform historical analysis over these tables.

Tools

Browser-based interfaces built on top of Hive allow users to compose and launch Hive queries (which in turn launch MapReduce jobs) using just a few mouse clicks.

Traditional RDBMS

We use Oracle and MySQL databases to publish these summaries. The volume of data here is relatively small, but the query rate is high and needs real-time response.

DataBee

An in-house ETL workflow software that is used to provide a common framework for reliable batch processing across all data processing jobs.

Data from the NFS tier storing Scribe data is continuously replicated to the HDFS cluster by copier jobs. The NFS devices are mounted on the Hadoop tier and the copier processes run as map-only jobs on the Hadoop cluster. This makes it easy to scale the copier processes and makes them fault-resilient. Currently, we copy over 6 TB per day from Scribe to HDFS in this manner. We also download up to 4 TB of dimension data from our MySQL tier to HDFS every day. These are also conveniently arranged on the Hadoop cluster, as map-only jobs that copy data out of MySQL boxes.

Hadoop configuration

The central philosophy behind our Hadoop deployment is consolidation. We use a single HDFS instance, and a vast majority of processing is done in a single MapReduce cluster (running a single jobtracker). The reasons for this are fairly straightforward:

- We can minimize the administrative overheads by operating a single cluster.
- Data does not need to be duplicated. All data is available in a single place for all the use cases described previously.
- By using the same compute cluster across all departments, we get tremendous efficiencies.
- Our users work in a collaborative environment, so requirements in terms of quality of service are not onerous (yet).

We also have a single shared Hive metastore (using a MySQL database) that holds metadata about all the Hive tables stored in HDFS.

Hypothetical Use Case Studies

In this section, we will describe some typical problems that are common for large websites, which are difficult to solve through traditional warehousing technologies, simply because the costs and scales involved are prohibitively high. Hadoop and Hive can provide a more scalable and more cost-effective solution in such situations.

Advertiser insights and performance

One of the most common uses of Hadoop is to produce summaries from large volumes of data. It is very typical of large ad networks, such as Facebook ad network, Google AdSense, and many others, to provide advertisers with standard aggregated statistics about their ads that help the advertisers to tune their campaigns effectively. Computing advertisement performance numbers on large datasets is a very data-intensive operation, and the scalability and cost advantages of Hadoop and Hive can really help in computing these numbers in a reasonable time frame and at a reasonable cost.

Many ad networks provide standardized CPC- and CPM-based ad-units to the advertisers. The CPC ads are cost-per-click ads: the advertiser pays the ad network amounts that are dependent on the number of clicks that the particular ad gets from the users visiting the site. The CPM ads, on the other hand, bill the advertisers amounts that are proportional to the number of users who see the ad on the site. Apart from these standardized ad units, in the last few years ads that have more dynamic content that is tailored to each individual user have also become common in the online advertisement industry. Yahoo! does this through SmartAds, whereas Facebook provides its advertisers with Social Ads. The latter allows the advertisers to embed information from a user's network of friends; for example, a Nike ad may refer to a friend of the user who recently fanned Nike and shared that information with his friends on Facebook. In addition, Facebook also provides Engagement Ad units to the advertisers, wherein the users can more effectively interact with the ad, be it by commenting on it or by playing embedded videos. In general, a wide variety of ads are provided to the advertisers by the online ad networks, and this variety also adds yet another dimension to the various kinds of performance numbers that the advertisers are interested in getting about their campaigns.

At the most basic level, advertisers are interested in knowing the total and the number of unique users that have seen the ad or have clicked on it. For more dynamic ads, they may even be interested in getting the breakdown of these aggregated numbers by the kind of dynamic information shown in the ad unit or the kind of engagement action undertaken by the users on the ad. For example, a particular advertisement may have been shown 100,000 times to 30,000 unique users. Similarly, a video embedded inside an Engagement Ad may have been watched by 100,000 unique users. In addition, these performance numbers are typically reported for each ad, campaign, and account. An account may have multiple campaigns with each campaign running multiple ads on the network. Finally, these numbers are typically reported for different time durations by the ad networks. Typical durations are daily, rolling week, month to date, rolling month, and sometimes even for the entire lifetime of the campaign. Moreover, advertisers also look at the geographic breakdown of these numbers among other ways of slicing and dicing this data, such as what percentage of the total viewers or clickers of a particular ad are in the Asia Pacific region.

As is evident, there are four predominant dimension hierarchies: the account, campaign, and ad dimension; the time period; the type of interaction; and the user dimension. The last of these is used to report unique numbers, whereas the other three are the reporting dimensions. The user dimension is also used to create aggregated geographic profiles for the viewers and clickers of ads. All this information in totality allows the advertisers to tune their campaigns to improve their effectiveness on any given ad network. Aside from the multidimensional nature of this set of pipelines, the volumes of data processed and the rate at which this data is growing on a daily basis make this difficult to scale without a technology like Hadoop for large ad networks. As of this writing, for example, the ad log volume that is processed for ad performance numbers at Facebook is approximately 1 TB per day of (uncompressed) logs. This volume has seen a 30-fold increase since January 2008, when the volumes were in the range of 30 GB per day. Hadoop's ability to scale with hardware has been a major factor behind the ability of these pipelines to keep up with this data growth with minor tweaking of job configurations. Typically, these configuration changes involve increasing the number of reducers for the Hadoop jobs that are processing the intensive portions of these pipelines. The largest of these stages currently run with 400 reducers (an increase of eight times from the 50 reducers that were being used in January 2008).

Ad hoc analysis and product feedback

Apart from regular reports, another primary use case for a data warehousing solution is to be able to support ad hoc analysis and product feedback solutions. Any typical website, for example, makes product changes, and it is typical for product managers or engineers to understand the impact of a new feature, based on user engagement as well as on the click-through rate on that feature. The product team may even wish to do a deeper analysis on what is the impact of the change based on various regions and countries, such as whether this change increases the click-through rate of the users in US or whether it reduces the engagement of users in India. A lot of this type of analysis could be done with Hadoop by using Hive and regular SQL. The measurement of click-through rate can be easily expressed as a join of the impressions and clicks for the particular link related to the feature. This information can be joined with geographic information to compute the effect of product changes on different regions. Subsequently one can compute average click-through rate for different geographic regions by performing aggregations over them. All of these are easily expressible in Hive using a couple of SQL queries (that would, in turn, generate multiple Hadoop jobs). If only an estimate were required, the same queries can be run for a sample set of the users using sampling functionality natively supported by Hive. Some of this analysis needs the use of custom map and reduce scripts in conjunction with the Hive SQL, and that is also easy to plug into a Hive query.

A good example of a more complex analysis is estimating the peak number of users logging into the site per minute for the entire past year. This would involve sampling page view logs (because the total page view data for a popular website is huge), grouping it by time and then finding the number of new users at different time points via a custom reduce script. This is a good example where both SQL and MapReduce are required for solving the end user problem and something that is possible to achieve easily with Hive.

Data analysis

Hive and Hadoop can be easily used for training and scoring for data analysis applications. These data analysis applications can span multiple domains such as popular websites, bioinformatics companies, and oil exploration companies. A typical example of such an application in the online ad network industry would be the prediction of what features of an ad makes it more likely to be noticed by the user. The training phase typically would involve identifying the response metric and the predictive features. In this case, a good metric to measure the effectiveness of an ad could be its click-through rate. Some interesting features of the ad could be the industry vertical that it belongs to, the content of the ad, the placement of the ad on the page, and so on. Hive is easily useful for assembling training data and then feeding the same into a data analysis engine (typically R or user programs written in MapReduce). In this particular case, different ad performance numbers and features can be structured as tables in Hive. One can easily sample this data (sampling is required as R can only handle limited data volume) and perform the appropriate aggregations and joins using Hive queries to assemble a response table that contains the most important ad features that determine the effectiveness of an advertisement. However, since sampling loses information, some of the more important data analysis applications use parallel implementations of popular data analysis kernels using MapReduce framework.

Once the model has been trained, it may be deployed for scoring on a daily basis. The bulk of the data analysis tasks do not perform daily scoring though. Many of them are ad hoc in nature and require one-time analysis that can be used as input into product design process.

Hive

Overview

When we started using Hadoop, we very quickly became impressed by its scalability and availability. However, we were worried about widespread adoption, primarily because of the complexity involved in writing MapReduce programs in Java (as well as the cost of training users to write them). We were aware that a lot of engineers and analysts in the company understood SQL as a tool to query and analyze data, and that a lot of them were proficient in a number of scripting languages like PHP and Python. As a result, it was imperative for us to develop software that could bridge this gap between the languages that the users were proficient in and the languages required to program Hadoop.

It was also evident that a lot of our datasets were structured and could be easily partitioned. The natural consequence of these requirements was a system that could model data as tables and partitions and that could also provide a SQL-like language for query and analysis. Also essential was the ability to plug in customized MapReduce programs written in the programming language of the user's choice into the query. This system was called Hive. Hive is a data warehouse infrastructure built on top of Hadoop and serves as the predominant tool that is used to query the data stored in Hadoop at Facebook. In the following sections, we describe this system in more detail.

Data organization

Data is organized consistently across all datasets and is stored compressed, partitioned, and sorted:

Compression
Almost all datasets are stored as sequence files using gzip codec. Older datasets are recompressed to use the bzip codec that gives substantially more compression than gzip. Bzip is slower than gzip, but older data is accessed much less frequently and this performance hit is well worth the savings in terms of disk space.

Partitioning
Most datasets are partitioned by date. Individual partitions are loaded into Hive, which loads each partition into a separate HDFS directory. In most cases, this partitioning is based simply on datestamps associated with scribe logfiles. However, in some cases, we scan data and collate them based on timestamp available inside a log entry. Going forward, we are also going to be partitioning data on multiple attributes (for example, country and date).

Sorting
Each partition within a table is often sorted (and hash-partitioned) by unique ID (if one is present). This has a few key advantages:

- It is easy to run sampled queries on such datasets.
- We can build indexes on sorted data.
- Aggregates and joins involving unique IDs can be done very efficiently on such datasets.

Loading data into this long-term format is done by daily MapReduce jobs (and is distinct from the near real-time data import processes).

Query language

The Hive Query language is very SQL-like. It has traditional SQL constructs like joins, group bys, where, select, from clauses, and from clause subqueries. It tries to convert SQL commands into a set of MapReduce jobs. Apart from the normal SQL clauses, it has a bunch of other extensions, like the ability to specify custom mapper and reducer scripts in the query itself, the ability to insert into multiple tables, partitions, HDFS, or local files while doing a single scan of the data and the ability to run the query on data samples rather than the full dataset (this ability is fairly useful while testing queries). The Hive metastore stores the metadata for a table and provides this metadata to the Hive compiler for converting SQL commands to MapReduce jobs. Through partition pruning, map-side aggregations, and other features, the compiler tries to create plans that can optimize the runtime for the query.

Data pipelines using Hive

Additionally, the ability provided by Hive in terms of expressing data pipelines in SQL can and has provided the much needed flexibility in putting these pipelines together in an easy and expedient manner. This is especially useful for organizations and products that are still evolving and growing. Many of the operations needed in processing data pipelines are the well-understood SQL operations like join, group by, and distinct aggregations. With Hive's ability to convert SQL into a series of Hadoop MapReduce jobs, it becomes fairly easy to create and maintain these pipelines. We illustrate these facets of Hive in this section by using an example of a hypothetical ad network and showing how some typical aggregated reports needed by the advertisers can be computed using Hive. As an example, assuming that an online ad network stores information on ads in a table named dim_ads and stores all the impressions served to that ad in a table named impression_logs in Hive, with the latter table being partitioned by date, the daily impression numbers (both unique and total by campaign, that are routinely given by ad networks to the advertisers) for 2008-12-01 are expressible as the following SQL in Hive:

```
SELECT a.campaign_id, count(1), count(DISTINCT b.user_id)
FROM dim_ads a JOIN impression_logs b ON(b.ad_id = a.ad_id)
WHERE b.dateid = '2008-12-01'
GROUP BY a.campaign_id;
```

This would also be the typical SQL statement that one could use in other RDBMSs such as Oracle, DB2, and so on.

In order to compute the daily impression numbers by ad and account from the same joined data as earlier, Hive provides the ability to do multiple group bys simultaneously as shown in the following query (SQL-like but not strictly SQL):

```
FROM(
   SELECT a.ad_id, a.campaign_id, a.account_id, b.user_id
   FROM dim_ads a JOIN impression_logs b ON (b.ad_id = a.ad_id)
   WHERE b.dateid = '2008-12-01') x
INSERT OVERWRITE DIRECTORY 'results_gby_adid'
   SELECT x.ad_id, count(1), count(DISTINCT x.user_id) GROUP BY x.ad_id
INSERT OVERWRITE DIRECTORY 'results_gby_campaignid'
   SELECT x.campaign_id, count(1), count(DISTINCT x.user_id) GROUP BY x.campaign_id
INSERT OVERWRITE DIRECTORY 'results_gby_accountid'
   SELECT x.account_id, count(1), count(DISTINCT x.user_id) GROUP BY x.account_id;
```

In one of the optimizations that is being added to Hive, the query can be converted into a sequence of Hadoop MapReduce jobs that are able to scale with data skew. Essentially, the join is converted into one MapReduce job and the three group bys are converted into four MapReduce jobs, with the first one generating a partial aggregate on unique_id. This is especially useful because the distribution of impression_logs over unique_id is much more uniform as compared to ad_id (typically in an ad network, a few ads dominate in that they are shown more uniformly to the users). As a result, computing the partial aggregation by unique_id allows the pipeline to distribute the work more uniformly to the reducers. The same template can be used to compute performance numbers for different time periods by simply changing the date predicate in the query.

Computing the lifetime numbers can be more tricky though, as using the strategy described previously, one would have to scan all the partitions of the impression_logs table. Therefore, in order to compute the lifetime numbers, a more viable strategy is to store the lifetime counts on a per ad_id, unique_id grouping every day in a partition of an intermediate table. The data in this table combined with the next days impression_logs can be used to incrementally generate the lifetime ad performance numbers. As an example, in order to get the impression numbers for 2008-12-01, the intermediate table partition for 2008-11-30 is used. The Hive queries that can be used to achieve this are as follows:

```
INSERT OVERWRITE lifetime_partial_imps PARTITION(dateid='2008-12-01')
SELECT x.ad_id, x.user_id, sum(x.cnt)
FROM (
  SELECT a.ad_id, a.user_id, a.cnt
  FROM lifetime_partial_imps a
  WHERE a.dateid = '2008-11-30'
  UNION ALL
  SELECT b.ad_id, b.user_id, 1 as cnt
  FROM impression_log b
  WHERE b.dateid = '2008-12-01'
) x
GROUP BY x.ad_id, x.user_id;
```

This query computes the partial sums for 2008-12-01, which can be used for computing the 2008-12-01 numbers as well as the 2008-12-02 numbers (not shown here). The SQL is converted to a single Hadoop MapReduce job that essentially computes the group by on the combined stream of inputs. This SQL can be followed by the following Hive query, which computes the actual numbers for different groupings (similar to the one in the daily pipelines):

```
FROM(
  SELECT a.ad_id, a.campaign_id, a.account_id, b.user_id, b.cnt
    FROM dim_ads a JOIN lifetime_partial_imps b ON (b.ad_id = a.ad_id)
    WHERE b.dateid = '2008-12-01') x
INSERT OVERWRITE DIRECTORY 'results_gby_adid'
  SELECT x.ad_id, sum(x.cnt), count(DISTINCT x.user_id) GROUP BY x.ad_id
INSERT OVERWRITE DIRECTORY 'results_gby_campaignid'
  SELECT x.campaign_id, sum(x.cnt), count(DISTINCT x.user_id) GROUP BY x.campaign_id
INSERT OVERWRITE DIRECTORY 'results_gby_accountid'
  SELECT x.account_id, sum(x.cnt), count(DISTINCT x.user_id) GROUP BY x.account_id;
```

Hive and Hadoop are batch processing systems that cannot serve the computed data with the same latency as a usual RDBMS such as Oracle or MySQL. Therefore, on many occasions, it is still useful to load the summaries generated through Hive and Hadoop to a more traditional RDBMS for serving this data to users through different BI tools or even though a web portal.

Problems and Future Work

Fair sharing

Hadoop clusters typically run a mix of production daily jobs that need to finish computation within a reasonable time frame as well as ad hoc jobs that may be of different priorities and sizes. In typical installations, these jobs tend to run overnight, when interference from ad hoc jobs run by users is minimal. However, overlap between large ad hoc and production jobs is often unavoidable and, without adequate safeguards, can impact the latency of production jobs. ETL processing also contains several near real-time jobs that must be performed at hourly intervals (these include processes to copy Scribe data from NFS servers as well as hourly summaries computed over some datasets). It also means that a single rogue job can bring down the entire cluster and put production processes at risk.

The fair-sharing Hadoop jobscheduler, developed at Facebook and contributed back to Hadoop, provides a solution to many of these issues. It reserves guaranteed compute resources for specific pools of jobs while at the same time letting idle resources be used by everyone. It also prevents large jobs from hogging cluster resources by allocating compute resources in a fair manner across these pools. Memory can become one of the most contended resources in the cluster. We have made some changes to Hadoop so that if the JobTracker is low on memory, Hadoop job submissions are throttled. This can allow the user processes to run with reasonable per-process memory limits, and it is possible to put in place some monitoring scripts in order to prevent MapReduce jobs from impacting HDFS daemons (due primarily to high memory consumption) running on the same node. Log directories are stored in separate disk partitions and cleaned regularly, and we think it can also be useful to put MapReduce intermediate storage in separate disk partitions as well.

Space management

Capacity management continues to be a big challenge—utilization is increasing at a fast rate with growth of data. Many growing companies with growing datasets have the same pain. In many situations, much of this data is temporary in nature. In such cases, one can use retention settings in Hive and also recompress older data in bzip format to save on space. Although configurations are largely symmetrical from a disk storage point of view, adding a separate tier of high-storage-density machines to hold older data may prove beneficial. This will make it cheaper to store archival data in Hadoop. However, access to such data should be transparent. We are currently working on a data archival layer to make this possible and to unify all the aspects of dealing with older data.

Scribe-HDFS integration

Currently, Scribe writes to a handful of NFS filers from where data is picked up and delivered to HDFS by custom copier jobs as described earlier. We are working on making Scribe write directly to another HDFS instance. This will make it very easy to scale and administer Scribe. Due to the high uptime requirements for Scribe, its target HDFS instance is likely to be different from the production HDFS instance (so that it is isolated from any load/downtime issues due to user jobs).

Improvements to Hive

Hive is still under active development. A number of key features are being worked on such as order by and having clause support, more aggregate functions, more built in functions, datetime, data type, and so on. At the same time, a number of performance optimizations are being worked on, such as predicate pushdown and common subexpression elimination. On the integration side, JDBC and ODBC drivers are being developed in order to integrate with OLAP and BI tools. With all these optimizations, we hope that we can unlock the power of MapReduce and Hadoop and bring it closer to nonengineering communities as well within Facebook. For more information on this project, please visit *http://hadoop.apache.org/hive/*.

—Joydeep Sen Sarma and Ashish Thusoo

Nutch Search Engine

Background

Nutch is a framework for building scalable Internet crawlers and search engines. It's an Apache Software Foundation project, and a subproject of Lucene, and it's available under the Apache 2.0 license.

We won't go deeply into the anatomy of a web crawler as such—the purpose of this case study is to show how Hadoop can be used to implement various complex processing tasks typical for a search engine. Interested readers can find plenty of Nutch-specific information on the official site of the project (*http://lucene.apache.org/nutch*). Suffice to say that in order to create and maintain a search engine, one needs the following subsystems:

Database of pages
> This database keeps track of all pages known to the crawler and their status, such as the last time it visited the page, its fetching status, refresh interval, content checksum, etc. In Nutch terminology, this database is called *CrawlDb*.

List of pages to fetch

> As crawlers periodically refresh their view of the Web, they download new pages (previously unseen) or refresh pages that they think already expired. Nutch calls such a list of candidate pages prepared for fetching a *fetchlist*.

Raw page data

> Page content is downloaded from remote sites and stored locally in the original uninterpreted format, as a byte array. This data is called the *page content* in Nutch.

Parsed page data

> Page content is then parsed using a suitable parser—Nutch provides parsers for documents in many popular formats, such as HTML, PDF, Open Office and Microsoft Office, RSS, and others.

Link graph database

> This database is necessary to compute link-based page ranking scores, such as PageRank. For each URL known to Nutch, it contains a list of other URLs pointing to it, and their associated anchor text (from HTML `<a href="..">anchor text</a>` elements). This database is called *LinkDb*.

Full-text search index

> This is a classical inverted index, built from the collected page metadata and from the extracted plain-text content. It is implemented using the excellent Lucene library (*http://lucene.apache.org/java*).

We briefly mentioned before that Hadoop began its life as a component in Nutch, intended to improve its scalability and to address clear performance bottlenecks caused by a centralized data processing model. Nutch was also the first public proof-of-concept application ported to the framework that would later become Hadoop, and the effort required to port Nutch algorithms and data structures to Hadoop proved to be surprisingly small. This probably encouraged the following development of Hadoop as a separate subproject with the aim of providing a reusable framework for applications other than Nutch.

Currently, nearly all Nutch tools process data by running one or more MapReduce jobs.

Data Structures

There are several major data structures maintained in Nutch, and they all make use of Hadoop I/O classes and formats. Depending on the purpose of the data, and the way it's accessed once it's created, the data is kept either using Hadoop map files or sequence files.

Since the data is produced and processed by MapReduce jobs, which in turn run several map and reduce tasks, its on-disk layout corresponds to the common Hadoop output formats, that is, `MapFileOutputFormat` and `SequenceFileOutputFormat`. So to be precise, we should say that data is kept in several partial map files or sequence files, with as many parts as there were reduce tasks in the job that created the data. For simplicity, we omit this distinction in the following sections.

CrawlDb

CrawlDb stores the current status of each URL, as a map file of <url, CrawlDatum>, where keys use Text and values use a Nutch-specific CrawlDatum class (which implements the Writable interface).

In order to provide a quick random access to the records (sometimes useful for diagnostic reasons, when users want to examine individual records in CrawlDb), this data is stored in map files and not in sequence files.

CrawlDb is initially created using the Injector tool, which simply converts a plain-text representation of the initial list of URLs (called the seed list) to a map file in the format described earlier. Subsequently, it is updated with the information from the fetched and parsed pages—more on that shortly.

LinkDb

This database stores the incoming link information for every URL known to Nutch. It is a map file of <url, Inlinks>, where Inlinks is a list of URL and anchor text data. It's worth noting that this information is not immediately available during page collection, but the reverse information is available, namely that of outgoing links from a page. The process of inverting this relationship is implemented as a MapReduce job, described shortly.

Segments

Segments in Nutch parlance correspond to fetching and parsing a batch of URLs. Figure 16-5 presents how segments are created and processed.

A segment (which is really a directory in a filesystem) contains the following parts (which are simply subdirectories containing MapFileOutputFormat or SequenceFileOutputFormat data):

content
> Contains the raw data of downloaded pages, as a map file of <url, Content>. Nutch uses a map file here, because it needs fast random access in order to present a cached view of a page.

crawl_generate
> Contains the list of URLs to be fetched, together with their current status retrieved from CrawlDb, as a sequence file of <url, CrawlDatum>. This data uses sequence file, first because it's processed sequentially, and second because we couldn't satisfy the map file invariants of sorted keys. We need to spread URLs that belong to the same host as far apart as possible to minimize the load per target host, and this means that records are sorted more or less randomly.

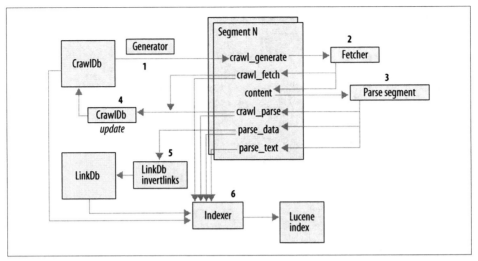

Figure 16-5. Segments

crawl_fetch
> Contains status reports from the fetching, that is, whether it was successful, what was the response code, etc. This is stored in a map file of <url, CrawlDatum>.

crawl_parse
> The list of outlinks for each successfully fetched and parsed page is stored here so that Nutch can expand its crawling frontier by learning new URLs.

parse_data
> Metadata collected during parsing; among others, the list of outgoing links (outlinks) for a page. This information is crucial later on to build an inverted graph (of incoming links—inlinks).

parse_text
> Plain-text version of the page, suitable for indexing in Lucene. These are stored as a map file of <url, ParseText> so that Nutch can access them quickly when building summaries (snippets) to display the list of search results.

New segments are created from CrawlDb when the Generator tool is run (1 in Figure 16-5), and initially contain just a list of URLs to fetch (the *crawl_generate* subdirectory). As this list is processed in several steps, the segment collects output data from the processing tools in a set of subdirectories.

For example, the *content* part is populated by a tool called Fetcher, which downloads raw data from URLs on the fetchlist (2). This tool also saves the status information in *crawl_fetch* so that this data can be used later on for updating the status of the page in CrawlDb.

The remaining parts of the segment are populated by the Parse segment tool (3), which reads the content section, selects appropriate content parser based on the declared (or detected) MIME type, and saves the results of parsing in three parts: *crawl_parse*, *parse_data*, and *parse_text*. This data is then used to update the CrawlDb with new information (4) and to create the LinkDb (5).

Segments are kept around until all pages present in them are expired. Nutch applies a configurable maximum time limit, after which a page is forcibly selected for refetching; this helps the operator phase out all segments older than this limit (because he can be sure that by that time all pages in this segment would have been refetched).

Segment data is used to create Lucene indexes ([6]—primarily the *parse_text* and *parse_data* parts), but it also provides a data storage mechanism for quick retrieval of plain text and raw content data. The former is needed so that Nutch can generate snippets (fragments of document text best matching a query); the latter provides the ability to present a "cached view" of the page. In both cases, this data is accessed directly from map files in response to requests for snippet generation or for cached content. In practice, even for large collections the performance of accessing data directly from map files is quite sufficient.

Selected Examples of Hadoop Data Processing in Nutch

The following sections present relevant details of some Nutch tools to illustrate how the MapReduce paradigm is applied to a concrete data processing task in Nutch.

Link inversion

HTML pages collected during crawling contain HTML links, which may point either to the same page (internal links) or to other pages. HTML links are directed from source page to target page. See Figure 16-6.

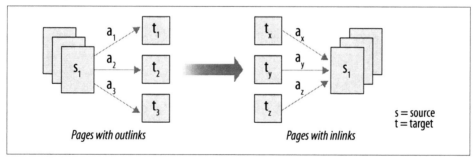

Figure 16-6. Link inversion

However, most algorithms for calculating a page's importance (or quality) need the opposite information, that is, what pages contain outlinks that point to the current page. This information is not readily available when crawling. Also, the indexing process benefits from taking into account the anchor text on inlinks so that this text may semantically enrich the text of the current page.

As mentioned earlier, Nutch collects the outlink information and then uses this data to build a LinkDb, which contains this reversed link data in the form of inlinks and anchor text.

This section presents a rough outline of the implementation of the LinkDb tool—many details have been omitted (such as URL normalization and filtering) in order to present a clear picture of the process. What's left gives a classical example of why the MapReduce paradigm fits so well with the key data transformation processes required to run a search engine. Large search engines need to deal with massive web graph data (many pages with a lot of outlinks/inlinks), and the parallelism and fault tolerance offered by Hadoop make this possible. Additionally, it's easy to express the link inversion using the map-sort-reduce primitives, as illustrated next.

The snippet below presents the job initialization of the LinkDb tool:

```
JobConf job = new JobConf(configuration);
FileInputFormat.addInputPath(job, new Path(segmentPath, "parse_data"));
job.setInputFormat(SequenceFileInputFormat.class);
job.setMapperClass(LinkDb.class);
job.setReducerClass(LinkDb.class);
job.setOutputKeyClass(Text.class);
job.setOutputValueClass(Inlinks.class);
job.setOutputFormat(MapFileOutputFormat.class);
FileOutputFormat.setOutputPath(job, newLinkDbPath);
```

As we can see, the source data for this job is the list of fetched URLs (keys) and the corresponding ParseData records that contain among others the outlink information for each page, as an array of outlinks. An outlink contains both the target URL and the anchor text.

The output from the job is again a list of URLs (keys), but the values are instances of inlinks, which is simply a specialized Set of inlinks that contain target URLs and anchor text.

Perhaps surprisingly, URLs are typically stored and processed as plain text and not as java.net.URL or java.net.URI instances. There are several reasons for this: URLs extracted from downloaded content usually need normalization (e.g., converting hostnames to lowercase, resolving relative paths), are often broken or invalid, or refer to unsupported protocols. Many normalization and filtering operations are better expressed as text patterns that span several parts of a URL. Also, for the purpose of link analysis, we may still want to process and count invalid URLs.

Let's take a closer look now at the map() and reduce() implementations—in this case, they are simple enough to be implemented in the body of the same class:

```
public void map(Text fromUrl, ParseData parseData,
    OutputCollector<Text, Inlinks> output, Reporter reporter) {
  ...
  Outlink[] outlinks = parseData.getOutlinks();
  Inlinks inlinks = new Inlinks();
  for (Outlink out : outlinks) {
```

```
            inlinks.clear(); // instance reuse to avoid excessive GC
            String toUrl = out.getToUrl();
            String anchor = out.getAnchor();
            inlinks.add(new Inlink(fromUrl, anchor));
            output.collect(new Text(toUrl), inlinks);
        }
    }
```

You can see from this listing that for each Outlink, our map() implementation produces a pair of <toUrl, Inlinks>, where Inlinks contains just a single Inlink containing fromUrl and the anchor text. The direction of the link has been inverted.

Subsequently, these one-element-long Inlinks are aggregated in the reduce() method:

```
    public void reduce(Text toUrl, Iterator<Inlinks> values,
        OutputCollector<Text, Inlinks> output, Reporter reporter) {
      Inlinks result = new Inlinks();
      while (values.hasNext()) {
        result.add(values.next());
      }
      output.collect(toUrl, result);
    }
```

From this code, it's obvious that we have got exactly what we wanted—that is, a list of all fromUrls that point to our toUrl, together with their anchor text. The inversion process has been accomplished.

This data is then saved using the MapFileOutputFormat and becomes the new version of LinkDb.

Generation of fetchlists

Let's take a look now at a more complicated use case. Fetchlists are produced from the CrawlDb (which is a map file of <url, crawlDatum>, with the crawlDatum containing a status of this URL), and they contain URLs ready to be fetched, which are then processed by the Nutch Fetcher tool. Fetcher is itself a MapReduce application (described shortly). This means that the input data (partitioned in N parts) will be processed by N map tasks—the Fetcher tool enforces that SequenceFileInputFormat should not further split the data in more parts than there are already input partitions. We mentioned earlier briefly that fetchlists need to be generated in a special way so that the data in each part of the fetchlist (and consequently processed in each map task) meets certain requirements:

1. All URLs from the same host need to end up in the same partition. This is required so that Nutch can easily implement in-JVM host-level blocking to avoid overwhelming target hosts.

2. URLs from the same host should be as far apart as possible (i.e., well mixed with URLs from other hosts) in order to minimize the host-level blocking.

3. There should be no more than *x* URLs from any single host so that large sites with many URLs don't dominate smaller sites (and URLs from smaller sites still have a chance to be scheduled for fetching).

4. URLs with high scores should be preferred over URLs with low scores.

5. There should be, at most, *y* URLs in total in the fetchlist.

6. The number of output partitions should match the optimum number of fetching map tasks.

In this case, two MapReduce jobs are needed to satisfy all these requirements, as illustrated in Figure 16-7. Again, in the following listings, we are going to skip some details of these steps for the sake of brevity.

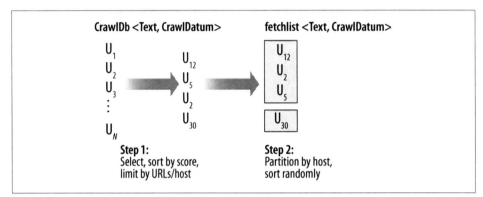

Figure 16-7. Generation of fetchlists

Step 1: Select, sort by score, limit by URL count per host.   In this step, Nutch runs a MapReduce job to select URLs that are considered eligible for fetching and to sort them by their score (a floating-point value assigned to each URL, e.g., a PageRank score). The input data comes from CrawlDb, which is a map file of <url, datum>. The output from this job is a sequence file with <score, <url, datum>>, sorted in descending order by score.

First, let's look at the job setup:

```
FileInputFormat.addInputPath(job, crawlDbPath);
job.setInputFormat(SequenceFileInputFormat.class);
job.setMapperClass(Selector.class);
job.setPartitionerClass(Selector.class);
job.setReducerClass(Selector.class);
FileOutputFormat.setOutputPath(job, tempDir);
job.setOutputFormat(SequenceFileOutputFormat.class);
job.setOutputKeyClass(FloatWritable.class);
job.setOutputKeyComparatorClass(DecreasingFloatComparator.class);
job.setOutputValueClass(SelectorEntry.class);
```

The Selector class implements three functions: mapper, reducer, and partitioner. The last function is especially interesting: Selector uses a custom Partitioner to assign URLs from the same host to the same reduce task so that we can satisfy criteria 3–5 from the previous list. If we didn't override the default partitioner, URLs from the same host would end up in different partitions of the output, and we wouldn't be able to track and limit the total counts, because MapReduce tasks don't communicate between themselves. As it is now, all URLs that belong to the same host will end up being processed by the same reduce task, which means we can control how many URLs per host are selected.

It's easy to implement a custom partitioner so that data that needs to be processed in the same task ends up in the same partition. Let's take a look first at how the `Selector` class implements the `Partitioner` interface (which consists of a single method):

```
/** Partition by host. */
public int getPartition(FloatWritable key, Writable value, int numReduceTasks) {
  return hostPartitioner.getPartition(((SelectorEntry)value).url, key,
    numReduceTasks);
}
```

The method returns an integer number from 0 to `numReduceTasks` - 1. It simply replaces the key with the original URL from `SelectorEntry` to pass the URL (instead of score) to an instance of `PartitionUrlByHost`, where the partition number is calculated:

```
/** Hash by hostname. */
public int getPartition(Text key, Writable value, int numReduceTasks) {
  String urlString = key.toString();
  URL url = null;
  try {
    url = new URL(urlString);
  } catch (MalformedURLException e) {
    LOG.warn("Malformed URL: '" + urlString + "'");
  }
  int hashCode = (url == null ? urlString : url.getHost()).hashCode();
  // make hosts wind up in different partitions on different runs
  hashCode ^= seed;

  return (hashCode & Integer.MAX_VALUE) % numReduceTasks;
}
```

As you can see from the code snippet, the partition number is a function of only the host part of the URL, which means that all URLs that belong to the same host will end up in the same partition.

The output from this job is sorted in decreasing order by score. Since there are many records in CrawlDb with the same score, we couldn't use `MapFileOutputFormat` because we would violate the map file's invariant of strict key ordering.

Observant readers will notice that as we had to use something other than the original keys, but we still want to preserve the original key-value pairs. We use here a `Selector Entry` class to pass the original key-value pairs to the next step of processing.

`Selector.reduce()` keeps track of the total number of URLs and the maximum number of URLs per host, and simply discards excessive records. Please note that the enforcement of the total count limit is necessarily approximate. We calculate the limit for the current task as the total limit divided by the number of reduce tasks. But we don't know for sure from within the task that it is going to get an equal share of URLs; indeed, in most cases, it doesn't because of the uneven distribution of URLs among hosts. However, for Nutch this approximation is sufficient.

Step 2: Invert, partition by host, sort randomly. In the previous step, we ended up with a sequence file of <score, selectorEntry>. Now we have to produce a sequence file of <url, datum> and satisfy criteria 1, 2, and 6 just described. The input data for this step is the output data produced in step 1.

The following is a snippet showing the setup of this job:

```
FileInputFormat.addInputPath(job, tempDir);
job.setInputFormat(SequenceFileInputFormat.class);
job.setMapperClass(SelectorInverseMapper.class);
job.setMapOutputKeyClass(Text.class);
job.setMapOutputValueClass(SelectorEntry.class);
job.setPartitionerClass(PartitionUrlByHost.class);
job.setReducerClass(PartitionReducer.class);
job.setNumReduceTasks(numParts);
FileOutputFormat.setOutputPath(job, output);
job.setOutputFormat(SequenceFileOutputFormat.class);
job.setOutputKeyClass(Text.class);
job.setOutputValueClass(CrawlDatum.class);
job.setOutputKeyComparatorClass(HashComparator.class);
```

The SelectorInverseMapper class simply discards the current key (the score value), extracts the original URL and uses it as a key, and uses the SelectorEntry as the value. Careful readers may wonder why we don't go one step further, extracting also the original CrawlDatum and using it as the value—more on this shortly.

The final output from this job is a sequence file of <Text, CrawlDatum>, but our output from the map phase uses <Text, SelectorEntry>. We have to specify that we use different key/value classes for the map output, using the setMapOutputKeyClass() and setMapOutputValueClass() setters—otherwise, Hadoop assumes that we use the same classes as declared for the reduce output (this conflict usually would cause a job to fail).

The output from the map phase is partitioned using PartitionUrlByHost class so that it again assigns URLs from the same host to the same partition. This satisfies requirement 1.

Once the data is shuffled from map to reduce tasks, it's sorted by Hadoop according to the output key comparator, in this case the HashComparator. This class uses a simple hashing scheme to mix URLs in a way that is least likely to put URLs from the same host close to each other.

In order to meet requirement 6, we set the number of reduce tasks to the desired number of Fetcher map tasks (the numParts mentioned earlier), keeping in mind that each reduce partition will be used later on to create a single Fetcher map task.

`PartitionReducer` class is responsible for the final step, that is, to convert `<url, selectorEntry>` to `<url, crawlDatum>`. A surprising side effect of using `HashComparator` is that several URLs may be hashed to the same hash value, and Hadoop will call `reduce()` method passing only the first such key—all other keys considered equal will be discarded. Now it becomes clear why we had to preserve all URLs in `SelectorEntry` records, because now we can extract them from the iterated values. Here is the implementation of this method:

```
public void reduce(Text key, Iterator<SelectorEntry> values,
    OutputCollector<Text, CrawlDatum> output, Reporter reporter) throws IOException {
  // when using HashComparator, we get only one input key in case of hash collisions
  // so use only URLs extracted from values
  while (values.hasNext()) {
    SelectorEntry entry = values.next();
    output.collect(entry.url, entry.datum);
  }
}
```

Finally, the output from reduce tasks is stored as a `SequenceFileOutputFormat` in a Nutch segment directory, in a *crawl_generate* subdirectory. This output satisfies all criteria from 1 to 6.

Fetcher: A multithreaded MapRunner in action

The Fetcher application in Nutch is responsible for downloading the page content from remote sites. As such, it is important that the process uses every opportunity for parallelism, in order to minimize the time it takes to crawl a fetchlist.

There is already one level of parallelism present in Fetcher—multiple parts of the input fetchlists are assigned to multiple map tasks. However, in practice this is not sufficient: sequential download of URLs, from different hosts (see the earlier section on `HashComparator`), would be a tremendous waste of time. For this reason, the Fetcher map tasks process this data using multiple worker threads.

Hadoop uses the `MapRunner` class to implement the sequential processing of input data records. The `Fetcher` class implements its own `MapRunner` that uses multiple threads to process input records in parallel.

Let's begin with the setup of the job:

```
job.setSpeculativeExecution(false);
FileInputFormat.addInputPath(job, "segment/crawl_generate");
job.setInputFormat(InputFormat.class);
job.setMapRunnerClass(Fetcher.class);
FileOutputFormat.setOutputPath(job, segment);
job.setOutputFormat(FetcherOutputFormat.class);
job.setOutputKeyClass(Text.class);
job.setOutputValueClass(NutchWritable.class);
```

First, we turn off speculative execution. We can't run several map tasks downloading content from the same hosts because it would violate the host-level load limits (such as the number of concurrent requests and the number of requests per second).

Next, we use a custom InputFormat implementation that prevents Hadoop from splitting partitions of input data into smaller chunks (splits), thus creating more map tasks than there are input partitions. This again ensures that we control host-level access limits.

Output data is stored using a custom OutputFormat implementation, which creates several output map files and sequence files created using data contained in NutchWrita ble values. The NutchWritable class is a subclass of GenericWritable, able to pass instances of several different Writable classes declared in advance.

The Fetcher class implements the MapRunner interface, and we set this class as the job's MapRunner implementation. The relevant parts of the code are listed here:

```
public void run(RecordReader<Text, CrawlDatum> input,
    OutputCollector<Text, NutchWritable> output,
                Reporter reporter) throws IOException {
  int threadCount = getConf().getInt("fetcher.threads.fetch", 10);
  feeder = new QueueFeeder(input, fetchQueues, threadCount * 50);
  feeder.start();

  for (int i = 0; i < threadCount; i++) {          // spawn threads
    new FetcherThread(getConf()).start();
  }
  do {                                             // wait for threads to exit
    try {
      Thread.sleep(1000);
    } catch (InterruptedException e) {}
    reportStatus(reporter);
  } while (activeThreads.get() > 0);
}
```

Fetcher reads many input records in advance, using the QueueFeeder thread that puts input records into a set of per-host queues. Then several FetcherThread instances are started, which consume items from per-host queues, while QueueFeeder keeps reading input data to keep the queues filled. Each FetcherThread consumes items from any nonempty queue.

In the meantime, the main thread of the map task spins around waiting for all threads to finish their job. Periodically, it reports the status to the framework to ensure that Hadoop doesn't consider this task to be dead and kill it. Once all items are processed, the loop is finished and the control is returned to Hadoop, which considers this map task to be completed.

Indexer: Using custom OutputFormat

This is an example of a MapReduce application that doesn't produce sequence file or map file output—instead, the output from this application is a Lucene index. Again, as MapReduce applications may consist of several reduce tasks, the output from this application may consist of several partial Lucene indexes.

Nutch Indexer tool uses information from CrawlDb, LinkDb, and Nutch segments (fetch status, parsing status, page metadata, and plain-text data), so the job setup section involves adding several input paths:

```
FileInputFormat.addInputPath(job, crawlDbPath);
FileInputFormat.addInputPath(job, linkDbPath);
// add segment data
FileInputFormat.addInputPath(job, "segment/crawl_fetch");
FileInputFormat.addInputPath(job, "segment/crawl_parse");
FileInputFormat.addInputPath(job, "segment/parse_data");
FileInputFormat.addInputPath(job, "segment/parse_text");
job.setInputFormat(SequenceFileInputFormat.class);
job.setMapperClass(Indexer.class);
job.setReducerClass(Indexer.class);
FileOutputFormat.setOutputPath(job, indexDir);
job.setOutputFormat(OutputFormat.class);
job.setOutputKeyClass(Text.class);
job.setOutputValueClass(LuceneDocumentWrapper.class);
```

All corresponding records for a URL dispersed among these input locations need to be combined to create Lucene documents to be added to the index.

The Mapper implementation in Indexer simply wraps input data, whatever its source and implementation class, in a NutchWritable, so that the reduce phase may receive data from different sources, using different classes, and still be able to consistently declare a single output value class (as NutchWritable) from both map and reduce steps.

The Reducer implementation iterates over all values that fall under the same key (URL), unwraps the data (fetch CrawlDatum, CrawlDb CrawlDatum, LinkDb Inlinks, Parse Data and ParseText) and, using this information, builds a Lucene document, which is then wrapped in a Writable LuceneDocumentWrapper and collected. In addition to all textual content (coming either from the plain-text data or from metadata), this document also contains a PageRank-like score information (obtained from CrawlDb data). Nutch uses this score to set the boost value of Lucene document.

The OutputFormat implementation is the most interesting part of this tool:

```
public static class OutputFormat extends
    FileOutputFormat<WritableComparable, LuceneDocumentWrapper> {

  public RecordWriter<WritableComparable, LuceneDocumentWrapper>
    getRecordWriter(final FileSystem fs, JobConf job,
                    String name, final Progressable progress) throws IOException {
    final Path out = new Path(FileOutputFormat.getOutputPath(job), name);
    final IndexWriter writer = new IndexWriter(out.toString(),
                    new NutchDocumentAnalyzer(job), true);

    return new RecordWriter<WritableComparable, LuceneDocumentWrapper>() {
      boolean closed;
      public void write(WritableComparable key, LuceneDocumentWrapper value)
```

```
            throws IOException {                          // unwrap & index doc
                Document doc = value.get();
                writer.addDocument(doc);
                progress.progress();
            }

            public void close(final Reporter reporter) throws IOException {
                // spawn a thread to give progress heartbeats
                Thread prog = new Thread() {
                    public void run() {
                        while (!closed) {
                            try {
                                reporter.setStatus("closing");
                                Thread.sleep(1000);
                            } catch (InterruptedException e) { continue; }
                            catch (Throwable e) { return; }
                        }
                    }
                };

                try {
                    prog.start();
                    // optimize & close index
                    writer.optimize();
                    writer.close();
                } finally {
                    closed = true;
                }
            }
        };
    }
```

When an instance of `RecordWriter` is requested, the `OutputFormat` creates a new Lucene index by opening an `IndexWriter`. Then, for each new output record collected in the reduce method, it unwraps the Lucene document from `LuceneDocumentWrapper` value and adds it to the index.

When a reduce task is finished, Hadoop will try to close the `RecordWriter`. In this case, the process of closing may take a long time, because we would like to optimize the index before closing. During this time, Hadoop may conclude that the task is hung, since there are no progress updates, and it may attempt to kill it. For this reason, we first start a background thread to give reassuring progress updates, and then proceed to perform the index optimization. Once the optimization is completed, we stop the progress updater thread. The output index is now created, optimized, and is closed, and ready for use in a searcher application.

Summary

This short overview of Nutch necessarily omits many details, such as error handling, logging, URL filtering and normalization, dealing with redirects or other forms of "aliased" pages (such as mirrors), removing duplicate content, calculating PageRank scoring, etc. You can find this and much more information on the official page of the project and on the wiki (*http://wiki.apache.org/nutch*).

Today, Nutch is used by many organizations and individual users. Still, operating a search engine requires nontrivial investment in hardware, integration, and customization, and the maintenance of the index; so in most cases, Nutch is used to build commercial vertical- or field-specific search engines.

Nutch is under active development, and the project follows closely new releases of Hadoop. As such, it will continue to be a practical example of a real-life application that uses Hadoop at its core, with excellent results.

—Andrzej Białecki

Log Processing at Rackspace

Rackspace Hosting has always provided managed systems for enterprises, and in that vein, Mailtrust became Rackspace's mail division in Fall 2007. Rackspace currently hosts email for over 1 million users and thousands of companies on hundreds of servers.

Requirements/The Problem

Transferring the mail generated by Rackspace customers through the system generates a considerable "paper" trail, in the form of around 150 GB per day of logs in various formats. It is extremely helpful to aggregate that data for growth planning purposes and to understand how customers use our applications, and the records are also a boon for troubleshooting problems in the system.

If an email fails to be delivered, or a customer is unable to log in, it is vital that our customer support team is able to find enough information about the problem to begin the debugging process. To make it possible to find that information quickly, we cannot leave the logs on the machines that generated them or in their original format. Instead, we use Hadoop to do a considerable amount of processing, with the end result being Lucene indexes that customer support can query.

Logs

Two of our highest volume log formats are produced by the Postfix mail transfer agent and Microsoft Exchange Server. All mail that travels through our systems touches Postfix at some point, and the majority of messages travel through multiple Postfix servers. The Exchange environment is independent by necessity, but one class of Postfix machines acts as an added layer of protection and uses SMTP to transfer messages between mailboxes hosted in each environment.

The messages travel through many machines, but each server only knows enough about the destination of the mail to transfer it to the next responsible server. Thus, in order to build the complete history of a message, our log processing system needs to have a global view of the system. This is where Hadoop helps us immensely: as our system grows, so does the volume of logs. For our log processing logic to stay viable, we had to ensure that it would scale, and MapReduce was the perfect framework for that growth.

Brief History

Earlier versions of our log processing system were based on MySQL, but as we gained more and more logging machines, we reached the limits of what a single MySQL server could process. The database schema was already reasonably denormalized, which would have made it less difficult to shard, but MySQL's partitioning support was still very weak at that point in time. Rather than implementing our own sharding and processing solution around MySQL, we chose to use Hadoop.

Choosing Hadoop

As soon as you shard the data in a RDBMS system, you lose a lot of the advantages of SQL for performing analysis of your dataset. Hadoop gives us the ability to easily process all of our data in parallel using the same algorithms we would for smaller datasets.

Collection and Storage

Log collection

The servers generating the logs we process are distributed across multiple data centers, but we currently have a single Hadoop cluster, located in one of those data centers (see Figure 16-8). In order to aggregate the logs and place them into the cluster, we use the Unix syslog replacement syslog-ng and some simple scripts to control the creation of files in Hadoop.

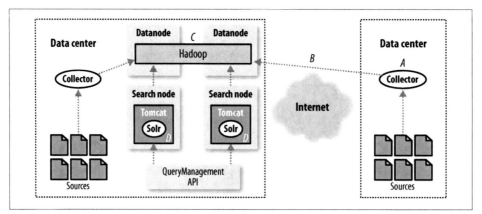

Figure 16-8. Hadoop data flow at Rackspace

Within a data center, syslog-ng is used to transfer logs from a *source* machine to a load-balanced set of *collector* machines. On the collectors, each type of log is aggregated into a single stream and lightly compressed with gzip (step A in Figure 16-8). From remote collectors, logs can be transferred through an SSH tunnel cross-data center to collectors that are local to the Hadoop cluster (step B).

Once the compressed log stream reaches a local collector, it can be written to Hadoop (step C). We currently use a simple Python script that buffers input data to disk and periodically pushes the data into the Hadoop cluster using the Hadoop command-line interface. The script copies the log buffers to input folders in Hadoop when they reach a multiple of the Hadoop block size or when enough time has passed.

This method of securely aggregating logs from different data centers was developed before SOCKS support was added to Hadoop via the `hadoop.rpc.socket.fac tory.class.default` parameter and `SocksSocketFactory` class. By using SOCKS support and the HDFS API directly from remote collectors, we could eliminate one disk write and a lot of complexity from the system. We plan to implement a replacement using these features in future development sprints.

Once the raw logs have been placed in Hadoop, they are ready for processing by our MapReduce jobs.

Log storage

Our Hadoop cluster currently contains 15 datanodes with commodity CPUs and three 500 GB disks each. We use a default replication factor of three for files that need to survive for our archive period of six months and two for anything else.

The Hadoop namenode uses hardware identical to the datanodes. To provide reasonably high availability, we use two secondary namenodes and a virtual IP that can easily be pointed at any of the three machines with snapshots of the HDFS. This means that in a failover situation, there is potential for us to lose up to 30 minutes of data, depending on the ages of the snapshots on the secondary namenodes. This is acceptable for our log processing application, but other Hadoop applications may require lossless failover by using shared storage for the namenode's image.

MapReduce for Logs

Processing

In distributed systems, the sad truth of unique identifiers is that they are rarely actually unique. All email messages have a (supposedly) unique identifier called a *message-id* that is generated by the host where they originated, but a bad client could easily send out duplicates. In addition, since the designers of Postfix could not trust the message-id to uniquely identify the message, they were forced to come up with a separate ID called a *queue-id*, which is guaranteed to be unique only for the lifetime of the message on a local machine.

Although the message-id tends to be the definitive identifier for a message, in Postfix logs, it is necessary to use queue-ids to find the message-id. Looking at the second line in Example 16-1 (which is formatted to better fit the page), you will see the hex string 1DBD21B48AE, which is the queue-id of the message that the log line refers to. Because information about a message (including its message-id) is output as separate lines when it is collected (potentially hours apart), it is necessary for our parsing code to keep state about messages.

Example 16-1. Postfix log lines

```
Nov 12 17:36:54 gate8.gate.sat.mlsrvr.com postfix/smtpd[2552]: connect from hostname
Nov 12 17:36:54 relay2.relay.sat.mlsrvr.com postfix/qmgr[9489]: 1DBD21B48AE:
from=<mapreduce@rackspace.com>, size=5950, nrcpt=1 (queue active)
Nov 12 17:36:54 relay2.relay.sat.mlsrvr.com postfix/smtpd[28085]: disconnect from
hostname
Nov 12 17:36:54 gate5.gate.sat.mlsrvr.com postfix/smtpd[22593]: too many errors
after DATA from hostname
Nov 12 17:36:54 gate5.gate.sat.mlsrvr.com postfix/smtpd[22593]: disconnect from
hostname
Nov 12 17:36:54 gate10.gate.sat.mlsrvr.com postfix/smtpd[10311]: connect from
hostname
Nov 12 17:36:54 relay2.relay.sat.mlsrvr.com postfix/smtp[28107]: D42001B48B5:
to=<mapreduce@rackspace.com>, relay=hostname[ip], delay=0.32, delays=0.28/0/0/0.04,
dsn=2.0.0, status=sent (250 2.0.0 Ok: queued as 1DBD21B48AE)
Nov 12 17:36:54 gate20.gate.sat.mlsrvr.com postfix/smtpd[27168]: disconnect from
hostname
Nov 12 17:36:54 gate5.gate.sat.mlsrvr.com postfix/qmgr[1209]: 645965A0224: removed
Nov 12 17:36:54 gate2.gate.sat.mlsrvr.com postfix/smtp[15928]: 732196384ED: to=<m
apreduce@rackspace.com>, relay=hostname[ip], conn_use=2, delay=0.69, delays=0.04/
0.44/0.04/0.17, dsn=2.0.0, status=sent (250 2.0.0 Ok: queued as 02E1544C005)
Nov 12 17:36:54 gate2.gate.sat.mlsrvr.com postfix/qmgr[13764]: 732196384ED: removed
Nov 12 17:36:54 gate1.gate.sat.mlsrvr.com postfix/smtpd[26394]: NOQUEUE: reject: RCP
T from hostname 554 5.7.1 <mapreduce@rackspace.com>: Client host rejected: The
sender's mail server is blocked; from=<mapreduce@rackspace.com> to=<mapred
uce@rackspace.com> proto=ESMTP helo=<mapreduce@rackspace.com>
```

From a MapReduce perspective, each line of the log is a single key-value pair. In phase 1, we need to map all lines with a single queue-id key together, and then reduce them to determine if the log message values indicate that the queue-id is complete.

Similarly, once we have a completed queue-id for a message, we need to group by the message-id in phase 2. We Map each completed queue-id with its message-id as key and a list of its log lines as the value. In Reduce, we determine whether all of the queue-ids for the message-id indicate that the message left our system.

Together, the two phases of the mail log MapReduce job and their InputFormat and OutputFormat form a type of *staged event-driven architecture* (SEDA). In SEDA, an application is broken up into multiple "stages," which are separated by queues. In a Hadoop context, a queue could be either an input folder in HDFS that a MapReduce job consumes from or the implicit queue that MapReduce forms between the Map and Reduce steps.

In Figure 16-9, the arrows between stages represent the queues, with a dashed arrow being the implicit MapReduce queue. Each stage can send a key-value pair (SEDA calls them events or messages) to another stage via these queues.

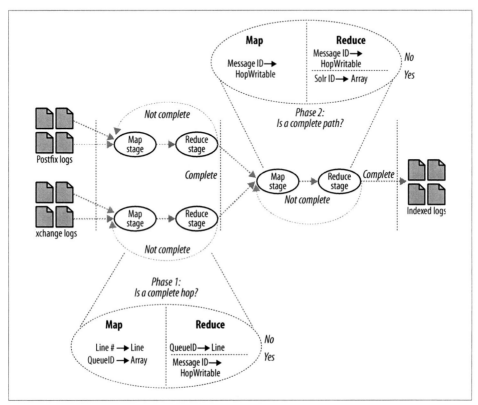

Figure 16-9. MapReduce chain

Phase 1: Map. During the first phase of our Mail log processing job, the inputs to the Map stage are either a line number key and log message value or a queue-id key to an array of log-message values. The first type of input is generated when we process a raw logfile from the queue of input files, and the second type is an intermediate format that represents the state of a queue-id we have already attempted to process but that was requeued because it was incomplete.

In order to accomplish this dual input, we implemented a Hadoop `InputFormat` that delegates the work to an underlying `SequenceFileRecordReader` or `LineRecordReader`, depending on the file extension of the input `FileSplit`. The two input formats come from different input folders (queues) in HDFS.

Phase 1: Reduce. During this phase, the Reduce stage determines whether the queue-id has enough lines to be considered completed. If the queue-id is completed, we output the message-id as key and a `HopWritable` object as value. Otherwise, the queue-id is set as the key, and the array of log lines is requeued to be Mapped with the next set of raw logs. This will continue until we complete the queue-id or until it times out.

 The `HopWritable` object is a POJO that implements Hadoop's `Writable` interface. It completely describes a message from the viewpoint of a single server, including the sending address and IP, attempts to deliver the message to other servers, and typical message header information.

This split output is accomplished with an `OutputFormat` implementation that is somewhat symmetrical with our dual `InputFormat`. Our `MultiSequenceFileOutputFormat` was implemented before the Hadoop API added a `MultipleSequenceFileOutputFormat` in r0.17.0, but fulfills the same type of goal: we needed our Reduce output pairs to go to different files depending on characteristics of their keys.

Phase 2: Map. In the next stage of the Mail log processing job, the input is a message-id key, with a `HopWritable` value from the previous phase. This stage does not contain any logic: instead, it simply combines the inputs from the first phase using the standard `SequenceFileInputFormat` and `IdentityMapper`.

Phase 2: Reduce. In the final Reduce stage, we want to see whether all of the `HopWritables` we have collected for the message-id represent a complete message path through our system. A message path is essentially a directed graph (which is typically acyclic, but it may contain loops if servers are misconfigured). In this graph, a vertex is a server, which can be labeled with multiple queue-ids, and attempts to deliver the message from one server to another are edges. For this processing, we use the JGraphT graph library.

For output, we again use the `MultiSequenceFileOutputFormat`. If the Reducer decides that all of the queue-ids for a message-id create a complete message path, then the message is serialized and queued for the `SolrOutputFormat`. Otherwise, the `HopWritables` for the message are queued for phase 2: Map stage to be reprocessed with the next batch of queue-ids.

The `SolrOutputFormat` contains an embedded Apache Solr instance—in the fashion that was originally recommended by the Solr wiki (*http://wiki.apache.org/solr/Embedded Solr*)—to generate an index on local disk. Closing the `OutputFormat` then involves compressing the disk index to the final destination for the output file. This approach has a few advantages over using Solr's HTTP interface or using Lucene directly:

- We can enforce a Solr schema (*http://wiki.apache.org/solr/SchemaXml*).
- Map and Reduce remain idempotent.
- Indexing load is removed from the Search nodes.

We currently use the default `HashPartitioner` class to decide which Reduce task will receive particular keys, which means that the keys are semirandomly distributed. In a future iteration of the system, we'd like to implement a new `Partitioner` to split by sending address instead (our most common search term). Once the indexes are split by sender, we can use the hash of the address to determine where to merge or query for an index, and our search API will only need to communicate with the relevant nodes.

Merging for near-term search

After a set of MapReduce phases have completed, a different set of machines are notified of the new indexes and can pull them for merging. These Search nodes are running Apache Tomcat and Solr instances to host completed indexes, along with a service to pull and merge the indexes to local disk (step D in Figure 16-8).

Each compressed file from `SolrOutputFormat` is a complete Lucene index, and Lucene provides the `IndexWriter.addIndexes()` methods for quickly merging multiple indexes. Our `MergeAgent` service decompresses each new index into a Lucene `RAMDirectory` or `FSDirectory` (depending on size), merges them to local disk, and sends a `<commit/>` request to the Solr instance hosting the index to make the changed index visible to queries.

Sharding. The Query/Management API is a thin layer of PHP code that handles sharding the output indexes across all of the Search nodes. We use a simple implementation of consistent hashing to decide which Search nodes are responsible for each index file. Currently, indexes are sharded by their creation time and then by their hashed filename, but we plan to replace the filename hash with a sending address hash at some point in the future (see phase 2: Reduce).

Because HDFS already handles replication of the Lucene indexes, there is no need to keep multiple copies available in Solr. Instead, in a failover situation, the Search node is completely removed, and other nodes become responsible for merging the indexes.

Search results. With this system, we've achieved a 15-minute turnaround time from log generation to availability of a search result for our Customer Support team.

Our search API supports the full Lucene query syntax, so we commonly see complex queries like:

```
sender:"mapreduce@rackspace.com" -recipient:"hadoop@rackspace.com"
  recipient:"@rackspace.com" short-status:deferred timestamp:[1228140900 TO 2145916799]
```

Each result returned by a query is a complete serialized message path, which indicates whether individual servers and recipients received the message. We currently display the path as a 2D graph (Figure 16-10) that the user can interact with to expand points of interest, but there is a lot of room for improvement in the visualization of this data.

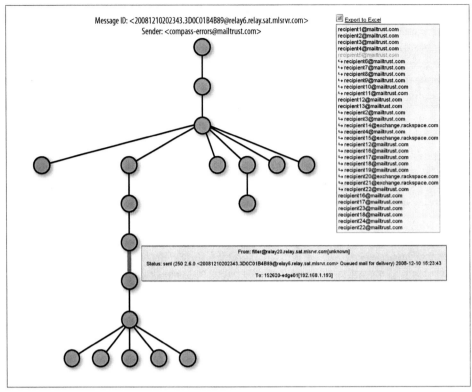

Figure 16-10. Data tree

Archiving for analysis

In addition to providing short-term search for Customer Support, we are also interested in performing analysis of our log data.

Every night, we run a series of MapReduce jobs with the day's indexes as input. We implemented a `SolrInputFormat` that can pull and decompress an index, and emit each document as a key-value pair. With this `InputFormat`, we can iterate over all message paths for a day and answer almost any question about our mail system, including:

- Per domain data (viruses, spam, connections, recipients)
- Most effective spam rules
- Load generated by specific users
- Reasons for message bounces
- Geographical sources of connections
- Average latency between specific machines

Since we have months of compressed indexes archived in Hadoop, we are also able to retrospectively answer questions that our nightly log summaries leave out. For instance, we recently wanted to determine the top sending IP addresses per month, which we accomplished with a simple one-off MapReduce job.

—Stu Hood

Cascading

Cascading is an open source Java library and application programming interface (API) that provides an abstraction layer for MapReduce. It allows developers to build complex, mission-critical data processing applications that run on Hadoop clusters.

The Cascading project began in the summer of 2007. Its first public release, version 0.1, launched in January 2008. Version 1.0 was released in January 2009. Binaries, source code, and add-on modules can be downloaded from the project website, *http://www.cascading.org/*.

"Map" and "Reduce" operations offer powerful primitives. However, they tend to be at the wrong level of granularity for creating sophisticated, highly composable code that can be shared among different developers. Moreover, many developers find it difficult to "think" in terms of MapReduce when faced with real-world problems.

To address the first issue, Cascading substitutes the "keys" and "values" used in MapReduce with simple field names and a data tuple model, where a tuple is simply a list of values. For the second issue, Cascading departs from Map and Reduce operations directly by introducing higher-level abstractions as alternatives: Functions, Filters, Aggregators, and Buffers.

Other alternatives began to emerge at about the same time as the project's initial public release, but Cascading was designed to complement them. Consider that most of these alternative frameworks impose pre- and post-conditions, or other expectations.

For example, in several other MapReduce tools, you must preformat, filter, or import your data into the Hadoop Filesystem (HDFS) prior to running the application. That step of preparing the data must be performed outside of the programming abstraction. In contrast, Cascading provides means to prepare and manage your data as integral parts of the programming abstraction.

This case study begins with an introduction to the main concepts of Cascading, then finishes with an overview of how ShareThis (*http://www.sharethis.com/*) uses Cascading in its infrastructure.

Please see the Cascading User Guide on the project website for a more in-depth presentation of the Cascading processing model.

Fields, Tuples, and Pipes

The MapReduce model uses keys and values to link input data to the Map function, the Map function to the Reduce function, and the Reduce function to the output data.

But as we know, real-world Hadoop applications are usually more than one MapReduce job chained together. Consider the canonical word count example implemented in MapReduce. If you needed to sort the numeric counts in descending order, not an unlikely requirement, it would need to be done in a second MapReduce job.

So, in the abstract, keys and values not only bind Map to Reduce, but Reduce to the next Map, and then to the next Reduce, and so on (Figure 16-11). That is, key-value pairs are sourced from input files and stream through chains of Map and Reduce operations, and finally rest in an output file. When you implement enough of these chained MapReduce applications, you start to see a well-defined set of key/value manipulations used over and over again to modify the key/value data stream.

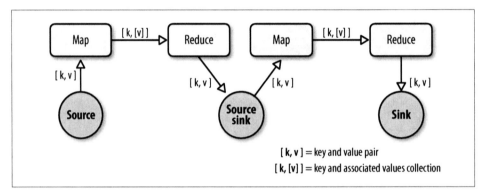

Figure 16-11. Counting and sorting in MapReduce

Cascading simplifies this by abstracting away keys and values and replacing them with tuples that have corresponding field names, similar in concept to tables and column names in a relational database. And during processing, streams of these fields and tuples are then manipulated as they pass through user-defined operations linked together by pipes (Figure 16-12).

So, MapReduce keys and values are reduced to:

Fields

Fields are a collection of either String names (like "first_name"), numeric positions (like 2, or –1, for the third and last position, respectively), or a combination of both, very much like column names. So fields are used to declare the names of values in a tuple and to select values by name from a tuple. The latter is like a SQL select call.

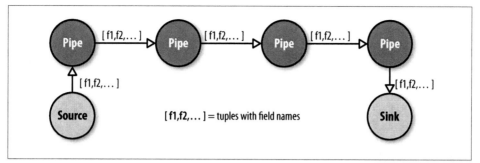

Figure 16-12. Pipes linked by fields and tuples

Tuple

A tuple is simply an array of `java.lang.Comparable` objects. A tuple is very much like a database row or record.

And the Map and Reduce operations are abstracted behind one or more pipe instances (Figure 16-13):

Each

The `Each` pipe processes a single input tuple at a time. It may apply either a `Func tion` or a `Filter` operation (described shortly) to the input tuple.

GroupBy

The `GroupBy` pipe groups tuples on grouping fields. It behaves just like the SQL group by statement. It can also merge multiple input tuple streams into a single stream, if they all share the same field names.

CoGroup

The `CoGroup` pipe both joins multiple tuple streams together by common field names, and it also groups the tuples by the common grouping fields. All standard join types (inner, outer, etc.) and custom joins can be used across two or more tuple streams.

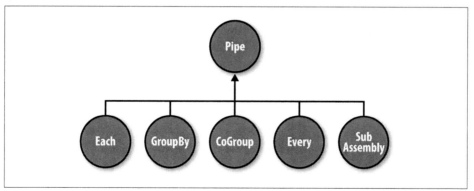

Figure 16-13. Pipe types

Every

The Every pipe processes a single grouping of tuples at a time, where the group was grouped by a GroupBy or CoGroup pipe. The Every pipe may apply either an Aggregator or a Buffer operation to the grouping.

SubAssembly

The SubAssembly pipe allows for nesting of assemblies inside a single pipe, which can, in turn, be nested in more complex assemblies.

All these pipes are chained together by the developer into "pipe assemblies" in which each assembly can have many input tuple streams (sources) and many output tuple streams (sinks) (see Figure 16-14).

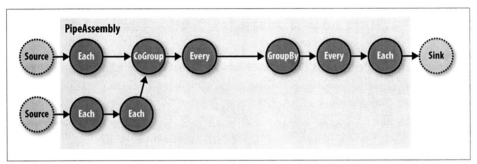

Figure 16-14. A simple PipeAssembly

On the surface, this might seem more complex than the traditional MapReduce model. And admittedly there are more concepts here than Map, Reduce, Key, and Value. But in practice, there are many more concepts that must all work in tandem to provide different behaviors.

For example, if a developer wanted to provide a "secondary sorting" of reducer values, she would need to implement Map, Reduce, a "composite" Key (two Keys nested in a parent Key), Value, Partitioner, an "output value grouping" Comparator, and an "output key" Comparator, all of which would be coupled to one another in varying ways and, very likely, nonreusable in subsequent applications.

In Cascading, this would be one line of code: new GroupBy(<previous>, <grouping fields>, <secondary sorting fields>), where previous is the pipe that came before.

Operations

As mentioned earlier, Cascading departs from MapReduce by introducing alternative operations that either are applied to individual tuples or groups of tuples (Figure 16-15):

Function

A Function operates on individual input tuples and may return zero or more output tuples for every one input. Functions are applied by the Each pipe.

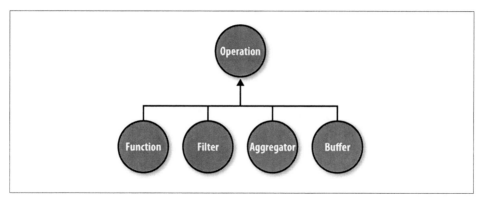

Figure 16-15. Operation types

Filter

A Filter is a special kind of function that returns a boolean value indicating whether the current input tuple should be removed from the tuple stream. A function could serve this purpose, but the Filter is optimized for this case, and many filters can be grouped by "logical" filters like And, Or, Xor, and Not, rapidly creating more complex filtering operations.

Aggregator

An Aggregator performs some operation against a group of tuples, where the grouped tuples are grouped by a common set of field values. For example, all tuples having the same "last-name" value. Common Aggregator implementations would be Sum, Count, Average, Max, and Min.

Buffer

A Buffer is similar to the Aggregator, except it is optimized to act as a "sliding window" across all the tuples in a unique grouping. This is useful when the developer needs to efficiently insert missing values in an ordered set of tuples (like a missing date or duration), or create a running average. Usually Aggregator is the operation of choice when working with groups of tuples, since many Aggregators can be chained together very efficiently, but sometimes a Buffer is the best tool for the job.

Operations are bound to pipes when the pipe assembly is created (Figure 16-16).

The Each and Every pipes provide a simple mechanism for selecting some or all values out of an input tuple before being passed to its child operation. And there is a simple mechanism for merging the operation results with the original input tuple to create the output tuple. Without going into great detail, this allows for each operation to only care about argument tuple values and fields, not the whole set of fields in the current input tuple. Subsequently, operations can be reusable across applications the same way Java methods can be reusable.

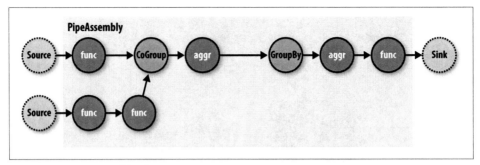

Figure 16-16. An assembly of operations

For example, in Java, a method declared as concatenate(String first, String second) is more abstract than concatenate(Person person). In the second case, the concatenate() function must "know" about the Person object; in the first case, it is agnostic to where the data came from. Cascading operations exhibit this same quality.

Taps, Schemes, and Flows

In many of the previous diagrams, there are references to "sources" and "sinks." In Cascading, all data is read from or written to Tap instances, but is converted to and from tuple instances via Scheme objects:

Tap

> A Tap is responsible for the "how" and "where" parts of accessing data. For example, is the data on HDFS or the local filesystem? In Amazon S3 or over HTTP?

Scheme

> A Scheme is responsible for reading raw data and converting it to a tuple and/or writing a tuple out into raw data, where this "raw" data can be lines of text, Hadoop binary sequence files, or some proprietary format.

Note that Taps are not part of a pipe assembly, and so they are not a type of Pipe.

But they are connected with pipe assemblies when they are made cluster-executable. When a pipe assembly is connected with the necessary number of source and sink Tap instances, we get a Flow. A Flow is created when a pipe assembly is connected with its required number of source and sink taps, and the Taps either emit or capture the field names the pipe assembly expects. That is, if a Tap emits a tuple with the field name "line" (by reading data from a file on HDFS), the head of the pipe assembly must be expecting a "line" value as well. Otherwise, the process that connects the pipe assembly with the Taps will immediately fail with an error.

So pipe assemblies are really data process definitions, and are not "executable" on their own. They must be connected to source and sink Tap instances before they can run on a cluster. This separation between Taps and pipe assemblies is part of what makes Cascading so powerful.

If you think of pipe assemblies like a Java class, then a Flow is like a Java Object instance (Figure 16-17). That is, the same pipe assembly can be "instantiated" many times into new Flows, in the same application, without fear of any interference between them. This allows pipe assemblies to be created and shared like standard Java libraries.

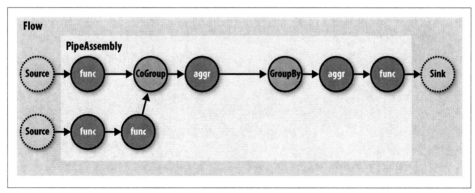

Figure 16-17. A Flow

Cascading in Practice

Now that we know what Cascading is and have a good idea how it works, what does an application written in Cascading look like? See Example 16-2.

Example 16-2. Word count and sort

```
Scheme sourceScheme =
  new TextLine(new Fields("line")); ❶
Tap source =
  new Hfs(sourceScheme, inputPath); ❷

Scheme sinkScheme = new TextLine(); ❸
Tap sink =
  new Hfs(sinkScheme, outputPath, SinkMode.REPLACE); ❹

Pipe assembly = new Pipe("wordcount"); ❺

String regexString = "(?<!\\pL)(?=\\pL)[^ ]*(?<=\\pL)(?!\\pL)";
Function regex = new RegexGenerator(new Fields("word"), regexString);
assembly =
  new Each(assembly, new Fields("line"), regex); ❻

assembly =
  new GroupBy(assembly, new Fields("word")); ❼

Aggregator count = new Count(new Fields("count"));
assembly = new Every(assembly, count); ❽

assembly =
  new GroupBy(assembly, new Fields("count"), new Fields("word")); ❾
```

```
FlowConnector flowConnector = new FlowConnector();
Flow flow =
  flowConnector.connect("word-count", source, sink, assembly); ❿

flow.complete();⓫
```

❶ We create a new Scheme that reads simple text files and emits a new Tuple for each line in a field named "line," as declared by the Fields instance.

❸ We create a new Scheme that writes simple text files and expects a Tuple with any number of fields/values. If more than one value, they will be tab-delimited in the output file.

❷ We create source and sink Tap instances that reference the input file and output
❹ directory, respectively. The sink Tap will overwrite any file that may already exist.

❺ We construct the head of our pipe assembly, and name it "wordcount." This name is used to bind the source and sink taps to the assembly. Multiple heads or tails would require unique names.

❻ We construct an Each pipe with a function that will parse the "line" field into a new Tuple for each word encountered.

❼ We construct a GroupBy pipe that will create a new Tuple grouping for each unique value in the field "word."

❽ We construct an Every pipe with an Aggregator that will count the number of Tuples in every unique word group. The result is stored in a field named "count."

❾ We construct a GroupBy pipe that will create a new Tuple grouping for each unique value in the field "count" and secondary sort each value in the field "word." The result will be a list of "count" and "word" values with "count" sorted in increasing order.

❿ We connect the pipe assembly to its sources and sinks into a Flow, and then execute
⓫ the Flow on the cluster.

In the example, we count the words encountered in the input document, and we sort the counts in their natural order (ascending). And if some words have the same "count" value, these words are sorted in their natural order (alphabetical).

One obvious problem with this example is that some words might have uppercase letters; for example, "the" and "The" when the word comes at the beginning of a sentence. So we might decide to insert a new operation to force all the words to lowercase, but we realize that all future applications that need to parse words from documents should have the same behavior, so we decide to create a reusable pipe SubAssembly, just like we would by creating a subroutine in a traditional application (see Example 16-3).

Example 16-3. Creating a SubAssembly

```java
public class ParseWordsAssembly extends SubAssembly ❶
  {
  public ParseWordsAssembly(Pipe previous)
    {
    String regexString = "(?<!\\pL)(?=\\pL)[^ ]*(?<=\\pL)(?!\\pL)";
    Function regex = new RegexGenerator(new Fields("word"), regexString);
    previous = new Each(previous, new Fields("line"), regex);

    String exprString = "word.toLowerCase()";
    Function expression =
      new ExpressionFunction(new Fields("word"), exprString, String.class); ❷
    previous = new Each(previous, new Fields("word"), expression);

    setTails(previous); ❸
    }
  }
```

❶ We subclass the SubAssembly class, which is itself a kind of Pipe.

❷ We create a Java expression function that will call toLowerCase() on the String value
in the field named "word." We must also pass in the Java type the expression expects
"word" to be, in this case, String. (*http://www.janino.net/* is used under the covers.)

❸ We must tell the SubAssembly superclass where the tail ends of our pipe subassembly
are.

First, we create a SubAssembly pipe to hold our "parse words" pipe assembly. Since this
is a Java class, it can be reused in any other application, as long as there is an incoming
field named "word" (Example 16-4). Note that there are ways to make this function
even more generic, but they are covered in the Cascading User Guide.

Example 16-4. Extending word count and sort with a SubAssembly

```java
Scheme sourceScheme = new TextLine(new Fields("line"));
Tap source = new Hfs(sourceScheme, inputPath);

Scheme sinkScheme = new TextLine(new Fields("word", "count"));
Tap sink = new Hfs(sinkScheme, outputPath, SinkMode.REPLACE);

Pipe assembly = new Pipe("wordcount");

assembly =
  new ParseWordsAssembly(assembly); ❶

assembly = new GroupBy(assembly, new Fields("word"));

Aggregator count = new Count(new Fields("count"));
assembly = new Every(assembly, count);

assembly = new GroupBy(assembly, new Fields("count"), new Fields("word"));
```

```
FlowConnector flowConnector = new FlowConnector();
Flow flow = flowConnector.connect("word-count", source, sink, assembly);

flow.complete();
```

❶ We replace the `Each` from the previous example with our `ParseWordsAssembly` pipe.

Finally, we just substitute in our new `SubAssembly` right where the previous `Every` and word parser function was used in the previous example. This nesting can continue as deep as necessary.

Flexibility

Take a step back and see what this new model has given us or, better yet, what it has taken away.

You see, we no longer think in terms of MapReduce jobs, or Mapper and Reducer interface implementations, and how to bind or link subsequent MapReduce jobs to the ones that precede them. During runtime, the Cascading "planner" figures out the optimal way to partition the pipe assembly into MapReduce jobs and manages the linkages between them (Figure 16-18).

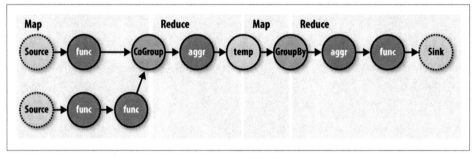

Figure 16-18. How a Flow translates to chained MapReduce jobs

Because of this, developers can build applications of arbitrary granularity. They can start with a small application that just filters a logfile, but then can iteratively build up more features into the application as needed.

Since Cascading is an API and not a syntax like strings of SQL, it is more flexible. First off, developers can create domain-specific languages (DSLs) using their favorite language, like Groovy, JRuby, Jython, Scala, and others (see the project site for examples). Second, developers can extend various parts of Cascading, like allowing custom Thrift or JSON objects to be read and written to and allowing them to be passed through the tuple stream.

Hadoop and Cascading at ShareThis

ShareThis is a sharing network that makes it simple to share any online content. With the click of a button on a web page or browser plug-in, ShareThis allows users to seamlessly access their contacts and networks from anywhere online and share the content through email, IM, Facebook, Digg, mobile SMS, etc., without ever leaving the current page. Publishers can deploy the ShareThis button to tap the service's universal sharing capabilities to drive traffic, stimulate viral activity, and track the sharing of online content. ShareThis also simplifies social media services by reducing clutter on web pages and providing instant distribution of content across social networks, affiliate groups, and communities.

As ShareThis users share pages and information through the online widgets, a continuous stream of events enter the ShareThis network. These events are first filtered and processed, and then handed to various backend systems, including AsterData, Hypertable, and Katta.

The volume of these events can be huge, too large to process with traditional systems. This data can also be very "dirty" thanks to "injection attacks" from rogue systems, browser bugs, or faulty widgets. For this reason, ShareThis chose to deploy Hadoop as the preprocessing and orchestration frontend to their backend systems. They also chose to use Amazon Web Services to host their servers, on the Elastic Computing Cloud (EC2), and provide long-term storage, on the Simple Storage Service (S3), with an eye toward leveraging Elastic MapReduce (EMR).

In this overview, we will focus on the "log processing pipeline" (Figure 16-19). The log processing pipeline simply takes data stored in an S3 bucket, processes it (described shortly), and stores the results back into another bucket. Simple Queue Service (SQS) is used to coordinate the events that mark the start and completion of data processing runs. Downstream, other processes pull data that load AsterData, pull URL lists from Hypertable to source a web crawl, or pull crawled page data to create Lucene indexes for use by Katta. Note that Hadoop is central to the ShareThis architecture. It is used to coordinate the processing and movement of data between architectural components.

With Hadoop as the frontend, all the event logs can be parsed, filtered, cleaned, and organized by a set of rules before ever being loaded into the AsterData cluster or used by any other component. AsterData is a clustered data warehouse that can support large datasets and allow for complex ad hoc queries using a standard SQL syntax. ShareThis chose to clean and prepare the incoming datasets on the Hadoop cluster and then to load that data into the AsterData cluster for ad hoc analysis and reporting. Though possible with AsterData, it made a lot of sense to use Hadoop as the first stage in the processing pipeline to offset load on the main data warehouse.

Cascading was chosen as the primary data processing API to simplify the development process, codify how data is coordinated between architectural components, and provide the developer-facing interface to those components. This represents a departure from more "traditional" Hadoop use cases, which essentially just query stored data.

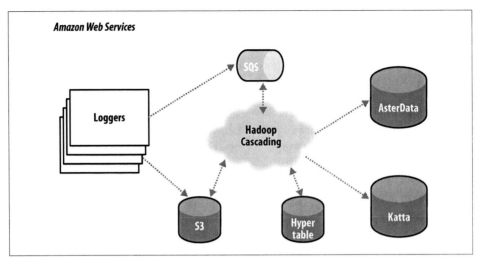

Figure 16-19. The ShareThis log processing pipeline

Instead, Cascading and Hadoop together provide better and simpler structure to the complete solution, end-to-end, and thus more value to the users.

For developers, Cascading made it easy to start with a simple unit test (by subclassing `cascading.ClusterTestCase`) that did simple text parsing and then to layer in more processing rules while keeping the application logically organized for maintenance. Cascading aided this organization in a couple of ways. First, standalone operations (Functions, Filters, etc.) could be written and tested independently. Second, the application was segmented into stages: one for parsing, one for rules, and a final stage for binning/collating the data, all via the `SubAssembly` base class described earlier.

The data coming from the ShareThis loggers looks a lot like Apache logs with date/timestamps, share URLs, referrer URLs, and a bit of metadata. To use the data for analysis downstream, the URLs needed to be unpacked (parsing query-string data, domain names, etc.). So a top-level `SubAssembly` was created to encapsulate the parsing, and child SubAssemblies were nested inside to handle specific fields if they were sufficiently complex to parse.

The same was done for applying rules. As every `Tuple` passed through the rules `SubAssembly`, it was marked as "bad" if any of the rules were triggered. Along with the "bad" tag, a description of why the record was bad was added to the `Tuple` for later review.

Finally, a splitter SubAssembly was created to do two things. First, to allow for the tuple stream to split into two, one stream for "good" data and one for "bad" data. Second, the splitter binned the data into intervals, such as every hour. To do this, only two operations were necessary: the first to create the interval from the *timestamp* value already present in the stream, and the second to use the *interval* and *good/bad* metadata to create a directory path (for example, "05/good/" where "05" is 5am and "good" means the tuple passed all the rules). This path would then be used by the Cascading

TemplateTap, a special Tap that can dynamically output tuple streams to different locations based on values in the Tuple. In this case, the TemplateTap used the "path" value to create the final output path.

The developers also created a fourth SubAssembly—this one to apply Cascading Assertions during unit testing. These assertions double-checked that rules and parsing SubAssemblies did their job.

In the unit test in Example 16-5, we see the splitter isn't being tested, but it is added in another integration test not shown.

Example 16-5. Unit testing a Flow

```
public void testLogParsing() throws IOException
  {
  Hfs source = new Hfs(new TextLine(new Fields("line")), sampleData);
  Hfs sink =
    new Hfs(new TextLine(), outputPath + "/parser", SinkMode.REPLACE);

  Pipe pipe = new Pipe("parser");

  // split "line" on tabs
  pipe = new Each(pipe, new Fields("line"), new RegexSplitter("\t"));

  pipe = new LogParser(pipe);

  pipe = new LogRules(pipe);

  // testing only assertions
  pipe = new ParserAssertions(pipe);

  Flow flow = new FlowConnector().connect(source, sink, pipe);

  flow.complete(); // run the test flow

  // verify there are 98 tuples, 2 fields, and matches the regex pattern
  // for TextLine schemes the tuples are { "offset", "line }
  validateLength(flow, 98, 2, Pattern.compile("^[0-9]+(\\t[^\\t]*){19}$"));
  }
```

For integration and deployment, many of the features built into Cascading allowed for easier integration with external systems and for greater process tolerance.

In production, all the SubAssemblies are joined and planned into a Flow, but instead of just source and sink Taps, trap Taps were planned in (Figure 16-20). Normally, when an operation throws an exception from a remote Mapper or Reducer task, the Flow will fail and kill all its managed MapReduce jobs. When a Flow has traps, any exceptions are caught and the data causing the exception is saved to the Tap associated with the current trap. Then the next Tuple is processed without stopping the Flow. Sometimes you want your Flows to fail on errors, but in this case, the ShareThis developers knew they could go back and look at the "failed" data and update their unit tests while the production system kept running. Losing a few hours of processing time was worse than losing a couple of bad records.

Using Cascading's event listeners, Amazon SQS could be integrated. When a Flow finishes, a message is sent to notify other systems that there is data ready to be picked up from Amazon S3. On failure, a different message is sent, alerting other processes.

The remaining downstream processes pick up where the log processing pipeline leaves off on different independent clusters. The log processing pipeline today runs once a day, so there is no need to keep a 100-node cluster sitting around for the 23 hours it has nothing to do. So it is decommissioned and recommissioned 24 hours later.

In the future, it would be trivial to increase this interval on smaller clusters to every 6 hours, or 1 hour, as the business demands. Independently, other clusters are booting and shutting down at different intervals based on the needs of the business unit responsible for that component. For example, the web crawler component (using Bixo, a Cascading-based web-crawler toolkit developed by EMI and ShareThis) may run continuously on a small cluster with a companion Hypertable cluster. This on-demand model works very well with Hadoop, where each cluster can be tuned for the kind of workload it is expected to handle.

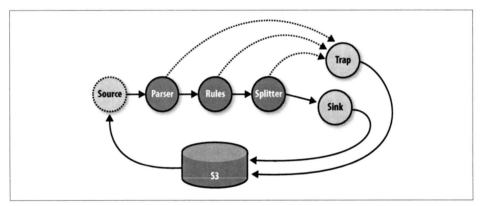

Figure 16-20. The ShareThis log processing Flow

Summary

Hadoop is a very powerful platform for processing and coordinating the movement of data across various architectural components. Its only drawback is that the primary computing model is MapReduce.

Cascading aims to help developers build powerful applications quickly and simply, through a well-reasoned API, without needing to think in MapReduce, while leaving the heavy lifting of data distribution, replication, distributed process management, and liveness to Hadoop.

Read more about Cascading, join the online community, and download sample applications by visiting the project website (*http://www.cascading.org/*).

—Chris K Wensel

TeraByte Sort on Apache Hadoop

This article is reproduced from http://sortbenchmark.org/YahooHadoop.pdf, which was written in May 2008. Jim Gray and his successors define a family of benchmarks to find the fastest sort programs every year. TeraByte Sort and other sort benchmarks are listed with winners over the years at http://sortbenchmark.org/. In April 2009, Arun Murthy and I won the minute sort (where the aim is to sort as much data as possible in under one minute) by sorting 500 GB in 59 seconds on 1,406 Hadoop nodes. We also sorted a terabyte in 62 seconds on the same cluster. The cluster we used in 2009 was similar to the hardware listed below, except that the network was much better with only 2-to-1 oversubscription between racks instead of 5-to-1 in the previous year. We also used LZO compression on the intermediate data between the nodes. We also sorted a petabyte (10^{15} bytes) in 975 minutes on 3,658 nodes, for an average rate of 1.03 TB/minute. See http://developer.yahoo.net/blogs/hadoop/2009/05/hadoop_sorts_a_petabyte_in_162 .html for more details about the 2009 results.

Apache Hadoop is an open source software framework that dramatically simplifies writing distributed data-intensive applications. It provides a distributed filesystem, which is modeled after the Google File System,[*] and a MapReduce[†] implementation that manages distributed computation. Since the primary primitive of MapReduce is a distributed sort, most of the custom code is glue to get the desired behavior.

I wrote three Hadoop applications to run the terabyte sort:

1. TeraGen is a MapReduce program to generate the data.
2. TeraSort samples the input data and uses MapReduce to sort the data into a total order.
3. TeraValidate is a MapReduce program that validates the output is sorted.

The total is around 1,000 lines of Java code, which will be checked in (*http://issues .apache.org/jira/browse/HADOOP-3402*) to the Hadoop example directory.

TeraGen generates output data that is byte-for-byte equivalent to the C version including the newlines and specific keys. It divides the desired number of rows by the desired number of tasks and assigns ranges of rows to each map. The map jumps the random number generator to the correct value for the first row and generates the following rows.

---

[*] S. Ghemawat, H. Gobioff, and S.-T. Leung. "The Google File System." In *19th Symposium on Operating Systems Principles* (October 2003), Lake George, NY: ACM.

[†] J. Dean and S. Ghemawat. "MapReduce: Simplified Data Processing on Large Clusters." In *Sixth Symposium on Operating System Design and Implementation* (December 2004), San Francisco, CA.

For the final run, I configured `TeraGen` to use 1,800 tasks to generate a total of 10 billion rows in HDFS, with a block size of 512 MB.

`TeraSort` is a standard MapReduce sort, except for a custom partitioner that uses a sorted list of N–1 sampled keys that define the key range for each reduce. In particular, all keys such that $sample[i–1] <= key < sample[i]$ are sent to reduce i. This guarantees that the output of reduce i are all less than the output of reduce $i+1$. To speed up the partitioning, the partitioner builds a two-level trie that quickly indexes into the list of sample keys based on the first two bytes of the key. `TeraSort` generates the sample keys by sampling the input before the job is submitted and writing the list of keys into HDFS. I wrote an input and output format, which are used by all three applications, that read and write the text files in the right format. The output of the reduce has replication set to 1, instead of the default 3, because the contest does not require the output data be replicated on to multiple nodes. I configured the job with 1,800 maps and 1,800 reduces and `io.sort.mb`, `io.sort.factor`, `fs.inmemory.size.mb`, and a task heap size sufficient that transient data was never spilled to disk other at the end of the map. The sampler used 100,000 keys to determine the reduce boundaries, although as can be seen in Figure 16-21, the distribution between reduces was hardly perfect and would benefit from more samples. You can see the distribution of running tasks over the job run in Figure 16-22.

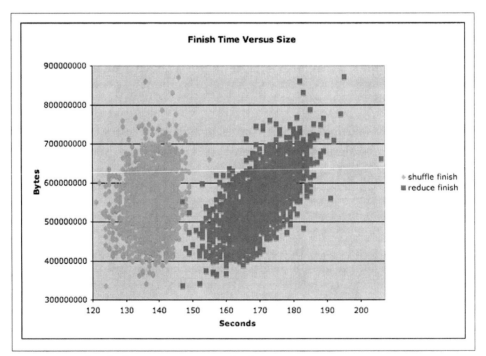

Figure 16-21. Plot of reduce output size versus finish time

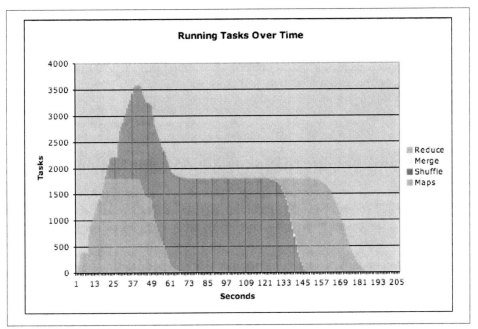

Figure 16-22. Number of tasks in each phase across time

`TeraValidate` ensures that the output is globally sorted. It creates one map per file in the output directory, and each map ensures that each key is less than or equal to the previous one. The map also generates records with the first and last keys of the file, and the reduce ensures that the first key of file *i* is greater than the last key of file *i*–1. Any problems are reported as output of the reduce with the keys that are out of order.

The cluster I ran on was:

- 910 nodes
- 2 quad core Xeons at 2.0 Ghz per a node
- 4 SATA disks per a node
- 8 G RAM per a node
- 1 gigabit Ethernet on each node
- 40 nodes per a rack
- 8 gigabit Ethernet uplinks from each rack to the core
- Red Hat Enterprise Linux Server release 5.1 (kernel 2.6.18)
- Sun Java JDK 1.6.0_05-b13

The sort completed in *209 seconds (3.48 minutes)*. I ran Hadoop trunk (pre-0.18.0) with patches for HADOOP-3443 (*http://issues.apache.org/jira/browse/HADOOP-3443*) and HADOOP-3446 (*http://issues.apache.org/jira/browse/HADOOP-3446*), which were required to remove intermediate writes to disk. Although I had the 910 nodes mostly to myself, the network core was shared with another active 2,000-node cluster, so the times varied a lot depending on the other activity.

—Owen O'Malley, Yahoo!

Using Pig and Wukong to Explore Billion-edge Network Graphs

Networks at massive scale are fascinating. The number of things they model are extremely general: if you have a collection of things (that we'll call nodes), they are related (edges), and if the nodes and edges tell a story (node/edge metadata), you have a network graph.

I started the Infochimps project, a site to find, share, or sell any dataset in the world. At Infochimps, we've got a whole bag of tricks ready to apply to any interesting network graph that comes into the collection. We chiefly use Pig (described in Chapter 11) and Wukong (*http://github.com/mrflip/wukong*), a toolkit we've developed for Hadoop streaming in the Ruby programming language. They let us write simple scripts like the ones below—almost all of which fit on a single printed page—to process terabyte-scale graphs. Here are a few datasets that come up in a search for "network" on infochimps.org:[‡]

- A social network, such as Twitter or Facebook. We somewhat impersonally model people as nodes, and relationships (`@mrflip` is friends with `@tom_e_white`) or actions (`@infochimps` mentioned `@hadoop`) as edges. The number of messages a user has sent and the bag of words from all those messages are each important pieces of node metadata.

- A linked document collection such as Wikipedia or the entire web.[§] Each page is a node (carrying its title, view count, and categories as node metadata). Each hyperlink is an edge, and the frequency at which people click from one page to the next is edge metadata.

- The connections of neurons (nodes) and synapses (edges) in the *C. elegans* roundworm.[‖]

[‡] *http://infochimps.org/search?query=network*

[§] *http://www.datawrangling.com/wikipedia-page-traffic-statistics-dataset*

[‖] *http://www.wormatlas.org/neuronalwiring.html*

- A highway map, with exits as nodes, and highway segments as edges. The Open Street Map project's dataset has global coverage of place names (node metadata), street number ranges (edge metadata), and more.#

- Or the many esoteric graphs that fall out if you take an interesting system and shake it just right. Stream through a few million Twitter messages, and emit an edge for every pair of nonkeyboard characters occurring within the same message. Simply by observing "often, when humans use 最, they also use 近," you can re-create a map of human languages (see Figure 16-23).

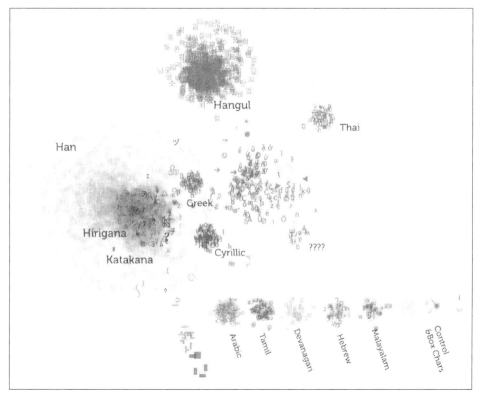

Figure 16-23. Twitter language map

#*http://www.openstreetmap.org/*

What's amazing about these organic network graphs is that given enough data, a collection of powerful tools are able to *generically* use this network structure to expose insight. For example, we've used variants of the same algorithm[*] to do each of:

- Rank the most important pages in the Wikipedia linked-document collection. Google uses a vastly more refined version of this approach to identify top search hits.
- Identify celebrities and experts in the Twitter social graph. Users who have many more followers than their "trstrank" would imply are often spammers.
- Predict a school's impact on student education, using millions of anonymized exam scores gathered over five years.

Measuring Community

The most interesting network in the Infochimps collection is a massive crawl of the Twitter social graph. With more than 90 million nodes, 2 billion edges, it is a marvelous instrument for understanding what people talk about and how they relate to each other. Here is an exploration, using the subgraph of "People who talk about Infochimps or Hadoop,"[†] of three ways to characterize a user's community:

- Who are the people they converse with (the @reply graph)?
- Do the people they engage with reciprocate that attention (symmetric links)?
- Among the user's community, how many engage with each other (clustering coefficient)?

Everybody's Talkin' at Me: The Twitter Reply Graph

Twitter lets you reply to another user's message and thus engage in conversation. Since it's an expressly public activity, a reply is a strong *social token*: it shows interest in what the other is saying and demonstrates that interest is worth rebroadcasting.

The first step in our processing is done in Wukong, a Ruby language library for Hadoop. It lets us write small, agile programs capable of handling multiterabyte data streams. Here is a snippet from the class that represents a twitter message (or *tweet*):[‡]

```
class Tweet < Struct.new(:tweet_id, :screen_name, :created_at,
                         :reply_tweet_id, :reply_screen_name, :text)
  def initialize(raw_tweet)
```

---

[*] All are steady-state network flow problems. A flowing crowd of websurfers wandering the linked-document collection will visit the most interesting pages the most often. The transfer of social capital implied by social network interactions highlights the most central actors within each community. The year-to-year progress of students to higher or lower test scores implies what each school's effect on a generic class would be.

[†] Chosen without apology, in keeping with the ego-centered ethos of social networks.

[‡] You can find full working source code on this book's website (*http://oreilly.com/catalog/0636920010388/*).

```
  # ... gory details of parsing raw tweet omitted
end

# Tweet is a reply if there's something in the reply_tweet_id slot
def is_reply?
  not reply_tweet_id.blank?
true
end
```

Twitter's Stream API lets anyone easily pull gigabytes of messages.§ They arrive in a raw JSON format:

```
{"text":"Just finished the final draft for Hadoop: the Definitive Guide!",
 "screen_name":"tom_e_white","reply_screen_name":null,"id":3239897342,
 "reply_tweet_id":null,...}
{"text":"@tom_e_white Can't wait to get a copy!",
 "screen_name":"mrflip","reply_screen_name":"tom_e_white","id":3239873453,
 "reply_tweet_id":3239897342,...}
{"text":"@josephkelly great job on the #InfoChimps API.
  Remind me to tell you about the time a baboon broke into our house.",
 "screen_name":"wattsteve","reply_screen_name":"josephkelly","id":16434069252,...}
{"text":"@mza Re: http://j.mp/atbroxmr Check out @James_Rubino's
  http://bit.ly/clusterfork ? Lots of good hadoop refs there too",
 "screen_name":"mrflip","reply_screen_name":"@mza","id":7809927173,...}
{"text":"@tlipcon divide lots of data into little parts. Magic software gnomes
  fix up the parts, elves then assemble those into whole things #hadoop",
 "screen_name":"nealrichter","reply_screen_name":"tlipcon","id":4491069515,...}
```

The reply_screen_name and reply_tweet_id let you follow the conversation (as you can see, they're otherwise null). Let's find each reply and emit the respective user IDs as an edge:‖

```
class ReplyGraphMapper < LineStreamer
  def process(raw_tweet)
    tweet = Tweet.new(raw_tweet)
    if tweet.is_reply?
      emit [tweet.screen_name, tweet.reply_screen_name]
    end
  end
end
```

The mapper derives from LineStreamer, a class that feeds each line as a single record to its process method. We only have to define that process method; Wukong and Hadoop take care of the rest. In this case, we use the raw JSON record to create a tweet object. Where user A replies to user B, emit the edge as A and B separated by a tab. The raw output will look like this:

---

§ Refer to the Twitter developer site (*http://dev.twitter.com*) or use a tool like Hayes Davis' Flamingo (*http://github.com/hayesdavis/flamingo*).

‖ In practice, we of course use numeric IDs and not screen names, but it's easier to follow along with screen names. In order to keep the graph-theory discussion general, I'm going to play loose with some details and leave out various janitorial details of loading and running.

```
% reply_graph_mapper --run raw_tweets.json a_replies_b.tsv
mrflip          tom_e_white
wattsteve       josephkelly
mrflip          mza
nealrichter     tlipcon
```

You should read this as "a replies b" and interpret it as a directed "out" edge: @watt
steve conveys social capital to @josephkelly.

Edge pairs versus adjacency list

That is the *edge pairs* representation of a network. It's simple, and it gives an equal
jumping-off point for in- or out- edges, but there's some duplication of data. You can
tell the same story from the node's point of view (and save some disk space) by rolling
up on the source node. We call this the *adjacency list*, and it can be generated in Pig by
a simple GROUP BY. Load the file:

```
a_replies_b = LOAD 'a_replies_b.tsv' AS (src:chararray, dest:chararray);
```

Then find all edges out from each node by grouping on source:

```
replies_out = GROUP a_replies_b BY src;
DUMP replies_out

(cutting,{(tom_e_white)})
(josephkelly,{(wattsteve)})
(mikeolson,{(LusciousPear),(kevinweil),(LusciousPear),(tlipcon)})
(mndoci,{(mrflip),(peteskomoroch),(LusciousPear),(mrflip)})
(mrflip,{(LusciousPear),(mndoci),(mndoci),(esammer),(ogrisel),(esammer),(wattsteve)})
(peteskomoroch,{(CMastication),(esammer),(DataJunkie),(mndoci),(nealrichter),...
(tlipcon,{(LusciousPear),(LusciousPear),(nealrichter),(mrflip),(kevinweil)})
(tom_e_white,{(mrflip),(lenbust)})
```

Degree

A simple, useful measure of influence is the number of replies a user receives. In graph
terms, this is the *degree* (specifically the *in-degree*, since this is a directed graph).

Pig's nested FOREACH syntax lets us count the distinct incoming repliers (neighbor
nodes) and the total incoming replies in one pass:[#]

```
a_replies_b = LOAD 'a_replies_b.tsv' AS (src:chararray, dest:chararray);
replies_in  = GROUP a_replies_b BY dest; -- group on dest to get in-links
replies_in_degree = FOREACH replies_in {
  nbrs = DISTINCT a_replies_b.src;
  GENERATE group, COUNT(nbrs), COUNT(a_replies_b);
};
DUMP replies_in_degree
```

[#]Due to the small size of the edge pair records and a pesky Hadoop implementation detail, the mapper may
spill data to disk early. If the jobtracker dashboard shows "spilled records" greatly exceeding "map output
records," try bumping up the io.sort.record.percent:

```
PIG_OPTS="-Dio.sort.record.percent=0.25 -Dio.sort.mb=350" pig my_file.pig
```

```
(cutting,1L,1L)
(josephkelly,1L,1L)
(mikeolson,3L,4L)
(mndoci,3L,4L)
(mrflip,5L,9L)
(peteskomoroch,9L,18L)
(tlipcon,4L,8L)
(tom_e_white,2L,2L)
```

In this sample, @peteskomoroch has 9 neighbors and 18 incoming replies, far more than most. This large variation in degree is typical for social networks. Most users see a small number of replies, but a few celebrities—such as @THE_REAL_SHAQ (basketball star Shaquille O'Neill) or @sockington (a fictional cat)—receive millions. By contrast, almost every intersection on a road map is four-way.[*] The skewed dataflow produced by this wild variation in degree has important ramifications for how you process such graphs—more later.

Symmetric Links

While millions of people have given @THE_REAL_SHAQ a shout-out on twitter, he has understandably not reciprocated with millions of replies. As the graph shows, I frequently converse with @mndoci,[†] making ours a *symmetric link*. This accurately reflects the fact that I have more in common with @mndoci than with @THE_REAL_SHAQ.

One way to find symmetric links is to take the edges in A Replied To B that are also in A Replied By B. We can do that set intersection with an inner self-join:[‡]

```
a_repl_to_b = LOAD 'a_replies_b.tsv' AS (user_a:chararray, user_b:chararray);
a_repl_by_b = LOAD 'a_replies_b.tsv' AS (user_b:chararray, user_a:chararray);
-- symmetric edges appear in both sets
a_symm_b_j  = JOIN a_repl_to_b BY (user_a, user_b),
                  a_repl_by_b BY (user_a, user_b);
...
```

However, this sends two full copies of the edge-pairs list to the reduce phase, doubling the memory required. We can do better by noticing that from a node's point of view, a symmetric link is equivalent to a paired edge: one out and one in. Make the graph undirected by putting the node with lowest sort order in the first slot—but preserve the direction as a piece of edge metadata:

```
a_replies_b = LOAD 'a_replies_b.tsv' AS (src:chararray, dest:chararray);
a_b_rels = FOREACH a_replies_b GENERATE
  ((src <= dest) ? src  : dest) AS user_a,
  ((src <= dest) ? dest : src)  AS user_b,
```

---

[*] The largest outlier that comes to mind is the famous "Magic Roundabout" in Swindon, England, with degree 10, *http://en.wikipedia.org/wiki/Magic_Roundabout_%28Swindon%29*.

[†] Deepak Singh, open data advocate and bizdev manager of the Amazon AWS cloud.

[‡] Current versions of Pig get confused on self-joins, so just load the table with differently named relations as shown here.

```
        ((src <= dest) ? 1 : 0)        AS a_re_b:int,
        ((src <= dest) ? 0 : 1)        AS b_re_a:int;
    DUMP a_b_rels

    (mrflip,tom_e_white,1,0)
    (josephkelly,wattsteve,0,1)
    (mrflip,mza,1,0)
    (nealrichter,tlipcon,0,1)
```

Now gather all edges for each node pair. A symmetric edge has at least one reply in each direction:

```
    a_b_rels_g    = GROUP a_b_rels BY (user_a, user_b);
    a_symm_b_all = FOREACH a_b_rels_g GENERATE
      group.user_a AS user_a,
      group.user_b AS user_b,
      (( (SUM(a_b_rels.a_re_b) > 0) AND
         (SUM(a_b_rels.b_re_a) > 0)     ) ? 1 : 0) AS is_symmetric:int;
    DUMP a_symm_b_all

    (mrflip,tom_e_white,1)
    (mrflip,mza,0)
    (josephkelly,wattsteve,0)
    (nealrichter,tlipcon,1)
    ...

    a_symm_b = FILTER a_symm_b_all BY (is_symmetric == 1);
    STORE a_symm_b INTO 'a_symm_b.tsv';
```

Here's a portion of the output, showing that @mrflip and @tom_e_white have a symmetric link:

```
    (mrflip,tom_e_white,1)
    (nealrichter,tlipcon,1)
    ...
```

Community Extraction

So far, we've generated a node measure (in-degree) and an edge measure (symmetric link identification). Let's move out one step and look at a neighborhood measure: how many of a given person's friends are friends with each other? Along the way, we'll produce the edge set for a visualization like the one above.

Get neighbors

Choose a seed node (here, @hadoop). First, round up the seed's neighbors:

```
    a_replies_b = LOAD 'a_replies_b.tsv' AS (src:chararray, dest:chararray);
    -- Extract edges that originate or terminate on the seed
    n0_edges    = FILTER a_replies_b BY (src == 'hadoop') OR (dest == 'hadoop');
    -- Choose the node in each pair that *isn't* our seed:
    n1_nodes_all = FOREACH n0_edges GENERATE
      ((src == 'hadoop') ? dest : src) AS screen_name;
    n1_nodes    = DISTINCT n1_nodes_all;
    DUMP n1_nodes
```

Now intersect the set of neighbors with the set of starting nodes to find all edges orig-
inating in n1_nodes:

```
n1_edges_out_j = JOIN a_replies_b BY src,
                      n1_nodes    BY screen_name USING 'replicated';
n1_edges_out   = FOREACH n1_edges_out_j GENERATE src, dest;
```

Our copy of the graph (with more than 1 billion edges) is far too large to fit in memory.
On the other hand, the neighbor count for a single user rarely exceeds a couple million,
which fits easily in memory. Including USING 'replicated' in the JOIN command instructs Pig to do a map-side join (also called a *fragment replicate join*). Pig holds the
n1_nodes relation in memory as a lookup table and streams the full edge list past.
Whenever the join condition is met—src is in the n1_nodes lookup table—it produces
output. No reduce step means an enormous speedup!

To leave only edges where both source and destination are neighbors of the seed node,
repeat the join:

```
n1_edges_j = JOIN n1_edges_out BY dest,
                  n1_nodes     BY screen_name USING 'replicated';
n1_edges   = FOREACH n1_edges_j GENERATE src, dest;
DUMP n1_edges

(mrflip,tom_e_white)
(mrflip,mza)
(wattsteve,josephkelly)
(nealrichter,tlipcon)
(bradfordcross,lusciouspear)
(mrflip,jeromatron)
(mndoci,mrflip)
(nealrichter,datajunkie)
```

Community metrics and the 1 million × 1 million problem

With @hadoop, @cloudera and @infochimps as seeds, I applied similar scripts to 2 billion
messages to create Figure 16-24 (this image is also hosted on this book's website (*http:
//oreilly.com/catalog/0636920010388/*)).

As you can see, the big data community is very interconnected. The link neighborhood
of a celebrity such as @THE_REAL_SHAQ is far more sparse. We can characterize this using
the *clustering coefficient*: the ratio of actual n1_edges to the maximum number of possible n1_edges. It ranges from zero (no neighbor links to any other neighbor) to one
(every neighbor links to every other neighbor). A moderately high clustering coefficient
indicates a cohesive community. A low clustering coefficient could indicate widely
dispersed interest (as it does with @THE_REAL_SHAQ), or it could indicate the kind of
inorganic community that a spam account would engender.

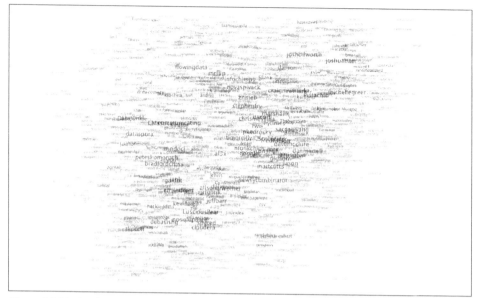

Figure 16-24. Big data community on Twitter

Local properties at global scale

We've calculated community metrics at the scale of a node, an edge, and a neighborhood. How about the whole globe? There's not enough space here to cover it, but you can simultaneously determine the clustering coefficient for every node by generating every "triangle" in the graph. For each user, comparing the number of triangles they belong to with their degree leads to the clustering coefficient.

Be careful, though! Remember the wide variation in node degree discussed above? Recklessly extending the previous method will lead to an explosion of data—pop star @britneyspears (5.2M followers, 420k following as of July 2010) or @WholeFoods (1.7M followers, 600k following) will each generate trillions of entries. What's worse, since large communities have a sparse clustering coefficient, almost all of these will be thrown away! There is a very elegant way to do this on the full graph,[§] but always keep in mind what the real world says about the problem. If you're willing to assert that @britney spears isn't *really* friends with 420,000 people, you can keep only the strong links. Weight each edge (by number of replies, whether it's symmetric, and so on) and set limits on the number of links from any node. This sharply reduces the intermediate data size, yet still does a reasonable job of estimating cohesiveness.

—Philip (flip) Kromer, Infochimps

[§] See *http://www.slideshare.net/ydn/3-xxl-graphalgohadoopsummit2010*—Sergei Vassilvitskii (@vsergei) and Jake Hofman (@jakehofman) of Yahoo! Research solve several graph problems by very intelligently throwing away most of the graph.

Installing Apache Hadoop

It's easy to install Hadoop on a single machine to try it out. (For installation on a cluster, please refer to Chapter 9.) The quickest way is to download and run a binary release from an Apache Software Foundation Mirror.

In this appendix, we cover how to install Hadoop Common, HDFS, and MapReduce. Instructions for installing the other projects covered in this book are included at the start of the relevant chapter.

Prerequisites

Hadoop is written in Java, so you will need to have Java installed on your machine, version 6 or later. Sun's JDK is the one most widely used with Hadoop, although others have been reported to work.

Hadoop runs on Unix and on Windows. Linux is the only supported production platform, but other flavors of Unix (including Mac OS X) can be used to run Hadoop for development. Windows is only supported as a development platform, and additionally requires Cygwin to run. During the Cygwin installation process, you should include the *openssh* package if you plan to run Hadoop in pseudo-distributed mode (see following explanation).

Installation

Start by deciding which user you'd like to run Hadoop as. For trying out Hadoop or developing Hadoop programs, it is simplest to run Hadoop on a single machine using your own user account.

Download a stable release, which is packaged as a gzipped tar file, from the Apache Hadoop releases page (*http://hadoop.apache.org/common/releases.html*) and unpack it somewhere on your filesystem:

```
% tar xzf hadoop-x.y.z.tar.gz
```

Before you can run Hadoop, you need to tell it where Java is located on your system. If you have the JAVA_HOME environment variable set to point to a suitable Java installation, that will be used, and you don't have to configure anything further. (It is often set in a shell startup file, such as ~/.bash_profile or ~/.bashrc.) Otherwise, you can set the Java installation that Hadoop uses by editing conf/hadoop-env.sh and specifying the JAVA_HOME variable. For example, on my Mac, I changed the line to read:

```
export JAVA_HOME=/System/Library/Frameworks/JavaVM.framework/Versions/1.6.0/Home
```

to point to version 1.6.0 of Java. On Ubuntu, the equivalent line is:

```
export JAVA_HOME=/usr/lib/jvm/java-6-sun
```

It's very convenient to create an environment variable that points to the Hadoop installation directory (HADOOP_INSTALL, say) and to put the Hadoop binary directory on your command-line path. For example:

```
% export HADOOP_INSTALL=/home/tom/hadoop-x.y.z
% export PATH=$PATH:$HADOOP_INSTALL/bin
```

Check that Hadoop runs by typing:

```
% hadoop version
Hadoop 0.20.2
Subversion https://svn.apache.org/repos/asf/hadoop/common/branches/branch-0.20 -r 911707
Compiled by chrisdo on Fri Feb 19 08:07:34 UTC 2010
```

Configuration

Each component in Hadoop is configured using an XML file. Common properties go in *core-site.xml*, HDFS properties go in *hdfs-site.xml*, and MapReduce properties go in *mapred-site.xml*. These files are all located in the *conf* subdirectory.

> In earlier versions of Hadoop, there was a single site configuration file for the Common, HDFS, and MapReduce components, called *hadoop-site.xml*. From release 0.20.0 onward, this file has been split into three: one for each component. The property names have not changed, just the configuration file they have to go in. You can see the default settings for all the properties that are governed by these configuration files by looking in the *docs* directory of your Hadoop installation for HTML files called *core-default.html*, *hdfs-default.html*, and *mapred-default.html*.

Hadoop can be run in one of three modes:

Standalone (or local) mode
> There are no daemons running and everything runs in a single JVM. Standalone mode is suitable for running MapReduce programs during development, since it is easy to test and debug them.

Pseudo-distributed mode
> The Hadoop daemons run on the local machine, thus simulating a cluster on a small scale.

Fully distributed mode
> The Hadoop daemons run on a cluster of machines. This setup is described in Chapter 9.

To run Hadoop in a particular mode, you need to do two things: set the appropriate properties, and start the Hadoop daemons. Table A-1 shows the minimal set of properties to configure each mode. In standalone mode, the local filesystem and the local MapReduce job runner are used, while in the distributed modes the HDFS and Map-Reduce daemons are started.

Table A-1. Key configuration properties for different modes

Component	Property	Standalone	Pseudo-distributed	Fully distributed
Common	`fs.default.name`	`file:///` (default)	`hdfs://localhost/`	`hdfs://namenode/`
HDFS	`dfs.replication`	N/A	1	3 (default)
MapReduce	`mapred.job.tracker`	local (default)	`localhost:8021`	`jobtracker:8021`

You can read more about configuration in "Hadoop Configuration" on page 266.

Standalone Mode

In standalone mode, there is no further action to take, since the default properties are set for standalone mode, and there are no daemons to run.

Pseudo-Distributed Mode

The configuration files should be created with the following contents and placed in the *conf* directory (although you can place configuration files in any directory as long as you start the daemons with the `--config` option):

```
<?xml version="1.0"?>
<!-- core-site.xml -->
<configuration>
  <property>
    <name>fs.default.name</name>
    <value>hdfs://localhost/</value>
  </property>
</configuration>

<?xml version="1.0"?>
<!-- hdfs-site.xml -->
<configuration>
  <property>
    <name>dfs.replication</name>
    <value>1</value>
```

```
    </property>
  </configuration>

  <?xml version="1.0"?>
  <!-- mapred-site.xml -->
  <configuration>
    <property>
      <name>mapred.job.tracker</name>
      <value>localhost:8021</value>
    </property>
  </configuration>
```

Configuring SSH

In pseudo-distributed mode, we have to start daemons, and to do that, we need to have SSH installed. Hadoop doesn't actually distinguish between pseudo-distributed and fully distributed modes: it merely starts daemons on the set of hosts in the cluster (defined by the *slaves* file) by SSH-ing to each host and starting a daemon process. Pseudo-distributed mode is just a special case of fully distributed mode in which the (single) host is localhost, so we need to make sure that we can SSH to localhost and log in without having to enter a password.

First, make sure that SSH is installed and a server is running. On Ubuntu, for example, this is achieved with:

```
% sudo apt-get install ssh
```

 On Windows with Cygwin, you can set up an SSH server (after having installed the openssh package) by running ssh-host-config -y.

On Mac OS X, make sure Remote Login (under System Preferences, Sharing) is enabled for the current user (or all users).

Then to enable password-less login, generate a new SSH key with an empty passphrase:

```
% ssh-keygen -t rsa -P '' -f ~/.ssh/id_rsa
% cat ~/.ssh/id_rsa.pub >> ~/.ssh/authorized_keys
```

Test this with:

```
% ssh localhost
```

If successful, you should not have to type in a password.

Formatting the HDFS filesystem

Before it can be used, a brand-new HDFS installation needs to be formatted. The formatting process creates an empty filesystem by creating the storage directories and the initial versions of the namenode's persistent data structures. Datanodes are not involved in the initial formatting process, since the namenode manages all of the filesystem's metadata, and datanodes can join or leave the cluster dynamically. For the same reason, you don't need to say how large a filesystem to create, since this is determined by the number of datanodes in the cluster, which can be increased as needed, long after the filesystem was formatted.

Formatting HDFS is quick to do. Just type the following:

```
% hadoop namenode -format
```

Starting and stopping the daemons

To start the HDFS and MapReduce daemons, type:

```
% start-dfs.sh
% start-mapred.sh
```

 If you have placed configuration files outside the default *conf* directory, start the daemons with the --config option, which takes an absolute path to the configuration directory:

```
% start-dfs.sh --config path-to-config-directory
% start-mapred.sh --config path-to-config-directory
```

Three daemons will be started on your local machine: a namenode, a secondary namenode, and a datanode. You can check whether the daemons started successfully by looking at the logfiles in the *logs* directory (in the Hadoop installation directory), or by looking at the web UIs, at *http://localhost:50030/* for the jobtracker and at *http://localhost:50070/* for the namenode. You can also use Java's `jps` command to see whether they are running.

Stopping the daemons is done in the obvious way:

```
% stop-dfs.sh
% stop-mapred.sh
```

Fully Distributed Mode

Setting up a cluster of machines brings many additional considerations, so this mode is covered in Chapter 9.

Cloudera's Distribution for Hadoop

Cloudera's Distribution for Hadoop (hereafter *CDH*) is based on the most recent stable version of Apache Hadoop with numerous patches, backports, and updates. Cloudera makes the distribution available in a number of different formats: source and binary tar files, RPMs, Debian packages, VMware images, and scripts for running CDH in the cloud. CDH is free, released under the Apache 2.0 license and available at *http://www.cloudera.com/hadoop/*.

To simplify deployment, Cloudera hosts packages on public yum and apt repositories. CDH enables you to install and configure Hadoop on each machine using a single command. Kickstart users can commission entire Hadoop clusters without manual intervention.

CDH manages cross-component versions and provides a stable platform with a compatible set of packages that work together. As of CDH3, the following packages are included, many of which are covered elsewhere in this book:

- HDFS – Self-healing distributed file system
- MapReduce – Powerful, parallel data processing framework
- Hadoop Common – A set of utilities that support the Hadoop subprojects
- HBase – Hadoop database for random read/write access
- Hive – SQL-like queries and tables on large datasets
- Pig – Dataflow language and compiler
- Oozie – Workflow for interdependent Hadoop jobs
- Sqoop – Integrate databases and data warehouses with Hadoop
- Flume – Highly reliable, configurable streaming data collection
- ZooKeeper – Coordination service for distributed applications
- Hue – User interface framework and SDK for visual Hadoop applications

To download CDH, visit *http://www.cloudera.com/downloads/*.

Preparing the NCDC Weather Data

This section gives a runthrough of the steps taken to prepare the raw weather data files so they are in a form that is amenable for analysis using Hadoop. If you want to get a copy of the data to process using Hadoop, you can do so by following the instructions given at the website that accompanies this book at *http://www.hadoopbook.com/*. The rest of this section explains how the raw weather data files were processed.

The raw data is provided as a collection of *tar* files, compressed with *bzip2*. Each year of readings comes in a separate file. Here's a partial directory listing of the files:

```
1901.tar.bz2
1902.tar.bz2
1903.tar.bz2
...
2000.tar.bz2
```

Each *tar* file contains a file for each weather station's readings for the year, compressed with *gzip*. (The fact that the files in the archive are compressed makes the *bzip2* compression on the archive itself redundant.) For example:

```
% tar jxf 1901.tar.bz2
% ls -l 1901 | head
011990-99999-1950.gz
011990-99999-1950.gz
...
011990-99999-1950.gz
```

Since there are tens of thousands of weather stations, the whole dataset is made up of a large number of relatively small files. It's generally easier and more efficient to process a smaller number of relatively large files in Hadoop (see "Small files and CombineFileInputFormat" on page 203), so in this case, I concatenated the decompressed files for a whole year into a single file, named by the year. I did this using a MapReduce program, to take advantage of its parallel processing capabilities. Let's take a closer look at the program.

The program has only a map function: no reduce function is needed since the map does all the file processing in parallel with no combine stage. The processing can be done with a Unix script so the Streaming interface to MapReduce is appropriate in this case; see Example C-1.

Example C-1. Bash script to process raw NCDC data files and store in HDFS

```bash
#!/usr/bin/env bash

# NLineInputFormat gives a single line: key is offset, value is S3 URI
read offset s3file

# Retrieve file from S3 to local disk
echo "reporter:status:Retrieving $s3file" >&2
$HADOOP_INSTALL/bin/hadoop fs -get $s3file .

# Un-bzip and un-tar the local file
target=`basename $s3file .tar.bz2`
mkdir -p $target
echo "reporter:status:Un-tarring $s3file to $target" >&2
tar jxf `basename $s3file` -C $target

# Un-gzip each station file and concat into one file
echo "reporter:status:Un-gzipping $target" >&2
for file in $target/*/*
do
  gunzip -c $file >> $target.all
  echo "reporter:status:Processed $file" >&2
done

# Put gzipped version into HDFS
echo "reporter:status:Gzipping $target and putting in HDFS" >&2
gzip -c $target.all | $HADOOP_INSTALL/bin/hadoop fs -put - gz/$target.gz
```

The input is a small text file (*ncdc_files.txt*) listing all the files to be processed (the files start out on S3, so the files are referenced using S3 URIs that Hadoop understands). Here is a sample:

```
s3n://hadoopbook/ncdc/raw/isd-1901.tar.bz2
s3n://hadoopbook/ncdc/raw/isd-1902.tar.bz2
...
s3n://hadoopbook/ncdc/raw/isd-2000.tar.bz2
```

By specifying the input format to be `NLineInputFormat`, each mapper receives one line of input, which contains the file it has to process. The processing is explained in the script, but, briefly, it unpacks the *bzip2* file, and then concatenates each station file into a single file for the whole year. Finally, the file is gzipped and copied into HDFS. Note the use of `hadoop fs -put -` to consume from standard input.

Status messages are echoed to standard error with a `reporter:status` prefix so that they get interpreted as a MapReduce status update. This tells Hadoop that the script is making progress and is not hanging.

The script to run the Streaming job is as follows:

```
% hadoop jar $HADOOP_INSTALL/contrib/streaming/hadoop-*-streaming.jar \
  -D mapred.reduce.tasks=0 \
  -D mapred.map.tasks.speculative.execution=false \
  -D mapred.task.timeout=12000000 \
  -input ncdc_files.txt \
  -inputformat org.apache.hadoop.mapred.lib.NLineInputFormat \
  -output output \
  -mapper load_ncdc_map.sh \
  -file load_ncdc_map.sh
```

I set the number of reduce tasks to zero, since this is a map-only job. I also turned off speculative execution so duplicate tasks didn't write the same files (although the approach discussed in "Task side-effect files" on page 187 would have worked, too). The task timeout was set high so that Hadoop didn't kill tasks that are taking a long time (for example, when unarchiving files, or copying to HDFS, when no progress is reported).

Last, the files were archived on S3 by copying them from HDFS using *distcp*.

Index

We'd like to hear your suggestions for improving our indexes. Send email to *index@oreilly.com*.

Q

query languages
    Hive Query Language, 513
    Pig, SQL, and Hive, 329
quorum (ZooKeeper), 457

R

rack awareness, clusters and, 262
rack-local tasks, 169
Rackspace, 531
    (see also log processing at Rackspace)
    log processing, 531–539
    Mailtrust division, 4
RAID (Redundant Array of Independent
    Disks), Hadoop clusters and, 260
RandomSampler objects, 240
RandomWriter objects, 288
RawComparator class, 88
    controlling sort order for keys, 234
    custom implementation, 100
    implementing (example), 99
RawLocalFileSystem class, 77
RCFile (Record Columnar File), 390
RDBMS (Relational DataBase Management
    Systems), 4
    extracting data with Sqoop, 477
    HBase versus, 431–435
        HBase characteristics, scaling and, 433
        typical RDBMS scaling story for
            successful service, 432
        use case, HBase at streamy.com, 433
    versus Hive, 368
    MapReduce versus, 5
    Pig versus, 328
read operations in ZooKeeper, 455
reader's schema, 113
reading/writing data in parallel to/from
    multiple disks, 3
RecordReader class, 199, 206
records, 198
    compression in sequence files, 122
    corrupt, skipping in task execution, 185
    logical records for TextInputFormat, 210
    processing a whole file as a record, 206
recoverable exceptions in ZooKeeper, 468,
    471
reduce functions
    general form, 189

secondary sort in Python, 246
reduce tasks, 28
    configuration properties for shuffle tuning,
        182
    number of, 29
    shuffle and sort, 179
    skipping bad records, 186
reduce-side joins, 249
    application to join weather records with
        station names, 251
    mappers for tagging station and weather
        records, 249
Reducer interface, implementation (example),
    21
reducers, 7
    default reducer, IdentityReducer, 195
    joining tagged station records with tagged
        weather records (example), 250
    specifying number in Pig, 361
    writing unit test for, 140
reflect mapping, 106
RegexMapper class, 257
RegexSerDe, 389, 391
regions in HBase tables, 413
regionservers (HBase), 414, 416
REGISTER operator, 345
regular expressions, using with PathFilter, 61
relational operators (Pig Latin), 332
relations (Pig), 326
    bags versus, 337
    propagation of schemas to new relations,
        341
    schema associated with, 338
remote debugging, 158
remote metastore configuration (Hive), 375
remote procedure calls (RPCs), 86
replicas, placement of, 67
replicated mode (ZooKeeper), 457, 473
replication factor, 44, 46, 168
Reporter class
    dynamic counters, 229
    purpose of, 189
reqs command, 443
reserved storage space, property for, 279
REST interface for HBase, 423
ResultSet interface (JDBC), 484
retries, ZooKeeper object, write( ) method,
    468
-ROOT- table, 415

About the Author

Tom White has been an Apache Hadoop committer since February 2007, and is a member of the Apache Software Foundation. He works for Cloudera, a company that offers Hadoop products, services, support, and training. Previously, he was an independent Hadoop consultant, working with companies to set up, use, and extend Hadoop. He has written numerous articles for oreilly.com, java.net, and IBM's developerWorks, and he speaks regularly about Hadoop at industry conferences. Tom has a B.A. in mathematics from the University of Cambridge and an M.A. in philosophy of science from the University of Leeds, UK. He lives in San Francisco with his family.

Colophon

The animal on the cover of *Hadoop: The Definitive Guide* is an African elephant. These members of the genus *Loxodonta* are the largest land animals on earth (slightly larger than their cousin, the Asian elephant) and can be identified by their ears, which have been said to look somewhat like the continent of Asia. Males stand 12 feet tall at the shoulder and weigh 12,000 pounds, but they can get as big as 15,000 pounds, whereas females stand 10 feet tall and weigh 8,000–11,000 pounds. Even young elephants are very large: at birth, they already weigh approximately 200 pounds and stand about 3 feet tall.

African elephants live throughout sub-Saharan Africa. Most of the continent's elephants live on savannas and in dry woodlands. In some regions, they can be found in desert areas; in others, they are found in mountains.

The species plays an important role in the forest and savanna ecosystems in which they live. Many plant species are dependent on passing through an elephant's digestive tract before they can germinate; it is estimated that at least a third of tree species in west African forests rely on elephants in this way. Elephants grazing on vegetation also affect the structure of habitats and influence bush fire patterns. For example, under natural conditions, elephants make gaps through the rainforest, enabling the sunlight to enter, which allows the growth of various plant species. This, in turn, facilitates more abundance and more diversity of smaller animals. As a result of the influence elephants have over many plants and animals, they are often referred to as a *keystone species* because they are vital to the long-term survival of the ecosystems in which they live.

The cover image is from the Dover Pictorial Archive. The cover font is Adobe ITC Garamond. The text font is Linotype Birka; the heading font is Adobe Myriad Condensed; and the code font is LucasFont's TheSansMonoCondensed.

CPSIA information can be obtained at www.ICGtesting.com
Printed in the USA
LVOW051602131211

259224LV00013B/13/P